The Imprint of Gender

courtly love - sonnet / Petrarchan
pastoral romance   p 117
complaint of mourning woman p 351 / Female complaint
                                    poems
chastity, beauty & proper womanhood

The
IMPRINT
of
GENDER

Authorship and *Publication*
in the
English Renaissance

Wendy Wall

CORNELL UNIVERSITY PRESS
Ithaca and London

First published 1993 by Cornell University Press.

Printed in the United States of America

Library of Congress Cataloging-in-Publication Data

Wall, Wendy, b. 1961
    The imprint of gender : authorship and publication in the English Renaissance / Wendy Wall.
      p.   cm.
    Includes bibliographical references and index.
    ISBN 0-8014-2765-7 (cloth : alk. paper). — ISBN 0-8014-8047-7 (paper : alk. paper)
    1. English literature—Early modern, 1500–1700—History and criticism. 2. Women and literature—England—History—16th century. 3. Women and literature—England—History—17th century. 4. Authors and publishers—England—History. 5. Literature publishing—England—History. 6. Authorship—Sex differences. 7. Authority in literature. 8. Renaissance—England.   I. Title.
PR418.W65W35   1993
820.9'003—dc20   93-22852

For my parents,
Harold and Martha Wall

CONTENTS

PREFACE   ix

INTRODUCTION:
To Be "A Man in Print"   1

1   TURNING SONNET:
The Politics and Poetics of Sonnet Circulation   23

2   AUTHOR(IZ)ING ROYAL SPECTACLE:
The Politics of Publishing Pageantry   111

3   PREFATORIAL DISCLOSURES:
"Violent Enlargement" and the Voyeuristic Text   169

4   IMPERSONATING THE MANUSCRIPT:
Cross-Dressed Authors and Literary Pseudomorphs   227

5   DANCING IN A NET:
The Problems of Female Authorship   279

AFTERWORD:
The Politics of Print   341

SELECTED BIBLIOGRAPHY   349

INDEX   369

PREFACE

IT IS DIFFICULT to write a preface for a book that devotes much of its time to critiquing book prefaces. As a female academic in a profession where "publish or perish" is the ever-present battle cry, I also find it difficult not to feel self-conscious about writing a book concerned with the gendered anxieties of publication and the masculinization of the domain of authorship. Rather than sending out my book as a coy maiden or a last will and testament, as did many Renaissance writers and publishers, I will simply preface this work by entertaining some of the questions that may immediately be raised by the tripartite subject evoked by the title: authorship, gender, publication.

What do authorship and publication have to do with each other, given that authors were around long before the Gutenberg invention? Why write a book about late sixteenth-century publication when the press had been operative for one hundred years? Why offer another book about Renaissance authorship at all? And isn't it old news that authorship is gendered?

To begin: I argue in this book that nondramatic texts written between 1557 and 1621 reveal in startling ways how publishers and writers negotiated Renaissance versions of authorship. Certainly print had been available in England since Caxton set up a press in 1476, but it was only in the latter half of the sixteenth century that print became popular and affordable enough to come into real conflict with the still burgeoning manuscript culture. This conflict generated political tensions even though publishing was still a limited endeavor at that time: often a print run would yield only five hundred copies of a book. It was not the sudden proliferation of books or a sudden increase in literacy rates that created an impact, I argue, but the way in which writers began to represent and perceive print's cultural, literary, and political potential. As publishing became cheaper, it promised to allow anyone with ready cash to have access to what had previously been a closed market. It thus played into a set of class politics that is distinctly sixteenth century. One result was that literary works began to put forth a provocative rhetoric of publication which described the relationship between writers, texts, and their readers by expressing problems of status as gendered issues.

Of course, authorship was hardly a Renaissance invention. Earlier writers had also articulated age-old anxieties about writing and formulated their own particular strategies for authorizing their works—for instance, we need only think of the medieval writer's claims to divine authority, spiritual modesty (*humilitas*), and the *auctoritas* of past writers. Certainly some of the strategies that sixteenth-century writers used form a continuum with past modes of presentation. But in this book I argue that the old problems of writing took on particular cultural and class valences during the Renaissance; inherited classical and medieval authorial roles were unavailable to contemporary writers, who expectedly created their own authorial presentations from a larger sixteenth-century conversation. Because gentlemanly amateurism was a vital part of court culture, writers from many social spheres, even those eager to publish, found it expedient to endorse the idea that publication made one common and vulgar. This "stigma of print," which flourished at midcentury before becoming a fashionable rhetoric in the 1590s, made it difficult for writers to declare publicly their ambition to appear to a large public audience. They thus had to invent their own system for presenting themselves as published writers and their texts as published commodities. In another sense, however, there were no Renaissance authors at all, at least in the modern sense of the word; writers did not have proprietary rights to the text at a time when copyright did not exist, and they could not govern the way in which texts were read, circulated, or classified.

Renaissance authorship becomes visible as a subtle and fascinating language designed to negotiate the status of writing. Authorship here is a concept vitally connected to the diverse politics of print—including the realm of sexual politics. This added dimension brings me to the issue of gender. While it is commonplace to observe that authors, like legal and political subjects, are gendered male by the evershifting institutions, traditions, and social codes of Western culture, my project looks to the precise cultural and textual coordinates of early modern English books in order to dramatize instances in which such gendering occurs. Even if the conclusion is hardly surprising—that authors were represented in ways that gendered the domain of writing as male—I think that it is important to trace this construction over a given time period lest it seem so stubbornly fixed as to be naturalized. As authorship became redefined in the wake of the print industry's collision with manuscript culture, it produced men in print. Most of us are aware of the force of that construction as we write today.

While conceptualizing this book, I profited from many different coteries of readers and friends who have proved that writing is truly collaborative, occasional, and collective. In my graduate studies, I was fortunate to discover an extraordinarily rich and diverse Renaissance group at the University of Pennsylvania. I especially thank Maureen Quilligan, whose intellectual energy sparked this work, and Margreta de Grazia, whose critical eye enabled me to envision its contours more deliberately. In giving me indispensable emotional and intellectual support, Phyllis Rackin taught me much that extends beyond the parameters of this project. I am also grateful to Rebecca Bushnell and Peter Stallybrass for shaping the project in important ways as it developed. Through the years I have benefited from numerous conversations with Gwynne Kennedy, Kim Hall, Jeff Masten, and Greg Bredbeck, which have changed how I think about Renaissance literature and made it an exciting subject for me to pursue. And Allyson Booth, James Krasner, Laura Tanner, Jennifer Green, and Susan Greenfield reminded me of life outside the Renaissance by offering a rewarding intellectual and social community.

My colleagues at Northwestern University have read various portions of this book and challenged me to be more attentive to my methods and claims. I thank in particular Sharon Achinstein, Paul Breslin, Helen Deutsch, Jules Law, Martin Mueller, and Barbara Newman. I owe special debts to Mary Beth Rose, Arthur Marotti, Ann Baynes Coiro, and Ann Rosalind Jones for reading sections of the manuscript at later stages and giving me invaluable advice and encouragement. If David Lee Miller unwittingly started the whole project years ago by teaching me how to read all over again, the two readers at Cornell University Press, Martin Elsky and Mary Ellen Lamb, made it possible for me to finish the project by helping me strengthen the argument and see its blind spots.

As for my mother, who is an English teacher, and my father, who is a printer, my subject matter makes my indebtedness to them embarrassingly clear. I deeply appreciate their enduring support. Undoubtedly the person who has shaped this project most is Juliet Fleming, whose unflagging energy, rigorous intelligence, and warm friendship have been, and are, indispensable to me. Mark Long reminded me daily of why it was important to integrate my beliefs and commitments with my research and teaching; his sheer patience and love enabled every single word of this book. And finally, I can't thank Jules Law enough for inspiring and sustaining me with his boundless emotional and intellectual generosity. He has made it all worthwhile.

Parts of this book have already appeared in print. A shorter draft of Chapter 3 was published as "Disclosures in Print: The 'Violent Enlargement' of the Renaissance Voyeuristic Text," in *Studies in English Literature* 29 (1989): 35–59. Chapter 5 contains material previously published in "Isabella Whitney and the Female Legacy," *ELH* 8 (Spring 1991): 35–62, and "Our Bodies, Our Texts?: Renaissance Women and the Trials of Authorship," in *Anxious Power: Reading, Writing and Ambivalence in Narrative by Women*, edited by Carol J. Singley and Susan Elizabeth Sweeney (Albany: State University of New York Press, 1993), 51–71. I thank the publishers for their permission to use revisions of this material.

WENDY WALL

Chicago

The Imprint of Gender

INTRODUCTION
TO BE "A MAN IN PRINT"

IN HIS 1604 INTRODUCTION to *Daiphantus*, Anthony Scoloker self-consciously mocks one of the conventions of published introductions. Ridiculing an author's feigned reluctance to appear in print, Scoloker tells his readers:

> He is A man in Print, and tis enough he hath under-gone a Pressing (yet not like a Ladie) though for your sakes and for Ladyes, protesting for this poore Infant of his Brayne, as it was the price of his Virginitie borne into the world in teares. . . . Thus like a Lover wooes he for your Favor, which if You grant then *Omnia vincit Amor.*[1]

Scoloker here makes fun of the artful and elaborate disavowals uttered by many published writers. "It is not my ambition," Thomas Dekker declares in one such representative statement, "to be a Man in Print."[2] By simultaneously identifying and satirizing the public author's conventional modesty, Scoloker teases out the bawdy implications of the word "press." In Elizabethan slang, to "undergo a pressing" is to act the lady's part and be pressed by a man, an act associated here with the loss of authorial virginity.

[1] Anthony Scoloker, *Daiphantus, or The Passions of Love*, STC 21853 (London: 1604), sig. A2ᵛ.
[2] Thomas Dekker, "To the Reader," in *The Gull's Hornbook* (London: 1609), reprint ed. R. B. McKerrow (London: Chatto and Windus, 1907), 3.

Publishing is widely represented, Scoloker claims, as if it were a bastardized birthing, a scandalous breach denoting forced entry into the public sphere. Breaking into print seemingly inspires the writer to present a highly confused gendered authorial position, paradoxically becoming vulnerable and impressionable while guarding against the effeminacy entailed in such a transformation ("not like a Ladie"). This entire procedure is nevertheless seen as expressly catering to women's desires and is described in the peculiarly feminizing language of modesty, seduction, and birth.

Scoloker also plays here with the multiple meanings of the phrase "a man in print." While obviously referring to a writer's appearance in publication, the term also implies a full masculinity, with "in print" meaning "thoroughly" or "completely."[3] The bizarre associations between publishing and gender roles that Scoloker so elaborately reproduces in his introduction become condensed into a punning phrase. Scoloker's further mockery merely draws out the slippages and contradictions that inform the gendering of writing. The declaration of full masculinity here is part and parcel of that gendering, for the writer can assert his manliness, despite the necessary feminizing that pressing implies, precisely by controlling his own effeminacy within a stylized and disingenuous language of seduction. Having been dangerously seduced by the press, the author plays out his seduction on the reader, thus establishing his thoroughly masculine power by professing to be a coy and reluctant lover. *Omnia vincit Amor.*

In bringing to light the perplexing mix of gendered roles evoked by the rhetoric of publication, Scoloker's mockery of prefatorial justifications raises a set of questions that this book addresses. What did it mean to be a "man in print" or to "undergo a pressing" in Renaissance England? What were the political climate of publication and the risks of public writing? Why did authors and printers justify their works through a highly sexualized language? How do these justifications shape authorship and the print medium? This book approaches these questions by mapping the complicated relationship between the gendered rhetoric of publication in late sixteenth- and early seventeenth-century England, the political stakes of printing, and the formation of a Renaissance version of literary authorship.

Scoloker's preface is fascinating because it both identifies and seeks to erode the reputed Renaissance "stigma of print" that other writers register so markedly.[4] In the preface to his satiric plague pamphlet *The Wonderfull Yeare*, Dekker again testifies to the dangers of publication and thus offers

---

[3]My thanks to Lawrence Lipking for calling to my attention the many resonances of this phrase.

[4]The classic article outlining this phenomenon is J. W. Saunders, "The Stigma of Print: A Note on the Social Bases of Tudor Poetry," *Essays in Criticism* 1 (1951): 139–64.

an example of exactly the kind of language that Scoloker found so irritating. For by complaining that writers pander to the tastes of scurrilous readers, Dekker legitimizes the authorial reluctance that Scoloker saw as unnecessary. But in doing so, Dekker also singles out for critique the fashion for disingenuous authorial poses:

> To mainteine the scurvy fashion, and to keepe Custome in reparations, [the writer] must be honyed, and come-over with Gentle Reader, Courteous Reader, and Learned Reader, though he have no more Gentilitie in him than Adam had (that was but a gardner) and no more Civility than a Tartar. . . . For he that dares hazard a pressing to death (thats to say, To be a man in Print) must make account that he shall stand . . . to be beaten with all stormes.[5]

Dekker's sense of the incivility of the public reader, expressed with regard to lines of race and class, marks just one complaint within a vast array of commentaries on the disreputable nature of the practice of publication. Here Dekker implies that true degradation lies in the baseness of readers who unfairly attack the valiant publishing author and render his noble efforts a physical form of torture (pressing). Other descriptions of the press attack the vulgarity of publishing writers. Together these different protests produce a general stigma attached to printing. Scoloker's words are particularly interesting because they suggest the fictitious nature of this stigma precisely by highlighting the way in which the scene of writing was eroticized and scandalized. In doing so, Scoloker produces a sarcastic version of what was in reality a conventional gesture: to use the axis of gender to encode anxieties about unauthorized social and textual circulation in early modern England.[6]

In this book I argue that Renaissance conceptions of authorship emerged in response to the social controversies surrounding print. As do existing studies of "the author," my book assumes that the seemingly timeless concept of authorship does indeed have a history to be told. Unlike authors of other such studies, however, I locate the formation of this literary category in the collision between manuscript and print practices on the one hand, and between aristocratic amateurism and the marketplace on the other. In

---

[5]Thomas Dekker, *The Wonderfull Yeare*, STC 6535.3 (1603), sig. A2ᵛ, reprinted in *The Plague Pamphlets of Thomas Dekker*, ed. F. P. Wilson (Oxford: Clarendon Press, 1925), 4.

[6]Joan Scott's commentary on gender is helpful in detailing what is meant by this complex term: "Gender is a constitutive element of social relationships based on perceived differences between the sexes, and gender is a primary way of signifying relationships of power." ("Gender: A Useful Category of Historical Analysis," *American Historical Review* 91 [December 1986]: 1067.)

arguing for a historical "stigma of print," scholars have noted that the four most influential books of Renaissance poetry—*Tottels Miscellany*, Sidney's *Astrophel and Stella*, Donne's *Songs and Sonnets*, and Herbert's *Poems*—were published only posthumously. It is easy to see the numerous prefaces, dedications, and commendatory poems that justified publication merely as confirmation of such a stigma. I see this rhetoric as more crucial, however, in articulating the concepts of the newly commodified book and its governing author. When writers, publishers, and printers adapted material for the press, they simultaneously activated an intertwined social, textual, and sexual politics and promoted a particular concept of literary authority. Because, as I argue, nondramatic works printed between 1557 and 1621 conceptualized the relationship between writer, text, and new reading public in particularly gendered terms, the developing concept of authorship was masculinized. While it is commonplace to observe that the author and the subject are male, I look to specific genres, strategies, and gestures through which that gendering occurred in early modern England.

In mapping the formation of English Renaissance literary authority, I am interested in giving attention to three important elements often neglected by scholarly accounts: the complexity of the printed book commodity, the variable of gender, and the social construction of the print medium. First, while following the recent work of new historicists and cultural materialists,[7] *The Imprint of Gender* emphasizes the importance of the text's

[7]I refer to historicist critics' attention to the social embeddedness of cultural forms, their belief that Renaissance culture can serve as a possible object of textual and discursive analysis, and their assumption that cultural forms and social relations are reciprocally produced. For a description of Renaissance historicist practices, see the introduction to *Shakespeare Reproduced: The Text in History & Ideology*, ed. Jean Howard and Marion F. O'Connor (New York: Methuen, 1987); Jonathan Dollimore's introduction to *Political Shakespeare: New Essays in Cultural Materialism*, ed. Jonathan Dollimore and Alan Sinfield (Ithaca: Cornell University Press, 1987); and Stephen Greenblatt's introduction to "The Forms of Power and the Power of Forms in the Renaissance," *Genre* 15 (1982). Louis Montrose outlines the professional politics of this methodology in "Professing the Renaissance: The Poetics and Politics of Culture," *The New Historicism*, ed. H. Aram Veeser (New York: Routledge, 1989), 15–36. Cultural materialism and new historicism acknowledge intellectual debts to the varied work of Raymond Williams, Louis Althusser, Pierre Macherey, Michel Foucault, and Clifford Geertz. For two of the more successful demonstrations of new historicist methodology, see Louis Montrose, "Shaping Fantasies: Figurations of Gender and Power in Elizabethan Culture," *Representations* 2 (1983): 61–94, reprinted in abridged form in *Rewriting the Renaissance: The Discourses of Sexual Difference in Early Modern Europe*, ed. Margaret W. Ferguson, Maureen Quilligan, and Nancy Vickers (Chicago: University of Chicago Press, 1986), 65–87; and "Of Gentlemen and Shepherds: The Politics of Elizabethan Pastoral Form," *ELH* 50 (1983): 415–59.

For a critique from a Marxist-feminist standpoint, and for an excellent bibliography of self-announcedly political work on Shakespeare, see Walter Cohen, "Political Criticism of Shakespeare," in *Shakespeare Reproduced*, 20–46. In "Are We Being Historical Yet?" *South Atlantic Quarterly* 87 (Fall 1988): 743–86, Carolyn Porter echoes Cohen's concerns about his-

material features to historicist critique. I rely on an expansive understanding of the "textual commodity" as an object that marks a juncture between the material and the symbolic, the historical and the textual. The physical features of the text—its prefatory apparatus, its title headings, its mode of distribution—figure prominently in my analysis, for these "trappings" construct protocols of reading and provide the grounds on which the text is authorized. In short, I read the text as an object as well as a symbolic form. While many critics have discussed the cultural negotiations prompted by, for example, *Astrophel and Stella*, I investigate how the very form itself of the published *Astrophel and Stella* had vital social stakes. Similarly I have found it possible to refine and problematize the representation of gender "within" a work by noticing that gender is an issue at the level of the commodity. In the case of *Gorboduc*, for instance, a text in which the consequences of the division of the kingdom are displaced rhetorically upon maternal monstrosity, the preface's eroticization of the text provides a layer that complicates the way gender functions in the play. When the publisher describes the book as a ravished, half-clad maiden, he suggests that the reader's very act of buying the text is complicitous in a power relationship dependent on the trafficking in female sexuality.[8] The text's "packaging," so frequently erased when a work's history is drained from it, speaks to the specific conditions by which meaning was and is transmitted. I pause in this study, then, to consider how a literary work becomes readable to its culture—to make visible the lens through which the "book" and the act of public writing are viewed.[9]

Extending my methodological concern with the relationship between the material and the symbolic, I argue that rhetoric itself can constitute crucial "evidence" for making historical claims about literature and culture. To understand the critically reputed Renaissance "stigma of print," for example, we need to look not only to whether something was licensed for publication or not, but also to the book's complex figures, tropes, and

toricism's political investments and its methodological premises, specifically taking practitioners of new historicism (namely, Stephen Greenblatt) to task for the unhistorical way in which they map the discursive field to be analyzed. See also Lee Patterson's comments on the political problems of new historicism in *Negotiating the Past: The Historical Understanding of Medieval Literature* (Madison: University of Wisconsin Press, 1987), 57–74.

[8]See my discussion of this preface in Chapter 2.

[9]For recent critical works that have given attention to the physical form of the book-commodity, see Leah Marcus, *Puzzling Shakespeare* (Berkeley: University of California Press, 1988); Timothy Murray, *Theatrical Legitimation: Allegories of Genius in Seventeenth-Century England and France* (Oxford: Oxford University Press, 1987); and Margreta de Grazia, *Shakespeare "Verbatim": The Reproduction of Authenticity and the 1790 Apparatus* (Oxford: Oxford University Press, 1991). While not foregrounding the book-commodity per se, Annabel

rhetorical self-identifications. If the text's "objectness" is vital to an understanding of its literary representations, its discursive features are equally important in making sense of its historical functions. I believe it is important to develop a paradigm for reading Renaissance poetry that looks both to its material production and to its encoding of that process.

Second, preeminent studies of Renaissance authorship often de-emphasize the gender politics on which such a concept rests.[10] Sixteenth-century writers draw on a gendered and sexualized language—replete with figures of courtly love, cross-dressing, voyeurism, and female desire—when they legitimate publication. My book unfolds the sexual ideologies embedded within these strategies, points to how publication and its attendant class issues motivated such identifications, and then queries how women's writing provided countermodels to dominant modes of authorization.

In writing this book, I have been made particularly aware of the often uneasy connection between feminist and materialist methodologies. New historicists have suffered rebukes from feminists who, while welcoming the return to history as a validation of the critical work they have been doing since the 1970s ("montage"), have also sensed that their theoretical contributions have been erased by the term "new" and by new historicism's self-identified genealogy.[11] Other scholars have also voiced their dissatisfactions with the professional and intellectual politics of new historicism, its tendency to reinscribe the canon while espousing commitment to multiculturalism, and its tendency to subordinate issues of gender to more traditional forms of power. Work by such critics as Peter Stallybrass, Catherine Belsey, Karen Newman, Mary Beth Rose, and Louis Montrose, however, offers a model for integrating the projects of feminist and historicist critique. These critics investigate constructions of gender in early modern England (through such avenues as the body, legal codes, maternity, racial ideology and representations of the female monarch), and their studies

---

Patterson's *Censorship and Interpretation: The Conditions of Writing and Reading in Early Modern England* (Madison: University of Wisconsin Press, 1984) offers an important analysis of the environment of public writing.

[10]The most compelling accounts of Renaissance authorship, which I discuss at the end of this Introduction, are by Richard Helgerson, *Self-Crowned Laureates: Spenser, Jonson, Milton, and the Literary System* (Berkeley: University of California Press, 1983); and Peter Stallybrass and Allon White, *The Politics and Poetics of Transgression* (Ithaca: Cornell University Press, 1986).

[11]See Judith Newton, "History As Usual? Feminism and the 'New Historicism,'" *The New Historicism*; Lynda E. Boose, "The Family in Shakespeare Studies; or—Studies in the Family of Shakespeareans; or—The Politics of Politics," *Renaissance Quarterly* 40 (Winter 1987): 707–42; and Carol Thomas Neely, "Constructing the Subject: Feminist Practice and the New Renaissance Discourses," *English Literary Renaissance* 18 (Winter 1988): 5–18.

make visible the discursive limits within which "woman" functioned.[12] Other scholars have complemented these studies by reading female-authored texts as proof that (male) cultural constructions did not directly dictate "female experience." In pointing out that women, like other subordinated groups, could resist cultural exhortations and proscriptions, these critiques have sought to replace a paradigm of victimization with one of enablement.[13] My book combines these approaches. I first articulate how the new literary marketplace inspired writers and publishers to define reading, writing, and publishing by generating various representations of women. The "feminine," it seems, often provided the unauthorized ground on which authorship could be established.[14] But in order to prevent the category of "woman" from becoming visible in this work solely as a metaphor for the insecurities of a patriarchal order, I conclude with an exploration of how women writers themselves tackled both the gritty problem of publication and the fact that cultural expressions of that problem relied on women as *tropes*. Gender thus provides a focal point throughout this work for querying the issues of authorship, privacy, and class energized by the spread of print technology.

Third, critics generally fall into two camps when analyzing the authority of print and writing in early modern England—the ideological and the metaphysical. In other words, scholars tend to interpret print in terms of

[12]For a collection of important feminist-historicist work outside the field of Renaissance studies, see *Feminist Criticism and Social Change: Sex, Class and Race in Literature and Culture*, ed. Judith Newton and Deborah Rosenfelt (New York: Methuen, 1985).

[13]One particularly fascinating study of women's writing is Ann Rosalind Jones, *The Currency of Eros: Women's Love Lyric in Europe, 1540–1620* (Bloomington: Indiana University Press, 1990). See also Maureen Quilligan, *The Allegory of Female Authority: Christine de Pizan's "Cité des Dames"* (Ithaca: Cornell University Press, 1991); Elaine Beilin, *Redeeming Eve: Women Writers of the English Renaissance* (Princeton: Princeton University Press, 1987); Gwynne Kennedy, "Lessons of the 'Schoole of Wysdome,'" in *Sexuality and Politics in Renaissance Drama*, ed. Carole Levin and Karen Robertson (Lewiston, New York: Edwin Mellen Press, 1991), 113–36; Margaret Hannay's anthology *Silent But for the Word: Tudor Women as Patrons, Translators, and Writers of Religious Works* (Kent, Ohio: Kent State University Press, 1985); and *Reading Mary Wroth: Representing Alternatives in Early Modern England*, ed. Naomi J. Miller and Gary Waller (Knoxville: University of Tennessee Press, 1991).

[14]While I argue that gender distinctions were generated in relation to other social negotiations, I realize that "gender" was itself a crucial and formative rather than a subordinate ideological category in early modern England; and I intend my account to be complemented by those that foreground organizations of the family and of desire as catalysts for socioeconomic change. For such accounts, see Mary Beth Rose, *The Expense of Spirit: Love and Sexuality in English Renaissance Drama* (Ithaca: Cornell University Press, 1988); and Catherine Belsey, *The Subject of Tragedy: Identity and Difference in Renaissance Drama* (New York: Methuen, 1985). For a study that gives priority to the complex circulations of homoerotic desire over other ideological structures in early modern England, see Valerie Traub, "Desire and the Differences It Makes," in *The Matter of Difference*, ed. Valerie Wayne (Ithaca: Cornell University Press, 1991).

its effects either on the political structure or on categories of thought. By paying attention to the competing notions of textuality engendered by manuscript and print media, most critical accounts tend to isolate one kind of "authority" as the object of their analysis: either the textually defined author or the socially defined role of authorship. I am interested in calling attention to the relationship between these two—in particular, to revealing how social and political pressures condition the medium's supposedly inherent textual features. Seemingly intrinsic features of print culture and textuality, I suggest, were in fact generated in response to specific cultural problems. By disclosing writers' and printers' strategies for presenting the newly commodified book, I hope to counter essentialist arguments, which imply that "print logic" necessitates a uniform movement toward fixity and totalization. I argue that neither authorship nor print, nor any set relationship between the two, is inevitable. Instead that relationship is created to fit the determinate needs of a specific historical situation. Conceptual shifts in the understanding of writing, authorship, and textuality were inextricably interwoven with political issues in early modern England.

I am eager in this book to consider how the findings of bibliographical study can be brought to bear on an investigation of the cultural politics of print. These two scholarly pursuits offer an interesting point of connection simply because they both rely heavily on the term "unauthorized" in their analyses, but with quite different meanings. Either print or manuscript can be seen as "unauthorized," depending on the particular way in which this term is used. In the late sixteenth and early seventeenth centuries, a writer could participate in either a healthy coterie manuscript culture or a newly burgeoning print industry. Manuscripts were unauthorized textually in the sense that they failed to designate "the author" as a central textual feature. To state the case somewhat schematically: Renaissance manuscripts were collectively produced and permeable texts, subject to editorial revision as they were passed from hand to hand. These works derived authority from their place in coterie circles—at court and in the satellite environments of the Inns of Court and the universities. Printed texts, on the other hand, can be said to be have been authorized by an appeal to their intrinsic textual features rather than to their status as occasional verse. Because they were linked to merchandising, however, printed texts had considerably less social authority. I argue that these common characterizations of the "closed" printed work and the "open" manuscript are, in fact, descriptions of particular textual interpretations that were socially constructed and perpetuated during this time period. In this precarious moment when print and manuscript cultures coexisted, writers, printers, and patrons negotiated and fashioned competing textual and cultural "authorities" through specific representations of publication. We see these negotiations in the highly gendered rhetorical self-identifications that Renaissance texts offer (in prefaces such as Scoloker's) and in changes in the typographical and physical format of the book itself. When examining texts with an eye to these elements, we uncover the sexual and social ideologies produced in the collision between coterie manuscript culture and print culture. This collision becomes especially pronounced in the love poetry that was so popular in courtly circles because this genre required more legitimation than sacred works. From within this intersection of competing authorities, I argue, we glimpse one site in which Renaissance authorship develops.

Rethinking conceptions of Renaissance texts and authors has been made possible by scholars who have charted the broad historical shift from manuscript to print culture on the one hand, and by those who have paid attention to the particular environment of Renaissance poetic circulation on the other. Critics have schematized the move from manuscript to print as one from "alterability" to "closure."[15] The monumental and seemingly highly finished medieval manuscript was "alterable," such critics claim, mainly in its use of precursor texts and its free incorporation of other literary material. Manuscripts texts were also alterable in their mode of production because they were subject to the conscious and unconscious revisions of the scribe.[16] In the principles by which they were constructed and read, coterie texts of the Renaissance share qualities with medieval manuscript works. The coterie text, as Arthur Marotti's groundbreaking work has made clear, was similarly "unfinished" until it circulated to its various

[15]Gerald L. Bruns, "The Originality of Texts in a Manuscript Culture," *Journal of Comparative Literature* 32 (Spring 1980): 113–29; Walter Ong, *The Presence of the Word* (New Haven: Yale University Press, 1967), *Rhetoric, Romance, and Technology* (Ithaca: Cornell University Press, 1971), and *Orality and Literacy: The Technologizing of the Word* (New York: Methuen, 1982); Jack Goody and Ian Watt, "The Consequences of Literacy," in *Literacy in Traditional Societies*, ed. Jack Goody (Cambridge: Cambridge University Press, 1968). For an application of some of these theoretical tenets, see Martin Elsky, *Authorizing Words: Speech, Writing, and Print in the English Renaissance* (Ithaca: Cornell University Press, 1989). Broadly concerned with examining how printed texts authorized themselves through an appeal to the inherited distinctions between speech and writing (orality, manuscript, and print), Elsky builds on Ong's argument about the spatializing effects of print. The most comprehensive survey of the effects of print is Elizabeth Eisenstein, *The Printing Press as an Agent of Change* (Cambridge: Cambridge University Press, 1979).

[16]For a discussion of how medieval writers circulated their texts, see Robert K. Root, "Publication before Printing," *PMLA* 28 (1913): 417–31; and H. S. Bennett, "The Author and His Public in the Fourteenth and Fifteenth Centuries," *Essays and Studies by Members of the English Association* 23 (1938): 7–24. For an overview of scribal and print practices, see Lucien Febvre and Henri-Jean Martin, *The Coming of the Book: The Impact of Printing, 1450–1800*, trans. David Gerard (London: Verso, 1990), first published as *L'apparition du livre* (Paris, 1958).

patrons and readers, from whom it took its full authorization. Responding to recent challenges to author-centered literary practices issued by critics of what has been termed the new bibliography,[17] Marotti demonstrates the importance of locating Renaissance poetry within the social milieu that dictated how it was written and distributed.[18] He has uncovered a fascinating array of archival materials that startlingly dramatize the collaborative and collective textual practices engendered by manuscript circulation. Although written more than one hundred years after the invention of the press, coterie texts, we learn, behaved as fluid "events" staged within circuits of social obligation and receipt.

According to print historians, such texts would necessarily become more fixed and closed as multiple reproduction gained force. It would be easy, then, to fit Marotti's findings about Renaissance literature within a narrative that details print culture's inexorable march toward stability and order. Sixteenth-century works would be said to display merely the residue of the dying world of manuscript culture. My book, however, argues that sixteenth-century poetic practices interrupt and complicate the evolutionary "logic" of this development. Seeing the Renaissance world as poised between manuscript and print cultures helps us begin to examine the complicated dynamic that ensued when coterie texts competed with and moved into the marketplace. The distinctions between these cultures, however, are ones that I will question and problematize within the scope of the

---

[17]See, for example, Stephen Orgel, "What Is a Text?" *Research Opportunities in Renaissance Drama* 2:4 (1981): 3–6; Joseph Loewenstein, "The Script in the Marketplace," in *Representing the English Renaissance*, ed. Stephen Greenblatt (Berkeley: University of California Press, 1988), 265–78; Murray, *Theatrical Legitimation*; and de Grazia, *Shakespeare Verbatim*. Jerome McGann's *A Critique of Modern Textual Criticism* (Chicago: University of Chicago Press, 1983) summarizes general innovations in bibliographical theory and indicates their ramifications for practitioners of literary interpretation. For a polemical argument about revisionist textual practice, specifically with regard to Renaissance texts, see Randall McLeod, "UnEditing Shakspeare," *Sub-Stance* 33/34 (1982): 26–55.

[18]Arthur Marotti, *John Donne: Coterie Poet* (Madison: University of Wisconsin Press, 1986), "'Love is not Love': Elizabethan Sonnet Sequences and the Social Order," *ELH* 49 (1982): 396–428, "John Donne, Author," *Journal of Medieval and Renaissance Studies* 19 (1989): 69–82, and especially his valuable essay "The Transmission of Lyric Poetry and the Institutionalizing of Literature in the English Renaissance," in *Contending Kingdoms: Historical, Psychological, and Feminist Approaches to the Literature of Sixteenth-Century England and France*, ed. Marie-Rose Logan and Peter L. Rudnytsky (Detroit: Wayne State University Press, 1991), 21–41. Together with Stephen Orgel's investigation of stage practices and scripting ("What Is a Text?"), Marotti's attention to the production of Renaissance poetry has prompted further inquiry into the social, textual, and legal ramifications of these modes of textual composition. See also J. W. Saunders, "From Manuscript to Print: A Note on the Circulation of Poetic MSS. in the Sixteenth Century," *Proceedings of the Leeds Philosophical and Literary Society* 6 (1951): 507–28.

book because their seeming differences are often an effect of the very language and forms created by writers and publishers.

Both broad and local studies of textual authority have been prompted and facilitated by poststructuralist challenges to the primacy of the author —namely, Michel Foucault's declaration that the author is a "function" and Roland Barthes's announcement that the author is dead. As we have become more and more aware that such features are historical constructs, we have been able to develop possible ways for rethinking the relationship between the author and the textual/social closures evoked by the work. The standard terms for characterizing print and manuscript cultures—as "closed" or "open"—find their extension, in fact, in Barthes's opposition between the "readerly" and "writerly" text.[19] This opposition provides a starting point for a more historical analysis of early modern poetic presentation, for it enables us to identify characteristics of Renaissance poems that approximate poststructuralist theories of textuality without remaking these poems in our own postmodern image.

My claims about authorship, gender, and print are premised on the now generally accepted idea that the two competing modes of literary transmission during the Renaissance carried strongly marked class implications.[20] Much attention has been paid to the way in which sixteenth-century English literature persistently makes visible a society obsessed with rank.[21] At a time in which the economic and cultural world was shifting to accom-

[19]Michel Foucault, "What Is an Author?" in *Textual Strategies: Perspectives in Post-Structuralist Criticism*, ed. Josué Harari (Ithaca: Cornell University Press, 1979); and Roland Barthes, "The Death of the Author," in *Image, Music, Text*, ed. Stephen Heath (New York: Hill and Wang, 1977).

[20]I use the term "class" here and throughout the book in an expansive sense, rather than in its narrow definition—as a self-conscious group operating within a capitalistic formation. Peter Laslett is representative of many critics who argue that despite obvious gradations in status and rank, the Renaissance world was a "one-class society," because there was "only one body of persons capable of concerted action over the whole area of society" (*The World We Have Lost* [New York: Scribner's, 1971], 23). In his definition, "class" signifies "a number of people banded together in the exercise of collective power, political and economic" (23). I use the category of "class" because it can also address the social relations of a precapitalist world as well as the emergent capitalist relations evident in the late sixteenth century. Raymond Williams notes that class can mean "(i) group; . . . social or economic category, at varying levels (ii) rank; relative social position; by birth or mobility and (iii) formation: perceived economic relationship; social, political and cultural organization" (*Keywords*, 3d ed. [New York: Oxford University Press, 1984], 69). "Class," then, can represent the more traditional issues of order, degree, and estate, as well as the developing protocapitalist social strata brought about by the "middling" level of society. See Keith Wrightson, *English Society, 1580–1680* (New Brunswick, N.J.: Rutgers University Press, 1982).

[21]See, for instance, Jean-Christophe Agnew, *Worlds Apart: The Market and the Theater in Anglo-American Thought, 1550–1750* (Cambridge: Cambridge University Press, 1986); and Frank Whigham, *Ambition and Privilege: The Social Tropes of Elizabethan Courtesy Theory* (Berkeley: University of California Press, 1984).

modate a "middling" class, people at many points on the social spectrum were concerned with both social mobility and the security of status indicators. Regardless of the actual cultural effects of printing, textual transmission became rhetorically tied to the symbolic codes that designated rank. Manuscript writing, particularly within the genres of romance and love poetry, was seen to constitute a bid for gentility, while publishing belied one's reliance on a "common" audience. Because it bridged socially differentiated readers, print played indiscriminately on real and perceived fears about the collapse of social difference. Renaissance texts air complaints that professional writers might ascend to the aristocracy and become the cultural trendsetters of their day or, alternately, that printing would render courtly practices obsolete because anyone with money could partake of social jokes, debates, and conversations. In reality, the press offered to make the precarious boundary between the aristocracy and the lower gentry more fluid, but this borderline was figured as a primary cultural linchpin, a privileged faultline on which the viability of widespread cultural changes was tested.[22] The press thus engendered outcries that far exceeded its apparent political force, for the circulation of texts created anxieties and benefits that tapped into vast cultural problems. In particular, publication became attached to the more threatening problem of social reorganization catalyzed by demographic, economic, legal, and administrative changes in early modern England.[23]

These changes meant that Renaissance writers could not easily identify themselves as "authors" in the modern or ancient sense of the term. Certainly past writers were well established within a more aesthetically defined literary canon: Dante, Virgil, Petrarch, Ovid, Chaucer. But classical and

---

[22]The resumption of outdated sumptuary laws testifies to the nobility's interest in preventing marginal gentry from encroaching on aristocratic privilege; numerous studies have documented these concerns about social mobility. See Lisa Jardine's summary of sumptuary laws in *Still Harping on Daughters: Women and Drama in the Age of Shakespeare* (1983; reprint, New York: Columbia University Press, 1989), 141–68. But for a critique of scholarly practices that validate this faultline, see Rosemary Kegl, "'Those Terrible Aproches': Sexuality, Social Mobility, and Resisting the Courtliness of Puttenham's *The Arte of English Poesie*," *English Literary Renaissance* 20 (Spring 1990): 179–208. For a broad if ahistorical study of the vital flow of information in a social system, see Harold Innis, *Empire and Communications* (Oxford: Clarendon Press, 1950).

[23]See Keith Wrightson's account of the growth of a national market and the shift in the highly stratified social makeup, in *English Society, 1580–1680*. While historians debate the extent of the dislocating effects of modernizing change during this period, they agree that the social, political, and economic order underwent some kind of transformation that necessitated rearranging social and institutional ties to accommodate new demographic and economic changes. In particular, there were precarious settlements between monarch and parliamentary powers, between growing merchant classes and fighting noble groups, and between various religious factions.

medieval authorial roles were not accessible to contemporary writers because of the prestige attached to poetic amateurism, the vitality of the institution of patronage, the court's curb on channels of ambition, and the special difficulties created by writing vernacular love poetry. Instead of banking on the legitimization offered by divine subject matter and Latin, gentlemen and aspirants to gentility wrote English poetic works as part of social commerce and entertainment in the domain of the private coterie, a group that J. W. Saunders describes as "a finishing school where members polished each other's art, which, like the taste for clothes, or the ear for a compliment, or the aptitude for dancing or fencing or riding, was very much a matter of doing the right things in the right way, in a game where every man tried to dazzle and outvie his competitors. More seriously a group restricted, ideally at least, to those who were equals or near-equals in social status . . . cooperated in the formulation of critical principles, a sense of values."[24] The political benefits of these "finishing schools" may now seem obvious: poetry, imagined as the product of an aristocratic social ethos, sustained and policed the social boundaries that defined "equals or near-equals in social status." Writing private poetry was thus an act of social classification.[25] In fact, it was Sidney's social credentials that created an ambiguous legacy for later writers: his refusal to publish set a powerful precedent for withholding poetry from the press, yet the posthumous publication of his works carved out a newly defined gentlemanly authorial role. Later writers had to tap-dance around this ambiguous cultural authorization. Spenser, who was in all probability eager to take advantage of the press, found it expedient to ratify the privilege associated with private texts when he begged his friend Gabriel Harvey to keep his verse "close." Even Thomas Nashe, an aspiring professional writer with seemingly few real qualms about appearing as "a man in print," voiced the language of authorial reluctance and shame.[26] Such writers confirmed the

---

[24]J. W. Saunders, *The Profession of English Letters* (London: Routledge and Kegan Paul, 1964), 43. See also Phoebe Sheavyn, *The Literary Profession in the Elizabethan Age* (Manchester: Manchester University Press, 1909).

[25]On the importance of rank, see Lawrence Stone, *An Open Elite? England, 1540–1880* (Oxford: Clarendon Press, 1984); Whigham, *Ambition and Privilege*; and Ruth Kelso, *Doctrine for the English Gentleman in the Sixteenth Century* (Gloucester, Mass.: Peter Smith, 1964). Louis Montrose documents the controversy over definitions and genealogies of gentility in "Of Gentleman and Shepherds."

[26]In the introductory apparatus to *Pierce Penilesse His Supplication to the Divell* (1592), Nashe tells his dedicatee: "Faith I am verie sorrie (Sir) I am thus unawares betrayed to infamie. You write me my book is hasting to the second impression: . . . It was abroad a fortnight ere I knewe of it, & uncorrected and unfinished it hath offred it selfe to the open scorne of the worlde." Reprinted in *Works*, ed. R. B. McKerrow, revised F. P. Wilson, 5 vols. (Oxford: Basil Blackwell, 1958), 1:153.

prestige given to the genteel system of manuscript exchange, a system that protected social capital through staged poetic rivalry among men.[27] If authorship was a vexed *textual* issue in both medieval and contemporary manuscript circulation, then its incompatibility with a gentlemanly amateurism made it *socially* problematic as well.

Despite such obstacles and prohibitions, writers began to find it advantageous to circulate their names and texts through a more far-reaching medium when print production became cheaper and the literacy rate increased at the turn of the century. According to H. S. Bennett, the output of printed titles almost doubled between 1558 and the 1580s; after 1580 there was a steady increase in book production.[28] Although the technology had been available for more than one hundred years, print became "Englished" only in the last half of the sixteenth century, when native printers began to cut their own type and produce their own paper.[29] Publishers and printers, eager to increase their markets, sought to devise a kind of book that was intelligible to their new audiences. The result of these changes was not only an increased awareness of the possibilities of commercially viable mass production and its new affordability, but also a crystallization of the social tensions that had made print a controversial avenue for midcentury writers to pursue.[30]

It is not surprising that publication figured in Renaissance mythography as a transgressive power. Legend has it, for instance, that when John Fust tried to distribute the first series of Bibles from the Gutenberg-Schoeffer

[27]The term "social capital" is from Pierre Bordieu, "Forms of Capital," in *Handbook of Theory and Research for the Sociology of Education*, ed. John G. Richardson (New York: Greenwood Press, 1986), 248. My work acknowledges that the coterie used the circulation of texts to consolidate the bonds formed among an elite and primarily male group. For a theorization of homosociality within the dynamic of male poetic rivalry, see Eve Sedgwick, *Between Men: English Literature and Male Homosocial Desire* (New York: Columbia University Press, 1985).

[28]H. S. Bennett, *English Books and Readers 1558–1603* (Cambridge: Cambridge University Press, 1965), 269–71. According to Bennett, the number of books increased from 125 to 202 between 1560 and 1580, and for every four items published in the first two decades of Elizabeth's reign, there were six published in the last two. In an earlier study, *English Books and Readers 1475–1557* (Cambridge: Cambridge University Press, 1952), Bennett notes that there were fifty-four books published in 1500, a figure that increased fourfold in the 1550s.

[29]Colin Clair, *A History of Printing in Britain* (New York: Oxford University Press, 1966), 1–2.

[30]Ann Baynes Coiro outlines how the dramatically different political climate of the 1630s and 1640s fostered new social meanings for manuscript and print circulation. During this time, Coiro argues, manuscript transmission was not solely or centrally identified as an elite practice, but as a potentially subversive mode of writing, determined as such simply by the fact that it evaded state censors. Coiro's study complements mine by offering a crucial explanatory narrative about the social valence of print and literary authorship later in the seventeenth century. "Milton and Class Identity: The Publication of *Areopagitica* and the 1645 *Poems*," *Journal of Medieval and Renaissance Studies* 22 (Spring 1992): 261–89.

press, the Parisian book guild, astonished that he had not one but twelve such valuable items, branded him a devil and ran him out of town. The yoking of demonry with the fantastic power to create multiple copies of the same book was matched by other, more positive associations between printing and divine power.[31] More commonly, however, writers registered their anxieties through earthly sets of oppositions, particularly those constructed along the axis of gender. Given that part of the threat of publication was its encouragement of a female readership, it is hardly surprising that gender served as an important idiom for managing and organizing anxieties about the press. One of John Harington's epigrams, for instance, voices the courtier's disdain for publication, noting of his Muse

> Myne never sought to set to sale her wryting
> In part her friends, in all her self delighting
> She cannot beg applause of vulgar sort,
> Free born and bred, more free for noble sport.[32]

Fending off the expanding marketplace that he felt would jeopardize the institution of patronage, Harington opts to preserve the "sport" of a private literary exchange that excludes the "vulgar sort," and he interestingly articulates this defense through an appeal to his Muse's female modesty. Manuscript culture offers his Muse a "free" arena in which she can conduct herself in a noble and dignified manner. Print, on the other hand, threatens to make her a prostitute.

In one of his poems, John Davies similarly expresses an aristocratic resistance to publication. Davies notes that publishing subjects the writer to the common and vulgar verse circulating in the marketplace:

[31]In *The Book of Martyrs*, for instance, John Foxe describes the press as a miraculous tool designed to facilitate God's redemptive plan in human history. "Through the light of printing," he claims, "the world beginneth now to have eyes to see, heads to judge. . . . By this printing, as by the gift of tongues, and as by the singular organ of the Holy Ghost, the doctrine of the gospel soundeth to all nations and countries under heaven." John Foxe, *Actes and Monuments of John Foxe*, ed. G. Townsend (London: Seeleys, 1885), vol. 3, pt. 2:720. Cited by John N. Wall, "The Reformation in England and the Typographical Revolution: 'By this printing . . . the doctrine of the Gospel soundeth to all nations,'" *Print and Culture in the Renaissance*, ed. Gerald P. Tyson and Sylvia S. Wagonheim (Newark: University of Delaware Press, 1986), 210–11. Elizabeth Eisenstein tells the anecdote about John Fust and the Paris book guild in *The Printing Press as an Agent of Change*, 49.

[32]John Harington, *Letters and Epigrams of Sir John Harington*, ed. Norman Egbert McClure (Philadelphia: University of Pennsylvania Press, 1930), no. 424, 320. See also his "A Comfort for Poore Poets" (164), a poem which similarly reveals Harington's anxiety that the amateur gentlemen has lost his place to the profiting author.

> . . . you well know the Presse so much is wrong'd,
>   by abject Rimers that great Hearts doe scorne
> To have their Measures with such Nombers throng'd,
>   as are so basely got, conceiv'd, and borne.[33]

In complaining that the press itself has been degraded by the outpouring of poor verse, Davies defends the print medium against its unfair stigmatization. But in doing so he unwittingly becomes circumscribed by his own language, for he portrays the literary marketplace as a site of social deterioration and sexual scandal. To publish is to place one's measured and civil self amid the vulgar "throng" of numbers (here both meter and crowds)—verse that is produced by illicit sexual behavior and that results in the contamination of family lineage: "basely got, conceiv'd, and borne." Davies's rich description of how bastard poetry wrongs the press has the paradoxical effect of reproducing the stigma against which he ostensibly writes. Like Harington, Davies makes bookselling a kind of brothel, a place of sordid mingling.

According to Harington's nervous commentary, the literary marketplace restricts texts by wresting away their free play; the movement from leisurely game to commodified product is carried out by a measure of control that cheapens the entire project of writing. In Davies's ill-conceived defense, publication remains tainted by the abjectness of the vulgar throng. These poetic commentaries constitute just two versions of the many different figurations of publication written during this time. While Harington's fears were in part unfounded—increases in print technology did not produce a sudden democratization of literary and social practices or a drastic change in literacy rates[34]—his articulation of the problem of textual authority, like Davies's, was crucial within the larger and ongoing reconceptualization of authorship and gender. Implicit in their comments on the press were particular constructions of gender difference itself.

[33]John Davies, *The Muses Sacrifice*, in *The Complete Works of John Davies*, ed. Alexander B. Grosart, 2 vols. (Edinburgh: Chertsey Worthies' Library, 1878), 2:l, 5.

[34]See David Cressy, *Literacy and the Social Order: Reading and Writing in Tudor and Stuart England* (Cambridge: Cambridge University Press, 1980). Cressy explains that while publication records, education, and book ownership are all inadequate ways to prove shifts in literacy, when taken together, they point to an increasingly literate population in the late sixteenth and early seventeenth centuries. Cressy makes this claim only after painstakingly qualifying the extent of that increase, pointing out, for instance, that "oral culture . . . with its traditions and tales, its proverbs and jokes, customs and ceremonies, offered enough in the way of entertainment and enrichment to sustain a satisfactory alternative" (13). I would suggest that because a relatively small but powerful portion of the population perceived printing as bound up with the larger question of social mobility, publication became vastly important in reconceptualizing the domain of knowledge, even if only a small percentage of the population was literate.

Ben Jonson's proud announcement of a new authorial role in the publication of his 1616 *Works* offers the most critically acclaimed and self-conscious version of the reconceptualization of Renaissance public writing. But it also serves as evidence that the political stakes of publishing had drastically changed since the mid-sixteenth century. It becomes clear that the "stigma of print" at the end of the century was curiously produced as much by the rhetoric of printed texts themselves as by the fact that texts were actually withheld from the press. The bizarre apologies, justifications, and dedications of the early modern printed text certainly indicate that publishing writers did indeed face a difficult problem: the fact that culturally sanctioned verse was "unauthored" while authored published works were socially "unauthorized." However, writers began to manipulate the "stigma of print" by encoding it in terms that allowed them other kinds of authorization; that is, they reproduced this stigma in published works as a way of safeguarding class distinctions and at the same time displaced it onto sexual ideologies that reinforced the writers' masculine authority. While responding in part to real and perceived class issues, writers, printers, and publishers used the rhetoric of publication to reshape notions of writing itself—to redeem the unauthorized nature of the manuscript and generate a new dispensation for textual production and governance.

In locating this dispensation within a matrix of social, political, technological, and typographical changes, I build on the important work of Richard Helgerson, whose monumental study of the "laureate" identity in the Renaissance has called attention to the social conditions of authorship.[35] I suggest that the emerging "laureate" can be seen as an extension of a reconceptualization of authorship itself, whose formation can best be understood by seeing the bizarre ways in which writers encoded class and gender when representing the materiality of their work. I also offer a nar-

[35]Richard Helgerson argues that the sixteenth century saw a newly dignified and enduring category of authorship rise from the normative crisis precipitated by Protestant reform, humanism, and a growing nationalist ideology. According to Helgerson, a group of young, elite Englishmen in the late sixteenth and early seventeenth centuries turned their attention to the collective project of rescuing poetry from its association with a disreputable and wasteful amateurism, and recruiting it in the service of a national literature. *Self-Crowned Laureates*, crucial for its unprecedented attention to self-identifying authorial strategies, has paved the way for further analysis of the precise configurations of rank and gender that went into that scripting. For the authority that Renaissance writers held was not just the result of a "self-crowning," but also part and parcel of the problems catalyzed by changes in patronage, print, and the marketplace. In noting that Renaissance poets worked to dismantle the view of poetry as a merely gentlemanly pastime, we may forget that "gentlemanly" pastimes had vast cultural value. The role of authorship becomes intertwined with the class politics of manuscript and print and the highly gendered language used to address that embraiding.

rative that complements important work on Ben Jonson's role in shaping authorship.[36] Recent critical attention to Jonson has tended to concentrate on the fact that theater served as a foil for the printed text. Precisely because the theater was viewed as heterogeneous and hybrid, collaborative in its mode of production and liminal in its cultural and geographical space, it proved a popular site for introducing and foregrounding the governing force of the author.[37] The theatrical script was considered both textually and socially unruly—unstable because it was multiply produced and illegitimate because it was connected with class hybridization and sexual license. Critics have thus argued that Jonson's active participation in the printshop and his editorial interventions allowed him to generate a "bibliographic ego" (Joseph Loewenstein) and a "textual sovereignty" (Timothy Murray) over and against the transgressive, unofficial force of theater. Jonson established himself as a central figure by highlighting the qualities of the printed artifact, to which he had more of a proprietary claim, over those of the collective performance (Stephen Orgel). By establishing a printed text set in contradistinction to the protean theatrical script, and by allegorically rejecting popular festivity and theatricality within his plays, Jonson presented the author as a powerful cultural and literary figure. Aware of both the textual and cultural inhibitions to theatrical "authority," Jonson published his folio *Works* to legitimate the author as both a stable textual function (through his control over textual architectonics) and a respectable social role (through strong evocations of classical precedent).

By explaining how Jonson constituted an identity against the theater, we may forget that he participated in a general modification of the idea of the book itself, not just the theatrical script. Looking at coterie textual practices reminds us that Jonson could not simply gather plays within the legitimate rubric of poetry; he had to redeem published poetry as well. Jonson's *Works* situated his writings not merely against "theatrical vulnerability" (Murray), but also against unauthorized and protean coterie textual

[36]See Murray, *Theatrical Legitimation*, especially 64–93; Don Wayne, "Drama and Society in the Age of Jonson: An Alternative View," *Renaissance Drama* 13 (1982): 103–29; Orgel, "What Is a Text?"; Loewenstein, "The Script in the Marketplace," 265–78; Richard Newton, "Jonson and the (Re-) Invention of the Book," in *Classic and Cavalier: Essays on Jonson and the Sons of Ben*, ed. Claude Summers and Ted-Larry Pebworth (Pittsburgh: University of Pittsburgh Press, 1982), 31–55; and Stallybrass and White, *The Politics and Poetics of Transgression*.

[37]For a study of collaborative practices, see Gerald Eades Bentley, *The Profession of Dramatist in Shakespeare's Time: 1590–1642* (Princeton: Princeton University Press, 1971); and Jeff Masten, "Beaumont and/or Fletcher: Collaboration and the Interpretation of Renaissance Drama," *ELH* 59 (1992): 337–59. On the theater's cultural place, see Steven Mullaney, *The Place of the Stage: License, Play and Power in Renaissance England* (Chicago: University of Chicago Press, 1988).

practices. While theatrical texts were more illegitimate than poetic ones (dramatic works were excluded, for instance, from Sir Thomas Bodley's Oxford library), they were not categorically more unstable than other kinds of texts. Nondramatic manuscript poems were just as alterable as the textually unstable and transitory scripts of the playhouse. Private transmission did not afford either an authorized text or a category of poetic authorship against which theatricality could neatly be pitted. Instead, both coterie texts and play texts were collaboratively produced, and both registered the permutations implicated in their individual modes of production. Jonson's editorial labor can thus be seen as an extension of the efforts made by other publishing poets as they tackled the tricky business of scripting literary authority. While absent from my analysis, Jonson occupies the margins of this work: he was exceptional in his self-conscious reformulation of authorship, but his self-monumentalizing was part of an ongoing revision of textual authority deeply enmeshed in the social controversies surrounding publication. If authorship was both enabled and haunted by the fantasized "low" of theatricality, as Peter Stallybrass and Allon White claim in *The Politics and Poetics of Transgression,* it was also enabled and haunted by the fantasized "high" of aristocratic coterie culture.

I employ a seemingly unstable and contradictory definition of authorship in this book for the simple reason that Renaissance authorship emerges in radically different ways—as the cumulative product of individual writers' "intentionalist" strategies and as a by-product of the social controversies surrounding the literary marketplace. In Chapters 1 and 2, for instance, I explore how authorship appears as a typographical effect when textual producers adapt ephemeral, collective, and highly social aristocratic texts—miscellaneous poems and panegyric pageants—for publication. Chapter 1 argues that certain gendered elements of Petrarchan rhetoric became central to poets and publishers when they put manuscript-identified love sonnets into print. The second chapter looks at courtly pageants to see how the eroticized political engagement between male courtier and female sovereign became important in shaping the literary authority of Philip Sidney and George Gascoigne. I then turn to consider the writer's agency in scripting a sanctioned authorial role through carefully designed modes of self-presentation. The first two chapters highlight the typographical authorizations produced in printed books, the next two emphasize the gendering of publication that occurs in prefatory material. Chapters 3 and 4 describe how writers devised two tropes—voyeurism and cross-dressing—as a means of deflecting the problems of literary and print authority onto more volatile cultural divides. Each of these chapters offers concrete examples of how versions of masculinized authorship were created. Chapter 5 analyzes the forms in which women published as they renegotiated the gender ideolo-

built into the concept of the "author." We can understand the problems that women writers faced in breaking into print more clearly, I argue, by reading their works within the context of widespread anxieties about authorship and publication. Conversely, it is time that accounts of authorship in early modern England include these writers' alternative models for fashioning literary authority. Throughout the book, I search typographical, rhetorical, and narrative figurations of public writing to see how they stage literary authority; what I have found is that a simple and fixed paradigm of Renaissance authorship is both ahistorical and inadequate.

Calling attention to the importance of rhetoric in assessing literary authority and print practices sends out a signal, I think, that we should move away from analyzing print solely in philosophical and abstract terms. Instead, the effects of the press can be understood most clearly when they are related to the press's contradictory social place at different moments in history. My work thus argues against technological determinism.[38] The new status of Renaissance authorship may have been enabled by print, but print certainly did not ensure a specific textual authority governed by the intrinsic logic of the technology itself. Rather the emergent "author" turns out to be merely one possibility among many for understanding literary works. Because authorship is now such a seductive and naturalized category of reading and because after the Renaissance it acquired status as the most enduring and characteristic means of interpretation, one can easily forget that this concept has a complicated history, in which it serves different textual and ideological functions. My reading can thus be counterposed to studies of "print logic," which claim that print transforms the social order into a uniform, fixed, and totalized world.[39] In this book I shy away from essentialist claims about the stabilizing nature of print, and work instead to make visible a set of "local histories" that illuminate the social place of literary publication and denaturalize the textual authority it affords. My interest is in complicating the humanist postulate that print's massive sin-

[38]One important foundationalist Marxist account is offered by Walter Benjamin, "The Work of Art in the Age of Mechanical Reproduction," in *Illuminations* (New York: Harcourt Brace and World, 1969), 217–52.

[39]One case in point is Elizabeth Eisenstein's monumental study of the epistemological and cognitive transformations brought about by print technology (*The Printing Press as an Agent of Change*). For print historians taking this line, see Marshall McLuhan, *The Gutenberg Galaxy: The Making of Typographic Man* (Toronto: University of Toronto Press, 1962); Ong, *Interfaces of the Word*; and Alvin Kernan, *Printing Technology, Letters, and Samuel Johnson* (Princeton: Princeton University Press, 1987). But for a critique of the essentialist notion of print, see Michael Warner, *The Letters of the Republic: Publication and the Public Sphere in Eighteenth-Century America* (Cambridge, Mass.: Harvard University Press, 1990), 1–19. Timothy Murray also questions the collision of writing and printing in McLuhanite works (*Theatrical Legitimation*, 61–62).

gle effect was to disseminate knowledge and spread literacy; instead, I want to make visible the various politics that defined and were defined by this medium.

Underlying this investigation is a belief that we can understand Renaissance authorship in its more elevated literary sense by seeing it as intricately linked to practices of textual transmission and to the ways in which those practices were understood and represented. I do not mean to suggest that the modern author really existed in an earlier period than is generally critically accepted, or to make the case that it was invented during the Renaissance.[40] Rather, I use the term "author" warily to indicate a set of provisional and sometimes contradictory roles that had not yet fully melded into our modern definition. I point to the importance of remembering the contingency, historicity, and instability of the very category of the "author," a concept that, in various permutations, goes on to become a critical and lasting literary convention. In the early modern period, writers, printers, and compilers rethought manuscript authority and printed literary wares through a wealth of tropes, forms, and textual apparatuses; as a result, they devised a language of justification and disavowal that activated various gendered dynamics and subsequently promoted gendered models of Renaissance authorship. "It is not my ambition," we hear Dekker declare, "to be a Man in Print." In disclosing some aspects of the historical formation of this literary concept, we make clear the ideological residue from early modern England that informs it. Because part of this residue involves gender difference, histories of authorship speak to the issue of women's writing, querying in particular the place of "the author" in feminist critique.[41] In more general terms, an examination of Renaissance publication vivifies how literary authority is inextricably bound up with political authority. Historicizing the author—investigating what it meant to be a Renaissance "man in print"—can allow us to comprehend the complexities attached to the author-figure and to see how versions of this figure are invented to fit the determinate needs of specific historical situations. It seems that authors are made and unmade in some form in every

[40]Although there is still critical debate over the precise date and cause, the appearance of the modern "author" is usually understood to be an epiphenomenon of the eighteenth-century institutionalization of letters, as Martha Woodmansee argues in "The Genius and the Copyright: Economic and Legal Conditions of the Emergence of the 'Author,'" *Eighteenth-Century Studies* 17 (1984): 425–48. In describing the types of authorial identity that became available in the late sixteenth century, I attempt to broaden and problematize both the notion of the author and the historical narratives to which it gave rise.

[41]For a lucid critique of Sandra Gilbert's and Susan Gubar's notion of authorship that demonstrates the problems this conceptual paradigm raises for feminist practices, see Toril Moi, *Sexual/Textual Politics: Feminist Literary Theory* (New York: Methuen, 1985), 57–69.

time period. By being conscious of the relationship between literary authorship and its past and present cultural authorizations, we can ideally unthink the seeming inevitability of our own critical categories and imperatives, and instead glimpse radically different ways of organizing, conceptualizing, and reading literary texts.[42]

[42]In her introduction to *Shakespeare Verbatim*, Margreta de Grazia explains her specific interest in unpacking the historicity of textual "authenticity" and thus countering interpretations that assume it as a critical imperative. The concept of Shakespearean authenticity was constructed, she argues, within the textual apparatus of Edmund Malone's 1790 edition. What de Grazia says of the apparatus can equally be applied to the category of authorship itself: "To recognize the synthetic and contingent nature of the Shakespearean apparatus is to allow for the possibility of its being otherwise. Once the apparatus is situated in relation to historical exigency, its conceptual grip begins to weaken. The very act of turning it into a subject of attention undermines its authority, for the apparatus can work only if it appears inert, optional; dispensable, even" (13). It is only by investigating the material, social, and textual conditions of Renaissance literary authority and thus seeing its relation to historical exigency that we can be self-conscious about the politics from which it emerged and the varied politics it can be made to support.

CHAPTER ONE

TURNING SONNET:
The *Politics* and *Poetics*
of *Sonnet Circulation*

Assist me, some extemporal god of rhyme, for I am sure I shall
turn sonnet. . . . Devise, wit; write, pen; for I am
for whole volumes in folio.
—*Love's Labour's Lost*

I have a sonnet that will serve the turn.
—*Two Gentlemen of Verona*

"IT IS A SIMPLE FACT of our reading experience," Neil Fraistat remarks in the preface to *Poems in Their Place*, "that poems take place . . . 'as a function of a Book.'" He goes on to explain: "That is to say that the book—with all of its informing contexts—is the meeting ground for poet and reader, the 'situation' in which its constituent texts occur. As such, the book is constantly conditioning the reader's responses, activating various sets of what semioticians call 'interpretative codes.'"[1] Fraistat's observation acts as a reminder that "texts" are consumed within physical forms that themselves possess and dictate meaning. This "simple fact" is obviously quite complicated in historical periods in which there are contradictory reading practices, some not at all dependent on the concept of the book. Sixteenth-century literature is a case in point; for these works are made to accommodate the interpretative codes generated by the "situation" of patronage as well as those expectations that evolved with the increased popularity of the book market.

Tottels Miscellany exemplifies in strong form the bizarre phenomenon that we call the English Renaissance book, for it reveals the difficulties publishers and writers faced in accommodating the diverse conditions of manuscript and print. The miscellaneous quality of *Tottels* can be disori-

---

[1]Neil Fraistat, introduction to *Poems in Their Place: The Intertextuality and Order of Poetic Collections*, ed. Neil Fraistat (Chapel Hill: University of North Carolina Press, 1986), 3.

enting to a modern reader who expects to find the conventional "informing context" of the modern book. The poems in *Tottels* alternate wildly in tone as well as genre. While comprised centrally of love poems and complaints, the text also indiscriminately collates epigrams, riddles, satires, psalms, elegies, and moral aphorisms. In presenting these different genres, the book serves as a virtual encyclopedia of metrical patterns and rhythmic forms. *Tottels* seems to be neatly divided into four sections that are classified by author—Henry Howard (Earl of Surrey), Thomas Wyatt, Nicholas Grimald, and "uncertain authors." But the book's four sections provide an organizational framework, which by its extraordinary permeability disorganizes and confuses the reading experience. Poems by various writers seep into these seemingly compartmentalized and categorized sections, and the book ends by recounting poems that were inadvertently omitted from the primary sections. The effect is a makeshift, authorially determined cataloguing format that fails to respect fully the classification system it offers. The format is not the only source of confusion for a modern reader. *Tottels* reveals irregularities in its pagination and title page as well. Surrey is advertised as the primary author, the book announces, but the reader finds that Surrey has written only 40 of the 213 poems in the collection, only half as many as were authored by Wyatt. The text thus offers no readily comprehensible generic, authorial, or structural order.

Given the apparent disorderliness of the book, it may be difficult for us to grasp just how easily *Tottels* found a niche in the literary market. First published in 1557, the text quickly went through three editions in just seven weeks, and was issued seven more times between 1557 and 1587. Rather than finding its format alien, contemporary readers were comfortable with its heterogeneous make-up. While it may or may not be one of the most important single volumes in the history of English literature, as some have claimed, it certainly was *the* handbook for Elizabethan poets. *Tottels* inspired a series of mid-Tudor poetic collections (including George Turberville's *Epitaphs, Epigrams, Songs, and Sonnets* and Barnabe Googe's *Eclogues, Epitaphs, and Sonnets*), served as the prototype for the outpouring of miscellanies for the next fifty years, and became a central literary model for the highly popular sonnet cycles later in the century.[2]

---

[2] *Tottels Miscellany* (*Songes and Sonettes*), STC 13860 (1557). In the introduction to his edition, Rollins analyzes the influence of *Tottels Miscellany* on Renaissance poetry, noting at one point that this text was "largely responsible" for the "magnificent outburst of lyricism" later in the century [*Tottel's Miscellany*, ed. Hyder Rollins, 2 vols. (Cambridge, Mass.: Harvard University Press, 1928–29) 2:107–24]. For other accounts of its influence, see Vere L. Rubel, *Poetic Diction in the English Renaissance from Skelton through Spenser* (Oxford: Oxford University Press, 1941); John Thompson, *The Founding of English Metre* (New York: Columbia University Press, 1961); and a negative evaluation by Raymond Southall, *The Courtly Maker:*

If we look at one feature of this heterogeneous and influential text—the "title" markers to the individual poems—we discover that Richard Tottel identifies his book both as a typographical printed object and as a socially embedded manuscript text. The poems are frequently named according to their original occasion ("N. Vincent to G. Blackwood agaynst wedding," "a song written by the earle of Surrey to a lady that refused to daunce with him"), although labeled as well by their subject ("the lover complaineth himself forsaken") and by their exemplification of conventional maxim ("the mean estate is best"). In the first of these groupings, the poems are introduced as textual traces identified by their placement in social transactions. Although formally finished in terms of meter and rhyme, the poems offer titles that define them more as active elements in social situations and less as freestanding literary artifacts. By introducing poems according to their utility, *Tottels Miscellany* stages a collision between poetry in its social environment and in its typographical form.

In his preface, Tottel praises the poems in terms that accentuate their liminal status. "To have well written in verse, yea and in small parcelles," he states, "deserveth great praise" (2). His use of the word "parcelles" to describe the poems is quite telling, not only because he points to the lyric poem's ability to straddle seemingly contradictory formal positions ("parcelle" meaning both an assemblage of diverse parts and a constituent portion of a larger whole), but also because he names poetry by its placement within coterie circuits: as "parcelles" to be sent.[3] *Tottels*, which by virtue of its published form necessarily subsumes the social within the typographical, nevertheless chooses to mark its poetry by a nonprint function. In fact, not only the foregrounding of the poetry's occasional status but also the work's very heterogeneous format aligns it with manuscript texts; for manuscript forms are deemed to be "open" in that they inspire the reader to reassemble literary material rather than to admire its cohesion within a totality.

In this miscellany we find evidence that the heterogeneity and openness of occasional verse had class implications in the sixteenth century. *Tottels* is a fascinating text because it makes visible, even as it challenges by virtue of its very existence, the "stigma of print" described in a now classic article

---

An Essay on the Poetry of Wyatt and His Contemporaries (New York: Barnes and Noble, 1964). These accounts and others are surveyed by Elizabeth Pomeroy in *The Elizabethan Miscellanies: Their Development and Conventions* (Berkeley: University of California Press, 1973), 31–35.

[3]According to the *Oxford English Dictionary*, the definition of "parcel" as a package to be sent was first used in the mid-sixteenth century, although it was not a central meaning for the word until later centuries, when with the development of the mail systems, the "parcel post" became a more common phrase.

by J. W. Saunders.[4] *Tottels* makes evident the existence of a real "stigma" at mid-century simply by the fact that it discloses to the public the poems circulating privately that writers had chosen to keep from the realm of print. This information suggests to us that print was not central for establishing the particular kind of authority that these writers sought. For the courtier, print could damage rather than enhance social status. *Tottels* retrospectively places such writers in a socially stigmatized zone, fashioning them as published authors who, while not in control of their poems' circulation, are nevertheless publicly identified with saleable books. But if Tottel makes writers into authors posthumously, he does not arrogate to them the sovereign authorial role of guiding the reader's perception of the poems. Instead, *Tottels* promotes a view of authorship as a flexible and provisional construct. Literary effort here is authorized as much by the poem's placement within the privileged circuit of presentation and receipt as by its status as personal utterance or finished craft. The poetic title markers emphasizing poetry's function in a system of reciprocal obligations point to occasions in which writers originally may have used, or did use, their poems. While *Tottels*'s appearance in print reveals its departure from the conventions of manuscript culture, it re-presents that culture through its organization of poetic material.

The controversial nature of publication is registered in the preliminary apparatus to the book. In his preface, Tottel feels compelled to justify his release of previously circulating private poems to a more general and undifferentiated public. "It resteth now, (*gentle* reder)," he announces, "that thou thinke it not evill doone, to publish, to the honor of the English tong, and for profit of the studious of English eloquence, those workes which the *ungentle* horders up of such treasure have heretofore envied thee" (2, my emphasis). In labeling the "horders" of such texts as "ungentle," Tottel reverses the class distinctions generated by coterie circulation, inscribing the act of publishing as the more noble, "gentle" mode of exchange and the book reader as the truly "gentle" kind of textual consumer. The economic metaphor here is especially resonant given that hoarding was a vice particularly repellant to members of the aristocracy. In order to set themselves apart from the growing merchant class, the nobility advertised ostentatious expenditure, lavish liberality, and conspicuous consumption. In short, they labored to be seen as "free of purse." In his preface, Tottel takes pains to equate liberality with the free circulation of texts. This restructuring of the typical coding—common print and no-

---

[4]See J. W. Saunders, "The Stigma of Print: A Note on the Social Bases of Tudor Poetry," *Essays in Criticism* 1 (1951): 139–64.

ble handwriting—is done within a nationalist project that set out to redeem English verse by validating the means by which the vernacular could be publicized. Tottel, who was both a scholar and a printer, sought to disclaim the reputed "evill" of publishing in order to safeguard the medium by which English poetry was to be proven.

By using an aristocratic value to criticize an aristocratic practice (the hoarding of private texts), Tottel employs a rhetorical move that later serves other writers. The prefatorial material to Barnabe Googe's 1563 poetic collection notes the "niggardly" character of private circulation.[5] And in the introduction to his 1581 translation of the courtesy handbook *The Civile Conversation of M. Steeven Guazzo*, George Pettie seeks to dignify publication through a similar strategy:

> Those which myslike that a Gentleman should publish the fruites of his learning, are some curious Gentlemen, who thynke it most commendable in a Gentleman, to cloake his arte and skill in every thyng, and to seeme to doo all thynges of his owne mother witte as it were: not considering how we deserve no prayse for that, which God or Nature hath bestowed upon us, but only for that, which we purchace by our owne industry: and if you shall chaunce to enter into reasonyng with them, they wyll at the seconde woorde make protestation that they are no Schollers: whereas notwithstanding they have spent all theyr tyme in studie. Why Gentlemen, is it a shame to shewe to be that, which it is a shame not to bee? . . . Alas you wyll be but *ungentle Gentlemen*, yf you be no Schollers: you wyll doo your Prince but simple service; you wyll stande your Countrey but in slender steade, you wyll bryng your selves but to small preferment, yf you be no Schollers. Can you counsayle your Prince wysely, foresee daungers providently, governe matters of state discreetly, without Learning? . . . To come lower, can you discourse with Strangers, inquire the state of forraine Countries, geve entertainement to Ambassadours, being no Schollers? . . . To come lowest of all, Can you so much as tell your Mistresse a fine tale, or delight her with pleasant device, beyng unlearned? . . . Therefore (Gentlemen) never deny your selves to be Schollers, never be ashamed to shewe your learnyng, confesse it, professe it, imbrace it, honor it: for it is it which honoureth you, *it is only it which maketh*

---

[5]Here L. Blundeston, the compiler of Googe's *Eclogues, Epitaphs, and Sonnets*, banks on the aristocratic value of expenditure in presenting the text. He tells the reader to "encourage others to make thee partaker of the like or far greater jewels, who yet doubting thy unthankful receipt niggardly keep them to their own use and private commodity, whereas being assured of the contrary by the friendly report of other men's travails, they could perhaps be easily entreated more freely to lend them abroad to thy greater avail and furtherance." Barnabe Googe, *Eclogues, Epitaphs, and Sonnets*, STC 12048 (1563), ed. Judith M. Kennedy (Toronto: University of Toronto Press, 1989), 38.

you men, it is onely it whiche maketh you Gentlemen. . . . And this I hope will satis-
fie those which mislike that Gentlemen should publish the fruit of their studies.
(emphasis mine)[6]

I quote this passage at length because it expresses more fully the concerns
mentioned elliptically in Tottel's preface. Pettie counters the stigma of
print by sarcastically exposing the hypocrisy of *sprezzatura*. He points out
the folly of dedicating time to scholarly pursuits only to devalue such learning disingenuously. Here publication is aligned with the dignity of work
itself; and gentility is redefined against the noble values of leisure and of
the "mother witte." In fact, the pretense of cloaking one's learning makes
one an "ungentle Gentleman," someone unfit to serve the needs of one's
country, monarch, or mistress. Publication becomes the imperative, rather
than the inhibiting factor, for establishing a claim to both social status and
manhood. But Pettie's argument seems to be undercut when he nervously
justifes his own previous poetic work. *A petite Pallace of Pettie his pleasure,* he
claims, was an unauthorized and trifling publication that "escaped" his private hand. Pettie's troubled justification for his own move into print, however, can be read as proof of the seriousness of his later claim—his impassioned cry for license to publish without the need for apology. In arguing
that literary display is compatible with the most noble of interests, Pettie
echoes Tottel's justification of the *Miscellany.* Both writers pit two values of
the good courtier against one another as a way of scrambling normative
social codes. Tottel's terms of justification, it seems, offer an important
rhetoric for legitimizing publication.

Tottel further authorizes his text by differentiating his work from those
appreciated by the "swinelike" consumers of "rude skill." Tottel's insistent
concern with clarifying the text's social status and establishing its legitimacy
only underscores the insecurities generated by print. His book enters the
public world at a time when textual transmission was linked with vexed
social problems—in essence, when printed books were compelled to address the stigma of print. In declaring that the book showers a hoarded
poetic cache upon a deserving public, Tottel's uneasy preface re-"class"-
ifies conventional marks of status, carefully framing that reclassification
within the nationalist project of "Englishing" letters. But in the structural
presentation of the poems and by their characterization as "parcelles,"
Tottels offers a poetry still indebted to a system of manuscript exchange.
The poems in his work are entities now bereft of, but named by, their
social context, and thus his text is marked by the noncommercial system

---

[6]George Pettie, "The Preface to the Readers," introduction to Steven Guazzo, *The Civile
Conversation of M. Steeven Guazzo,* STC 12422 (1581), trans. George Pettie, reprint ed.
Charles Whibley (New York: Alfred A. Knopf, 1925), 8–9.

of manuscript circulation from which it nevertheless consciously departs. *Tottels*'s "non-book"–oriented features can be seen as part of a formal bid for social status, even as its preface seeks to legitimate the practice of publication. While the form of *Tottels Miscellany* exists in tension with its publisher's stated values, both justification and miscellaneous format are compelling in vivifying poetry's troubled social and textual status.

It is more than coincidental that a book which so self-consciously marks the social and textual problems of literary transmission also delivers an Englished discourse of love to the reading public and inspires the proliferation of the amorous English sonnet. Proving that the English language was capable of both the beauty of poetic form and of expressing the most cherished truths, *Tottels* was seen as crucially important for the aspiring courtier's humanist education. Known specifically as the book of *Songes and Sonettes*, this miscellany became essential reading for the serious student of poetry as well for those interested in the overlapping activities of courtship and courtiership. Easily transcribed, framed within other contexts, attached to gifts, and read aloud in social settings, the physical size of the sonnet made it popular as coterie occasional verse and indispensable to both courtly love and the system of patronage. Numerous legends tell us how sonnets were used both to sue for favor in Elizabeth's court and to bargain for love. Obsessively concerned with courtly love, these poems became prime texts for acts of requesting and for displays of rhetorical and metrical prowess. Thus, the sonnet was crucial reading for the courtier who sought simultaneously to barter within the highly competitive court and to create an Englished version of the literarily sanctioned discourse of love. Because he lists courting as a skill that makes one a gentleman, Pettie's introduction gives an explicit statement of the compatibility of these practices. "Can you so much as tell your Mistresse a fine tale, or delight her with pleasant device, beyng unlearned?" he asks. Pettie goes on to answer his own question when he suggests that publishing the fruits of study confers masculinity as well as social prestige—"it is only it which maketh you men."

I begin this chapter with *Tottels* because it both introduces the problems surrounding manuscript and print transmission and documents how one printer responded to these problems through a complicated con̸f̸ tion of poetic motif and organizational frame. T̸ textual and social issues had points of connecti̸ ic transmission; it tells us that the "idea of the̸ modity" were entities being negotiated and fash̸ material format and through the rhetoric that w̸ to identify the social place of writing. I want to ̸ ments—the fact of publication, the use of occa̸

seemingly haphazard organizational framework, the rhetoric of social justification, and the presentation of highly influential love poetry—make *Tottels Miscellany* a publishing event that raises crucial questions regarding the social stakes of print and literary authority. In this chapter I tackle such questions by looking at how coterie poetic exchange informed the lyric poetry of the last half of the sixteenth century on many levels. I argue that writers design sonnets that interweave their poetry's manuscript status with the general presentation of authority and desire. When writers and publishers transform the sonnet from manuscript to print, they reinscribe the text's authority by searching out other principles of authorization, many of which rest on the gendered practices of reading and writing found within love poetry itself. In short, I see that inscriptions of exchange *within* sonnet themes prove important to understanding how they were viewed as manuscripts or as book commodities.

Recently, textual scholars have called into question the critical assumptions of the new bibliography, attacking in particular the privilege attached to the authored text. Finding a text that reflects the author's final intentions has historically overshadowed concern for the social conditions through which texts were produced, distributed, and read—for seeing other ways in which texts could be organized and classified in a given culture.[7] By seriously considering recent bibliographical and archival work that demonstrates the radically different manner in which Renaissance texts were produced, we are now in a position to understand the literary and social stakes posed by manuscript transmission and to see how these stakes changed during the move into print. Analyzing the intertwining of gender and authority in the English sonnet thus offers a way of fleshing out a conventional narrative in which the variability of the manuscript text gives way to the more literarily informed and "author(iz)ed" print commodity. I want to clarify, however, that this narrative hardly tells the entire story; nor does it confirm an ineluctable movement from manuscript to print. Therefore, at the end of the chapter I hold up the countermodel of the printed poetical miscellany, a form that places pressure on this ac-

[7]See Jerome McGann, *A Critique of Modern Textual Criticism* (Chicago: University of Chicago Press, 1983); Stephen Orgel, "What Is a Text?" *Research Opportunities in Renaissance Drama*, 2:4 (1981): 3–6; and Randall McLeod, "UnEditing Shak-speare," *Sub-Stance* 33/34 (1982): 26–55. In a talk for the Modern Language Association, Arthur Marotti offers a helpful summary: "Although the methods of author-centered editing and of analytic bibliography continue their usefulness, the idealism and scientism of both enterprises are gradually being replaced by a [mo]re social-historical conception of editing and bibliography, one which foregrounds the inter[activ]e work of editors and bibliographers." "Manuscript, Print, and the English Renaissance," [read] at a meeting of the Modern Language Association (Washington, D.C., 1989), 1–2.

count by making clear that the transformation into print, with its attendant constructions of authorship and gender, was hardly inevitable.

The Poetics of Exchange

The book was an alien environment for most sixteenth-century poetry, as Arthur Marotti explains: "In the Tudor and early Stuart periods, lyric poetry was basically a genre for gentleman-amateurs who regarded their literary 'toys' as ephemeral works that were part of a social life that also included dancing, singing, gaming, and civilized conversation. Socially prominent courtiers . . . essentially thought of poems as trifles to be transmitted in manuscript within a limited social world and not as literary monuments to be preserved in printed editions for posterity."[8]

In calling attention to the importance of nonprint literary production, Marotti uses J. W. Saunders's work on the social environment of sixteenth-century poetry to outline what I will call here a "poetics of exchange." Saunders documents how genteel English writers not only generated verse in friendly competition, but also improved and supplemented other poems when the writers so desired.[9] Barnabe Googe said he could not compose poems except in the company of friends; John Harington translated *Orlando Furioso* as a punishment exacted by the queen for his flirtation with the ladies of the court. Writing was not an individual activity performed by the romantic artist who carefully controlled the text's language. Instead, texts were seen as porous and variable scripts for performance. As lyric poems were transcribed repeatedly by various pens, they traveled into sundry households and were lodged within various other texts, attached to gifts, and made into albums and commonplace books. Numerous writers mention their carelessness in scattering their scribbled poems to friends; these writers were seemingly indifferent to their poems' circulation, readership, or preservation.[10] Certainly the trivialization of literary production

[8]Arthur Marotti, *John Donne: Coterie Poet* (Madison: University of Wisconsin Press, 1986), 3. Also see his "The Transmission of Lyric Poetry and the Institutionalizing of Literature in the English Renaissance," in *Contending Kingdoms: Historical, Psychological, and Feminist Approaches to the Literature of Sixteenth-Century England and France*, ed. Marie-Rose Logan and Peter L. Rudnytsky (Detroit: Wayne State University Press, 1991), 21–41. This portion of my argument draws significantly on Marotti's research on the compilation and circulation of Renaissance manuscript texts.

[9]See J. W. Saunders, "From Manuscript to Print: A Note on the Circulation of Poetic MSS. in the Sixteenth Century," *Proceedings of the Leeds Philosophical and Literary Society* 6 (1951): 507–28.

[10]Saunders notes that George Turberville called his poems "a handfull of written papers," while George Whetstone glibly remarked that he had abandoned his poems in loose sheets dispersed among his friends when he went abroad (514).

was part of the courtier's sprezzatura that Pettie decried—the courtier's ease in cutting the figure of a gentleman. Such characterizations, genuine or not, nevertheless generated a widespread perception of the poetic text that is incompatible with a more modern notion of the book.

When writers cite one another's unpublished works, they disclose a system of exchange operating independently from print circulation. Abraham Fraunce's in-knowledge of Sidney's yet unpublished *Arcadia*, made manifest by references in his *Arcadian Rhetoricke*, or Spenser's praise for Ralegh's unpublished *Cynthia* in the dedicatory sonnets of *The Faerie Queene*, are just two examples among many. More than merely an example of the intertextuality that characterizes all productions of meaning, these references point to the compositional practices encouraged by the lively system of textual transmission peculiar to the time period. Because Renaissance writers were trained according to principles of imitation, they collated the work that they circulated freely. By encouraging allegiance to a shared set of conventions and topoi, Renaissance humanistic training produced writing that explicitly functioned, as Germaine Warkentin explains, as "a dense network of common allusions." As an "individual variation on a set theme," she continues, the individual poem "distills the collected images of an entire tradition of culture."[11] This richly allusive mode of composition was underscored and subtended by the physical way in which texts were produced and exchanged. We need only look at the way in which commonplace books were fashioned to see the collective nature of textual production: readers compiled these books by piecing together circulated maxims, poems, and epigrams. We know from the surviving *Arundel Harington Manuscript*, for instance, that two sixteenth-century readers, John Harington father and son, assembled poems by such writers as Wyatt, Surrey, Sidney, and Queen Elizabeth, collating the various poems with each other and with the Haringtons' own poetic works. In gathering such poems into one book, readers frequently exercised their training in imitative practices. This manuscript thus exemplifies the operations of borrowing, amending, excerpting, and appropriating that constituted coterie transcription; it underscores in particular the liberties that the reader could take with literary material.[12]

Marotti offers perhaps the most striking example of the way in which a

---

[11]Germaine Warkentin, "The Meeting of the Muses: Sidney and the Mid-Tudor Poets," in *Sir Philip Sidney and the Interpretation of Renaissance Culture*, ed. Gary F. Waller and Michael D. Moore (Totowa, N.J.: Barnes and Noble, 1984), 18. In this essay, Warkentin analyzes Sidney's indebtedness to mid-Tudor poets such as Turberville, Googe, and Gascoigne.

[12]*The Arundel Harington Manuscript of Tudor Poetry*, ed. Ruth Hughey, 2 vols. (Columbus: Ohio State University Press, 1960).

specific manuscript poem could be reimagined and claimed by its Renaissance reader. While compiling his commonplace book, John Ramsey includes a poem of his own, "To the Fayrest. A Sonnett," which reproduces the blazon analogies from Spenser's *Amoretti* 64 almost verbatim.[13] After the first quatrain, Ramsey imports Spenser's exact tropes for describing the female beloved's lips, cheeks, brows, eyes, bosom, neck, breasts, and nipples.[14] While these similarities can in part be accounted for by the highly conventional nature of the conceits, Ramsey follows Spenser's precise ordering of the conventions and also includes the more idiosyncratic comparisons of "Gillyflowers" and "Cullambines." Today Ramsey's use of Spenser would be judged a blatant case of plagiarism. In the Renaissance, however, this transcription merely dramatizes in heightened form the acceptable and indeed privileged compositional methods employed by writers as they fashioned poetic works. Such imitative practices were part of a widespread system of reading and writing that prized the text as a catalyst for production and appropriation rather than as an autonomous finished artifact. Ramsey's re-presentation of Spenser's blazoned female body vivifies in its most obvious form what Marotti notes as the composite or communal authorship evident in Renaissance systems of writing, or what Walter Ong has termed the "participatory poetics" of manuscript culture.[15] Rather than the finished product of print culture, writing here is an intervention into other texts made possible by the fluid textuality of manuscript culture. The particular subject matter of this verse—the female body—points as well to the gendering of coterie writing, a subject to which I will return.

Coterie circles thus encouraged a "con-verse-ation" ("verse" from the Latin "vertere," meaning "to turn"), a turning back and forth of scripted messages between writers. Within this world of collective textual making, the reader exercised extensive control over the textual event. "In a system of manuscript circulation of literature," Marotti has summarized, "those

[13]Bodleian MS Douce 280, fol. 35ʳ. Cited by Arthur Marotti, "The Poetry of Feargod Barbaon, Edward Bannister, Nicholas Burghe, Peter Calfe, Sir Humphrey Coningsby, Margaret Douglas, John Finet, Lewison Fitzjames, John Lilliat, Andre Ransey, John Ramsey, Richard Roberts, William Skipwith, Henry Stanford, Thomas Wenman, and Others," presented at a meeting of the Modern Language Association (Washington, D.C., 1989), 15–16.

[14]Edmund Spenser, *Amoretti*, no. 64, in *The Yale Edition of the Shorter Poems of Edmund Spenser*, ed. William A. Oram et al. (New Haven: Yale University Press, 1989), 639. For a striking example of this appropriation/imitation in published works, see William Smith's *Chloris*, no. 12 (1596), which reproduces verbatim lines from Thomas Lodge's *Phillis*, no. 4 (1593).

[15]Arthur Marotti, "Shakespeare's Sonnets as Literary Property," in *Soliciting Interpretation: Literary Theory and Seventeenth-Century English Poetry*, ed. Elizabeth D. Harvey and Katherine Eisaman Maus (Chicago: University of Chicago Press, 1990), 143–73; Walter Ong, *Interfaces of the Word* (Ithaca: Cornell University Press, 1977), 274–79.

into whose hands texts came could, in a real sense, 'own' them: they could collect, alter, and transmit them." ("Shakespeare's *Sonnets*," 143). In a representative moment in *Delia*, Samuel Daniel dramatizes this practice when he beseeches his patron to accept his "humble rhymes," noting that they are *hers*: "Vouchsafe more, to accept them as thine own / Begotten by thy hand and my desire." The exchangeability of her hand and his points to a peculiar conception of authorship, one in which the dedicatee (as well as the subject) can own or seem to originate the work.[16] Shakespeare's dedication of *Lucrece* to the Earl of Southampton thus can simply affirm: "What I have done is yours, what I have to do is yours." These dedications are just two among many that imply an authorial claim in their language—"what I have done," "my desire"—only to defer to the greater claims of the reader —"yours," "thy hand." This gesture of deferral expresses the medieval and coterie practice whereby readers were authorized to edit the poems they read, to scribble answers in the blank white space of the page, and even to alter the poems themselves. In the envoi to "Dan Bartholomew of Bath" in George Gascoigne's *Posies*, the speaker characteristically orders the reader "To reade, to raze, to view, and to correct, / Vouchsafe (my friend) therein for to amend."[17] Seldom bound within a published book, individual poems behaved as textually permeable forms, editorially open to amendation, dialogue, and conversation.

The Dialogue of Courtship

How does understanding the collaborative and unfinished nature of manuscript textuality help us read the sonnets? I suggest that if we examine Renaissance sonnets with an eye to their place within this system of private production and distribution, we can discover how crucial the poems' self-identifications—as manuscript texts—are to their broader thematic concerns. In particular, we can find a startling phenomenon: sonneteers inscribing the exchangeability of their verse within the economy of desire that fuels the poems. Because sonnet writers use poetic transmission as a thematic topos in their verse and because their inscriptions are bolstered by longer prose narratives that allegorize poetic transmission in the same eroticized terms, we are able to see how poets pointed to the

[16]Samuel Daniel, *Delia*, STC 62531, now STC 6243.2 (1592), reprinted in *Samuel Daniel: Poems and A Defence of Ryme*, ed. Arthur Sprague (Chicago: University of Chicago Press, 1930).

[17]George Gascoigne, *The Whole woorkes of George Gascoigne Esquyre: Newlye compyled into one Volume*, STC 11638 (1587), reprinted as *The Complete Works of George Gascoigne*, ed. John W. Cunliffe, 2 vols. (Cambridge: Cambridge University Press, 1907–10), 1:137.

extraliterary functions of poetry—its ability to "turn"—as a means of establishing textual authority.

Many Renaissance narratives allegorize the creation and distribution of lyric poetry. One of the first of its genre (although not labeled as such until the nineteenth century when it was first published), Thomas Whythorne's *Autobiography* demonstrates how poems were created in both a social and a specifically collaborative environment. The writer prefaces his work by explaining that he literally builds his text from a group of sonnets; he composes the "story" from the autobiographical and occasional poems that he recorded in his miscellaneous manuscript. The fictional prose narrative thus serves to replace, or to reenact, the personal interchanges that first inspired the sonnets. But even his fictionalized account emphasizes the social context for verse making, as evidenced when Whythorne narrates the origin of one of his poems:

> As one day, coming into my mistress' chamber and finding there a pen, ink and paper, I wrote in a piece of the paper as thus following—
>
> > When pain is pleasure and joy is care
> > Then shall goodwill in me wax rare.
>
> This writing I left where I found the said implements to write withal; and coming the next day to her chamber, I found written as followeth—
>
> > For your goodwill look for no meed,
> > Till that a proof you show by deed.
>
> Unto the which when I had seen it, I replied as followeth—
>
> > When opportunity of time serveth,
> > Then shall you see how my heart swerveth.[18]

As he dramatizes such moments of exchange, Whythorne underscores how poetry functions not only as a tool for seduction but also as a discursive means of conversation between people who communicate through artfully fashioned "turns." Within Whythorne's commonplace book, the poem presumably stood as an integral whole, the alternating speakers joining together to produce a single verse. His account serves to return the poem to its initial polyphonic point of production.

Romeo and Juliet brilliantly stages a moment of collective sonnet making in a scene in which a poem is spread across alternating speakers. When

---

[18]Thomas Whythorne, *Autobiography*, ed. James Osborn (London: Oxford University Press, 1962), 44. I have transcribed his "new orthography."

Romeo and Juliet meet at the Capulets' feast, they speak a sonnet:

> *Romeo:* If I profane with my unworthiest hand
> This holy shrine, the gentle sin is this:
> My lips, two blushing pilgrims, ready stand
> To smooth that rough touch with a tender kiss.
> *Juliet:* Good pilgrim, you do wrong your hand too much
> Which mannerly devotion shows in this;
> For saints have hands that pilgrims' hand do touch
> And palm to palm is holy palmers' kiss.
> *Romeo:* Have not saints lips, and holy palmers too?
> *Juliet:* Ay, pilgrim, lips that they must use in pray'r.
> *Romeo:* O, then, dear saint, let lips do what hands do!
> They pray; grant you, lest faith turn to despair.
> *Juliet:* Saints do not move, though grant for prayers' sake.
> *Romeo:* Then move not, while my prayer's effect I take.
>
> (1.5. 94–107)[19]

Rather than a complete and crafted form written and sent by one lover to another, the sonnet is performed as a parleying of words between speakers. Of course, this highly dramatic moment offers no evidence that people spoke in sonnets spontaneously. Yet given the communal poetry making narrated by Whythorne and evidenced in commonplace books, Shakespeare's presentation of this highly contrived and structured form reveals a poetic conversation that merely exaggerates the collective and composite nature of literary production. The play's exaggeration lies mainly in its (mis)representation of the poem as an act of improvisation. By erasing the labor of poetic production, the play recasts a common mode of *written* discourse as speech.

Even when writers do not represent poetic making as collaborative, they nevertheless assume that poetry is resolutely occasional, produced through channels of exchange rather than through the force of a seemingly autonomous creative energy. In *Love's Labour's Lost*, for example, writing and trading sonnets are fundamental to social courtship. Sonnet writing is not only the natural act of the lover (who exists to "love, write, sigh, pray, sue, groan"—3.1.202), but also the crucial "conversation" within the process of seduction, as Berowne suggests: "I do love, and it hath taught me to rhyme" (4.3.11-12). When Armado declares his love for Jacquenetta, he expresses his conversion by evoking increasingly more durable forms of

---

[19] *The Complete Works of Shakespeare*, ed. David Bevington, 3d ed. (Glenview, Ill.: Scott Foresman and Company, 1980). All references to Shakespeare's dramatic works are to this edition.

writing: "Assist me, some extemporal god of rhyme, for I am sure I shall turn sonnet. . . . Devise, wit; write, pen; for I am for whole volumes in folio" (1.2.176). Likewise, in *Two Gentlemen from Verona,* Thurio plots to triumph in love by stylizing himself as a poet: "I have a sonnet that will serve the turn," he declares to Proteus (3.2.90-92). If "turn[ing] sonnet" and using sonnets to "serve the turn" imply a communal compositional practice used situationally, they also signify more specifically the rhetorical tools necessary for seduction. Benedick's complaint in *Much Ado About Nothing* that Claudio has "turn'd orthography" (2.3.20) by falling in love sets the terms by which Benedick's own love for Beatrice will be exposed at the end of the play; for what does Claudio produce as evidence of Benedick's "turn" but "a halting sonnet of his own pure brain" (5.4.86)?

When writers fictionally represent the act of "turning sonnet," they emphasize the labyrinthine ways in which writing is caught up in the illicit and artful negotiations of courtship.[20] Whythorne's *Autobiography* is a case in point, for this work dramatizes the role of poetry in the strategic maneuvers of courtship/courtiership. As music master in several aristocratic households, Whythorne is privy to the workings of an upper-class community. In describing the social life in these estates, he narrates how many of his poems originally were used for the purposes of flirtation. In one aristocratic home, for example, Whythorne discovers that he is pursued by an anonymous young woman who leaves verses hidden in his musical instrument: "She devised certain verse in English," he states, "and she did put them between the strings of a gittern, the which instrument . . . I then used to play on often" (30). In order to discover her identity, Whythorne forges a cautious reply and leaves it in the same hidden location. Eventually the woman is discharged for engaging the affections of the music tutor, for participating in a courtship that took place entirely in scattered verses. Using his scribbled poems as a focal point in the text, Whythorne details episode after episode in which he struggles to come to terms with the wily powers of women and their poetic love negotiations. Whythorne describes how his relationship with the mistress of the household is established and conducted through ambiguously phrased verses (53). Unsurprisingly, the overt artifice of verse provides the covert means for making flirtatious overtures without fear of repercussion. Whythorne explains to the reader that he sends his mistress a verse, noting "if she did dissemble, I, to re-

---

[20] Numerous other Renaissance narrative texts foreground the production and exchange of poetry, including Thomas Lodge's prose romance *Rosalynde* (1592), *The Complete Works of Thomas Lodge*, vols. 5–8 in the Hunterian Club Series (Glasgow: Robert Anderson, 1883); and Philip Sidney, *The Countess of Pembroke's Arcadia* (1590), ed. Maurice Evans (New York: Penguin, 1984).

quite her, thought that to dissemble with a dissembler was no dissimulation." He produces a verse "dark and doubtful of sense" in order to protect himself from possible scorn. When she finally rejects him in a verse that states, "the suds of soap shall wash your hope," he responds ambiguously: "the suds of soap shall wash no hope / That I have had in you," a phrase, he explains, that could indicate fortitude or mistaken identity (in that he had no hope in *her* at all). These games of courtship play a fundamental part in the music master's ability to make a living. Sonnet exchange, as his text makes clear, is a means of cementing vital social relationships. As in George Gascoigne's prose narrative "Master F.J.," which turns completely on the covert exchange of verse in a world of sexual intrigue and duplicitous machinations, poems in Whythorne's story function as artfully exchanged currency, necessary for the expression of sexual and economic aggression, desire, and anxiety.

What becomes apparent from these fictional narratives is that the active reader vital to the practice of coterie exchange is pervasively figured as the courted woman. The (coded) dialogue of the coterie is represented by the (coded) dialogue of heterosexual courtship. Certainly some women did participate in poetic game playing, and poetry could be employed in the service of courtship; but the more common mode of coterie exchange was "between men." Or we can say that texts presented to women were more frequently part of a play for economic rather than for sexual advantage. Extant manuscripts and historical reports make clear that men scribbled appropriate responses to other men's poetic wooing. This exchange created a network of homosocial rivalry, a dynamic that critics have exhaustively analyzed in terms of the trafficking of women.[21] Nancy Vickers describes

---

[21]The classic theoretical account of homosocial bonding is offered by Eve Sedgwick in *Between Men: English Literature and Male Homosocial Desire* (New York: Columbia University Press, 1985). Deriving a triangulated model of desire from René Girard, Sedgwick traces this pattern, although not in historical terms, in Shakespeare's sonnets. Other critics who have theorized about the trafficking of women include Gayle Rubin, "The Traffic in Women: Notes on the 'Political Economy' of Sex," in *Toward an Anthropology of Women*, ed. Rayna R. Reiter (New York: Monthly Review Press, 1975), 157–210; Patricia Joplin, "The Voice of the Shuttle Is Ours," *Stanford Literature Review* 1 (1984): 25–53; and Mary Jacobus, "Is There a Woman in This Text?" *New Literary History* 14 (1982): 117–54. For critics who read Renaissance texts through this lens, see Coppélia Kahn, "The Rape in Shakespeare's *Lucrece*," *Shakespeare Studies* 9 (1976): 45–72; Karen Newman, "Portia's Ring: Unruly Women and the Structures of Exchange in *The Merchant of Venice*," *Shakespeare Quarterly* 38 (Spring 1987): 19–33; Nancy Vickers, "'The blazon of sweet beauty's best': Shakespeare's *Lucrece*," in *Shakespeare and the Question of Theory*, ed. Patricia Parker and Geoffrey Hartman (New York: Methuen, 1985), 95–115; and Patricia Parker, *Literary Fat Ladies: Rhetoric, Gender, Property* (London and New York: Methuen, 1987), 126–54.

in her study of the text of *Lucrece*, for instance, the "potential consequences for being female matter for male oratory":

> The canonical legacy of description in praise of beauty is, after all, a legacy
> shaped predominantly by the male imagination for the male imagination; it
> is, in large part, the product of men talking to men about women. In *Lucrece*,
> occasion, rhetoric, and result are informed by, and thus inscribe, a battle
> between men that is first figuratively and then literally fought on the fields of
> woman's "celebrated" body. Here metaphors commonly read as signs of a bat-
> tle between the sexes emerge rather from a homosocial struggle . . . which
> positions a third (female) term in a median space from which it is initially
> used and finally eliminated.[22]

Renaissance fictions do occasionally give us glimpses of the triadic figuration of desire that motivated sonnet discourse. They do so by vivifying the
way in which "woman" is structured in that "median space," and thus making clear that the mistress's absence or unavailability constructs the terms
by which men can speak to one another. In the *Autobiography*, Whythorne
explicitly shows how a male community fashions itself by writing and
exchanging poems. True to Vickers's formulation, Whythorne and another
tutor build a friendship based on the exchange of poems, many ostensibly
addressed to their celebrated mistresses. Likewise, the "shepherds" in
Sidney's *Arcadia* compete with one another by singing songs addressed to
their mistresses, a competition that simultaneously confers masculinity
and membership within a privileged community. These texts merely allegorize the compositional practices between men that Ramsey's and
Spenser's lyric blazon document as part of the Renaissance courtly world.

Such allegorizations could easily have taken their cue from the complicated representations of sonnet exchange lodged within the numerous
sonnet sequences published in the last decades of the sixteenth century.
From Dante's own account of the "true" male audience for his love poems
to Thomas Watson's insistence that his sonnets are literary exercises, poets
have been forthright about the fictional status of their poetic mistresses.[23]

---

[22]Vickers, "'The blazon of sweet beauty's best,'" 96. Such a construction makes the wo-
man, in Hélène Cixous's terms, the "uncanny stranger on display." "The Laugh of the
Medusa," trans. Keith Cohen, in *New French Feminisms*, ed. Elaine Marks and Isabelle de
Courtivron (Amherst: University of Massachusetts Press, 1980), 250.

[23]Dante, for instance, reports that he sent his poems to three friends: "Since just recently I
had taught myself the art of writing poetry, I decided to compose a sonnet addressed to all of
Love's faithful subjects; and, requesting them to interpret my vision, I would write what I had
seen in my sleep. . . . This sonnet was answered by many, who offered a variety of interpretations. . . . This exchange of sonnets marked the beginning of our friendship." Cited by Carol

Within the scope of the poems, however, writers inscribe a double audience: the spectating and morally critical male public, and the cruel and resisting mistress who ostensibly receives the verse. Male readers become visible as the unwanted public, unfortunately witness to the more important gestures of seduction, praise, and blame that the poems dramatize. While some poems in *Astrophel and Stella,* for instance, admit the medicinal quality of the "rhubarb words" of friends—"Your words, my friend! (right healthful caustics!) blame / My young mind marred, whom love doth windlass so" (14; 21)—the speaker inevitably shuns advice against love, dismissing logical argument in favor of the inarguable and transcendent power of beauty.[24] In these poems, interlocutors are made to serve the purposes of seduction as they provoke witty defenses of love that will be offered to the mistress. The world outside the lovers comes into view only momentarily before the speaker elaborately justifies its subordination.

Renaissance sonnet writers generally depict poetry as the product of hetero-eroticized bantering; that is, they figure the homosocial network operating within coterie poetic exchange as courtship. By pointing out that the woman is used as a trope for solidifying male homosocial bonds, I realize that I come close to voicing a critical commonplace. My point, however, is that in the production and transmission of Renaissance sonnets, the female reader acts not only as a median space marking the forging of alliances, but more particularly as the *privileged* median space on which a specific class-identified understanding of reading and writing is expressed. Gender is the axis on which writers register a specific conception of the literary text, one which de-emphasizes the author in lieu of his role in a set of social relations and bonds. If we argue that the male speaker poetically imagines a sonnet mistress as a means of articulating a combined social and literary power, we make the faulty assumption that social and literary power were homologous in the coterie. "Authorship," in the modern sense of a singular writing origin who authorizes the work, was a construct largely outside the demands and rewards of the manuscript sys-

---

Thomas Neely, "The Structure of English Renaissance Sonnet Sequences," *ELH* 45 (1978): 364. For other critics who debate whether there was a real female reader of the sonnets and what her status would have been, see Clark Hulse, "Stella's Wit: Penelope Rich as Reader of Sidney's Sonnets," in *Rewriting the Renaissance: The Discourses of Sexual Difference in Early Modern Europe,* ed. Margaret W. Ferguson, Maureen Quilligan, and Nancy J. Vickers (Chicago: University of Chicago Press, 1986), 272–86; and Jacqueline Miller, "'What May Words Say': The Limits of Language in *Astrophil and Stella,*" in *Sir Philip Sidney and the Interpretation of Culture,* 95–109. Hallet Smith discusses the double audience for the sonnets in *Elizabethan Poetry* (Cambridge, Mass.: Harvard University Press, 1952), 147–48.

[24] All references to *Astrophel and Stella* are cited from *Sir Philip Sidney: Selected Poems,* ed. Katherine Duncan-Jones (Oxford: Oxford University Press, 1973).

tem. Instead, the discourse of courtly love marks and ensconces a *socially* authorized poetics of exchange by expressing patronage as an eroticized relationship. In this formulation, the woman represents the powerful recipient of the trafficked poem, rather than the shuttled textual object.

Sonnet writers construct this dynamic by superimposing two themes: the exchange of love and the exchange of texts. In the sonneteers' fictional world, reading, writing, and exchanging poems figure prominently within the articulation of desire. More particularly, frequent references to dialogue, hands, ink, and paper underscore the fact that acts of reading and writing take place within the highly present exchange of manuscript texts. This exchange becomes thoroughly conflated with the thematics of bodily desire that undergird the sonnet program. Writers develop what we might call a textual erotics through which other themes are expressed; that is, they create a textual/sexual logic dependent on a homology between the lover's and reader's desire. The manuscript economy of reading and writing becomes a central trope through which sonnet writers articulate other broader concerns: the limits of representation, the paradox of desire and loss, the variable and uncontrollable nature of emotion.

Sonnet writers most explicitly indicate the occasional extraliterary nature of their poems when they dramatize the fictional exchanges of courtship through an actual dialogue on the page. William Percy's *Coelia* is exemplary in this respect. After the speaker urges his beloved: "Relent, my dear, yet unkind Coelia / At length, relent, and give my sorrows end," he goes on to reproduce a mock dialogue in which her resistance ("must I relent?") initially wins a linguistic battle.[25] The next poem, however, reframes her previous victorious response as a tactic for the speaker's ongoing rhetoric of persuasion. The fourth poem in the collection alternates the mistress's objections with the speaker's responses:

> "What be men's sighs but cauls of guilefulness?"
> "They shew, dear Love! true proofs of firmity!"
> "What be your tears but mere ungraciousness?"
> "Tears only plead for our simplicity!"

Just as Stella's words frequently provide matter for Astrophel's witty commentary, Coelia's words, encompassed within the speaker's own, become part of the text ostensibly sent to her, although her language is necessarily refashioned within the terms of the speaker's desire. In representing poems as mobile texts caught up in the processive nature of conversation (albeit a conversation artfully controlled by the speaking voice), *Coelia* is

---

[25]William Percy, *Sonnets to the Fairest Coelia*, STC 19618 (1594), no. 17.

hardly exceptional: sonnet sequences turn on this very identification. When justifying his decision to circulate his poetry, for instance, Astrophel orchestrates a dialogue on the page:

> "Art not ashamed to publish they disease?"
> Nay that may breed my fame, it is so rare.
> "But will not wise men think they words fond ware?"
> Then be they close, and so none shall displease.
>
> (34)

Astrophel's mock debate appropriately links the form of dialogue with the "shame" of publication. If the poem calls attention to the way dialogue underpins the conception of the poetic artifact through its implication within a sustained conversation, it also explicitly makes the difference between "close" coterie circulation and the publication of "fond ware" part of its subject matter.[26]

When sonnet writers present a literal dialogue between speaker and mistress, they merely display in extreme form their general concern with the fictional acts of reading and writing that condition the poems. Sidney, Spenser, Michael Drayton, and Samuel Daniel signal the importance of textual reception in the opening poems to their sequences. More precisely, they introduce issues of emotional excess and poetic crafting by representing those issues as structured and determined by the mistress/reader's response. Although I risk pointing out the obvious, I want to unpack what it meant for the mistress to be represented specifically as a *reader*: for the poems are inscribed as artifacts sent to persuade, or as records of the speaker's emotional overflow dramatized for his lover's benefit. The speaker portrays himself as unfulfilled in desire and hence incomplete, thus analogous to his incomplete text, which is similarly unfinished because it lacks her response. Even in poems not addressed to the mistress, she is identified as the text's true reader. Sidney defines his poetic collection in terms of the possible effects reading can have on Stella's sen-

---

[26]William J. Kennedy sees these inscriptions of dialogue as part of a general technique of voice and address that writers employed as a means of fending off the objectifying power of print. Through such strategies, the speaker was able, Kennedy suggests, to manipulate Petrarchan rhetoric so as to create an authorial presence within the dead literary object. While I agree that the inscription of dialogue in these poems is, in fact, partially generated in response to print technology, I do not assume, as Kennedy does, a coherent authorial subject position that print threatens to erode. Instead, I want to call attention to the way in which a writer's decision to move into print allowed for the construction of an authorial role as much as it deteriorated the presence of oral culture that still left its residue in manuscript culture. William J. Kennedy, "Petrarchan Audiences and Print Technology," *Journal of Medieval and Renaissance Studies* 14 (1984): 1–20.

sibilities: "Pleasure might cause her read, reading might make her know, / Knowledge might pity win, and pity grace obtain" (1). It is the anticipated act of reading that becomes privileged as the moment of potential fulfillment. In exploring the limits and possibilities of representation in this initial sonnet, Sidney differentiates between the "natural" (body, native, truth) and the "artificial" (study, feigning, painting, writing), only to collapse these oppositions finally through a series of overlapping organic and artificial images. By marking out the field of inquiry, the poet first and foremost establishes a causal link between reading and loving, with Stella's reading functioning as the contingent act.

Other sequences follow *Astrophel and Stella* in calling attention to the power of reading in the text's introductory moment. In Spenser's *Amoretti* 2, the problem of the text's success precedes an outlaying of the origin of the speaker's love; in fact, love seems constructed from the desire for a good *textual* reception. Transforming the aesthetic challenge of his poem into an erotic quest, the speaker directs his verse: "grace for me entreat / Which if she grant, then live, and my love cherish: / If not, die soon; and I with thee will perish."[27] Spenser had already established a vital association between the livelihood of poem and speaker in the *Amoretti*'s introductory poem, which includes an extended description of how his text would be held in his mistress's hands. Drayton's *Ideas Mirrour* similarly opens with a directive for handling the text: "Reade heere (sweet Mayd) the story of my wo," the speaker sternly commands, " The drery abstracts of my endles cares."[28] Finally, Daniel opens *Delia* by identifying his poems as subject to the magnetic force of the reading lover:

> Unto the boundless ocean of thy beautie
> Runs this poore river, charg'd with streames of zeale:
> Returning thee the tribute of my dutie,
> Which heere my love, my youth, my playnts reveal.[29]

Punning on the tributive nature of the text through the metaphor of the river (a figure to which Daniel will return in the last sonnet when he characterizes his poems as "tributary plaintes"), the speaker suggests that the flow of energy to the reader is the poetic project's privileged dynamic. It is only after identifying this moment of *return* that the speaker establishes his own relationship to his poems: "Heere I unclaspe the booke of my charg'd soule" (1). The speaker's active assertion—"I unclaspe"—and his identifi-

---

[27]References to Edmund Spenser's *Amoretti* (1595) are cited from *The Yale Edition of the Shorter Poems of Edmund Spenser.*

[28]Michael Drayton, *Ideas Mirrour*, STC 7203 (1594).

[29]References to *Delia* (1592) are cited from *Samuel Daniel: Poems and A Defence of Ryme.*

cation of the text with his interiority—"my charg'd soule"—constitutes a secondary and belated claim subordinate to and originating from the mistress's more crucial power. These initial poems reveal that sonneteers go to extraordinary lengths to define their poems as invitations to love issued within a manuscript system of exchange, with the mistress's awaited response serving as the raison d'être for the verse.

The remainder of these sonnet sequences play out the associations forged by their initial poems; for they dramatize in various ways how the conversation between lovers takes place through exchanged verse. Sonnet writers are conventionally self-conscious about their poetry's place in a "non-book"–oriented textual system based on the desire for, and failure of, sexual/textual reciprocity between mistress and speaker. The speaker characteristically alternates between instructing his verse about the proper behavior for serving its powerful reader and announcing that reader's refusal of the text and thus the speaker's desire. In this way, the poems generate a strange chronology, for they seemingly recognize and contain their own (eventual) moment of reading within the rhetoric of seduction they offer. Of course, poets in these instances logically refer to previously sent poems, building on the poem's past circulation as part of the discourse of love itself. Yet the result is still a paradoxical dynamic whereby the texts' anticipated moment of reception rests at the core of the speaker's presentation of poetic creativity and erotic desire. In Thomas Lodge's *Phillis*, the speaker sorrowfully describes the failure that ensues when he sends his "moaning lines" to his "love's queen"; he complains that "Phillis sits, and reads, and calls them trifles" (4). The *Amoretti* everywhere marks the mistress's response: she has an unyielding hardness (18); she unweaves his meaning with her own artistry (23); she offers a playful refusal to his requests (25); and she assertively refuses to accept the interpretations of her own desire offered by the speaker (29).

Sonnet speakers generally posit a fictionalized economy of exchange centered around the circulation of texts and words. In Bartholomew Griffin's *Fidessa*, the speaker dramatically portrays his text as a mirrorlike surface in which the mistress sees both his longing and her own disdain:

> She takes the Glass, wherein herself She sees,
> In bloody colours cruelly depainted;
> And her poor prisoner humbly on his knees,
> Pleading for grace with heart that never fainted
> She breaks the Glass.[30]

---

[30]Bartholomew Griffin, *Fidessa, more chaste then kinde*, STC 12367 (1596), no. 19.

Here the sonnet takes as its very subject the mistress's violent refusal of the poet's self-representation as wooing lover. Although sonnets conventionally name poetry as a glass, this poem offers not an hourglass or a mirror in which virtue, beauty, and truth are reflected, but a device that holds to view the private moment of presentation on which the poems depend (the "poor prisoner humbly on his knees"). It thus particularizes and makes visible the fact that the reader's response is fundamental to the speaker's presentation of himself and his artful craft. Not only are the interchanges between lovers cast as scenes of reading and writing, but the two acts—her reading and his writing—become conflated in the rhetoric of the poems. He writes because she refuses to read properly, and his writing is everywhere marked by that refusal. The poems are represented as poised against the possibility of transformation, awaiting the negative aesthetic judgment ("Phillis . . . calls them trifles," Fidessa "breaks the glass"), which is completely interwoven with a sexual refusal. The dialectic of response then becomes a vital part of the poem's subject matter.

The formal sonnet structure, with its tight and coherent rhyme scheme, is constantly offset by its insistent reminder of a world beyond the sonnet, of its informal material existence as paper and ink passed from hand to hand. Sonneteers emphasize the intimacy of this exchange when they emphasize the physical nature of reading and writing. In his highly influential sequence, Sidney not only associates writing with the body in the very first poem, but he continues to trace myriad permutations of the body-text identification throughout the next 107 sonnets. Most obvious are the poems that represent Stella as a written and therefore readable "fair text": she appears as a book written by nature, as a text erotically misread, as "letters of bliss" (3; 11; 56; 67; 71; Eighth Song). As the opening poem signals, however, the poems can also be represented as the writer's surrogate body rather than the mistress's, because he has access to and contact with Stella through her act of reading him. Astrophel's identification with his own written page reaches its culmination in the famous lines of Sonnet 45 where he authorizes his full transformation into writing itself, albeit with seeming resignation: "I am not I: pity the tale of me." The mistress, herself often allegorized as a poem, is thus invoked in the argument of the sonnet to "read" the "tale" of the lover/speaker. Astrophel and Stella's consummation is imagined in the fantasized moment of reading ("reading might make her know," Astrophel puns initially). Sonnet 45 asks that Stella render a positive aesthetic/sexual judgment about the speaker by seeing him as identical to his poem—accepting his manuscript, usually synecdochally represented as his "hand" but here portrayed as his "tale"/"tail."

This conflation of the bodily hand and the handwriting of the text operates most explicitly in the first lines of Spenser's opening poem to the *Amoretti*:

> Happy ye leaves when as those lilly hands,
> which hold my life in their dead doing might
> shall handle you and hold in loves soft bands,
> lyke captives trembling at the victors sight.

The speaker self-referentially identifies his lines as tangled between delicate "lilly hands" that gently hold the paper, hands whose murderous capacity poses a threat to the very work that they lovingly fondle. The "trembling" poems become alive as flickers of paper, whose fragility is registered in their precarious and hopeful exchange and whose quivering signifies the presence of the sexually powerful reader.[31] The pages of the sequence thus act as a synecdochic figure for the speaker's body, and reading is the site of physical contact between speaker and mistress. This figuration, which amplifies the implied eroticism harbored in the uttered "might" of Astrophel's initial sonnet, suggests the way the text functions as both sublimated erotic energy and surrogate sexuality. The double meanings of the word "hand" highlight both the physicality of writing and reading and the intimacy of the private exchange of personal poetry. In the remaining lines of this opening sonnet, the poem traces a circuit of interwoven desire cast through the shifting agencies of reader and text: the poem at first standing in for the speaker's body kneeling in servitude, then being cast as the object of the mistress's fantasized gaze, and finally actively beholding in the mistress the reflection of the speaker's desire, here expressed as the urge to consume her. (She is the speaker's "long lacked foode, [his] heavens blis.") The "happy" or satisfied text thus contrasts with the speaker's decidedly unhappy frustration, but it also enacts his longing through its route of transmission. Issued from his body—with "teares in harts close bleeding book"—the poem is sent out with a command to offer the mistress private pleasure: "seeke her to please alone," the speaker urges. The speaker's desire is inscribed on the materiality of the poem—with blood and tears for ink—and it unfolds within the instance of reading. By introducing the poem's very writing ("happy lines") and internal structure ("happy rhymes") through reference to the material page ("happy leaves"), the poet calls attention to the text's manuscript sta-

---

[31]In his sequence *Phillis* (STC 16662 [1593], sig. A4ᵛ), Thomas Lodge also creates this sexualized dynamic between text and reader when he instructs his poem: "Kiss Delia's hand for her sweet prophet's sake / . . . / Then lay you down in Phillis' lap and sleep / Until the weeping read and reading weep."

tus, corporeally imagined as passed to delicate but threatening "lilly hands." The poem is identified as a trace of a transaction, the poet's trembling, desiring body registered in his fetishized "hand," a term that surfaces again with condensed anatomical, erotic, and scriptive meanings later in the sequence (see 4, 47, and 73).

Spenser is not exceptional in fashioning a dynamic of eroticized textual exchange through the foregrounding of the poems' materiality and through inscriptions of bodily desire. Sidney's *Astrophel and Stella* is riddled with specific references to to "ink," "paper," and "pen" (see 19, 93, 102, 50, 58, 70, and 34); and Daniel's *Delia* animates the text by paradoxically calling attention to its "objectness" (see 36, 49, 35, 39, and 37). Both poets employ the word "hand" in its anatomical, erotic, paleographic, and textual registers;[32] the result are sequences that everywhere announce their status as physical objects placed within circuits of exchange. Paper and ink become registers of bodily fluids and emotive states, as Astrophel notes in one instance when cataloguing various poets' failed methods:

> To some a sweetest plaint a sweetest style affords,
> While tears pour out his ink, and sighs breathe out his words,
> His paper, pale despair, and pain his pen doth move.
>
> (6)

Writing oozes from the body, created from the disordered physiology of the lover; and it makes its way to physical contact with the "fair soft hand" of the beloved, whose fingers are detailed in one poem as "Cupids shafts" (83, Fifth Song). The poems in these sequences are presented as intricately personal, highly present, and determinedly physical objects, whose identity rests in their linkage with the hands and bodies of writers and recipients.

[32]In *Astrophel and Stella* Sidney generally plays out the association made strikingly clear in Spenser's fetishization of the "lilly hands" at the site of reading. Sidney's first poem establishes a link between the speaker's body and the body of the poem; the scene of writing is one of birthing and castration (a double image echoed in Sonnet 50's evocation of abortion and writing). *Astrophel and Stella* presents the hand as a condensed image that points to the act of writing, the body that writes, the reader's point of contact with the speaker's words, and, finally, the idealized female body described and adored in the poems. In short, frequent references to the hand pull together issues of eroticized reading and surrogate sexuality. Note, for instance, Astrophel's wistful and elusive complaint about triumphant fools: "what their hands do hold, their heads do know" (24:6); his gesture of sincerity: "Look at my hands for no such quintessance" (28); his description of the poetic and erotic register of writing as he disclaims ambition: "all my words thy beauty doth endite / And love doth hold my hand, and makes me write" (90); and the designation of his hand as more true than mere writing (70). For a fascinating analysis that uses references to the "hand" and pedagogical handwriting manuals to open up complex questions concerning the status of representation and its materiality, see Jonathan Goldberg, *Writing Matter: From the Hands of the English Renaissance* (Stanford: Stanford University Press, 1990).

Even the mistress's violent or harsh refusal can be represented as a surrogate or displaced consummation, for it is her act of reading—which necessitates her taking his "hand" within hers—that is erotically charged. In the Eighth Song, for example, Astrophel self-referentially narrates his struggle of desire:

> There his hands in their speech fain
> Would have made tongue's language plain:
> But her hands, his hands repelling,
> Gave repulse, all grace excelling.

While the exchange of hands on one level notes the failure of seduction (she slaps his hand away), it alludes to the more successful exchange of handwriting that marks its substitute success (she understands the import of his received speech, represented through his poetic "hand"). Spenser picks up Sidney's method of dramatizing the mistress's rejection by referring to the struggle of hands. In Sonnet 48, the speaker describes the mistress's violent refusal of his poetry, when her "cruell hand" consigns his "innocent paper" to the fire. Spenser implies that the poem's status as martyr ironically transforms it into a seemingly more accurate simulacrum of the speaker's burning desire. The drama of this moment is heightened by the representation of the sexual struggle as one between hands—her "cruell hand" and his "innocent paper"/body. As does *Astrophel and Stella*, this poem in the *Amoretti* reveals a sonnet convention in which the play of fair and cruel hands marks an intertwined sexual and textual struggle.

Such associations between body and text highlight a poetic concern for the reader's agency in generating what Clark Hulse calls the "language of bliss" ("Stella's Wit," 282). Through corporeal representations of their poems, sonnet writers repeatedly name their work as desire incarnate in material form, textual and sexual interrogatories seeking completion. Not only is desire registered within and constituent of poetic exchange, but also the speaker's persistent confession of his own "lack" calls attention associatively to the poem's lack. In this sense, the poetry seems to "desire" its reader, formally and thematically. Richard Lanham rightly comments that "*Astrophel and Stella* begins and ends in the begging mode";[33] the act of persuasion, "begging," is an intricate part of the sonnet sequence structure. If manuscript circulation implies a certain contract of collaboration, as Gascoigne's *Posies* suggest (where the reader is urged to "reade, to raze, to view, and to correct, / Vouchsafe (my friend) therein for to amend"),

---

[33]Richard A. Lanham, "*Astrophil and Stella*: Pure and Impure Persuasion," *English Literary Renaissance* 2 (1972): 100–115.

then that act of emendation is registered in the thematic of the sonnet as an acceptance or rejection of both the "text" of physical desire and the poet's aesthetic craft. The failure of desire paradoxically produces more writing, which, while it only enacts desire's failure once again, translates the failed personal relationship into a collaborative exchange system of writers and readers.

The poems' inscription of their own function thus corresponds to the function of the coterie text as we have seen it: the poem is written for exchange and given to a reader who has the power to amend or "finish" the lover's deficient text by granting it a complete meaning. Although formally finished, the poems take their full meaning through the interactive and eroticized moment between writer and reader, the "conversation" that constructs the sonnet text. Working through the central tropes of loss and desire, sonnet speakers *perform* texts through extended acts of poetic deferment; their linguistic utterances foreground the mistress's private editorial power (or figure female sexuality, it could be said, as an editorial power). On one level, of course, this deferral mystifies the speaker's own assertion of control generated by the poem itself: the seeming centrality of the mistress/reader may constitute her subordination to his more powerful linguistic authority. But we can understand the woman's subordination only by reading past the poet's inscription of the poem as subject to her ultimate and invincible power. Rather than evaluating the female character's "real" power within this dynamic, or a female reader's "real" cultural power within courtly love, I am here concerned with how the woman functions within a particular representation of reading. For we find the curious fact that the governance of volatile emotion and volatile text is established as the prerogative of the female reader.

Sonnet writers thus rewrite the functions of poetic exchange in Renaissance culture—the coterie bonding that solidifies class boundaries—as the dialogue of courtship. The economy of manuscript exchange underpins and is interwoven with broader investigations of desire, subjectivity, and language in sonnet sequences. What becomes clear is that the exchanged textual object becomes a fruitful and complex figure within the fictive universe of the poems: as tributary rivers circling back to the privileged reading origin, as personified body parts fondled by the mistress's hands, as signs of the deferred nature of writing, as operations enacting the contradictory logic of desire itself. It may well be that writers in an age of print construct an eroticized authorial and readerly presence within these poems precisely in order to combat the distance publication seemingly conferred on writing. But such inscriptions could as easily contradict the idea that writers felt this distance at all, suggesting instead that these erotic exchanges mimetically reproduce the losses and gains incurred by the actual exchange of manuscript texts. While it is impossible to decide between these two readings, we can assuredly say that the sonnets include a blueprint for reading and writing that informs their subject matter and signals the value of a specific set of reading practices. The editorial open-endedness and social embeddedness that characterize manuscript texts become important parts of the thematic play of Petrarchan love in the poems.

Readers of these poems find themselves positioned as the sonnet mistress, or rather the real reader writes over and subsumes the mistress's place in the economy of exchanged poems (holding the text in now embarrassed hands, deciding, for example, whether the poems are trifles, or whether they are persuasive in other senses). The discourse of love repeats and consolidates by reformulating in erotic terms the operations of reading that comprised the politics of poetic exchange. If writing poetry was a humanist proving ground, then gender difference became the axis on which that ground was articulated. Courtly love interestingly became the "turn" or trope for the conversation of the Renaissance coterie. Many scholars have described the vast changes in familial organization, marriage, and gender ideology that took place in early modern England.[34] Sonnets certainly speak to these concerns in ways independent from their focus on textual exchange and erotic interchange. What I am suggesting is that the volatile discourse of love, in addition to the other cultural work that it did, was used as a means of registering a particular textual practice. As "parcelles" seeking love, offering praise and rehearsing moments of linguistic exchange between readers, sonnets both describe and enact the poetics of exchange that motivated their production. Quite tellingly, they do so through a highly gendered and sexualized rhetoric.

The Author Function, Poetic Function, and Class

When representing and dramatizing their poetry's unfulfilled social and sexual functions, sonnet writers create the impression that their texts are frustratingly incomplete. Critics have frequently discussed the ways in which sonnet sequences exhibit a lack of closure, solicit an active reader, turn on metapoetic and self-conscious moments, and prompt attention to their intertextuality and polysemicity. Many studies have attempted to account for the "writerly" features of the sonnets—their seeming incom-

herine Belsey, "Disrupting Sexual Difference: Meaning and Gen- 1 *Alternative Shakespeares*, ed. John Drakakis (London: Methuen, h Rose, *The Expense of Spirit: Love and Sexuality in English Renaissance* Jniversity Press, 1988); and the important anthology *Rewriting the* s *of Sexual Difference in Early Modern Europe*, ed. Ferguson, Quilligan,

pleteness and their construction of an unusually active reader.[35] Stephen Booth discloses the "multitude of different coexistent and conflicting patterns—formal, logical, ideological, syntactic, rhythmic, and phonetic"— that invigorate and frustrate a reading of the sonnets.[36] Gary Waller argues that sonnets are particularly demanding texts because they consciously exploit inherent qualities of language—its play of difference and its instability of meaning—in creating richly elusive rhetorical structures.[37] Because *Astrophel and Stella* issues rhetorical invitations for readerly play, he explains, it is "less a definable literary 'text' than a field of potential meaning" (23). These arguments, which we can crudely call the formalist and poststructuralist, take their cue in part from Renaissance poets' own rhetorical identifications of their sonnets. The hermeneutical complexity and textual tractability of the sonnet, identified so eloquently by Booth and Waller, are somewhat scripted by its self-identification as a construct functioning elusively within a specific material circuit of exchange. While a sonnet's textual elusiveness is, of course, generated by complex formal patterns and wordplay, it is also promoted, I argue, by the inscription of its ability to "turn." The poems' resistance to closure, then, is not only a mimetic rehearsal of the theme of unconsummated desire, but also an assertion of a kind of textuality familiar to manuscript culture, a textuality that gestures toward the extraliterary (the reader, the translator, or the occasion) as the means of poetic realization.[38]

[35]Jacqueline T. Miller concurs with the critical consensus that the sonnets encourage an extraordinarily active reader, only with this qualification: "Once Stella's position as defined by the poem is recognized, we may, I think, see that while the sequence may acknowledge that its reader takes an unusually active role in the assembling of meaning, it does not necessarily encourage this—at least, not without reservations. . . . Sidney uses Stella's role as audience and Astrophil's as poet to display, I think, his own uneasiness about what Waller calls the 'reciprocity' that exists between readers and writers." ("'What May Words Say,'" 98.) Miller suggests that Sidney stages the speaker's encounter with the governability of meaning, and thus her argument runs counter to my claim that Sidney activates the reader's response by dramatizing the poetics of exchange.

[36]Stephen Booth, *An Essay on Shakespeare's Sonnets* (New Haven: Yale University Press, 1969), ix.

[37]Gary Waller, "Acts of Reading: The Production of Meaning in *Astrophil and Stella*," *Studies in the Literary Imagination* 15 (1982): 23-35. In a later essay, Waller historicizes his earlier argument by noting that "the 'undecidability' of Sidney's poems is not simply the undecidability of textuality so beloved by deconstruction. While it may be true that *Astrophil and Stella* is a powerful example of a collection of poems where contradictory codes force each other into strange shapes, nonetheless these contradictions are inseparable from the contradictory codes of his society," namely, Waller argues, those of Petrarchism and Protestantism. ("The Rewriting of Petrarch: Sidney and the Languages of Sixteenth-Century Poetry," in *Sir Philip Sidney and the Interpretation of Renaissance Culture*, 79).

[38]In a fascinating essay, Marion Campbell mentions the poem's social function when

In one sense, contemporary theoretical practices that decenter, deauthorize, and deconstruct the fixity of texts find striking examples for their theories in the sonnets. Sonnets act as verbal signs whose meanings are always deferred (although not endlessly) to dynamic circulations between senders and receivers. As the poets insist on a model of poetic production dependent more on social and intertextual relationships than on inherent authorized meanings, they create poems that stage the "unfixing" strategies so prevalent in numerous poststructuralist methodologies. Barthes's and Foucault's work on the author and reader, for instance, have made these concepts visible for analysis and critique. In "The Death of the Author," Barthes argues for a dispensation of the modern capitalist invention called the "author" in order to access a historically remote mode of reading and to free the modern text from a restrictive mode of interpretation: "We know now that a text is not a line of words releasing a single 'theological' meaning (the message of the Author-God)," Barthes explains, "but a multidimensional space in which a variety of writings, none of them original, blend and clash. The text is a tissue of quotations drawn from the innumerable centres of culture. . . . To give a text an Author is to impose a limit on that text, to furnish it with a final signified, to close the writing."[39] According to Barthes, the author and reader are antithetical ways of organizing reading; and with the author safely dead (or in the case of Renaissance texts, not yet fully constructed), the text's unity and meaning can be generated by its reader. Sixteenth-century sonnets can be seen as "writerly" texts rather than authored "works" because they constitute a "field of meaning" rather than an "object of consumption" (Barthes, 157). Without the stabilizing signature of the author, these manuscript poems fully display their multiplicity and openness. Foucault's classic essay on the author function, which amplifies Barthes's schematic presentation of the clash between the unlimited free play of the text and the limiting factor of authorial command, theorizes this multiplicity more fully. Rather than serving simply as a sign of attribution, the author functions, Foucault suggests, to characterize the existence and operation of discourses within a society.[40] Within this governing force, Renaissance poems become characterized by other means, namely their complex operations within their social world.

---

explaining the relationship between *Astrophil and Stella*'s resistance to closure and its rewriting of Petrarchan desire. "Unending Desire: Sidney's Reinvention of Petrarchan Form in *Astrophil and Stella*," in *Sir Philip Sidney and the Interpretation of Renaissance Culture*, 84–94.

[39]Roland Barthes, "From Work to Text," in *Image, Music, Text* (New York: Hill and Wang, 1977), 146, 147.

[40]Michel Foucault, "What Is an Author?" in *Textual Strategies: Perspectives in Post-Structuralist Criticism*, ed. Josué Harari (Ithaca: Cornell University Press, 1979), 159.

Because Barthes and Foucault have been instrumental in challenging literary critics to rethink authorial control in general, their work is helpful in drawing out the implications of the textuality produced by Renaissance coterie exchange. But I do not want to equate Renaissance poetry's intertextuality and lack of closure with a general polysemicity unless such concepts are adequately historicized.[41] In two central ways sonnets fail to fit into the models of liberatory flux described by Barthes and Foucault: their linguistic instability and lack of fixity do not point to an antitheological and radical indeterminacy, and they do not signify a democratic play of language associated with political nonauthoritarianism. The reader's power in sonnet circulation, as I describe in the following pages, works instead to consolidate the restrictive social boundaries that protected an empowered social group. While the lack of a defined author function cannot be explained unreservedly by theories used to fuel an oppositional politics, the work of Barthes and Foucault can be instructive in providing a language through which we can identify characteristics of these poems that approximate poststructuralist theories of textuality.[42] Once the complicated relationship between author function and text has been recognized and charted, we are free to employ these conceptual rubrics in other kinds of analyses, namely those concerned with the cultural valences of poetry.

Instead of accounting for the sonnets' stylized and sexualized writerly qualities—their tractability, permeability, and lack of closure—by seeing them as demonstrations of postmodern textuality, I suggest that we interpret these features by framing them within the institution of patronage and the codes of manuscript exchange it promoted. In generating a logic of desire in the poems that was everywhere interwoven with their exchangeability, sonnet writers reproduced the conversation of the coterie

[41]But see Jonathan Goldberg's account of the compatibility of new culturally oriented textual procedures and poststructuralist practices. "One must recognize that post-structuralism and the new textual criticism coincide, historically—and theoretically. Both have called the criterion of authorial intention into question, thereby detaching the supposed sovereign author from texts open to and constituted by a variety of interventions" (213). Goldberg goes on to criticize readings that cast Derridean "free play" as antihistorical and overly simplistic. "Textual Properties," *Shakespeare Quarterly* 37 (1986): 213–17.

[42]Barthes uses the language of social liberation in describing the text's release from the author: In "refusing to assign a 'secret,' an ultimate meaning, to the text (and to the world as text)," literature "liberates what may be called an anti-theological activity, an activity that is truly revolutionary since to refuse to fix meaning is, in the end, to refuse God and his hypostases—reason, science, law" ("Death of the Author," 147); the writerly text can be used "to escape the patrilineal system of textual filiation," he argues ("From Work to Text," 161); to counter consumer logic; and to free language to a sexual/social pleasure. He further explains, "As for the Text, it is bound to jouissance, that is to a pleasure without separation. . . . The Text participates in its own way in a social utopia; . . . The Text is that space where no language has a hold over any other, where languages circulate" ("From Work to Text," 164).

in poetic form. This reaffirmation of elite practice was necessitated in part by the weakening in lines of division in the latter part of the century, owing primarily to the shift from a feudal to a protocapitalist economic system. The possibility of social mobilization produced, as Lawrence Stone points out, "an obsessive anxiety about rank and status," evidenced by the popularity of heraldry and genealogical tables, and by the bolstering of medieval sumptuary and precedent laws.[43] Indeed, critics have persuasively argued that the loud and sustained outcry against social breakdown and the widespread nervousness about masterless men were indicators of a more particular anxiety concerning the slippage of a crucial social fault line—that between the merchant and noble classes.[44] While aspiring writers were, of course, interested in appealing to actual patrons through their poetry, they also used inscriptions of this kind of exchange as a means of resettling the bounds of social circulation that were somewhat at risk of being blurred within the culture. Poets were concerned not only with personal economic gain, but also with consolidating the familiar system in which such gains were issued and dispensed. By inscribing an exclusive social world through the fictional exchange of love sonnets—one that was increasingly threatened by the more inclusive realm of print publication— a threatened coterie system attempted to reproduce itself through its cultural productions. In this way, the participatory poetics of exchange vali-

[43]Lawrence Stone, *An Open Elite? England, 1540–1880* (Oxford: Clarendon Press, 1984), 7. See also Stone's *The Crisis of the Aristocracy, 1558–1641* (Oxford: Clarendon Press, 1965), 21–39. Whitney Jones explores the problematic crumbling of social distinction in *The Tudor Commonwealth, 1529–1559* (London: Athlone Press, 1970). See also Keith Wrightson, *English Society, 1580–1680* (New Brunswick, N.J.: Rutgers University Press, 1982), and Susan Amussen, *An Ordered Society: Gender and Class in Early Modern England* (Oxford: Basil Blackwell, 1988), for varying views on the threats posed by social mobility and the stability of order in early modern England.

[44]In his analysis of the correspondence between market systems and the theater in early modern England, Jean-Christophe Agnew discusses the way in which the "widening maelstrom of England's social mobility" in the sixteenth century was evidenced in the replacement of estate literature with cony-catching, or rogue, pamphlets. He explains: "In the face of the accumulating pressures of enclosure, disestablishment, and demobilization, new forms of social, political, and imaginative order were improvised to keep people and things in their place. Like the estates literature that preceded it, rogue literature served as a figurative act of settlement: exposing, dissecting, and classifying all that threatened to confuse the social relations of Elizabethan England, tying the loose ends of commerce and crime back to the frayed fabric of society" (65). Agnew cites as evidence Philip Stubbes's *Anatomie of Abuses* (1583), which complained of the growing difficulty "to knowe who is noble, who is worshipfull, who is a gentleman, who is not" (74). Agnew, *Worlds Apart: The Market and the Theater in Anglo-American Thought, 1550–1750* (Cambridge: Cambridge University Press, 1986). Agnew's work acknowledges a debt to Ruth Mohl, *The Three Estates in Medieval and Renaissance Literature* (New York: Columbia University Press, 1933).

dated a more intense social classification, rather than merely celebrating the free play of a collaborative poetry.

The inscription of texts as situational and appropriable objects should have logically disappeared when the poems were commodified within the public marketplace. It seems peculiar, then, that the trace of private circulation registered in the sonnets continued to be produced in printed works. When Sidney circulated *Astrophel and Stella* within the coterie, his medium of transmission corresponded neatly and appropriately to the exchange of courtly love within the text. Sidney's fictionalized wooing quite accurately identifies his poems as exchanged manuscripts: the works could have been passed privately to the "interlocutors" or to the mistress that the poems describe. But writers such as Spenser and Drayton, who were highly influenced by Sidney but who wrote explicitly for publication, continued to design poems identified with manuscript culture. Their poems formed a continuum with, rather than a break from, their exchanged manuscript counterparts. In this sense, these writers chose to produce poetry that de-authorized themselves as writing subjects in lieu of displaying their accessibility to a socially authorized practice of writing. What this choice suggests is that writers after Sidney used courtly love as a topos for misidentifying their texts' system of transmission; that is, for claiming to write within a network of patrons and readers rather than for the marketplace. The creation of writerly texts thus constituted a bid for social inclusion. By appealing to the enervated codes of manuscript writing, writers could legitimate a foray into print and, more important, suggest the compatibility of print and patronage. Writers created texts that appropriated the traces of privilege from the coterie in order to encroach on (and then, of course, to protect) those bounds.

This practice of appropriation helps to explain in part why printed books continue to retain the trappings of private manuscript texts in their paratextual apparatuses. The preliminary features of published books—commendatory sonnets, prefaces, and dedications—represent poetry as the product of the aristocratic sitting room, where courtiers invented verse in leisurely game-playing and conversation. In the numerous dedicatory and commendatory poems that precede their works, publishers and writers emphasize the compatibility of the privately dedicated manuscript and the publicly sold book; the book could be written in gratitude for (or in hopes of) preferment, but could also be addressed to the general reader.[45] During a time in which people were scrambling to secure a place within a

[45]The seven commendatory and ten dedicatory poems belatedly introducing *The Faerie Queene* (1590), for example, present the text through a simulated conversation of collective voices rather than by highlighting the authority of the single author. (The number of dedica-

more socially fluid world, poetic forms offered a means of signifying status. More important, the reproduction of these marks of privilege revealed the writers' concern that marks of status themselves not become obsolete. Critics have rightly pointed out that Renaissance poets sought to legitimate and to redeem the enterprise of writing by countering the notion that poetry was merely a wasteful gentlemanly pastime (Helgerson, *Self-Crowned Laureates*). I am suggesting that many poets felt compelled to inscribe their works precisely as *gentlemanly* pastimes as a means of acquiring social, if not literary, legitimation.

Promoting a view of poetry writing as collective and occasional can thus be read as a doubly encoded feature of many sonnet writers' agendas, drawn on by would-be aristocrats as well as the more firmly ensconced elite. We find that the seemingly trivial and amorous sonnet offers not only a trace of the material life of the world of the courtiers, but also a site where writers sought to reconfigure and enlarge the cultural field from which they produced their poems.[46] Because print and private circulation were symbolically identified with social hierarchy (common print and noble writing), the writer's presentation of a "poetics of exchange" within the poems refashions even as it reflects the fault line differentiating social groups. In this act of refashioning we see the way in which social, textual, and gender issues coalesce. For sonnets re-create that social fault line as a gendered binary between male sonnet speaker and female patron/reader. An apparent textual concept—the perception that texts are governed more by their context and function than by their author—is intricately tied to both the sixteenth-century controversy over the place of public writing and the disparate cultural inscriptions of gender roles. A real stigma of print, clearly operative at mid-century when Wyatt and Surrey did not think to publish, evolves into one that is rhetorically produced and con-

---

tory poems is expanded to seventeen in later printings.) Emerging from a prefatorial exchange of poems, the work retains the trappings of sustained courtly conversation in the arena of print: for instance, when Ralegh's poem praising Spenser as the next "Petrarke" is followed by a Spenserian verse praising *Cynthia* and asking for Ralegh's inspiration. Ralegh's double presence in this material suggests a reciprocity between writer and reader; the narrative not only springs from a circle of praise but also carries the textual baggage of the circular scene of reading as well. These poems are reproduced in Edmund Spenser's *The Faerie Queene*, ed. Thomas P. Roche (New York: Penguin, 1987), 19–33; see 1072–73 for a discussion of their printing history.

[46]In pointing out the way in which poets reflected and and reconfigured social codes, I participate in the ongoing and larger theoretical investigation that preoccupies many Renaissance historicist and Marxist critics, one concerned with elasticizing the lines of determination between the Renaissance text and the culture from which it was generated. For an example of a historicist practice that convincingly shows how Renaissance culture was itself dialectically and discursively produced, see Louis Montrose, "Shaping Fantasies: Figurations of Gender and Power in Elizabethan Culture," *Representations* 2 (1983): 61–94.

trolled in the sonnet of the 1580s and 1590s. Here we see sonnet writers emphasizing their text's erotic exchangeability while deliberately placing these works in print.

The Poetics of Print

"The Presse hath gathered into one," William Habington writes in the introduction to his poetic collection *Castara*, "what fancie had scattered in many loose papers."[47] Habington here suggests that the difference between manuscript and print practices rests primarily on an opposition between dispersal and unification. If coterie sonnets were identified by collective and collaborative methods of production—represented as situational and occasional, produced through dialogue and conversation, and characterized by textual diversity and openness—how could these poems operate as book commodities within a literary marketplace? Habington describes this transformation as a movement toward unification and fixity. When "the Presse . . . gathered into one" disparate texts, it countered not just *fancy*, as Habington suggests, but also an established and loaded set of reading practices.[48] For despite many writers' protests to the contrary, printing held the possibility of superseding the circuit of patronage that fostered this brand of textuality. If writers labored to highlight their poems' noncommercial and collectively authorized character, they did so within a more book-oriented environment at the end of the century. Thus, even if sonnet themes remained largely the same when they were published, the poems themselves as book objects became subject to various formal and physical arrangements that changed the way texts were understood and governed.

We have abundant evidence that writers worried about the possible changes that could be instigated by an expanding publishing industry. Witness to the increasing popularity of print practices, John Harington, for instance, frequently commented in his verse on the plight of courtly poets. In one such poem, "Of his Muse," Harington portrays the move-

---

[47]William Habington, *Castara*, STC 12585 (1640), no. 5.

[48]The printer's introduction to Spenser's *Complaints* also uses this thering. In this preface, William Posonby describes how he labored to "get into Poemes of the same Authors, as [he] heard were disperst abroad ir easie to be come by." "Of the which I have," he continues, "by together these fewe parcels present, which I have caused to bee ir that they al seeme to containe like matter of argument in them." In resent to his audience "the New Poet." STC 23078 (1591), reprint *Shorter Poems of Edmund Spenser*, 223–24.

ment from manuscript to print in terms of a wrenching away of poetic liberty. "Let others Muses fayne," he declares:

> Myne never sought to set to sale her wryting;
> In part her friends, in all her self delighting,
> She cannot beg applause of vulgar sort,
> Free born and bred, more free for noble sport.[49]

Harington here contrasts the genteel and free activities of well-bred coterie poems engaged in a world of sporting exchange with the poverty, baseness, subjugation, and prostitution of the published text. In "A Comfort for Poore Poets," Harington again bemoans the fact that "Verses are growne such merchantable ware, / That now for Sonnets, sellers are, and buyers" (*Letters*, 164). Harington's complaints not only signal a collision between the manuscript and print media, but also interpret that collision as a struggle between liberty (Barthes' free play, perhaps) and the strictures of the commodity (as mere "ware"). Having been appraised by values that inspired conspicuous consumption—liberality, excess expenditure, things that made them "free for noble sport"—texts entered an economy in which value partially rested on the ability to be accountable and purchasable ("set to sale"). If in a manuscript culture, poems were governed by social transaction rather than by singular author, poems in the literary marketplace had yet to be defined and classified.

The publication of *Astrophel and Stella* in 1591 inspired an outpouring of sonnet sequences at the end of the sixteenth century: Samuel Daniel's *Delia* (1592), Henry Constable's *Diana* (1592), Michael Drayton's *Ideas Mirrour* (1594), Thomas Lodge's *Phillis* (1593), Giles Fletcher's *Licia* (1593?), Barnabe Barnes's *Parthenophil and Parthenophe* (1593), William Percy's *Coelia* (1594), the anonymous *Zepheria* (1594), Spenser's *Amoretti* (1595), Richard Barnfield's *Cynthia* (1595), William Smith's *Chloris* (1596), and Bartholomew Griffin's *Fidessa* (1596).[50] As they presented these sequences to a larger reading public, publishers, writers, and printers reconceptualized the manuscript idea of the book by devising new principles of authorization, namely those based on an appeal to the structure and unity of the work itself. Because they could not easily authorize their works according to manuscript principles—by evoking the social bonds in which the text was situated and empowered—they looked for

---

[49]John Harington, *The Letters and Epigrams of Sir John Harington*, ed. Norman Egbert McClure (Philadelphia: University of Pennsylvania Press, 1930), 320.

[50]*Delia*, STC 6243.2; *Diana*, STC 5638; *Idea*, STC 7203; *Phillis*, STC 16662; *Licia*, STC 11055; *Parthenophil*, STC 1469; *Coelia*, STC 19618; *Zepheria*, STC 26124; *Amoretti*, STC 23076; *...thia*, STC 1483; *Chloris*, STC 22872; and *Fidessa*, STC 12367.

other, less socially oriented means of presenting published works. Through changes in rhetorical identifications and in the text's format, publishers fashioned the book into a less manuscript-identified object. In submitting previously variable and miscellaneous poems to a set order, publishers of sonnet cycles reformulated the textual, theoretical, and social relations evidenced by these coterie forms. The presentation of poems within published books thus articulated new relationships between writer, text, and reader.

On a simple level, the commodification of sonnets meant that individual texts had to be presented as forms that could be bought and sold rather than as assemblages of diverse and freely circulating parcels. In this sense, the transformation from manuscript poem to printed book tells us a familiar story, one in which the shift to print technology privileged a more aesthetically isolated text. While printed sonnet sequences did not, in fact, effect a widespread and radical transformation of the idea of textuality itself, I argue that the reformatting of the sonnet into the printed sequence signaled a shift in how the reading public was asked to imagine textual authority.[51] This invitation was necessitated by the fact that publishers could not tap into the inscription of authority within the sonnets themselves—as exchanged manuscripts sent out in the service of seduction—and merely use this topos as a means of authorizing the print commodity.

While type did not necessarily confer fixity on its more widely distributed and multiply reproduced objects, it began to be interpreted, even as early as the Renaissance, as an art necessarily concerned with stabilization. In a prefatorial letter to Thomas Watson's *Hekatompathia*, John Lyly describes print in just these terms: "I will shortly make your pryvie to mine [writings], which I woulde be lothe the printer shoulde see, for that my fancies being ever so crooked he would put them in streight lines, unfit for my humor, necessarie for his art."[52] By suggesting that print has the ability to harness inchoate emotions to a fixed form, Lyly (perhaps somewhat idiosyncratically) puts forth a more modern meaning for type. He

[51]That is, seventeenth-century readers often felt free to read according to manuscript principles—to reassemble printed material within their commonplace books and produce collaborative work. For a fascinating discussion of the royalist micropolitics of manuscript exchange and print in the mid-seventeenth century, see Ann Baynes Coiro, "Milton and Class Identity: The Publication of *Areopagitica* and the 1645 *Poems*," *Journal of Medieval and Renaissance Studies* 22 (Spring 1992): 261–89. In arguing that the move into print can be seen as a demystification of courtly elitist circles, Coiro describes a dynamic remarkably similar to the one I have traced in the publication of earlier printed miscellanies. Her study makes clear, however, the very different political resonances produced in marketing gentrification during this later time period. In the postwar era, she explains, private manuscript exchange constituted an act of social critique and an evasion of government surveillance systems.

[52]Thomas Watson, *The Hekatompathia, or Passionate Century of Love*, STC 25118a (1582), ed. S. K. Heninger, Jr. (Gainesville, Fla: Scholars' Facsimiles and Reprints, 1964), 8.

articulates a conception of print as more hermeneutically stable and less flexible handwriting. In noting that mechanical reproduction produces a unified and finished artifact, Lyly distinguishes between the art of print and manuscript forms. Like Habington, who sensed that the press's drive toward unity and singularity contradicted the play of fancy, Lyly opposes imaginative disorder with printed stability. Discovering that it was advantageous for the reading public to perceive texts as books rather than assemblages, writers, printers, and publishers struggled to gather into one the convertible and fanciful texts of the coterie. In doing so, textual producers devised formal and rhetorical strategies that converted unruly "crooked" poems into more fixed commodities. It is testimony to their success that writers such as Lyly and Habington read this art as a function of the medium itself.

The Authority of Flesh

Given the prominence of bodies in Petrarchan discourse, it is not surprising that publishers drew on corporeality as an important rhetorical trope when they sought to make exchangeable sonnets into merchandisable books. Corporeal metaphors were widespread in the Renaissance (in the phrase the "body politic," for instance), often used to designate a unified system of integral and yet stratified parts. When printers and writers characterized their newly popular published books, they employed the text-as-body analogy as a means of generating a new authorizing principle, one that pointed more to the intrinsic qualities of the text rather than its privileged route of circulation. By doing so, writers and publishers highlighted one particular thematic inscription of the body in sonnet discourse—the vision of the mistress as "fair text"—rather than the equally prevalent association between the speaker's body and poem. Renaissance writers turned to bones and flesh to naturalize a conception of the stable and saleable text. In submitting the text to incorporation as a principle of unity, they also presented a book commodity that had less permeable and provisional borders.

This strategy was hardly unique to writers in print. One of the most vociferous amateur writers, John Harington, similarly relied on personification as a technique for presenting a manuscript work to the Countess of Bedford (1600). In justifying his audacity in mixing his own poems with those of the Countess of Pembroke, he writes: "I have presumed to fill up the emptie paper with some shallowe meditations of myne owne; not to conjoine theis with them; for that were to piece sattin with sack-cloth, or patch leade upon gold; much lesse to compare them; that are but as foyle to a dyamond: but as it were to attend them. So as being bothe of meaner matter, and lighter manner, yett maie serve to waite as a wanton page is admitted to beare a torche to a chaste matrone."[53] Harington's words impose gender and hierarchy on the physical composition of the text. Drawing on a language common within the domain of patronage, he figures his poems as servants attending to the chaste woman, who here stands for both female author and recipient/patron. Harington plays with the notion that his poems are "wanton pages" (both in the sense of servants and texts) as a means of charting the power relations between his errant poems and her more magisterial verse. Harington's palpable shapes fashion the political terms of exchange, for his poems are already engaged in the client/patron relationship that he seeks.

This embodiment also unwittingly serves to mark the text in another way, to protect against the "participatory poetics" (in Ong's description of manuscript textuality) that necessarily de-emphasizes textual singularity and thus blurs authorial distinction. Harington's simile guards against the possibility that the poems may promiscuously collide on the page. Personification bolsters the rhetorical structures of difference used to suggest the impropriety (especially in this rank-conscious world) of gold being mixed with lead, of richly textured cloth being mixed with the cheaper text/ile. Bodies here serve as classifying barriers, and while Harington's wanton pages humbly deprecate themselves by attending the other more gentle poems, they also rely on that deference to mark themselves as separate, identifiable, and noteworthy. Any mingling would prove indecorous.

In drawing on bodies as a vocabulary for designating and classifying the relations between poems in terms of their social standing, Harington blends poetic reflexes associated with both Petrarchan discourse and the medieval envoi. Harington's preface introduces the embodied text through a moment of social obligation and deference. Renaissance writers and printers widely used this technique as a means of commodifying their books in the marketplace, because this trope could register the uneasy alliance between the text's physical autonomy and its placement within the social network. Sonnet collections are unified centrally through their transformation from scattered pages into an embodied and singular woman. Curiously, sonnet sequences are endowed with female titles. The names chosen for these works—*Diana, Coelia, Phillis, Fidessa, Licia, Delia, Caelica, Chloris, Zepheria, Cynthia*—place a corporeal grid over the texts. Disparate poems are made to coalesce into the figure of a particular woman, who acts as the unifying principle for governing the disparate and seemingly

---

[53]Petyt MS 538.43.1 in the Inner Temple Library. The letter is printed in Gary Waller's *Mary Sidney, Countess of Pembroke: A Critical Study of Her Writings and Literary Milieu* (Salzburg: Univeristät Salzburg Institut für Anglistik und Amerikanistik, 1979), 142–43.

scattered rhymes. Even sonnet collections with several addressees often bear a singular title; *Caelica,* for example, includes poems written to Mira and Christ as well as the title figure. And those collections that officially boast two names—a man's and a woman's—were commonly renamed by their readers to reflect the force of this gendered entitlement. Harington mentions Sidney's "sonets of Stella," and William Percy refers to Barnabe Barnes's poems as "those of Parthenophe."[54] As we shall see, this embodiment served to map the terrain of a more literary poetic corpus, and thus it was one technique among many that aided in replacing the convention of anonymity with the practice of the signature.

Literary history proves that it was not uncommon, of course, for texts to be personified. But writers at the end of the sixteenth century exaggerated traditional envoi personifications, highlighting the way the female title could authorize printed works. These exaggerations were further magnified by the novelty and increased significance of titles themselves. We have to remember that titles were exceptionally important during this time because title pages served as the only means of advertising books. If a book buyer were to stroll through the courtyard of St. Paul's, he or she would see title pages posted everywhere on booksellers' stalls. This flurry of papers acted as a sixteenth-century version of a cinematic preview for the book. Booksellers thus chose their titles carefully so as to maximize their ability to market their wares.[55] When stationers brandished female titles for their works, they drew on the appeal of a feminized good. One effect of this representation was, of course, a consolidation of the woman's proscribed subordinate position in Renaissance culture. Naming books as women constituted a mutually reinforcing moment of commodification, in which the overt display and objectification of equivalent merchandisable goods policed a woman's cultural standing, while at the same time identifying the book within a sanctioned existing cultural definition: as a *femme covert* necessarily in need of supervision by the more authoritative and masculine force of the writer and/or publisher.

In the introduction to *Phillis,* Thomas Lodge demonstrates the complexity of this identification when he tells the reader: "May it please you to looke and like of homlie Phillis in her country caroling, & to countenance

---

[54]John Harington, introduction to *Orlando Furioso,* ed. Robert McNulty (Oxford: Clarendon Press, 1972), 183; Percy, *Coelia,* Madrigal.

[55]Descriptions of bookselling practices can be found in Marjorie Plant, *The English Book Trade: An Economic History of the Making and Sale of Books* (London: George Allen and Unwin, 1939); and Edwin Haviland Miller, *The Professional Writer in Elizabethan England: A Study of Nondramatic Literature* (Cambridge, Mass.: Harvard University Press, 1959).

her poore and affectionate Sheepheard."[56] Through this directive, Lodge works, on one level, simply to introduce the "characters" in the sonnet sequence—the speaker and the beloved—and to ask for the reader's good will in learning of their "lives." But the conflation of text and woman gives his introduction a double edge, so that Lodge's simple identification calls attention to the relationship between the writer and his "homlie" written product. Instead of sending a female text out with the highly conventional instruction to defer to her patron, Lodge uses this mode of address to emphasize the pleasures afforded in imagining the text as modestly receiving the reader's gaze. As I discuss in Chapter 3, there is a prurient air to this display of the "country" woman; while implying merely that she is humbly rustic, the lewd pun (the same that Hamlet so glibly uses in addressing Ophelia) hints at her wantonness and paves the way for her necessary discipline by a governing authority. Combined with the announced title, this prefatory introduction primarily serves to extract from the sequence two subject positions for the author and now unified text. The reader is asked to empathize with the author's desire for his own "homlie" book, and thus to enrich the "poore" coffers of the humble writing shepherd whose affections are unanswered by other means. Exactly what is being shepherded here is slightly ambiguous. (Phillis could strangely be positioned as a sheep in one reading of these lines.) Less speculatively, however, we can see that the book *Phillis* becomes the object of the reader's gaze ("please you to looke and like") while the author asks for approval and *acceptance* on the grounds of his affection and desire.

William Smith's *Chloris* similarly presents the text as a personified figure. In the last poem, the speaker apologizes to Colin Clout for the book's publication, protesting that he had been supremely content that the poems remain private, "obscur'd from light." "But that it pleased thy grave Shepherdhood," the speaker explains, "the Patron of my maiden verse to bee, / When I in doubt of raging Envie stood, / And now I waigh not who shall Chloris see" (50, sig. A3). While Smith's words constitute a conventional appeal to Spenser for protection and a conventional justification of publication as accommodating a willing patron, the doubling of woman and book allows the same prurient punning evident in *Phillis* to surface.

[56]Thomas Lodge, *Phillis* STC 16662 (1593), sig. A2. The fact that this introduction is contained within an address to a female patron confuses the terms of presentation even more. The reader is made to inhabit unstable gender positions—as the female reader who can grant the poet the "affections" that the mistress withholds, and as a male buyer who takes pleasure in sharing the author's gaze. This doubleness marks the point of strain between the private dedication and the printed work. That is, the two readers point to the possible incompatibility of print and patronage within publishing practices.

Smith and Spenser confer together to display the "maiden verse" for potentially envious readers. The text is thus Smith's first poetical essay (his maiden), and is a maid herself previously seen by Colin, a meaning that establishes the collection of poems as a single object whose trafficking between writer and patron is now made visible to a larger public. The author's decision to publish his manuscript is explained in terms of the overtly erotic relationship between sonnet speaker and mistress, now extended to the economy of publication via the mediating figure of the patron. We have only to look at the way in which the word "Chloris" is employed differently in the previous sonnet (49) and this poem (50) in order to observe the power of this doubling; for while the speaker conventionally pleads with Chloris in Sonnet 49 to requite his love, he interprets her as his book artifact in the last poem (which contains both her refusal and his plea), a book that he displays to a public audience that may be equally inhospitable. In this move from mistress to text, the entitling word "Chloris" is transformed from a reading agent into a textual object.

Given these textual introductions and identifications, even the most innocuous allusion to the sonnet mistress can serve as self-referential commentary on the literary enterprise itself. When, in a commendatory poem to *Cynthia*, T.T. conventionally asserts the mistress's divinity ("Faire Cynthia lov'd, fear'd, of Gods and men"), the words carry an implicitly ambitious statement about the quality of the book embodied under her name. The titling of sonnet sequences when they moved into print makes Shakespeare's line more resonant and obviously commercial: "I will not praise that purpose not to sell" (Sonnet 102), for such titles generally make the speakers' praise and blame of the mistress sound more like a business negotiation. They create a network of puns within the sonnets so that when male speakers call out to the beauty of Diana, Phillis, and Fidessa, they praise and implicitly conceptualize their own disparate poetic works as a single praiseworthy female body. The intriguing fact that so many sonnet sequences bear a woman's name can partially be accounted for by the fact that this conflation allowed writers and buyers to see the book as a stable artifact—one that was more readily identified, signed, and commodified.

When introducing their sonnet collections as personified women, writers follow one of Queen Elizabeth's own strategic political uses of the idealized female body. In her famous speech to the troops at Tilbury, Elizabeth evoked the inviolate female body to suggest that her commitment to protecting the bounds of England was ensured by her gender: "I know I have the body of a weak and feeble woman," she said while rallying the troops on the eve of the Armada, "but I have the heart and stomach of a king, and of a king of England too. And I think foul scorn that Parma or

Spain, or any Prince of Europe, should dare to invade the borders of my realm." Elizabeth's words conflate geographical and biological borders in asserting her resistance against personal and military violation. In doing so, she appeals to an understanding of the idealized woman as an entity sealed, contained, and enclosed within herself.[57] In their use of titled personifications, writers enact a similar strategy. Dramatizing Mary Douglas's general notion that the "body's boundaries can represent any boundaries which are threatened or precarious," these writers produce from the body /text analogy more fixed textual, rather than national or class, borders.[58] One consequence is the implicit presentation of a writer as a powerful patriarch who governs, protects, and cautiously displays his highly contained, idealized, and weaker text.

The use of female personification as a technique for authorial presentation was evidently quite successful. Many commendatory poets praise the texts' authors in ways that call attention to the strange but compelling interdependence of textual mistress and writing subject. Richard Barnfield, for instance, notes how frequently a poet's *fama* rests in the name and body of a woman. "Live Spenser ever, in thy Faerie Queen," he announces at the beginning of one of these poems, and then he goes on to praise other poets specifically for their textual women:

> And Daniell, praised for thy sweet-chast Verse:
> Whose fame is grav'd on Rosamonds blacke Herse
>
> . . .
>
> And Shakespeare though, whose hony-flowing Vaine,
> (Pleasing the World) thy praises doth obtaine.
> Whose Venus and whose Lucrece (sweete and chaste)
> Thy Name in fames immortall Booke have plac't.[59]

Rosamond, Lucrece, and Venus provide the corporeal terrain on which these poets' "fame is grav'd." If publishers and writers used incorporation as a principle of authorization, their identification between female beloved and text offered a language through which an authorial claim was implicitly made. Barnfield tellingly accentuates the homology between "sweet-chast

[57]See Peter Stallybrass, "Patriarchal Territories: The Body Enclosed," in *Rewriting the Renaissance*, 123–44. Queen Elizabeth's speech at Tilbury is quoted in *English Women Writers Before 1800*, ed. Mary Mahl and Helene Koon (Bloomington: Indiana University Press, 1977), 48–49.

[58]Mary Douglas, as quoted by Louis Montrose in "The Elizabethan Subject and the Spenserian Text," in *Literary Theory/Renaissance Texts*, ed. Patricia Parker and David Quint (Baltimore: Johns Hopkins University Press, 1986), 315.

[59]Richard Barnfield, "A Remembrance of Some English Poets," in *Poems: In Divers Humors* (1598), reprinted in *The Poems of Richard Barnfield* (London: Fortune Press, 1936).

Verse" and the "sweet and chaste" female poetic subject. Inscriptions of the modest and inviolate woman paradoxically create a textual product that can reciprocally re-engrave its author, in "fames immortall Booke" no less. The entitling woman thus entitles the writing author. Spenser can live "in" the enclosed *Faerie Queene* because his text is staked out as a chaste corporeal domain worthy of bearing an authorial inscription.

The way in which writers discussed "feminized texts" clues us in to their awareness of the power of commodification exercised through such titles. We see this mode of identification, for instance, when Gabriel Harvey compares Spenser's epic and satiric work: "Mother Hubbard in the heat of chollar, forgetting the pure sanguine of her sweete Faery Queene, wilfully over-shot her malcontented selfe."[60] One effect of Harvey's decision to evaluate satire in terms of the disparities between two textual women is that both books are imaged as consolidated entities set apart by personal differences. After the success of Daniel's *Complaint of Rosamond,* which alluded explicitly to his complaint of Shore's wife as well as repopularized the complaint genre, Thomas Churchyard republished his complaint poem with an introduction predicated on a related strategy of authorization: "Because Rosamond is so excellently sette forth . . . I have somewhat beautified my Shore's wife."[61] If Harvey critiques Spenser's books by coding them in terms of feminine decorousness and excess, Churchyard figures textual revision as the application of cosmetics to another man's wife who is now claimed as his own. Churchyard's explanation is even more resonant because it falls on the heels of an indignant assertion of a paternally defined authorship; he condemns the reader who "denies [him] the fathering of such a worke that won so much credit." Robert Wilmot's preface to *Tancred and Gismund* suggests that a similar rhetoric could be used to justify the publication of dramatic works as well. When explaining his decision to print this twenty-five-year-old play, Wilmot tells his readership: "I am bold to present Gismund to your sights, and unto yours only, for therefore have I conjured her, by the love that hath bin these 24 yeres betwixt us, that she waxe not so proude of her fresh painting, to stragle in her plumes abroad, but to contein her self within the walls of your house."[62] Wilmot represents Gismund as his beloved mistress whom he reluctantly displays in her wanton (painted) form to the print audience "abroad." I

[60]Gabriel Harvey (1592), cited in *The Yale Edition of the Shorter Poems of Edmund Spenser,* 327.

[61]Thomas Churchyard, *Churchyards Challenge,* STC 5220 (1593), sig. T1ᵛ.

[62]Robert Wilmot, *The Tragedies of Tancred and Gismund* (1591), reprinted for the Malone Society Reprints, ed. W. W. Greg (London: Oxford University Press, 1914). In Chapter 3, I analyze in more detail how writers and publishers use the female body to scandalize the site of reading and writing.

offer this array of references to point out generally how writers figured books as unruly women (malcontented, painted, and beautified) who necessarily relied on the care and supervision of their publishing authors. The publishers and writers of sonnet sequences merely make this culturally widespread gesture a more constitutive feature of the form through the convention of female titles.

When writers use the woman/text analogy, they draw on and intensify one descriptive technique that is shot through the discourse of Petrarchan love so popular in literary works. As critics have repeatedly disclosed, Renaissance romances, plays, and poems make evident the implicit connection between bodily dismemberment and Petrarchan love, revealing, in fact, that the program of the sonnets turns on an array of dismembered bodies as well as scattered rhymes.[63] The *Arcadia* tells how the love-spurned wrath of King Tiridates led him to full-fledged slaughter: he "spared not man woman and child; but . . . wrote, as it were, the sonnets of his love in the blood and tuned them in the cries of [his beloved's] people" (303). Martial combat here makes common Petrarchan metaphors literal; that is, combat actually carves a name on the heart, generating the wounds of Cupid's arrow.[64] This overtly violent assault finds its nonviolent formal counterpart in the clipped sonnets and broken columns of poetic language that were commonly used by poets in their description of the female body.[65] In the miscellany *Love's Martyr* (1601), "Rosalin's Complaint" serves as the most extreme example of this widespread poetic technique; for this poem provides a seductive marginal gloss that labels each stanza as a body part. The reader is encouraged to linger on and sweep down the woman's body from forehead to feet, observing her head, hair, eyes, cheeks, chin, lips (with, of course, a conspicuous absence, the *nota*, in the

---

[63]Nancy Vickers, "Diana Described: Scattered Woman and Scattered Rhyme," in *Writing and Sexual Difference*, ed. Elizabeth Abel (Chicago: University of Chicago Press, 1986), 95–110.

[64]For another canonical instance, we can look to the episode at the House of Busyrane in *The Faerie Queene*, when Britomart seemingly stumbles into a Petrarchan poem. Negotiating her way through a set of literalized trappings of love, she finds Amoret with her heart cut out and the "arch Petrarchan poet," as one critic calls Busyrane, attempting to write on her heart; here the metaphor of the woman inscribed on the lover's heart is made graphically literal and rendered in its most violent form. See Maureen Quilligan, "Words and Sex: The Language of Allegory in *De planctu naturae*, *La Roman de la Rose*, and Book III of *The Faerie Queene*," *Allegorica* II (1977): 195–216.

[65]For examples of poems that enact the dispersion of body parts in its typographical format, see Ralegh's poem in *The Phoenix Nest* where "hir face, her tong, hir wit" are written in short, staccato lists in separate columns, dividing the poem into segments (71), and "My bonie Lasse thine eie" (60). *The Phoenix Nest*, ed. Hyder E. Rollins (Cambridge, Mass.: Harvard University Press, 1961), 71.

middle).[66] "Rosalin's Complaint" formally enacts a set of correspondences between female body parts and the disjunct nature of the poetic form.

Barnabe Barnes and Anthony Scoloker both explicitly comment on the conflation of texts and limbs that are dramatized in poetic form and allegorized in Renaissance narratives. In short, they suggest a crucial link between this poetic mode of description and the scattering of body parts. In Barnes's *Parthenophil*, the speaker demands:

> Where shall I Sonnets borrow
> Where shall I finde brests, sides and tong,
> Which my great wrongs might to the world dispence?[67]

Barnes's poem suggests the interchangeability of scattered rhyme and bodily limb. In his preface to *Daiphantus*, Scoloker mockingly says of Sidney's *Arcadia*: "The Prose and Verce, (Matter and Words) are like his Mistresses eyes, one still excelling another and without Corivall."[68] As metaphors for generic rivalry and for variant sonnet posturing, and as thematic counterparts to formal catalogs, blazoned body parts—breasts, sides, and tongues—neatly complemented the dispersed and disjunct poetry of coterie exchange. One legacy of Petrarch was a descriptive technique of bodily fragmentation that was enacted formally in English sonneteers' own *rime sparse* and linked metaphorically to the exchangeability of their poetic forms. In these instances, the blazon serves as an intensification of the synecdochic mode of representing femininity that pervaded not just love poetry but also Renaissance sermons, legal codes, and historical narratives.[69]

If the blazoned body functions as a thematic and formal expression of the unfixed, unruly, and disjunct nature of coterie texts, the less exchangeable published poetic forms that rolled off the printing presses had to be troped through other bodily representations. Rather than presenting scattered bodies and rhymes, writers, printers, and publishers held these texts tenuously together through embodying titles. The use of the highly conventional figure of personification thus throws into relief a primary feature of the sequence. When the sonnet cycle gathers the poems under the

---

[66]*Love's Martyr* (London, 1601), reprinted by the Shakespeare Society, ser. 8, nos. 1–4 (Klaus Reprint, 1965). For other instances of this conventional mode of poetic description, see Sidney's poem from the *Arcadia*, "What Tongue can her Perfections Tell," reprinted as "Pyrocles Praises Philoclea," in *Sir Philip Sidney: Selected Poems*, 47.

[67]Barnabe Barnes, *Parthenophil and Parthenophe*, STC 1469 (1593), ed. Victor Doyno (Carbondale: Southern Illinois University Press, 1971), Madrigall 1.

[68]Anthony Scoloker, *Daiphantus, or The Passions of Love*, STC 21853 (1604), sig. A2.

[69]See Karen Newman's discussion of "body politics" in *Fashioning Femininity and English Renaissance Drama* (Chicago: University of Chicago Press, 1991), 1–12.

name of the woman, it unites the poetic parcels circulating in manuscript and creates a re-membered book. Writers represent their texts as flesh in order to forge a new principle of authorization; in doing so, they code manuscript texts as a poetic disarray of scattered rhymes (associated with Petrarchan bodily scattering) and offer instead more fixed, commodified, embodied books. Foucault has suggested in peculiarly pathological terms that authorship is a "functional principle" that "impedes . . . the cancerous . . . proliferation of significations"; the publishers of sonnet sequences also interestingly recognized the connection between attribution and containment in terms of corporeal metaphors. Their presentation of printed sonnet sequences drew on a discourse of power and the body that countered Petrarch's dispersed representations of alternating breasts, tongues, and sonnets. Instead, these writers and publishers seized on and reversed the logic of the blazon in the arena of publication, reproducing its reflex of reification but creating a set of binary object relations instead of presenting collectable miscellaneous poems. In effect, writers and publishers extracted the positions of Petrarchan sonnet speaker and his displayed female mistress as the terms for defining the book in the marketplace economy. As a result, they strengthened the connection between writer and literary object.

Gender difference thus became crucial to both manuscript and publishing writers when they figured their text's mode of transmission and its subsequent social standing. As the printed book arrogated to itself the social power generated between men, publication created a gendered median third term—the female text—to be trafficked among readers. So feminized, the book became an appropriate object of male desire: desirable in its own right in the marketplace of sonnet sellers and buyers. Petrarchan poetry particularly accommodated the institution of patronage, as I have noted, because it expressed desire through reference to the exchange of physically convertible texts. By commodifying texts, writers, publishers, and printers picked up other formal and thematic Petrarchan codes, particularly those that authorized subject and object on the basis of gender. In other words, by catering to the needs of print technology, textual producers downplayed the ostensible power given to the female mistress as a figure for the patron/ reader and instead activated the power of reification found in blazoning the female body. One effect of presenting the book as an idealized mistress figure was the production of a masculinized author as a counterpart to the Petrarchan sonnet speaker—a figure produced in distinction to the inviolate feminized text that he governed and who profited from the textual stability, security, and unity offered by that analogy. In conceptualizing and authorizing the "idea of the book" against more socially authorized manuscript "parcels," writers and publishers relied on and reproduced a set of gendered roles embedded within reading practices. This move was double-edged, in that it feminized the text as well as recoded femininity. Cultural anxieties about the social and literary authorization of book commodities thus became inextricably embroiled in a discourse concerned with shifting gender ideologies. The presentation of published books partook of a rhetoric that embraided textual, cultural, and gender issues.

The Fixity of Form

In authorizing sonnet sequences when they placed them into print, publishers not only appended these personifying titles, but they also altered the physical presentation of the poems in ways that bolstered the textual unity provided by such figurative titles. In particular, they designed title pages that advertised the writing agent more prominently, arranged the poetic material within a more structured format, and highlighted the typographical features that stabilized the text. As a result, the printed sonnet sequence appeared to be a more stable and fixed artifact than any of its individual poems. These printed works dictated and controlled the reading experience more protectively than that of manuscript texts circulating within coterie circles. A book's reidentification was not dependent on whether the author did or did not supervise the text's actual publication, for she or he became the recipient of the newly emphasized textual authority that different textual producers arrogated to the book. Like the corporeal metaphors used in the presentation of sonnet sequences, the physical features of the book called attention to principles of authorization independent of the socially prestigious poetics of exchange.

This change in authorization is seen most obviously in the arrangement of poems on the page. If we look at two editions of *Astrophel and Stella*, one published in 1591 and the other in 1598, we see this text's evolution into a more ordered form.[70] Not only did the publisher include poems by Daniel in the first printed edition, but he also arranged the poems on the page so that they seemed to collide and connect more easily: more than one poem appeared on a page, the poems were broken in the middle of their stanzas by page breaks, and they were not separated either by borders, titles, or numbers (fig. 1). By placing the poems within this format, the publisher accentuated their miscellaneous quality and thus suggested the affinity of this work to a manuscript. In the later edition, the publisher saw fit, however, to impose a chronological order on the collection by

---

[70]Philip Sidney, *Syr P. S. His Astrophel and Stella*, STC 22536 (1591); *Astrophel and Stella* in *The Countess of Pembrokes Arcadia*, STC 22541 (1598).

separating the individual poems with numerals (fig. 2). Coterie readers had taken liberties in imposing a particular order of their own choosing on the poems they transcribed into commonplace books. The printed numerals in this later edition of *Astrophel and Stella* constrained this process; the protocols of reading established by this presentation suggest that the reader had editorial discretion only by countering the directives issued by the intervening numbers, directives that intensified the order always present when one reads a book. Rather than accentuating the poems' status as extraliterary occasional verse, numerical titles strengthened the autonomy of the book artifact by indicating that the sonnets' primary relationships were to the other poems within the text. Page numeration, itself a new feature of the printed book, heightened the linear nature of the reading experience. The sequences thus proscribed and encouraged a linearity that amplified the figurative "re-membering" performed through their titles.

If *Astrophel and Stella,* one of the first collections of its kind and certainly the most influential, underwent a tentative evolution toward a more uniformly presented chronological order, later sequences designed for publication bore such formatting devices when they were initially put into print. Samuel Daniel's *Delia* (fig. 3), Edmund Spenser's *Amoretti* (fig. 4), and Richard Barnfield's *Cynthia* (fig. 5) framed the individual poems through a simple but uniform page border. The printer's signaling word constituted the only moment in which that border was crossed. Numbers and borders served to create the effect of a closed and complete poetic unit, finished without the reader's collaborative aid. In this way, sonnet sequences revised the method of presentation used in miscellanies such as *Tottels,* where the poems were introduced according to their social situation and utility. Here numerical designations called attention to the reading experience rather than the social world in which the poem could function. Numeration occupied the slot where miscellanies had placed contexts ("a young lover to use in wooing," "a sonnet upon the mistress's eyes"). The sequences thus called attention to the poems' place in the reading path of the book rather than its use for wooing courtiers. Through these changes in format, publishers constructed the "closure of print" that scholars sometimes assume print inherently foments, and they contributed to the denigration of the reader's power (the "marginalization of the margin") that critics have noted.[71]

At the end of the century, engraved title pages became more common as well. During the medieval period, portraits of authors were placed on

---

[71]Jennifer Summit argues that print was instrumental in constructing a privatized personal space in distinction to the authority of typeface ("The Gloss That Mars: Gabriel Harvey's Marginalia," talk delivered at the Medieval Congress at Kalamazoo, Michigan, May 1992).

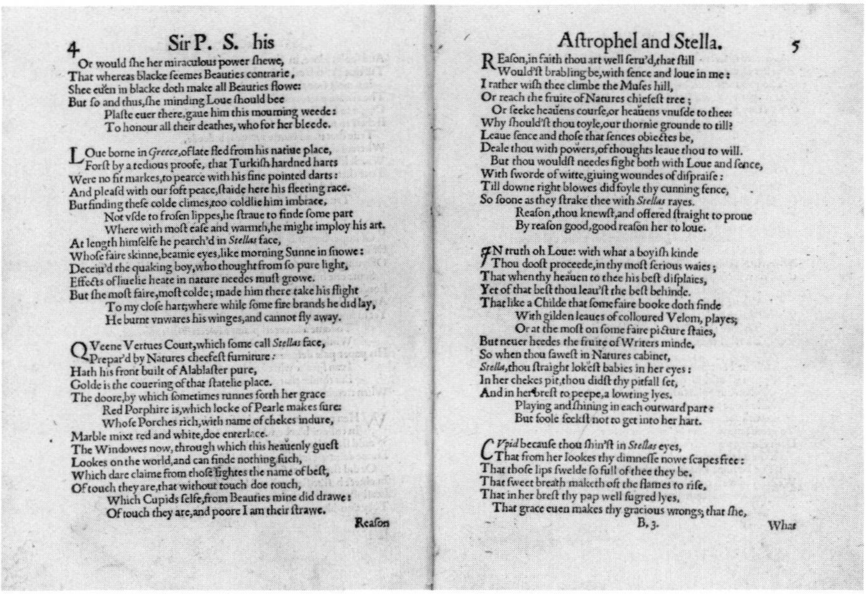

Figure 1. Astrophel and Stella, STC 22536 (1591). By permission of the British Library.

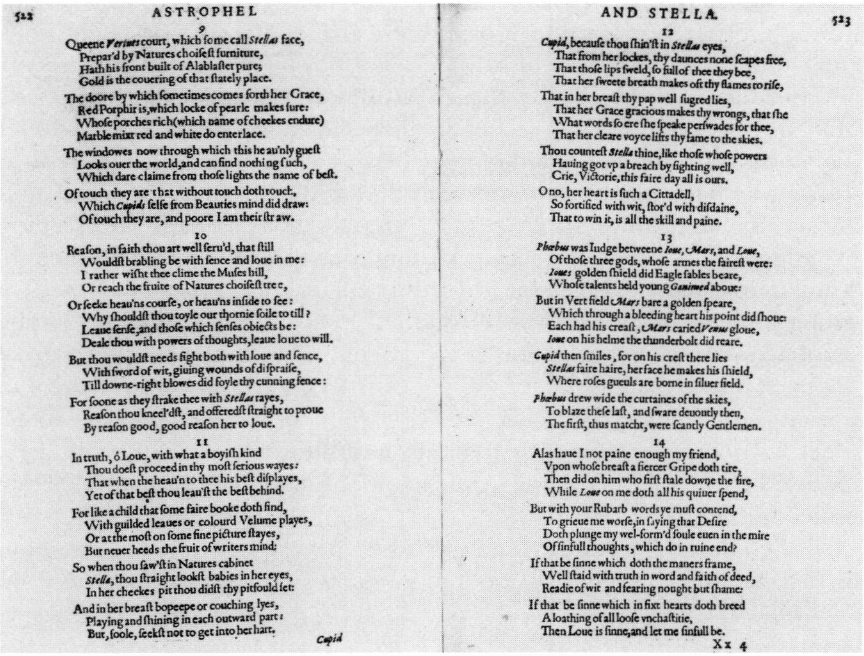

Figure 2. Astrophel and Stella, in *The Countess of Pembrokes Arcadia*, STC 22541 (1598). Courtesy of the Newberry Library.

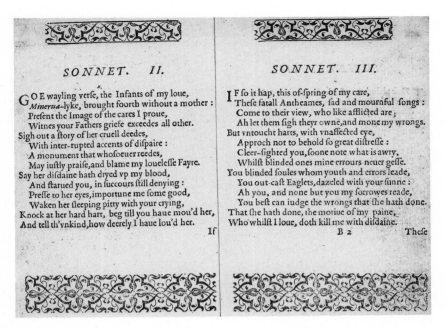

SONNET. II.

GOE wayling verſe, the Infants of my loue,
Minerua-lyke, brought foorth without a mother :
Preſent the Image of the cares I proue,
Witnes your Fathers griefe exceedes all other.
Sigh out a ſtory of her cruell deedes,
With inter-rupted accents of diſpaire :
A monument that whoſoeuer reedes,
May iuſtly praiſe,and blame my loueleſſe Fayre.
Say her diſdaine hath dryed vp my blood,
And ſtarued you, in ſuccours ſtill denying :
Preſſe to her eyes,importune me ſome good,
Waken her ſleeping pitty with your crying,
Knock at her hard hart, beg till you haue mou'd her,
And tell th'ynkind,how deerely I haue lou'd her.

If

SONNET. III.

IF ſo it hap, this of-ſpring of my care,
Theſe fatall Antheames, ſad and mournful ſongs :
Come to their view, who like afflicted are ;
Ah let them ſigh theyr owne,and mone my wrongs.
But vntoucht harts, with vnaffected eye,
Approch not to behold ſo great diſtreſſe :
Cleer-ſighted you,ſoone note what is awry,
Whilſt blinded ones mine errours neuer geſſe.
You blinded ſoules whom youth and errors leade,
You out-caſt Eaglets,dazeled with your ſunne :
Ah you, and none but you my ſorrowes reade,
You beſt can iudge the wrongs that ſhe hath done.
That ſhe hath done, the motiue of my paine,
Who whilſt I loue, doth kill me with diſdaine.

B 2   Theſe

Figure 3. Samuel Daniel, *Delia*, STC 6254, now STC 6243.4 (1594). Reproduced by permission of The Huntington Library, San Marino, California (RB 58732).

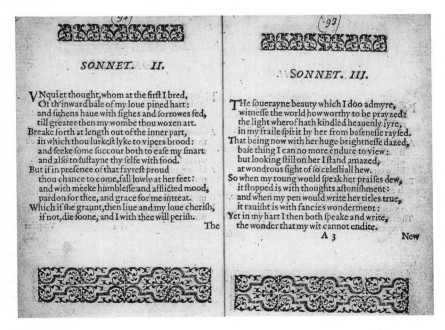

SONNET. II.

VNquiet thought,whom at the firſt I bred,
Of th'inward baſe of my loue pined hart :
and ſithens haue with ſighes and ſorrowes fed,
till greater then my wombe thou woxen art.
Breake forth at length out of the inner part,
in which thou lurkeſt lyke to vipers brood :
and ſeeke ſome ſuccour both to eaſe my ſmart
and alſo to ſuſtayne thy ſelfe with food.
But if in preſence of that fayreſt proud
thou chance to come, fall lowly at her feet :
and with meeke humbleſſe and afflicted mood,
pardon for thee, and grace for me intreat.
Which if ſhe graunt,then liue and my loue cheriſh,
if not, die ſoone, and I with thee will periſh.

The

SONNET. III.

THe ſouerayne beauty which I doo admyre,
witneſſe the world how worthy to be prayzed :
the light wherof hath kindled heauenly fyre,
in my fraile ſpirit by her from baſeneſſe rayſed.
That being now with her huge brightneſſe dazed,
baſe thing I can no more endure to view :
but looking ſtill on her I ſtand amazed,
at wondrous ſight of ſo celeſtiall hew.
So when my toung would ſpeake her praiſes dew,
it ſtopped is with thoughts aſtoniſhment :
and when my pen would write her titles true,
it rauiſht is with fancies wonderment :
Yet in my hart I then both ſpeake and write,
the wonder that my wit cannot endite.

A 3   New

Figure 4. Edmund Spenser, *Amoretti*, STC 23076 (1595). Reproduced by permission of The Huntington Library, San Marino, California (RB 69571).

SONNET. II.

Beauty and Maiefty are falln at ods,　　　(chin,
Th'one claimes his cheeke, the other claimes his
Then Vertue comes, and puts her Title in.
(Quoth fhe) I make him like th'immortall Gods.
(Quoth Maieftie) I owne his lookes,his Brow,
His lyps,(quoth Loue) his eyes, his faire is myne.
And yet (quoth Maieftie) he is not thyne,
I mixe Difdaine with Loues congealed Snow.
I, but (quoth Loue) his locks are mine (by right)
His ftately gate is mine (quoth Maieftie,)
And mine (quoth Vertue) is his Modeftie.
Thus as they ftriue about this heauenly wight,
　At laft the other two to Vertue yeeld,
　The lifts of Loue,fought in fayre Beauties field.
　　　　　　　　　　　　　　　　The

SONNET. III.

The Stoicks thinke, (and they come neere the truth,)
That Vertue is the chiefeft good of all,
The Academicks on *Idea* call,
The Epicures in pleafure fpend their youth,
The Perrepateticks iudge felicitie,
　To be the chiefeft good aboue all other,
　One man,thinks this : and ỹ conceaues another :
So that in one thing very few agree.
Let Stoicks haue their Vertue if they will,
　And all the reft their chiefe-fuppofed good,
　Let cruell Martialifts delight in blood,
And Myfers ioy their bags with gold to fill :
　My chiefeft good, my chiefe felicity,
　Is to be gazing on my Loues fayre eye.
　　　　　　　　　　　　　　　　Two

Figure 5. Richard Barnfield, *Cynthia*, STC 1483 (1595). Reproduced by permission of The Huntington Library, San Marino, California (RB28503).

presentation copies, but in print these portraits were presented in the form of the title page, a feature that arose to accommodate the new desire to identify the text for a larger public.[72] The practice of using title pages and elaborate accompanying frontispieces provided ground for identifying the textual commodity and its governing forces. If the preliminaries to books gradually began to emphasize the text's relationship to a writing subject, these engravings provided visual and iconic representations that supplemented the presentation of the author.

A look at the title pages from the various editions of Daniel's poems testifies to both an evolution of the authorial name and a reconstitution of what that name signified. As successive editions of *Delia* were published, the name "Samuel Daniel" gradually figured more prominently.[73] The title

---

　[72]In *The Comely Frontispiece: The Emblematic Title Page in England, 1550–1660* (London: Routledge and Kegan Paul, 1979), Margery Corbett and Ronald Lightbown offer a descriptive analysis of a range of Renaissance frontispieces, placing these forms particularly within the traditions of the emblem and the device.

　[73]Samuel Daniel, *Delia*, STC 6253, now STC 6243.2 (1592); *Delia*, STC 6254, now STC 6243.4 (1594); *The Works of Samuel Daniel*, STC 6236 (1602); *The Whole Workes of Samuel Daniel Esquire in Poetrie*, STC 6238 (1623).

page to the 1592 edition (fig. 6) simply placed the title within an architectural buttress made up of classical Corinthian columns accompanied by a motto and the printer's identification. Figures roughly corresponding to the appended complaint text's fictional characters of Rosamond and Henry II occupy the upper corners of the woodcut, while a floral border forms the lower boundary. In the 1594 edition, the page presents a magnification of the middle portion of the previous title page, enlarging the arch and eliminating the outer portion of the edifice (fig. 7). Thus the characters and the natural symbols disappear, and more space is devoted instead to the linguistic description of the text enclosed within the columns. But this description of the text is modified as well; most notably, Daniel's name replaces the description of the text and another poem, *Cleopatra*, is added. When *Delia* was published in Daniel's *Works* in 1602, Daniel's name became part of the title itself (fig. 8). The entire title page in this later edition is bordered by an elaborately ornate frame that monumentalizes the text and celebrates its writing origin. The icons of shepherd and king, designed to lean casually against the edifice's columns, point to the disparate genres that are contained within this collection and unified in part by an appeal to Daniel's family crest (displayed at the top of the border). This classicizing and heraldic frame packaged the coterie-identified sonnets like the classic texts that readers could find in the Bodleian; through these trappings, contemporary poetry was presented less as an ephemeral trifle and more as a contribution to a newly emerging institutionalization of English letters. Amorous sonnets are introduced by a different set of preliminaries in part because they are grouped with other literary genres (history, panegyric, elegy), all of which now become readable together through the unifying rubric of the author. Although it serves as a compilation of diverse material, Daniel's *Works* is a collection organized by a specific criterion that serves as the conceptual lens through which the various works are interpreted. The textual apparatus highlights the poems' singular origin, rather than their occasional status. The classicizing trappings of authority reimagine, reconstitute, and validate the new terrain of the writer's poetic corpus. "Turning sonnet" in this text is not an act of courtship, and writing is not centrally defined as a carrier of social relationship and obligation; instead, the exchange of courtly love becomes subsumed within the more general display of the writer's literary talents and wares. The architectonics of the folio volume in effect serve to monumentalize the poems.

The 1623 folio volume of Daniel's *Workes* includes a frontispiece reprinted from Daniel's *The Civile Wares* that presents his portrait embedded within the classifying icons of a pictorial border (fig. 9). This figure reveals the extent to which the personalized author has become important to the

Figure 6. Samuel Daniel, *Delia*, STC 6253, now STC 6243.2 (1592). Reproduced by permission of The Huntington Library, San Marino, California (RB 58734).

DELIA
and
ROSAMOND
augmented.
CLEOPATRA

By
Samuel Daniel.

*Ætas prima ca-
nat Veneres postre-
ma tumul-
tus.*

1594.

Printed at London for *Simon Waterson*; and
are to be sold in Paules Church-yarde at the
signe of the Crowne.

Figure 7. Samuel Daniel, *Delia*, STC 6254, now STC 6243.4 (1594). Reproduced by permission of The Huntington Library, San Marino, California (RB 58731).

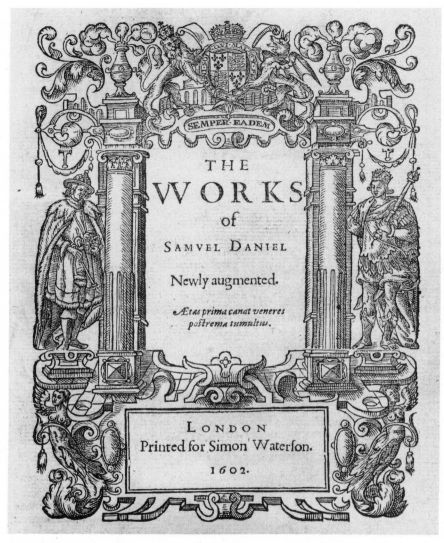

THE
WORKS
of
SAMVEL DANIEL

Newly augmented.

Ætas prima canat veneres
postrema tumultus.

LONDON
Printed for Simon Waterson.
1602.

Figure 8. The Works of Samuel Daniel, STC 6236 (1602). By permission of the
Houghton Library, Harvard University.

reader's interpretative process. As the words "Samuel Daniel" are expanded
to represent a corporeal figure, the author emerges as a personalized and
particularized emblem that intervenes in the reading process, if for no
other reason than that the book offers more information about the writing subject. The poems in the *Whole Workes* seem, in one sense, to emanate
from Daniel's very stare, for the author appears in this format to be surveying the title page that announces his authority. Daniel's portrait, in effect,

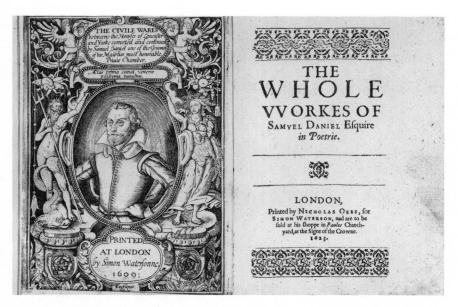

Figure 9. The Whole Workes of Samuel Daniel Esquire in Poetrie, STC 6238 (1623). Reproduced by permission of The Huntington Library, San Marino, California (RB 60945).

becomes the title to the work, for the title page is expanded to two full pages. If the title *Delia* first conjured up a female body that unified a highly miscellaneous poetry, that nomination gives way to the author's own name and corporeal representation. The sonnet sequence *Delia* becomes a constitutive part of *The Whole Workes of Samuel Daniel Esquire in Poetrie*, and Samuel Daniel becomes authorized as the writer of *Delia*, among other poetic texts.

The early publication history of Drayton's sonnet sequence *Ideas Mirrour* reveals a similar textual evolution.[74] The title page to the 1594 edition of the poems presents the title without ornamentation or the author's name (fig. 10). This edition primarily emphasizes the formal qualities of its poetry—"Amours in Quatorzains." Even the printer's mark serves to accentuate the amorous theme of the verse. Drayton becomes identified as the writer of these quatorzains only through his subsequent dedicatory poem to Anthony Cooke. When the sequence is republished in his collected *Poems* in 1608, however, the title page boasts not only the author's name

---

[74]Michael Drayton, *Ideas Mirrour*, STC 7203 (1594); *Poems by Michael Drayton Esquire*, STC 7218 (1608); *Poems by Michael Drayton Esquyer*, STC 7223 (1619); *Poems by Michael Drayton Esquyer*, STC 7225 (1637).

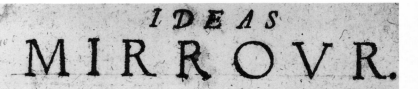

IDEAS
MIRROVR.

AMOVRS
IN QVATORZAINS.

Che ſerue é tace aſſai domanda.

AT LONDON,
Printed by *Iames Roberts*, for *Nicholas Linge*. *Anno*. 1594.

Figure 10. Michael Drayton, *Ideas Mirrour*, STC 7203 (1594). Reproduced by permission of The Huntington Library, San Marino California (RB51353).

and his gentlemanly status, but also an assurance that Drayton has "newly corrected" and revised the work (fig. 11). The authorization offered by this claim is underscored by its typographical presentation, for the title page is carefully framed by a border that augments the presentation of the

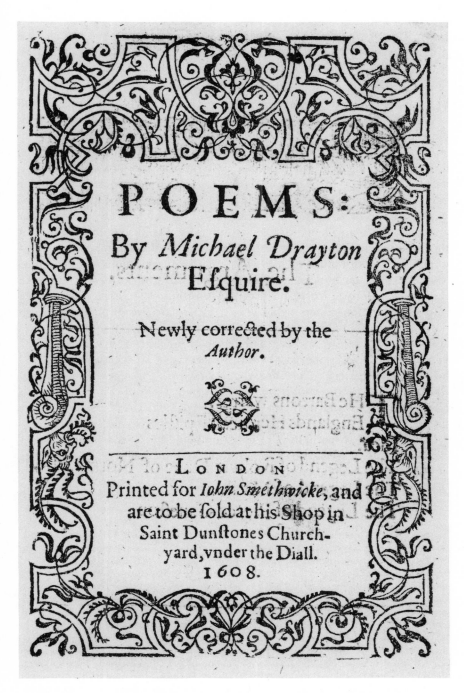

Figure 11. *Poems by Michael Drayton Esquire*, STC 7218 (1608). Reproduced by permission of The Huntington Library, San Marino, California (RB 60207).

title. The 1620 edition offers a more elaborate and stylized double title page, constructed as an edifice comprised of the representative emblems of the genres found in the volume—the satyr, the shepherd, Calliope, and Belona (fig. 12). As in the presentation of Daniel's collected poems, the book includes a frontispiece woodcut that faces the pictorial title page. Here Drayton makes an appearance in contemporary dress with a laurel adorning his authorial head. Unlike the portrait of Daniel, however, this figure is strangely rendered, in ways both natural and highly literary: natural in that it represents him in a pose common for individuals sitting for private portraits, but artificial in that this portrait is double framed to highlight the mythic and pictorial quality of the representation. The attached motto and laudatory verse only make the reader more aware of the monumentalizing effect of this framing. In the 1637 reprint, Drayton's face, now disembodied into the form of statuary, blends into the somewhat more seriously rendered classical icons that make up the pictorial title page (fig. 13). As his portrait is repositioned to share prominence with the mythological icons that depict the very origins of poetry, Drayton becomes more closely associated with the title designation and the mythic authority that these icons bear. The figure of the author, now more than a name or merely a personal portrait, functions as an interpretative focal point for the reader.[75] The title page to Drayton's *Poems* goes further than Daniel's by suggesting that the writer's claim to importance lies in his placement within the transcendent sphere of poetry and literary history rather than through his social status. The laurel that rests on Drayton's crown and the easy conflation of his disembodied face with potent literary icons not only suggests the scope of his ambitions, but also heightens the power of his textual function.

It would be a mistake to think that the authorial figure presented

[75]Several critics have commented on Ben Jonson's use of engravings on his title pages. See Corbett and Lightbown, *The Comely Frontispiece*, 145–50; Timothy Murray, *Theatrical Legitimation: Allegories of Genius in Seventeenth-Century England and France* (Oxford: Oxford University Press, 1987), 64–70; and Leah Marcus, *Puzzling Shakespeare* (Berkeley: University of California Press, 1989), 2–32. In *Shakespeare Verbatim: The Reproduction of Authenticity and the 1790 Apparatus* (New York: Oxford University Press, 1991), Margreta de Grazia reads Jonson's authorial folio engraving against that of Shakespeare's, arguing that while the architectonics of both folios fashion textual coherence by entitling these folio works to the lineage of the author, the textual apparatuses rely on two disparate modes that generate the very different cultural identities these figures have come to represent. Particularly in the Heminges and Condell folio, links between the bibliographical and biographical establish Shakespeare as the poet of nature and Jonson as the scholar. De Grazia persuasively makes this case in her analysis of how the 1623 Shakespearean folio performs the cultural and textual operation of stabilizing transitory theatrical texts. Her book is broadly concerned with how Malone's 1790 edition of Shakespeare constructed Shakespeare's particular "author effect."

through these preliminaries is severed completely from social relations or exists independently of issues of status. We have only to note other features evident on the title page to Daniel's *Workes*—the queen's motto and heraldic family crest, the designation "Esquire" placed after the writer's name—to see that the author remains defined in part by his ties to established social and cultural institutions. What are striking about these features, however, are their coexistence with a literary iconography that increasingly overshadowed and superseded the more socially oriented textual codes.

Modern editions that delete original title pages efface this narrative of the evolution of authorial prominence. As Margreta de Grazia says with regard to the 1623 Shakespearean folio apparatus, "The modern introduction assumes the identity of both the corpus and its author that the preliminaries are in the business of constituting" (*Shakespeare Verbatim*, 42). The transformation of Daniel's and Drayton's title pages highlights the gradual but active constitution of the author as a more powerful cultural sign, and it reveals the way in which authorship itself is reimagined in relationship to genre and mythology. While these changes in format were partially due to the individual writer's growing popularity (and thus the economic viability of publishing a collected *Works*), the fact that such popularity was expressed in authorial command over the text indicates a new impetus in the culture to link contemporary texts more solidly to their authors. In other words, print allowed a wider circulation, which produced a popularity that allowed this (reactive) physical format. Thus the writer's prominence (culturally) and the author's prominence (textually) functioned as mutually reinforcing events enabled by the publishing industry. When publishers chose to display the author's portrait in the introductory material to their books, they asked their audience to read the work not only through the rubric of a singular writer, but also according to a specified visual, often emblematic, and embodied perception of that writer. To the modern reader, this understanding of the text is so deeply engrained that it seems completely natural. What these title pages vivify, however, is the construction of that seemingly natural mode of reading. In the more specific case of the sonnets, these title pages show us how the authorial figure supersedes the titled mistress figure as the text's primary mode of identification. The world of sonnet speaker and mistress, and their subsequent figuration of publishing author and text, become inadequate to introduce the more inclusive collection of literary genres found in these editions. And the decision to read a host of works through the figure of the writer necessarily severs that figure from the authorial role of wooing courtier.

In making the claim that these typographical innovations accentuated

EFFIGIES MICHAELIS DRAYTON ARMIGERI POETÆ CLARISS. ÆTAT. SVÆ L. A. CHR. cɪɔ. ɔc.XIII

Lux Hareshulla tibi (Warwici villa, tenebris,
Ante tuas Cunas, obsita) Prima fuit.
Arma, Viros, Veneres, Patriam modulamine dixti;
Te Patria resonant Arma, Viri, Veneres.

{84}

POEMS
by
MICHAEL DRAYTON
Esquyer.

Collected into
one Volume.

With
sondry peeces
inserted

neuer before Imprinted

LONDON
printed for
John
Smethwick.

Figure 12. Poems by Michael Drayton Esquyer, STC 7223 (1619). By permission of the British Library.

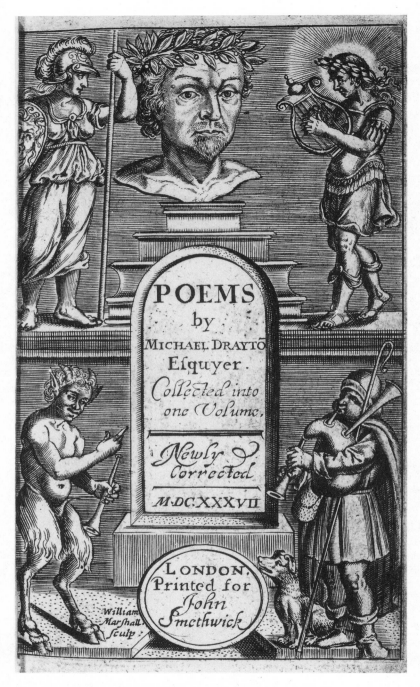

POEMS
by
MICHAEL DRAYTON
Esquyer.
Collected into
one Volume,

Newly
Corrected

M·DC·XXXVII

William
Marshall
Sculp:

LONDON,
Printed for
John
Smethwick

Figure 13. Poems by Michael Drayton Esquyer, STC 7225 (1637). Reproduced by permission of The Huntington Library, San Marino, California (RB 59021).

the function of the book format, however, I do not want to assign to this figure the traits only later ascribed to the modern author. These title pages certainly demanded that the reader acknowledge the writer as a presence when mentally cataloging the text. But this invitation did not, I think, produce a figure who authenticated the work; nor did it put forth a romantic genius who was thought to invent "from within" and give expression to authentic, interior, (and, contradictorily, transcendent) truths.[76] Instead, these portraits put forth a less defined writing origin who nevertheless personalized a realm previously identified by social function. In the case of Daniel and Drayton, classical emblems provide perhaps the only means possible for imagining an "authorizable" aesthetic realm, although the iconography's depersonalization is somewhat offset by the localization of the figure through dress and bearing. Generally, however, we can say that these frontispieces provided a governing center in the figure of the writer that coexisted with other forms of attribution seen in Renaissance books. This figure is important because it will become invested in later years with a cultural authority that makes it the locus of the text's universal and historical meanings.[77]

[76]In comparing the frontispiece of the Shakespearean folio to other folio texts in *Puzzling Shakespeare*, Leah Marcus claims that the Shakespearean edition creates this kind of tension by introducing a Shakespeare who refuses localization and who instead resides in the "starry" transcendent realm of Art. Marcus makes a case by appealing to omissions; that is, she argues that the folio lacks historical referents evident in other engravings. While sympathizing with the questions Marcus asks and with her attention to preliminary material in pursuing this field of inquiry, I am hesitant to claim that the folio engraving marks a departure from a fixed set of frontispiece conventions. In my view, rather than demonstrating a refusal to identify a historical author, the folio makes one of many kinds of provisional and exploratory gestures toward an undefined space of authorial intervention.

[77]For an account of the emergence of the more modern author figure in the eighteenth century within the context of the legal advance of copyright in Germany, see Martha Woodmansee, "The Genius and the Copyright: Economic and Legal Conditions of the Emergence of the 'Author,'" *Eighteenth-Century Studies* 17 (1984): 425–48. Woodmansee broadly outlines a shift in the conception of the writer as craftsperson to that of inspired genius, and discusses the complications in the legal definition of intellectual property.

I want to uncouple definitions of Renaissance authorship from issues of intellectual property. When the notion of literary property was raised in Renaissance England, it was framed in distinctly premodern terms: the notion applied centrally to the stationer's right to a text and was implicated in a language of social hierarchy. The introduction to the miscellany *England's Helicon* makes this concept of social property clear. Here the problem of correct attribution bleeds over into a discussion of proper social standing. It is important to understand that debates about textual property were implicated in the language of social receipt and hierarchy rather than in a discourse of individualism, and that such debates afforded no special privilege to the writer, but instead focused alternately on the multiple producers of the text—stationer, publisher, compiler, and writer. *England's Helicon* (1600), ed. Arthur Bullen (London: Lawrence and Bullen, 1899).

As well as emphasizing and rescripting the role of the author, these title pages were significant because they framed coterie poems within elaborately wrought pictorial woodcuts and borders. Because these borders seal the linguistic signs on the page and demarcate more rigidly the boundaries of the poetic material, they produce a more finished and "closed" artifact, insulated from the readerly alterations invited by manuscript exchange. The array of title pages that I have displayed here indicates that the introductory apparatus to these published poetry collections usurped what had previously been the prerogative of the reader. The move into print, as Paul Saenger and Michael Heinlen argue, did alter the balance of power between reader and writer: "The perfection of printing techniques divested the reader of the last vestiges of his ancient role as textual clarifier and planted seeds for modern book etiquette, which views the printed page as sacrosanct and consequently all handwritten additions to the printed page as personal notes, detrimental to subsequent common use."[78] This appropriation from reader to writer was not, of course, an arrogation of power from a mass reading public to a monumental authorial ego, but an encroachment on a rich and powerful group of private readers. Certainly the printed form (and the author it often established) offered a counterclaim to the reader's editorial power at the very moment that the book was distributed to a larger audience, but I want to guard against a nostalgic impulse to see these formal designs as paving the way for a concept of intellectual property by enclosing a previously free and shared textuality. Instead, we must acknowledge that while the exchangeability of texts rendered them writerly events, such events were confined within the domain of an exclusive social group.

In designing books that bore these symbolic codes, I argue, publishers signaled the book's transformation from permeability to stability. Recent critical work on the theatrical script in the marketplace has identified a related transformation. At the end of the sixteenth century, plays, emerging from complicated processes of transmission, were being published in great number. Scholars have labored to describe these processes as they have hypothesized about memorial reconstruction, cataloged compositors' errors, and speculated on "good" and "bad" quartos. While the intricate textual and social issues evident in publishing scripts were very different from those that arose when coterie poems were placed in print (the

---

[78]Paul Saenger and Michael Heinlen, "Incunable Description and Its Implication for the Analysis of Fifteenth-Century Reading Habits," in *Printing the Written Word: The Social History of Books, Circa 1450–1520*, ed. Sandra L. Hindman (Ithaca: Cornell University Press, 1991). Jennifer Summit summarizes Saenger and Heinlen's argument and places it within a larger argument about the revaluation of textual margins ("The Gloss That Mars").

theatrical work, for instance, being constituted from distinct compositional practices), this process of commodification often turned on a common grammar. I think it crucial to mention that publishers developed editing practices to counter the script's instability that were strikingly similar to the strategies used in printing poetic texts. Although located in very different cultural sites, coterie sonnets and play texts began to be presented as unruly bulks of language, whose collaborative process of creation complicated their status as marketable commodities. Theatrical texts were even more unauthorized than poetic texts, for exactly opposite reasons: they were seen as illegitimate and vulgar trivial events rather than as elite but trivial noble "sport." Theatrical scripts circulated in a manner that made their preservation even more difficult than that of poetic ones (not only unbound or loosely stitched, but also in variant partial scripts held by acting companies). Legitimating the authority of the theatrical book was an even more arduous task than the business of legitimating the private forms of printed poetry. For the theatrical script was not only subject to multiple sites of production and protean textual practices, but it was also associated with a socially suspect cultural domain. From opposite ends of the social spectrum, these nonfixed, nonprint texts elicited concern over issues of textual stability and authority when placed in print. Certainly the gathering of quartos into folio form (performed in Jonson's 1616, Shakespeare's 1623, and Beaumont and Fletcher's 1647 collected works) can be seen as analogous to the project of integrating miscellaneous poems into a single volume. Both textual endeavors use a similar authorizing preliminary format. William Hole created the engravings, for instance, that announced both Jonson's and Drayton's collected works. Both kinds of textual publications—poetic and dramatic—involved unifying and stabilizing a disparate and transitory set of socially transacted events.

The gestures made by the publishers of Drayton's *Poems* and Daniel's *Workes* were intensified by their more durable folio form, books whose cost hardly allowed them to be seen as "parcelles" sent carelessly between diffident senders and receivers. Instead, these collected editions stand at the end of a process of evolution in which publishers presented the book more as a monumental literary artifact inhering within itself and its origin and less as a process-oriented function that harkened toward more powerful readers and patrons.

The Conventions of the Book

While the need for an authorial copyright was not even articulated until one hundred years later, the author presented by published sonnet sequences acts as a more important category for defining what Harington sneeringly terms the "merchantable ware" of the literary marketplace. Drayton's sonnet sequence *Idea*, revised and republished late in the vogue of sonnet writing, recognizes this shift of authority in promissory form when it accentuates the writing figure as an authorizing principle. By suggesting that his poems are circumscribed within the confines of his own psyche, Drayton reconceptualizes the concept of *varietio* that informs poetic collections. The speaker notes that his pen strives to "eternize" his beloved, but in his struggle with tyrannical time to make his lover young and beautiful again, it is himself whom he declares to be immortal:

> And though in youth, my youth untimely perish,
> To keep Thee from oblivion and the grave;
> Ensuing Ages yet my Rhymes shall cherish,
> Where I entombed, my better part shall save;
> And though this earthly body fade and die,
> My Name shall mount upon Eternity!
>
> (44; 1619)

Drayton's authorial figure on the title page makes these words doubly resonant; his "entombed . . . earthly body" does occupy at least one representative form not subject to mortal decay. Even his language of entombment is cagey; although the speaker initially generates a correspondence between his mistress's immortality and his untimely perishing youth (suggesting his own sacrifice as necessary for her transcendence), he goes on to replace her immortality with his own by framing them together within a transcendent cultural memory that combats death. The praised mistress and the speaker's "better part" both become exempt from the grave. His sacrifice of youth becomes a reinscription of himself within his eternal "Rhymes." The speaker thus strays from the conventional argument that verse will keep his beloved from the grave to a declaration of his own engraved/imprinted status. Promising and claiming a textual immortality, Drayton is clearly "impressed" by, and with, his poetic artifacts. The sense that the work is originally unified (through its authorial origin) pervades the texture of the work, so that the "Name" of the writer, now more visible and ornately framed on the title page, is scripted as ascending into the timeless heavens through his poetic receptacle.

The establishment of an authorial consciousness becomes a more fundamental part of Drayton's sequence generally, as his introductory sonnet, "To the Reader," makes clear:

> My verse is the true image of my Mind,
> Ever in motion, still desiring change:
> And as thus to variety inclined;

> So in all humours sportively I range
> My Muse is rightly of the English strain,
> That cannot long one fashion entertain.
> ("To the Reader," 1619)

When Drayton locates diversity within the consciousness of the writer
rather than in the makeup of the text itself, he chooses to emphasize Petrarch's opening identification of his fragmented sonnets as psychological
experience: Petrarch's *Rime Sparse* points to the dispersed emotional state
of the speaker.[79] Drayton's articulation of this poetic difference-in-unity is
consolidated by the characterization of his sportive mental ranging as
decidedly "English." His verse is thus a mimetic replication of his mutable
will ratified by national identity. The second sonnet, similarly addressed to
the reader in the 1605 edition, recapitulates this identification. Like his
own libertine fancy, Drayton states:

> My wanton verse nere keepes one certain stay,
> But now, at hand; then, seekes invention far,
> And with each little motion runnes astray,
> Wilde, madding, jocund, and irregular.
> (1605, sig. B5)

Here the verse's metrical and thematic irregularities reflect neatly the ardent poet's own unruly desires. The discontinuities of the text thus become explicable in terms of the poet's own "wanton" nature.

Drayton furthers this set of associations in the 1619 edition when he follows the introductory poems with a sonnet in which he figures himself as a
traveler called to tell of his explorations: "Like an adventurous seafarer am
I / Who hath some long and dangerous voyage been; / And called to tell
of his discovery." Using the metaphor of the voyage, Drayton presents his
poems as the cartographical depictions of his heart's emotional sojourn,
the book's variety explained by the divergent experiences the single traveler
encounters. While other sonnet sequences emphasize their organizing
principle of *varietio*, Drayton's frame verse suggests that instability is not
primarily a structural feature of the text, but a description of the inchoate
feelings associated with love. Variety becomes the characteristic of the
modern subject, rather than a mark of the missing social transaction that
had occasioned the verse. Of course, these two dimensions, formal and

[79]Petrarch, *Petrarch's Lyric Poems*, ed. and trans. Robert Durling (Cambridge, Mass.:
Harvard University Press, 1976). For a different reading of the effects of print on Petrarch-
anism, see William J. Kennedy, "Petrarchan Audiences and Print Technology."

thematic, always correspond in the sonnet collections: the varieties and incoherency of love maintaining the varieties and incoherency of the text. But Drayton's collection shifts the emphasis to accentuate the guiding "I" that can contain and embody the disorders of the form. When the penulti-mate sonnet in the sequence recalls that initial travel metaphor as a means of explaining the paradox of desire, it reconfirms the difference-in-unity paradigm subtending the sequence and establishes a circularity to the book that can frame its contradictions: "When first I ended, then I first began; / Then more I *travelled* further from my rest" (62;1619). Caught in a tantalizing feedback loop of desire and frustration, the speaker chooses poetic metaphors that account for the lack of closure by appealing to the vagaries of desire. Miscellaneous poetry is, in fact, the product of the mis-cellaneous experiences of love.

J.C., author of the sonnet collection *Alcilia* (1595, rpt. 1613), offers a similar claim in his introduction: "These Sonnets following were written by the Authour . . . at divers times, and upon divers occasions, and there-fore in the forme and matter they differ, and sometimes are quite contrary to one another, considering the nature and qualitie of LOVE, which is a Passion full of varietie, and contrariety in it selfe."[80] The diversity of the work, as the writer suggests, registers love's forceful ability both to pro-duce and to catalogue miscellaneous passions. As does Drayton, J.C. resitu-ates the variety of the work by placing it within the definition of one tur-bulent and contrary emotion, making it an identity "in it selfe." This redef-inition serves as a means of containing the disparate verses within the ex-perience and scope of the writing origin. If for Petrarch, the "act of falling in love is a fragmentation of the personality, an emotional dispersal under the pressure of desire," as Marion Campbell claims ("Unending Desire," 87), then the increasingly popular published sonnet sequences reproduce the fragmentation predicated on the finished form of Petrarch's *Rime Sparse* (rather than use Petrarch as a handbook for creating miscellaneous scattered rhymes). The published sonnet sequences, unlike the miscella-nies we shall discuss later, mark a return to Petrarch's (always already for-mulated) representation of difference within the psyche. While Petrarch generally lent to sixteenth-century English writers a poetics of unity/frag-mentation (disseminated in various ways thematically in mid-Tudor poetic miscellanies), that poetics becomes vital *as a formal principle* in single-authored sequences that stress the integrating possibilities of poetic and

---

[80]J.C., *Alcilia, Philoparthens loving folly*, STC 4274 (1595), reprint STC 4275 (1613), B2. Germaine Warkentin cites this passage in a different context in "'Love's sweetest part, vari-ety': Petrarch and the Curious Frame of the Renaissance Sonnet Sequence," *Renaissance and Reformation* 11 (1975): 20.

psychic fragmentation. The controlled formal disarray acts as a simula-crum of the poet's disordered psyche—"turning sonnet" as the artful con-versation *between* becomes that enacted *within*. Rather than the exchange of critical taste in elite circles, the "turn" implied by J.C. and Drayton marks the thematic of the divided self, the display of a passion "full of . . . contrariety in it selfe." It is quite telling that the highly popular printed sequence appeals to desire as a means of turning the "turn" of the son-nets. If the various exchanges of desire and writing in the poems empha-size their indebtedness to social relations, desire here enables a recogniz-ably modern speaking figure, riven but unified, who emerges from those exchanges.

Closures

While it may seem natural to argue that print generates a realm of objectivity and thus distances the writer from his or her own work (the "hand" of the manu-script), I suggest that print allows instead for the construction of the writing figure. In Renaissance manuscript works, this figure was defined as a participant in a sociotextual event rather than as the text's origin. The rhetori-cal and typographical identifications offered by sonnet sequences de-empha-sized the bonds of social obligation that held the text within a system of patronage and instead emphasized the incorporated and static book object and its monumental writing figure. In these particular kinds of presentations, the book seems to constitute for itself its place in the poetics of print, a mode of textuality that informs much of our twentieth-century critical assumptions. For we generally take our critical cues from Drayton's representation of the sonnet and from the shifts in typography that consolidated that representa-tion. We see the poems in light of their relationship to a speaking subject rather than as a social transaction; we look for what Barthes calls the "inscrip-tion of the Father," the patriarchal figure who is shadowed within the speak-ing subject ("From Work to Text," 161). The dominant way in which these works have been read for centuries is, in fact, as *sonnet sequences* rather than as miscellaneous collections of poems, sequences governed by a flickering and discontinuous writing subject who acts as a forerunner of modern subjectivity. Discussing Petrarch, John Freccero argues that "the extraordinary innovation in the *Canzoniere* is rather to be found in what the verses leave unsaid, in the blank spaces separating these lyric 'fragments,' as they were called, from each other. The persona created by the serial juxtaposition of dimensionless lyric moments is as illusory as the animation of a film strip."[81] Drawing on

---

[81]John Freccero, 'The Fig Tree and the Laurel: Petrarch's Poetics," *Diacritics* 5 (1975): 34.

Augustinian poetics, Freccero argues that the string of poems, "like pearls on an invisible strand," create a surface of mirrors in which the poet can self-referentially create himself. The Petrarchan lover, composed of shards and fragments, perpetually re-creates himself through ever-shifting postures that generate his (discontinuous) identity.[82]

Many critics have activated a similar paradigm when reading English sonnets: interpreting the work with an expected textual coherence allows critics to posit the formation of the postmodern subject within disjunct poetic moments. This subject acts as the point of access for assessing psychic and formal discontinuities and continuities. Waller, for instance, argues that along with Protestantism, Petrarchism "provide[s] complex mechanisms whereby the desiring subject [is] permitted to speak, put under observation, and articulated in the presence and under the power of an Other (a mistress or a God), through which speaking wells up as a seemingly obligatory truth-bearing act and which asserts or desires to reveal a stable, given, pre-existent, autonomous and originating self" ("The Rewriting of Petrarch," 70). In making this argument, Waller relies on a modern notion of the integral text to argue ironically for the construction of the modern subject. Rather than suggesting that such readings are misguided, I am concerned with pointing out that they respond to only one set of reading cues within the poems.

Governed by the category of "author," the text more easily offers itself as a narrative representation of the "story" of love's experience. The self becomes the absent presence that catalogs the text and motivates a precarious "plot." Critics have come to see the poems as the expression of the solitary lover/poet lost in his own torment—and some have gone on to inform this poet with biographical specificity. Literary scholars have made sonnet cycles reveal a full story, one in which Lady Rich and the "dark lady" play central roles. The genealogy of the sonnets' critical history reveals a progressively more engaged attempt to "fix" the text by filling in what are seen as elliptical spaces with biographical, historical, and structural narrative. A sample of titles makes this point strikingly clear: *The Secret Drama of Shakespeare's Sonnets Unfolded, The True Order of the Sonnets, The Answer to the Mystery of W. H.* As Stephen Orgel points out, postromantic criticism tends to read these works anachronistically as narratives that hover around a particular authority, a mode of reading that presupposes a fixed text, an origin, and a controlling speaking subject.[83] At the begin-

---

[82]Marion Campbell offers an important key for understanding Sidney's complex inscription of the reading process: "To see fragmentation as a principle of structuration provides a means of connecting thematics and poetics," "Unending Desire," 94.

[83]Stephen Orgel, "The Authentic Shakespeare," *Representations* 21 (1988): 1–25.

ning of the twentieth century, for instance, critic and biographer Sir Sidney Lee evaluated the sonnet sequences based on their expression of the writer's personal authenticity and candor, a romantic expressivist criterion that persists in variant forms in many critical strains.[84] The history of sonnet criticism thus constitutes an increasingly complex and divided response to the terms effected in part by the rhetorical self-identifications and new formats of printed books, both of which de-emphasized the social, sexual, and economic ideologies played out within textual exchangeability and instead emphasized the authority of the writer and the autonomous text. This emphasis is perhaps nowhere more evident than in textual practices, where the author has for many years been the sole determinant in matters of classification (for instance, the Short Title Catalogue exasperatingly lists by author), and of editing, where the "authorized" text has been privileged over collaborative work even when the collaborative or unauthorized versions were more socially and literarily influential. Critics of Renaissance sonnets have ironically chosen to take their cue, it seems, from the reading imperatives and textual authorizations offered by publishers when they put Renaissance sequences into print.

Miscellaneous Privileges and Pleasures

Sonnet sequences were not the only form in which lyric poetry was published for the increasingly literate sixteenth-century audience. In the wake of *Tottels Miscellany*, anthologies presenting didactic and amorous verse, broadside ballads, psalm translations, epigrams, satires, pastorals, and maxims flooded the market. Miscellanies were such popular literary forms, in fact, that one was published or republished every year of Elizabeth's reign. A partial list of these works includes *A Handful of Pleasant Delights* (1566); *A Small Handful of Fragrant Flowers* (1575); *The Paradise of Dainty Devices* (1576); *A Gorgeous Gallery of Gallant Inventions* (1578); *The Forrest of Fancy* (1579); *A Banquet of Dainty Conceits* (1588); *Brittons Bowre of Delights* (1591); *The Phoenix Nest* (1593); *The Arbor of Amorous Devices* (1597); *The Passionate Pilgrim* (1599); *England's Helicon* (1600); *Belvedere, or The Garden of the Muses* (1600); *Loves Martyr or Rosalins Complaint* (1601); and *A Poetical Rhapsody* (1602). While publishers defined printed sonnet sequences, as opposed to collective writing, by employing an author-oriented

---

[84]In *Critical Contexts of Sidney's "Astrophil and Stella" and Spenser's "Amoretti"* (Victoria: University of Victoria, 1989), Janet MacArthur surveys several twentieth-century interpretive paradigms (romantic expressivist criticism, modernism, numerological formalism, reader-response criticism, new historicism, and feminism) and their applicability for analyses of these sonnet sequences.

mode of textual attribution and organization, they emphasized the miscellanies' heterogeneity (as our modern genre title so clearly signals) rather than the text's coherence under the rubric of the author. Because they look strikingly like personal commonplace manuscript books, miscellanies consolidate the value of poetic amateurism in the realm of print.

I began this chapter by noting how alien and assorted *Tottels Miscellany* can appear to the modern reader. Given the social investment in seeing texts as exchangeable manuscripts, the published book's miscellaneous quality becomes socially significant. For the structural variety in published works forged that text's relationship to the textual economy of manuscript culture rather than to the newly popular literary marketplace. We might expect that the physical fact of mechanical reproduction would ensure that published works be modern—that is, be characterized by fixity and uniformity rather than fluidity. Early printed Renaissance books, however, like many of their medieval and contemporary manuscript counterparts, were permeable artifacts, not only subject to the considerable vagaries of composition in the printshop, but also constituted by a principle of variety. Such books flaunt textual assortment and flexibility rather than textual coherence. Gascoigne's *Posies*, for instance, boasts a commendatory poem jumbled into the middle of the volume. Similarly, the seemingly prefatorial "Fraunces Flower in the Commendation of the Authour" finds itself lodged in the middle of Thomas Howell's *The Arbor of Amitie* (Saunders, "From Manuscript to Print"). Rather than acting as signs of a new system fostered by the logic of print culture (which is supposedly linear, frozen, and stable), these printed texts register marks of circulation in their disorderly collation. The Elizabethan miscellany thus bears an odd relationship to other printed books: on the one hand, it highlights the possibility of representing manuscript practices in print and, therefore, chooses to ignore revisionary modes of authorization and attribution; on the other hand, it simply exemplifies in strong form the permeability displayed generally by most early printed books.

Unlike individual sonnet writers, the publishers of miscellaneous anthologies were not concerned with their own social status when they reduplicated coterie practices. For in disseminating manuscript-like texts to a larger and more assorted reading audience, publishers participated in an economy separate from the system of courtly reward and preferment; they were not publishing these anthologies to find patrons. Because they failed, in fact, to emphasize their own authority in composing these collections, the producers and compilers of miscellany texts are often unknown. More likely, publishers sought to trade on the prestige attached to privately circulated works as a means of securing patents for more publications; they marketed exclusivity. Such a project ironically had the effect of placing pressure on one of the very reasons for a popular reception: the privilege these texts generated by being withheld from view. Printed miscellanies functioned as conduct books, I argue, because they demonstrated to more common audiences the poetic practices entertained by graceful courtly readers and writers. Rather than merely teaching poetic manner and decorum through their content, these books demonstrated *formally* the various ways in which poetry could be made to serve social functions. Staging intratextual exchange in a way that dramatized the permeability and exchangeability of their poems, miscellany compilers invited participants to join in the noble sport of poetic camaraderie that upheld the coterie. These highly popular texts, then, replicated manuscript practices in print by playing out the poetics of exchange through the texts' rhetorical self-identifications and formal structuring.

Like their manuscript counterparts, miscellanies were indifferent to establishing a stable authorial signature to authorize or govern the work. In the first popular miscellany, which we with our name-dependent practices identify as *Tottels Miscellany*, but which was known in the Renaissance as the *Book of Songes and Sonettes*, authorial markers are used only in a provisional manner. It is fitting, however, that the text was later retitled with the printer's name in the nineteenth century, for it would have been in keeping with the Renaissance notion of textuality that a work be marked by the name of the printer rather than the author's. The *Norton Anthology* series serves as the most prominent contemporary vestige of this type of attribution, one in which commercial authority takes precedent in the text's presentation.

While *Tottels Miscellany* did boast a title page that claimed Surrey as the text's primary author ("Songes and Sonettes, written by the ryght honorable Lorde Henry Haward late Earle of Surrey, and other"), the individual attributions within the book make clear that Surrey wrote less than a fifth of the 213 poems. His place of importance on the title page seems to be a function of his social, rather than authorial, status. As the book presents sections signed by various authors, it offsets Surrey's place of prominence on the title page. The initial nomination on the title page, then, contradicts the text that follows, or rather, Renaissance readers saw no contradiction in multiple names and attributions. The authorship of the poems is announced *within* the work in a nonuniform and variable manner; in the first two sections, the author's name follows the poems, as if secondary to a reading of the text. The last sections offer a headnote that identifies the verse as by "Grimald" and "uncertain authors." Tottels thus does not use the author's name as a stabilizing factor, one that takes a prominent place typographically and serves as a crucial locus of meaning in the classification and interpretation of the text. Without this force of stability in early miscellanies, the poems could be read with more latitude on the readers' part, for attribution is here a discontinuous and provisional indicator. Proper names are shuffled about so much that the text becomes referenced without an authorial marker. In *The Merry Wives of Windsor*, when Slender calls out, "I'd give 40 shilings to have my *Book of Songs and Sonets*," he employs a now common (but relatively empty) phrase that had specific significance at this time. As the volume circulates to a wider audience, the proper names "Surrey" and "Tottel" fail to become the predominant means of reference, and the book is free to become the "property" of the reader ("*my* Book," Slender states). The book's physical presentation of its poems, as well as this reference by a later reader, indicate a text open to identification within multiple sites of production.

Later miscellanies employ authorship as an even more flexible term of classification and designation. No other anthology until *A Poetical Rhapsody* (1602) is even divided into sections named by author. While four of the anthologies published between *Tottels* and *A Poetical Rhapsody* name a primary author, they erode the centrality of that figure within the book's format. The most popular miscellany published after *Tottels*, *The Paradise of Dainty Devices* (1576), claims on the title page to be "written for the most part by M. Edwards," but only fourteen of the ninety-one poems are signed by Richard Edwards, and the printer's dedicatory address to Henry Compton in fact takes great pains to point out that the verse has been "penned by divers learned Gentlemen" for "private use."[85] The preliminary material to *Colin Clouts Come Home Againe* (1595) gives every indication of Spenser's authorship: his name appears on the title page, and the work opens with his dedication to Ralegh. But the text that follows contains poems by Mary Sidney and Fulke Greville as well as Spenser. Likewise, *The Passionate Pilgrim* (1599), attributed to William Shakespeare, presents only five of his poems and includes well-known poems by Christopher Marlowe, Sir Walter Ralegh, and Bartholomew Griffin. When Richard Jones published *Brittons Bowre of Delights* (1591), Nicholas Breton, the supposed author, printed a retraction in his *Pilgrimage to Paradise* (1592), arguing that many of the poems were not written by him. While this retraction might seem to indicate that in the span of time between 1557 and 1591 concern for "proper" attribution had increased, this conclusion could be hasty; for the retraction was in all probability a publicity stunt, a concocted pretext for a later edition. Given that Breton printed another text with Jones in the next few years, it is likely that the produc-

---

[85] *The Paradise of Dainty Devices*, ed. Hyder E. Rollins (Cambridge, Mass.: Harvard University Press, 1927), 3–4. Elizabeth Pomeroy discusses this edition in *The Elizabethan Miscellanies*, 53–70.

tion of the "corrupt" text was indeed a marketing strategy. In any case, the *Bowre*'s attribution through the title page was not an uncontested one; while the introduction mentions an author—singularly—several poems are signed by other authors, and some would have certainly been recognized as well-known poems by other writers.[86] Today we, with our author-centered textual practices, see as evident the voice of the individual author marked with the authorial name, but Renaissance readers engaged in textual practices that persistently discouraged that recognition. Instead, a singular author was frequently mentioned only as a means of advertisement. As well-known poems circulated under variant names without scandal, distinctions among individual writers were blurred in lieu of making other social and textual distinctions.[87]

Instead of establishing the author as a central controlling feature of the miscellany's poems, compilers and printers designated the verse as a function of the particular collection's contextualization and placement. *The Passionate Pilgrim* presents five Shakespearean poems—two published later in slightly different form in the 1609 *Sonnets* and three from *Love's Labour's Lost*—but the poems are not presented in a manner that distinguishes their original site of production. Despite the fact that the poems from *Love's Labour's Lost* were extracted from a narrative and made to take on radically different new meanings, these poems are not identified in a distinctive manner. In the play, the poems are undercut by the ladies' valuation that these verses are "a huge translation of hypocrisy, / Vilely compounded simplicity." When placed in the miscellany, the avowal of "perjury" in the poems—activated as a literal breaching of a particular oath in the play—signifies the general agony imposed by love's emotional contradictions. The poems "authored" by courtier characters (who are ridiculed in the fictional context) are not distinguished from those "authored" by "William Shakespeare" (who now seems to utter such poems unselfconsciously and excessively). Or rather, there is no attempt to connect the utterance with an "author." Despite the attached name, the poems are

---

[86]*Brittons Bowre of Delights*, STC 3633 (1591), ed. Hyder E. Rollins (New York: Russell and Russell, 1968). No. 40, for instance, is signed by the Earl of Oxford (47). No. 51, which had been published in *Tottels*, would surely have been known as a poem by Surrey (55). Although attributed to Breton as well, *The Arbor of Amorous Devices*, STC 36331 (1597), contains other authors' works; it includes, for instance, "A Lover's Complaint," a poem from the *Arcadia* that was republished in Abraham Fraunce's *Arcadian Rhetorick*, ed. Hyder E. Rollins (Cambridge, Mass.: Harvard University Press, 1936), no. 12.

[87]"The presumed universality of individuated style," Jeff Masten observes, "depends on a network of legal and social technologies specific to post-Renaissance capitalist culture (e.g., intellectual property, copyright, individuated handwriting" ("Beaumont and/or Fletcher: Collaboration and the Interpretation of Renaissance Drama," *ELH* 59 [1992]: 342).

centrally defined by their link to the Ovidian theme of Venus and Adonis, recently popularized in Shakespeare's published narrative poem. The added subtitle to the 1612 addition makes this topos clear: *The Passionate Pilgrim, or Certaine Amorous Sonnets betweene Venus and Adonis.* Both the poems from *Love's Labour's Lost* and the more privately exchanged sonnets become framed by this overarching theme. If authorship is, as Foucault argues, a construct that "impedes the free circulation, the free manipulation, the free composition, decomposition and recomposition of the text," then the lack of a stable author in these miscellanies makes visible the way in which Renaissance poetry did circulate *freely* in the culture, open to both recomposition and reframing ("What Is an Author?" 141).

The Phoenix Nest (1593) employs this practice more generally, as it broadcasts the *subject* of the entire book as the text's center of gravity. Because no authorial names are provided for the book's seventy-eight poems (which critics have ascertained to be authored by such writers as Walter Ralegh, Edward Dyer, George Peele, the Earl of Oxford, Thomas Watson, Robert Greene, and Fulke Greville) and the compiler is identified only by the initials R. S. with a subsequent testimony to his gentility, the text's identity rests in sympathy with the Protestant political faction. The preface sets up this pattern in its commendation of Leicester; and the text opens with an elegy to Sidney, the first of several poems written to eulogize him. The authority lent to the text stems not from the originator of the poems or their collector, but instead from the poetic subject, the dead cultural hero known as the "phoenix" of his time.[88] Grief for Sidney authorized the publication of *The Phoenix Nest* and provided its only provisional organizational format. If, as Foucault says, the author function constitutes a principle of unity that neutralizes contradictions within works or separates texts from each other, these miscellanies do indeed offer an authorless discourse, loosely unified by various and contradictory elements (148–53). Here miscellaneous poetry is loosely given a context as an extended and disjunct elegy. In doing so, *The Phoenix Nest* intensifies the hints given by *Brittons Bowre of Delights*, published four years earlier. For the *Bowre* opened with a pastoral elegy to Sidney by Breton and went on to present five other short epitaphs to him scattered throughout the volume. *The Phoenix Nest* carries this tentative thematic connection further by highlighting it in the title.[89]

This is not to say that the writer was an unacknowledged or unimpor-

---

[88]The fact that only a third of the poems in *The Phoenix Nest* are marked by a set of initials throws into relief the prominence given to the names of Sidney and Leicester, who are evoked and elegized throughout the work.

[89]*England's Helicon* (1600) unites a group of previously published poems through the pas-

tant feature of the text. Renaissance readers often knew very well what Sidney or Spenser had written, and they celebrated these figures as talented poets. But Renaissance authors did not fully authorize their works in ways with which we are familiar. In other words, even prestigious writers did not become the central rubric through which the text was known; they were not given special license to control the circulation of their writing, and the authorial signature did not secure properties of the text in a modern sense. This lack of authorial control explains why it was common practice for texts to be so frequently unattributed, misattributed, and altered. Writers sometimes protested that their works were borrowed or printed without their permission, but their complaints were a rhetorical strategy as much as a claim to intellectual property. Certainly these protestations had no corresponding authority in legal codes or within the conventions of the publishing industry.

By generating rubrics for understanding and reading poems that are distinct from an "author," the miscellany producers call attention to the reader's power in determining the meaning of a poetic collection. The way in which Richard Jones identifies and labels the poems in *Brittons Bowre of Delights* demonstrates that Renaissance readers understood a radically different circuitry between names and texts. This circuitry is seen most clearly when Jones manufactures a "signature" for the individual poem by extracting the name from acrostic poems. Although the capital letters seem obviously to spell out the name of the text's subject rather than its author, they are made to serve as signatures for the poems. One poem's acrostic forms the name "Anne Parker," which then serves as an authorial signature (*Bowre*, 2); its status as a signature is suggested by its placement on the page (number 40, for instance, is signed "Finis. E. of Ox."), and by the tag "finis" (which proximates the authorial name for the book itself—"finis. N.B. Gent"). Likewise poems 3 and 4 are "signed" by the subjects of the poems—"Trentame" and "Garet." The miscellany thus blends the poems' subjects and sources. It is ironic that there was a controversy over Nicholas Breton's authorship of the entire collection, for the miscellany itself reveals the instability of names internally.

By playfully demonstrating the making of the author's name from within the intrinsic features of the poem itself, Jones acts out every manuscript reader's prerogative in strong form. As a genre, miscellanies held out an

---

toral theme. It is believed that Nicholas Ling edited the work with the patronage of John Bodenham. Ling not only collected lyrics from various romances, plays, and poetic collections, but also altered them (adding titles, attributing shepherd speakers, etc.) to make them reflect more clearly the pastoral convention.

invitation to their readers to recompose the poetic material they presented; they solicited readers to imitate the patterns of organization and reorganization that they demonstrated in their use of previously published material and their refashioning of the poems' contexts. That such demonstrations were successful in luring readers to impose their own order on the text is evidenced by the ways in which many Renaissance readers used these poems in fashioning their own commonplace books. Marotti explains that one such reader formed his or her own "plot" by drawing together poems by various authors and by marking their points of connection through carefully crafted titles, such as "then the lover responds to his mistress" (*John Donne*, 13). The temporal organization ("then") is imposed by the active reader who rearranges poems from various texts, trespassing (in modern terms) the boundaries of authorial signature as a means of constructing a new work. The fact that the poems were authored by different hands in different contexts becomes secondary to the poems' malleability, their ability to be reconstructed in new contexts and even made to form the reader's (rather than the writer's) "plot."

In creating these miscellanies, compilers and publishers followed protocols of reading dictated by medieval and coterie manuscript practice. Miscellany editors assumed the role of the privileged scribe or patron, who had the authorization to amend and edit the work to complete its full meaning. Miscellany editors thus thought nothing of regularizing meter, deleting stanzas, and changing the poems' titles. Elizabeth Pomeroy describes in detail how Tottel revised the verse to fit his editorial designs.[90] By doing so, he was merely acting out in a more permanent and visible forum the rhetorically constructed role of Renaissance dedicatee. Instead of securing a new authorized and permanent text, these editorial designs extend to miscellany readers the privilege of participating in the text's creation.

With an understanding of the exchangeability of poems within the miscellanies, we can return to the issue raised by the miscellaneous titles given to the individual works. If *Tottels* displays the collision of typography and social context when it highlights the poem's initial occasion, it also dramatizes the way in which poems can be labelled through a variety of

---

[90]"Rough lines were altered into regular iambic movement. Words or phrases were inserted or omitted; phrases or even whole lines were sometimes transposed. Refrains were omitted in several of Wyatt's poems, and three of his rondeaux were changed into fourteen-line poems resembling sonnets. Besides these well-known changes in meter, the editor also substituted contemporary words for some archaic ones, occasionally eliminated end rhymes, censored references that were thought imprudent in the year 1557. . . ." (Pomeroy, *The Elizabethan Miscellanies*, 35).

classification systems within the same book. Following Tottel's use of multiple structural categories, *A Handful of Pleasant Delights* (1566) presents
and organizes poems through a wide range of labels: we see the descriptive, "wherein Danea welcommeth home her lord Diophon from the war";
the occasional, "A proper new Song made by a Student in Cambridge";
the prescriptive, "An nosegaie always sweet, for lovers to send for tokens of
love, at Newyeres tide"; the universalizing, "A proper sonet, wherein the
Lover dolefully sheweth his greif"; and the simple evaluation, "A proper
Sonet, Intitled Maid, will you marrie." The intermixture of identifying
markers confers variety rather than fixity; they are used to illuminate the
text's radically different possibilities—named by potential use, by author,
by subject. Rather than offering a taxonomy of associated aesthetic
objects, the miscellanies offer multiple paradigmatic frames for governing
the meaning of the poems. Therefore, it is not just the titled designations
referring specifically to social occasion that register a manuscript textuality;
the heterogeneity of the designations themselves point to a non-book–
oriented and more permeable concept of poetry. The structure of miscellanies encouraged readers to accommodate poems to other contexts. Even
when the sonnet was placed within the book form, its placement was identified as provisional, and the poems thus remained discrete and collectable entities. In the sonnet sequences, of course, this open-ended textuality was closed by the more linearly defined numeration and was increasingly bound by the figure of the author.

The titles and prefatory material to the miscellanies reinforce the fluidity
of their structure and organization, for the preliminary apparatus often
calls attention to the provisional unity of the work by designating the book
as a gathering of disparate material. H. C., the probable author of *The
Forrest of Fancy*, remarks that he had "gathered together in one small volume diverse devises" (cited by Saunders, "From Manuscript to Print," 514).
In John Bodenham's *Belvedere* (1600), the text is alternately figured as a
garden path displaying myriad flowers, a casket containing jewels, a hive
housing bees, and a sea absorbing thousands of rivers. The titles of miscellanies themselves interestingly encode the book as a set of collected
objects that either imitate natural groupings (*The Forrest of Fancy, A Small
Handful of Fragrant Flowers, Brittons Bowre of Delights*), social gatherings (*A
Banquet of Dainty Conceits*), or spaces for meeting (*A Gorgeous Gallery of
Gallant Inventions, The Arbor of Amorous Devices*). This last classification is
perhaps the most provocative, as it implies partially covered spaces in which
people casually stroll and make secret rendezvous. To a Renaissance person, a gallery was distinct because of its relative open and closed nature. It
was only secondarily a place in which works of art were exhibited. Like the
more ambiguously blended artificial and natural "bowre" and "arbor," the

gallery connotes both the private and secret space of lovers and the more public place in which beauty is displayed and admired. In picking these titles for his miscellanies, Richard Jones generated figurative textual identifications that gestured toward the now absent human community that occasioned coterie poetry. Primarily a gesture toward the ambiguous space of gathering, these titles ask us to hear echoes of the murmured voices that constituted coterie poetry. Through these textualized spaces, miscellanies replicate the poetic exchanges of manuscript culture in printed form. These forms re-present the spirit of a manuscript polyphony by creating poetic collections as surrogate conversations and social events. As a result, the book is imagined as a momentary stopping place, a provisional grouping that holds together discrete and assorted poems. Instead of being publications that move poetry further from acts of social occasion, miscellanies bring those frames of reference into print.

Publishers of miscellanies thus asked their reading public to imagine these works in very different ways from sonnet sequences. To explain this difference a bit schematically, miscellanies were not personified as idealized integral female bodies, intrinsically unified and in need of male authorial supervision; they did not trade heavily on the writer's popularity or stake an identity through a highly ornate frontispiece celebrating the author; and they were not unified through the psychic unities and discontinuities of love. Although these collections frequently reproduced the very love poetry found in sonnet sequences, they were not defined as commodities by the relationship between sonnet speaker and mistress. Instead, miscellanies translated the social bonds that produced and motivated occasional verse into the figure of an analogous, precariously gathered text.

Such gatherings not only were associated with social occasion, but also were self-announcedly provisional. The provisional relationship between verse and book is evident in the way in which poems were reproduced and recycled in various publications throughout the last decades of the sixteenth century. *Belvedere* published already printed verse by such writers as Sidney, Ralegh, Greville, Harington, Spenser, Daniel, and Drayton. Like its counterpart, *Politeuphuia. Wits Commonwealth* (1597), *Belvedere* functions as an encyclopedia, categorizing poems by subject—"Of Jealousie," "Of Wit and Wisdom"—and captioning each group with a summary didactic epigram. In this way, poems are identified through, and subsumed within, an overarching subject matter. Unlike modern collections of quotations, however, *Belvedere* acknowledges its poems' authors by prefatorially listing authorial names without matching them to specific poems. The attribution is casual and collective; for the individual poems are centrally understood within this new work, their reappropriation more important than their origin. Similarly, two-thirds of the poetry in *England's Helicon* had previously been published, and it advertises its verse by emphasizing their new framing within the pastoral topos rather than through a claim to poetry's novel status. As lyric poems were detached from and reattached to a number of collections, the courtly practices of exchange were demonstrated to readers, and appropriated by them, at a distance from the site of those practices.

C. S. Lewis once said that "a good sonnet . . . [is] like a good public prayer: the test is whether the congregation can 'join' and make it their own."[91] Although Lewis merely suggests that the poet articulates the common experience rather than the particular, his words unwittingly point to a property both of the sonnet text and of the system in which it was created and read. "Making it one's own" was an intricate part of the poetics of exchange, as Harington attests:

> When Lynus thinkes that he and I are frends,
> Then all his Poems unto me he sends:
> His Disticks, Satyrs, Sonnets, and Exameters,
> His Epigrams, his Lyncks, his Pentameters.
> Then I must censure them, I must correct them,
> Then onely I must order, and direct them.
> ("Of Lynus Poetrie," *Letters*, No. 67, 173)

The collaborative nature of this exchange, as Harington makes clear, rests on a supposed intimacy (Lynus "thinkes that he and I are frends"). As miscellanies demonstrated the re-formation and refashioning of manuscripts, they courted readers to become directing members within this circle of "frends." Miscellanies, in short, played into the class dimension of reading. In his opening address to the *Bowre*, for instance, Jones urges "Gentlemen" readers to appreciate the works not only for "the well penning of them, but *especially,* for the Subjet and Worthinesse of the persons they doo concerne." Equally insistent to emphasize the fact that *The Arbor of Amorous Devices* opens up the province of an elite world, Jones's title page describes the text as a work "[w]herin, young Gentlemen may reade many plesant fancies, and fine devices: And thereon, meditate divers sweete Conceites, to court the love of faire Ladies and Gentlewomen." The text has been trimmed up, Jones adds in his address to the Gentleman readers, "for gentlemen to recreate them selves" as well within the artificial "arbor" of "trades" in London as they do within "your pleasant Arbors of the countrie" (sig. A2r). "Recreate" here signifies both "entertain" and "remake."

[91]C. S. Lewis, *English Literature in the Sixteenth Century (Excluding Drama)* (Oxford: Clarendon Press, 1954), 491.

Gentility can thus be reproduced through the leisure of social compliment associated here with the country estate. Harington's description of his relationship to Lynus's works as one of friendly circulation becomes vivified in Jones's introduction to these miscellanies. The invitation to love in the sonnets becomes paralleled through the invitation to poetic play in the miscellaneous form and structure, a play given a local habitation and name in the London bookselling trade. Given that Pettie's extended justification of print calls attention to the fact that wooing was a requisite skill for a gentleman, it is not surprising that in the miscellanies love was not simply reducible to amorous courting but also served a means of gentrification, a tool for becoming courtly. While miscellanies obviously appealed to anyone who could read, they offered the promise of interpellating such readers as gentlemen—here defined as genteel men familiar with the intimate exchange of poems that re-created and displayed manliness and gentility.

"Making it one's own" is a principle of reading and writing that links Renaissance miscellanies to the ethos of medieval manuscript textuality. Having looked at the way in which miscellanies were presented, structured, and read, we must remember the schematic differences that scholars attribute to print and manuscript. Gerald L. Bruns argues that the manuscript text of the medieval and early Renaissance period did not function as a "closed text":

> By a closed text, I mean simply the results of an act of writing that has reached a final form. . . . Print closes off the act of writing and authorizes its results. The text, once enclosed in print, cannot be altered—except at considerable cost and under circumstances carefully watched over by virtually everyone: readers, critics, the book industry, the legal profession, posterities of every stripe, and so on. There are numerous (numberless) complicated forces of closure in a print culture.[92]

In a manuscript culture, Bruns explains, where such "forces of closure" are not evident, the reader has more latitude: "we are privileged to read between the lines, and not to read between them only but to write between them as well, because the text is simply not complete" (125). If the presentation of printed sonnet sequences calls our attention to the labor required to imagine the text as more complete and finished, the Renaissance miscellany complicates this manuscript/print distinction further; for it instances how the "open" text can proliferate within the supposed "closure" of print culture. Miscellany publishers continued to identify

---

[92]Gerald L. Bruns, "The Originality of Texts in a Manuscript Culture," *Journal of Comparative Literature* 32 (Spring 1980): 113.

their works as invitations to collaborate, embellish, and emend. The individual poems that surface in various collections during the last half of the sixteenth century document how readers as well as readers-turned-editors answered these invitations readily, choosing to recontextualize and reauthor poetry in manuscript commonplace books and in print.[93] Bruns asks us to think of the "open" text in relation to "the medieval concept of *translatio*, or turning, which is more than the turning of a text into another language because it implicate[s] the notion of metaphorical turning as well" (125). We have seen that coterie practice encourages a "turning" of poetry in order to realize the true potential of the poetic work; miscellanies stand as proof that printing itself did not require a different "turn." In representing coterie principles of composition to a larger more undifferentiated audience, miscellany publishers did not simply create a makeshift hybrid form destined to disappear inevitably when the properties of the print medium became more realized. In such an interpretation, the miscellany would simply be an unwitting compromise between manuscript and print as Renaissance texts moved to a more developed print culture. I argue instead that miscellanies intervene in this conventional narrative, revealing that the closed readerly text named by its author function is not the inevitable product of commodification itself. Miscellanies were startlingly elusive and variable works that asked readers to take poetry and "make it their own." Poised beside the sonnet sequence, they offered a more socially oriented and less explicitly gendered mode of authorization. Their invisibility in literary history may have to do with the fact that this mode of authorization never acquires the cultural and literary power that authorship attains.

Tottels Miscellany entered the market as a handbook for love, codifying the graceful maneuvers of courtship while also explaining and amplifying the practices of courtiership through a remarkable and ingenious display of poetic exchange. The numerous miscellanies that flourished in the next fifty years offered myriad variations on the playful structural composition and recomposition of poems found in *Tottels*. While the discourse of love found in these miscellanies often offered the mistress's body, being, and response as a topos through which social solidarity could be established, the display of the rules governing that discourse offered miscellaneous privileges and pleasures to a more public reading audience. By altering the perimeters of the system of literary circulation, miscellanies offered to their readers the collaborative and proprietary power of "turn-

---

[93]Hyder E. Rollins thoroughly documents the variant versions of poems within these miscellanies and argues their possible authorship in his introductions.

ing" that was crucial both to the medieval ethos of literary authority and coterie notions of social authority.

In sorting out ways in which texts were perceived within the different political economies of writing generated by publication and coterie exchange, it becomes clear that our own interpretive and literary categories have developed from within historically specific struggles to understand and to manipulate the social place of reading and knowledge.[94] Poised against the socially defined possibilities offered by published miscellanies, the Renaissance author emerged as a governing textual force within the context of controversies about print and status; and the Renaissance book commodity came into being invested in the problematic of cultural distinction and sexual division. Authorship was interestingly bound up with the competing claims of other authorizations, namely with the conflict over determining the precise social status of different kinds of writing at the end of the sixteenth century. This conflict, I argue, was voiced on one front through the eroticized language of Petrarchan discourse. In my account of how sonnets were rhetorically, formally, and typographically scripted in Elizabethan culture, we find a subnarrative of a more broad and pervasive history of the institutionalization of English letters, the movement toward economic reorganization and the development of print culture.

In *A Treatise of Commerce*, John Wheeler announces that "there is nothing in the world so ordinarie, and naturall unto men, as to contract, truck, merchandise and trafficke one with another . . . so that all things come into Commerce and passe into traffique."[95] One version of Renaissance authorship was, in fact, tailored when poetic texts "came into commerce" through the typography of the newly fashionable printed sonnet sequence. This contracting was articulated, on the one hand, through the extraction of a feminized book commodity from the landscape of courtly love, and on the other, through the containment of textual unruliness by formal devices and psychic metaphors. If the Renaissance author was produced partially in contradistinction to a transgressive theatricality, as recent critical studies have suggested, it was also generated in opposition to a collective and elite process of poetic exchange. This point will be vivified further in the next chapter, where I analyze how another notable aristocratic form, the courtly pageant, became authorized in print. In the case

[94]For a discussion of the relationship between the author and the "political economy of writing," see Raymond Williams, *Marxism and Literature* (Oxford: Oxford University Press, 1977), 192–98.

[95]John Wheeler, *A Treatise of Commerce* (1601), reprint facsimile (New York: Columbia University Press, 1931), 6.

of the sonnet, however, we see that writers, publishers, and printers chose as one option to transform the textuality of the open manuscript coterie culture into a protoliterary masculine closed authority when they commercialized Renaissance poetic texts. If writers "turned sonnet" to express their erotic and social desires, this very turn was strikingly reframed in the literary marketplace in ways that consolidated a new, often gendered, relationship between writer, text, and reading public.

CHAPTER TWO

AUTHOR(IZ)ING ROYAL SPECTACLE:

The *Politics* of *Publishing Pageantry*

Wordes do flye, but wryting dothe remayne.
—Richard Mulcaster, *The Quenes Maiesties Passage Through the Citie of London* . . .

ONE OF QUEEN ELIZABETH'S most famous sayings was her comment that *Richard II* was performed as propaganda for the Essex rebellion. "Know ye not," Elizabeth is reported to have exclaimed, "I am Richard II." The queen's words have recently been cited in numerous investigations of Renaissance theater and politics to document the tremendous power that English sixteenth-century theater held in encoding and containing highly inflammatory political issues. Certainly the context of this performance—its connection with the attempted rebellion—indicates that many within the culture were aware of theater's political possibilities. It is important to see that these possibilities, however, were not just a function of the performance's status as spectacle. Printed versions of the account of Richard II were also deemed controversial. As Leeds Barroll has noted, when a prose history of Richard's reign was circulated before the rebellion and *dedicated to Essex*, the printer and seller were called to court for treason.[1] While the players in the more famous theatrical incident received a warning and were dismissed, the printer of the history was imprisoned and threatened with torture.[2] The published account of the history was perceived by the crown as potentially more seditious than the performance. The medium of print, then, added a set of social variables that altered the subject matter's political impact. Queen Elizabeth's identification, "Know ye not, I am Richard II," was realized more dramatically within the economy of the printed book.

---

[1] Leeds Barroll's detailed excavation of the context for this quote has done much to debunk the perceived role of the play in staging the rebellion. "A New History for Shakespeare and His Time," *Shakespeare Quarterly* 39 (1988): 441–64.

[2] I refer to the history by John Hayward. This incident is described by Phoebe Sheavyn in *The Literary Profession in the Elizabethan Age* (Manchester: Manchester University Press, 1909), 47.

THE IMPRINT OF GENDER

I am not here interested in debating which medium—print or theater—was considered a more socially radical symbolic channel. Rather I call attention to how publication sheds light on this canonical example of the politics of theatricality as a means of considering the relationship between Elizabethan authorship and pageantry. Rooted in the discrepancy between spectacle and its representation in printed form is not only an intertwined politics, I argue, but also a specific model of Renaissance authority produced when writers translated spectacle into writing and print. When a writer created and recorded royal spectacle, he inscribed a particular dynamic between sovereign and body politic.[3] When these spectacular inscriptions were published, an "author function" was defined emphatically from within that inscribed dynamic. In this chapter, I investigate how the private negotiations that were carried out between courtier and queen through spectacle became a blueprint for defining literary authority in print.

By analyzing display events in terms of their authorization in print, my work veers from the more critically popular analyses of spectacle's power itself. In the 1980s, various Renaissance critics, the most influential perhaps being Stephen Greenblatt, have called attention to the intricately woven connections between power and theatricality in the Renaissance.[4] Interest in the cultural place of spectacle has been important in expanding the range of "texts" singled out for study: for instance, we now "read" processions, jousts, and tilts. But it also has allowed us to generate theories about the way in which power operates within the dynamic of performance. In particular, recent critical arguments suggest that the power of the Tudor monarch lay squarely in theatricality, in the sovereign's ability to disseminate a vision of monarchal power through magisterial display. The conditions of the Renaissance state, it seems, were maintained by consummate and vital acting. Relying on Foucault's theorization of spectacle, Greenblatt explains that the subversions generated by the medium of theater were contained by the dominant ideology of the court. If critics have departed somewhat from Greenblatt's unified vision of power, many have nevertheless ratified his assertion of theater's particular embeddedness in cultural negotiations.[5]

---

[3]I use "he" advisedly. I know of no account of a pageant by a Renaissance woman; and, as I shall discuss in this chapter, the authorship of the pageant writer becomes gendered through the symbolic codes he uses to engage the queen.

[4]Stephen Greenblatt, *Renaissance Self-Fashioning: From More to Shakespeare* (Chicago: University of Chicago Press, 1980); and his *Shakespearean Negotiations* (Berkeley: University of California Press, 1988); Stephen Orgel, *The Illusion of Power: Political Theater in the English Renaissance* (Berkeley: University of California Press, 1975); Roy Strong, *The Cult of Elizabeth* (London: Thames and Hudson, 1977); and his *Splendour at Court* (London: Weidenfeld and Nicolson, 1973).

[5]See Louis Montrose, "The Purpose of Playing: Reflections on a Shakespearean An-

Drawing from Foucault's *Discipline and Punish*, Leonard Tennenhouse's *Power on Display* opens by articulating a connection between theatricality and power. Tennenhouse portrays a culture in which "power worked more effectively through theatrical display rather than through writing."[6] In such a culture, he continues, ". . . with neither police force nor standing army to enforce the law, the representation of punishment was itself an important form of power. Performed in public places, often on raised platforms for all to see, the criminal's torture was carefully designed to be spectacularly horrible, out of all proportion to the crime. Such a scene was supposed to create a visible emblem of the king's absolute authority over the body of the condemned" (13). Tennenhouse concludes by stating that it was not "the punishment so much as the *spectacle* of punishment that enforced the power of the state" (14). Foucault's explanation of spectacular punishment provides us with a crucial way of rethinking power in terms of its horrendous and visually explicit control over the body rather than in terms of justice. Tennenhouse assumes, however, that Foucault's "scaffold-power" implies a theory of the spectacular itself. His comparison is important here: it is a power that channels itself, he states, "through theatrical display *rather* than through writing." Yet as we have seen in the account of Richard II, the form of the book had a unique power separate from the spectacle it represented. In fact, the force of spectacle was in many ways given meaning and license by its anticipated transference into the channel of print. Even while accepting the highly corporeal and spectacular nature of power, we still must query the multiple ways in which that power was played out in a culture.[7]

Such critiques are vital in pointing out that Renaissance pageants performed important political functions because they allowed the public audience, the courtier, and the sovereign to generate settlements about

---

thropology," *Helios* 7 (1980): 51–74; his "Celebration and Insinuation: Sir Philip Sidney and the Motives of Elizabethan Courtship," *Renaissance Drama* 8 (1977): 3–35; and Leonard Tennenhouse, *Power on Display: The Politics of Shakespeare's Genres* (New York: Methuen, 1986). Since the publication of *Renaissance Self-Fashioning*, numerous critics have sought to qualify the "totalizing" component of Greenblatt's conception of Foucauldian power. For commentary on this debate, see Jonathan Goldberg's sympathetic corrective in "The Politics of Renaissance Literature: A Review Essay," *ELH* 49 (1982): 514–42; and Theodore Leinwand, "Negotiation and New Historicism," *PMLA* 105 (May 1990): 477–90.

[6]Tennenhouse, *Power on Display*, 13. The theoretical groundwork for many of these studies is found in Michel Foucault's *Discipline and Punish: The Birth of the Prison*, trans. Alan Sheridan (New York: Vintage, 1979).

[7]While one of its central critical legacies has been attention to theatricality, Stephen Greenblatt's *Renaissance Self-Fashioning* does explore the potent force of the printed Bible by examining it within a psychological arena of self-creation.

the terms of rule. By extending this inquiry to take into account the pageant as writing, we see how pageant accounts enacted another set of negotiations by virtue of their place within coterie circuits or within the economy of the marketplace. The possibility that pageants could be further reproduced for public reading changed the stakes of the cultural practices embedded in acts of spectacle. While we see that the printed version of Richard II's fall translates a mild political threat into a seditious publication, it becomes evident that other accounts alter, contest, and reverse—rather than merely amplify—the political terms set up by the display event, although they do so, almost without exception, within the larger project of disseminating monarchal authority. In short, writing and publishing add a variable that complicates in disparate ways a reading of pageantry's politics. Like the pageant itself, the written account records a set of negotiations that cannot simply be labeled "subversive" or "hegemonic." Unlike the dramatization of a pageant, however, the translation of the event into a printed narrative fits spectacle within the existing social codes attending to print; the spectacle becomes subject not only to the specific formal requirements and conditions of writing, but also to the social problems attached to publication. While pageants were structured episodically and often produced collectively, printed accounts often established a more accessible focal point for the event, whether through narrative unity or through the writer's function in memorializing the event. Regardless of the specific changes in the political valences of a pageant event, it is the writer's necessary *moment of intervention* in controlling those valences that becomes important for an analysis of authorship. For we see that in the process of imagining and distributing official power, writers necessarily express their role in representing pageantry and thus define themselves as the required satellite power that must record the queen's graceful royal presence.

Some pageant writers went on to become prominent Elizabethan authors. In these cases, authorship emerged from a complicated two-step process: the writer came to light textually as the necessary narrative and editorial subject ("I") who controlled the act of description; that is, the writer emerged almost as an excess textual energy produced when the aspiring courtier set out to offer his monarch the service of translating her spectacular display into a written commodity. Writers such as George Gascoigne and Philip Sidney craftily used that energy to their political advantage. When placing these accounts into the medium of print, writers and publishers had the option of reframing those authorizing gestures, with the result that they scripted the writer more particularly as an author figure and the act of narrative and editorial control more specifically as a literary effect. I argue that when the common practices of the courtier (wooing, celebrating, and influencing the monarch through verse and performance) were shifted into another form of representation, this shift generated possibilities for different kinds of textual authorization.

This shift in authorization does not mean that pageant writers self-consciously sought to reconceptualize authorship in early modern England. When writers such as Gascoigne and Sidney designed and transcribed pageants, they did so with an eye to social reward rather than literary fame; generating courtly entertainments was standard fare for those aspiring to a career in statecraft and diplomacy. These highly ambitious courtiers, however, sought to secure a role within the court by counseling the queen through pageantry and therefore insinuating themselves in the knotty affairs of state. Sixteenth-century writers more readily turned to other genres when they sought to fashion themselves as epic poets, to inscribe themselves as immortal, or to rethink the way in which a poetry should be imagined. In the case of pageantry, it was ironically the publisher who primarily "authorized" the writer's claim to the work and his status as an author. The publisher strengthened the link between writer and pageant text by emphasizing the author's name over the event that occasioned the pageant. Significantly, the posthumous publication of elaborate editions—Gascoigne's 1587 *Works* and Sidney's 1598 *The Countess of Pembrokes Arcadia*—contributed most substantially to the construction of these men as authors.[8] These works also elevated pageantry to the category of literature.

The publisher's control over authorial presentation, however, did not nullify the writer's part in determining and shaping the way in which the author would later be perceived by a reading public. Instead, as we shall see, Gascoigne's and Sidney's particular stylization and recasting of royal power offered the language and the social authority through which their authorship was later expressed. In recording royal theatricality in written form, Sidney and Gascoigne combined their literary interests with a political critique of the queen's policies. This combination provided them with a leverage that was not found in the spectacle itself; there they played the part of the good courtier and presented verses publicly to their monarch. The written account allowed for an editorial control over this moment of presentation and receipt. When these written accounts were later placed in print—bound with other genres, prefaced with explanations of the writer's skill, and framed by title pages—the courtier's social and textual

---

[8]When discussing the construction of the literary Donne, Arthur Marotti notes, "The posthumous 1633 edition of Donne's poetry was the watershed event leading to Donne's conversion from coterie poet to English author." "John Donne, Author," *Journal of Medieval and Renaissance Studies* 19 (1989): 72.

control became articulated more specifically as an authorial claim. Although it was not until much later that the full effects of this framing were registered (in the shift from gentlemanly amateurism to professional author), published pageantry can be seen as one form among many that allowed sixteenth-century writers to be categorized as authors. If, as critics have argued, Ben Jonson self-consciously sought to fashion himself as an author by holding spectacle at bay, Gascoigne and Sidney used the transference of royal spectacle into writing as their access to a less radical self-assertion, one that was nevertheless continued, amplified, and given stronger form after their deaths. Although publication partially underpinned a poetics of spectacle, the nascent concept of the "author" was partially dependant on the power of publishing display.[9] Authorship here is a by-product of the political vying that occurred when writers scripted and edited royal display events.[10]

In Chapter 1, I discussed how authorship was defined in the relationship between the sonnets' eroticized themes, their textual practices, and general cultural markers of social status. The sprawling and formless pageant entertainment paradoxically shares features with the highly formal coterie sonnet. Like the coterie sonnet, the pageant was an ephemeral, collective, collaborative, and often anonymous textual event generated within private courtly and aristocratic circles. When writers wrote and circulated Petrarchan lyric poems, they made a bid for inclusion within a privileged social rank; similarly the queen herself comprised a privileged "text" to be written only by those who had access to her royal presence. Publicizing both the private poetic or theatrical text (one produced within elite coterie circles or aristocratic festivities) created the same paradoxical

---

[9]Timothy Murray describes the ways in which Ben Jonson created an authorial presence through strategic editing of his plays. In arguing that Jonson initiated a radically new sense of authorship, Murray claims for Jonson a role that I hesitate to claim for these earlier pageant writers. Sidney and Gascoigne did not conceive of governing the text in the way Jonson did, nor did they seek to be defined by a "bibliographic ego." But when Murray articulates Jonson's strategic authorial maneuvers, he does touch on many techniques for self-presentation that these pageant writers also used. See *Theatrical Legitimation: Allegories of Genius in Seventeenth-Century England and France* (Oxford: Oxford University Press, 1987), 50–63.

[10]In positing a definition of "authorship" that was primarily an effect generated by a commercial process rather than the product of a writing agent's self-stylization, this chapter locates one process among many by which an ambivalent and contradictory concept of authorship comes into being in early modern England. In this historical moment, authorship has a provisional and processive nature. This chapter seeks to expand on and, in one sense, critique a definition of authorship based solely on the "intentionalist" authorial moves evident in, for instance, Spenser's and Whitney's stylization of a literary career (see my respective discussions in Chapters 4 and 5).

transgression and consolidation of privilege. The publication of royal and coterie texts allowed for the expression of a writing authority dependent on, but distanced from, that courtly world, for it advertised aristocratic and royal practices to a larger public. As part of this distribution, a particular writer could claim these anonymous and collective events. Pageants lent an authority predicated on direct petitioning of the queen within the encomiastic language of royal celebration. If the stigma of print made it socially hazardous for would-be gentlemen to appear in print, then basking in the presence of the queen safeguarded one's social station. Obviously, the magnificent nature of the written subject required circulation beyond the confines of a noble enclave. The outpouring of printed pageants during the reign of Elizabeth thus benefited both monarch and courtier. It allowed the writer to publish his talents to prospective patrons and readers while the queen could gracefully receive the flattering symbolic roles that expressed her power. If sonnet writers relied on the coterie status of their works, the author of pageantry was a figure constructed from the court and protected by that construction. The writer's place in the socially undifferentiated realm of the publishing industry was secured through his familiarity with the elite world of royal progress. As they also do in the sonnets, gendered literary codes and genres provide the terms by which this privileged authority was expressed.

The writer's presence in the narrative account of the pageant not only changed the cultural resonances of spectacle (both its theatrical power and its aristocratic stamp), but also marked a site where personal assertion and social legitimation became expressed as literary authorization. By examining George Gascoigne's published account of the festivities of royal progress, *The Princely Pleasures at Kenelworth Castle* (1576) and Sidney's coterie pageant *The Lady of May* (1578?), published after his death, we are able to see the way in which the writer's textual inscription of the pageant became a fulcrum for interpreting these authors and their social and literary place in Elizabethan culture. In particular, we see how these writers rely on the highly gendered discourses of pastoral romance and courtly love to inveigh the queen and to question the terms of her rule. In putting these spectacular negotiations into writing, courtiers assert an authority that becomes masculinized, if for no other reason than because it is predicated on interpreting Elizabeth's sovereignty in terms of female desire and refusal.

Mulcaster's Account of the Coronation Procession

Before examining the gendered construction of authorial power in Gascoigne's and Sidney's works, we must first understand the conventions established by previous writers for recording royal pageantry. Richard Mulcaster's anonymously published account of the queen's coronation procession in 1558, *The Quenes Maiesties Passage Through the Citie of London . . .* , provides us with an important starting point, for Mulcaster's tract records the inaugural and most canonical act of spectacle in Elizabeth's reign. His pamphlet was a highly influential publication that popularized various rhetorical techniques for "writing" the text of the queen. While Mulcaster was pointedly not concerned to establish an authorial identity for himself—by which I mean that he did not seek to advertise his reputation as a writer through this account—his pamphlet nevertheless served as an important model for authorizing the queen, one that Gascoigne and Sidney followed in spirit in their later and more literary pageant entertainments. In particular, they repeated Mulcaster's tactic of emphasizing his own labor in generating a state mythology. Through his epideictic and encomiastic writing, Mulcaster reminded the queen that her consummate acting of royal authority depended on textual interpretations and more far-reaching and durable modes of dissemination than spectacle. While Mulcaster's rhetorical and narrative strategies for controlling and defining the court-sanctioned event rested on the highly public condition of the printed text, any bid for authority that he might have devised through this service was a private one: his name does not appear on his account of the procession, and thus the work's publicity furthered his authority only in the sense that it increased the text's (and text writer's) value in the queen's eyes. The fruits of writing were limited to those granted by the royal reader.

Mulcaster's tract records the spectacular event that announced Elizabeth's rule, legitimized her claim to the throne, and set up the terms by which her reign could be envisioned by a justifiably suspicious and nervous public. Comprised of five elaborately decorated tableaux interspersed with the presentation of verse, money, and other gifts to the royal train, this visual and verbal event authorized Elizabeth's claim to the throne through an array of representations. These tableaux included a genealogy that attempted to restore Anne Boleyn to the royal lineage and thus erase Elizabeth's stain of illegitimacy; a representation of Deborah as prototype of the maternal monarch; a comparison of flourishing and decaying commonwealths; and allegorical depictions of the virtues of a good ruler. With a well-adorned entourage of thirty noblemen and thirty gentlewomen, Elizabeth processed from the Tower of London through the city streets toward the palace of Whitehall, pausing at each of these display events and receiving the compliments and gifts presented by the city.[11]

[11]Accounts of the procession are found in John Nichols, *The Progresses and Public Processions of Queen Elizabeth*, 3 vols. (1823; reprint, New York: Burt Franklin, 1966), 1:38–60;

The expression of overwhelming and awe-inspiring royal power seen in the symbolic depictions of Elizabeth's rule, however, was complicated by the fact that this event called for more interaction between the spectators, presenters, and royal ensemble than previous coronation processions had. Traditionally, the royal party's movement from one point to another was spotlighted as the central feature of the event. The core of the festivity rested in the motion and gesture of the monarch. Motion itself—processus—signified power; the audience remained static. Elizabeth's procession contained vestiges of this structure: the queen sat elevated on a litter surrounded by sixty noble persons and framed by the hundreds of tradesmen from different guilds who lined the street. This particular enactment of the royal entry, however, was designed to offer a second and competing focal point. The presentation of elaborate tableaux shifted the focus away from the sovereign as spectacle to the sovereign as audience. Beginning with Mary's procession in 1553 and created more intricately in Elizabeth's procession, the city erected elaborate pageantry along the route. One effect was that the royal train's movement could no longer be linear, but instead was interrupted by displays that foregrounded the margins of the route. The power that inhered in processing became suspended as the pageant forced the queen to defer her own performance momentarily to a representation (of herself and her state) and thus relinquish the spotlight of the spectacle event. In other words, the dynamic changed from one of singularity and continuity to what John Neale calls the "picture of Queen and citizens courting one another with delightful ardor."[12] As the center was transferred to the margins, the cheering audience participated more actively in the power dynamic of "courting." In moments when former spectators performed, the queen was scripted as passive: she had to watch, thank, applaud, and receive. In this sense, the procession enacted a mode

---

Richard Mulcaster, *The Quenes Maiesties Passage Through the Citie of London* . . . , ed. James Osborne (New Haven: Yale University Press, 1960); and Arthur F. Kinney, *Elizabethan Backgrounds* (Hamden, Conn.: Archon Books, 1975), 7–14. My citations are from Nichols's edition. Commentary on the procession has been made by Sydney Anglo, *Spectacle, Pageantry, and Early Tudor Policy* (Oxford: Clarendon Press, 1969): 344–59; David Bergeron, *English Civic Pageantry, 1558–1642* (London: Edward Arnold, 1971), 11–23; Robert Withington, *English Pageantry: An Historical Outline*, vol. I (Cambridge, Mass.: Harvard University Press, 1918), 199–202; Mark Breitenberg, "'. . . the hole matter opened': Iconic Representation and Interpretation in 'The Quenes Majesties Passage,'" *Criticism* 28 (1986): 1–25; and Clifford Geertz, "Centers, Kings, and Charisma: Symbolics of Power," in *Local Knowledge* (New York: Basic Books, 1983), 125–29.

[12]John Neale, introduction to the facsimile of *The Quenes Maiesties Passage Through the Citie of London* . . . , 11.

of power relations more like those later found in the Jacobean masque, a complex form in which monarchal authority was partially articulated through the powerful gaze of the royal spectator.[13] This mode of authorization had not yet become conventional; instead, the scripting of Elizabeth marked a revision in the procession dynamic.

This structural shift was accompanied by a more rigorous program of instructing the monarch; that is, the traditional *laudando praecipere* was peculiarly prominent in Elizabeth's coronation procession. Sydney Anglo explains that while advice in the display event was traditional, "there is one feature of the pageants for Elizabeth which marks them off from their predecessors. This is the degree to which they not merely praise the monarch, or exhort her to behave well toward her people, but also give advice on a right course of action" (*Spectacle*, 357). The presentation of a Bible during the entry corroborates Anglo's point. It might seem appropriate that Queen Elizabeth, the Protestant symbol of rebirth, would be presented with a Bible by the allegorical figure of Truth at the climax of the coronation procession. When we consider, however, that Richard Grafton, who had been on the planning committee for the procession, had previously devised the Grafton Bible depicting a very different monarchal presentation of the Holy Word, we begin to question the appropriateness of the procession's "gift" to Elizabeth. The Grafton Bible boasted a frontispiece portraying Henry VIII handing the Bible down to the bishops. The procession shifts the lines of biblical endowment by making Elizabeth the recipient of Truth's counsel. The pageant brought the engraving to life but reversed the direction of the presentation: the father gave; the daughter received. This double-edged "gift" constituted just one of many political challenges waged by the event: the Deborah tableau instructed Elizabeth to listen to her counselors; the mayor's reminder that the city had paid for the whole event created a coercive sense of obligation that had to be acknowledged by the queen publicly; and the presented poetic verses continually exhorted Elizabeth to bind her tongue and heart. In a time of social instability when power was being invested in a new Protestant female monarch, it was certainly not strange that English subjects wanted to have a say about the terms of the queen's rule. Given the structural shift in focal point away from the queen, however, this advice became peculiarly insistent and emphatic. It constituted a revision in the genre of royal entry.

Mulcaster's memorialization of the procession was listed in the Stationers' Register just nine days after the event. From the city's records, we know

---

[13]See Jonathan Goldberg, *James I and the Politics of Literature: Jonson, Shakespeare, Donne, and Their Contemporaries* (Baltimore: Johns Hopkins University Press, 1983; reprint, Stanford: Stanford University Press, 1989); and Orgel, *The Illusion of Power*.

that Mulcaster was solicited to write the document and was paid by the queen for its production. Corporation records indicate that he was given "his reward for makying of the boke conteynynge and declarying the historyes set furth by the Cyties pageants at the tyme of the Quenes Highnes comyng thorough the Cytye to her coronacion."[14] The court's sponsorship of the pamphlet and its haste to issue a printed account indicate that publication was seen as necessary for the official event to be disseminated and, in light of the strange shifts in convention, reinterpreted.

When reinterpreting the royal entry, Mulcaster, in part, sought to revise the significance of passivity and movement suggested by the event itself. He argues, for instance, that the halting of the royal litter signified the queen's volition rather than her deference to a greater power. By emphasizing Elizabeth's command over movement, Mulcaster weakens the challenge posed by the restructuring of royal display—the image presented of monarch and public as equal partners in an active courtship. Mulcaster instead depicts these interruptions as moments when the queen voluntarily stops for interaction with her beloved people, an arrest that reveals her truly aristocratic, "most gentle," and charitable nature. Mulcaster argues for Elizabeth's "loving Behaviour" based on the fact that "she did not only shew her most gracious love toward the people in generall, but also privately, if the baser personages had offered her Grace any flowers or such like as a signification of their good wyll, or moved to her any sute, she most gently . . . staid her chariot and heard theyre requestes" (39). In essence, Mulcaster reinterprets the relationship between power and motion in the procession, showing that the truly "gentle" character of the queen was revealed when greatness halted for the "baser" spectator. In keeping with Theseus's later account of noblesse oblige in *A Midsummer Night's Dream,* Mulcaster reads noble character in the queen's ability to see value in baseness.[15] The pamphlet specifies that the magnanimity of her loving gestures overshadows any indication that her rule is contingent, dependent, or inadequate. It is not the requests by the people that are privileged, but the swelling generosity displayed when the sovereign *allows* her power to be interrogated. Greenblatt has suggested that the power of the Renaissance state included its ability to generate and contain its own sub-

---

[14]Anglo, 346. Bergeron has documented the court's involvement in the production of the event, thus revealing both text and procession as intertwined in a web of royal authorization. *English Civic Pageantry,* 12.

[15]In act 5, scene 1, Theseus tells Philostrate that he will hear the mechanicals' play despite Philostrate's warning that the performance is "nothing, nothing in the world": "I will hear that play; / For never anything can be amiss / When simpleness and duty tender it" (82–84).

versions.[16] Mulcaster hints that Elizabeth's power is made most evident when it responds to inquiry. In the printed text, the dialogue of spectacle is governed by princely consent.

As part of his reinterpretation, Mulcaster exploits the qualities peculiar to narrative to unify the procession's disparate messages. By glossing the moments of hesitation and interruption in the pageant, Mulcaster makes the queen the event's central theme. In doing so, he provides a stronger narrative logic to the display event. "The matter of this Pageant dependeth on them that went before," he states in summing up the procession event (1:51). Throughout the pamphlet, he calls attention to the "unitie of the thing" by emphasizing thematic links that rest on the tableaux's relevance to the queen. In this way, the narrative seems more interconnected than the pageant could have appeared to any of its observers, save perhaps to the queen herself. By positioning the reader as royalty rather than as spectator, Mulcaster de-emphasizes the margins that the pageant had foregrounded. Il Schifanoya, a Venetian diplomat who also recorded the procession in letters to the Mantuan ambassador, bears witness to the fact that the entirety of the pageant could not have been experienced by any single person.[17] As a static spectator, he could only see fragments of the procession. His account of the event consequently omits many display scenes and all of Elizabeth's verbal quips. It is up to the official narrative to create the unified effect of theatricality and to align the reader's view with that of the queen.

As subsequent accounts of the procession indicate, Mulcaster's text was extremely successful in projecting to a larger audience an image of the queen as commanding and confident. Rather than the scenes along the route, the queen's responses became fetishized texts in numerous history books. *The Sayings of Queen Elizabeth* is an entire book devoted to reproducing these sacrosanct utterances. The very fact that I can quote them verbatim within this book suggests their entrenched place in the historical/literary canon. Yet how do we know these words? Mulcaster's repeated descriptions of the crowd's noise and the lapses in Il Schifanoya's text verify the impossibility of hearing these speeches. During the performance, the queen could not even hear the verses read to her and had to ask the crowd several times to be quiet in order to hear the verses repeated. Be-

---

[16]Stephen Greenblatt, "Invisible Bullets: Renaissance Authority and Its Subversion," *Glyph* 8 (1981): 40–61. Published in revised form in *Political Shakespeare: New Essays in Cultural Materialism*, ed. Jonathan Dollimore and Alan Sinfield (1985; reprint, Ithaca: Cornell University Press, 1987), 18–47.

[17]Il Schifanoya's account is recorded in the *The Calendar of State Papers and Manuscripts, Relating to English Affairs* . . . , vol. 7, 1558–1580, ed. Rowden Brown and Cavendish Bentinck (London, 1890), 11–31.

cause Elizabeth's responses were uttered in an arena filled with noise, the written account *had* to re-present them to the people at large (or present them, if we believe that an official tract had the authority to fictionalize royal language). For much of her audience, then, the queen was constituted by the language of the pamphlet. The tremendous power of spectacle and her "impromptu" words were retrospectively written into the event when they were printed.

The procession event became a text that was reproduced, re-presented, and reduplicated numerous times in the next four hundred years. Thomas Heywood's history of Elizabeth's reign (1631) offers one such description of the procession. His account evidences how these reproductions could indulge in elaboration and fictionalization. He reports, for instance, that the queen responds to the allegorical display of virtues. "I have taken notice of your good meaning toward mee, and will endeavor to Answere your severall expectations," she is reputed to have said.[18] Heywood qualifies his text by noting that he tells "what *supposedly* was the Queen's verbal response." When the queen saw the children lining the streets, Heywood reports that she called out, "Wee are Orphans all; let me enjoy your Prayers and you shall be sure of my assistance" (114). Finally, he describes how Elizabeth offers her appreciation for the Bible presented to her: "I thank the Citie for this guift above all the rest; it is a Booke which I will often and often read over" (113). Yet none of these responses are registered either in Mulcaster's official tract nor in Il Schifanoya's more private letter. They appeared in print *for the first time* eighty years after the procession. As the historical text circulated new anecdotes about the queen in print, it reproduced the power of her presence years after the event. Writers such as Heywood also used the procession to consolidate the illusion that the royal presence was more accessible through spectacle events.[19]

---

[18]Thomas Heywood, *England's Elizabeth: Her Life and Troubles* (1631), ed. Philip R. Ryder (New York: Garland, 1982), 112.

[19]A more recent instance of this fictional theatricalization of political pageantry occurred in a 1985 Geneva summit. The headline to the Tuesday, 12 April 1988 *Boston Globe* discloses this episode: "Speakes, in book, says he fabricated Reagan quotes" (vol. 233, no. 103). These words caption a story that explains how Larry Speakes, a White House spokesperson, fictionalized quotations by President Ronald Reagan at a 1985 Geneva summit with Soviet leader Mikhail Gorbachev in order to assign Reagan more quotable words. Speakes confesses that he was worried that Gorbachev was too successful in courting the press at this highly theatrical event; the spokesperson intuited what the president felt and reported those intuitions to the press as verbatim quotes: "I polished the quotes and told the press that, while the two leaders stood together at the end of one session, the president said to Gorbachev: 'There is much that divides us, but I believe the world breathes easier because we are talking here together'" (1). While it is common practice for political figures and candidates to have speech writers design their quips, it was considered scandalous for the press secretary

Because print enabled a larger textual distribution, it encouraged the expansion of the theatrical event in its various representations. The queen's overwhelming presence is constituted retroactively by the printed accounts of later writers. Heywood's words thus legitimate themselves by filling in the elliptical gaps created by the pageant, amplifying further Elizabeth's "spontaneous" theatrical voice.

By locating this text within the hegemonic practices of the Tudor throne and thus reading it as propaganda, however, we are in danger of simplifying the relationship of printed artifact to the social and political system from which it was produced. While Mulcaster may realign the reader's perception of the event to match that of the official Tudor view, or perhaps fashion a more theatrical Elizabeth through print, he also creates a text that underscores his power as a reporter. When Mulcaster calls attention to his role in governing the flow of the text's interpretation, he appropriates the pageant's power for his own ends. His printed account supplements, in the double sense that Derrida teases out of the term when discussing the function of the sign itself, the social force of spectacle.[20] Because the supplement adds to something that is ostensibly already complete and whole, it is an unnecessary and troubling addition; but because it also completes that entity, it calls attention to the inherent lack that makes the addition necessary. Mulcaster's text makes evident the inadequacies of the procession event, even as he labors both to compensate for possible unofficial interpretations and to identify the pageant as fully complete in meaning.[21]

---

to misreport the conversation between world leaders, as evidenced by the outcry that followed in the wake of Speakes's disclosure (see *Boston Globe*, 13 April 1988, 3; and 14 April 1988, 3). Ironically, in this case, the print media demystified the mythologization that print itself had endowed on this spectacle event.

[20]In the "movement of supplementarity," Derrida writes in his reading of Lévi-Strauss, the sign "replaces the center, which supplements it, taking the center's place in its absence—this sign is added, occurs as a surplus, as a supplement. The movement of signification adds something, which results in the fact that there is always more, but this addition is a floating one because it comes to perform a vicarious function, to supplement a lack on the part of the signified." This duality of surplus and requisite addition describes printed pageantry's relationship to the pageant itself. Jacques Derrida, "Structure, Sign, and Play in the Discourse of the Human Sciences," in *Writing and Difference*, trans. Alan Bass (Chicago: University of Chicago Press, 1978), 289.

[21]As I have mentioned, Mulcaster continually foregrounds the slippage between the event and its meaning. In "'. . . the hole matter opened,'" Breitenberg argues that this concern speaks to the principle of similitude: the iconic codes in the work point to a process by which meaning is conveyed not so much by interpretation as by repetition and imitation. Meaning is "immanent in what is seen"; it is not "produced by an interpretative code." Instead, Breitenberg argues, the written text carefully repeats the significances that were themselves repeated incessantly in the procession. When the queen demands to have the "hole

Divergent interpretive glosses of the pageant, seen in later histories as well as in Il Schifanoya's contemporaneous account, make strikingly visible the slippage in meaning that made the official account so necessary. Mulcaster, for instance, validates his interpretative role by noting the queen's own insistence on having the "matter" interpreted: "because she feared, for the Peoples noyse," he states, "that she shoulde not heare the child which dyd expounde the same, she enquired what that Pageant was ere that she came to it" (1:44). At five different points, he notes, "she required the matter somewhat to be opened unto her" (1:47). When Mulcaster tells of the queen's demand for an explanation, he implicitly legitimates his own critical practice as a response to the sovereign's needs. Throughout the pamphlet he calls attention to this practice through his abrupt transitions from mere description to interpretation: "the ground of meaning was," he states; "the matter of this pageant was," he begins. Timothy Murray has suggested that Ben Jonson created "typographical disruptions," learned marginal glosses appended to the text that were designed to stage and contain overlapping modes of reading (*Theatrical Legitimation*, 89). Mulcaster, relying less on the typography of the page than on narrative itself, displays his own hermeneutic activity through a series of obvious narrative intrusions. These intrusions have a two-fold effect: Mulcaster controls evident slippages in meaning and thus singles out his own voice from the collective authorship of the procession event.[22] By calling attention to his presence in the text, Mulcaster reiterates the necessity for written explanations and justifies his pamphlet's role in unfolding the significance of vital political fictions. If he initially justifies his text by noting the queen's call for explanations, Mulcaster ultimately offers interpretations that far exceed the queen's demands, for he introduces the possibility, however academic, that the interpreter can refuse to perform these celebratory investitures. Sidney, as we shall see, stages this exact moment of refusal in his pastoral masque.

In attenuated form, then, Mulcaster participates in that same inquiry of

---

matter opened to her," Breitenberg asks, "could there be even the slightest doubt in anyone's mind, much less the Queen's, about what the allegory means?" (15) If we look at Il Schifanoya's contemporary account, we must allow for this doubt. Because the Venetian ambassador interprets the allegories slightly differently than does Mulcaster, he makes evident that there *is* room in this layering of meaning for mis- or re-interpretation. Mulcaster does not merely participate in a harmonious repetition of self-evident meanings. My reading differs from Breitenberg's in that I see Mulcaster as actively asserting authority when he calls attention to his own role in *articulating* state power.

[22]Mulcaster was part of the forty-four-person team that divided into smaller committees when they produced the display events. For a description of the planning of the coronation procession, see David Bergeron, *English Civic Pageantry*, 12; and Sydney Anglo, *Spectacle*, 346.

royal power that his own text has more overtly sought to deflect. This incongruity may become explicable when we consider that it was by virtue of righting/writing the pageant's meaning that Mulcaster was able to promote his own talents. He thus renders a theme articulated in the pageant event into material form: "Wordes do flye, but wryting dothe remayn" (50). The brief period of time allowed to elapse between event and official printed description vivifies this theme within the book marketplace. Mulcaster, however, finds it in his interest to point to the gap between event and its meaning and to the insufficiency of spectacle's mere words. In doing so, he not only justifies his own text, but also demarcates the spaces in which an unofficial response to the official voice can be heard. In short, Mulcaster authorizes his own language in conjunction with the queen's, with the result that monarchal authority becomes contingent on other textual authorities and spectacle becomes contingent on publication.

Mulcaster's account of the coronation procession did not launch a literary career. He never sought a less court-bound means of reward for his efforts by printing the text under his name, nor did he produce a more literarily defined body of writing with which his pageant text could be published. The narrative authority he so craftily generated in his account never contributed to his reputation as a writer. By rendering service to the queen through this publication, Mulcaster instead solidified his place within the court. He went on to produce humanist tracts of pedagogy and is remembered chiefly for his expositions on knowledge and rhetoric. His pamphlet was important because it offered the first representation of Elizabeth as queen and thus publicized a way of reading her place within the royal display event. As Mulcaster dutifully translated Elizabeth into the object of written narrative, he disclosed a set of bargaining strategies within the act of narration itself, strategies that many writers—Gascoigne and Sidney among them—found useful in their more literary accounts of royal progress pageantry.

For much of her reign, Queen Elizabeth undertook annual progresses from court to country. As the court made its rounds to various aristocratic estates, it demanded to be presented with a wealth of extravagant and spectacular entertainment. Many writers and artists were called forth to participate in designing the masques, poetic presentations, games, gifts, and festivities that became part of these entertainments.[23] Like the coro-

---

[23]For discussions of Elizabethan pageantry and iconography, see Anglo, *Spectacle;* Robert Withington, *English Pageantry*; Marie Axton, "The Tudor Mask and Elizabethan Court Drama," in *English Drama: Forms and Development*, ed. Marie Axton and Raymond Williams (Cambridge: Cambridge University Press, 1977), 24–47; Frances A. Yates, *Astraea: The Imper-*

nation procession, progress events were often produced anonymously, attributed, if at all, to the owner of the estate or the occasion of the royal visit. When writers created the lavish entertainments performed on royal progresses, they shaped the rituals and practices of the Crown through their own imaginative rhetoric. When recording these events, they could intervene more emphatically in the space between event and its textual representation and thus establish a role for the writer within the world of spectacle. Both George Gascoigne and Philip Sidney participated in progress events that were sponsored by Robert Dudley, the Earl of Leicester. When they translated these highly public theatrical events into written texts, Gascoigne and Sidney followed Mulcaster's lead in calling attention to their role in editing and interpreting these malleable scripts of royal pageantry. While their face-to-face engagements with the queen became the ground for expessing their views on statecraft, Gascoigne's and Sidney's *written* accounts provided them with another opportunity; for in contesting the queen's policies through the medium of writing, these courtiers generated a cultural and narrative role for themselves that had an effect on the way they would posthumously be figured as early modern English authors.

Gascoigne's "Deep Desire" and the Spectacle of Queenly Authority

When the queen arrived at Leicester's castle at Kenilworth for a two-week stay during the summer progress of 1575, she was greeted and entertained by a range of figures from classical mythology and medieval folklore. Gascoigne was part of the large courtly crew brought in by Leicester to design the lavish festivities that summer. The end product of this planning included poetic presentations to the queen as well as short skits, musical productions, water "inventions" (including one in which Proteus rode across a lake on a dolphin's back), chivalric battles, animated landscapes, and fireworks. Unlike many of the other contributors to the entertainment, Gascoigne did not remain anonymous or unrewarded for his efforts. His service to the queen was apparently deemed worthy of recognition, for he received a commission to write an account of another pageant that had been performed at Woodstock that same summer. Perhaps encouraged by this approbation, Gascoigne then published in 1576 an

---

ial Theme in the Sixteenth Century (Harmondsworth: Penguin, 1977), 88–94; Roy Strong, *The Cult of Elizabeth*; Elkin Calhoun Wilson, *England's Eliza* (1939, reprint, London: Frank Cass, 1966); Glynne Wickham, *Early English Stages, 1300–1600*, 3 vols. (New York: Columbia University Press, 1959–1981); and Enid Welsford, *The Court Masque* (New York: Russell and Russell, 1962).

account of the display events he had helped to create the year before at Kenilworth.[24] Involved in these theatrical events in many capacities, Gascoigne found in royal pageantry a means of both experimenting stylistically and furthering his ambitions within the highly competitive world of the court.

Gascoigne's two pageant accounts circulated during his lifetime, marked either with his well-known motto or his name. From these texts, we see that Gascoigne was aware of the narrative and political possibilities to be found in translating officially authorized pageantry into print. This particular interest can be linked to his general concern with the place of the poet and of poetry within English Renaissance culture, evidenced not only by the many amorous and didactic poems, plays, and essays that he wrote, but also by his laborious attempts to justify and explain his own intentions in creating imaginative works. Writing, it seems, often got Gascoigne into trouble with court and state authorities. The ill-success of his poetry collection *A Hundreth Sundrie Flowres* (1573) throws into relief the limited success he achieved from creating and editing display events. His career clearly dramatizes the way in which pageantry provided the opportunity for self-promotion within court culture. Pageantry became the page on which he could inscribe his own social and poetic authority.

Gascoigne's first venture in recording spectacle came when Elizabeth commissioned him to translate the pageant at Woodstock into a written text.[25] Although he had not participated in creating the festivities at Woodstock, Gascoigne retrospectively became their sole "author" by virtue of translating the masque into writing. In response to the queen's request, Gascoigne produced an elegant and learned volume, *The Tale of Hemetes*

---

[24]While we know that Gascoigne's first pageant account, *The Tale of Hemetes the Heremyte* was signed by him, we have no way of determining if *The Princely Pleasures at Kenelworth Castle* was attributed explicitly to him; the only remaining title page was destroyed by fire in the nineteenth century. Because *The Princely Pleasures* was signed, however, with Gascoigne's well-known motto, it is safe to say that the written text was connected to him in a way that the pageant itself was not, and that the connection was solidified when the printed account was republished in his 1587 *Works*. Entitled "A briefe rehearsall, or rather a true Copie of as much as was presented before her Majestie at Kenelworth," the pageant is reprinted in *The Complete Works of George Gascoigne*, ed. John W. Cunliffe, 2 vols. (Cambridge: Cambridge University Press, 1907–1910), 2:91–131. Gascoigne's *The Tale of Hemetes the Heremyte*, published in 1579 and 1585, is also reprinted in Cunliffe's edition of the *Works*, 2:472–501.

[25]Just as Mulcaster was commissioned to publish the coronation procession, Gascoigne was asked to turn the Woodstock entertainment into book form. Elizabeth commanded "that the whole in order as it fell, should be brought to her in writing." "The Queen's Majesty's Entertainment at Woodstock," ed. A. W. Pollard (1903); rpt. (Oxford: H. Daniel and H. Hart, 1910), xxviii. Cited by Richard McCoy, "Gascoigne's 'Poēmata castrata': The Wages of Courtly Success," *Criticism* 27 (1985): 30.

the Heremyte (1575), which not only presents the pageant's plot, but also provides translations in three other languages, interpretative glosses, and emblematic drawings. *The Tale of Hemetes* is a material object that sets itself far apart from either progress or spectacle by emphasizing the distinct qualities of the book form—drawings, glosses, translations, a dedicatory poem, and a lengthy prefatorial statement. As part of his interest in using the book format as a means of self-presentation, Gascoigne carefully engraved a frontispiece for the pageant (fig. 14). In this image, he kneels gallantly before the queen presenting his work to her. With a spear held in one hand, he clasps a sword by his side and kneels beneath his well-known motto, "Tam marti quam Mercurio" (as [devoted] to Mars as Mercury). Through this image, Gascoigne depicts himself as the book's origin, but the authority that he appropriates from the pageant to himself is one that rests on his deferral and deference to the queen. His placement of this preliminary drawing in a prominent location is sanctioned by his equal emphasis on the text's destination and origin. The martial aspect of the engraving declares a similar willingness to lay down his arms, or to pick them up, for the queen. Gascoigne here reveals an act of courtly grace, declaring his intention that the phallic sword be wielded only at the whim of his female sovereign. This deference may seem a particularly meek way for Gascoigne to declare his textual authority, for the picture predicates the power of the writer squarely on that of the royal reader.[26]

The humility of this essentially medieval gesture is complicated by the simultaneous threat it expresses. For the martial allusions in the engraving become magnified when they are interpreted in light of the dedicatory poem that follows:

> Beholde (good Quene) A poett with a Speare
> (straundge sightes well markt are understood the better)
> A soldyer armde, with pensyle in his eare
> With penn to fighte and sworde to wryte a letter.
>
> (*Works*, 2:473)

[26]In "Gascoigne's 'Poēmata castrata': The Wages of Courtly Success," Richard McCoy reads Gascoigne's posture in this frontispiece as evidence of Gascoigne's gradual loss of autonomy and "creative ingenuity" in the face of oppressive social institutions. McCoy inteprets this image in light of Gascoigne's supposed decline into "abject flattery" and a loss of artistic integrity. The *Hemetes* pageant reveals the necessity of literary compromise; "[Gascoigne] had to present a text," McCoy argues, "which was not his own, relinquishing his poetic authority while ceding control to a higher power" (30). I would qualify McCoy's argument to offset the modern bias regarding "original" poetic authority. Trained in patterns of imitation, Renaissance writers did not necessarily assume orginality to be prerequisite to literary authority.

Figure 14. George Gascoigne, *The Tale of Hemetes the Heremyte.* By permission of the British Library.

The "straundge sightes" refer ambiguously to the man of letters bearing arms and the spectacle that the text will go on to describe, both of which are sights that equally need to be "markt" on these pages.[27] In vivifying the linkage between writing and weaponry, Gascoigne self-reflexively comments on the potential violence of the letter. The phrase "well markt" condenses these meanings: as a noun, "mark" signifies a limit, a target aimed at with a weapon, a sign or trace, a written symbol; as a verb—the act of remarking, the act of striking. When Gascoigne writes that the poet/soldier should be "well markt," he suggests the oddity of connecting the sword and the pen, items that should designate two distinct vocations. Through his pun on "markt," however, he points to their necessary linkage, as these differences and similarities must be remarked by the writer who controls their meanings and who also marks the pageant by transforming it into writing and demarcating its message. The engraving implies that writing and weaponry are naturally connected in their equal potential for rendering service to the queen. So, too, the violence implicit in "marking" his text is suggested and then subdued, for in the next lines, he notes that his gown is "haulffe of, his blade not fully bownde." Poised, almost but not quite ready to take up arms (perhaps with his "penn to fighte"), Gascoigne unveils his blunted instrument and thus stages his own potential emasculation for his readership. The moment of displayed private presentation has a strangely combative and confessional air, as the power of writing is both heralded and denied through a textual transmission that seems laden with sexual anxiety. On a simple level, Gascoigne merely asks for Elizabeth's patronage: "peereles prince, employe this willinge man / In your affayres to do the beste he canne" (2:473). His petition, however, is complicated by the ambiguous "danger" that everywhere surrounds his service.

The combination of aggression and deference that is expressed through the sword/pen analogy gathers force in the dedicatory letter that follows the poem. In this epistle, Gascoigne plots his career through a highly conventional prodigal narrative.[28] "Behold me," he cries, "not as I am, but as I would be" (2:477). In renouncing, as he states, "my youth myspent, my substaunce ympayred, my credytt accrased, my tallent hydden" (2:476), he obviously promotes his own substance, credit, and talent. Gascoigne then goes on to apologize for his lengthy self-absorbed and immodest narrative: "I fynd in my self some suffycyuency to serve your highnes / which causeth

[27]C. T. Prouty, *George Gascoigne: Elizabethan Courtier, Soldier, and Poet* (New York: Columbia University Press, 1942).

[28]In *Elizabethan Prodigals* Richard Helgerson details the complex mechanisms that went into this highly stylized and conventional mode of presentation (Berkeley: University of California Press, 1976).

me thus preseumpteowsly to present you with theis rude lynes / having turned the eloquent tale of Hemetes the Heremyte (wherewith I saw your lerned judgment greatly pleased at Woodstock) into latyne, Italyan and frenche" (2:476–77). Gascoigne is fully aware that it is his position as translator that allows him to disclose his "tallent hydden" to the queen and his readership at large. He is equally aware that his book caters to the tastes of the queen's "lerned judgment" as it was revealed at the pageant. In admitting that his "arrogant speeches" constitute a "bold" enterprise (2:478), Gascoigne makes visible the potency and force implicit in the seemingly humble posture of dedication in the engraving. Thus read, the soldier's state of disarray implies a potency barely masked.

Gascoigne's earlier work "The Adventures of Master F.J." (1573) explicitly equated sword, pen, and penis throughout, as evidenced when the powerful mistress whom the main character Ferdinando woos is raped /seduced by his "naked sword" and eventually leaves him for her secretary because he has a better "pen."[29] Gascoigne's verbal associations between writing, wounding, and sexuality in this earlier text cast a peculiar light on the authority that he asserts through his pen reference in the later preface. For his engraving represents him laden with phallic power standing before the female queen, who must drop her symbols of power (her smaller scepter—drastically overshadowed by his two weapons) to accept his writing. The spectacular nature of the pageant allows him to combine the flattering obsequiousness of epideictic language and Christian humility with the boldness of writing, a boldness coded in martial and sexual imagery. In the frontispiece and preface, Gascoigne creates a pre-text that threatens to swallow the actual tale. With the apparatus—the preface, gloss, engravings, poems, and translations—he multiplies the size of the spectacle four times over. By tailoring the pageant to the form of the book, Gascoigne is able to highlight his own humbly ambitious presence and script his reputation. The pageant, authored by someone else, becomes subsumed within his written account, now the Tale of Gascoigne.

It is no surprise that gender becomes part of Gascoigne's coding of authority in this prefatory material, for it was equally important in his previous pageant at Leicester's estate at Kenilworth. Gascoigne's project of fashioning power through editing becomes even more apparent in the Kenilworth account. His introduction and packaging of the *Hemetes* pageant throws into relief some of the issues he considered in his own pageant writing. In preparation for a two-week long progress visit by the court, Gascoigne and other courtiers designed displays based on Arthur-

[29]George Gascoigne, "The Adventures of Master F.J.," in *Works*, 1:436.

ian legend and classical mythology as a means of welcoming and allegorically lauding the queen: a porter presents Elizabeth with keys to the castle; the lady of the lake is freed from imprisonment, and a savage man is civilized by her presence; Echo charms her with verses of praise, and Diana appears to her in a masque. At the conclusion Gascoigne, dressed as the woodsman Silvanus, trots beside the queen's litter begging her in stylized prose to allow "Deep Desire" (personified as a holly bush) to enter into her heart. This last maneuver, which raises the highly controversial issue of the queen's chastity and the marriage question, draws to a close when the poet suggests that the queen's acceptance of desire will insure the support of her realm. If she grants desire its due, the woodsman states, "the heaven will smile, the earth will quake, men will clap their hands, and I will always continue an humble beseecher for the flourishing estate of your royall person" (2:131). Just as Puck's and Prospero's epilogues later bargain with the theater audience for their "hands," Silvanus here offers applause to the royal actress only if she grants his suit. Gascoigne's finale thus puts in suspension the loyalty and support of the English people and makes their approval for the royal display event contingent on the success of the negotiations between courtier and sovereign. The coronation procession had established this dynamic in its representation of the queen and her subjects engaged in a process of mutual courting.

In drawing on an erotic discourse to represent the struggle for mastery between royal mistress and ardent courtier, Gascoigne as Silvanus calls attention to the question of the queen's marriage and her possible vulnerability to foreign and native aristocratic factions. Although the queen was adamant against direct advice on this issue, the pageant's indirect insinuations seem to have escaped censure. At a previous pageant sponsored by Leicester in 1565, the queen had taken exception to a staged marriage debate.[30] In the Kenilworth pageant, however, Gascoigne's exhortations are perhaps offset by the poet's comic appearance. Dressed as Silvanus, he runs breathlessly beside the queen's horse, beseeching her to accept an emotion personified as a bush. Gascoigne's final injunction to marriage thus comically stages the queen's refusal of correct desire and unmasks the pageant's political interests.

The service that Gascoigne rendered in placing the event in print apparently gave him license to include more controversial material. As Mulcaster's tract suggests, the queen relied on written accounts to pro-

---

[30]When the 1565 entertainment dramatized a debate between Juno and Diana in which Jupiter declares in favor of matrimony, the queen is said to have turned to the Spanish ambassador and said, "This is all against me." Quoted by Louis Montrose in "Gifts and Reasons: The Contexts of Peele's 'Araygemement of Paris,'" *ELH* 47 (1980): 441.

duce her mythologized and theatrical presence to her subjects. In his published record, Gascoigne finds it possible to include a mythological play that interrogates the relationship between marriage and sovereignty and thus intensifies Silvanus's implied critique of the queen's lack of "Deep Desire."[31] This masque is peculiar in that it explains the origins of royal power as a trick. Elizabeth (Zabeta) is seemingly trapped into her reign by a rival goddess. As if this odd account of sovereign power were not problematic enough, Gascoigne links it to it a debate over the issue of marriage. Iris argues that Queen Zabeta neglects her duties in not marrying:

> How necessarie were
> for worthy Queenes to wed
> That know you wel, whose life alwayes
> in learning hath beene led.
>
> (2:119)

The play concludes with a highly controversial assessment: "Yet never wight felt perfect blis, / but such as wedded beene" (1:120). Happiness and true learning, it seems, were only available to the married queen.

The narrator mentions that although this "shewe" was "prepared and redy," it "never came to execution"; "the cause whereof," he continues, "I cannot attribute to any other thing, then to lack of opportunitie and seasonable weather" (2:120). The narrator is, of course, a bit disingenuous in not acknowledging why a show advocating the necessity of marriage for the ruler was never performed. Even his phrasing—"I cannot attribute to any other thing"—seems self-consciously strained to the point of sarcasm. The printed text, however, not only performs this show publicly but also disingenuously calls attention to its suppression. By including this censored show in his written account, Gascoigne risks the queen's disapproval. Eventually she did tire of challenges to her judgment in this matter. In 1581 she issued the so-called "Statute of Silence" that stifled public commentary on her behavior, particularly on the issue of marital questions.[32] Gascoigne's record of the pageant boldly approaches this very question. The subtitle to his text claims that it presents "a brief rehearsall or rather a true Copie of as much as was presented before her Majestie at Kenelworth during her last abode there" (2:91). Yet Gascoigne does not produce a copy, a mere repetition, if such a transcription were possible.

---

[31]For a reading of the ending to this pageant, see Joseph Loewenstein, *Responsive Readings: Versions of Echo in Pastoral, Epic, and the Jonsonian Masque* (New Haven: Yale University Press, 1984), 61–73.

[32]Annabel Patterson discusses this statute in "'Under . . . Pretty Tales': Intention in Sidney's *Arcadia*," *Studies in the Literary Imagination* 15 (1982): 14.

Instead, he self-consciously exploits the interpretative slippage between event and report, capitalizing on the process of editing to refashion and remake the event. If Mulcaster flaunted his ability to reinstate the queen as the narrative center of the royal entry, Gascoigne declares his ability to uncensor his performance when translating the pageant into print.

It is more than coincidental that the most controversial moment of the pageant occurs when the entertainment focuses on the issue of marriage. Gascoigne's mythological play targets the vulnerability of the queen's gender, probes the basis of her rule, questions her suppression of her courtier's ambitions ("desire"), and criticizes her decision to remain a virgin queen. Through these tactics, Gascoigne identifies himself as an ambitious Protestant courtier who craves to employ his overlapping talents as soldier, writer, and counselor. We must remember that Gascoigne wrote this pageant under the auspices of Leicester, who headed a powerful Protestant faction continually at odds with Elizabeth's policy and who was known for his intermixed erotic and political interest in the queen. Gascoigne implores her to alter her conservative policy so as to profit from the group of highly ambitious, humanistically trained courtiers who sought more active service within the court. Gascoigne's decision to risk the queen's disfavor by placing the controversial material in print calls attention to the distinct authority that publication afforded. Because he undertakes this negotiation precisely at the moment in which the queen's erotic desire is at issue, the authority he garners for himself in translating pageantry into print is colored by the gender coding that structures his request. The queen is asked to admit proper "desire" (that is, the ambitions of motivated courtiers as well as her own need for masculine "affection" and advice) into the world of her court.

Gascoigne's reporting of the pageant also reveals the gender coding of his own peculiar generic and stylistic choices. Because we have Robert Laneham's epistolary account of the same pageant, we are able to identify moments when Gascoigne submitted the published account to his own specific editorial designs.[33] By comparing Gascoigne's and Laneham's texts, we see the different generic expectations each writer imposed on the disparate entertainments. Laneham presents a *commedia rusticale*, shaped by several rural shows and a mock wedding between caricatured peasants. Gascoigne, however, strings together episodic scenes into a loose structure framed by the topos of Arthurian romance: the queen quests through a romantic landscape of knights, giants, and fairy queens, her

[33]Robert Laneham's account of the Kenilworth pageant is reprinted in John Nichols, *Progresses*, 1:426–84.

presence magically rescuing damsels, taming savages, and reconciling warring knights. Gascoigne's printed pageant produces that quest by condensing and unifying a week's disparate events. As the story line conflates time and space into the flow of written narrative, the queen seems to move continuously from adventure to adventure. Unlike Laneham, Gascoigne does not interrupt the queen's adventures to describe her physical setting or to inventory the library. Instead, the text falls into a loose adventure "plot." Silvanus's final show abruptly shifts the gender coding of this romance structure so that Elizabeth is no longer figured as the second Arthur, but as the damsel wooed by the questing knight. Gascoigne thus designs a frame for the entertainment that absorbs the queen's figuration of herself as an autonomous heroine into Leicester's insistent wooing of the queen and his injunction to marriage. In other words, the queen moves from powerful male quest figure to the Petrarchan heroine who understands her power as predicated on the refusal of desire. Gascoigne's *Tale of Hemetes*, in fact, concluded with an acknowledgement that he, as an aspiring courtier, was made to play the role of Petrarchan lover to the queen: "Ye god wolde deigne to make, a Petrarks heirs of me the coomlyest Queene that ever was, my Lawra nedes must be" (2: 510). In the Zabeta marriage skit at Kenilworth, Gascoigne problematizes this position by exposing its limitations as well as its advantages, just as he has exposed the potential violence of servitude on the frontispiece engraving. His pageant account positions the queen to expose the limitation of her own powerful literarily informed representations.

In editing the pageant, Gascoigne also deletes portions of the entertainment that might distract the reader from the more crucial exchanges between Elizabeth and her courtiers. He thus follows Mulcaster's strategy in unifying and focusing the pageant event so as to accentuate its continuity and cohesion. Laneham's version narrates moments edited from Gascoigne's more public account: a mishap in which a tree branch falls on the queen and a full description of Gascoigne's unflattering comic trot beside Elizabeth's horse. Not surprisingly, Gascoigne chooses to omit these fiascoes and to create in writing a more orderly and tidy pageant than could be produced by the performance. Gascoigne's deletions serve not only to correct mishaps, however, but also to create a general focal point for the week's festivities. Deleting from the script an episode that relies on the rapid sword fighting of Sir Bruse and a dramatic chase, Gascoigne substitutes instead a series of static poetic addresses to the queen. Stephen Orgel notes that this shift recenters the pageant on Elizabeth,[34] but it also accentuates the craft

[34]Stephen Orgel, *The Jonsonian Masque* (Cambridge, Mass.: Harvard University Press, 1965), 42.

of the poet rather than the performer. In narrating the display events so that they emphasize the dynamic between courtier and queen, Gascoigne, like Mulcaster, foregrounds the importance of writing and print to the creation and dissemination of a fully intelligible spectacle. Only in the reported accounts can the full spectacular force of royal display be truly realized. Gascoigne's posturing in the frontispiece to *The Tale of Hemetes* appropriately complements this double inscription of the queen as textual cynosure and unrelenting Petrarchan mistress. While deferentially offering his text to his queen, Gascoigne keeps one hand poised beside his critical sword/pen as well. He thus implies that he is as capable of defiantly challenging royal authority as he is of celebrating its majestic force. The threat of emasculation that he airs on the frontispiece to *Hemetes* serves paradoxically as an apt counterpart to his published display of the queen's refusal of his "Deep Desire." In both cases, the published representation recasts the courtier's unrealized potential.

In the engraving for the *Hemetes* pageant, Gascoigne presents himself as a man caught unsteadily between love and war, writing and weaponry, and acquiescence and resistance. These tensions are evident in the Kenilworth masque as well. Here he not only invokes the queen (unsuccessfully) to rethink her sovereign judgment, but also edits the entire pageant to intensify the force of that critique. The "straundge sight" on which Gascoigne comments in the *Hemetes* tale is the image of the soldier using a "penn to fighte." While his publication of the Kenilworth entertainments certainly displays his literary wares to prospective patrons, it also stages more publicly the political negotiations between courtier and queen. Gascoigne insists on the queen's need for masculine advice and counsel by framing that critique within a theatrical celebration of imperial mythology designed to legitimate Elizabeth's rule. His editorial designs declare the importance of writing to event, print to spectacle, and courtier to sovereign.

It is more than coincidental that Gascoigne's account of the entertainment simultaneously orders the disparate episodes into a coherent narrative and establishes an author for the event. In *The Princely Pleasures at Kenelworth Castle*, Gascoigne attributes many of the displays, poems, and performances to their writers; thus, he insists on the collaborative nature of the progress entertainment. But in doing so, Gascoigne becomes the author of the *account* itself, and the events at Kenilworth become categorized and classified through reference to him. His authorship is made nowhere more apparent than by the text's inclusion within Gascoigne's collected *Works*, published after his death in 1587. While we have no way of knowing if the first published account was signed by Gascoigne or merely stamped with his motto, we find that publishers assigned a permanent retrospective signature to the progress festivities when they incorporated the entertainments within his oeuvre. The events at Kenilworth thus became known as his literary accomplishment.

The Whole woorkes of George Gascoigne Esquyre: Newlye compyled into one Volume (1587), which included this masque as well as two plays, satires, amorous narratives, and didactic poetry, indexed and created a profile of the courtier and writer. *The Whole woorkes* is introduced by Gascoigne's lengthy epistle to the Reverend Divines, which was reprinted from his poetic collection *The Posies.* In this letter, Gascoigne declaims against the unjust criticisms to which he has been subject and protests the censorship of his writing. While serving the queen in Holland, Gascoigne explains, his youthful and wanton poems were published without his consent and deemed to be immoral and seditious by powerful readers. Gascoigne then offers numerous elaborate justifications for his books: they promote English nationalism, they signify a prodigal lad now matured, they innocently document gentlemanly amateurism, and they serve as a moral negative example to the young men of the realm. While obviously evidencing Gascoigne's continual trouble with Elizabethan authorities, the letter is equally important in interpreting his trouble in the best light: Gascoigne presents himself as a man of good will who suffers egregious injustices at the hands of the administration. He is depicted as a man of promise and faith, whose potential is squelched by those who have willfully misconstrued his innocent meanings.

Other prefatory material to the edition consolidates this presentation by ambiguously alluding to perils that await the writer and courtier. In an address to the "Young Gentlemen" readers, for instance, Gascoigne says that his work has been misunderstood because "the doubtfulnes of some darcke places have . . . seemed heretofore daungerous" (sig. **1).[35] While centrally justifying his work on moral grounds, Gascoigne acknowledges the controversial political interpretations (the danger) that the work inadvertently encountered. R.S.'s commendatory poem suggests that Gascoigne's martial and defensive postures were less a response to hostile critics than an offer of valiant service to the Crown; Gascoigne yields, the poem states, "His pen, his sword, himselfe and all his might / To Pallas schoole, and Mars in princes right." The prefatory material thus indicates that the court world forced Gascoigne to become embattled and frustrated in interrelated ways; his gallant offer of martial service *to* the Crown bleeds over into his confrontation *with* state authority. Gascoigne's famous autobiographical poem, "Woodmanship," explicitly constructs this view of himself—a man foiled by misdirected ambitions and by unfair censure: "wonder not / To

---

[35]George Gascoigne, *The Whole woorkes of George Gascoigne Esquyre: Newlye compyled into one Volume,* STC 11638 (1587).

see your woodman shoote so ofte awrie," Gascoigne writes (*Works*, 1:348). In metaphorically associating the thwarted goals of courtiership with the failed hunt, Gascoigne reestablishes the connection between martial and literary accomplishment that is evident in his pageant texts. Such an association makes his prominently displayed but bowed weapon in the *Hemetes* engraving more striking and threatening. We must remember that Gascoigne himself provided a gender coding for these phallic instruments in his narrative work. In unfolding the linkage between pen, sword, and penis in "Master F.J.," Gascoigne exposed how his conflicting roles of soldier and writer betrayed a sexual anxiety. The commendatory poem hints at this conflation in its parallel structure: "His pen, his sword, himselfe." Shooting awry and writing dangerously become tentatively yoked to his forced service to an unappreciative female sovereign. The dangers that await the courtier, soldier, and writer become associated with threats to masculinity itself.

The metaphor of hunting found in "Woodmanship" also recalls Gascoigne's pageant performance of the woodman Silvanus, who tried so desperately to get Elizabeth to open her heart to desire. The pageant offers in condensed form, then, the verbally connected desires and defeats of the courtier. In presenting Gascoigne as an embattled and frustrated soldier /courtier/poet, whose talents were not appreciated by royal and state authorities, the collected works magnifies Gascoigne's own presentation of himself as Silvanus, the woodsman whose "mark" was missed although he wielded his weapons (his phallic pen and sword) with the best of intentions and the greatest of skill. In celebrating his imperial queen, Gascoigne certainly challenges her wisdom in refusing his offer of desire. The violence implied in these unrealized ambitions pervades Gascoigne's authorial persona. Suffering from the capriciousness of fortune within a dangerous world of court intrigue, the poet necessarily writes through defensive and combative postures. His editing of royal pageantry serves as only one instance among many of the potential violence of the letter.

It is fitting that Gascoigne's pageant account be introduced through the prefatory material of the entire *Works*. By presenting the Kenilworth pageant to a larger public, Gascoigne magnified the narrative control he had over the political challenges he launched and the defeats he suffered. The inclusion of the pageant text in the *Works* heightens the general presentation of Gascoigne's foiled literary career by giving it a distinctly political edge. If the pageant material underscored the half-defeated, half-threatening, and half-emasculated stance that the pleading courtier sought to control, the other texts reciprocally endowed the pageant with a literary quality. In linking the pageant texts with poetic and dramatic genres, publishers reframed the narrative and editorial power Gascoigne garnered in editing the "text" of the queen specifically as a literary authority. The image of Gascoigne as a man caught unsteadily between writing and warfare is bolstered by the representation that introduces his satire *The Steele Glass* (1575). The text is prefaced by a woodcut in which Gascoigne poses between books and guns. While obviously designed to display the writer's equal talents in martial combat and literary endeavor, the woodcut brings to life Gascoigne's frustration as a man of letters. As in the *Hemetes* engraving, the emblematic weapon/pen identifies points of affinity between seeming opposites: the potency and aggression evidenced in the Elizabethan courtiers' project of creating celebratory symbolic forms. Gascoigne's presentation of himself as an ambitious man shooting awry is reinforced by this engraving's duality; and these authorial trappings become more resonant when seen in light of Gascoigne's courtly negotiations with his monarchal "Lawra." *The Steele Glass*'s woodcut interestingly became the primary modern emblem for presenting Gascoigne's authority; a replication of this image was bound together with one copy of the *Whole woorkes* sometime after the seventeenth century, and the same image was used as the frontispiece to Cunliffe's early twentieth-century edition of Gascoigne's collected works (fig. 15). Gascoigne's spectacular and editorial engagements with Elizabeth, cast within the discourse of Petrarchan desire, produced a contest that later publishers recast when they stylized Gascoigne's authorship in terms of his frustration and besiegment as a courtier.

Sidney's Staging of the Queen's Desire

Unlike Gascoigne's published account of the festivities at Kenilworth, Sidney's *Lady of May* circulated only in manuscript within the coterie during his lifetime. It became a public text only when printed posthumously with his opus. Commissioned by Leicester, Sidney designed this masque-like pageant to celebrate Elizabeth's presence while she was on progress in Wanstead in either 1578 or 1579.[36] As she strolled the grounds of the estate, Elizabeth was seemingly "spontaneously" accosted by a May Lady, who described the two suitors, Espilus and Therion, who sought her hand in marriage. The May Lady informed Elizabeth that Espilus is a wealthy shepherd of "mild disposition" (25). Therion, however, is a "livelier" forester, who, the Lady reports, "doth me many pleasures, as stealing me venison out of these forests, but withal he grows to such rages, that sometimes he strikes me, sometimes he rails at me" (25). The May Lady reported

---

[36] *The Lady of May* is reprinted in *The Miscellaneous Prose of Sir Philip Sidney*, ed. Katherine Duncan-Jones and Jan Van Dorsten (Oxford: Clarendon Press, 1973), 21–32.

that she had to decide between "the many deserts and many faults of Therion, or the very small deserts and no faults of Espilus" (25). Following the tradition of the eclogue, the two engage in a poetic singing contest, which is extended to the community at large when Dorcas and Rixus (a shepherd and a forester) argue about the relative merits of their professions. In the most general terms, the debate becomes one of contemplation against action, the life of pastoral ease judged against the gallant activity of the woodsman. When the Lady is asked to choose, she defers her choice to the queen, who decides on the contemplative shepherd Espilus. In the final speeches, however, it appears that Elizabeth's decision was not the expected or, rather, the prescribed choice. Even though the correct victor poetically declares his triumph, it is obvious that the speeches have merely been switched to accord with the queen's choice. For in exclaiming his triumph, Espilus calls on the forest god, Silvanus, as the victor. By virtue of this reference, we see that Therion had been intended to win the lady's hand, and Pan's representative was to have been beaten by the more ambitious courtier figure who dared to "rail" at his beloved. The pageant had favored a choice that the queen did not pick. Just as Gascoigne's final injunction to marriage dramatized the pageant's eroticized political contestation, Sidney's attempt to determine the queen's choice is unmasked by the mismatched ending verses. Stephen Orgel cogently argues that Sidney's masque questions the pastoral ideal of otium, a critique that the queen ignores when she chooses the more generically conventional pastoral hero for the May Lady's nuptials.[37]

Louis Montrose has demonstrated how the pageant's scripting of the queen as royal actor constitutes Sidney's attempt to test the queen and to query her criteria for assessing her subjects.[38] Operating within the highly competitive and dangerous world of court machinations, Sidney includes in his royal entertainment an attempt to persuade the queen of the value of his own dearly held beliefs. Sidney uses pastoral and royal encomium to convince Elizabeth that she should choose his type of courtier and thus affirm the ambitions and civic values of the Protestant, humanistically trained man of action.[39] The pastoral entertainment presents a micro-

[37]Stephen Orgel, "Sidney's Experiment in Pastoral: *The Lady of May*," *Journal of the Warburg and Courtauld Institutes* 26 (1963): 198–203.

[38]Montrose, "Celebration and Insinuation," 3–35. My discussion of the pageant is indebted throughout to Montrose's important reading of this text.

[39]Montrose goes on to read a later entertainment at the tiltyard at Whitehall (*The Triumph of the Fortress of Perfect Beauty*, 1581) in terms of Sidney's renewed attempt to negotiate with Elizabeth through spectacle. In this pageant, the "foster" children of desire, played by Sidney and Fulke Greville, punningly enact the willful and impetuous forester qualities that the queen rejected ("Celebration and Insinuation," 23–28).

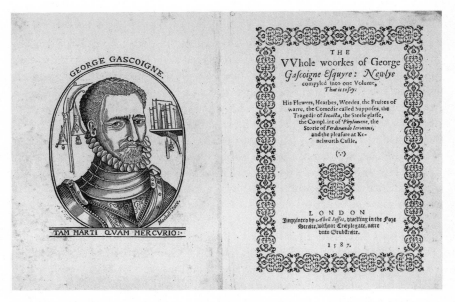

Figure 15. The Whole woorkes of George Gascoigne Esquyre: Newlye compyled into one volume, STC 11638 (1587), with the subsequent inserted copy (by Machell Stace) of the 1570 frontispiece to *The Steele Glass*. Reproduced by permission of the Huntington Library, San Marino, California (RB 49980).

cosm of the Elizabethan court, with the queen judging her courtiers' merits for preferment. In privileging the character of Therion, Sidney asks her to modify her conservative policy and acknowledge the benefits of a courtier whose impetuosity and bluntness may lead to an occasionally harsh critique of policy. Writing from his precarious social position on the bottom tier of the aristocracy, Sidney asks Elizabeth to imagine the possible advantages of encouraging the new generation of courtiers.[40] The pageant, then, dramatizes one courtier's attempt to petition the queen, and it registers that courtier's failure when Elizabeth does indeed write her authority against that of the text's and chooses the safer Espilus. Montrose's work on Elizabethan pastoral has made it easier for us to see why Sidney chose the pastoral form to celebrate the queen's splendor and to

[40]Alan Sinfield discusses Sidney's bizarre and confusing class position in "Power and Ideology: An Outline Theory and Sidney's *Arcadia*," *ELH* 52 (1985): 259–77. In *Elizabethan Prodigals*, Richard Helgerson makes the case for a new generation of ambitious young men caught in a social world that refuses to reward their skills and knowledge. Historical work on the new generation of men born between 1552 and 1563 has been done by Anthony Esler, *The Aspiring Mind of the Elizabethan Younger Generation* (Durham, N.C.: Duke University Press, 1966).

insinuate himself into the state apparatus, for he engages pastoral in a way that George Puttenham found appropriate—to "glaunce at greater matters" through "rude speeches."[41] The May Lady ominously and prophetically hints at the seriousness of this "glaunce" when she states, "in judging me, you judge more than me in it" (30). She implies that the queen's decision will be a self-judgment. By making her choice, Elizabeth rewrites Sidney's script and asserts her own wisdom over his advice.

Sidney's attempt at instruction is intricately woven within a web of royal praise. The majesty of the queen is written into the script so that she merely steps into an already lauded role. The masque is designed to herald her wise decision no matter what lines she assigns herself; she is praised as "Juno, Venus, Pallas et profecto plus [and certainly more] " (31).[42] Sidney thus follows Mulcaster's tactic of creating ellipses in which the queen can offer her own valued words to the display event. All Elizabeth had to do was play herself, and a mythology was guaranteed to be built around her. As does Mulcaster, however, Sidney curiously emphasizes the writer's role in constructing that queenly authority. The pageant, for instance, is structured on a succession of deferred powers: Master Rombus, though shown subsequently to be a pedantic fool, is initially introduced as an eloquent and fair adjudicator. After he announces that he has failed to arbitrate the dispute, the focus then shifts to the May Lady, who yields her decision to Elizabeth. In presenting the queen's authority as the product of a series of deferrals rather than as an innate or essential force, the pageant shows the construction necessary to buttress her power. This revelation makes resonant the May Lady's opening words: "Most fair lady; for as for your other titles of state, statelier persons shall give you" (30). Here Sidney's humility disguises a strong assertion—that the queen is *given* titles, just as she is handed the Bible in the coronation procession during that moment of peculiar historical revision. The power of the royal interpreter is thus simultaneously presented and undercut by the privileging of the pageant maker himself, who advertises his importance to political authority. In short, Sidney calls attention to what is always evident, but not readily or

[41]George Puttenham, *The Arte of English Poesie* (1589), ed. Gladys Doidge Willcock and Alice Walker (Cambridge: Cambridge University Press, 1936): 38–39. Louis Montrose discusses Puttenham and the ideology of pastoral form in "Of Gentlemen and Shepherds: The Politics of Elizabethan Pastoral Form," *ELH* 50 (1983): 415–59; and "'Eliza, Queene of Shepheardes,' and the Pastoral of Power," *English Literary Renaissance* 10 (1980): 153–82. The progress itself, in fact, was pastoral in the largest sense, as it enacted the movement from city to country.

[42]David Lee Miller traces Spenser's use of a similar inscription of self-reflexive approbation in "Authorship, Anonymity, and *The Shepheardes Calender*," *Modern Language Quarterly* 40 (1979): 219–36.

easily emphasized—the *act* of fictively proffering titles and praise. Certainly, the queen was aware that her power was not absolute: she relied on Parliament for funds and an extensive bureaucratic structure for administrative work. Yet pageantry was precisely the place where a fiction of innate power, grace, and merit was expected to be generated.

I would like to further Montrose's analysis of the politics of this masque by paying attention to how those transactions were registered when Sidney turned the event into writing. Frank Whigham suggests that ambitious young men in the late sixteenth century often designated for themselves the "lucrative role of intercessor, of translator, of priest to these secular [bureaucratic] mysteries" by knowing some skill that was mystified within the government structure (such as church Latin or the legal code).[43] The fashioning of royal mythology played a crucial role within the mystified network that Whigham describes. Sidney's pageant foregrounds his authority by interceding between sovereign and cheering masses. Writing furthered this process by allowing the poet to step forth from his anonymous and mystified position as the producer of courtly spectacle into the more public realm of authorship.

When the pageant is recorded, Sidney writes the queen's words out of the play. At the most climactic moment in the drama, the moment when the sovereign is to decide the ending of the debate and add her speech to the script, the poet draws attention away from her to himself. Inscribed instead is a silence. Sidney makes an ambitious assertion through this humble statement: "It pleased her Majesty to judge that Espilus did the better deserve [the May Lady]; but what words, what reasons she used for it, this paper, which carrieth so base names, is not worthy to contain. Sufficeth it that upon the judgement given, the shepherds and foresters made a full consort of their cornets and recorders" (30). The queen's role is undercut by this elision. Sidney hints that certain royal opinions were spoken and that they constituted the judgment that resolved the masque's entire conflict; but in a stroke of simultaneous humility and assertion, he presents a work that "sufficeth" without Elizabeth's monumental words. In a moment characterized by Montrose as one of "cryptic brevity" (19), the author remains at the forefront of the narrative and the "base" name he humbly denounces is left to define the text. If the queen was unwilling to validate Sidney's energetic forester/courtier within the pageant, Sidney was unwilling to cede his written narrative to the queen.

This omission might not seem important. After all, it could have been

---

[43]Frank Whigham, *Ambition and Privilege: The Social Tropes of Elizabethan Courtesy Theory* (Berkeley: University of California Press, 1984), 30.

an oversight or a trivial absence. As Mulcaster's coronation procession emphasized, however, the written account occupies a powerful site that is unavailable to spectacle—"wordes do flye, but wryting dothe remayn." The fact that the queen's words were endlessly fetishized as texts only emphasizes this point. John Nichols's monumental gathering of Elizabethan spectacle uncovers her words scattered in a variety of cultural forms—etched in corporation records, quoted in competing pamphlets, peppered throughout historical accounts. Her anecdotes have acquired a sense of canonicity,[44] as John Neale ratifies when he writes, "few of the queen's sayings are so choice . . . as are those connected with her progresses."[45] By omitting Elizabeth's words, Sidney denies material for the cult of worship that seized on the queen's every phrase. Orgel's reading of *The Lady of May* is here relevant: "If it was a fiasco in production," he observes, "its success, for those who care to look, is apparent on the page" (203). Although he locates this "success" in aesthetic terms—in Sidney's clever experimentation with pastoral form—Orgel's words could point as well to the political dimension of the pageant that is registered so clearly *on the page*. In the wake of the "fiasco" created by the queen's unintended choice, Sidney used the slippage evident in the script's transformation into written representation to write his own authority against the queen's (who wrote hers against that of his script). Although his text was written only for manuscript circulation, Sidney exercised the prerogative of the editor in order to consolidate his status within a circle of his peers.[46]

Sidney's deletions can be seen as an extension of Gascoigne's editing procedures. Gascoigne's inclusion of the unperformed Zabeta skit in his account of the festivities at Kenilworth paradoxically constitutes a deletion because it omits the queen's presence. The progress as a genre is unified only by the perimeters of the estate and the queen's being. By showing the hypothetical progress without the queen's attendance or performance, Gascoigne erases the event's raison d'être. In choosing to transmit the *intended* (but not performed) script to the public, Gascoigne modifies the ostensible reason for pageant writing: capturing a moment of the queen's splendor as made manifest in entertainments. Instead, he indicates that the script is worthy of print because of its own merits. By deleting the conventional point of reference, Gascoigne challenges a fundamental generic

[44]For evidence, see the following passages in John Nichols, *Progresses*, 1:215, 2:155, 2:159, and 1:338.

[45]John Neale, "Sayings of Queen Elizabeth," *History*, n.s. 10 (October 1925): 220.

[46]J. W. Saunders describes the elaborate and extended network of coterie systems that allowed for the building and tearing down of poetic reputations. In "From Manuscript to Print: A Note on the Circulation of Poetic MSS. in the Sixteenth Century," *Proceedings of the Leeds Philosophical and Literary Society* 6 (1951): 507–28.

assumption of royal pageantry: he implies that the royal entertainment can be valuable without any royalty at the occasion at all. While Sidney represents Elizabeth's presence and splendor at Wanstead, he uses the opportunity to publicize his ability to suppress her language. Both courtiers choose to alter the performances by tinkering with the representation of the queen.

In 1579, contemporaneous with the performance of *The Lady of May*, Sidney circulated his ill-advised protest to the queen regarding her potential marriage to Alençon, "A Letter written by Sir Philip Sidney to Queen Elizabeth, touching Her Marriage with Monsieur." As in the pageant, Sidney challenges the queen precisely on the delicate issue of her desire. If the masque touched on the issue of the queen's wooing practices in an indirect and open-ended way, the letter was rash enough to warrant Sidney's banishment from court. The boldness of his counsel in this matter confirms his interest in targeting a particular point of vulnerability for the queen—her "second" body's gender. Elizabeth's sex surfaced continuously in debates about succession and rule, in the erotic mythologization of the queen, and in discussions of her potential dual role as sovereign and wife. We must remember that what Sidney chose to erase in his pageant account are the exact words with which Elizabeth named the May Lady's desire. As a figure for female authority who exceeded the limited domain of the May Lady (the May Lady's "transcendent Idea," in Montrose's terms), Elizabeth was asked in this moment of adjudication to name her own political desires within the framework of romantic love. Sidney's use of pastoral romance to question the queen's policy is thus more than another Renaissance example of how "love is not love"; for here Sidney not only inveighs the queen through the terms of courtly love, but also calls attention to the importance of her desire exactly at the moment that he demonstrates his own ability to reshape her opinions.

Sidney appeals to traditional literary tropes by questioning the queen about her courtly practices. The shepherd and forester's debate in the masque is articulated as an exploration of Petrarchan metaphor's limits and advantages (Orgel, 200-202). As a surrogate Petrarchan mistress, Elizabeth is granted the opportunity to name her favored wedding partner and to reinstate the conventional pastoral schema within the pageant, but Sidney shows her up by foregrounding her inability to recognize the problems inherent in playing the part of the sonnet mistress. Within his script, Espilus, her choice, can only express love by preaching the value of worldly wealth and thus naming his beloved as a possession that he deserves by virtue of his station. Therion, on the other hand, explicitly states that he never seeks to own the deer, or the beloved, that he ardently desires. Instead, the forester mocks conventional pastoral and Petrarchan tropes.

Sidney not only sets up a problematic set of alternatives for the queen, but when she resists the critique of Petrarchan/pastoral courtship that Therion offers, he also edits her language. Because Sidney frames the singing match in distinctly Petrarchan terms, the leverage he gains in articulating his own political agenda becomes inextricable from the binary opposition of male lover and female mistress. The rejected suitor has the last say. In making her judgment, the queen holds up for critique her own chosen gendered role: that of the Petrarchan mistress who negotiates with the idealizing lyrical shepherd. Sidney's superior position, established by his narrative control of the queen's choice, becomes aligned with the masculine Petrarchan poet's prerogative of petitioning and linguistically fashioning his sonnet mistress.

Like Gascoigne, Sidney frames his political negotiations within the topos of courtship. Gascoigne stages a mythological play that questions Elizabeth's statecraft and marital policy, and he performs in the entertainments as a suitor to the queen. Sidney offers Elizabeth control over another woman's desire in order to extract from the queen a statement about her intentions in awarding preferments to courtiers. Sidney makes Elizabeth's acquiescence or refusal part of the dramatic play; he turns her, in effect, into Gascoigne's Zabeta and instructs her about the terms of her own desire. Like Gascoigne, Sidney gleans narrative and political authority by besting the female sovereign in a theatrical contest of wills, a contest that becomes most heated and pronounced when the queen's erotic desire is at issue. The authority that these writers gain in translating pageantry into writing is informed by the gender coding implicit in their addresses.

We know that *The Lady of May* circulated privately because Elizabethan miscellanies incorporated verse from the pageant text, referenced as part of Sidney's masque for the queen and signed with his name.[47] After his death, however, when *The Lady of May* was published in the 1598 folio edition of *The Countess of Pembrokes Arcadia*, Sidney's strategic editing became more public and more integrated with his other literary endeavors. As critics have noted, the *Arcadia* was a highly influential manual of style, a handbook for courtly practices.[48] After 1598, however, it consisted of much more than the bulky romance, because it included, among other works, the sonnets, his defense of poetry, and this slight pageant text. The 1598 *Countess of Pembrokes Arcadia* was centrally important as a textual monu-

[47]For one example, see John Bodenham's *Belvedere, or the garden of the Muses*, STC 3189 (1600; reprint, New York: Burt Franklin, 1967), no. 78.

[48]For a discussion of the *Arcadia*'s influence, see Victor Skretkowicz's introduction to his edition of *The Countess of Pembroke's Arcadia: The New Arcadia* (Oxford: Clarendon Press, 1987).

ment that marked Sidney's place in literary history and contributed to his growing reputation as a cultural legend and symbol of the new age of English letters. In fact, a bizarre and contradictory "cult of Sidney" was created after his death, orchestrated in part by his sister (see Chapter 5). His lavish funeral celebrated him as both a rebellious Protestant martyr and an emblem of the flowering of Elizabethan chivalry. Elizabeth obviously found it in her interest to foreground the latter view, while others identified Sidney in terms of the tragedy of his life's failures, his death merely serving as the culmination of the overwhelming loss England suffered because of this courtier's unrealized, though almost universally recognized, potential.[49] Sidney became known, like Gascoigne, as a man whose career was thwarted because of his inability to succeed at court. The *Arcadia* placed Sidney's literary achievements in print, along with the outpouring of published elegies that mythologized him as a highly ambitious and learned man of promise who was nevertheless frustrated in his career. Trained to be a leader in English statecraft and diplomacy, Sidney found himself either languishing at court or exiled from it because of royal disfavor. Through the *Arcadia*, Sidney was posthumously endowed with an authorial role that framed his contradictory cultural reputation within his literary endeavors.

The Lady of May offers a condensed version of the trials of Sidney's life; it particularizes his courtly exploits and failures into an actual bargain with Elizabeth herself. Although his courtly "wooing" of the queen in the *The Lady of May* might have been a peripheral literary labor, it encapsulated his overlapping literary and political interests and disclosed his continual struggles with authority. In the masque, Sidney scripts the theatrical power of the sovereign while refusing to accord the queen's exact desires. In a sense, what he inserts into the repetition of power is difference itself, a moment of resistance that allows his politicized presence as a writer to be expressed. Sidney's critique of pastoral's political mythography, seen in strong form when he editorially chastises the queen's overly simple validation of pastoral, positions him simultaneously as an ardent and defiant courtier and as a talented man of letters.

The masque joins Sidney's other works in projecting an image of his cultural and authorial power. Rather than offering a random assortment of writing, the 1598 volume presents a set of texts that share philosophical, literary, and linguistic concerns. *The Lady of May,* for instance, picks up a number of themes that are articulated in Sidney's other works. Orgel

---

[49]For a discussion of Sidney's literary sublimation and repetition of courtly failure, see Richard McCoy, *Sir Philip Sidney: Rebellion in Arcadia* (New Brunswick, N.J.: Rutgers University Press, 1979).

describes this relationship nicely when he comments on Sidney's use of pastoral in the masque:

> "The Lady of May" is concerned with only a single aspect of the pastoral mode, the assumption that the contemplative life is intrinsically more virtuous than the active life. We may see the critique extended and deepened in the larger pastoral world of *Arcadia*, that wild country where the retired life of the contemplative man is full of deception and misery, and the innocent lover, that indispensable figure of pastoral, is met with sudden and violent death. *Arcadia* is about what happens if we consider the real implications of pastoral romance, about the abrogation of responsibility in a world where nature is not friendly nor chance benign. Similarly, Sidney creates in a Petrarchan sonnet sequence, a beloved who is literally unattainable, and a lover for whom the sense of loss and separation approaches the Calvinist sense of original sin. Both *Arcadia* and *Astrophel and Stella* are obviously serious in a way in which the Queen's entertainment at Wanstead cannot be. Nevertheless, the same intelligence is at work, the same sorts of questions are being asked.
>
> (199)

Orgel argues that the relationship between the masque and Sidney's other writings is founded on their shared concern with "basic questions of [their] own form" (199). He explains this concern specifically in terms of Sidney's particular preoccupation with drawing out the cultural and political implications of literary genres. In *The Lady of May*, Sidney makes light of the queen's desire for complacent shepherd-like courtiers. The masque thus offers a more highly politicized version of the conflict staged between pastoral ease and sovereign responsibility in the *Arcadia*. There is a two-fold effect produced when the masque is incorporated into his other writings: the pageant's topical reference charges the other works with the political meaning, and the masque is reclassified as a literary work rather than a courtly spectacle. In other words, its inclusion in the volume highlights the fact that the pageant is pastoral in nature and thus appropriately aligned with the more sweeping world of Arcadian shepherds. Because the singing debate in the masque turns on the advantages and limitations of Petrarchan discourse, the text offers a sketch of the issues that *Astrophel and Stella* explored in depth. In this sense, Orgel's observation that the masque played out a dynamic found throughout Sidney's works shows us how the pageant joined the other works in shaping the writer's renown.

Sidney's coterie masque authorized his mourners and followers, many of whom elegized him as a means of criticizing the queen's failure to value her (usually more militantly Protestant) courtiers' services. If he inherited from Mulcaster a rich sense of the latitude that the writer held in representing royal spectacle, Sidney directed other writers more particularly on how to challenge the sovereign's theatrical self-representations through literary forms. Sidney's legacy was, in part, a demonstration of how a writer could manufacture his own presence from within representations of the sovereign's splendor and power. As *The Lady of May* testified to both Sidney's growing literary reputation and his skirmishes with authority, it offered to other writers particular strategies for manipulating Elizabeth's self-fashioning.

Spenser made his allegiances clear by dedicating his inaugural poem, *The Shepheardes Calender*, to Sidney and naming Sidney as the ultimate source of inspiration in his pastoral elegy, "Astrophel." His indebtedness to Sidney is made evident in one place when he rehearses Sidney's strategy of erasure by substituting Gloriana for a mere mortal woman in the Mount Acidale scene of *The Faerie Queene* (book 6, canto 10). This canto opens with Spenser's mild critique of pastoral idleness, because Calidore's trek into the countryside is said to constitute his truancy from his more important quest. While indulging his desires and being distracted by female fancy, Calidore disrupts the gorgeous but precarious vision of the artist/shepherd piping among the graces. In the ensuing dialogue between Calidore and Colin, the shepherd Colin lauds the fourth grace as the source of true poetic inspiration, and then apologizes to Elizabeth for this seeming slight:

> Great Gloriana, greatest Maiesty,
> Pardon thy shepheard, mongst so many layes,
> As he hath sung of thee in all his dayes,
> To make one minime of thy poore handmayd.[50]

Spenser's apology only calls attention to the transgressive nature of this substitution, one that replicates Sidney's humble explanation for his omission of the queen's words in the masque. If Sidney had pointed to social decorum as a reason for his silence—to the prohibition against mingling queens with clowns—Spenser humbly asks leave to write a "minime" (a short musical note) that will only throw into relief the greatness of other poetic lays written to Elizabeth. As in Sidney's masque, the oddity of the representation of the queen is highlighted by the writer's explanation. Sidney's coterie negotiation in his slight pastoral progress, it seems, provided a model for writers such as Spenser in their more public and published literary representations. One of the commendatory poems to *The Faerie Queene* interestingly names Sidney as the authorizing and inspiring force for Spenser's writing, which here is depicted as the daring and dangerous task of blazoning Elizabeth's glory. After comparing Spenser to

---

[50]Edmund Spenser, *The Faerie Queene*, ed. Thomas P. Roche (New York: Penguin, 1987), 995, stanza 28.

Achilles, W.L. states,

> So Spencer was by Sidneys speaches wonne,
> To blaze [the Faerie Queene's] fame not fearing futures harm:
>
>   . . .
>
> What though his taske exceed a humaine witt,
> He is excus'd, sith Sidney thought it fitt.

                                  (22)

This poem offers an extraordinary account of the relationship between the two writers, one in which Sidney epitomizes both the bold and overly ambitious poet who dares to write the queen and the authoritative precursor figure who grants absolution for Spenser's brazen overreaching. The 1598 publication of the masque with other genres cemented the intersection between Sidney's literary and political reputation.

    The trappings of the 1598 *Arcadia*—the title page and the two prefaces—helped to create and monumentalize the literary reputation that the combined works established. The title page to the *Arcadia* (reprinted from the 1593 edition) not only projects a particular image of Sidney, but also serves as a new and apt introduction for his courtly masque. The title page is telling in its triadic representation of social status, gendered confrontation, and literary authority (fig. 16).[51] Within this iconography, the Sidney family emblem, the boar, takes a central place in the ornate classical frame surrounding the title. The pig and marjoram device at the bottom of the page preemptively denounces the unappreciative reader whose porcine nature prohibits him or her from recognizing the sweet riches of this literary herb. In his *Miscellany* Tottel had described this exact emblem in his attempt to protect his text from the socially undifferentiated and porcine audience of print.[52] While the pig emblemizes an undesirable aesthetic and moral response, it also represents the common nature of the people publication necessarily courted, the "unlearned." These animals—the aristocratic boar and the common pig—become the poles by which Sidney's textual authority is fashioned. The iconography of the title page thus reveals the publisher's concern to preserve the work's social status in print, a status that the courtly masque only consolidated. In his account of the pageant performed at his uncle Leicester's home, Sidney displayed his social position by virtue of his ability to accost the queen while she casually

[51]Philip Sidney, *The Countess of Pembrokes Arcadia*, STC 22541 (1598). The 1598 title page is considerably revised from the 1590 edition, which printed the first three books of the *Arcadia*. In that first publication, Sidney's family emblem was centered on a page that had none of the heraldic trappings of literary genre or classical iconography.

[52]Richard Tottel, "The Printer to the Reader," in *Tottels Miscellany*, (*Songes and Sonettes*), 2 vols., ed. Hyder E. Rollins (Cambridge, Mass.: Harvard University Press, 1928–1929), 1:2.

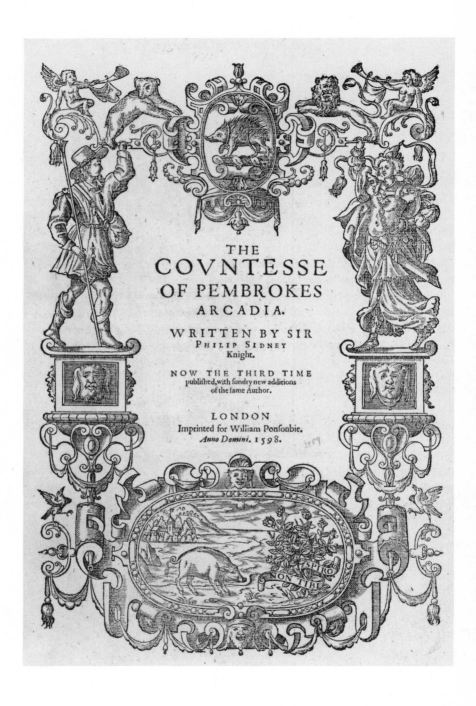

THE
COVNTESSE
OF PEMBROKES
ARCADIA.

WRITTEN BY SIR
PHILIP SIDNEY
Knight.

NOW THE THIRD TIME
published,with sundry new additions
of the same Author.

LONDON
Imprinted for William Ponsonbie.
Anno Domini. 1598.

Figure 16. Phillip Sidney, *The Countess of Pembrokes Arcadia*, STC 22541 (1598). Reproduced by permission of The Huntington Library, San Marino, California (RB 69477).

{152}

strolled the grounds of an estate. The coterie manuscript masque thus becomes valuable because of its exclusivity at the very moment that it appears to a public readership. At the same time, Sidney's inclusion within the aristocratic elite safeguards the royal critique that his masque offers. Sidney's courtiership and family lineage become important in defining his authorial position.[53]

More important is the title page's presentation of the figures of the shepherd and the amazon on opposite sides of the pictorial frame. These icons obviously introduce the central characters from the *Arcadia*—Musidorus and Zelmane—two noble princes who cross-dress as a shepherd and a woman respectively. They also point generally to thematic concerns of this romance, namely the otium of pastoral life as it comes into conflict with the heroism of the soldier and active governor. In the 1598 edition, however, these figures not only introduce the *Arcadia* but also the pageant masque that follows. I want to suggest that this inclusion alters slightly the political valence of these icons; for in the 1598 presentation, these figures are not simply representations of Musidorus and Zelmane, but also the gendered binary of male suitor and May Lady, or male courtier and female sovereign. Poised ready to clash, these figures become classicized into the literary forms that adorn the monumentalizing frame. While Gascoigne's text appropriately presents him as torn between the arts of martial combat and literary endeavor, Sidney's poetic opus introduces him through the opposition between male shepherd and female Amazon. These emblems, each bearing phallic instruments and separated tellingly by symbols of family heraldry and rude print audience, seem to square off on the title page, elegantly transfigured into a skirmish between literary genres.

This iconography was reinforced and interpreted more particularly by the two prefaces to the 1598 edition: Sidney's private dedication of the *Arcadia* and the publisher's address to the reader. In "To My Deare Lady and Sister, The Countess of Pembroke," Sidney expresses his concerns about his work's merit and readership by describing the process of writing as a thwarted infanticide that is staved off in part by his sister's special relationship to his text:

---

[53]Sidney's position in Elizabethan social hierarchy had protected him in his bouts with authority all his life. He was only banished from court when he wrote his controversial and risky "A Letter written by Sir Philip Sidney to Queen Elizabeth . . . ," while the appropriately named John Stubbes, who had no such lineage to safeguard him, lost his hand for similarly attempting to advise the queen against marriage. For a discussion of this episode, see Edwin Haviland Miller, *The Professional Writer in Elizabethan England: A Study of Nondramatic Literature* (Cambridge, Mass.: Harvard University Press, 1959), 171–74.

Here now have you (most deare and most worthie to bee most deare Ladie) this idle work of mine: which, I feare (like the Spiders webbe) will bee thought fitter to bee swept away, then worne to any other purpose. For my part, in very trueth (as the cruell fathers among the Greeks, were wont to doe to the babes they would not foster) I could well find in my hearte, to cast out in some desert of forgetfulnes this child, which I am loth to father. But you desired me to do it, and your desire, to my heart is an absolute commandement. Now, it is done only for you, only to you: if you keepe it to your selfe or to such friends, who will weigh errors in the balance of goodwill, I hope, for the fathers sake, it will be pardoned, perchance made much of, though in it selfe it have deformities. . . . [I]f it had not been in some way delivered, [it] would have growne a monster. . . . But his chiefe safety, shall be the not walking abroad; and his chiefe protection, the bearing the liverie of your name.

(fol. *3-*3^v)

In order to protect his work from criticism and social stigmatization, Sidney asks that it circulate only privately ("not walking abroad") and be guarded by Mary Sidney ("bearing the liverie of your name"). Sidney's dedication portrays his writing as a monstrous and involuntary pregnancy rendered acceptable only by the text's circumscribed viewership. The *Arcadia* is ennobled (birthed and dressed) by its placement within the confines of family and social group. Sidney interestingly figures himself as both the text's loving mother and violent father; he assumes the dual roles of male and female authority, the mother in him combining with the female influence of his sister to triumph over the father's destructive impulses. Sidney not only places the text in circulation within the family itself—as a private and trivial gift to his sister—but he also uses familiar metaphors to describe its production and worth.[54] His dedication thus suggests that his pastoral text caters to female desire and is protected by female authority. "It is done only for you, only to you"; "you desired me to do it, and your desire, to my heart is an absolute commandement," he tells the the Countess. Her authority comes to represent the insulated world of the coterie, here shrunk to the perimeters of the sibling relationship. The Countess's authority becomes emblematic of the social hierarchy that ensures and protects his writing. His trivialization of his text ("this idle work") bespeaks the gentlemanly amateurism and *humilitas* that commonly defined aristocratic writing. His textual "child" thus emerges as part of the glorious Sidney family. Sidney's deferral to female authority everywhere within this familial network enables him to announce his authorship in terms of the private nature of his text and the prestige of his

---

[54]Mary Ellen Lamb reads Sidney's presentation within her more encompassing analysis of female authorship within the Sidney family. In *Gender and Authorship in the Sidney Circle* (Madison: University of Wisconsin Press, 1990), 72–75.

family. If the animals on the title page are used to construct the text's social identity, Sidney's preface recasts that identity within the familial relationship of humble brother and powerful matriarchal patroness.

Sidney's private dedication is followed by Hugh Sanford's uneasy explanation for why the text has been printed despite the explicit desires of the author. In his address, Sanford re-presents and recasts Sidney's own rhetoric to validate his public authorship.[55] The publisher, for instance, identifies the text's deformity (its "defect") as both its incompletion and its previous corrupt printing in the 1590 edition: "The disfigured face, gentle Reader, wherewith this worke not long since appeared to the common view, moved that noble Lady, to whose Honour consecrated, to whose protection it was committed, to take in hand the wiping away those spots wherewith the beauties thereof were unworthily blemished" (fol. *4). Sanford trades on Sidney's language of deformity but rejects his assessment that the book's defect is its intrinsic lack of merit. He also indicates that Mary Sidney fulfills her role as the text's protector by putting it into print; for rather than breaching Sidney's explicit command, she can correct the "blemishes" of the previous publication. In direct contradiction to the codes of gentlemanly amateurism found in the dedication, Sanford suggests that Sidney's greatness and stature calls for the publication of his equally noble "child." By arguing that Sidney's and the reader's social status and shared cultural values will safeguard the text, he stretches the Countess's "liverie" of aristocratic and moral honor so that it enfolds Sidney and his larger print readership. Sanford thus twists the language of coterie manuscript circulation to accommodate the literary marketplace.

Sanford expresses his desire that

> the noble, the wise, the vertuous, the courteous, as many as have had any acquaintance with true learning and knowledge, will with all love and dearenesse entertaine it, as well for affinitie with themselves, as being childe to such a father. Whom albeit it doe not exactly and in every lineament represent; yet considering the fathers untimely death prevented the timely birth of the childe, it may happily seeme a thanke-worthy labour, that the defects being so few, so small, and in no principall part, yet the greatest unlikenes is rather in defect than in deformity
>
> (fol. *4ᵛ, emphasis mine)

Sanford uses Sidney's own textual description against itself, amplifying the metaphors of paternity and deformity in a way that bends them to serve

---

[55]Annabel Patterson notes this oddity: "there is a remarkable conflict between the discretion invoked in the letter, the emphasis on the text's 'safetie' in 'not walking abroad,' and its appearance as the preface to a *published* work." In "'Under . . . Pretty Tales,'" 6.

the ends of publication and the public author. Sidney's evocation of thwarted infanticide is recast as a kind of Caesarian posthumous birthing performed by Mary Sidney and the publisher. In Sanford's account, the father does not threaten the textual child, but instead ensures its safe public acceptance; and Sidney's ominous words about infanticide re-emerge in the reference to his own untimely death that prevented the text's true birth. The metaphor of lineament (clothing and genealogy) is used to establish the lineage of the author and his "gentle" text. The publisher thus foregrounds how the text's privileged rather than abject birth safeguards its circulation. Sanford reframes Sidney's expression of hostility to his text to suggest that the writer's unfortunate death was the reason for the text's neglect. He also authorizes Sidney's literary career by restoring to him the praise he heaped on the female protector of his work. Sanford highlights the circular nature of this endowment by creating a set of strategically placed verbal echoes. He opens his address with the claim that Mary Sidney is the person "to whose Honour [the text is] consecrated," and closes it with a statement of how "the love of her excellent brother, will make her consecrate [other works] to his memory" (fol. *4-*4ᵛ). Sidney's dedication of his trivial amateur labors to his sister is thus recast as her dedication to him of the published monumental folio.

When *The Lady of May* follows this introduction, its representation of the engagement between male suitor and female authority bleeds into the relationship between deferential brother and the powerful woman who posthumously endows that suitor with authority. In *The Lady of May*, Sidney reveals his humility in preserving the queen's language from baseness. He modestly declares that the trivial nature of his writing allows him to offer his work only to the private female reader for her adjudication. Editing royal spectacle allowed Sidney to use his writing talents to critique the queen in performance. In the introduction to the *Arcadia*, his engagement with female authority also confirms his achievements, this time with the woman's powerful approbation rather than her refusal. The odd pair of conflicting prefaces become important in announcing Sidney's public authorship because they suggest a transition from the private network of preferment and reward into the more public world of print. When the publisher uses Sidney's protest that he is a gentleman, not a poet, to announce a poetic identity, he follows in the broadest sense Sidney's own paradoxical tactic in his pageant. In the masque, Sidney announces himself to be an active courtier rather than a poetic shepherd, but he does so through his role as editor and writer. The prefatory material thus places Sidney's confrontation with female authority in the masque within the larger context of his private and public literary productions. When Sidney becomes constructed as a cultural hero and literary model by his survivors, his own prefatorial dedication and his royal spectacle offer the terms through which that construction could take place.

It is not surprising that Sidney became memorialized through one of the literary roles he had shaped. Spenser elegized "Astrophel" as both the disappointed "gentle shepherd" and the Petrarchan lover:

> Young Astrophel, the pride of shepheards praise,
> Young Astrophel, the rusticke lasses love;
> Far passing all the pastors of his daies,
> In all that seemly shepheard might behove:
> In one thing onely fayling of the best,
> That he was not so happie as the rest.[56]

Extracted from the *Arcadia* (and bolstered by the widespread conventions of pastoral), the shepherd figure on the title page places Sidney's literary and cultural authority against his disappointed hopes as the heroic military figure of English statecraft. Just as Gascoigne's stylization of himself as a frustrated woodsman (in "Woodmanship") becomes a symbol for his unrealized potential as author and courtier, Sidney's title page represents him through the poles of contemplation set against action. It thus transforms him into Espilus, whose forced idleness enabled him to render little service to his queen and community. In print, traces of Sidney's political pastoral in the masque combine with his other self-presentations to form an authorial and cultural persona.

Rather than arguing that *The Lady of May* was included in the impressive and monumental 1598 volume simply because it was the work of the eminent Sidney, I call attention here to how this work participated in generating that eminence. *The Lady of May* was certainly authorized by the trappings of the folio edition, but it also retrospectively charged the title page and preface with social and political meanings. By portraying Sidney in the presence of royal authority, wooing the queen as lover and courtier, and stubbornly refusing to bend his words to her desires, the masque advertises him as a man accustomed to the presence of royalty, but rarely to its graces; it thus consolidates his growing reputation. When absorbed into the more literary world of Arcadian pastoral, the masque foregrounds the political negotiations and the social authorization found in conventional literary genres

---

[56]Edmund Spenser, "Astrophel. A Pastorall Elegie on the Death of the Most Noble and Valorous Knight, Sir Philip Sidney," in *Colin Clouts Come Home Again* (1595). In *The Poeticall Workes of Edmund Spenser*, ed. J. Payne Collier, 5 vols. (London: Bickers and Son, 1873), 5:68. In a poem in *The Phoenix Nest*, Matthew Roydon places Sidney within the idyllic landscape of Arcadian pastoral and announces his fame when he demands: "who knew not Astrophil?" *The Phoenix Nest*, ed. Hyder E. Rollins (Cambridge, Mass.: Harvard University Press, 1961).

and referenced by the prefatory material. The dual figures on the *Arcadia*'s title page, marked everywhere by the privilege of social birth and the contest between gendered subjects, name Sidney's public authorship in terms of the anxieties of courtiership and the gendered struggles evident throughout his work: *The Lady of May*'s conflict between female sovereign and male suitor; the dedication's depiction of a loving brother's deferral of power to his sister (who, as the "principal ornament to the family of the Sidneys," consolidates his own social authority); and *Astrophel and Stella*'s meditation on the parts played by Petrarchan male suitor and female beloved. The title page hints at this whole jumble of overlapping oppositions: action/contemplation, arms/pastoral, male/female, aristocrat/commoner, heraldic boar /vulgar pig. The prefaces and title page blend the opposition between male and female authorities into the larger context of the poet's social status and cultural identity. The writer's engagement with spectacle becomes part of the trappings that institutionalized Sidney as an author.

Sidney's and Gascoigne's pageant texts "mark" the queen in the exegetical and martial sense that Gascoigne suggests in his frontispiece to *Hemetes*. Both writers translate the trappings of Elizabeth's power into written symbols and call attention to the interpretive layering that necessarily conditions this process. Yet the language of praise endemic to pageantry produces the classic paradox: it asserts an autonomy dependent on royal encomium. Through epideictic verse, the poet forges an authority by riding on the glory of the queen's coattails. In a discussion of *The Faerie Queene*, Thomas Cain points out the ways in which Spenser uses praise to promote a powerful humanist vision of the place of the poet: "whenever Spenser praises Elizabeth he concomitantly asserts his role as encomiast, often with implicit reference to the archetypal poet Orpheus."[57] Spenser, like Gascoigne in the frontispiece kneeling before the queen, ensures his authority though deferral. In his 1581 courtesy book, *Civile Conversation*, Steven Guazzo articulates the reflexive potential locked within royal praise: "Who ought not to bee glad to honor another, for so much as . . . he honoureth, hee receiveth more honour, then hee which is honoured, for like unto the Sunne, the beames of honour by reflexion, as it were doo shine back again upon him."[58] In this politicized exposition of the golden rule, humble addresses to patron and queen reveal the writer's attempt to gain from granting magnificence.

In this mirroring dynamic, the writer occupies a dual position similar to

---

[57]Thomas Cain, *Praise in "The Faerie Queene"* (Lincoln: University of Nebraska Press, 1978), ii.
[58]Steven Guazzo, *The Civile Conversation of M. Steeven Guazzo*, STC 12422 (1581), trans. George Pettie, reprint ed. Charles Whibley, 2 vols. (New York: Alfred A. Knopf, 1925), 1:165.

that of the Petrarchan lover. Both exist as courtly suitor and rhetorical master,[59] and thus it is not surprising that Sidney's *The Lady of May* and Gascoigne's pageant of "Deep Desire" both engage the queen in acts of wooing. Gascoigne makes the literary and cultural coding of this enactment strikingly clear when he names Queen Elizabeth as his "Lawra" and himself as "Petrarks heirs" in his pageant (*Works*, 1:510). The eroticized Petrarchan relationship allows the speaker to pit himself against a central power (the queen as "Lawra") from which he derives validation. Through these pageant texts, writers fashion themselves as satellite subjects who are persistently defined in terms of their frustrated desire and the queen's seemingly perverse representation of her power through the rhetoric of courtly love. Sidney authorizes himself by manipulating the queen's counter-articulation of her desire, while Gascoigne more directly challenges the sovereignty of the unmarried female monarch. Both writers' construction of authority becomes gendered by their use of the discourse of courtly love and by the fact that these particular cultural forms were produced for a female monarch. The writers name their power to rewrite the "text" of the queen precisely by reference to the subject positions of the familiar Petrarchan and pastoral paradigms; these genres provide the imaginative landscape through which the courtier can negotiate within the court world. The courtier supplements the queen's text by identifying himself as a necessary mediator, but that identification is highly gendered. The writer's power is that of the male lover who, although circumscribed within the sphere of female authority, steps forth to offer a verbal account that points to his sovereign's lack. Fostered by the institution of patronage, the language of courtly love informed completely the symbolic forms of Elizabethan culture. So it is not surprising that the authority generated when these writers' written pageants were transformed into print was predicated not only on a monarchal authority that it tried to hold at bay, but also on a specifically female monarchal authority that was coded in eroticized terms.

The Politics of the Book

How was it possible for these men to establish political and authorial leverage within the celebratory royal display event? How did they manage to generate this initial ambivalence that was later to tural and authorial valences? I began this chapter wi

---

[59] For a discussion of the dual power position in the Petrarch Waller, "The Rewriting of Petrarch: Sidney and the Languages of in *Sir Philip Sidney and the Interpretation of Renaissance Culture*, ed. Moore (Totowa, N.J.: Barnes and Noble, 1984), 69–83.

performed and printed accounts of Richard II because they vivified the distinct political resonances attached to the different media. As Mulcaster's tract makes clear, the importance of printed royal displays rests not only in print's more durable form, but also in its retrospective creation of the monarch's theatrical presence. Here we return to the important Foucauldian insight acknowledged in much Renaissance critical work: that Elizabeth, like her father before her, was keenly aware of her dependence on the symbolic encodings of rule and the theatricality of power; and thus she relied on courtiers such as Sidney and Gascoigne to generate and disseminate the theatrical force of her sovereignty. Elizabethan writers fashioned an imperial mythology, shot through with the conventions of Petrarchism and a secularized version of the iconography of the "cult of Mary." In creating royal display events that sanctioned the incarnation of power within the body of the monarch, Sidney and Gascoigne banked on Elizabeth's recognition of her dependency on these representations. Otherwise, they could not have underscored the crucial role of the writing figure to the process of disseminating and preserving royal spectacle. In keeping with their humanist training, these men used their writing in the affairs of state.

As creators of Elizabethan spectacle and majesty, courtiers served as functionaries of their royal patroness. As writers of pageantry, Sidney and Gascoigne sought to master the condition of their own functional status as courtiers. In doing so, they offered to the queen the advantages to be gleaned from the literary marketplace: the dissemination of her presence to a more far-reaching audience and the preservation of her presence within a more enduring medium. Mulcaster, we must remember, was rewarded for "the making of the book." In equally material terms, Queen Elizabeth commanded that the "whole order" of the Woodstock pageant "as it fell, should be brought to her in writing." The first and foremost display of royal power in Elizabeth's reign, her procession, signaled the importance of this translation: "wordes do flye, but wryting dothe remayn." Writers who recorded Elizabeth's royal pageantry throughout her reign revealed the truth of this adage. In performing common courtly tasks, they shaped an authority predicated on their ability to make performance into something material. In print, the particular relationship between courtier and sovereign was recast, as a larger reading public usurped the queen's role as judge and audience to the display event.[60]

***

[60]Louis Montrose writes of Spenser's authorial presentation: "The 'Laureate' authorial persona . . . authenticates through print the subjectivity of a writer whose class position ght otherwise have rendered him merely the anonymous functionary of his patron. . . . er's authorial self-fashioning proceeds by the constitution of the writer as a subject of

The dire necessity of inscribing theatricality into published form becomes evident in other kinds of Elizabethan spectacle. We see that in translating display festivities into printed accounts, writers and publishers simultaneously endowed these events with new meaning and multiplied the political stakes of the transactions such events held. Publication, for instance, impacted in particular on the theatrical power produced by the spectacle of the scaffold. Let me describe one case. On February 27, 1585, William Parry was convicted and executed for treason, a spectacle that was probably, like many of its day, a bloody and dramatic event. Letters were produced that implicated the criminal in treason; he confessed under "questioning." And then, as we are told in a pamphlet that duly notes this chain of events, he was led to the tower and executed. Although a large number of people could have attended this spectacle, and word of mouth would have allowed the details to spread even more, many people relied on the sensational pamphlet to provide the details. Among the sensational ballads and broadsides that flooded the booksellers' markets (describing witches, strange hybrid animals, hatchet murders, or hieroglyphics in the sky) were tracts describing the executions and confessions of traitors. "A true report of the Araignement and execution of the later Popishe Traitour, Everard Haunce" was one such text.[61] In these pieces, criminals conventionally confessed their crimes against God and queen and recanted their seditious beliefs.[62] This repentance frequently occurred with a dramatic flair, as loyalty was transferred back to the state as part of the act of punishment ("God save the queen"). The pamphlet describing William Parry's execution participated in this outpouring of written spectacle, focusing mainly on his crimes but mentioning his last days. The work, however, was registered *three days before the execution*. In other words, the published tract seems to be a fictionalized account of the spectacle.[63] It is likely, of course, that the printer could have just registered the piece earlier to beat his

---

and in his own discourse; and also by the insertion of his text into the economy of courtly service and reward—that is, by its constitution as a book, a tangible commodity that functions as a vehicle of the writer's social and material advancement." "The Elizabethan Subject and the Spenserian Text," in *Literary Theory/Renaissance Texts*, ed. Patricia Parker and David Quint (Baltimore: Johns Hopkins University Press, 1986), 319–20.

[61]These texts are mentioned in H. S. Bennett's *English Books and Readers, 1558–1603* (Cambridge: Cambridge University Press, 1965), 226–27.

[62]For a discussion of these dying set speeches, see J. A. Sharpe, "'Last Dying Speeches': Religion, Ideology, and Public Execution in Seventeenth-Century England," *Past and Present* 107 (May 1985): 144–67. Frances Dolan discusses representations of women's speech during public executions. "'Gentlemen, I have one thing more to say': Women on Scaffolds in England, 1563–1680," *Modern Philology*, forthcoming.

[63]Lennard Davis cites Defoe as commenting that criminals accused of capital crimes in the

competition and not have written the tract until after the execution. Yet this strange inversion of time suggests that the text did not have to rely on the drama of the spectacle; it could produce that moment of display on its own authority.

There were many other apparently hasty publications. The account of murderer Arnold Cosby's fall from grace, which mentions his demise in the past tense, appeared two days before his death. A description of the queen's state entry into London in 1588 and an account of the Prince of Wales's funeral in 1612 were both entered into the register the day before the actual event.[64] Even if the printers were merely trying to establish an early claim to the topic, their hasty entries raise questions about the relationship of the spectacular event to the written description. These "pretexts" point to a system of communication in which the power of the spectacle relies on printed publication; the writing of the event seems to precede the event itself. The Parry case merely points to how inconsequential or inadequate the actual spectacle was. Certainly, those who saw it were impressed by its raw power. But more people, even in this highly illiterate nation, may have heard of the event from the ballads and broadsides that were sung and read aloud in public markets. These pamphlets often bore engravings for the illiterate signaling the type of matter described. Those who heard about these events from others were in all probability influenced by the interpretations generated through the descriptive pamphlets.

And, of course, we have the peculiar case of Richard II. When we recall the different treatment given to the performers and the printer of this seditious history, we can gauge the importance placed on publication for the dissemination of performance. In the Parry case, writing and spectacle are intricately connected; the execution almost becomes an event by virtue of its registration, when it was chosen as a subject for a text. The case of Richard II does not point to the priority of writing over event, but merely suggests the political significance invested in the written text. In both cases, however, the written account of spectacle seems to be the representation more crucial to the state. The many accounts of pageantry,

---

early eighteenth century became so outraged that their last words were being consistently misquoted or fictionalized that they wrote out their dying speeches before their executions and left them with friends and relatives. If this bizarre observation is true, we see a reclamation of the right to speak by the dying person, an attempt to seize power back from those responsible for circulating the kind of textual accounts that I am discussing. This later move by accused criminals calls attention to how writers appropriated the aura of the "last words" when they circulated descriptions of the execution spectacle in textual form. Davis, *Factual Fictions: The Origins of the English Novel* (New York: Columbia University Press, 1983), 127.

[64]Marjorie Plant, *The English Book Trade: An Economic History of the Making and Sale of Books* (London: George Allen and Unwin, 1939), 238.

progresses, and processions—penned by Sidney, Gascoigne, and numerous others—function in the same way as the accounts of executions. The decreasing costs of print technology revised the already complex power of the court by multiplying the sites in which authority was sought, distributed, interpreted, and protected. Spectacle was not a singular means of creating obedience; it needed supplemental help from textual tracts. While the critically heralded power of display was certainly a real force in the Renaissance, it was, in part, fashioned by written words. The writer could empower himself in making spectacle "readable" (both in the sense of devising it into a narrative complete with interpretative gloss and turning it into print). In some ways, then, writing, and particularly printing, enabled the politics of spectacle.[65] Precisely because print was necessary to create the theatrical nature of royal power, it provided the ground for the simultaneous construction of authorship.

Print's ability to inscribe the force of theatricality rested in several of its features. Both pageantry and the printed text could reduplicate the state's magnificent presentation of itself, but published accounts could also scatter local spectacle across the realm and ensure the reputation of the author (or of the aristocrat who staged the event). The published text's power rested in its breadth, as it amplified across the nation the words uttered in Suffolk. Thomas Churchyard notes this amplification when he makes this statement about one of his published pageants: "I will boldly hold on my matter which I have penned, for those people that dwell farre off the Court, that they may see with what majestie a Prince raigneth, and with what obedience and love good subjects do receive hir" (Nichols, 2:180). Churchyard establishes his authorial claim for the work at the same moment that he articulates its advantages to the queen. He can "own" a previously unsigned script ("boldly hold on my matter") because he releases the message of the work from local confinement to allow it to reach people who "dwell farre off the Court."[66] Henry Goldwell, who "collected gath-

---

[65]In arguing that spectacle functioned through writing, I am not addressing the complex social issues that surrounded carnivals, festivals, Ascension Day festivities, and parades—events that obviously did important cultural work without, for the most part, being printed or recorded. For the relationship of popular festivity to authorship, see Peter Stallybrass and Allon White, *The Politics and Poetics of Transgression* (Ithaca: Cornell University Press, 1986).

[66]When Thomas Churchyard published the entertainments at Suffolk and Norfolk in 1578, he bragged that his pamphlet would make this entertainment a "mirror and shining glasse, that all the whole land may loke into, or use it for an example in all places." "I can do no lesse . . . than to use my peene," he continued, "to [the people's] greate glory" (Nichols, 2:179). He then praised the townspeople "especially in Norwich where the entertainmente was so greate." This was self-serving praise considering that he had created the "greate" entertainment, but it was a necessary assertion if he was to claim publicly his role in devising the festivities. Churchyard published this text, in part, to place a retrospective signature on

ered, penned and published" the devices at the tiltyard also emphasizes this aspect of his project. He indicates that he immortalizes displays of power in order to make them readable by a larger populace, to "lay" them "open." He then tells his readers that he has written the text so that "thou maiest, being farre off, peradventure knowe more than they that were present and eye-beholders of the same" (Nichols, 2:329). To know more than the spectators? As we have seen through the editing practices of Gascoigne and Sidney, the written text not only affords a front-row seat that few spectators could have had, but it also provides a completely new view of the event.[67]

The commodification of spectacle was crucial for preservation as well; for while ephemeral spectacles vanished as soon as performed, or lay as barren scripts in aristocratic or city archives, the written text could reactivate the pageant perpetually. Henry Goldwell thus justifies his authorial boldness by acknowledging his insufficiency and the possibility of misreporting, but still arguing that the display is "better badly laid open than quite forgotten." He concludes, "rather than oblivion should diminish [the pageant participants'] merits, I have attempted the writing" (Nichols, 2:310). By making entertainments durable and marketable objects, pageant writers performed a vital task for the dissemination of spectacle, a powerful but ephemeral form "better badly laid open than quite forgotten." These writers produced public commodities that gained force as social and political memory registers, monuments to both the sovereign and the authorial enterprise itself.

For the modern reader, this concern for preserving spectacle through publication reflects writers' recognition of those qualities that distinguished print from mere writing or performance. Publication not only allowed courtly spectacle to be distributed to a larger reading audience, but also seemed to provide an orderliness that exceeded the hasty scrawls of writing. Even in a time in which printing practices ensured that each book rolling off the press was different from every other book, type could be seen as having an orderliness that granted the published work an authority that spectacle did not have. Like photographs today, which harbor so much mimetic power within them that they are admitted as evidence in a court of law, the new form of the typed text was understood by some as a

---

the anonymous progress event, and he justified his claim by pointing to the way in which writing can amplify a local event.

[67]The Archbishop of York's epistolary response to the Archbishop of Canterbury verifies the success of reproducing the theatrical moment in private written form: "Your Grace's large description of the Entertainment at Canterbury did so lively set forth the matter, that, in reading thereof, I almost thought myself to be one of your guests there, and, as it were beholding the whole order of all things done there" (Nichols, 1:346).

more modern characterization of print: as cool and objective, removed from the hasty scribbles of human emotion. We remember John Lyly's observation that print necessarily submitted inchoate and unruly experience to a more fixed form.[68] Because it was seen as having the power to standardize experience and thus render it more official, print could mask courtly negotiations behind the seeming order of the printed report.

In order to filter out our modern assumptions about print's uniformity and precision, however, we can look to *Love's Labour's Lost*'s ambivalent use of the term "print." In one scene, Berowne sends a love sonnet to Rosaline through Costard, who promises to fulfill his assigned task: "I will do it, sir, in print." What he means, according to the notes to the text, is "most exactly." The word "print," functioning as a synonym for precision, promised uniformity, completeness, and accuracy. The negotiations of authority that writers entered into while changing spectacle into object form were shielded and supported by the seeming exactness of print. Gascoigne's promise to deliver an "exact rehearsall" of the events at the aristocratic estate offers a credibility crucial for the success of Tudor propaganda.[69] But such promised hermeneutic precision is, of course, impossible, because there is necessarily a slippage between event and published account. Shakespeare acknowledges this slippage when he has Costard's message in *Love's Labour's Lost*—supposedly delivered "in print"—misdelivered, or accidentally exchanged with another letter. Costard's use of the printing metaphor and the confusion of texts that ensues comically exposes the miscommunications that that run rampant beneath the seeming accuracy of the printed page. Ironically, then, the seeming *objectivity* of print only mystified the intrusive *subjectivity* of the writer. If it seemed to distance the hand—the "mano" or manuscript—from its author, print allowed spectacle to be marked with an authorial signature.

Print did have an impact on how royal spectacle was reported. Gascoigne's highly public printed pageants, for instance, are strikingly different from those accounts reported in more private media, Sidney's text standing as an exception. The descriptions of numerous pageants in Nichols's collection derived from private letters, manuscripts, and city archival records—texts never circulated—lack the authorial "I" that generally intrudes into the printed accounts. Although, of course, personally inflected

---

[68]"I will shortly make your pryvie to mine [writings], which I woulde be lothe the printer shoulde see, for that my fancies being ever so crooked he would put them in streight lines, unfit for my humor, necessarie for his art." John Lyly makes this statement in his prefatory letter to Thomas Watson's *The Hekatompathia, or Passionate Century of Love*, STC 25118a (1582), ed. S. K. Heninger, Jr. (Gainesville, Fla.: Scholars' Facsimiles and Reprints, 1964), 8.

[69]John Neale, introduction to *The Quenes Maiesties Passage Through the Citie of London . . .*, 15.

in the choice of materials reported, the less public accounts instead look more like catalogs of the events with few narrative intrusions by the mediating writer. As one example, the description of the devices presented by the Earl of Essex, a manuscript found only in the private memorials of the Sidney family, has no narrative "glue" or plot that unifies the disparate episodes of the entertainment; instead, these episodes remain uninterpreted and disjunct (3:371–79). Similarly, the unpublished entertainments at Bisham and Sudely lack both narration and a gloss on the events (3: 130–43). When the written work was more widely circulated, the spectacle became a more powerful ground for narrative intervention. Through this intervention, the writer could announce his own role in molding the spectacle of the queen. The future publicity of the written pageant text, then, seems to have informed the negotiations performed by the courtier when he lent his courtly considerations and authorial voice to his pageant record.

Because publication reproduced and partially underpinned the politics and poetics of spectacle, publishers, writers, and printers became important to Elizabethan display. When writers created political pageantry and translated it into writing, their authority exceeded that produced within the courtly network of service and reward. Their literary authority became posthumously intertwined with the politicized stance of the critical narrator in these spectacle texts. Tracing the monumentalization of Sidney's privately circulated deletions and Gascoigne's more public editorial revisions, we see that these writers emerge as authors, in part, because of Elizabeth's need for representations of her spectacular image. Officially sanctioned power is always obviously vulnerable to the process by which it becomes legitimated and circulated. While the authority of these authors was, of course, produced by their creation of a vast range of literary genres and strategic postures, it was also partly dependent on Elizabeth's double vulnerability—her reliance on courtiers to write her highly coded theatrical presence and her difficulty in articulating female authority. Sidney's and Gascoigne's authorship emerges ambiguously: a product authorized by the state and a by-product of the fact that the writers took liberties with the state's representation of itself. Thus when Elizabeth so fervently read herself within the narrative of Richard II, she not only located the force of the performed drama, as critics are wont to claim, but also unwittingly pointed to the volatile function of writing within the politics of theatricality. We must remember that it was part of the physical format of the printed text—the dedication to Essex in the account of Richard II—that underscored the seditious implications within that history. Elizabeth's nervous yet magisterial identification with Richard, then, points to a set of unstable relationships between Crown, spectacle, writing subject, and text: she not only heralds the cultural power of spectacle and her own stately position as royal actress, but also throws into relief the monumental power, and the concomitant threat attached to it, that editing pageantry offered the male courtier. The next chapter takes us into a discussion of the eroticized tropes used to introduce the new book commodity. In Sidney's and Gascoigne's editorial designs for royal pageantry, Elizabeth's and their own power came into being through the negotiation of desire itself.

CHAPTER THREE

PREFATORIAL DISCLOSURES:
"Violent Enlargement" and the *Voyeuristic Text*

The experience of transgression . . . is indissociable from the consciousness of the limit or prohibition it violates. . . . The characteristic feeling accompanying transgression is one of intense pleasure (at the exceeding of boundaries) and of intense anguish (at the full realization of the force of those boundaries). And nowhere is this contradictory heterogeneous combination of pleasure and anguish more acutely present than in the interior experience of eroticism.
—Susan Suleiman, "Pornography, Transgression, and the Avant-Garde"

Est Virgo Hec Penna: Meretrix Est Stampificata.
(The pen is a virgin, the printing press a whore.)
—Filippo di Strata

IN BRUSSELS IN 1543, Andreas Vesalius published the first inclusive illustrated book of human anatomy, a work commonly referred to as the *Fabrica*.[1] In its display of more than two hundred anatomical illustrations made from copper plates, the *Fabrica* put into public view a virtual atlas of the human body. While much could be said about how this revolutionary text contributed to the social formation of the body and its relationship to the public world, I want here to comment only on one of its provocative features. The title page consists of a full-page engraving depicting a crowd of men in a classically styled arena gathered around a table (fig. 17). The audience strains eagerly to peer onto a central object of focus, a naked female corpse who is sprawled in the center of the frame and whose entrails spill from her dissected midsection. This illustration serves as a peculiar introduction to the book: only five of the illustrations in the entire text show identifiably female bodies, and the book is concerned with represent-

---

[1] Andreas Vesalius, *De humani corporis fabrica libri septem* (1543; facsimile, Brussels: Gabriel Lebon, 1964). Glenn Harcourt offers commentary on this text in "Andreas Vesalius and the Anatomy of Antique Sculpture," *Representations* 17 (Winter 1987): 28–61. For general information on Vesalius's life, see Charles D. O'Malley, *Andreas Vesalius of Brussels: 1514-1564* (Berkeley: University of California Press, 1964). Vesalius's illustrations were distributed in England with an English text in Thomas Geminus, *Compendiosa totius anatomie delineatio*, STC 11714 (1545).

ing isolated body parts rather than dramatizing the theatrical scene of public dissection. Despite its nonrepresentative nature, this engraving proved immensely popular, appearing as the title page in the 1555 edition and in Vesalius's subsequent text, the *Epitome*. Luke Wilson cryptically comments that because Vesalius rarely used female corpses, the fact that this illustration figures in a place of such prominence is "certainly remarkable."[2] I would like to unfold this curiosity: the fact that this odd image should be chosen to announce and to bear the ornate title for this culturally significant work.

In order to do so, we might turn to England several decades later, when Thomas Nashe's preface to the inaugural publication of the 1591 *Astrophel and Stella* encases the text in a similarly curious package. In his lengthy prefatorial statement, Nashe decries the coterie exchange that conceals literary works from public view and relishes that he is able to display Sidney's private poems to a larger audience. Tottel also charges that manuscript participants niggardly refused to share their literary bounty, but Nashe expresses his protest against coterie circulation through a set of bizarre and contradictory sexual metaphors.[3] Poetry, he warns, "although it be oftentimes imprisoned in Ladyes casks, & the president bookes . . . yet at length it breakes foorth in spight of his keepers, and useth some private penne (in steed of a picklock) to procure his violent enlargement."[4] His words describe poetry as a volatile force locked within women's treasure chests and hidden in commonplace books (which offered a model or "president" for poetic imitation). Nashe's linking of women's casks and commonplace books acquires particular resonance from the fact that the words "casket"

---

[2]Luke Wilson, "William Harvey's *Prelectiones*: The Performance of the Body in the Renaissance Theater of Anatomy," *Representations* 17 (1987): 71, note 15. In her reading of the juxtaposed male and female bodies that preface Helkiah Crooke's anatomy, *Microcosmographia, A Description of the Body of Man* (1615), Karen Newman similarly discusses the way in which female modesty and exposure become the topos through which the book is announced. *Fashioning Femininity and English Renaissance Drama* (Chicago: University of Chicago Press, 1991), 1–12.

[3]"It resteth now, (gentle reder)," Tottel says, "that thou thinke it not evill doone, to publish, to the honor of the English tong, and for profit of the studious of English eloquence, those workes which the ungentle horders up of such treasure have heretofore envied thee" (2). *Tottels Miscellany (Songes and Sonnettes)*, ed. Hyder E. Rollins, 2 vols. (Cambridge, Mass.: Harvard University Press, 1928–1929). I discuss Tottel's introduction in Chapter 1.

[4]Thomas Nashe, introduction to Philip Sidney, *Syr P.S. His Astrophel and Stella*, STC 22536 (1591). Nashe goes on to proclaim: "Long hath Astrophel (Englands Sunne) Withheld the beames of his spirite, from the common view of our darke fence" (A3ᵛ). I should mention that publication became a social force with which to be reckoned much earlier on the continent than it did in England. Sidney's text may well be contemporary with the *Fabrica* in terms of the points at which English and continental cultures were experiencing the disparate effects of print to roughly the same degree.

Figure 17. Andreas Vesalius, *De humani corporis fabrica libri* (Brussels, 1543).
Courtesy of The Newberry Library, Chicago.

and "case" were often used as code names for the female genitalia. In *The Merry Wives of Windsor*, for instance, Mistress Quickly confuses "Jinny's case!" (genitive case) with promiscuity.[5] The substitution of pen and pick-lock is notable as well, because lock-picking had bawdy overtones.[6] Nashe's imprecise yoking of coterie poetry with both women's genitalia and a male force (*"his* keepers") freed from female enclosure through an act of sexual violence figures the "picklocking" act of publication as both a rape and as a wanton textual display. Through these odd overlapping metaphors of male and female sexuality, Nashe describes how poems burst forth from their imprisonment with the ambiguous aid of a "private penne" that swells them to a "violent enlargement" into the "common" view. He thus figures the process by which the text is amplified to a larger audience in multiple sexually resonant images: as the swelling pregnancy of an unruly woman and the trajectory of male sexual tumescence. The fervency and energy with which he imagines poetry's embattlement against courtly limitations point to a transgressive violence bound up with poetic publication. The extremity of Nashe's language and his indiscriminate blending of metaphors of sexuality set a strange tone for this highly influential publication—the first appearance of Philip Sidney's well-known sonnet sequence in the medium of print.

Like the woman's body in the *Fabrica*'s engraving, Nashe's provocative image seems an erotic oddity, an excessive and troubling beginning. I would like to suggest that these two very different texts, the *Fabrica* and *Astrophel and Stella*, both vastly important publishing events in their respective social milieu, demonstrate a pervasive cultural phenomenon in which writers and publishers ushered printed texts into the public eye by naming that entrance as a titillating and transgressive act. The preliminary apparatus of engravings and prefaces—formats engendered by print technology itself—testifies that publishers and writers constructed a language of intrusion that designated reading as a prurient activity. They did so, I argue, as a means of addressing the vexed class concerns that were bound up with the act of publication. In this way, readers and writers could safeguard the social boundaries that relied on the coterie network by translating that boundary

---

[5]William Shakespeare, *The Merry Wives of Windsor* (4.1.59–61), *The Complete Works of Shakespeare*, ed. David Bevington, 3d ed. (Glenview, Ill.: Scott Foresman and Company, 1980). All other references to Shakespeare's plays are to this edition. See also Mistress Quickly's suggestive complaint in *2 Henry IV*: "My exion is entered, and my case so openly known to the world" (2.1.28). Patricia Parker cites these passages when discussing various puns on female genitalia in *Literary Fat Ladies: Rhetoric, Gender, Property* (New York: Methuen, 1987), 103–7.

[6]Iachimo equates the seduction/rape of a woman with having "pick'd the lock and ta'en / The treasure of her honor" (*Cymbeline*, 2.2.41–2). See also *Love's Labour's Lost*, 4.1.28: "Were beauty under twenty locks kept fast, / Yet love breaks through and picks them all at last."

into sexualized terms. The view of the author that emerges from this metaphoric inscription is one defined against a wanton and feminized textual commodity. As many early modern books indicate, Nashe's introduction and Vesalius's engraving were not unique in offering startling preludes to their subject matter.

Nashe's statement suggests that he felt the cultural anxieties generated by printing when it encroached on a more socially established mode of textual production. As the sixteenth-century press created a bridge between courtly aristocratic audiences and a growing literate populace, it catalyzed the general and age-old anxieties of writing—embarrassment at appearing in public, fear of criticism, worries about the control of meaning—into the more specific class anxieties of publishing. In previous chapters, I explained that the author became a more pronounced textual feature when sonnets and pageants were put into print. In this chapter and the next, I look to how publishers and writers responded to print's ability to occlude social difference by characterizing the relationship among authors, texts, and their reading public in particular ways. Publication seemed dangerous precisely because it threatened to render manuscript circulation and the patronage network obsolete. Instead, publication made "common" the flow of information that up to this time had been guarded within private channels. Therefore, printing had to be imagined in ways that made it acceptable to audiences who understood and valued the text within the patronage system of manuscript exchange.

Hundreds of prefaces were designed to perform the arduous task of explaining and justifying printed texts. Writers created a vast array of strategies that quickly became conventional: they withheld their names, claimed that the text was a youthful exercise, and emphasized their gentility. Such strategies had the effect of reinforcing the stigma of print even as they ostensibly sought to lessen its hold. Even those on the margins of the social world, would-be aristocrats, found it advantageous to mimic a disdain for print in order to indicate their "proper" position. The most common means for the writer or printer to ease the text into the public eye was for him to suggest that publication did not have full authorial consent. This strategy of dissociating text and author created a skewed vision of printed texts; they seemed to be private words snatched away from their producers and offered for sale to the public. Discourse was written as private and secretive matter unveiled in a moment of transgression. Reading became figured as an act of trespass.

Prefatorial Disclaimers/Sexualizing Frames

Renaissance prefaces repeatedly call attention to the impropriety of the printed literary texts they introduce. Important because they mark the threshold of the work, these addresses—letters to the reader, dedications to potential patrons, commendatory sonnets, and notes from the printer—form a lens through which the reader views the text and assesses its relationship to its public audience. In the late sixteenth century, it became common for these addresses to declare that the author was not complicitous in putting the work into print. William Percy's *Coelia* (1594), for instance, opens with an assurance that the published text that follows is a mistake: "Whereas I was fullie determined to have concealed my Sonnets, as thinges privie to my Selfe," he states, "yet of courtesie having lent them to some, they were secretlie committed to the Presse, and almost finished, before it came to my knowledge."[7] Percy here announces his gentlemanly status: he reports that he not only tried to keep his poems in manuscript, but that his "courtesie" betrayed him to the mercenary marketplace. With the text already in press, Percy states, he can only resignedly offer his dedication to the reader. The text is thus presented through the bizarre lens of an author who is declaring the text's lack of authorization. Percy's language cloaks the text in secrecy; the poems are private, and their exposure rests on an act of betrayal.

R.B., the publisher of George Pettie's *A petite Pallace of Pettie his pleasure* (1576), similarly confesses that the author did not give permission for the text to be published:

> May it please you to understand, that the great desire I have to procure your delight, hath caused me somewhat to transgresse the boundes of faithfull freindship: for havinge with great earnestnesse obtained of my very freinde Master George Pettie a copie of certaine Histories by himselfe upon his owne and certaine of his freinds private occasions drawn into discourses. I saw sutch wittie & pithie pleasantnes contayned in them, that I thought I could not any way do greater pleasure or better service . . . then to publish them in print, to your common profit & pleasure.[8]

As if to make sure that the reader understands that the work is indeed unauthorized, R.B. says further: "I am sure hereby to incur [Pettie's] displeasure, for that he willed me in any wise to keepe them secret" (sig. A2). The publisher documents his claim by enclosing a letter from Pettie that contains this directive: "I pray you only to use [the verses] to your owne private pleasure. . . . let them bee an object only for your owne eyes" (sig. A3). Like Percy, Pettie vividly describes the private nature of his work, which is ostensibly written for intimate friends rather than common profit. As Percy's

---

[7]William Percy, *Sonnets to the Fairest Coelia*, STC 19618 (1594), sig. A2.

[8]George Pettie, *A petite Pallace of Pettie his pleasure*, STC 19819 (1576), sig. A2. The publisher could possibly be Barnabe Rich, whose initials would here be inverted.

and Pettie's prefatorial words indicate, publication breaks the closed circle of communication between friends; the text's value lies in its limited visibility ("for your owne eyes"), a value that is obviously lost when the work is multiply reproduced as a public object of display. R.B.'s language explicitly names this act of display as a transgressive disclosure of a secret.

This type of disclaimer became so common that it functioned as a conventional frame for introducing the text. Scores of other writers, including Thomas Lodge and Edmund Spenser, claimed that their texts were published without their consent. The 1582 edition of Thomas Watson's *The Hekatompathia*, for instance, inscribes publication as an act of betrayal. It presents a prefatorial letter by John Lyly in which he thanks the author for allowing him to see the work privately. "Seeing you have used mee so friendly, as to make me acquainted with your passions," he states, "I will shortly make you pryvie to mine, which I woulde be loth the printer should see."[9] This letter's denunciation of printing suspiciously accompanies the text in its publication. It thus suggests an artful ploy by printer, author, or both. Certainly Lyly, Percy, and Pettie point to the private nature of their imaginative creations as a means of justifying the fact that they lowered themselves to merchandise their literary wares. Their disclosures, however, have the extra effect of highlighting the act of reading as an affront. The text stands as an invasion into the "pryvie" dialogue between friends and equals.[10] Other writers merely registered their authorial reluctance. John Dowland comments on the difficulty of "going public" when he says of his text, *The first book of songes or ayres*: "I had conceald these my first fruits. . . . How hard an enterprise it is, in this skilfull and curious age, to commit our private labours to the publike view."[11]

Samuel Daniel's preface to *Delia* (1592) perhaps serves as the consummate text for representing this sense of disclosure. He begins: "Although I rather desired to keep in the private passions of my youth, from the multitude, as things utterd to my selfe, and consecrated to silence: yet seeing I was betraide by the indiscretion of a greedie Printer, and had some of my secrets bewraide to the world uncorrected: doubting the like of the rest, I am forced to publish that which I never ment."[12] Daniel goes on to say that

[9]Thomas Watson, *The Hekatompathia, or Passionate Century of Love*, STC 25118a (1582), ed. S. K. Heninger, Jr. (Gainesville, Fla.: Scholars' Facsimiles and Reprints, 1964), 8.

[10]The introduction to Robert Tofte's sonnet sequence *Laura the Toyes of a Traveller* (STC 24097 [1597], sig. A3v) narrates the same act of betrayal. The printer, Valentine Simmes, states that he received the text in manuscript from a friend who had sworn to keep it private: "I must confesse we are both too blame, that whereas he having promised to keep private the originall, and I, the copie, secret: we both have consented to send it abroad, as common."

[11]John Dowland, *The first book of songes or ayres*, STC 7091 (1597), sig. *r.

[12]Samuel Daniel, *Delia* (1592), reprinted in *Samuel Daniel: Poems and A Defence of Ryme*, ed.

his work is "thrust out into the world" and his Muse is forced to appear nakedly, "rawly." The preface presents *Delia* as a work composed of private, sacred words that suddenly find themselves dangled before the public eye. The author claims indignantly that his "private passions" are made the object of public discussion and scrutiny. The text is figured as a bundle of "secrets," stolen and held to view because "of a greedie Printer"; they are the fruits of an offense. In Daniel's preface and in those by Lyly, Pettie, and Percy, the site of publication is, at the least, one of anxiety and often a place in which violation and betrayal is said to have occurred.

Prefaces that construct and display a sphere coded as private cast the reader into the role of voyeur, one who partakes of forbidden discourse and is complicitous in stealing a glance at clandestine words. These introductions also have the effect of positing a notion of privacy itself. It is important to note that the word "privacy," so commonly evoked in these prefaces, was a term under interrogation in the sixteenth century. Social historians have documented the lack of a modern sense of privacy in the Renaissance due to cramped living spaces (for the lower strata of society) and wide public rooms in country estates (for the upper). Lawrence Stone suggests that the fully formulated conception of "private" as opposed to "public" did not take root until the seventeenth century when a more modern notion of self was consolidated; for in early modern England, the notion of a private, individual self was fraught with contradictions.[13] During the late sixteenth and early seventeenth centuries, we see a series of phenomena that point to the gradual emergence of the conception of privacy.[14] Among the various cultural markers that indicate a new interest in privacy and the personalized self, Stone lists the self-revelatory diary, the autobiog-

---

Arthur Sprague (Chicago: University of Chicago Press, 1930), 9. Citations to *Delia* will be made to this edition and marked by poem number.

[13]Lawrence Stone, *The Family, Sex, and Marriage in England: 1500-1800* (London: Weidenfeld and Nicolson, 1977). Stone's well-known but controversial thesis suggests that the eighteenth century witnessed the formation of the nuclear modern family, a unit that has four main features: intensified affective bonding at the expense of neighbor and kin; a strong sense of individual autonomy and the right to personal freedom; a weakening of the association of sexual pleasure with sin and guilt; and a growing desire for physical privacy.

[14]Stone argues that interest in introspection and the private self was spurred on by Puritanism's insistence on the individual conscience, private prayer, confession, and literacy. He notes that the space of reserve that we define as a "self" was developed as much in the interests of monitoring individual rights as in protecting them. "The interest in the self sprang from the urgent need to discipline the self," a need advocated by Puritanism. Literacy, privacy, and introspection emerged within "a suspicious and inquisitorial society, constantly on the watch to spy out the sins of others, and to suppress all deviations from the true way" (224).

raphy, and the love letter.[15] Accompanying an understanding of the particularized individual were architectural changes that enhanced privacy: cor-
ridors and hallways made it possible for servants and guests to shuffle past
rooms rather than processing through them en route to a waiting chamber; bedrooms were transferred upstairs, leaving the ground floor for living
quarters; smaller rooms proliferated; apprentices and servants begin to live
in separate chambers. But as Mark Girouard points out, historians have
been too quick to make these changes seem completely novel. The
medieval home offered a certain amount of seclusion, he explains, that gradually expanded throughout the Renaissance.[16] The language surrounding
publication marks this change, pointing to a tentative exploration of
spheres designated as "private" and "public." In fact, the force of making
something public (publication) could even create the sense of an inner
space, privacy becoming an acknowledged or even privileged category in
opposition to the formulation of publicity. As conceptions of the individual
were reformulated, the term "private" was subjected to negotiation in the
early modern period. Rather than signifying something merely singular,
privacy began to register a new concern for valuing those secret spheres
inaccessible to the public.

Through their particular representations of text's controversial movement from one domain into another, published literary works participated
broadly in constructing a concept of privacy. Preface writers not only narrate the ostensible betrayal that enabled publication, but also use spatial
metaphors to figure the relationship between text and reader. In many
cases, the book buyer seems to invade an enclosed or secret sphere (such
as the court or the home) simply by reading the book itself. For example,
in Robert Greene's *Groats-Worth of Witte* (1592), published immediately
after the author's death, the printer William Wright states, "Nowe hath
death given a period to his pen: onely this happened into my handes which
I have published for your pleasures. Accept it favourably because it was his
last birth and not least worth."[17] A second prefatorial letter heightens the
sense that the text is a deathbed utterance: "The Swan sings melodiously
before death. . . . Greene though able inough to write, yet deeplyer serched
with sickness than ever heeretofore, sendes you his Swanne like songe" (7).
Through this framing device, the reader enters the text as if escorted into

---

[15] Thomas Whythome produced one of the first autobiographies in 1576. See Wayne
Shumaker, *English Autobiography* (Berkeley: University of California Press, 1954).

[16] Mark Girouard, *Life in the English Country House: A Social and Architectural History* (New
Haven: Yale University Press, 1978).

[17] Robert Greene, *Groats-Worth of Witte* (1592), reprinted in Bodley Head Quartos, ed. G.
B. Harrison (New York: E. P. Dutton and Company, 1923), 5.

the private bedchamber to hear the dying man's last words. The sanctity of the scene is marked by the finality and intimacy of death. Another address, "A letter writen to his wife, founde with this booke after his death," (50) tells the reader that his intimate material has been extracted from personal correspondence. These words are equally powerful because of their success in calling up the image of a fresh corpse and a grieving wife. When Greene pours forth his grief over his wife's absence—"I cannot (as I ought) to thy owne selfe reconcile my selfe, that thou mightest witness my inward woe at this instant" (50)—he utters his final legacy. The reader thus purchases the deathbed directive from husband to wife, a text that is explicitly named as a personal confession. The book as a physical artifact highlights its exposure of intimacy; the multiple preliminary addresses (four prefatorial letters) make the act of reading seem to be a move inward—through public casings toward a secluded interiority, the "inward woe" of a dying man.

In his miscellany *Belvedere* (1600), John Bodenham introduces his work by stating that it gives the reader the opportunity to "peep" at the language of the court—more explicitly, at the language directed to courtly ladies. Unnoticed, the common book reader is allowed to observe the love poems, suits, and Petrarchan complaints that were trafficked between courtiers and mistresses, the circulation of courtship as well as courtiership.[18] Love poems topically connected to members of the court become a spectacle for a larger public through works such as Bodenham's. He states that he reveals "the privat Poems, Sonnets, Ditties, and other wittie conceits, given to her Honorable Ladies and vertuous Maids of Honour; according as they could be obtained by sight, or favour of coppying."[19] Readers imagine themselves as privy to a precious sight, the exclusive and "privat" social life of the ladies of the court. Anne Ferry calls attention to the fact that architectural metaphors were commonly used for creating the sense of an internal realm because words like "consciousness" and "individual" were not available.[20] By promising that reading would offer the opportunity to spy inside the enclosed domestic space of the aristocratic home, publishers and writers constructed a "private" moment for the nonaristocratic public.

As we have seen, the editorial practices and typography of printed poetic texts corresponded in striking ways to those of play texts, even though each form had a distinct place in the culture and a set of problems peculiar to its

[18]See Ann Rosalind Jones and Peter Stallybrass, "The Politics of *Astrophil and Stella*," *Studies in English Literature* 24 (1984): 53–68.

[19]John Bodenham, *Belvedere, or the garden of the Muses*, STC 3189 (1600; reprint, New York: Burt Franklin, 1967).

[20]Anne Ferry, *The "Inward" Language: Sonnets of Wyatt, Sidney, Shakespeare, Donne* (Chicago: University of Chicago Press, 1983), 53.

site of production. The prefaces written to accompany dramatic works demonstrate that the placement of the already highly public theatrical text
into print sometimes occasioned the same rhetoric of privacy that was used
in presenting the ostensibly private poetic one. Printed plays can be said to
have borrowed the discourse of privacy central to the production of printed
poetic forms. In his preface to *Tancred and Gismund* (1591), for instance,
Robert Wilmot labels his text as matter for the "Students of the Inner
Temple," an inner sanctum of the satellite gentry found in the Inns of
Court. Like Bodenham's text, which unfolds to view a private circle of
ladies, Wilmot's preface signals that he has opened up one of the exclusive
circles of gentlemen for public viewing. In a second preface, he changes
strategies and gestures toward the thrill that awaits the patron/reader; he
personifies his work as Gismund, the loved but "painted" lady that must be
exhorted not to walk in public. "I am bold to present Gismund to your
sights," he tells his friend, "and unto yours only, for therefore have I conjured her, by the love that hath been these 24 years betwixt us, that she
waxe not so proud of her fresh painting, to stragle her plumes abroad, but
to contein her self within the walls of your house."[21] Just as Nashe characterizes the coterie text as bound within "Ladyes casks," Wilmot seeks to
guard and imprison his mistresslike ("painted") text within a domestic
space. The restrictive relationship between patron and reader, first imagined as a shared but private gaze, is recast metaphorically as the space of
the home. The privacy of the text is thus created by reference to the private
gentleman's club, a sphere that seemingly extends to the reader's private
dwelling when the book is sold. Wilmot's words make *Gismund*'s "prison-
break"—her circulation in the public marketplace of St. Paul's booksellers—all the more scandalous. The image of the unruly woman becomes
blended with the double image of the sanctity of domestic enclosure and
the prestige of gentleman's clubs.

It is not difficult to account for these figurations of publication when we
remember that the Renaissance manuscript text was deeply embedded in a
network of social relations. J. W. Saunders explains: "Poetry was an instrument of social converse and entertainment. . . . [It] could be used as a compliment or comment on virtually every happening in life, from birth to
death, from presentation of a gift to the launching of a war; it was the
agent of flattery, ego titillation, love-making, condolence. Poetry was the
medium of the communication of experience."[22] As one Renaissance writer's
bitter complaints make clear, this mode of communication was reserved for

[21]Robert Wilmot, *The Tragedies of Tancred and Gismund* (1591), reprinted in The Malone
Society Reprints, ed. W. W. Greg (London: Oxford University Press, 1914).

[22]J. W. Saunders, "From Manuscript to Print: A Note on the Circulation of Poetic MSS. in

select circles. "In publishing this Essay of my Poeme," Drayton says at the beginning of his monumental *Poly-Olbion*, "there is this great disadvantage against me; that it commeth out at this time, when Verses are wholly deduc't to Chambers and nothing is esteemed in this lunatique Age, but what is kept in Cabinets."[23] Drayton reaffirms his protest against the insularity of private circulation in a poem to Henry Reynolds that justifies his refusal to comment on courtly foppish works:

> For such whose poems, be they nere so rare,
> In private chambers that encloisterd are,
> And by transcription daintyly must goe;
> As though the world unworthy were to know,
> Their rich composures, let those men that keepe
> These wondrous reliques in their judgement deepe;
> And cry them up so, let such Peeces bee
> Spoke of by those that shall come after me,
> I passe not for them.[24]

Drayton expresses his frustration with transcribed manuscript works by drawing on a set of spatial metaphors. He denounces the snobbish, cowardly, and exclusive character of works kept hidden "in Cabinets" or "private chambers." These "rich composures" are most objectionable, Drayton states, because they are kept invisible, buried within the "judgement deepe" of their writers. Snatching poetry away from these elite recesses thus constitutes both a transgression and an enticement for readers. Preface writers conjure up the image of reading as an act of opening closed cabinets, hearing confessions from within bedroom chambers, and watching unruly women in a patron's home. Spatial metaphors reinforce the image of publication as a volatile but liberating invasion into exclusive spheres. The title of one of our contemporary texts, *Penthouse,* reveals the same yoking of illicit sexuality and the upper-class domain; it promises not just a lavish display of female bodies, but also a peek at the culture that can afford such an exclusive and luxurious living space.

If Renaissance writers and publishers generally convey a sense of social scandal by naming publication in terms of spatial metaphors, narratives of authorial reluctance, and deathbed scenes, they more particularly repre-

---

the Sixteenth Century," *Proceedings of the Leeds Philosophical and Literary Society* 6 (1951): 509.

[23]Michael Drayton, "To the Generall Reader," in *Poly-Olbion* (1622), reprinted in Publications of the Spenser Society, n.s., 3 vols. (Manchester: Charles S. Simms, 1889), 1: sig. A.

[24]Drayton, "To My most dearely-loved friend Henery Reynolds Esquire, of Poets & Poesie," in *Minor Poems of Michael Drayton,* ed. Cyril Brett (Oxford: Clarendon Press, 1907), 112–13.

sent published books as bodies lavishly displayed to a public audience. Within the larger context of the language of privacy that Renaissance prefaces constructed, we find a set of texts that emphasize the erotic nature of public display in print. Thomas Heywood, for instance, draws a corporeal analogy when he tells his readers in *The Golden Age* that he is loath "to see [his book] thrust naked into the world."[25] The preface to *England's Helicon* compares the text to a woman who braves censure by showing herself in public. The fear of appearing vulgar is evident in a later poem addressed to the bookseller:

> I have common made my book; 'tis very true;
> But I'd not have thee prostitute it too:
> Nor show it barefaced on the open stall
> To tempt the buyer; nor poast it on each wall
>
>   . . .
>
> No: profer'd wares do smel; I'd have thee know
> Pride scorns to beg: modestie fears to wooe.[26]

According to one Italian writer, as the epigraph at the beginning of the chapter reveals, the pen was a virgin, while the press was branded a whore. Cast in this light, the emerging composite portrait of the printed artifact is startling: texts appear as frail, naked, and immodest human flesh, endangered by their "barefaced" exposure to the ravishing eyes of reading strangers.

Even the common metaphor of writing as reproduction becomes resonant when seen in the context of the vast array of prefaces that rely on a sexualized language. In the opening to Sidney's *Apologie for Poetry* (1595), for instance, editor Henry Olney represents writing as childbirth and the site of writing as the female genitalia. Olney implores the reader to act as nurse to the birthing process, to "help to support me poore Midwife, whose daring adventure hath delivered from Oblivions wombe this ever-to-be-admired wits miracle."[27] Once again ushered metaphorically into the bedchamber, the reader is given a glimpse of the text in the moment of its public birth, produced from a female body that is positioned in the indelicate posture of labor. Oblivion's feminized body is evoked only as the op-

[25]Thomas Heywood, *The Golden Age* (1601), reprinted in *The Dramatic Works of Thomas Heywood* (New York: Russell and Russell, 1964), 3.

[26]R. Heath, "To My Bookseller," in *Epigrams* (1650). Cited by Marjorie Plant, *The English Book Trade: An Economic History of the Making and Sale of Books* (London: George Allen and Unwin, 1939), 249.

[27]Philip Sidney, *The Complete Works of Sir Philip Sidney*, ed. Albert Feuillerat, 4 vols. (Cambridge: Cambridge University Press, 1923), 3:377.

positional entity from which the male producer of the work will extract the textual child. While the metaphor of parthenogenetic authorship was a common one (used by Sidney in his address to the *Arcadia,* for instance), it is here put forth with the realist details of the midwife and womb. These remarks allow the publisher to amplify a general trope so that it vivifies the scene of multiple textual production as human reproduction.

The oddity of such images did not go unnoticed. As I noted in the introduction, Anthony Scoloker's preface to *Daiphantus* (1604) comments on these widespread and highly sexualized introductions. Scoloker mocks the publishing author who feigns postures of reluctance or fear; he offers a sample of these pretenses for his readers: "He is A man in Print, and tis enough he hath under-gone a Pressing (yet not like a Ladie) though for your sakes and for Ladyes, protesting for this poore Infant of his Brayne, as it was the price of his Virginitie borne into the world in teares."[28] Scoloker satirizes the kind of prefaces we have seen thus far: those texts in which the author modestly denies his complicity in appearing in print. Scoloker also registers his awareness of how these disclaimers can be gendered and sexualized. Writers who complain that they want to keep their passions hidden from the print audience play the part of the coy virgin, Scoloker suggests. His use of the Elizabethan slang, "to undergo a pressing," suggests that the male writer always trades on his vulnerability when he agrees to play the female role and be "pressed" for the public. Authors capitalize on this pun when they represent their move into print as a sexual sacrifice, as if "it was the price of his Virginitie." Scoloker's satiric version of the author's disclaimer furthers the association among justification, modesty, seduction, and birth that these prefaces offer; he foregrounds the sexual and corporeal metaphors that are embedded in the presentation of many public texts.

Scoloker could easily have been commenting on the introductory language used in Thomas Sackville and Thomas Norton's *Gorboduc* (1570). The stationer opens this work by comparing the text's previous corrupt printing to a ravished virgin. In his address, the scenes of writing and reading are fraught with images of sexual violation and wantonness. In particular he condemns the irresponsible printer who put the book forth "exceedingly corrupt as if by meanes of a broker for hire, he should have entised into his house a faire maide and done her villanie, and after all to bescratched her face, torne her apparell, berayed and disfigured her, and then thrust her out of dores dishonested."[29] The stationer first uses the metaphor of the ravished maiden to describe the text's victimization: she has been ruined by the vicious printer who rakishly seduced and aban-

---

[28]Anthony Scoloker, *Daiphantus, or The Passions of Love,* STC 21853 (1604), sig. A2ᵛ.
[29]Thomas Sackville and Thomas Norton, *Gorboduc,* retitled in this edition as *The Tragidie of*

doned her. In the latter part of his preface, however, the publisher begins to attribute the text's "wantoness" to her inability to stay within chaste boundaries:

> In such plight after long wandring she came at length home to the sight of her frendes who scant knew her but by a few tokens and markes remayning. They, the authors, I meane, though they were very much displeased that she so ranne abroad without leave, by which she caught her shame, as many wantons do, yet seing the case as it is remedilesse, have for common honestie and shamefastnesse new apparelled, trimmed and attired her in such forme as she was before.
>
> (sig. A2)

As the stationer draws out this analogy, he shifts the blame from the rapist printer to the wanton text. She is cast as the erring maiden who shows herself in public without the permission of her guardians. Somehow the violation done to the text becomes a sign of the text's own desire, for *Gorboduc* is named as a common wanton who does not know her proper place.

The publisher concludes his preface by simultaneously declaring the woman/text "loosed" once again and by urging the reader to follow the authors' lead and reprivatize the book within the safety of the home. "If not," the writer states, "the poore gentlewoman will surely play Lucreces part & of her self die for shame, and I shall wishe that she had taried still at home with me."[30] When cast as the raped Lucrece, the text appropriately

---

Ferrix and Porrex, STC 18685 (1570), sig. A2. As I discussed in the first chapter, the text's authorization was not at all a readily comprehensible or even a necessarily desirable status within the various Renaissance textual economies. Because copyrights did not yet exist and coterie writers were largely indifferent to signing their own works, it is difficult for us to understand what force an authorized text would carry. This printer's assumption that Renaissance readers, printers, and writers naturally sought an authentic and uncorrupt text was hardly a well-established tenet within publishing practices. We can account for these occasional denunciations of "bad" texts as either an articulation of the more modern notion of the text, or as a strategy of presentation that has little backing legally or economically in sixteenth-century England.

[30]The publisher's simultaneous concern with textual and sexual purity, as evidenced in his use of the Lucretia myth, can be said to exemplify what Stephanie Jed has described as "chaste thinking," a figure of thought, which, she argues, "functions as a figure by means of which the linguistic material representing Lucretia's rape and the materials of writing by which her story is transmitted can be related to the circumstances in which interpretation takes place" (8). Jed reads actual representations of the Lucretia myth as these "materials of writing " disclosing important connections between philological concerns about textual contamination, the reading and writing practices of humanism, and the subject of rape and revolution; but her findings make it easier to understand why the publisher expresses his concern

becomes a contested cultural figure: both a symbol of excessive pride and the epitome of modesty. The preface furthers this dichotomy by contradictorily identifying the book both as a "gentlewoman" who longs for her home and as a wanton textual object who performs falsely (she can only "play Lucreces part").[31] Given that the text fell from grace when she "ranne abroad," the publisher's final permission smacks of the unseemliness he ostensibly denounces: "I have now geven her to goe abroad among you withall." In this extraordinary preface, the publisher calls up the image of sexual violation to describe the text's emergence into the public eye. The wanton woman's disheveled body here functions as a means of defining authorship and textual purity. Although the printing of the authorized text supposedly erases its wayward and lewd history, the publisher's lengthy analogy indelibly inscribes the text as a promiscuous and immoral object. By boasting that the author has "re-dressed" and redeemed the text by re-establishing her "forme," the publisher titillates his audience with the image of the text in its previously disheveled state. As de-formed rather than re-formed, the book immodestly appears momentarily in the guise of her prodigal past—as unauthorized and half-clothed. The reader must finish this process of redemption by rescuing the book from the public literary marketplace, taking her lovingly into the private home, and guarding the text so that she does not run abroad delinquently again. Given that the etymological definition of the word "pornography" is "writing about prostitutes," this preface conflates the two parts of the definition: it mingles the sexual/textual and provides a text that *has itself* become wanton.

Gorboduc carries to a logical extreme the rhetoric of disclosure that other writers use so easily. Percy, Lyly, and Pettie, for instance, all hint at the titillating possibilities for figuring publication when they describe how their passions were so indecorously made public. Other writers rely on the *Gorboduc* publisher's more specific tactic of textual feminization as a means of announcing their literary wares. In the preface to *Volpone*, Ben Jonson describes his authorial function as that of stripping and redressing poetic precedent in order to redeem verse from corruption. He states that he will "raise the despised head of poetry again and, stripping her out of those rotten and base rags wherewith the times have adulterated her form . . .

---

for the text's "chastity" by general reference to Lucrece. *Chaste Thinking: The Rape of Lucretia and the Birth of Humanism* (Bloomington: Indiana University Press, 1989).

[31]For a reading of Lucrece as a female object of exchange trafficked between men, see Nancy Vickers, "'The blazon of sweet beauty's best': Shakespeare's *Lucrece*," in *Shakespeare and the Question of Theory*, ed. Patricia Parker and Geoffrey Hartman (New York: Methuen, 1985), 95–115; and Coppélia Kahn, "The Rape in Shakespeare's *Lucrece*," *Shakespeare Studies* 9 (1976): 45–72.

restore her to her primitive habit, feature, and majesty."[32] The "adulter-ation" used to describe poetry's lack becomes the legitimating ground for Jonson's reputable authority, here exercised in his redemptive act of laying the text bare. Likewise, in a dedicatory poem to *Musophilus*, Samuel Daniel both expresses his authorial vulnerability and preempts possible censure by raising the specter of the unruly woman. Building on a theatrical meta-phor, he writes: "I doe not here upon this hum'rous Stage, / Bring my transformed Verse, apparelled / With others passions, or with others rage."[33] Daniel here personifies his writing as a means of clarifying his authorial status; the work is "the form of mine own heart," he states. Daniel can only imagine the publication of his "own heart," however, as per-formed by the actress Muse, who is inclined "with motions of her owne, t'act her owne part." This Muse figure has a strange independent streak that may incline her to "fall from," among other things, "Vertue": "She might repent the course she began; / And with these times of disolution, fall / From Goodnesse, Vertue, Glory, Fame and all." The text's circulation is characterized in terms of the uncontrollable female Muse upon the stage of the public, and female reputation is again at stake in portraying public writing. These writers' figurations are, of course, distinct—Jonson uses the language of investiture when meditating broadly on the debased state of poetry, while Daniel issues disclaimers and claims to his readers through the trope of spectacle. Both writers, however, rely on the image of the dis-played woman as a tactic for scandalously authorizing their works. In doing so, they project in attenuated form, the scene of scandal so vividly narrated in the preface to *Gorboduc*. Worries about unlicensed, unauthorized, textu-ally corrupt or indiscriminantly circulated poems coalesce in the emblem of the wanton Muse, whose possible disrepute and erotic allure act as a vital cultural idiom for expressing the anxieties generated by the print medium.

In his dedication to *Scillaes Metamorphosis* (1589), Thomas Lodge modu-lates from a conventional disclaimer for the work to the more specific fig-ure of the female text who has a spotty past. He tells "Master Rase Crane and the rest of his most entire well willers, the Gentlemen of the Innes of Court" that his publication was unintended:

> I had not thought at this instant to have partaked my passions with the print, . . .
> but the base necessities of an extravagant melancholie mate . . . made my

---

[32] Ben Jonson, *The Works of Ben Jonson*, ed. C. H. Herford Percy and Evelyn Simpson, 11 vols. (Oxford: Clarendon Press, 1925–1952), 5:17–21.

[33] Samuel Daniel, *Musophilus* (1602–1603), *Works*, ed. Alexander B. Grosart, 5 vols. (London: Hazell, Watson, and Viney, 1885–1896; reissued, New York: Russell and Russell, 1963), 1:223.

unperfit Poems (in spite of waste paper) to hazard an apprenteship in Poules: so that that which in the first peeping foorth was wholie predestinate to your friendship by an underhand marte, is made the mercenarie recreation of everie ridiculous mate. Our wits now a daies are waxt verie fruitefull, and our Pamphleters more than prodigall: so that the postes which strode naked a tedious *non terminus,* doo vaunt their double apparrell as soone as ever the Exchequer openeth.[34]

As Lodge declares his intentions that the text remain the manuscript property of his patron and friend, he falls into a language replete with images of the human body; the text is seen first as a "peeping foorth" that subsequently becomes the "apparrell" to clothe the "naked" posts of bookselling shops at St. Paul's. After protesting the literary outpouring of the prodigal writing masses, Lodge speaks more particularly of the corrupt printing of his own work. He personifies the title characters as separated and shipwrecked lovers:

> For transformed Scilla however she hapned now to bee disjoyned from disdainfull Charybdis: thinke not but if they have good shipping they wil meete ere long both in one shop: and landed they had at this instant, in one and the selfe same bay, if *Scilla* (the unfortunater of the two) had not met with a mudie pirate by the way. Arived shee is, though in a contrary coast, but so wrackt, and weatherbeaten, through the unskilfulness of rough writers, that made their poast haste passage by night, as *Glaucus* would scarce know her, if he met here; yet my hope is Gentlemen, that you wil not so much imagine what she is, as what shee was: insomuch as from the shope of the Painter, shee is falne into the hands of the stainer.
>
> (xiv–xv)

Releasing the story of Scilla from that of Charybdis pulls the text from her mythological roots into the literary marketplace. Lodge argues that his poor Scilla has also lost her lover Glaucus to another printshop, and the two remain to be reunited in better form in a more reputable place of textual production. Lodge's apology serves two purposes: he can justify the poor form of the text by claiming that it was, like *Gorboduc,* pirated without his consent and printed in corrupt form. He can then redeem the polluted textual woman by presenting her in a more legitimate form to the public, calling her gentlemanly reader to imagine her in a previous and more virginal state. In this sexually fraught representation of the book, the author nostalgically visualizes his text's unstained nature while at the same time describes with relish her fall into a "wrackt and weatherbeaten" condition.

[34]Thomas Lodge, *Scillaes Metamorphosis* (1589), reprinted in *Glaucus and Silla with Other Lyrical and Pastoral Poems* (Chiswick: C. Whittingham, 1819), xiii–xiv.

Writing and bookselling are portrayed by Lodge in terms of thwarted love, sexual infidelity, and erotic display.

Publication was imagined by numerous writers and publishers throughout the culture as an act implicated with sexual scandal. One writer summarized the spirit of many of these figurations of public writing when he explained, "To come in print is not to seeke praise, but to crave pardon."[35] Many proclaimed boldly that publishing offered only shame and ignominy. This presentation of literary texts is, as I have suggested, a strategy for avoiding the responsibility of crossing social boundaries. In this sense, the voyeuristic reader is merely a by-product of writers' and printers' attempts to avoid admitting a desire for public display. Yet the persistence with which publication is made into a sexual act and the relish with which scandal is described hints that there is another more obvious motive involved in this representation: the producers of these texts exploit a sense of prohibition in order to titillate and entice their audiences to buy new commodities. Narrating the many ways in which writers "crave pardon" functions as a marketing strategy.

Works that depend on this odd representation of public display were more readily available than texts that we would define as pornographic. Texts such as Nashe's "Choice of Valentines," which details sexual and scatological acts, were rare. Instead, plays, poems, and pamphlets circulated bawdy verbal play freely. Barnabe Barnes's *Parthenophil and Parthenophe* (1593), however, stands as an exception. In these poems, the speaker enviously describes the wine that his mistress drinks and urinates, the details of his erect penis, and the rape of his mistress. One of our few bits of information about Barnes notes that he paraded around the court in a pair of "Babilonian britches, with a codpisse as big as a Bolognian sawcedge," an action which prompted ridicule.[36] The image of Barnes seeking favor by such a hyperbolic breach of decorum acts as a correlate to his poetic sequence. Barnes's inappropriate literary and courtly displays were unsuccessful in helping him obtain courtly favor. Robert Merrix explains this failure by arguing that Renaissance audiences preferred poems that "depict the sexual process metaphorically."[37] Prefaces, I argue, participated in a metaphorical eroticism that was socially sanctioned. By inserting a bizarre

---

[35]Henry Chettle, *Kind-Hartes Dream* (1592), reprinted in Bodley Head Quartos, ed. G. B. Harrison (London: John Lane, 1923), 5. Chettle interestingly begins his preface by commenting on the well-established practice of writing prefaces: "It hath beene a custome Gentle men (in my mind commendable) among former Authors . . . to begin an exordium to the Readers of their time" (5).

[36]Thomas Nashe, *Have With You to Saffron-Walden* (1596), in *Works*, ed. R. B. McKerrow, revised F. P. Wilson, 5 vols. (Oxford: Basil Blackwell, 1958), 3:109.

[37]Robert Merrix, "The Vale of Lillies and the Bower of Bliss: Soft-core Pornography in

type of pornography into representations of the materiality of the text, these prefaces provided a layer of erotic mediation that was crucial to the newly flourishing marketplace of book buyers and sellers.

The Spectacle of Sonnet Disclosures

The outburst of these prefatorial disclaimers was tellingly accompanied by the watershed production of sonnet sequences, forms whose central literary model was Petrarch. Both sonnet cycles and the prefatorial conventions that figured publication as a disclosure flourished in the last decades of the sixteenth century and then virtually disappeared. Critics who speculate on the popularity of the sonnet sequence usually give particular attention to the queen's cultivation of love poetry as a means of negotiating for political advantage and offering political opinion within the court world. Sonnets provided a vocabulary for addressing the issues of suit and service that arose in a court ruled by a woman. I suggest that printed sonnets were also popular because they foregrounded the emerging distinctions between public and private, and in doing so, they expressed a set of general cultural changes enhanced by print. The excessive popularity of the amorous sonnet rather than its unique representation of courtly love is of interest to my argument, for that popularity was accompanied by a complementary language of disclosure in the architectonics of the printed book. While there are distinctions to be made, Renaissance versions of Petrarchan love are not radically different from their medieval counterparts. What does become significant in the Renaissance is the widespread popularity of Petrarchan love lyrics and their emergent centrality for the aspiring writer. Writing sonnets was a proving ground for the serious poet; these forms suggest that Petrarchan love occupied a prominent place in the culture at large.

As coterie poems circulated among courtiers, they functioned within a highly circumscribed arena. As Arthur Marotti has pointed out, the courtly audience recognized that intimate verse between lovers addressed overtly political and social concerns ("'Love is not Love'"). Because the coterie charted a pathway that identified class boundaries, it reinforced a peculiarly socially defined sense of privacy. The social enclosure and exclusivity generated by the circulation of manuscript texts could be discussed thematically as "the personal." Social privacy, when threatened by technological innovation, became articulated in Renaissance English culture as erotic intimacy. The popularity of the sonnet tradition could well be linked to the insecuri-

Elizabethan Poetry," *Journal of Popular Culture* 19 (Spring 1986): 3–4.

ties produced by this newly popular and affordable system for transmitting literary texts. It is not merely coincidence, then, that the coterie-identified sonnet and the eroticized rhetoric of disclosure flourished in the same moment in which the print medium was revamping the culture's under-standing of the relationships between writer, text, and reader.

The conventions of Petrarchan courtly love found in the sonnet tradi-tion tell us that the form is one that thrives on the contradiction between public and private. These love lyrics are ostensibly written by the powerless and abject lover in pursuit of his mistress's favors. Occasional addresses to other men within the sequences, however, as well as the fact that these poems were frequently exchanged among *men* as part of courtly competi-tion, indicate that the female subject of the poem is displayed by and pos-sessed within the verse, rather than merely pursued ardently by the sonnet speaker. Within the competitive network of the court, the poetry of pas-sionate love served as an important means of advertising poetic and diplo-matic skills. Both in their thematic representations and in their social func-tions, sonnets were implicated in a system that produced voyeurs at every point: men who read what was supposedly written as the private suit be-tween one man and his mistress.

Love's Labour's Lost comically allegorizes this aspect of the sonnet pro-gram. In this play, Shakespeare sets up successive layers of voyeurs, hidden audiences who watch and comment on the private love lyrics unwittingly displayed by their authors. Because the courtiers in the play have taken an oath against courtship, their poetic declarations of passion serve as embar-rassing and mischievous undertakings that must be concealed from their peers. The audience, like many of the characters, is frequently given access to poetic expressions of love only when they are eavesdropped or acciden-tally discovered: Holofernes mistakenly reads Berowne's love sonnet, and the princess intercepts Armado's love letter. The thematic culmination of all these misdelivered poems is found in the third scene of act 4, a scene that dramatizes a four-part layering of eavesdroppers formed when each courtier recites a sonnet "privately" only to be discovered by his friends. As the audience is made to spy on the practices of courtship, it becomes situated as another one of the successive layers of hidden listeners in the scene. Be-rowne highlights his own role as a voyeur when he calls himself a "demigod" who "secrets heedfully o'er-eye" (4.3.75-76). The king himself heightens the connection between poetry and transgression when he refers to the newly exposed poems as "guilty rhymes." He then demands of Berowne, "Are we betrayed thus to thy overview?" (4.3.170). The women to whom the poems are addressed are, in fact, not present at most of the sites of reading in the play. While the play writes this reception as a mishap, it unwittingly points to a courtly reality. For we might wonder why Marlowe's poignant love poem "Come Live with Me and be my Love" was answered by Ralegh rather than any mistress. The play's "mistake" reveals that the seemingly private appeal to the female mistress was staged within a complicated game of titillating homosocial bonding.

Nancy Vickers argues that voyeurism was actually an intricate part of the program for the Renaissance sonnet. She details how Petrarch left the Renaissance a "poetics of fragmentation," a descriptive technique that allows the male speaker to present his own unified subjectivity through linguistic dismemberment of the female.[38] She argues that the process of projected identity formation and scattering that is performed by the sonnet speaker within his verse is particularly inscribed in sonnet tradition within an overwhelmingly popular narrative of voyeurism, the Diana-Actaeon myth. Actaeon suffers dismemberment by his own hounds for spying on Diana's naked flesh. The speaker in Petrarch's *Rime Sparse* acts as a self-conscious Actaeon who has been voyeur to his powerful female mistress and who constructs his subjectivity by dispersing her as a means of staying his own potentially destructive metamorphosis.[39] The speaker does so centrally through the literary blazon. Through this mode of description, the woman is idealized by being cataloged into bits and pieces: a beautiful leg, eye, or hand that is lovingly compared to the earth's natural wonders or the zodiac of mythololgical beauty. The myth speaks to the issue of privacy, because Diana dismembers Actaeon precisely because she does not want to be published. By publicizing (blazoning) Diana's secret in verse, the speaker then scripts the sonnet reader as a fellow transgressor and voyeur caught within a perpetual moment of agonistic sexual confrontation. Renaissance sonneteers, who saw Petrarch as a central authority, expanded his lyric program's particular mode of figuring the female body within poetry. The Diana-Actaeon myth thus indexes the sonneteers' general interest in questions of subjectivity, illicit viewing, and the problematic distinctions between public and private.[40]

Vickers's argument becomes more compelling when we see how important this multivalent myth was within the culture at large. Leonard Barkan

[38]Nancy Vickers, "Diana Described: Scattered Woman and Scattered Rhyme," in *Writing and Sexual Difference*, ed. Elizabeth Abel (Chicago: University of Chicago Press, 1986), 95–110. Vickers takes the phrase "poetics of fragmentation" from Giuseppe Mazzotta, "The *Canzoniere* and the Language of the Self," *Studies in Philology* 75 (1978): 274. In Chapter 1, I draw on Vickers's argument in "Diana Described" to explain how corporeal metaphors provided a principle of unification for the text.

[39]Petrarch makes the myth the subject of his *Rime Sparse* 23 and 52. *Petrarch's Lyric Poems*, ed. and trans. Robert Durling (Cambridge, Mass.: Harvard University Press, 1976).

[40]The Renaissance was a time in which sight and visibility had an uncertain and less central place in the culture. People still *heard* plays in the Renaissance, while we *see* them today. Texts were just as often read in public spaces as in sequestered corners. Even when reading

documents how the Diana-Actaeon myth functioned as "a powerful crux in the work of creative artists" of the late middle ages and Renaissance (325).[41] In accommodating a wide range of complex ideas and truths, the myth produces an Actaeon who becomes "virtually overburdened with significances" in Renaissance mythography (359). Barkan explains the conflicting neoplatonic, political, and rationalist interpretations of this story through which the culture syncretically read the sexual/sacred components of visionary experience, the vexed issues of accountability and guilt, the vicissitudes of fortune and politics, and the knotty problem of mirrored but destructive identities. As a "working out of that problem of self-consciousness" (322), Actaeon's mythic crimes become intertwined into an "amalgam of blasphemy, voyeurism, lust, ingratitude, and sedition" (335). Barkan, like Vickers, is sensitive to Petrarch's particular role in interpreting and popularizing the Ovidian myth for the Renaissance. Vickers concentrates, however, on how this "drama of embarassment" functions in psychoanalytic terms, as mediating the crucial structuring of identity seen in the sonnet speaker's uncanny encounter with the female mistress, and as redressed through the speaker's role as a *writer* of the "text" of his beloved. I want to suggest that this "drama of embarassment" also spoke to the public/private issues that were prevalent in the sonnets and prefaces and tied to the more class-oriented issue of publication.

Sonnet cycles are insistently concerned with disclosure, privacy, interiority, and public representation, issues that find their culmination in the theme of illicit sight. In Spenser's *Amoretti*, the speaker persistently raises the problem of representing emotion in language and grounding this signification within the "private self." As in the prefaces, Spenser's speaker exploits the text-as-body metaphor in investigating the limits of visual representation itself. In the first sonnet of the *Amoretti*, the poet identifies the text as an extension of his body so that he will not be jealous when his mistress folds the poem within her loving fingers. After dwelling on her "lilly hands, / which hold [his] life in their dead doing might," he constructs the text as "written with teares in harts close bleeding book."[42] In the next poem, the

---

alone in private, people often pronounced the words aloud. If we consider this period a shift to an era in which plays are seen and reading is a private visual act, then the sonnets' preoccupation with seeing makes sense. Renaissance works generally exploit the destabilizing transition to a more sight-oriented culture. In the sonnets, writers refocus this newly important visual force by rendering it frighteningly desirable and perverse.

[41]Leonard Barkan, "Diana and Actaeon: The Myth as Synthesis," *English Literary Renaissance* 10 (1980): 317–59.

[42]Edmund Spenser, *Amoretti and Epithalamion*, STC 23076 (1595), reprinted in *The Yale Edition of the Shorter Poems of Edmund Spenser*, ed. William A. Oram et al. (New Haven: Yale University Press, 1989), 600.

speaker scolds his text for involuntarily bursting forth from his mental womb:

> Unquiet thought, whom at the first I bred
> Of th'inward bale of my love pined hart:
> and sithens have with sighes and sorrowes fed,
> till greater then my wombe thou woxen arte:
> Breake forth at length out of the inner part.
>
> (2)

In imagining the process of writing, the reader is asked to bear witness to the interior of a body opening for public view.[43] As the speaker appropriates for himself the female act of childbirth, he calls up a particular image of the female anatomy, legs spread apart birthing a private language. The placement of the pages as within the "harts close bleeding book" heightens the sense that the words are born from within the speaker's invisible "inner part," a private bodily writing that Spenser stakes out later in architectural terms, buried "deepe in the closet of my parts entyre" (84). We can recall the scorn Drayton expressed in *Poly-Olbion* that the age only valued coterie work which was "kept in Cabinets." Here the "cabinet" or "closet" of the body harbors the passions that constitute amorous lyric poetry. Spenser's depiction of the text as folded within the mistress's hands in the first sonnet is merely a reembodiment of the sonnet's moment of production: the poems are sent from the interior cupboard of one human body into the enclosure of another anatomy.

At points in the *Amoretti* when language seems to fail the speaker, he claims the body as a ground for meaning. In the third sonnet, the poet argues that he is dazed beyond language by the "huge brightenesse" of the mistress, a sight that silences him: "when my pen would write her titles true, / it ravisht is with fancies wonderment." The solution to this linguistic paralysis is to contain discourse within the body so that the speaker may claim: "in my hart I then both speake and write" (3). While the speaker suggests that his solution, in part, involves transforming the physicality of his "pen's" ravishment into the more spiritual experience of emotion, he also charts a move from a spectacular visionary mode of expression to an invisible corporeal and enclosed writing. Repeatedly he argues that the mistress circumscribes his existence, forcing him to recede into interiority.

---

[43]Leonard Barkan's *Nature's Work of Art: The Human Body as Image of the World* (New Haven: Yale University Press, 1975) is also helpful here generally because his study takes seriously the idea of body as microcosm and shows how it served as a crucial idiom for expressing the dearest-held cosmic and social truths of Renaissance thought.

"You frame my thoughts and fashion me within," the poet declares; "You stop my toung, and teach my hart to speake" (8). What Spenser gestures toward is a highly private language, one in which the heart holds within it what the tongue cannot express outwardly. The reader thus becomes an eavesdropper to passionate and private words that emerge painfully from the lover's "inner" soul. The result is a language that seems to shy away from representation; the speaker's passions are best imagined within the hidden depths of the human body. Of course, the poststructuralist reader knows that the subject always evades representation, maintaining its existence in a pattern of endless deferral; this evasion necessarily occurs because of the slippage in the process of signification.44 The sonnets, however, accentuate this slippage by foregrounding an arena inaccessible to language. They do so by drawing our attention to a bodily layer of meaning that is seemingly secreted away from public view.

Daniel's *Delia* suggests not only the lover's *inability* to represent this secret corporeal passion, but also the *undesirability* of such an outward show. In the first sonnet, the speaker tells of a reserve of self that must be concealed from representation; he thus extends the preface's depiction of publication as a breach of secrecy into the poems themselves. "Who can shewe all his love, doth love but lightly," he asserts. Not only does the speaker refer to his "hidden griefe" and "silent art" (8), but he scorns the outward representation that necessarily "bewraies [his] love, with broken words halfe spoken, . . . / And layes to view [his] Vultur-gnawne hart open" (15). Once again the act of exposure is portrayed in graphic bodily terms through the image of the written word feasting on a love-worn heart. Publication becomes conflated with the wound that exposes the bloody heart. The speaker worries that his text performs a similar (though less violent) act of betrayal against the mistress by pressing her into language: "O be not griev'd," the speaker pleads, "that these my papers should, / Bewray unto the world howe faire thou art" (36). In these words, we hear echoes of Daniel's description of the publication of his own work in the preface: "I rather desired to keep in the private passions of my youth, from the multitude, as things utterd to my selfe, and consecrated to silence: yet seeing I was betraide by the indiscretion of a greedie Printer . . . I am forced to publish that which I never ment" (*Poems*, 9). The problems that arise from revealing love are registered in Daniel's poems as well as in his description of the text's move from manuscript to print.

Because the disclosure of speech is figured as sacrilege, the index to the

---

44Catherine Belsey succinctly articulates this now common point in *The Subject of Tragedy: Identity and Difference in Renaissance Drama* (New York: Methuen, 1985).

speaker's love becomes the reticence of the poems. If the preface suggests that publication is a betrayal of trust, the poems themselves emphasize that language is a measure of defective feeling. True discourse remains unpublished, buried within "the booke of my charg'd soule," the speaker declares (1). The sonnets thus complicate and extend the preface's construction of invasive reading through their division of experience into interior/exterior. *Delia* offers poems that both mourn the inability of language to capture true feeling and grieve at hidden emotions involuntarily made visible. Both of these rhetorical moves construct a distinct private subject that resists exposure, a core of meaning that recedes first from language itself and then from the more public circulation of that representation. In discussing this gesture in a different context, Patricia Fumerton notes, "Again and again in *Astrophel and Stella*, we proceed through public 'casings' of conventional rhetorical display toward a private and sincere vision that is never attained."[45] It is this repeated, although thwarted, movement that makes the sonnets seem so seductively private. Daniel's sequence thus appropriately concludes by naming his own textual display as improper. In the final sonnet, he recedes into his own emotions and lapses into silence: "I say no more / I feare I saide too much" (50). If the writer has presented the text as a series of painful revelations and disclosures, then he makes it fold in on itself at the conclusion. This complex move invites attention to, as it covers over, the illicit nature of the sonnets' language.

Delia provides a heightened articulation of a theme that was common in many sonnet collections: the problematics of representation and display. Sonnet writers registered their concern with this issue through a systematic denunciation of visual and verbal display. In Henry Constable's *Diana*, for instance, the speaker declaims first against his eyes and then his speech:

> Woe to mine eyes! The organs of mine ill;
> Hate to my heart! for not concealing joy;
> A double curse upon my tongue be still!
> Whose babbling lost what else I might enjoy.[46]

Continuing the censure of his own unruly language, the speaker scorns his "tell-tale tongue, in talking over bold." In the opening sonnet to Percy's *Coelia*, the speaker introduces his work by expressing the worry that "every

---

[45]Patricia Fumerton, "'Secret' Arts: Elizabethan Miniatures and Sonnets," *Representations* 15 (Summer 1986): 81.

[46]Henry Constable, *Diana, or, The excellent Conceitful Sonnets of H.C.* (1594), reprinted in *Elizabethan Sonnets: An English Garner*, ed. Sidney Lee, 2 vols. (New York: Cooper Square Publishers, 1964), 2:90, Third Decade, Sonnet 9.

silly eye may view [his passions] most plain." The speaker in Bartholomew
Griffin's *Fidessa* suggests that his greatest burden is the turmoil that has
become registered in his verse: "all my privat griefe her publique shame."[47]
The juxtaposition of these two phrases allows the reader to trace the evolution caused when the speaker expresses his unrequited desire; when the
private is transformed into the public, the lover's passionate "griefe" becomes the mistress's "shame." When Sidney stages a mock dialogue in which
a friend demands of the love-stricken Astrophel, "Art not ashamed to publish thy disease?" Astrophel responds by explaining that his disgrace will be
mitigated if the circulation of the text remains "close"—that is, within a
coterie of friends (34). As these examples suggest, poets identify their poems
as emblems of an unwise blazoning. Sonnet readers are made to feel that
they have not only participated in the guilt of publication, but also spied
on the act of courtship, an event so private that it is best imagined within
the interior of the body. The poet's general self-consciousness about his
poem's status as verbal artifact heightens an awareness of the process of
reading itself; for the poems call attention to the reader's role in intruding
on a passion that is expressly described as private, covert, and resistant to
outward expression.[48]

Although Shakespeare modifies the traditional binary opposition between male speaker and the female object of desire through his particular
representation of triangulated love within the *Sonnets*, he still draws heavily
on the tensions created from the contradictory impulses to conceal and
display emotion. His poems record the experience of love as the disclosure
of interiority, a space described as "a closet never pearst with christall eyes."[49]
The sonnets' economic metaphors, however, complicate this figuration. In
the first nineteen sonnets, the speaker pleads that the young man stop
"having traffike with [him]selfe alone" (4). Through metaphors of usury

---

[47]Bartholomew Griffin, *Fidessa, more chaste than kinde,* STC 12367 (1596), Sonnet 52.

[48]Stephen Greenblatt, Patricia Fumerton, and Anne Ferry all grapple with the question of
the Renaissance private self, trying to locate its contours and its capacity for representation at
this time. I am not suggesting that poets disclose or fail to disclose a private self in their
works. Nor am I addressing the dilemma of the constitution of the private self through a public vocabulary. I am suggesting that Renaissance poets create the *trappings* of disclosure that
mold a certain relationship between text and reader as well as text and writer. The "self" that
they withhold and display certainly may not be equivalent to our understanding of the subject defined by interiority, but the works certainly create a problematic *gesture* toward an
inward self. I explore the sexual and political ramifications of that gesture. See Greenblatt,
Renaissance Self-Fashioning: From More to Shakespeare (Chicago: University of Chicago Press,
1980); Ferry, *The "Inward" Language;* and Fumerton, "'Secret' Arts."

[49]William Shakespeare, *Shakespeare's Sonnets,* ed. Stephen Booth (New Haven: Yale
University Press, 1977), no. 46. All references to Shakespeare's sonnets are drawn from the
unmodernized quarto side of this edition.

and expenditure that laud circulation and denounce withholding, the speaker protests the young man's self-love as masturbatory. In Sonnet 11, the speaker suggests that these economic metaphors have a correlate in tropes of printing. Arguing generally for an amplification that stands for both reproduction and circulation, he advises, "Thou shouldst print more, not let that coppy die." In these sonnets, Shakespeare portrays publication as a vital and necessary means for preserving youthful beauty rather than as a betrayal of private emotion. The act of amplification becomes problematized, however, at other points in the collection. In Sonnet 17, for instance, the speaker bewails the fact that his verse shrouds its beloved subject: "though yet heaven knowes [my verse] is but as a tombe / Which hides your life, and shewes not halfe your parts." The urge to extend circulation sexually, economically, and textually is made problematic by the metaphors of enclosure and death that the speaker evokes in describing his own sonnet creations. Sonnet 17 points to an equally prevalent set of metaphors in the sonnets that depict representation and public circulation in less positive ways than Sonnet 11 and the first nineteen poems.

In Sonnet 48, the speaker yokes betrayal and publication more conventionally. Here the poet represents sexual jealousy by activating the vocabulary Nashe uses to describe the erotics of coterie poetry's imprisonment:

> How carefull was I when I tooke my way,
> Each trifle under truest barres to thrust,
> That to my use it might un-used stay
> From hands of falsehood, in sure wards of trust?
> But thou, to whom my jewels trifles are,
> Most worthy comfort, now my greatest griefe,
> Thou best of deerest, and mine onely care,
> Art left the prey of every vulgar theefe.
> Thee have I not lockt up in any chest,
> Save where thou art not though I feele thou art,
> Within the gentle closure of my brest,
> From whence at pleasure thou maist come and part,
>   And even thence thou wilt be stolne I feare,
>   For truth prooves theevish for a prize so deare.

While the speaker guards his emotional "trifles" by putting them in "wards" (chests, caskets, or cases) for safekeeping, he gives free license to the object of his desire, safeguarding only his beloved's image within his own breast. He adds, however, that even this tenuous enclosure creates a resistance that makes it possible for the lover to be "stolne," to be "the prey of every vulgar theef." In his notes to the text Stephen Booth glosses "vulgar" as meaning "generally circulating," "base," "public," and "widely dissemi-

nated."[50] The refusal to contain the beloved completely makes him susceptible to a shared circulation. But because the beloved lives in the speaker's
immortalizing and public lines, as the poems generally assert, the sonnets
themselves invite such a theft. The sexual implications of locking and picklocking riddle this sonnet, as the lover speaks of "jewels" and the "gentle
closure" of "chests," common double entendres for "private parts." The
poems draw on these sexual metaphors, as Nashe does, to link acts of disclosure and circulation with sexual promiscuity.

Sonnet 102 more explicitly frames the problem of disclosure/enclosure
in terms of publishing:

> I love not lesse, thogh lesse the show appeare,
> That love is marchandiz'd, whose ritch esteeming,
> The owners tongue doth publish every where.[51]

In arguing that "sweets growne common loose their deare delight," the
speaker places pressure on his own earlier assertion that the beloved "shall
shine more bright" in the poems themselves because these artifacts submit
the partner to a public view that threatens to make him "common" (55).
By suggesting that public display cheapens emotion, Sonnet 102 thus reverses the argument made through the economic and printing metaphors
in the first nineteen poems. If, in these earlier sonnets, printing ensured
the preservation of youthful beauty, these later poems suggest that the
commodified text produced by the press degrades the emotion that fuels
celebratory love poetry.

Sonnet 26 queries the connections between erotic and textual exposure
by conflating Petrarchan language with the obsequious language commonly
seen in the dedications written from poet to patron:

> Lord of my love, to whome in vassalage
> Thy merrit hath my dutie strongly knit;
> To thee I send this written ambassage

---

[50]Stephen Booth's notes to *Shakespeare's Sonnets*, pp. 212, 362.

[51]The circulation of language and love is also written as guilty betrayal in Sonnet 110, a
poem in which the speaker confesses his infidelity through metaphors of display. "Alas 'tis
true, I have gone here and there, / And made my selfe a motley to the view, / Gor'd mine
own thoughts, sold cheap what is most deare." Although many critics read this sonnet as
commentary on the profession of the actor, the economic language ("sold," "cheap,"
"deare") connects this display with the sonnets themselves, texts in which the beloved is
repeatedly described as "dear," and in which the speaker has promised not to "praise that
which I would not sell." Before the speaker goes on to name that display as redemptive, he
offers us a moment of illicit viewing.

To witnesse duty, not to shew my wit.
Duty so great, which wit so poore as mine
May make seeme bare, in wanting words to shew it;
But that I hope some good conceipt of thine
In thy soules thought (all naked) will bestow it:
Til whatsoever star that guides my moving,
Points on me gratiously with faire aspect,
And puts apparell on my tottered loving,
To showe me worthy of their sweet respect,
   Then may I dare to boast how I doe love thee,
   Til then, not show my head where thou mayst prove me.

The outer layers of the text—those addresses that introduce the book to the public—seem to have spilled over into the poems themselves. The prefatorial and dedicatory language of service becomes part of the discursive rhetoric of the amorous poem. Or, rather, this correspondence merely documents the way in which the prefatory language found in published works began to rely on the sonnets' language of courtly love. In describing how his text performs an exhibition, the speaker conflates the display of the text with the display of the sexual organs. Words such as "wit," "bare," "naked," and "head" imprecisely create an aura of sexuality, as Booth notes (176–77). By drawing on the metaphor of investiture to throw into relief the sparsity of his own text, the speaker informs the word "loving," which seems to be both "tottered" and "naked," with a peculiarly sexual resonance. Similarly, the speaker's teasing and playful reluctance—"to shew [his] wit"—absorbs these puerile overtones. In replicating the language of presentation found in so many texts, the sonnet transforms these words into provocative overtures full of mock reluctance at a potentially erotic moment of display, an illicit spectacle viewed by the book reader as well as the private patron.

If the sonnet writers are generally fascinated and troubled by the translation of private experience into publicly represented visual scandal, they express that interest particularly through frequent reference to the Diana-Actaeon myth. Petrarch called on this myth when he sought to explain the complex psychology of love and to introduce the sonnet speaker's duel role as lover and writer. Barkan notes that the myth, which was given its distinct place in lyric poetry and its most popular interpretation by Petrarch, was an important topos for Renaissance sonneteers. "Once the goddess becomes the unattainable object of an amorous hunt, the story of Actaeon acquires enormous psychological power," he comments. "The tormenting but fatally remote sight of a beautiful women realizes the beastliness of the lover and atomizes him into his destructive desires as represented by the devouring hounds" ("Diana and Actaeon," 339). In *Parthenophil and*

Parthenophe, Barnes describes the self-torture and "thralldome" produced by his own desires, portraying himself as the doomed mythic hunter: "Behold, one to his fancies made a praye, / A poore Actaeon with his houndes devour'd" (Elegy 3). Likewise, Bartholomew Griffin tells Fidessa of the agony his desires cause: "These breed such thoughts as set my heart on fire, / And like fell hounds, pursue me to my death" (8). Many other sequences, including William Smith's *Chloris* and the anonymous *Zepheria,* introduce us to speakers who find a mythic soulmate in Actaeon, for the failed hunter is seen as vividly portraying the predicament of unjust emotional torture [52]

A sonnet from Daniel's *Delia* provides us with a more complete retelling of the myth:

> Whilst youth and error led my wandring minde,
> And set my thoughts in heedeles waies to range:
> All unawares a Goddesse chaste I finde,
> Diana-like, to worke my suddaine change.
>   For her no sooner had my view bewrayd,
> But with disdaine to see me in that place:
> With fairest hand, the sweet unkindest maide,
> Castes water-cold disdain upon my face.
>   Which turn'd my sport into a Harts dispaire,
> Which still is chac'd, whilst I have any breath,
> By mine owne thoughts: set on me by my faire,
> My thoughts like houndes, pursue me to my death.
>   Those that I fostred of mine owne accord,
> Are made by her to murther thus their Lord
>
> (5)

This poem offers us many of the standards of sonnet writing: highly wrought paradox, extended conceit, hyperbolic analogy. Daniel conventionally and unsurprisingly employs the Diana-Actaeon myth as an analogue for the emotional conflict produced by desire. The sonnet thus relies on the story as a means of investigating the complex psychology of love—its destructive potential and its gendered coordinates. In this poem, the sight of the woman catalyzes the speaker's emotional transformations. Delia paradoxically orchestrates the speaker's self-torture.

In his punning suggestion that the mistress is "chaste" while the speaker

---

[52]See William Smith, *Chloris, or the complaint of the passionate despised shepherd,* STC 22872 (1596), reprinted in *The Poems of William Smith,* ed. Lawrence A. Sasek (Baton Rouge: Louisiana State University Press, 1970), Sonnet 10, p. 46; and *Zepheria,* STC 26124 (1594), reprinted in Publications of the Spenser Society (Manchester: Charles S. Simms, 1869), Canzon 7, p. 11.

is "chac'd, Daniel draws out the striking mirror of identity that many other Renaissance artists found so provocative in the myth. Actaeon's guilt or innocence becomes at issue in the ambiguous blending of happenstance and intent. The words "wandring," "heedeles," and "unawares" suggest the speaker's innocence as he meanders into this state of emotional chaos. But the verbs also imply another story: the speaker has purposely transgressed sanctioned limits by daring to possess the sight and heart of the beloved. Youth and error "led" the ostensibly wandering lover, and "set" his thoughts in a certain direction; such influence prompted him to "finde" the object that he unconsciously sought in his "sport." Daniel constructs this same duality through the ambiguous phrase —"my view bewrayd"—which could imply either that Actaeon's innocent act of seeing was betrayed by the unsought sight, or that he did indeed betray the goddess by stepping into her private bower and gazing on her naked flesh. Actaeon's problematic accountability becomes important here and throughout the sonnets, which spin out a contradictory language of praise and blame directed at the sonnet mistress. As a goddess, huntress, and woman, she holds significant power over her wooing lover. When the speaker notes that his mistress turns his "sport into a Harts dispaire," he hints at the potential violence that becomes explicit in the next lines. The threat of dismemberment found in the "dis-pairing," or breaking asunder of the heart, gives way to a more definitive image of the hunt's reversed destruction: "My thoughts like houndes, pursue me to my death." Daniel thus uses the myth to trace the volatile and dangerous psychic turmoil produced by the love relationship; his version of the story particularly explores Actaeon's ambiguous responsibility for his threatening metamorphosis into the object of violence.

The sight of forbidden flesh is represented in terms that echo Daniel's description of publication in the preface—as a "bewrayal." This association implicitly constructs the reader as a voyeur who, like Actaeon, has ventured into a "private" domain simply by buying the book. This general association is played out in the sonnets themselves as well as through the preface's figuration of book and reader. Sonnet 5's retelling of the Actaeon myth, for instance, is followed by a poem that describes the very sight that is said to pose the threat of dismemberment. Sonnet 6 offers a blazoned description of the Diana-like mistress. The reader is invited to visualize the beloved's body and thus to repeat the mythic crime of Actaeon as translated into the act of reading. The book's title already sets up a correspondence between reading and loving (possessing Delia); this sonnet endows that correspondence with criminality.

Delia was another name for Diana, who was born at Delos. Lars-Hakan Svensson's modern critical commentary and edition of *Delia* reinforces the title's association with the myth when he locates an interpretative crux in the fifth sonnet.[53] As if to reiterate how crucial the Diana-Actaeon myth is for this sequence, Svensson uses Jean Mignon's engraving of Actaeon and Diana as the frontispiece for his facsimile reproduction. Because there is no explanation given for this addition, Svensson seems to think it natural that this icon should be selected as the image that introduces the sequence. By displaying Diana's naked body at the outset, he thus unwittingly reproduces the prefatorial voyeurism that Vesalius's engraving and the prefaces create, forging an Actaeon-like reader through the text's preliminary apparatus. While this modern addition points, of course, to the idiosyncratic work of one editor, it also draws out more fully Daniel's interest in issues of disclosure, publication, and illicit viewing.

Svensson's use of the engraving can also be seen as a reduplication of many Renaissance writers' own tactics for presenting their works. In his book of love sonnets, *The Tears of Fancie* (1593), Thomas Watson alludes to the Diana-Actaeon in both his amorous poems and in the envoi to the text. Sonnet 49 draws on the myth to show how the lover's predicament is actually much worse than Actaeon's, for Actaeon was accorded the minimal respect of being allowed to die. The speaker complains that he instead must suffer perpetual and unrepresentable psychic distress. But if the myth proves useful when Watson represents unrequited love, it also becomes his means of introducing the entire sequence. In the envoi, he alludes to the Diana-Actaeon myth in order to dramatize for the public reader the poem's engagement with its most important and intimate reader, the female mistress:

> Go idle lines unpolisht rude and base,
> Unworthy words to blason beauties glory:
> (Beauty that hath my restless *hart in chase,*
> Beauty the subiect of my ruefull story.)
> I warne thee shunne the bower of her abiding,
> *Be not so bold ne hardy as to view her:*
> Least shee inraged with thee fall a chiding
> And so her anger prove thy woes renewer.
> Yet if she daigne to rew thy dreadfull smart,
> And reading laugh, and laughing so mislike thee:
> Bid her desist, and looke within my hart
> Where shee may see how ruthles shee did strike mee
> If shee be pleasde though shee reward thee not,
> What other say of me regard it not.[54]

---

[53]Lars-Hakan Svensson, *Silent Art: Rhetorical and Thematic Patterns in Samuel Daniel's "Delia"* (CWK Gleerup, 1980).

[54]Thomas Watson, *The Tears of Fancie*, STC 25122 (1593), sig. A2, emphasis mine.

Conventionally sending out his poem with instructions for proper textual behavior (certainly as a means of preempting criticism), Watson calls on central features of the Actaeon myth: the dramatization of reciprocal and dangerous looks, the enclosed secret bower, the way in which venturing on this domain could be construed as blasphemous and arrogant, the hart/heart pun that vivifies the self-destructive nature of passion, and the concern with reputation and just reward. Like the poem's speaker, the author scripts himself as Actaeon, who can knowingly warn his own text against the hazards of display and public viewing. Having suffered the fate of Actaeon by falling in love, Watson seeks to prevent his book from being subject to the criticism of the Diana-like reader. The book thus takes on the role of the overly bold Actaeon as it sallies forth to meet its public. The reader becomes the exposed female Diana, who may punish the writer/text for his hardiness. The sonnets' general concerns about publicity and transgressive representation find their apt expression in Watson's envoi and Daniel's preface.

Sonnets are everywhere marked by their troubling concern with public display. Sonnet writers initiate their readers into an understanding of the anxieties of public viewing through their creation of readerly voyeurs. This prevalent dynamic is seen in its most literal form when poets compare themselves to Actaeon and link their poetic outpourings with an episode that involves spying and metamorphosis. The myth becomes an allegory for the reader/text relationship that the sonnets create through their pervasive exploration of the dangers of exposure and representation.

The Erotics of the Commodified Book

Sonnets are thus prime texts for helping us to see the eroticized rhetoric of disclosure that so many published works use in their prefaces. Sonnet writers self-consciously foreground and comment on the bizarre fact that public writing was introduced to its larger readership by being scandalized. In a sense, Vesalius's introductory engraving to the *Fabrica* stands as an emblem not only for the general erotic imagery that pervades book preliminaries, but also for the specific gendered program that Vickers retrieves from the sonnets. In its display of the dissected, sprawled female body, the engraving acts as a visual blazon. Vesalius garners authority by presiding over the dissection with his sharp penlike instrument. Like the sonnet speaker who controls the linguistic fragmentation of his beloved mistress, Vesalius prominently displays his own mastery vis-à-vis this inert female body. The voyeuristic eavesdropper to the passionate outpourings of the sonnet speaker becomes represented here as a throng of onlookers. The title page to the *Fabrica* is itself an appropriate blazon, given that the word also means "to herald, to proclaim, to publish to the world." The engraving's function is to announce the text, to herald its contents, and to proclaim the import of the disparate illustrations in the anatomy. The text and author are heralded through this multifaceted image of female dismemberment and display. By casting the book reader in the role of voyeur, and particularly in the role of the male voyeur viewing the female body, this prefatory image, like so many others used to announce Renaissance books, plays out a dynamic also prevalent in the popular and celebrated Petrarchan sonnet sequences that were rolling off the presses in great numbers.

It is not surpising, then, that sonnet sequences themselves were packaged to foreground the voyeuristic aspect of authorial display and book buying. In the preliminary layers to their books, publishers identified their works as sonnet mistresses. This identification is reflected most evidently in their choice of titles: *Diana, Coelia, Phillis, Delia, Licia, Caelica, Fidessa, Chloris*. Through this publishing practice, the text became synonymous with the female body, which was now multiply reproduced and displayed for a larger reading audience. By mass-producing portable and compact textual women for the male gaze, printing offered its readers the thrill of acquiring, owning, and viewing the erotics of love coded as a woman.

The trope of voyeurism became particularly important to publishers and writers when they sought to conceptualize the published sonnet sequence, a practice inspired undoubtedly by the convention of using female names as titles for these books. As I have discussed, the strategy of naming sonnet sequences for the poetic mistress allowed for the unification of disparate poetic texts (see Chapter 1); this embodiment contributed as well to the published book's erotic appeal and social scandal. William Smith, for instance, coyly displays his "maiden verse," *Chloris*, calling on the public to "see" her as she sallies out from the private exchange between the writer and patron Colin Clout:

> But that it pleased thy grave Shepherdhood,
> The Patron of my maiden verse to bee,
> When I in doubt of raging Envie stood
> And now I waigh not who shall Chloris see.
>
> (sig. A3)

Here the relationship between male patron and writer is dramatized for the public reader's benefit. The private relationship becomes scandalized when it is staged as the exchange of the "maiden" textual woman between men. This eroticized exchange is held out to inspire the reader's envy and desire. In fact, the desire for the beautiful woman becomes indistinguishable from the reader's desire for the book. Like Thomas Lodge, who asks the public to gaze on his "country" woman/text *Phillis*, Smith draws on the text's femininity in order to formulate the relationship between writer, object/text, and reading public. When Lodge displays his shepherdess/text, he tells about the pleasures available in watching the text receive the reader's gaze.[55] He introduces his sonnet sequence by lewdly punning on her "countrie" status, one that makes his act of display a salacious auction for the book and woman. In both of these introductions, the reader is lured into identifying with the author's desire for his feminized book— asked to enter into the private, exclusive, and eroticized relationship between author, text, and patron. If this figuration creates a subject position for the author, as I have argued, it also represents the reader as a voyeur to a scandalous exchange.

Renaissance readers and writers were aware of the commodification exercised through the female title, as is made clear in Samuel Rowlands's *Tis Merrie when Gossips meete*.[56] The work opens with a mock introductory scene in which a bookseller/printer desperately tries to peddle his wares. When the prospective male customer protests that the title, "A Merrie meeting heere in London betweene a Wife, a Widdow and a Mayde," is hardly novel and that he is certain he has already seen such a book anyway, the seller argues that *owning* the text offers the truly riveting and novel experience: "You have not seene it . . . . For I am sure you are in Love, or at least will bee, with one of these three: or say you deale but with two, the Widdow and the Mayde: because the Wife is another mans commoditie: is it not a prettie thing to carry Wife, Mayde, and Widdow in youre pocket, when you may as it were conferre and heare them talk together when you will? nay more, drinke togither: yea, and that which is a further matter: utter their mindes, chuse Husbands and censure complections" (sig. A4). The enticement to buying the book is the possibility of mastering three women, holding them in the private space of a pocket at will ("when you may"), listening to them articulate their desires about men, as well as taking liberties with another man's "commoditie." This dialogue trades on the conflation of text and woman, appealing to the reader's prurient interest not in reading about sexually stimulating matter, but in the seductiveness of *merely owning the book*. The seller's suggestion details the puerile appeal that the title implicitly suggests: the reader will be able to buy private female discourse, eavesdrop on a meeting that is exclusively female, and fall in love with his book. The seller's parting advice—to "sit alone privately in your Chamber [when]

---

[55]Thomas Lodge, *Phillis*, STC 16662 (1593), sig. A2. In the introduction to *Phillis*, Lodge tells the patron/reader: "May it please you to looke and like of homlie Phillis in her country caroling, & to countenance her poore and affectionate Sheepheard."

[56]Samuel Rowlands, *Tis Merrie when Gossips meete*, STC 21409 (1602).

reading of it"—recalls the spatial tropes used to depict those threatened coterie, erotic, and bodily enclosures: chambers, cabinets, and closets. The seller, in essence, argues that the buyer should reprivatize the woman, redeeming her by becoming a prudent and watchful book owner. Like Wilmot, who argued that Tancred should be confined within the walls of the private library, the bookseller urges that the reader ultimately bring the feminized book to safety within the redemptive domestic space. The reader is thus invited to bear witness to the woman's promiscuous circulation and then to aid in her rescue. As the scene dramatizes the transaction of the book as a sullied commodity changing hands, it opens up the issue of voyeurism fully. Books are presented as physical objects that are circulated within a market of salacious buyers and sellers. When the issues of disclosure and concealment, the concern of so much Renaissance literature, are activated in these prefaces, they help to mediate the commodification of the written word. Shakespeare's line—"I will not praise that purpose not to sell" (Sonnet 21)—unfolds the coalescing notions of display, praise, and commodification that become evident when writers and publishers seek to identify their own acts of blazoning and publishing.

This scene from Rowlands's text is important because it teases out the gendered and erotic ramifications of the practice of giving books female titles. In dramatizing how a printer personifies his text to tout the advantages of possessing another man's female writing, Rowlands exposes the game of titillation and sexual rivalry that underscored the marketing of books. Barnabe Barnes reveals another way in which the writer can make a prurient appeal to his reader. Barnes conjures up the conventional female muse as a means of negotiating his text's entrance into the public sphere. In the first commendatory poem to his sonnet sequence *Parthenophil and Parthenophe*, Barnes narrates his muse's "drama of embarrassment" as she modestly presents herself to her prospective patron. He urges the Earl of Northumberland to

> Deigne (mightie Lord) these verses to peruse
> Which my blacke mournfull muse presenteth here,
> Blushing at her first entrance in for feare,
> Where of her selfe, her selfe she doth accuse,
> And seeking Patronage, bold meanes doth use.[57]

Barnes compares his text to a bashful woman who blushes at the forwardness of her appearance. His analogy serves as a means of deferentially ask-

[57]Barnabe Barnes, *Parthenophil and Parthenophe,* STC 1469 (1593), ed. Victor A. Doyno (Carbondale: Southern Illinois University Press, 1971), 131.

ing Northumberland to accept this lowly work into such a worthy and noble home. But Barnes's apology also draws on feminine modesty and boldness to describe the text's reception in the public sphere. This coy dramatization of the coquettish woman as she reluctantly offers herself to her patron is, after all, published to all book readers. The muse's self-accusation, then, seems to reflect the fact that the text wanders promiscuously into the public as a "bold meanes" of finding her gentle patron. Barnes asks Northumberland to "peruse" these now feminized lines, but in doing so, he displays his private request and the narrative of the embarrassed muse to a voyeuristic public audience.

This commendatory poem merely hints at the narrative of female fall and redemption that underlies the prefaces to *Gorboduc* and *Scillaes Metamorphosis,* and the bookseller's strategy in Rowlands's representation. The muse's self-accusation gives the barest hint of her transgression in using "bold meanes" to seek her patron. Barnes's next commendatory poem to Essex, however, quite explicitly identifies his book's appearance with a breach of sexual decorum:

> My bashfull muse (which lost her mayden-head
> In too deare travell of my restless love)
> To you my Lord her first borne babe presentes,
> Unworthie such a patrone for her lightnesse.
>
> (131)

This verse comes as no surprise, given that Barnes's own envoi to *Parthenophil* represents his writing as a bastard child abandoned by the father who protects himself through anonymity.[58] The verse is also unsurprising, given how common it was for writers to represent their relationship to their work in paternal terms. But Barnes here stretches convention when he suggests that the book is the bastard offspring of his wanton muse, whose passionate experience in crafting the poet's throes of love has made her lose her virginity and conceive illegitimately. Barnes's amorous verse is vivified when he scandalously deflowers his own modest muse. As in the preface to *Gorbo-*

---

[58]The envoi opens: "Go barstard Orphan packe thee hence, / And seeke some straunger for defence" (2). In this introduction, Barnes acknowledges the moral levity of his poetry and suggests that only a socially powerful patron can protect him from criticism for his wayward text. As he instructs his book on proper textual decorum, he portrays the moment of textual production as one of shame and scandal. His bastard son/text is told, for instance, to "be secrete, wise, and circumspect, / And modesty sometimes affect" (2). In keeping with Nashe's strange blend of male and female sexuality in his preface to *Astrophel and Stella,* Barnes figures his text as both a wanton muse and a bastard boy—each tainted with the sexual improprieties he has committed in writing.

duc, the female text now must accept responsibility for her seduction/rape; here Barnes charges her with "lightnesse" for her part in the sexual scandal that produces the sonnet sequence. By creating a lens through which the reader can view the newly commodified book, Barnes tells a story of immodest display, sexual transgression, and the loss of virginity.

When the publisher of a narrative poem entitled *Willobie his Avisa* (1594) put together an engraving and a set of prefaces designed to introduce the book, he highlighted the alluring nature of female display through direct reference to the Diana-Actaeon myth.[59] The title page offers a dense voyeuristically encoded image. The subtitle, "The true Picture of a modest Maid, and of a chaste and constant wife," promises to represent a "modest maid" to the public, a woman who should, by definition, shy away from such dangerous displays. This promise is curiously reinforced by a pictorial image within the circular frame of the bottom border. Lodged within the elaborate adornments of angels, flowers, and classical figures, the naked Diana and her nymphs, spied on by the reader, splash water onto the already transformed Actaeon. Like Avisa, the nymphs are clearly modest, a characteristic evidenced as they attempt to pull garments around their exposed bodies. If the publisher chose this emblem to suggest that Diana was the supernatural counterpart to the ideal mortal maid Avisa, he strangely represents the epitome of female virtue by reference to an episode in which her virtue is challenged. This odd title page stages a moment of voyeuristic transgression while it claims to present the story of exemplary feminine ideals.

To complicate matters further, the engraving is accompanied by the following command: "Read the preface to the Reader before you enter further." On reading this preface, we find a standard disclaimer written by Hadrian Dorrell, who claims that he took the poem from his friend Willobie's study while his friend was abroad. Dorrel thus presents the conventional authorial disclaimer that we have seen in numerous prefaces. Using Nashe's terminology, he notes that Willobie had provided him with a "key" to his library, so he, in effect, is the private picklock who unleashes this text to a violent enlargement. Dorrel frees the text from its imprisonment in the aristocratic domain of manuscript circulation. The modest maid Avisa is thus stolen from her enclosure and displayed to the world as Diana. The

---

[59] *Willobie his Avisa,* STC 25755 (1594), reprinted in Bodley Head Quartos, ed. G. B. Harrison (New York: E. P. Dutton, 1926). It not surprising that the Diana engraving disappears in the 1635 edition. The disappearance of the engraving from the title page is accompanied by a gradual decline in the number of prefatorial disclaimers published with texts generally. By this time, publication had either gained more legitimacy and prestige, or its status was negotiated by other figurations.

prominence of these emphatic prescriptive words, "Read the preface to the Reader before you enter further," self-consciously foregrounds the process by which the reader preconceptualizes the book before enjoying the imaginative fiction it presents. When yoked with the portrait of the naked Diana and the authorial disclaimer, this command reminds readers of the crucial role these oddly gendered beginnings play in representing commodified books within the literary marketplace.

Because it links the Diana myth, a statement of unauthorized publication, and a commentary on the importance of prefatory material, *Avisa* is an exceptional and unique text. Its manner of presentation, however, is merely a highly condensed example of a general cultural practice: the process by which printers and authors titillated their reading audiences within the physical feature of the printed book. Often publishers generated this enticement by staging their own refusal to identify an author, therefore endowing the text with a mysterious quality. In many early English books, signatures were cryptic—often a set of bare initials or the generic terms "Immerito," "Anon.," or "Incognito." These marks acted as both a signature and an anti-signature, ciphers that pretended to give information while in reality shrouding a secret identity. By using initials, publishers teased the audience into playing word games that involved constructing possible meanings for these enigmatic codes (for example, as critics still do for the infamous W. H.). Acrostics, puns, riddles, and autobiographical references suggest that a hidden, private discourse lay beneath the text, one that could be found when the outer layer was stripped away.[60]

Indeed, the covert wordplay evident in the packaging of published books was fueled by the detective games surrounding publication itself. The state, constantly on guard for treasonous or heretical material, hired state decipherers to subject written works to careful scrutiny. These decipherers made a living by unscrambling codes in books, attempting to detect seditious or immoral meanings buried within the seemingly innocent story, ballad, or play. As a result, writers and printers lived in a milieu defined by suspicion and fear. Nashe, in typically hyperbolic terms, lashes out at these state censors: "Let one but name bread, and they will interpret it to be the town of Bredan in the low countreyes."[61] Nicholas Breton similarly complains that "points and commas, oftentimes misread, / Endanger oft the

---

[60]In "'Love is not Love': Elizabethan Sonnet Sequences and the Social Order," *ELH* 49 (1982): 396–428, Arthur Marotti demonstrates the political nature of the sexual courtship game. In *Censorship and Interpretation: The Conditions of Writing and Reading in Early Modern England* (Madison: University of Wisconsin Press, 1984), Annabel Patterson discusses the coded language that Renaissance writers were forced to use.

[61]Thomas Nashe, dedication to the 1594 edition of *Christs Teares Over Jerusalem*, in *Works*, 2:182.

harmless writer's head."[62] When Jonson in *Bartholomew Fair* calls these decipherers the "politic pick-lock," he echoes Nashe's sexually laden description of the release of coterie poetry. In protesting this surveillance, writers
unwittingly represent a seething underside to their works able to be discovered. Books become figured as material entities, "cases" that contain
volatile significations that can be stolen and exposed. By advertising their
texts so cryptically, printers and authors tapped into this general air of suspicion, twisting a threatening force into a strategy of advertisement. In the
late sixteenth century, a work was already scripted as potentially transgressive before it was written; publishers reframed the text's mysterious quality
by playing word games with the reader or by figuring the text's scandal as
sexual rather than seditious. Anxiety about the text's uncontrollable or
incriminating meanings became translated into an appeal to the prurient
interest of the reader.

Concealment and mystery surrounded the packaging of published
texts. Barnes's *Parthenophil and Parthenophe* and Francis Davison's miscellany *A Poetical Rhapsody* (1602), for instance, were put forth with self-
conscious anonymity. The publishers of these works not only withheld
each author's name, but also called attention to that act of suppression:
"My friendes name I concealed, mine owne and my brothers, I willed the
Printer to suppresse," Davison states.[63] This playful act of concealment
could be carried out by an author as well. Rather than suppressing his
own identity, George Pettie confesses that his work alludes to a private
clique of people. In the prefatory letter to *A petite Pallace of Pettie his pleasure,* Pettie claims that his tales "touch neerely divers of my nere freindes:
but the best is, they are so darkely figured forth, that onely they whom
they touch, can understand whom they touch" (sig. A3). Pettie cloaks his
text in an innocent but elite secrecy, acknowledging that covert matters
are "darkely figured forth" and that only the initiated reader can comprehend these meanings. Giles Fletcher similarly teases the reader about
possible biographical meanings underlying his work: "for the matter of
love, it may bee I am so devoted to some one, into whose hands these
may light by chance."[64] Fletcher's conditional "may" makes the reader
guess about the gossip that surrounds the poems. Like the self-consciously
cryptic signatures that publishers used, Fletcher's ploy whets the reader's

---

[62]Nicholas Breton, *No Whipping, but a Tripping,* in *Works,* ed. Alexander B. Grosart, 2 vols.
(Edinburgh: Chertsey Worthies, 1879), 1:32.

[63]Francis Davison, "To the Reader," in *A Poetical Rhapsody* (1602), ed. Hyder E. Rollins
(Cambridge, Mass.: Harvard University Press, 1931), 4.

[64]Giles Fletcher, *Licia, or Poemes of Love,* STC 11055 (1593?), reprinted in *The English Works
of Giles Fletcher, the Elder,* ed. Lloyd E. Berry (Madison: University of Wisconsin Press, 1964), 78.

appetite. He continues this game by cataloging "possibilities" for the mistress's identity. Fletcher thus both seduces the reader and manipulates him or her into the position of voyeur, someone who must read to glean information that is labeled as forbidden, to discover what the text insists must remain hidden. When information about the text is tantalizingly acknowledged and suppressed, the publisher or the writer engages the reader in a game of power and desire.

The representation of reading as voyeurism served, as I have suggested, to disavow authorial responsibility for the work, to entice readers to buy the product, and to negotiate the complicated move from manuscript to print. Such representations also had the effect of displacing the potential transgressions of writing from author to reader. The creation of voyeuristic reading, then, addresses anxieties, as many critics have pointed out, that stemmed from the dangers that the Renaissance public writer faced. Marjorie Plant notes that "hidden meanings were looked for in the most innocent of publications, so that the printer who was considering the issue of a new work had to calculate not only the risks of monetary failure but also the possibility of losing his life as a result of his project."[65] One writer, Ludwick Lloyd, took the opportunity in his preface to romanticize the writer's job by comparing his risk in publishing with the mythological quests and battles of past heroes. Lloyd hyperbolically declares: "Greater is the attempt of any simple booke writer to hazarde himselfe to present perile to encounter with divers men with a pen in his hande, then that that valiaunt Perithus with Cerebus, or Theseus with Minotaurus, yea, of Hercules with Antheus . . . for that they fought with one a peece, and that before their faces, & the simple writer with thousandes, and they behinde his backe slaunder him. Architas the Philosopher . . . was in no such daungers in his warres."[66] If Lloyd runs the gamut of legendary heroes in searching for the representative analogy, other writers protest against the risks of print by using a language that makes publication sound strangely akin to Actaeon's ominous hunt. Francis Sabie pleads with vicious critics not to dismember his works: "let them not, like angrie dogs, also beslaven with their jawes the stone cast at them, I meane, teare in sunder my faultlesse Papers."[67] John Northbrooke is even more blunt about the severity of book critics. "I am not the first," he warns, "that their venemous tongues . . . have torne in pieces."[68] And Spenser concludes the second installation of

---

[65]Marjorie Plant, *The English Book Trade*, 31.

[66]Ludwick Lloyd, preface to *The pilgrimage of princes*, STC 16624 (1573), sig. **2ᵛ.

[67]Francis Sabie, preface to *Flora's Fortune*, STC 21536 (1595), sig. A2ᵛ. H. S. Bennett lists Lloyd's and Sabie's protests in his broader analysis of the hazards of publication. *English Books and Readers, 1558–1603* (Cambridge: Cambridge University Press, 1965), 6–7.

[68]John Northbrooke, *A Treatise wherein Dicing, Dauncing, vaine playes or Enterludes . . . are*

his epic *Faerie Queene* with the image of the backbiting Blatant Beast ("like a fearfull dog"), who escapes Calidore's bondage and infiltrates the courtly world in the form of the "venemous" critic:

> Barking and biting all that him doe bate,
> Albe they worthy blame, or cleare of crime:
> Ne spareth he most learned wits to rate,
> Ne spareth he the gentle Poets rime,
> But rends without regard of person or of time.[69]

To publish means to risk Actaeon's fate. Appearing as a man in print makes the author vulnerable to critical, physical, and social dismemberment. The portrayal of criticism as animal attack may sound hyperbolic, but as Phoebe Sheavyn and H. S. Bennett have shown, Renaissance writers did indeed face exorbitant problems that justified these representations. We must remember John Stubbes's literal dismemberment; he had his hand cut off for printing a letter that attempted to advise the queen against marriage. More generally, writers and printers kept their limbs but suffered economic hardship, social ridicule, and dangerous entanglements with the state. They could be "dismembered" (made nonmembers) by being excluded socially from enclaves of power. By shifting the perspective so that the guilty crime lies with the spectator/reader, the author's guilt for writing and the printer's guilt for displaying such writing are shielded. When voyeurism becomes a trope for reading, it makes the reader complicitous in the more insidious act of display involved in public writing.

Allegories of Reading and Textual Display

Renaissance culture obsessively dramatized scenes of voyeurism in general and the Diana-Actaeon myth in particular. Renaissance visual art is filled with myriad examples that demonstrate the problem of seeing, not only in their conscious direction of the viewer's gaze to the human body, but also in their choice of scenes. Titian's several Venus pictures, for instance— *Venus with a Mirror, Venus with an Organ Player, Venus at Urbino*—show us men spying on Venus's naked body.[70] One could hardly escape reference to the Diana-Actaeon myth in the various statuary, tapestries, masques, jokes, cuckoldry rituals, engravings, and emblem books of sixteenth-

---

reproved, STC 18670 (1577), sig. A3v.

[69]Edmund Spenser, *The Faerie Queene.* Book 6, ed. Thomas P. Roche (New York: Penguin, 1987), VI. xii. 40 (1023).

[70]See Edward Lucie-Smith's *Eroticism in Western Art* (New York: Praeger Publishers, 1972), Chap. 9.

century England.[71] According to Leonard Barkan, at least two of the queen's residences presented pictorial representations of the myth.[72] The Petrarchan sonnet sequence, then, condenses the culture's absorption of the logic of voyeurism and metamorphosis, a widespread thematic that informed virtually all the symbolic forms of the period.

It was not unusual for literary works to offer intricate and involved narrative descriptions of voyeuristic moments.[73] Sidney's *Arcadia* and Shakespeare's *Rape of Lucrece* present two such moments, significant because these representations self-consciously allegorize the relationships between reader and writer as the text circulates. In the *Arcadia* we see the how a character's act of spying becomes related to the descriptive Petrarchan blazon that he composes.[74] Because Pyrocles has cross-dressed as the Amazon Zelmane precisely in order to gain entrance into the home of Philoclea, his presence at the ladies' bath in this particular scene bespeaks the more general trespasses he undertakes throughout the work. Zelmane's disguise allows her/him to be admitted into restrictive female spaces, including the private site where the ladies bathe, "a place upon pain of death as nobody durst presume to come thither" (285). While watching Philoclea and the other women disrobe, Zelmane is moved to pick up a lute and fashion a lyrical song. Sidney's contextualization of the blazon lends striking force to Vickers's argument about the psychodynamics of the Diana-Actaeon myth —its connection both to voyeurism and the fragmenting impulses it plays out through the poetic blazon. Sidney clearly suggests that the song is the product of the hero's agitation at the sight of his naked beloved: "Zelmane . . . was taken with such a quivering that she thought it more wisdom to lean herself to a tree and look on, while Miso and Mopsa, like a couple of foreswat melters, were getting the pure silver of their bodies out of the ure of their garments" (285); "Zelmane . . . had the coals of her affection so kindled with wonder and blown with delight that now all her parts grudged that her eyes should do more homage than they to the princess of them"

---

[71]Walter Davis discusses the myth's popularity and its appearance in numerous cultural forms in "Actaeon in Arcadia," *Studies in English Literature* 2 (1962): 95–110.

[72]Barkan argues that the myth had special import for Elizabeth who becomes represented as the virtuous woman surrounded by overly ambitious and imprudent courtiers such as Essex ("Diana and Actaeon," 333).

[73]In *Milton's Spenser: The Politics of Reading* (Ithaca: Cornell University Press, 1983), Maureen Quilligan discusses the Faunus episode in the Mutability Canto as a rewriting of the Diana-Actaeon myth (166–69).

[74]Philip Sidney, *The Countess of Pembroke's Arcadia* (1590), ed. Maurice Evans (New York: Penguin, 1984), bk. 2, 285–95. In "Actaeon in Arcadia," Davis suggests that the myth is the key to reading Gynecia's attempted seduction of Pyrocles in the cave scene. This episode not only foregrounds the collision of art and nature within a scene of prohibition and desire, but it also offers a parody of the Diana-Actaeon confrontation.

(287). When overwhelmed by the illicit sight of the women's naked splashing bodies, Zelmane composes a song that inventories his beloved's anatomical parts, poetically cataloging Philoclea from head to toe for 150 lines. This poem tellingly opens and closes with a question: "What tongue can her perfections tell, / In whose each part all pens may dwell?" Zelmane's verse doubly indicates the linkage between sexuality and writing, both in his overly elaborate and highly fetishized description of Philoclea's body and in his initial association of poetic ineffability with phallic possession. Sidney clearly associates obsession concerning the woman's displayed "parts" with Zelmane's covert and anxiety-ridden act of voyeurism. What is enacted throughout the sonnets is dramatized quite vividly in this episode of the *Arcadia*: the readerly gaze is invested with criminality. We hear a lengthy description of the women's disrobing, we are told that no one enters this spot on pain of death, and we understand Philoclea's translation into poetry as a repetition of a prohibited sight.

Zelmane's discovery of another male character, Amphialus, lying secretly nearby in the woods doubles the anxiety that undergirds the scene. Confronting a mirrored version of himself caught in the act of violation, Zelmane disingenuously warns Amphialus of the impropriety of spying on women. In the subsequent fight between them, Zelmane symbolically castrates Amphialus when he punishes him for his infraction by stabbing him in the thigh. The doubling of identities in the Diana-Actaeon myth and the potential violence that results from that doubling thus becomes triangulated. Amphialus suffers the bodily wound for Zelmane, whose disguise protects him from full censure. Interestingly, this entire confrontation between the Actaeon figures comes to the fore because Amphialus's dog steals a glove and a piece of paper from the women, thereby exposing his hidden stance in the woods. In light of the fact that voyeurism figures publication in the culture, it seems appropriate that the illicit transference of a private text from the royal ladies to a then-unknown gentleman becomes a crucial part of this confrontation. The paper is endowed with intimacy because it is paired with the glove, which was a typical love token.[75] Amphialus's illicit vision is represented synedochically in this scene through the slip of paper that has scandalously been taken beyond its acceptable place.

[75]The illicit nature of the letter is heightened by its alliance with Philoclea's glove, a piece of intimate clothing, which, as Richard Barnfield's sonnet to the glove indicates, can act as a token of love or a permission for erotic advances. Sonnet 14 states: "If thou from glove do'st take away the g, / Then glove is love; and so I send it thee." *The Poems of Richard Barnfield* (London: Fortune Press, 1936), 63. See also Tarquin's encounter with Lucrece's glove as an analogue for his intended rape (Shakespeare, *The Rape of Lucrece*, in *The Complete Works*, 316–29); and "To his love from whom he hadd her gloves," no. 56 in *Tottels Miscellany*.

As in Nashe's preface, the secret domain of writing is here associated with female privacy. Sidney aligns the scandal of a man's forbidden access into an eroticized female cloister with the sudden publication of a private text. As in the prefaces, a social boundary is defined in terms of its gendered demarcations of private and public. This scene was interestingly absent in the *Old Arcadia*, which was never published.[76]

The *Arcadia* demonstrates how the culturally popular scene of transgressive viewing played within the agon of public/private. Actaeon's offense is here decriminalized, covered over by Zelmane's disguise and by the women's subsequent pardon of the spying Amphialus. The scene does, nevertheless, suggest that a moment of scandal and deception constitutes the blazon (meaning both a specific descriptive technique and the broader act of publishing and displaying). Amphialus, acting as a double for Zelmane, absorbs the potential punishment that can be leveled against the Actaeon-like transgressor. In representing this scene, Sidney magnifies and overstates the anxieties of public display that are articulated in the prefaces. Authors and printers, after all, were not literally castrated for their public representations, and readers were asked only to imagine themselves as vicarious intruders. The scene is striking, however, in revealing how the Diana-Actaeon myth could be reconfigured within sixteenth-century narrative to address the more historically specific concerns of lyric blazoning and textual transmission within its amalgam of the broader issues of gazing, trespass, metamorphosis, and destabilized identity.

In *The Rape of Lucrece*, Shakespeare goes to greater lengths to establish a connection between publication and sexual shame as he forces the reader to be complicitous in encroaching on private feminized territory. In this narrative poem, Shakespeare projects the anxieties of writing and display onto the reader both formally and thematically. *The Rape of Lucrece* strikingly stages the unauthorized trafficking of the sexual and the textual. It provides an access point for seeing how publication is bound up with illicit see-

---

[76]In the *Old Arcadia*, a coterie manuscript not published until 1911, this poem is introduced at the end of Book 3 as Pyrocles is about to consummate his relationship with Philoclea. In the revised and published *Arcadia*, the love song no longer marks the site of shared sexuality between hero and heroine, but instead is displaced onto a scene in which it is associated with voyeurism. While the revision was certainly intended to cleanse the text of the lovers' moral indiscretion and while we don't know if Sidney intended the revised version to be published, I want to think about the possibility that the different status of the texts (for a more private viewing or more public) affected this specific representation. When Fulke Greville edited and published the work after Sidney's death, he suggested that the revised work, rather than the first text, was obviously more appropriate for a public audience. Both Greville and Mary Sidney judged the revised version to be more appropriate for print. Regardless of Sidney's intentions, the revised *Arcadia* marked its public function in a way that made it amenable for public consumption.

ing, erotic display, and sexual guilt. In *Lucrece*, Shakespeare offers commentary on the pervasive verbal associations and tropes that publishers and writers used in introducing printed works to the public.

As Vickers has demonstrated, the rhetoric of display is crucial in determining Lucrece's fate. Vickers argues cogently that the poem both exposes the mediatory function of the woman in Petrarchan rhetoric, and reveals the consequences for Lucrece of being female matter for male oratory: "Rape is the price Lucrece pays for being described" ("'The blazon of sweet beauty's best,'" 102). Vickers's reading allows us to understand why Shakespeare changed his source to heighten Collatine's complicity in his wife's rape. It is the "name of chaste" (spoken by Collatine) that inflames Tarquin's desire. In the first lines of the poem, the narrator indicts Collatine explicitly for telling what he should have kept secret:

> . . . why is Collatine the publisher
> Of that rich jewel he should keep unknown
> From thievish ears, because it is his own?[77]

Collatine's unwitting publication of his "jewel" makes Lucrece the exchanged object of speech between men. This unwise description haunts the remainder of the poem, surfacing in Tarquin's thoughts as he marches toward Lucrece's bed and infecting the narrator's description of events.[78] Through the attention that he places on Collatine's initial bragging, Shakespeare makes Lucrece an emblem of the dangers and pleasures of circulation itself. It is no wonder that the publisher of *Gorboduc* referred specifically to Lucrece when he narrated his work's shameful entry into the public sphere. Lucrece was an apt metaphor for the danger of display itself.

After attributing Tarquin's motivation to Collatine's "publication" of his wife's body, the poem goes on to meditate broadly on the problems bound up with narration, fame, rumor, slander, and public language. Tarquin, when debating with himself over whether or not to commit the rape, is

---

[77]Shakespeare, *The Rape of Lucrece*, 1544–66, lines 33–35. Subsequent references are to line numbers.

[78]The poem makes Collatine's speech into a critical event: Tarquin views Lucrece through the lens of her husband's language, noticing the heraldry in her face when he first meets her and then seeing her colors of red and white when he views her sleeping body before the rape (256). In the representation of the Trojan War that Lucrece interprets, Sinon is described in these same terms: the traitor emblemizes the heraldic red and white that is a sign of Collatine's unwise construction of Lucrece. In the final scene, Collatine bathes his face in Lucrece's blood, thus producing a mixture of red and white on his own skin; he ironically becomes his own descriptive language. The entire text, then, dilates on Collatine's opening words, which are rehearsed in the final moments of the poem—his boasts become literalized on his own flesh.

haunted by the stubborn problem of reputation, the possible disgraceful stories that could stain his genealogy: "Yea, though I die, the scandal will survive, / And be an eyesore in my golden coat" (204–5). By attempting to convince Lucrece to submit to him, Tarquin translates his own fears of scandal into a tactic of persuasion. His argument here squarely rests on the importance of reputation, for he threatens to slander Lucrece and disgrace all her kinsmen: "And thou, the author of their obloquy," he threatens, "Shalt have thy tre[s]pass cited up in rhymes, / And sung by children in succeeding times" (523–5). If Lucrece resists, she will be slandered; if she acquiesces, she can buy her privacy. "But if thou yield," Tarquin states, "I rest thy secret friend" (526). In offering Lucrece the choice of being infamous or violated, Tarquin reiterates the association between speaking and desire that motivated him to commit his offense. Collatine's previous speech had threatened Lucrece's chastity simply by making her the object of public representation. Whether housed within the enclosed or permeable body, in the terms that Peter Stallybrass has suggested of idealized womanhood in the Renaissance, Lucrece's desirability powerfully figures the dangers of circulation.[79] This highly rhetorical poem is clearly suspicious of the dangers posed by rhetoric and language; that suspicion is cast in terms of rhetoric's link to sexual violation.

After the rape, Lucrece meditates on the intricacies of fame and shame as she tells the personified Night that her blemish will become publicly visible. "Make me not object to the tell-tale Day," she begins:

> The light will show, character'd in my brow,
> The story of sweet chastity's decay,
> The impious breach of holy wedlock vow.
> Yea, the illiterate, that know not how
>   To cipher what is writ in learned books,
>   Will quote my loathsome trespass in my looks.
>   (806–12)

Lucrece's fears that her rape is already published on her very articulate flesh is followed by a fantasy in which she imagines herself as a shamed narrative: nurses will sing songs of her; orators will use her name for ornament. Having argued that Tarquin has made "fair reputation but a bawd" (621), she absorbs his fears about publicity. Lucrece casts her grievances in terms of the horrors of exposure and disclosure—shunning daybreak and read-

---

[79]Peter Stallybrass, "Patriarchal Territories: The Body Enclosed," in *Rewriting the Renaissance: The Discourses of Sexual Difference in Early Modern Europe*, ed. Margaret W. Ferguson, Maureen Quilligan, and Nancy J. Vickers (Chicago: University of Chicago Press, 1986), 123–42.

ability, those things that make the private public. If Collatine unwisely made his wife a publicized text, Lucrece conjures up a worse fate by imagining herself as a highly readable tale of shame. In her view, the rape has made her eminently quotable: reading is associated with the detection of scandal.

Lucrece was Shakespeare's second publication and one of his few known premeditated forays into the world of print. In shifting from the sphere of theater to that of print, Shakespeare interestingly chooses to narrate a tale that fixates on a sexual shame and betrayal that is everywhere linked to dangerous speech. The well-known narrative of Lucrece's defilement provides a vehicle for meditating on the vexed problems surrounding public writing, particularly the problem of negotiating between the public and private. *Lucrece* reveals an uneasiness about textual display and circulation, and it initiates readers into an understanding of that uneasiness by making them complicitous to those illicit sights. Through the structure of the text, Shakespeare positions the reader as Tarquin, who slowly makes his way in the first part of the poem toward Lucrece's vulnerable bed. The penetration of her body begins rhetorically as Tarquin moves through the house —journeying rapaciously toward an interior through various barriers. He marches past "the locks between her chamber and his will," encountering obstacles—locks, the wind, the glove—that impede his progress. He chooses to interpret these obstacles as temporary setbacks that only enhance his desire (302). When the narrator states, "and with his knee the door he opens wide" (359), it becomes embarrassingly clear that the journey through the house constitutes an architectural rape. The reader thus is drawn into participating in this imitation rape through the structure of narrative movement itself.

The reader first encounters Lucrece through the eyes of the spying Tarquin. In describing how she is "admir'd of lewd unhallowed eyes," the narrator implies that Lucrece is subject to both the rapist's and our own readerly gaze (392). Indeed, the narrator lingers over the site of the sleeping, corpselike Lucrece for one hundred lines, sustaining a gaze that the text emphatically curses and denounces. Because Tarquin and the narrator begin to share puns, on "color," for instance, the rapist's consciousness consumes the work and becomes the overarching lens through which the action is presented. All structural elements—narrator, character, and reader— blend into a voyeur, who tiptoes quietly toward Lucrece's bed. Ian Donaldson points out that traditional Renaissance pictorial versions of the story highlight the voyeurism within the legend by both aligning the viewer's gaze with the fully clothed Tarquin, who watches the naked Lucrece, and including a servant, who watches the action from behind a curtain. When Lucrece complains to Daybreak after the rape—"O eye of eyes, / Why pry'st thou through my window? Leave thy peeping"—she merely calls our attention to the acts of spying, tattling, peeking, and exposing that the story has implicitly dramatized throughout, an undercurrent that is drawn out more explicitly in the pictorial versions of the myth (1088–89).[80] Lucrece could well be reprimanding the reader who has also become privy to the private sight of her sleeping body.

After the rape, the story shifts to the consciousness of Lucrece, and the reader's position as Tarquin-like voyeur is realigned to reveal the consequences of the former view. In Lucrece's complaints, we are reminded of the effects of this horrendous violation and her fear of its being publicly narrated. She complains to Opportunity that "Thy secret pleasure turns to open shame, / Thy private feasting to a public fast, / Thy smoothing titles to a ragged name" (892). Her words articulate an anxiety that is partially realized within the context of the poem itself. After all, the poem exposes her "open shame" to public view. We participate in a narrative that not only casts the reader as a violator, but also translates the secret of that violation into an "open shame" through its poetic account. As Coppélia Kahn notes, the central metaphor in this poem is the stain, and that stain becomes linked to the criminality of telling the tale. Consuming the text of *Lucrece*, then, involves a necessary alliance with the unstable textual dynamic of transgression, desire, and violence. The reader is indicted as an unwanted listener and spy, for Shakespeare's text expressly identifies itself as the future story that Lucrece fears. Until the 1616 edition, the text was simply called *Lucrece*. This original title produces a darker version of the effect created by the titles of the sonnet sequences: the reader grasps a book that is personified as a raped maiden, whose violation stems from her rhetorical objectification and wrongful "publication" to Tarquin by her "owner." While the last scene in the text goes far in redeeming the act of publication, it does not erase the troubling associations that the entire poem establishes between sexual shame and public display.[81]

The mythical figure of Lucrece, I suggest, stands as a sign for the sexual/

---

[80]See Ian Donaldson, *The Rapes of Lucretia: A Myth and Its Transformations* (Oxford: Clarendon Press, 1982). For a fascinating analysis of how textual materiality and representations of the story of Lucrece fit into the development of European humanism, see Stephanie Jed, *Chaste Thinking*.

[81]The problem of guilty publication is rewritten in the last scene, when the overthrow of the usurper is predicated on another act figured as publication. After the men vow revenge, they carry Lucrece's corpse through the city "to show her bleeding body through Rome, / And so to publish Tarquin's foul offense" (1851–52). The husband's guilty publication of the woman is redeemed through this rehearsal of language; exposure becomes the means for political and sexual purification. Kahn and Vickers both comment on the repeated male rivalry in the final scene that complicates a reading of this purification.

symbolic economy of the world of print. Within the logic that Joel Fineman sees as central to the poem, Collatine's description of his wife is both an allowance and a forebearance: "Collatine unwisely did not let / To praise the clear unmatched red and white" of Lucrece's beauty, the narrator states (10–11).[82] As Tarquin points out when he stumbles across the hindrances that block him from the object of his desire, such obstacles generate pleasure precisely by their seeming prohibition:

> . . . these lets attend the time,
> Like little frosts that sometime threat the spring,
> To add a more rejoicing to the prime.
>
> (330–32)

If Collatine's "let" of publication inaugurates Tarquin's rapacious desire and sets into motion a chain of violence, it also figures the perverse way in which exposure to public view becomes conceptualized in this poem and in the culture at large. Collatine whets Tarquin's appetite precisely by constructing an enticing prohibition. After all, he has bragged not only about his wife's beauty, but also her chastity. Like Collatine's description itself, Lucrece functions as a "let" for Tarquin. The poem thus calls our attention to the tremendous dangers of representing "texts" in ways that construct them as inviting transgressions. While Shakespeare self-consciously critiques the potential violation of publication and its concomitant production of shame, his critique acts as a "let" that simultaneously allows and forebears its own production. That is, the poem's narrative strategy relies on the reader's absorption into the dynamic that it criticizes. Shakespeare allegorically situates his poem as a work beyond the rhetoric of exposure, yet one that depends on that very rhetoric as a way of managing its place in the economy of published material books. After all, he has repeated Collatine's unwise decision to publish the text of *Lucrece*. Giving the text her name extends that ominous engagement to the reader.

If Shakespeare comments in this poem on the complexity of the erotic figurations that name public writing, he also creates a narrative that merely plays out a set of common verbal associations that stigmatize printed works. To be "pressed," as Renaissance texts suggest, is to "play the ladies part," to undergo the "press" of the male body during sexual intercourse. Published texts are thus already gendered: the page is encoded as feminine while the

---

[82]Joel Fineman argues that the poem configures Shakespeare's unique signature through its construction of a complex system of readerly resistances and allowances. The ambiguous status of the "let" is important in his argument. "Shakespeare's *Will*: The Temporality of Rape," *Representations* 20 (Fall 1987): 25–76.

machinery of the press, the writer, and the ink are depicted as masculine. These gendered codes become the subject of numerous bawdy jokes and allusions in the sixteenth century. Textual impressionability is always already scandalized. The printed page is always a fallen woman because it is, by definition, highly public and common. If the character Lucrece complains about her reputation and fall, she offers a complaint that speaks as well to her status as a book object pressed in the shop and publicly displayed within the marketplace. When publishers and writers create prefaces that elaborately construct the text's shameful entry into the public, they play out the bawdy connotations of the act of "pressing." Therefore, it is not surprising that so many prefaces use the narrative of female fall and redemption to explain their works' perilous journey in the socially unsanctioned world of print.

Social Privacy

Writers and publishers figured the class problems of publication by constructing a highly gendered rhetoric of disclosure. By sexualizing reading, writers overshadowed and recoded the trespass of class boundaries that printing seemed to foster. In this sense, the bizarre prefatorial disclaimers and eroticized prefatorial images were designed to forestall the crumbling of social distinctions. The writer represented the act of reading as a voyeuristic impulse to divert the spotlight from his own hazardous position in print. In this way, socially distinct writers and readers could exchange information and stories in the space of the text without authorizing such blending. The book as a physical object marked a site of exchange, but the book's presentation of itself reconstructed the barriers between those worlds by reformulating, in terms of gender, the unauthorized nature of textual circulation and its social transgression. In the late sixteenth century, a rhetoric of shame was constructed as a means of managing and organizing anxieties about the breakdown of social hierarchy. This rhetoric became embroiled in the Diana-Actaeon myth and its staging of illicit viewing. Thus, voyeurism was a trope that mediated a complex set of cultural anxieties.

The language of disclosure was often riddled with an indiscriminately gendered sexuality. We can think of Nashe's bizarre mixing of female and male sexuality when he described the swelling of the private text into the public sphere. More frequently, however, this erotically charged dynamic took on specific gendered coordinates, for it largely turned on the analogy of the female body as text. The sex of that body was crucial to this idiom because the trafficked woman could consolidate the largely male group that made up book readers. But the female body was more important because the idealized woman was by nature more private. Modesty, containment, and silence defined the traits of the paradigmatic virtuous Renaissance woman (Stallybrass, "Patriarchal Territories"). Queen Elizabeth's rally to the troops on the eve of the Armada's invasion, which conflated her sex's insularity with the security of her nation's borders, depended on this cultural ideal. Conduct books typically underscored the woman's privatization and domestic enclosure in language that makes sense of *Gorboduc*'s presentation of the unauthorized text as wanton. In *My Ladies Looking Glasse* (1616), Barnabe Rich argues that a good woman, as defined by Solomon, "should be a home housewife": "shee must looke to her children, her servants and family: but the pathes of a harlot . . . are mooveable, for now shee is in the house, now in the streetes, now she lieth in waite in every corner, she is still gadding from place to place . . . shee is ever more wandring: her feete are wandring from place to place, from person to person, from companie to company: from custome to custome."[83] Rich's equation of harlotry with public movement echoes the language of Renaissance prefaces, which describe the "wandring" of the text in terms of its sexual degradation. The doubleness within the representation of femininity, then, makes the woman a useful figure for expressing these transgressive authorizations. The harlot, like the enclosed maiden, was crucial to the articulation of social circulation and containment in general. Serving as an inverse of the idealized female body, the harlot could encode the problems involved when a previously elite private discourse moved into the public arena, when it was allowed to wander "gadding from place to place." In order to represent powerfully the text's entry into the public sphere, writers drew on the modesty and the lack of public exposure stereotypically associated with femininity. The publication of the shy male text would not have been as disruptive or culturally fraught.

Within the titillating rhetoric of disclosure, the subject positions of both reader and author become coded as male. The trope of the female body is used to describe the stakes involved in publishing "private" books, and that use creates a perception of writers and readers as embarrassed men who spy on the objects of their desire. Of course, throughout literary history, the "feminine" has served as a vehicle through which male psychocultural anxieties are expressed. What we see in the sixteenth century is one specific configuration of this dynamic, in which the general anxieties of writing become particularized into the social anxieties of printing. Henry Constable comments on this very process in *Diana*. Here the speaker describes

---

[83]Barnabe Rich, *My Ladies Looking Glasse*, STC 20991.7 (1616), 43. Patricia Parker discusses Rich's passage in a different context in *Literary Fat Ladies*, 105.

the creation of love poetry as a Promethean theft that metamorphoses feminine beauty into male desire:

> Prometheus for stealing living fire
> From heaven's king, was judged eternal death
>
> . . .
>
> So I, for stealing living beauty's fire
> Into my verse, that it may always live;
> And change his forms to shapes of my desire.
>
> (Fifth Decade, X)

The creation of poetry, aligned here with theft, is strangely portrayed as an event prior to the erotic alliance, which appears to be a product of that violation. The speaker is caught in a hellish punishment of his own making, burning in love because he has dared to subject his beloved to poetic form. Constable's depiction of sonnet writing as a transgressive act of appropriation unwittingly points to the larger network of desire and repulsion that surrounded the creation and packaging of printed poetry. Writing was represented as a shameful act both within the poems and in the way in which their status as material objects was defined within the literary marketplace. Constable's poem interestingly frames the violation of writing as a theft of the "feminine" that is made to serve the artist's purposes.

In recent years, critics have written about the significance of the Renaissance woman as a crucial trope for mediating cultural disruptions, particularly those that involved social mobility.[84] The "gadding" and unstable harlot was a convenient figure for absorbing many of the culture's concerns about change itself. While the analogy of the text as an unruly woman functioned as a barrier against the breakdown of social boundaries, this figure was also used to shield the culture from the overwhelming power of representation itself. A host of activities and objects suddenly multiplied and were made visible throughout the social world as the affordability of printing inaugurated an era of disclosure. The outburst of "how-to" manuals made previously invisible segments of society highly visible. Mundane

---

[84]To mention just a few: Leonard Tennenhouse reads the aristocratic female body as marking the terrain of blood lineage and thus the entire property of the nobility (*Power on Display: The Politics of Shakespeare's Genres* [New York: Methuen, 1986]); Jean Howard shows that Renaissance fears of theatricality often focused on women's ability to mimic identity, specifically with regard to face painting ("Renaissance Antitheatricality and the Politics of Gender and Rank in *Much Ado About Nothing*," in *Shakespeare Reproduced: The Text in History & Ideology*, ed. Jean Howard and Marion F. O'Connor [New York: Methuen, 1987], 163–87, especially 168–72); and Peter Stallybrass argues that the female body, the home, and social place used interchangeable figures of permeability ("Patriarchal Territories: The Body Enclosed").

processes, such as cooking, leather-making, and limning, suddenly became worthy of representation and multiple reproduction. Prosaic parts of daily life became objects of wonder: the gear, the pulley, the spinner. The many medical treatises that circulated allowed people to peer into the workings of the human body, to see blood pumping from chamber to chamber. These texts were billed as the instigators of grand revelations; they boasted titles that foregrounded the revelatory nature of their information or the secretive nature of their subject: *The treasury of commodious conceits and hidden Secretes and may be called the good huswives closet; The ladies cabinet opened: wherein is found experiments in preserving, cookery and huswifery; A Closet for Ladies and Gentlewomen.*[85] The language of disclosure emerged in all types of texts. When George Gascoigne described the wars in the Netherlands, he recounted the horrors of mutilated bodies in the terms of an exposé: "some their head and shoulders burnt of," he wrote, "so that you might looke down into the bulk and brest and there take an Anatomy of the secrets of nature."[86] In Gascoigne's words, the mutilated body afforded a means of finding secret and hidden views. This passage reveals a lurid fascination with revelation; the scene is an obscene parody of medical texts like the *Fabrica*, which unveiled the human body's interior to the public.

The outcry against the printing of special information suggests that some people in the culture were concerned about the revelation of such information to the "un-elite": "Secretes of phisicke ought not to bee participated unto the common sorte," one writer of a medical tract reported that others said, "but onely knowne of such as be professors of the arte."[87] There were similar protests against the translation of classics into the vernacular: "What should Plinie . . . bee read in English, and the mysteries couched in his books divulged?"[88] If translation demystified these mysteries, printing cheapened them further. Interestingly, these reports of dissent were reproduced by the very publishers who had divulged such mysteries to the public. In other words, publishers often claimed special privilege precisely by boasting about the ways in which printed books overcame vast odds as they dramatically faced down opponents of learning and knowledge. Many of the ballads, poems, plays, and pamphlets of the period also represented

---

[85]John Partridge, *The treasury of commodious conceits and hidden Secretes and may be called the good huswives closet*, STC 19427 (1584); Anonymous, *The ladies cabinet opened: wherein is found experiments in preserving, cookery and huswifery*, STC 15119 (1639); *A closet for Ladies and Gentlewomen*, STC 5434 (1602).

[86]George Gascoigne, *The Spoyle of Antwerp*, STC 11644 (1577).

[87]Leonard Mascall, *Prepositas his Practise*, STC 17977 (1588), sig. A2. Quoted by Bennett, *English Books and Readers, 1558–1603*, 180.

[88]Philemon Holland's introduction to Pliny, *The Historie of the World*, STC 20029 (1601), sig. 3ᵛ.

their appearance in print as extraordinary and revelatory; they claimed to be able to unfold a new world for their readers.

In the narrowest sense, what was threatening to unfold was a firm sense of class barriers. As printing pushed the boundaries of a highly circumscribed manuscript culture into the more democratic marketplace, books worked "too lay foorth things plainlie . . . too the understanding of many" rather than "indyt[ing] things curyously too the pleasing of a fewe."[89] In doing so, publication responded to the increasing social mobility evident in the culture. As Wallace MacCaffrey notes, "In the intensely rank-conscious world of late Tudor England there was an increasing scramble to cross the dividing line which separated gentlemen . . . from the mere yeoman or freeholder."[90] And, of course, there was equal energy spent in trying to ward off that encroachment. Published material in its very format ironically testifies to this social blending. In poetical miscellanies, for example, the poems of pamphleteers sit closely and familiarly with those of the nobility. Frances Davison's defense of this mingling in his introduction to *A Poetical Rhapsody* indicates that this blending of classes was viewed as a threat: "If any except against the mixing . . . of diverse thinges written by great and learned Personages, with our means and worthles Scriblings, I utterly disclaime it, a being done by the Printer" (5). The preface to *England's Helicon* defends against this intermeshing as well: "if any man whatsoever, in prizing of his owne birth or fortune, shall take in scorne, that a far meaner man in the eye of the world shal be placed by him, I tell him plainly . . . that mans wit is set by his, not that man by him."[91] Apparently, the text itself stood as an embarrassing evidence of the disintegration of social borders. One way of controlling and harnessing this social flux was by introducing texts according to an "aesthetics of transgression"—a term connected with the avant-garde pornographic fictions of this century.[92] If the language of

[89]Henry Golding, preface to *The Psalmes of David and Others*, STC 2389 (1591), sig.*5.

[90]Wallace MacCaffrey, introduction to William Camden, *History of the Most Renowned and Victorious Princess Elizabeth* (Chicago: University of Chicago Press, 1970), xiii–xiv. Cited by Frank Whigham, "Interpretation at Court: Courtesy and the Performer-Audience Dialectic," *New Literary History* 14 (1983): 624.

[91]"To the Reader, If Indifferent," in *England's Helicon*, ed. Arthur Bullen (London: Lawrence and Bullen, 1899), 6.

[92]Susan Suleiman discusses the "aesthetics of transgression" in "Pornography, Transgression, and the Avant-Garde: Bataille's *Story of the Eye*," in *The Poetics of Gender*, ed. Nancy K. Miller (New York: Columbia University Press, 1986), 117–36. Bound up with the sense of voyeuristic reading is a sense of writing as an act of cross-dressing, as Juliet Fleming describes in "*The French Garden*: An Introduction to Women's French," *ELH* 56 (1989): 19–51. Fleming notes that *The French Garden*, written specifically for women, is a "cross-dressed text"; "that is, although it seems to offer itself to women, and is, as it were, dressed as a woman, in other ways it is a male text, designed specifically for the enjoyment of men. . . . It sets out

disclosure enabled the public to perceive, in the broadest sense, the mechanisms of culture that suddenly became objects of representation, it also spoke specifically to the social permeability print seemed to promise.

While emblem books interpret the Diana-Actaeon myth variously (most frequently, perhaps, as a struggle between the forces of reason and passion), Abraham Fraunce reads the myth as concerned with establishing and overreaching limits: "We ought not to be over curious and inquisitive in spying and prying into those matter which be above our reache, lest we be rewarded as Actaeon was."[93] Fraunce's "moral" tells us that the myth speaks to concerns about the breakdown and reinforcement of set areas of prohibition. George Sandys's edition of Ovid reinforces this reading by particularizing the matter "above our reache" into the female figure of the queen: "this fable was invented to shew us how dangerous a curiosity it is to search into the secrets of Princes or by chance to discover their nakedness."[94] According to Sandys, the tale proves the barrier between royalty and the rest of the realm. The political as well as personal "secrets" of the monarch are represented as fleshly nakedness. Sandys's interpretative gloss is highly eroticized and politicized: one should not dis-cover (undress) the queen or search into her "secrets" (open her case to the world).[95] Barkan comments on this politicized reading when he documents the vast and contradictory range of interpretations given to the myth. "What was forbidden knowledge of the gods," Barkan states, "becomes (very logically) espionage" (328).[96] Actaeon, according to this gloss, is a typical Renaissance

---

to create and display the language of female separatism, which it grounds in the domestic scene. Then, perhaps for no reason other than that it is specifically female, women's French immediately becomes the object of erotic interest" (19). In her catalog of books written for women, Suzanne Hull includes texts that allow men to possess the female domain of domesticity. In one pamphlet, for instance, the male author claims that although he has never actually cooked, he is qualified to write a book of recipes. Through such books, male writers could cross-dress, discursively entering a private, demarcated space of femininity. *Chaste, Silent, and Obedient: English Books for Women, 1475-1640* (San Marino, Cal.: Huntington Library Press, 1982).

[93]Abraham Fraunce, *The Third Part of the Countess of Pembrokes Yvychurch, Entitled Amintus Dale* (1592), fol. 43ʳ.

[94]George Sandys, trans. *Ovids Metamorphosis Englished, Mythologiz'd and Represented in Figures* (Oxford: I. Lichfield, 1632), ed. Karl K. Hulley and Stanley Vandersall (Lincoln: University of Nebraska Press, 1970), 151.

[95]Jonathan Goldberg brilliantly outlines the construction of state secrets. He notes that Robert Filmer opens his *Patriarcha* by disclaiming that he "meddle[s] with mysteries of the present state. Such arcana imperii, or cabinet councils, the vulgar may not pry into." *James I and the Politics of Literature: Jonson, Shakespeare, Donne, and Their Contemporaries* (Baltimore: Johns Hopkins University Press, 1983; reprint, Stanford: Stanford University Press, 1989), 85. See 55-112 for a discussion of the collision of private, state, and public.

[96]Ovid himself used the plight of Actaeon to describe the alienation he felt when ban-

overreacher, but one who enacts a highly sexualized version of the crime. While there are numerous myths that condemn overreaching—those of Prometheus, Icarus, Pandora, Adam and Eve—Actaeon's story is distinguished by its sexual dimension. In these readings of Ovid, seeking knowledge above one's class is an act of voyeurism, an intrusion into upper-class flesh.

Buried within the strange language of the prefaces—within metaphors such as the one Nashe evokes in his preface to *Astrophel and Stella*—we find a clue to the bizarre illustration that announces the *Fabrica* by making readers into voyeurs of a female corpse. The resonant image of an editor wielding his phallic picklock to pry into ladies' casks and release private poetry to a "violent enlargement" "opens" the text in more than one sense. As Patricia Parker suggests, opening the closed text is a kind of "dilation," a term similarly fraught with sexual meanings.[97] Given that Nashe's language suggests that the "Ladyes casks, & the president bookes" are wedged open with a phallic pen, then the dilation of the text may also be its publication—its multiplication and amplification as it extends and becomes violently larger. The female body is used to "open" the text by way of a preface.

As public writing and illustration exposed, stripped away, and uncovered the most secret parts of the body, home, and political enclave, the culture sought a vocabulary that could mediate the shock of that release, the "violent enlargement" of both social circles and literary readership. In reading these prefaces, we see that a vocabulary was discovered in a sexually laden language of transgression. This language finds its most popular and intense literary expression in the sonnet sequence, a form intricately connected to the anxieties of desire and display. It is remarkable but not inexplicable, then, that a female cadaver could become a marketing strategy. The public dissection of the woman's body employed in publicly announcing this new text was merely one example of the widespread erotics of commodification that constructed Renaissance publication as an enticing and dangerous cultural event.

---

ished for a political indiscretion. In the *Tristia*, he complains: "Why did I see anything? Why did I make my eyes guilty? Why was I so thoughtless as to harbour the knowledge of a fault? Unwitting was Actaeon when he beheld Diana unclothed: none the less he became the prey of his own hounds." *Tristia*, trans. Arthur Leslie Wheeler, Loeb Classical Library (Cambridge, Mass.: Harvard University Press, 1965), 2:103–6. Barkan cites this passage in "Diana and Actaeon," 321, n. 6.

97See Patricia Parker, "Shakespeare and Rhetoric: 'Dilation' and 'Delation' in *Othello*," in *Shakespeare and the Question of Theory*, 54–74.

CHAPTER FOUR

IMPERSONATING THE MANUSCRIPT:
Cross-Dressed Authors and Literary Pseudomorphs

> I am not he whom slaunderous tongues have tolde,
> (False tongues in dede, & craftie subtile braines)
> To be the man, which ment a common spoyle
> Of loving dames, whose eares wold heare my words
> Or trust the tales devised by my pen.
> I n'am a man, as som do thinke I am,
> (Laugh not good Lord) I am in dede a dame,
> Or at least a right Hermaphrodite.
> —George Gascoigne, *The Steele Glass*

THE 1590 *FAERIE QUEENE* boasts a curious and fascinating commendatory poem, one in which an unknown poet named W.L. compares Spenser's emergence into the public eye to Achilles' transformation from cross-dressed coward on Skyros to the martial hero of the Trojan War:

> When stout *Achilles* heard of *Helens* rape
> And what revenge the States of Greece devisd:
> Thinking by sleight the fatall warres to scape,
> In womans weedes him selfe he then disguisde:
> But this devise *Ulysses* soone did spy,
> And brought him forth, the chaunce of warre to try.
>
> When *Spencer* saw the same was spredd so large,
> Through Faery land of their renowned Queene:
> Loth that his Muse should take so great a charge,
> As in haughty matter to be seene,
> To seeme a shepheard then he made his choice,
> But *Sydney* heard him sing, and knew his voice.
>
> And as *Ulysses* brought faire Thetis sonne
> From his retyred life to menage armes:
> So *Spencer* was by *Sidneys* speaches wonne,
> To blaze her fame not fearing future harmes:

For well he knew, his Muse would soone by tyred
In her high praise, that all the world admired.

Yet as *Achilles* in those warlike frayes,
Did win the palme from all the *Grecian* Peeres:
So *Spencer* now to his immortall prayse,
Hath wonne the Laurell quite from all his feres.
What though his taske exceed a humaine witt,
His is excus'd, sith *Sidney* thought it fitt.[1]

While quite appropriately apologizing for Spenser's hubris in undertaking
the literary feat of writing an epic, this commendatory verse announces
the monumental *Faerie Queene* by asking readers to imagine the text through
an odd, perhaps inappropriate, set of images. Achilles serves as a problematic figure for poetic authority, despite the fact that the poet here evokes
and then suppresses Achilles' cowardice by rewriting the motivation for
disguise as simple humility. In this verse Achilles' fear is wittily translated
into Spenser's modesty. In depicting Spenser's career as a movement from
disguised shepherd to epic poet, W.L. inscribes poetic authority as contingent on acts of impersonation, acts that are unraveled by canny readers:
Ulysses spies Achilles' deception, while Sidney brings Spenser out of the
pastoral closet. The poet is created by a screen that paradoxically discloses
his talents and his "true" identity by first hiding his name and being. Spenser becomes an epic poet through games of pretense in which he, like
Achilles, generates a false identity (seeming a shepherd, as Achilles dressed
in "womans weedes") in order to cast off such masks at a later time.[2] By
calling to mind this legendary incident, the poet converts questions of
genre into those of gender. Spenser's cross-dressing, which in reality was
his indulgence in the humble otium of pastoral, becomes conflated with
the baseness of feminine disguise. The poem cleverly redefines this apparent transgression; it suggests that Spenser's embarrassing pastoral disguise
warrants more of an apology than his ambitious epic task does. As the
move from pastoral to epic *and* from anonymity to publicity are simultaneously cast as shifts from femininity to masculinity, the bravado of Spenser's

[1]Edmund Spenser, *The Faerie Queene*, ed. Thomas P. Roche (New York: Penguin, 1987),
21–22.

[2]Ovid's *Metamorphoses* is one text that describes Achilles' cross-dressing. This episode provides many of the key elements in the strategy of authorial presentation that this chapter
unfolds. In particular, the scene at Skyros dramatizes the affirmation of Achilles' "manhood,"
which is revealed by the instinctive way he grasps his shield while he is costumed as a woman.
Achilles gives away his identity when he chooses his weapon from a set of womanly trifles presented by Ulysses. This allusion is particularly resonant given the persistent representation of
courtiership and amateur love poetry as effeminizing, foppish trifles. (Trans. Mary M. Innes
[Harmondsworth: Penguin Books, 1955], book 13, lines 162–80, 289–90.)

writing comes to be associated with the assertion of correct gender.[3] In the last chapter, we saw that publication was glossed as an erotic disclosure to a voyeuristic public. Here the founding moment of authorship is troped through another "interested representation," this time in terms of an investiture and revelation that legitimates poetry by scandalizing and then descandalizing public writing.[4]

A second issue raised by this commendatory poem is the dimension of detection. In Ovid's *Metamorphoses*, Ulysses stakes a claim to Achilles' shield by telling how he wittily discovered Achilles' feminine disguise. As recounted in Arthur Golding's 1567 edition, Ulysses tests Achilles by baiting him to pick up his shield from a group of "womens tryflyng toyes."[5] Ulysses argues that he deserves the heralded shield primarily because his detection of Achilles' heroic "manly hart" beneath the feminine disguise

[3]Leonard Barkan gives a particularly compelling reading of how poets use the myth of Achilles' disguise to express buried anxieties about sexual and poetic authority. Barkan discusses how Dante's dream about Ganymede bleeds into the poet's identification with Achilles as he goes to Skyros: "The drama of sexual ambivalence, which has been completely suppressed in the Ganymede narrative, sneaks back in through the absent telos of the Achilles story." *Transuming Passion: Ganymede and the Erotics of Humanism* (Stanford: Stanford University Press, 1991), 66.

[4]I use the term "interested representation" in the way that Jean Howard and Marion F. O'Connor suggest in their introduction to *Shakespeare Reproduced: The Text in History & Ideology*, ed. Jean Howard and Marion F. O'Connor (New York: Methuen, 1987): "In speaking of 'interested' representations, we do not imply that there is a conscious conspiracy on the part of particular social groups to distort (misrepresent) reality through dramatic fictions. Rather, we mean that reality is knowable only through the discourses which mediate it, and that there is a constant, if subterranean, struggle over whose constructions of the real will gain dominance" (3).

[5]Foreknowing that her sonne shoule dye, The Lady Thetis hid
Achilles in a maydes attyre. By which fyne slyght shee did
All men deceyve, and Ajax too. This armour in a packe
With other womens tryflyng toyes I caryed on my backe,
A bayte too trye a manly hart. Appareld like a mayd
Achilles tooke the speare and sheeld in hand, and with them playd.
Then sayd I: O thou Goddesse sonne, why shouldst thou bee afrayd
Too raze great Troy, whoose overthrowe for thee is only stayd?

The .xv. Bookes of P. Ovidius Naso, entytuled Metamorphosis, translated oute of Latin into English meeter, by Arthur Golding, gentleman (1567), reprinted in *Shakespeare's Ovid*, ed. W. H. D. Rouse (London: Centaur Press, 1961), 256, xiii, lines 200–207.

spurred the hero into battle. Sidney is likewise presented as having recognized the true voice of the epic poet beneath Spenser's shepherd's weeds. Just as Ulysses argues that his detective work be rewarded, W.L. reciprocally nominates Sidney as the important precursor who legitimates Spenser's ambitious laureate status. Spenser writes because Sidney "thought it fitt." The poem's placement as a commendatory verse, however, tellingly constructs itself as a double in this process of detecting greatness. Because the inaugural moment of authorial fashioning is one of disguise and revelation, the smart reader knows to see past formal and thematic masquerades to recognize the value of the text. W.L.'s scripting of Spenser's career as the move from the feminine to the masculine simultaneously instructs the reader and lauds the power of knowledge itself. Images of the legendary feats of the battlefield become superimposed onto literary exploits, and the recognition of manliness becomes the reader's task. Both Sidney and W.L. are identified as model readers for those who venture into the confusing epic landscape of this romance. If Actaeon allegorized the practices of reading and writing in a culture suddenly conscious of the repercussions of public display, Achilles here allegorizes the evolution of the writer who casts off anonymity and emerges as a man in print. The true reader can appreciate that moment of authorial revelation: the disclosure of the author's "manly hart."

This mythologization obviously validates the authority of the Virgilian formal progression, which places pastoral at the bottom of a privileged career track. When the commending poet writes of Achilles' transformation, he wittily frames that myth in terms of the generic evolution charted by Virgil's model—from pastoral to georgic to epic. But the hierarchical progress that the poet charts also addresses the stubborn social problems surrounding the issue of publication: after pretending to be a lowly shepherd, Spenser now thrusts off a disempowered role and steps forth as an author. Through this analogy, the stigma attached to print undergoes a metamorphosis into a narrative of heroic possibility. The risk of becoming déclassé or downwardly mobile is reversed in this representation because the emergence into print is scripted as a movement away from a disempowered state rather than a fall into the common lot. That discredited status is curiously portrayed as femininity itself, a displacement that suppresses the class issues that made publishing socially hazardous in order to emphasize the highly gendered shame and redemption to which the great author can fall prey.

A raid of the classics was not the only response from writers and publishers when they sought to address the stigma of print. In addition to mythologizing and troping publication in various ways, writers also dealt with the move from manuscript to print by devising particular kinds of published forms. Coterie exchange, as I have described, was a mode of literary transmission that produced heterogeneous, collaborative, and socially oriented texts (see Chapter 1.) The commonplace book epitomizes this dimension of manuscript writing most clearly. We remember that in these private books readers designed their own texts by piecing together other people's circulating poems. By collecting, embellishing, and altering existing poetic works, as well as adding their own commendatory verses, marginalia, and answer poems, readers exerted their prerogative as editors. The works they produced offered an extreme form of the "open" texts seen in manuscript culture, works that were not governed by a central authority but instead characterized by a plurality of voices.

When gentlemanly writers began to find it advantageous to enter the public marketplace—if only to attract patrons—they found that the world of public authorship required new modes of authorization. If, as I have argued, writers negotiated their entrance into public circles by figuring publication in terms of sexual scandal, they also devised published forms that replicated the characteristics of manuscript works. It is certainly not surprising that early printed books looked like manuscript texts. After all, readers had set expectations when they approached books that did not disappear when print technology was founded or when it became more popular. But while books begin to take on a different character in response to the demands of the printshop, some writers self-consciously held on to and modified manuscript features in their literary works. These writers were not simply reproducing the vestiges of an older system of reading within a newer medium; instead, they played the competing modes of literary transmission against one another by carefully designing books that staged literary authority. In doing so, writers were able to capitalize on the familiarity of past forms but could bend them to new use in the process.

We might call these new forms "literary pseudomorphs." In *Technics and Civilization*, Lewis Mumford calls forth Oswald Spengler's concept of the cultural pseudomorph—an invention that retains the outward shape of the mechanism whose function it replaces—to denounce a culture's lack of imagination and its resistance to change. "New forces, activities, institutions, instead of crystallizing independently into their own appropriate forms, may creep into the structure of an existing civilization," Mumford explains.[6] Because the first car, for instance, retained some of the features of the horse and buggy, even though those features served no apparent purpose, it stands as a prime example of a cultural pseudomorph. Mumford sees this phenomenon as the result of a culture's dangerous and un-

---

[6]Lewis Mumford, *Technics and Civilization* (New York: Harcourt, Brace, 1934), 225.

acceptable reliance on obsolete thinking, mainly because these creations seem to be mindless reproductions of past cultural ideas. When Renaissance writers generated literary pseudomorphs by creating manuscript-identified printed texts, however, they did so not because they were trapped in an outdated mode of thinking. Instead, they created these forms consciously and with an eye to altering the culture's perception of the written work, a task demanded by the fact that the Renaissance culture did not offer a stable definition of literary authority for contemporary writers. The books that these writers designed thus bore a striking resemblance to those hand-scrawled bits of poetry passed among friends and acquaintances within the networks of the coterie. In the broadest sense, writers used these forms to impersonate the textuality of elite amateurism. By importing Mumford's notion of the pseudomorph into my discussion of the move from manuscript to print, I do not mean to imply that these published texts were inauthentic or unimaginative works formed in contradistinction to "true" kinds of writing. Rather, the operation of "seeming" (pseudo) becomes the very language through which writers imagined the design of "true" textual possibilities. The creation of pseudomorphs revealed a writer's vital interest in rethinking the authority of written books within an acceptable cultural language.

The commendatory poem to *The Faerie Queene* allegorizes this formal architectonics when it bizarrely names the move from anonymity to authorship—and thus from the manuscript-identified *Calender* to the grand epic—as a renunciation of transvestism, the move from the "seeming" to the real. The inauthentic entity in this representation comes to be represented by the feminine disguise that is overlaid onto Spenser's manuscript-like text. W.L. associates the falsity of womanly camouflage with Spenser's pseudomorphic pastoral, a text that was studiedly anonymous. Sidney was, of course, extraordinary in "hearing" Spenser's voice not only because it was disguised as a shepherd's, but also because Spenser's pastoral was not signed. In other words, his identity had to be revealed later publicly. This commendatory poem, then, helps us to unfold the complicated dynamic of literary pseudomorphs; for we can read texts by Spenser, Gascoigne, and Daniel as instances of how writers constructed manuscript forms from which they dramatized their entrance into the public sphere as authors. I am curious about how these formal disclosures helped to bring into being an extremely particularized conception of authorship, one that positioned authority by an appeal to gender difference. Therefore, I argue that when the introductory poem to *The Faerie Queene* suggests that Spenser's choice of epic genre constitutes a renunciation of his feminine disguise, it does not necessarily forge an eclectic association. Instead, its use of the Achilles myth merely offers a more explicit example of a general cultural strategy for "staging" the gender of public authorship.

In following *The Faerie Queene*'s conflation of literal and metaphorical cross-dressing, in which Spenser's assumed pastoral persona is written as Achilles' costuming, I do not mean to mystify distinctions between rhetorical figures and material acts. Dressing as a member of the opposite sex in the Renaissance social world was a transgression that bore harsher penalties than verbal impersonation. Textual forms and dress were intricately connected, however, in the polemics produced from the controversy surrounding social mobility. As Jean Howard has discussed, assigned dress— enforced by sumptuary laws and biblical prohibitions affirmed in the pulpits—played an integral role in maintaining a normative social order.[7] While clothing helped to articulate codes that distinguished correct social place, written forms were equally valid, if more ambiguous, social indicators. Both texts and dress were privileged sites of struggle over the meaning of social order and practice in the sixteenth century. So we should not be surprised if *The Faerie Queene* aligns fiction and fashion when describing the emergence of something as important as authorship itself. This alignment was part of a rhetoric that flirted with crucial cultural issues, even while it attenuated them. If voyeurism was a cultural trope that made print more compatible with the patronage system, then the narrative of authorial disguise and revelation functioned in a similar way to announce the author's negotiation between two systems of textual transmission.

Spenser's Pastoral Masquerade

The Shepheardes Calender is now popularly read as Spenser's carefully orchestrated poetic debut. In *Self-Crowned Laureates*, Richard Helgerson describes how the *Calender* played a significant part in shifting the system of authorial roles that existed in late sixteenth-century England. According to Helgerson, writers such as Spenser, Jonson, and Milton successfully fashioned a laureate identity from the normative crisis precipitated by Protestant reform and humanism. Central to this project was the attempt to dignify the literary enterprise so that it could contribute to the founda-

[7]See Jean Howard, "Crossdressing, the Theatre, and Gender Struggle in Early Modern England," *Shakespeare Quarterly* 39 (1988): 418–40. Howard argues that polemics about the gender codes of clothing "signal a sex-gender system under pressure and that crossdressing, as fact and as idea, threatened a normative social order based upon strict principles of hierarchy and subordination, of which women's subordination to man was a chief instance. . . . As part of a stage action, for example, the ideological import of crossdressing was mediated by all the conventions of dramatic narrative and Renaissance dramatic production. It cannot simply be conflated with crossdressing on the London streets" (418).

tion of a national literature and thus allow the writer to comply with the civic demands of humanism. As part of this project, the *Calender* was a carefully planned literary event that paved the way for the laureate status of the "New Poet," for in this text Spenser presents and critiques the conventional view of a poet indulging in youthful folly. Although this method may seem an odd way to validate poetry, Helgerson explains that such a critique was necessary:

> To write only in youth and only of love and neglect, to accept a definition that denied poetry any hope of affecting the world in a significant way, a definition that allowed poetry only by trivializing it, this a laureate poet could not do. The New Poet thus had his task clearly laid out for him. He had to redefine the limits of poetry, making it once again (if in English it ever had been) a profession that might justifiably claim a man's life and not merely the idleness or excess of his youth.[8]

The *Calender* thus stages the age-old battle between duty and love.[9] Although Helgerson largely sees its effort to define a new poetic role as a failed one, he acknowledges that the *Calender* critiques the poet-as-lover in order to upgrade the state of poetry, to "make of a gentleman's toy something of unspeakable profit" (21). We remember that Ulysses proved Achilles' manly worth by getting him to reveal his instinctual rejection of "womens tryflyng toyes." In Helgerson's account, writers were enjoined to redeem effeminizing literary amateurism by a similar act of poetic valor.

David Lee Miller also sees *The Shepheardes Calender* as central to Spenser's

---

[8]Richard Helgerson, *Self-Crowned Laureates: Spenser, Jonson, Milton, and the Literary System* (Berkeley: University of California Press, 1983), 60. "Rife with intimations of failure, breakdown, and renunciation," the *Calender*, Helgerson claims, is caught within the self-defeating poetic role that it so stridently criticizes (69). Helgerson argues that Spenser is able to fuse the ideals of humanist active duty with poetic talent in the first three books of *The Faerie Queene*, while Book 6 reintroduces the split between poetic and worldly commitment. On Mount Acidale, he explains, the union between heroic activity and amorous contemplation breaks down. Spenser's staging of the conflict, Helgerson concludes, enables a new authorial identity, one from which writers such as Daniel and Drayton profit. As will become clear, my argument differs from Helgerson's in that I tease out the specific social and gender implications of this emergent authorial identity, and I attend to the typographical, formal, and printed status of the text within this construction. In one sense, I am making visible certain features that give social character to Helgerson's larger claim; for Spenser's production of his career was staged not just from the collision between civic humanism and poetic desire, but also from the specific class entanglements of print.

[9]What Louis Montrose says of the cultural values in the poem apply equally to the aesthetic values it debates in moral terms: "In both *The Shepheardes Calender* and *The Faerie Queene*, Spenser attempts to transcend the cultural opposition that he is articulating; the poems repeatedly evidence the strains and contradictions involved in this attempt" (37). "'The perfecte paterne of a Poete': The Poetics of Courtship in *The Shepheardes Calender*," *Texas Studies in Literature and Language* 21 (1979): 34–67.

rescripting of poetic vocation in Elizabethan England. Miller suggests that
Spenser manipulated the textual apparatus as well as the thematics of the
poem by cleverly engaging medieval textual practices.[10] Combating an unre-
ceptive, perhaps even hostile, social milieu and a culture informed by the
medieval concept of anonymity, Spenser had to devise a strategy through
which he could display his signature and create his place within the socioit-
erary world. Using anonymity as a "literary device" allowed writers to assume
"a role not yet fully created, or instituted, within their culture" (Miller, 220).
For Spenser, this general career problem was intensified; for he wanted not
only to mold a place for the poet, but also to fashion himself as the Virgilian
national poet for the dynastic English state. The *Calender* thus works to produce an imperial public role for the humanist poet.

What Spenser does in his first text, then, is to concoct a form that artfully
presents its author. The *Calender* is full of strategems designed to acceler-
ate its own reception: it not only is a pastoral text, but its range of allusions to the chief models of classical and canonical literature place it firmly
within a carefully defined literary canon. When he alludes to Virgil, Marot,
and Skelton in the first set of glosses, E.K. gives us the correct exegetical
tools for locating the work in a well-established tradition of pastoral. The
book comes into print, as Miller notes, as "a kind of grand summary and
contemporary rebirth of the genre's distinguished ancestry" (221). The
layered folds of language within the *Calender*—the gloss, envois, woodcuts,
and poems within the text—create the effect that the text is already a classic worthy of careful annotation. What E.K. suggests of Spenser's archaic
poetic diction is true for the multiple layers within the entire text: it is designed to "bring . . . auctoritie to the verse."[11]

Through the framing envois, Spenser lifts the question of the poem's
origin into a place of central importance. The opening verse introduces
the issue of authorship in each of its three sestets:

> Goe little booke: thy selfe present,
> As whose parent is unkent:
>
> . . .
>
> And asked, who thee forth did bring,
> A shepheardes swaine saye did thee sing,
>
> . . .

[10]David Lee Miller, "Authorship, Anonymity, and *The Shepheardes Calender*," *Modern Language Quarterly* 40 (1979): 219–36. In *The War Against Poetry* (Princeton: Princeton University
Press, 1970), Russell Fraser broadly discusses the attacks levied against poetry in the sixteenth century.

[11]Edmund Spenser, *The Yale Edition of the Shorter Poems of Edmund Spenser*, ed. William A.
Oram et al. (New Haven: Yale University Press, 1989), 14.

But if that any aske thy name,
Say thou wert base begot with blame.

(12)

This opening verse portrays the text as a bastard, a wandering poem whose author-father is "unkent" or unknown. The next stanza foregrounds the question of origins once again by positing a correlation between the author and his fiction; the writer here takes on the role of his character and becomes a shepherd. Thus, the pastoral is not only a genre, but also an assumed persona for the author. The final sestet "names" the text only by designating its lowly status; the envoi simply stages the mystery of the author's identity. This query of origins concludes with the writer's promise to "name" himself and thus rescue his poem from bastardy after the text has been well received—when it is "past jeopardee." The envoi offers a crafted apology for the baseness of the poem, which blushes with shame because it lacks a father, because it inhabits the humble form of a pastoral and also, perhaps, because it is published and thus "begot with blame." The opening verse calls attention to the author's concealed status by putting forth the sign "Immerito" with the suggestion that this nonsignature is merely provisional. The final envoi goes on to complete this dramatic unfolding. In continuing E.K.'s persistent construction of Immerito's poetical success, the concluding envoi ends with a bold statement: "Lo I have made a Calender for every yeare." This is a presumptuous statement for a text "begot with blame." The opening and closing envois, then, narrate the text's maturation, its realization of greatness as it overcomes temporal and mortal hindrances (unknown paternity and the decay of time itself). In addition to its pastoral features, the *Calender* narrates its own poetic ascendancy up the ranks into the realm of the transcendent.

If the *Calender* is framed to highlight the absent presence of its author, its subject matter brings the question of poetic authority and agency to the fore as well. In the "April," "October," and "August" eclogues, Spenser dramatizes debates about the proper function of the poet. Colin's well-known encomium to Elizabeth in the "April" eclogue defines the poet by reference to his place in creating an imperial mythology. Colin here specifically figures the queen as a poem. By suggesting that she is the product of the union of Syrinx and Pan, Colin aligns Elizabeth with the song that was the result of that mythological coupling. As in Sidney's and Mulcaster's accounts of royal pageantry, this figuration foregrounds the poet's tremendous power in "making" both sovereign and verbal artifact. The song goes on to emphasize the potency of artistic creation when Colin boldly points out that he orchestrates the adornment of the queen: "Now ryse up Elisa, decked as thou art, / in royall aray," he commands, thus making clear his own role in performing this "decking." Spenser intensifies his claim to poetic power by making Elizabeth the symbol of England's imperial destiny, for he becomes the Virgilian poet whose responsibilities include the consolidation of England as well as its royal embodiment. The ambitiousness of this claim is made apparent in the poem's disclaimer about its royal subject: "I will not matche her with Latonaes seede, / Such follie great sorow to Niobe did breede" (74). Because the *Calender* and Elisa are his acknowledged children, Colin is able to use Niobe as an emblem for the dangers of artistic presumption (Miller, 231). The poet's misgivings about the scope of his ambition throw into relief the tremendous power implied by his claim to forge state mythologies. The "October" eclogue links this political function with the moral responsibilities that accompany poetic power. Piers tells Cuddie that the true poet works to "restraine / The lust of lawlesse youth with good advice" (171); and the argument to the eclogue announces as well that poetry is a "worthy and commendable . . . arte." In describing the moral, political, and social functions of the poetic endeavor, the characters in these eclogues give definition to the free-floating authority created by the framing devices of the gloss and envois.

By narrating the failures and triumphs of the poet Colin, the *Calender* glorifies the poetic vocation in general and Spenser's success in particular. In the "August" eclogue, for instance, Spenser stages a poetic competition, a "contro-versie" between Perigot and Willye, which is followed by Cuddie's performance of Colin's rondelay. Although the singing match is between Perigot and Willye, Colin's song retrospectively wins the match. Like Spenser himself in this anonymous book, Colin is an absent author, present only through the voicings of others. Spenser's identification with Colin becomes a way of shaping the reader's response to the *Calender*. When one character exclaims, "O Colin, Colin, the shepheardes joye, / How I admire ech turning of thy verse" (145), for instance, he offers thinly veiled praise for Spenser's own metrical dexterity. Hobbinol similarly heralds the writer's skill when he narrates how Calliope and the muses were stunned by Colin's artistry: "They drewe abacke, as halfe with shame confound, / Shepheard to see, them in their art outgoe" (111). By self-consciously exploring its own status as a poetic artifact, the book announces the "art" of the "New Poet." Colin, often invisible but persistently audible in the work, is lauded and proxied in many of the eclogues. He thus serves as a double for the anonymous poet Immerito, whose presence in the *Calender* is announced but mystified. In the concluding envoi, Immerito severs this identification by stepping out of his role as lover/poet and superceding Colin. Immerito differentiates himself from Colin by emerging as a poet capable of making "a Calender for every yeare," a poet far superior to the shepherd who is caught within the vicissitudes of the seasons and the emotional entanglements of love (Montrose, "'The perfecte paterne'").

While Miller argues that Spenser "overgoes" the medieval tradition of anonymity by inscribing a poetic role through the eclogue debates and the textual apparatus, Michael McCanles interprets the auctoritie of the gloss as the text's construction of its own historicity.[12] The poem not only presents a pastoral, but also, through its dense and myriad textual layers, monumentalizes itself within a built-in literary history of the pastoral. While Miller sees the *Calender* as set in relation to medieval practices, McCanles argues that the text fictionally imitates the humanist annotations of classical works. Both Miller and McCanles are convincing in their suggestions that the *Calender* artfully reveals its layers of construction; it produces meaning but also presents traces of how that meaning is constructed. By placing Spenser's self-consciously designed authorship within the framework of the cultural anxieties surrounding public writing, I would like to inflect these critical arguments a bit differently. In particular, I see the *Calender* as responding to the intertwined issues of social distinction and the practice of signing works. Anonymity was not only a medieval legacy but also a contemporary convention associated with manuscript writing. Because the circulation of texts at court designated the boundaries of a social sphere, works that eschewed marks of origin and that were multivoiced staked a claim to gentility. In other words, the *Calender* reveals that Spenser was aware that privilege was afforded to anonymous and exchanged texts rather than "named" published books.

The textual layers of *The Shepheardes Calender*—its multiple genres, scattered poems, proem, envois and gloss—imitate the annotations of a classical text, but they also inform the work with the heterogeneity associated with coterie writing. Because Spenser's *Calender* was published with E.K.'s scholarly gloss, it enters the public domain as if already engaged in a dialogue. It is formally packaged with the trappings of conversation. Ironically, then, the classical work and the ephemeral occasional verse look similar in their specific physical formats.[13] E.K.'s extensive commentary in the outer

[12]Michael McCanles, "*The Shepheardes Calender* as Document and Monument," *Studies in English Literature* 22 (1982): 5–19.

[13]In reading the gloss as a sign of coterie amateurism, I mean to point to its construction of a multivocal form. I recognize, however, that E.K.'s gloss, the subject of much critical commentary, also raises complex questions about the limits of humanist knowledge (i.e., exegetical practices and textual uncertainty) and about crises in political, moral, and ecclesiastical authority. For a discussion of these issues, see Richard Halpern, *The Poetics of Primitive Accumulation: English Renaissance Culture and the Genealogy of Capital* (Ithaca: Cornell University Press, 1991), 176–214; and Annabel Patterson, *Fables of Power: Aesopian Writing and Political History* (Durham, N.C.: Duke University Press, 1991), 59–66.

layer of the poem provides an uncanny mirroring of the fictional characters' own enthusiastic responses to Colin's poetry. Through the complex
strata of the book, the *Calender* generates a screen of coterie poetic forms.
The reader confronts multiple voices and multiple forms in this debut text,
as Jonathan Goldberg explains: "On the title page . . . no author appears,
and the only proper name is Sidney's. On the verso, a poem, addressed
'To His Booke,' signed Immeritô. Prefatory prose follows, directed not (as
one might expect) to Sidney but to 'Mayster Gabriell Harvey,' and not
from the author but from someone signed E.K. (and who is that?). Then,
finally—one might say—the text itself. Or, rather, a palimpsest: woodcut,
argument, monologue or dialogue, emblem, gloss."[14] By employing these
diverse layers of text and image, Spenser cross-dresses in pastoral form,
like Musidorus in the *Arcadia*, but he does so in the dress of pastoral collectivity. From this impersonation, he prepares for his emergence as heroic
and singular in the concluding moments of the poem, where he will throw
off the old identity that has strengthened his claim to a new authority.
Spenser designs a text that looks as if it were collectively and multiply produced, but the text does not remain caught within a network of plural
voices and social transactions.

Spenser conceals the *Calender* as a coterie text in order to differentiate
it, finally, from those works produced in the sphere of private circulation.
When Immerito's authorial voice resounds at the conclusion, "Lo I have
made a Calender for every yeare," he not only stabilizes the dialogue of
the text, but also goes beyond the endeavors of the courtly gentleman, the
love-struck youth, or the leisurely shepherd to argue for a moral vocational
duty. This self-consciously staged anonymity is discarded after serving its
purpose; for while the lack of a name on the *Calender* (besides that of
Sidney and the printer—both cultural signs pointing to a Protestant identity) first disperses authority to readers and critics, Spenser's later acknowledgment of the text allows him to step into the role he has created and

---

[14]Jonathan Goldberg, *Voice Terminal Echo* (New York: Methuen, 1986), 38. My argument
runs counter to Goldberg's in that I believe that the text does construct the "abiding fictions"
of the "Author selfe." Like Goldberg, I believe that the text disperses authority onto numerous unstable voices; but unlike him, I see this dispersion as orchestrated by the author, who
announces his own name in his subsequent text. According to Goldberg, the scattered play
of language is infinitely disseminated and disseminating, a play so powerful that it consumes
even character and author. In his reading, the text is a "deconstructive literary act" that swallows everything within its economy of sliding differences (39). The *Calender* becomes one
more utterance that traces its own slippage, that "speaks to unsay itself," and that sets up an
"exchange in which the poet is always already depleted by the one to whom the text, for
whom the text is written" (66). I want to historicize that slippage by placing it in the context
of manuscript reading practices, the inflections of class within those practices, and the
writer's stylization of his career.

thus appropriate the force of that collective power. The *Calender* acts as a pre-text for a subsequent work: "I will send more after thee" is a promise that the "New Poet" made good with his later epic. In *The Faerie Queene*, "Immerito" identifies himself, thus retrospectively reclaiming his previously published anonymous work and the role it devised:

> Lo I the man, whose Muse whilome did *maske*,
> As time her taught in lowly Shepheards *weeds*,
> Am now enforst a far unfitter taske,
> For trumpets sterne to chaunge mine Oaten reeds.
>
> (39, emphasis mine)

The multiple voices that disperse the pre-text are solidly unified in the bold claim announcing the epic poem. The *Calender* is one kind of literary pseudo-morph designed to mediate the tensions surrounding the place of poetry and print at the end of the century: the text inhabits coterie forms ("maskes"), but then it sheds them in order to locate itself within the commercial marketplace as a public and authorized epic work. Spenser hides in and renounces not only the pastoral or female clothing, but also the guise of manuscript textuality. As W.L.'s commendatory poem to *The Faerie Queene* implies, Spenser disguises himself as a shepherd, barely hiding his Virgilian ambitions beneath the lowly formal dress of the pastoral, a guise, I suggest, that figures the elite dress of collectivity as well. When the narrator nostalgically asks in Book 6, "Who knows not Colin Clout?" he comments on the success of this strategy of authorization.

   In casting off coterie forms, the writer simultaneously renounces the conventional feminizing role of the poet-as-lover. When Spenser differentiates himself from the time-bound Colin, he levies a critique at Colin's imprisonment within his own bodily desire and romantic self-indulgence (Montrose, "'The perfecte paterne'"). Colin's artistry is harnessed by his desire, as Thenot exclaims, "And hath he skill to make so excellent, / Yet hath so little skill to brydle love?" (71). Thenot's criticism of Colin is later made more damning by Colin's confession: "I play to please my selfe, all be it ill" (112). The poetic role advocated by Thenot and the shepherds in the *Calender* stands strikingly in contradiction to the amateur poet's perception of himself as a maker of trifles. Like Colin, whose songs to Rosalind are designed to please himself, court poets represented their verse as ditties spun by ladies and gentlemen seeking entertainment. In *The Arte of English Poesie* (1589), George Puttenham designates a chapter on the poetic figures that adorn language to "Ladies and young Gentlewomen, or idle Courtiers, desirous to become skilful in their owne mother tongue . . . for their private recreation to make now and then ditties of pleasure."[15] He thus

---

[15]George Puttenham, *The Arte of English Poesie* (1589), ed. Gladys Doidge Willcock and

describes a poetic study that is particularly associated with both courtliness and the feminine. Spenser's book is replete with such occasional poetry (the complaint of Dido's death, Colin's laments to Rosalind), but his "ditties" are framed by textual layers that qualify and supersede them by pointing to another view of poetic crafting as "a divine gift and heavenly instinct . . . poured into the witte by . . . celestiall inspiration" (170). In the final envoi, Spenser claims that he has assumed a newly respectable role by making a text that will "teach the ruder shepheard how to feede his sheepe, / And from the falsers fraud his folded flocke to keepe" (213). Immerito, then, becomes the poet that Piers describes in the "October" eclogue when he instructs Cuddie: "Lyft up thy selfe out of the lowly dust: / And sing of bloody Mars, of wars, of giusts" (172). This is, of course, the shape of Spenser's career: he lays down the love text to pick up the heroic and moral song. In making that substitution, Spenser defeminizes the poetic enterprise, moving beyond Puttenham's leisurely "ditties of pleasure." More specifically, he constructs a text that responds to criticism levied by his friend Gabriel Harvey: "Credit me," Harvey writes, "I will never linne baiting at you, till I have rid you quite of this yonkerly and womanly humor."[16] Spenser's own printed coterie text, filled with poetic "ditties" and "womanly humor," is ultimately legimated by the counterclaim to a moral poetic duty, one that is masculinized for no other reason than that it exists in opposition to the "feminine" manuscript circulation at court, customarily associated with "womanly" and foppish love poetry. It is no wonder that W.L. narrates his transition in gendered terms; his epic is merely the culmination of the process he begins in the *Calender* where he hears the battle cry and discards feminine courtly trifles.

It is interesting to note that the "weeds" that Spenser expels formally and metaphorically in the 1590 *Faerie Queene*'s opening moment reappear in variant form in the proem to Book 4 in the 1596 edition. Here, as Spenser addresses the stern Burghley, who was praised in the 1590 text as a man "of most grave affaires," he apologizes for the seeming fancifulness of his poem. His work, he explains, has been criticized for

---

Alice Walker (Cambridge: Cambridge University Press, 1936). Elaine Beilin cites this passage in explaining the prohibitions on women's learning in *Redeeming Eve: Women Writers of the English Renaissance* (Princeton: Princeton University Press, 1987), 8.

[16] Edmund Spenser, *Works of Edmund Spenser*, ed. Edwin Greenlaw et al., 11 vols. (Baltimore: Johns Hopkins University Press, 1932–1957), 10:444. Spenser himself registers his worry about being emasculated because of his preoccupation with the aesthetic: "Nought under heaven so strongly doth allure / The sence of man, and all his minde possesse, / As beauties lovely baite, that doth procure, / Great warriours oft their rigour to represse, / And mighty hands forget their manlinesse" (*The Faerie Queene*, ed. Roche, bk. 5, canto 8, 1:1–4).

> . . . magnifying lovers dear debate;
> By which fraile youth is oft to follie led,
> Through false allurement of that pleasing baite,
> That better were in vertues discipled,
> Then with vaine poemes *weeds* to have their fancies fed.
>
> (FQ, bk. 4, proem; emphasis mine)

Although Spenser goes on to justify his apparent "weeds," his use of the word signals its double signification; the fanciful "dress" of the epic tale of heroic love becomes associated with those things irrelevant, excessive, and dispensable. George Gascoigne, who, I suggest, uses a similar authorial strategy of coterie impersonation, also relies on the garden metaphor in morally categorizing his more "serious" work: *The Posies* is divided into "flowers," "herbs," and "weeds." The process of "weeding," then, revolved not only around metaphors of investiture, particularly that of casting off lowly "woman's weeds," but also on tropes of gardening that had implicit evaluations attached. If Spenser states that he cast off pastoral costume in writing the epic, he also demands that the reader sort through the amorous and fanciful "weeds" that hide the text's more serious concerns. As in the myth of Achilles, the power of disguise and detection go hand in hand.

W.L.'s commendatory poem can thus be seen as a very smart rehearsal of Spenser's own strategies of authorization in the publication of *The Shepheardes Calender* and *The Faerie Queene*. In his pastoral debut Spenser presented a flawed poet in the figure of Colin, from whom he distinguished his more reputable authorial role; he renamed the privilege associated with coterie forms as a mere pretext to true public and civic authority. Part of his renaming involves redeeming "womanly" love poetry as a manly heroic enterprise. When introducing his epic, he presents an image that has all the ingredients used by the commendatory poem—the pastoral "maske," the shepherd "weeds," the "unfitter taske." W.L.'s use of the story of Achilles' feminization and redemption merely redramatizes the process of concealment and disclosure that Spenser evokes in the move from pastoral to epic. As the commendatory poem implies, Spenser's pastoral functions as a disguise; he is always aware that it is a prelude to a greater project, and he makes maturation and renunciation part of the text's formal and thematic dynamic. Spenser designs a poem that formally dresses as a manuscript text, although he reverses the meaning attached to this elite form by linking it to the lowly and humble pastoral "begot with blame." The promised text, *The Faerie Queene*, constitutes a strange "undressing" of his career, one in which the author announces his published and public identity by renouncing his former text, his former persona, and the stance of collectivity (with its association to a gentlemanly poetic amateurism) that concealed his true epic authorial pretensions.

Gascoigne's Scandalous "Anthology"

Rather than an isolated case of authorial impersonation, the *Calender* offers us a singularly successful example of a literary strategy that was used in a slightly different way by George Gascoigne in *A Hundreth Sundrie Flowres*.[17] When the *Flowres* was published in 1573, six years earlier than the *Calender*, it appeared to be the work of many writers, one of whom was Gascoigne. As did *The Shepheardes Calender*, Gascoigne's pseudomorphic anthology laid the groundwork for a later text that could announce his public authorship and renounce the levity and triviality of his previous poetic amateurism.[18] The *Flowres* is presented as a manuscript work that the printer intercepts when it is sent from a man identified as G.T. to one called H.W. The exchange of letters between these gentlemen, printed in the preliminary material to the work, defines the text's private and privileged site of production. H.W. explains that the poems are largely occasional works written by various people, which G.T. has simply gathered together:

> In August last passed my familiar friend Master G.T. bestowed upon me the reading of a written Booke, wherin he had collected divers discourses & verses, invented uppon sundrie occasions by sundrie gentlemen. . . . And herewithal my said friend charged me, that I should use them onely for mine owne particuler commoditie, and eftsones safely deliver the originall copie to him againe, wherein I must confesse my self but halfe a marchant, for the copie unto him I have safely redelivered. But the worke (for I thought it worthy to be published) I have entreated my friend A.B. to emprint.[19]

[17]For a reading that posits an inverse relationship between Spenser's and Gascoigne's debut texts, see Paul Alpers, "Pastoral and the Domain of Lyric in Spenser's *Shepheardes Calender*," *Representations* 12 (1985): 83-100. Alpers argues that unlike Gascoigne's *Flowres*, Spenser's presentation of his lyric-pastoral poem "gives no sign of diffidence about appearing in print" (165). Alpers suggests that the *Calender* "stands on its own terms" rather than relying on the "elaborations and evasions" that Gascoigne's work displays (176). My reading, on the other hand, interprets the gloss and the textual apparatus as mediating devices that produce an effect similar to those employed by Gascoigne in the *Flowres*.

[18]For a discussion of the strange presentation of *A Hundreth Sundrie Flowres*, see Arthur Marotti, "Patronage, Poetry, and Print," *The Yearbook of English Studies* 21 (1991): 9-15; and Richard McCoy, "Gascoigne's 'Poëmata castrata': The Wages of Courtly Success," *Criticism* 27 (Winter 1985): 33-34.

[19]The introductory material to the *Flowres* is reprinted in the appendix of *The Complete Works of George Gascoigne*, ed. John W. Cunliffe, 2 vols. (Cambridge: Cambridge University Press, 1907–1910), 1:490–92. All references to *The Posies* (1575) are also cited from this text (1:1–137).

What we encounter when reading the *Flowres*, then, is a surreptitiously printed commonplace book. H.W. accentuates the transgression involved in putting forth this work when he hints of his amusement at exposing these writers' private fantasies to the world without their knowledge. The printer next presents G.T.'s letter requesting that his friend keep this book private. The printer's deliberate presentation of G.T.'s disclosure forms a screen through which the reader encounters the poems. While this prefatorial strategy certainly banks on the desirability of the forbidden (as did the more explicit tropes of voyeurism that we have seen in Renaissance prefaces), it also calls on the text's private status as a means of emphasizing the manuscript features of the book. The presentation of this heterogeneous text as a commonplace book is so convincing, in fact, that one twentieth-century editor insists on omitting the prose links between the verse on the grounds that they "obscure" the poems. The *Flowres*, he vehemently claims, is *supposed* to be an anthology rather than a narrative authored by a single writer.[20] The book's rhetorical self-fabrication as a manuscript was, it seems, somewhat successful.

If the editorial apparatus to *The Shepheardes Calender* creates the effect of manuscript anonymity, the editorial apparatus to the *Flowres* opts to reinforce the manuscript collectivity of the project. The dispersion of authority effected by H.W. and G.T. is consolidated by the title page and the variety within the work itself (which is comprised of two plays; two prose "autobiographical" narratives interspersed with poems; translations; miscellaneous anonymous verse; and works signed by Gascoigne). The title page declares that the work is "A Hundredth sundrie Flowres bounde up in one small Poesie, gathered partely (by translation) in the fyne outlandish Gardins of Euripides, Ovid, Petrarke, Ariosto, and others: and partly by invention, out of our owne fruitefull Orchardes in Englande." The printer suggests that the reader, in sampling the variety of classical and contemporary writers, should savor the principle of difference that governs the text: "you shall not be constreined to smell of the floures therein conteined all at once, neither yet to take them up in such order as they are sorted: But you may take any one flowre by itselfe" (1:476). The *Flowres* thus unfolds before us as a mass of poetic language assembled from various origins and offered for the reader to assemble and reassemble. Flaunting its textual assortment rather than its textual coherence, the book urges the reader to

---

[20]When editing the text, B. M. Ward leaves out the prose links, merely reproducing the poetry because, he states, they "were out of place in a poetical anthology." He retains only enough of the prose plot "as is necessary to serve as explanation for the poems." George Gascoigne, *A Hundreth Sundrie Flowres*, ed. B. M. Ward (London: Frederick Etchells and Hugh MacDonald, 1926), viii.

pick and choose portions of the work to read. The metaphor within the title both figures the diversity of its own textual form and registers the flexibility and provisionality of the book's physical arrangement of its literary material.

Despite the encoded gentlemanly amateurism that identifies the work as ephemeral and provisional, the prefatory material asks the reader to place the text within a literary canon. G.T.'s letter tellingly compares the writing of contemporary Englishmen to Chaucer and to the "poets of antiquitie." Arthur Marotti remarks on this contradiction: "Despite the many statements denigrating the collection as trivial, immature, and occasional, Gascoigne clearly wishes the publication to constitute a significant cultural achievement, to join the editions of classical authors and of the first canonized English author, Chaucer" ("Patronage," 11). We see in the *Flowres* the same strange contradiction found in Spenser's pastoral debut; both texts brilliantly perform the poetic codes of coterie verse, only to insist on the limitations of that brand of poetry. How can the text be both an ephemeral commonplace book designed for private viewing and a literary monument to be inserted within a particular canon? This bifurcation appropriately lays the groundwork for the construction of an author who will triumphantly appear from within the very codes of manuscript culture. In Spenser's case, the author emerges from anonymity; Gascoigne accepts authorial responsibility for an apparent gentlemanly anthology. Both writers become retrospectively identified by a text that studiedly downplayed authorship in lieu of dramatizing the book's multiple authorizations.

Two years after his anthology appeared, Gascoigne republished the work as *The Posies* under his own name. In the preliminary material to the new edition, Gascoigne directs his remarks more attentively to the scandal and controversy apparently sparked by his previous text. Gascoigne's apology thus overshadows his bolder feat of unifying the work and authorizing it as his own writing rather than that of "sundrie" gentlemen.[21] In *The Posies*, Gascoigne stages his own personal and poetic conversion within a conventional prodigal narrative: he argues for "the reformation of [his] minde" (1:7). In his youth, Gascoigne explains, he, like many others before him, did fall into "some snares of the Divell, and temptations of the flesh" (*Works*, 1:9). This second publication is presented through the lens of an apology for both his past life and his past text. In this way, Gascoigne

---

[21] The palinode was, of course, a conventional tactic used by Renaissance writers in establishing their authority. See, for example, Spenser's heavenly hymns, which renounce the two previous secular ones, and Thomas Watson's *Hekatompathia*, a sonnet collection that has a break in the middle in which the poet renounces the stance of love. These writers generally follow Petrarch in creating the secular/heavenly division in their amorous works.

produces a pseudomorph that inverts Spenser's more famous reclamation of his pseudomorph in *The Faerie Queene*, although W.L.'s apology for Spenser's potentially "unfitt" publication and Spenser's own scripting of the *Calender* as "begot with blame" hints at this same strategy. Gascoigne emerges in the wake of his previous semi-anonymous fame, or rather from the notoriety and scandal generated by the pre-text. Under the rhetoric of apology, which broadly encompasses both his youthful sins and the possible political and moral misconstructions laid on his text, lies the implicit staking of a claim. After all, when he tells his readers, "I have not published the same to the intent that other men hereafter might be infected with my follies forepassed," he defends *his* follies and thus *his* text (1:13). Just as Spenser's envoi established his text as a bastard only to set up its reunion with its legitimate authorial father, Gascoigne's confession of scandal glosses a buried but important authorial claim.

Gascoigne's claim is formally consolidated by the exorbitant number of commendatory poems that precede his revised text—twenty verses that not only identify him as the author of the newly "beautified" and corrected work, but also place him in the tradition of moralizers like Virgil, Galen, and Ovid (1:28). This preliminary material signals a shift in the spirit of the book, but it also marks Gascoigne's transition from lesser to more important literary genres. He indicates his awareness of the moral and poetic gradation of the work by dividing it into the evaluative categories of "flowers," "herbs," and "weeds." In a verse entitled "The Opinion of the aucthor himselfe after all these commendations," Gascoigne "humbly" revels in his own glory: "What neede I speake my self, since other say so much? / Who seme to praise these poesies so, as if ther wer none such?" (1:33). If Gascoigne uses his own artful silence to defer to the voices that authorize him, he later speaks in a poetic envoi that dispatches the text to his audience:

> Kinde Erato, and wanton Thalia,
> (Whose name my muze, devoutly did invoke)
> Adieu deare dames, Caliope sings alia,
> Which are more worth.
>
> (1:34)

Gascoigne's dismissal of wanton goddesses and his welcome instead to the muse of history signals the final transformation of his career. *The Posies*, then, marks his authorial control not only because it offers an explicit signature to previously unsigned material, but also because it interprets what that signature means through a complex, intertwined narrative of personal conversion and formal progression.

Gascoigne uses his elaborate justification and apology as an emphatic means of asserting authority over his book. While the *Flowres* did apparently irritate the Privy Council, the text did not produce a scandal of the magnitude that Gascoigne describes. We can assume that he found it in his interest to overemphasize the controversy produced by his publication as a means of presenting the second signed work as new and improved. Under the cover of a confession, he is able to anchor collective voices and heterogeneous forms to an authored text. The flimsiness of his claim of conversion is made evident by the fact that the second book is quite similar to the first, although it claims to be considerably altered. Gascoigne assures the Reverend Divines that "this second imprinting [is] so turquened and turned, so clensed from all unclenly wordes, and so purged from the humor of inhumanitie, as percase you woulde not judge that it was the same tale" (7). But the trappings of presentation rather than the substance have primarily been altered. Gascoigne, for instance, changes many of the disparate mottos used to sign the poems to his favorite, "Tam Marti quam Mercurio." He also deletes the letters explaining the fictional origin of the book, the supposed narrator, and all references to England (instead identifying the work as based on an Italian story by a writer named Bartello). Through these minor revisions, Gascoigne appropriates the authority of those who had staked a claim to the text in the first edition—the editor, the writer, the reporter, and the various poets within. He is able to demonstrate his authorial virtuosity by merely erasing the few words that mediated between writer and story, i.e., "as I heard him say." The cleansing to which he subjects the text centrally consists of a formal consolidation of his authority rather than a purification of morally or politically suspect subject matter. *The Posies* does reframe the poetic material significantly; it calls attention, for instance, to the literary rather than the occasional nature of its poems, and thus it introduces a more important authorial role in the work. Although Spenser and Gascoigne construct very different second texts—one merely a revised miscellany and the other a magisterial epic poem—both writers employ the same strategic reflex for self-presentation, which Richard McCoy describes as the "evasions of courtly discourse in which desire and identities are revealed through displacement and disguise" (33). Each pre-text disperses the authorial self onto the more socially acceptable collective, anonymous, or multivocal text, while the later work amalgamates that dispersion and reclaims these displaced authorities.

As in the *Calender*, where E.K. comments so fully on the triumphs and failures of Colin Clout, the *Flowres* has an editor who interprets and glosses the performance of various poetic figures. This fictional editor, whom we can almost assuredly identify as Gascoigne, provides a vantage point from which to critique the poet who merely sings love songs and paves the way for the re-presentation of the author as a didactic reformer. Throughout the *Flowres,* editor G.T. lavishly applauds the poetic endeavors of the fictional F.J. Indeed, the narrative, as the editor states, is merely included to frame the poems, which are the central texts on display. By analyzing the strengths and weaknesses of the inscribed poems—that is, pointing out the problems in rhyme or the success of the well-placed stanza—the editor authorizes the work as a verbal artifact worthy of intent intellectual study. At the same time, however, he splinters the work into two layers. The book takes shape through the interaction between these two layers, which praise the poetics of the text while calling attention to the limitations of this kind of verse.

Through the privileged position of editor, Gascoigne can distance himself from F.J., the failed poet, and thus supersede him. This formal distancing is bolstered by the narrative line of the story, which amply displays the vexed problems the courtly poet faced. In "Master F.J.," the central character fervently writes poems to establish a secret liaison with his host's daughter-in-law, but his attempts to win love are, like Colin Clout's, unsuccessful. As F.J.'s poems escape his control literally and figuratively (one is dropped on the floor, found by Elinor, and made the object of ridicule), his own verse-making becomes the channel through which others insult and mock him. Like Colin, who hung up his pipes in resignation, F.J. abandons his verse-making when he fails at courtship. In a later verse narrative in the *Flowres,* "Dan Bartholomew of Bath," the lover/poet similarly resigns his love pursuits when his mistress is found to be fickle. His outbursts of passion modulate into doleful poems of distress that conclude with a poetic last will and testament. When the poet ceases writing, the editor steps in to tell of the poet's illness, his recovery, and his decision to go to war (136). Both of these tales are thus enveloped within a formal structure that allows the editor to comment on the limitations of love and poetry. In this sense, the work provides a critique of the courtly, manuscript-identified versifier. By simultaneously exploiting and renouncing the role of lover/poet, the writer can contradictorily disavow the conception of writing as occasional and amateur play from *within the ranks.* He establishes his claim to gentility in the form of the work and proves his ability to cut a gentlemanly figure through the verse that is included; but at the same time, he articulates a new social and moral function for the poet.[22]

[22]In arguing that repentance served as the privileged position from which a writer could script his career, I am indebted to Richard Helgerson's *Elizabethan Prodigals* (Berkeley: University of California Press, 1976), a book that investigates five authors' obsessive preoccupation with the story of prodigal rebellion. Helgerson notes that this paradigmatic plot allowed

Gascoigne's prefatorial justification in *The Posies* completes the project he began in his earlier publication. Here he performs that double gesture again by contradictorily underscoring and disavowing the fact that his first work was a coterie commonplace book. His text is not written for profit, he assures his readers, nor because he wishes to be a "pleasaunt Poet . . . or a cunning lover" (4). The repudiation of both profit and pleasure places Gascoigne in the liminal position of a nonprofessional poet who nevertheless shuns the connection between poetry-making and otium. Although he moves from the overtly occasional to the professedly literary in his revised edition, the poet writes against his own professional status, screening his debut in the literary marketplace in revisionary terms. Spenser's final emblem to *The Shepheardes Calender*—"merce non mercede" ([for] reward not for hire)—displays the same double attempt to redraw the lines of distinction that separated the available categories of a literary career.

Gascoigne's renunciation of the poetic erotics of courtly love and his establishment of a moral tenor for his work is accompanied by his arrangement of *The Posies* into a more unified tale. When *The Posies* introduces a fictional source figure, Bartello, to mediate between Gascoigne and his writing, that introduction ironically consolidates the literariness of the work and thus emphasizes Gascoigne as an author rather than a mere commonplace book editor. Although we might think that a source would mitigate the authority of the writer, Gascoigne evokes Bartello as the absent governing force that unifies the text and dissolves the pretense that the story is a narrated true event. When the tale announces its own fictionality—its status as a created artifact rather than a mere record of the intrigues of courtly play—it necessarily makes room for a more prominent governing "origin." Thus, it is no surprise that Gascoigne replaces many of the mottos in the text with his own. In *The Posies*, Gascoigne self-consciously figures his work as a devised and structured form rather than a set of occasional verse.

Richard McCoy argues that the text's republication evidences Gascoigne's unwilling submission to the powerful forces of higher authority. In an

---

writers to indulge in a rebellion from "paternal expectation" (67) and thus to justify their decision to counter the dictates of public service issued in humanist study. Like Helgerson, I believe that the stance of repentance is bound up with the production of the role of author; and like him, I argue that the writer uses this plot structure to combat social criticisms that allied the poet with wantonness, idleness, and women. This preoccupation is, furthermore, bound up with vexed social issues that are exacerbated by the act of publishing. The "weight of the humanist tradition" that Helgerson rightly sees as impinging on Elizabethan writers was also crucial to the elite conception of writing as amateuristic play, a view that the writer was forced to contradictorily maintain and disavow in forging a public role for himself in print.

argument that falls along the lines of what has been dubbed as the "containment theory" associated with some brands of new historicism, McCoy suggests that Gascoigne's career dramatizes the gradual effacement of personal and poetic autonomy within the Elizabethan court ("'Poëmata castrata'"). But if we read the second publication as evidence of Gascoigne's poetic impotence, we fail to take into account the possibility that Gascoigne had some measure of control in stylizing his own career. In other words, part of our evidence for his submission is the rhetoric of humility that he self-consciously fashions as a means of constructing an authorial identity not yet fully articulated within his culture. Although writers were certainly subject to social ridicule and economic hardship as well as limited by manuscript notions of writing, they could exploit that position for political advantage. Why otherwise would Spenser subscribe to a stigma of print? Both Spenser and Gascoigne depend on the very conception of the writer that they criticize in order to shape a place for themselves and their professions. From their literary pseudomorphs, they become men in print. The role of lover/poet is a necessary stance for them to assume and renounce; and the palinode is a necessary means for both *establishing* themselves as poets who can prove their worth on inherited terms and *refashioning* those very terms by reshaping the poet's relationship to his public text.

Those Complaining Women

Like Gascoigne and Spenser, Samuel Daniel reshaped and introduced a new authorial career by developing a literary pseudomorph that he could supersede, but Daniel used a different strategy to revise poetic authority in Elizabethan England. In particular, he devised a pseudomorphic form by yoking the genres of sonnet sequence and complaint poem rather than by concealing his authorial identity in a conspicuously edited debut text. When Daniel published *Delia* with the appended *Complaint of Rosamond*, he offered a model for other writers to use in scripting textual and social authority. It is first important to point out that in writing this complaint, Daniel was extending a popular literary trend. Following a tradition marked by Boccaccio and *The Mirror for Magistrates*, writers in the 1580s and 1590s saw a renewed interest in the genre of the complaint poem, a verse that told of an illustrious victim's fall from greatness. The *Mirror* (1559), first published as the joint enterprise of a group of writers headed by William Baldwin, went through numerous editions until its final publication in 1610. This book consisted of a continuously expanding array of monologues voiced by historic male leaders, a pattern disrupted by the 1563 edition's inclusion of Jane Shore as a female complaint speaker. This apparent encroachment ushered in a literary trend. Female characters began to serve as the principal speakers in the complaint poems at the end of the century. Writing the complaint of the fallen woman became a literary craze; as Hallet Smith notes, "it was in the last decade of the century that the story of the sinning woman developed into a fad."[23] Ballads about such figures as Rosamond Clifford (mistress of Henry II) and Jane Shore (mistress of Edward IV) flooded the market. Thomas Deloney's *Garland of Good Will*, Anthony Chute's *Beauty Dishonested*, Michael Drayton's *Matilda*, Thomas Lodge's *Complaint of Elstred*, Thomas Middleton's *Ghost of Lucrece*, and Shakespeare's *A Lover's Complaint* testify to the popularity of this tradition. These works formed a distinct and self-identifying body of literature. Shakespeare draws from this tradition in *The Rape of Lucrece*, for instance, although he situates the heroine's rhetorical complaint in a story of rape and political revolution. Indeed, the plight of infamous women became so popular that Giles Fletcher felt he had to justify his complaint poem about Richard III simply because his subject was male. Fletcher describes himself as engaged in a tennis match with fortune, which allows him to ridicule those poets who

> Like silly boates in shallowe rivers tost,
> Loosing their paynes, and lacking still their wage,
> To write of women, and of womens falles,
> Who are too light, for to be fortunes balles.

As Fletcher charges that women's misfortunes are simply "too light" a subject matter for serious poets, he unwittingly testifies to the popularity of this body of writing.[24]

Female complaint poems are highly conventional. They tell of a legendary figure who returns from the dead to recount her misfortunes through an extended monologue, one that wavers in tone between vindication, shame, and vengeance. The choice of this form signaled a writer's affiliation with Ovid, whose *Heroides* offered the classic text of lamenting and forlorn

---

[23]Hallet Smith, "*A Woman Killed With Kindness*," *PMLA* 53 (1938): 145. For an interesting discussion of the genre of the female complaint in a postmodern context, see Lauren Berlant, "The Female Complaint," *Social Text* 19/20 (Fall 1988): 237–59. Berlant sees this form as marking a moment in which postmodern feminism grapples with the problem of difference within its ranks. She also explores the form's usefulness for articulating disenfranchisement and the concomitant problem of cultural appropriation of that articulation. Her work charts how the female complaint shaped American romance, feminism, and contemporary pop culture; and it throws into relief some of the strategies Renaissance writers used in negotiating an authorial identity by producing the voice of the discontented woman.

[24]Giles Fletcher, *Licia, or Poemes of Love whereunto is added the Rising to the Crowne of Richard the third*, STC 11055 (1593?), reprinted in *The English Works of Giles Fletcher, the Elder*, ed. Lloyd E. Berry (Madison: University of Wisconsin Press, 1964), 124.

heroines. But these Renaissance complaints are not grounded through reference to Ovid, nor do they simply reproduce Ovidian heroines. For in these works, the female speaker is not simply portrayed as a lamenting and powerless paramour pleading to win back an unfaithful love or to offer herself as an example of sin and frailty. Instead, she moves in a complicated fashion between justification and penitence. The female character thus acts as a more complex literary figure than in the *Heroides*, and through that complication she voices issues crucial to poetic authority itself.

Ballads about sinning women not only proliferated, but also became the site of male rivalry, competition, and debate as these textual women strangely began to quarrel and compete among themselves. Rosamond, for instance, scoffs that in Churchyard's representation, Jane Shore "passes for a Saint," while Rosamond herself, who is more deserving, rests in infamy.[25] Churchyard responds by reissuing his complaint text: "because Rosamind is so excellently sette forth . . . I have somewhat beautified my Shore's wife, not in any kind of emulation, but to make the world know my device in age is as rife and reddie, as my disposition and knowledge was in youth."[26] In his text, Jane Shore disagrees with her author by scorning Rosamond's claim to beauty, claiming that she is not so "excellently set forth." Drayton's complaining Matilda criticizes "looser wantons" such as Elstred and Jane as unworthy of literary immortalization at all, charging that Daniel's Rosamond, in particular, has flawed her poet's craft: "Though all the world bewitched with his ryme, / Yet all his skill cannot excuse her cryme."[27] In the public at large, Thomas Nashe and Gabriel Harvey characteristically fought over *whose* Jane Shore was superior. Writing the text of female "experience," therefore, provided the structural ground for asserting poetic mastery. These complaining women generated a discursive site for literary competition and authorization. In one sense, writing such a complaint constituted a poetic dare: to "stellify" a whore, as Drayton says; to vindicate a concubine. The triumph of these poems, while somewhat bizarrely connected to both the immorality and beauty of their speaking subjects, finally rested on the writer's ability to garner sympathy for a woman's injustices and misfortunes and thus to criticize one of the courtly poet's favorite stances as ardent wooer.

When Daniel published *The Complaint of Rosamond*, which was appended

[25]Samuel Daniel, *The Complaint of Rosamond* (1592), reprinted in *Samuel Daniel: Poems and A Defence of Ryme*, ed. Arthur Sprague (Chicago: University of Chicago Press, 1930), 11. 22–28.

[26]Thomas Churchyard, *Churchyards Challenge*, STC 5220 (1593), sig. T1ᵛ.

[27]Michael Drayton, *Matilda*, in *The Works of Michael Drayton*, ed. J. William Hebel, 5 vols. (Oxford: Basil Blackwell, 1931–1941), 1: 214.

to his sonnet sequence *Delia* (1592), he not only contributed to this growing body of literature, but he also initiated a publishing trend, a way of textually framing the well-worn form. While this first grouping may have been inspired by the physical conditions of publication—the necessity to "make up" the text by including a shorter work at the end—its subsequent popularity and the way in which Daniel positions the poems to reflect and comment on each other creates a paradigm for their interconnection. A year later, Thomas Lodge's *Phillis* (1593) greeted the public eye trailed by the story of the complaining Elstred. A decade before *Delia*'s publication, Henry Constable's *Diana* (1584) had concluded with "diverse poems by various honorable personages." Fifteen years after *Delia*, the chosen model for concluding Shakespeare's 1609 *Sonnets* was the echoing female complaint text *A Lover's Complaint*.[28]

I want to suggest that the dialogue between sonnet sequence and complaint poem generates a literary pseudomorph that functions like Spenser's and Gascoigne's doubled debut texts. Here the woman's voice absorbs the role of the pseudomorphic editor in carving out a particular poetic role for the writer. In short, the sonnet sequence/complaint combination stages the writer's emergence into the public through two primary means: by blending genres (having one poetic form comment on another) and by dislocating gender (assuming the female voice). In constructing this text, Daniel can be said to "cross-dress," following the Achillean gesture of taking on a female disguise—which was, in W.L.'s account, really the assumption of a literary genre. This disguise functions as the legitimating ground for articulating literary authority.

We remember that Daniel's *Delia* emerged bearing protestations of authorial reluctance. It made its way into print, Daniel assures us in his confessional preface, only because the poems had appeared incorrectly as part of the 1591 *Astrophel and Stella*. *Delia* thus became public, as did *The Faerie Queene* and *The Posies*, through a pre-text. Because it was published with Sidney's work, *Delia* was indebted to *Astrophel and Stella* in ways that exceeded mere literary influence. This collision of textual voices provided Daniel with an excuse to republish a corrected and reauthorized text, all done, of course, in the service of humility; his "private passions" could not dare to be confused with those of the masterful Sidney. Complaining that

---

[28]Daniel's text became a model for other types of appended texts as well. Giles Fletcher's *Licia* (1593?) is followed by the story of Richard III's rise to the Crown; Richard Lynche's *Diella* (1596) concludes with "The amorous poem of Dom Diego and Gyneura"; and Spenser's *Amoretti* (1595) is closed by the *Epithalamion*. It can be argued that these texts played an important formal role in providing closure to the widely heralded anticlosure of the sonnet sequence, a form that rests on frustrated desire and incompletion.

he was "betraide by the indiscretion of a greedie Printer," Daniel went public with his signed work, writing to remedy the dishonor given to Sidney's name (*Poems*, 9). His status as an author, then, was born from an act of impersonation, whether manipulated by him or not.

Daniel's presentation of himself as an unwilling author disappears in the 1594 edition of his sonnets, which includes *Cleopatra*. Here he criticizes the frivolity of the sonnet genre, boasting that he has been lifted from "low repose /. . . tragicke notes to frame." Discarding the lowly form of his "humble song," Daniel now ascends the ladder of literary genre to labor for posterity. We recognize the narrative of authorial progression that was put forth by W.L.'s mythological analogy and Gascoigne's prefatorial confession, a progression that is charted here spatially as an ascension from a "low" or base state into the more rarified realm of tragedy. Daniel's potent and more serious literary voice can be heard because of the groundwork laid by his humble and reluctant public disclosure. Acting out the inherited ladder of the Virgilian progression of forms, I argue, not only evidenced his genteel modesty, but also glossed the stigma associated with print. Daniel's stylization of his career ensures that the reader in the marketplace sees that the writer has abandoned, rather than fallen into, a position of "low repose."

In order to understand the success of this ascension, we must first look to the book that announced Daniel publicly, the 1592 *Delia* that was issued with an echoing verse in the tradition of the Propertian and Ovidian female complaint poem. Daniel opens his complaint by telling us that it has been written at the demand of Rosamond, the fallen mistress of Henry II, who has returned from the dead to ask the poet to bewail her loss and vindicate her reputation. When Propertius's Cynthia returns from the dead, she asks him to burn his books and rewrite her identity through a new verse, one that she willingly dictates.[29] In Daniel's complaint, the woman speaks from the dead in a way that positions her not only as the mistress of Henry II, but also specifically as a fictional character within Daniel's work, one who knows his other fictions and is aware of the dilemmas he faces as a Renaissance writer. She emerges as a self-conscious reader of the sonnets that precede her in the text. Initially, the fallen woman reaffirms the logic of the sonnet text as she validates the poet's role as amorous pursuer and the sonnet speaker's own coded language.[30] Rosamond seemingly legitimates the Petrarchan poet's wants and desires when she

---

[29]Propertius, *The Poems*, ed. and trans. W. G. Shepherd (New York: Penguin Books, 1985), bk. 4, 7. I want to thank Helen Deutsch for calling this poem to my attention.

[30]The sonnet speaker's insistent representation of himself as a writer and of writing as an integral part of the process of courtship forges a solid cultural link between poet and Petrarchan lover.

incorporates his goals and ambitions within her own project. She explains that only the sympathy of lovers can rescue her from her imprisonment in purgatorial limbo and deliver her safely to the life thereafter. Rosamond is in dire need of a poet's skills; "No Muse suggests the pittie of my case," she laments, "Each penne dooth overpasse my just complaint" (23). In keeping with the pattern established by Churchyard in *The Mirror for Magistrates*, the ghostly woman introduces her author as a man already read, one worthy of the fame he will accrue by this publication. But Rosamond appeals to Daniel not only because of his talents, but also because of the emotional loss and unfulfilled desire he displays in the sonnets. She thus sets up an apparent reciprocity: she needs the sighs of lovers to redeem her, while Daniel desperately seeks Delia's pity. The common remedy—Delia's sympathy—becomes the ground on which Rosamond suggests their identification:

> Thy joyes depending on a woman grace,
> So move thy minde a woefull womans case.
>
> . . .
>
> Delia may happe to deygne to read our story,
> And offer up her sigh among the rest.
>
> (41–44)

Indeed, Rosamond clearly says that it is precisely Daniel's precarious position as a lover that makes him a better mediator for her story; he has, after all, shown himself to be sensitive to women's graces. The female speaker and the Petrarchan lover thus have the compatible goal of winning Delia's heart. "She must have her praise, thy pen her thanks," the character bargains with her writer (735). Daniel accepts this task, acknowledging that Rosamond's "griefes were worthy to be knowne," but qualifying his approval of his female subject by suggesting that her arguments are somewhat questionable.[31] Instead, Daniel is primarily interested in Rosamond's laments because they displace his own woes. By "telling hers, [I] might hap forget mine owne," the narrator admits (63). Yoking "hers" and "mine owne" implies the peculiar identity of sorrows that Rosamond suggests when she deems the text "our" story, for here Daniel acknowledges that his act of writing the female complaint allows him to suppress or

---

[31] In keeping with the way in which Jane Shore is introduced in the 1563 edition of *The Mirror for Magistrates*, the opening lines of *Rosamond* ostensibly affirm women's speech, even as they question its appropriateness. See the preface to Jane Shore's complaint in *The Mirror for Magistrates*, ed. Lily B. Campbell (1938; reprint, New York: Barnes and Noble, 1960), 371–73.

reveal his own interests.[32] In this sense, Rosamond's complaint reinforces the poetic function named by the sonnet text that precedes her story.

Although Rosamond initially suggests a collaborative project with her author, one in which she and the poet labor together to win Delia's good graces, it soon becomes evident that her agenda runs counter to that of the sonnet speaker's. By the course of her story, Rosamond critiques the poet's role as lover by discrediting the language of seduction that can produce fallen women. She becomes, in essence, a double for Delia, the mistress who supposedly receives the love sonnets. By urging other women not to be seduced by slippery rhetoric, she exposes the power dynamic within the sequence, making visible the logical consequence of succumbing to male desire. In doing so, she functions as a voice of commentary like E.K. and Gascoigne's "editor," one who turns the sonnet sequence into a more multivocal text governed, in part, by its appended reader.

Rosamond thus functions as a mechanism through which her writer can distance himself from his demonstrated poetics of love. Through his female complaint text, Daniel ruptures the identification set up in *Delia* between author and lover. Following on the heels of the sonnet sequence, the complaining woman's words allow the poet to prove himself on grounds other than the Petrarchan stage of love. In *The Shepheardes Calender*, Cuddie accomplishes the same task when he praises the moral and didactic functions of the poet and thus implicitly criticizes Colin's shortcomings. Gascoigne's "prodigal" narrative allows him to levy a similar critique of wasteful poetic indulgence. The female complaint speaker criticizes the limitations and dangers of poetry that operates within the eroticized sphere of literary amateurism; at the same time she creates a manuscript-identified, multivocal text that bears all the class privileges associated with that medium. Capitalizing on the tension created by the interstices of these two combined works, the poet colonizes the voice of Rosamond as a means of scripting himself as the restorer of fallen womanhood.

After her initial appeal to Daniel as a lover, Rosamond validates his new authorial role by contrasting the tremendous power of Daniel's poetic monument to the "little lasting" architectural one built by her ineffectual kingly lover (707). According to Rosamond, Henry II had promised to build a monument to memorialize his mistress: "I will cause posterity shall know,"

---

[32]This identity is curiously formed within the texture of the language as the two texts exhibit a series of verbal echoes. When Rosamond describes her submission to the king as the time when "dreadfull black, had dispossess'd the cleere," for instance, she echoes the sonnet writer/lover's description of his state of self-dispossession (431). Rosamond's description of the labyrinthine palace Henry built to imprison her also reflects tellingly on Daniel's description of love as "this thoughts maze" (Sonnet 17).

he states, "How faire thou wert above all women kind" (689–90). But Rosamond complains that this marble and brass structure is "little lasting" because it does not serve to memorialize her beauty properly. A more durable edifice can be found in Daniel's verse, as she exclaims to the poet:

> And were it not thy favourable lynes,
> Reedified the wracke of my decayes:
> And that thy accents willingly assignes,
> Some farther date, and give me longer daies,
> Fewe in this age had knowne my beauties praise
>   But thus renewd, my fame redeemes some time,
>   Till other ages shall neglect thy rime.
>
> (715–21)

Rosamond craftily forges a connection between her fame and her poet's. In applauding Daniel's favorable "accents" and urging that they be read, Rosamond reinvests herself in Daniel's new poetic role; for his text can do what her kingly lover within the story could not—project her beauty into posterity. Her inscriptions of Daniel's authorial role thus index his shift in poetic persona from lover to didactic writer. First validating his Petrarchan goal of attaining female sympathy, and then critiquing the language of courtly love on which his stance as lover rests, Rosamond finally compliments his poetic skill in moralizing historical wrongs. Henry's failed efforts become the foil to Daniel's successful creations.

Rosamond establishes herself as a reader not only of the sonnets, but also of her author's career. She solicits Daniel specifically because of his poetic skill; therefore, she demands that the reader rethink the place of the famed poems that she follows. In suggesting that "Delia may hap to read our story," she acknowledges the success of the previous work and implicitly applauds Daniel's talents in singing of his own loss and desire. The peculiarity of Rosamond's remarks lies in the fact that both *Delia* and *Rosamond* were published simultaneously. Daniel could not yet be a well-established love poet. Instead, by interpreting Daniel's training as a lover to be beneficial to her narrative, Rosamond creates a privileged place for the sonnets that she overtly criticizes. In short, she makes the sequence into a pre-text like the *Calender* or the *Flowres*, which is designed to give way to a more serious literary endeavor. Daniel's status as unfulfilled lover and as consummate artisan becomes the ground for qualifying him as the author of her more serious and tragic tale. Like E.K., Rosamond inscribes her author as famous, and thus he enters the public world, as does Immerito, as if he has already been read. He is known through his connection to Sidney and the acknowledgments of the infamous fallen woman who comments appreciatively but critically on his oeuvre. If *Delia* emerged from the pre-text of *Astrophel and Stella*, it also acts as a pre-text for the female complaint.

Daniel's sophisticated construction of authority was imitated by other writers. Thomas Lodge's publication of the *Complaint of Elstred* with the sonnet sequence *Phillis* follows the structure that Daniel established. While lamenting his own complaint, the poet encounters a vision of two women, Elstred and her daughter, who testify to their unfortunate fall from power. First mistress of Humber and then captured as a spoil of battle by Locrinus, Elstred provokes a political fracas that ends in Locrinus's overthrow and the death of herself and her daughter. The two women's spirits return to inscribe the story of their illustrious and sinful lives for posterity.[33]

Lodge's complaint poem, like Daniel's, alternately blurs and distinguishes between the malleable roles of poet, lover, and fallen woman. The text opens with a series of doublings, as the speaker's complaints blend into those of the "woeful vision" he discovers. The fact that there are two women complaining within this already doubled frame creates a network of echoes and reverberations. One effect of this mirror device is that an identity is forged between the principal characters and the writer himself, all of whom suffer from torturous woes. But Elstred ruptures that identity in the course of her tale when she undermines male language and the power of women in the machinations of courtship and chivalric exploit. When Elstred condemns her lover's "honny speech / Delivered by a trick Herculean tongue" (71), for instance, her words refer back to the playful rhetoric found in the poems of seduction in *Phillis*. The authority of the poet/narrator is thus qualified by, or held in tension with, the authority of the complaining woman.

As in Rosamond's text, Elstred's condemnation of the duplicity of courtly love is accompanied by a meditation on the importance of marking events through writing. Both works thus critique the discourse of love in order to make room for the poet to redeem his own profession. Elstred narrates how she and her daughter are transformed into historical texts justified by their didactic purpose; they present "the Annals of mishap / Wherein woe-tempted men may read theyr fortune" (83). Elstred thus offers herself as a negative moral example that can, she states, "teach successions to avoyde my fall" (59). The poet's new role—as the moral choric voice pronouncing on sin and tragedy, rather than as a seducer—is thus announced and demonstrated in the complaint text. As the women evaporate into ghosts, they become ephemeral poetic visions whose durability is deter-

---

[33]Thomas Lodge, *Complaint of Elstred*, in *The Complete Works of Thomas Lodge*, vols. 5–8 in the Hunterian Club Series (Glasgow: Robert Anderson, 1883), 5:59–84.

mined by the writer's more lasting poem. Lodge relies on the narrative of betrayal as a means of establishing a poetic vocation independent from that of the Petrarchan seducer, and he juxtaposes the transient laments on love with the lasting power of writing. After being enmeshed in the language of courtly love, Lodge emerges as someone able to fashion the moral "Annals of mishap" caused, in part, by the problems of erotic desire.

The publication of Shakespeare's *A Lover's Complaint* with the 1609 *Sonnets* also performs this operation of distantiation/authorization, but it goes to thematize the text's own doubleness more extensively. While it is difficult to sort out whether Shakespeare had any part in the decision to print these two genres together, we do know that he reaped the benefits of this publication because its effect was to validate a new authorial identity. As in the other poems, this text makes audible the woman's voice as she criticizes the practices of seduction, indicting the "deep brained sonnets" of the false Petrarchan lover. In *A Lover's Complaint*, however, the doubling of poet and vision occurs on multiple levels.

> From off a hill whose concave womb reworded
> A plaintive story from a sist'ring vale
> My spirits t'attend this double voice accorded,
> And down I laid to list the sad-tun'd tale.
> (1–4)

The image of doubleness is here built into the physical environment as the speaker listens to the echoes from the valley around him. The "tale" that he hears is not the complaint, as we might expect, but the "sist'ring" echoes produced from this "womb." This already doubled voice proliferates when the woman tells her story to the religious man. The reader, like the speaker, eavesdrops on a highly mediated tale surrounded by echoes against the backdrop of the weeping and reflective river. The complaining woman creates another embedded layer of dialogue when she gives voice to her seducer's words within her own story. The text then abounds with "re"'s—things told again, filtered, repeated, reverberating. As in Daniel's text, replication and echo become the techniques through which the Petrarchan poet and female auditor are associated and dissociated as complaining publishers. And again this complaint adds a layer of voices to the sonnet book that renders the work more plural and multivocal.

In the complaint/sonnet texts, authorial identity is shaped through the artful dialogue that strategically generates the role of the author through a simulated dispersal of speaking voices. The authority of the work is split between many doubles, as *Elstred* and *A Lover's Complaint* vivify in their exaggerations of this bifurcation. The complaint text allows the writer to gather these splintered layers together in a way that renders the author a more central and legitimate figure. In other words, the poet ironically emerges from his impersonation of discredited voices, an impersonation that, again ironically, simulates the privileged forms of manuscript writing. The female respondent becomes one of the doubles that the writer uses, like the role of editor or presenter of the work, to introduce his own authority through masquerade. The fallen woman's critique becomes a central part of the architecture of poetic authority, as it establishes an acceptable idiom through which the new poet can be presented and formally contained.

"Re-dressing" Authorial and Sexual Shame

The patterns of authorial emergence that I have described are frequently cast in a language that relies on sexual difference. W.L., for instance, tropes the class tensions surrounding publication as a heroic scene of cross-dressing, and Daniel and Lodge each devise authority by taking on the voice of a fallen woman. We remember that Gascoigne merely created what seemed to be an anthology when generating his public persona. A careful examination of Gascoigne's own descriptions of his career, however, reveals that he narrated the poetic progression and authorial emergence produced from that anthology in gendered terms. In his prefatorial apology to the Reverend Divines in *The Posies*, for instance, Gascoigne ex-plains that his revised text is "gelded" of all lascivious matter.[34] When promising a sexual purification of his work, a chastening of its taint of lust, Gascoigne associates masculinity with the previous illicit and scandalous text.

In *The Steele Glass*, Gascoigne further articulates the progression of his career in gendered terms. Here he suggests that as "Philomene" he has been subject to violation from a slanderous public and from hostile censuring authorities. He opens the text with an invocation to the infamous Nightingale,

> ... whose happy noble hart,
> No dole can daunt, nor feareful force affright,
> Whose chereful voice, doth comfort saddest wights,
> When she hir self, hath little cause to sing,
> Whom lovers love, bicause she plaines their greves,
> She wraies their woes and yet relieves their payne.
> (*Works*, 2:143, lines 1–6)

[34]Likewise, the printer of George Pettie's *A petite Pallace of Pettie his pleasure* (1576) figures his editorial practices as "gelding." STC 19819, ed. Herbert Hartman (London: Oxford University Press, 1938).

Gascoigne's words inadvertently point to the tumultuous connection between the woes of lovers and writers because Philomela is a paradoxical
emblem of both silence and speech. The narrator, in fact, calls on Philomela precisely for aid in writing his own verse, for she offers both poets
and lovers an indispensable vehicle for expressing themselves cathartically:
"she wraies their woes, and yet relieves their payne." Gascoigne suggests
that he learns from this bird "to sing a song, in spight of [his critics] de-
spight" (143). He furthers this analogy, in fact, by stating that he feels
more than mere sympathy for the raped bird; instead, he fully identifies
with the female subject position. Like Philomela, Gascoigne has been ravished by a Tereseus-like public, subject to the harsh rape and silencing of
Vain Delight and Slander. The raped woman's voice is used to articulate
the cultural pressures that could suppress the authorized poet and to
grant the homeopathic relief they need.[35] Gascoigne thus registers the
healthy amount of anxiety that the Elizabethan writer necessarily had in
betraying his woes to a powerful public body.

Casting himself as a hermaphroditic combination of male writer and
female subject, Gascoigne becomes Satyra who, like Philomela, sings to
reprove wretchedness. If he initially portrays himself as victim to implicitly
masculine forms of power, his text later playfully but forcefully comments
on this strange shift in gender:

> I am not he whom slaunderous tongues have tolde,
> (False tongues in dede, & craftie subtile braines)
> To be the man, which ment a common spoyle
> Of loving dames, whose eares wold heare my words
> Or trust the tales devised by my pen.
> I n'am a man, as som do thinke I am,
> (Laugh not good Lord) I am in dede a dame,
> Or at the least, a right Hermaphrodite.
>
> (2:144 , lines 46–53)

35Shakespeare's raped Lucrece also voices the shared problems of writing, ignominy, and
violation. In *Lucrece*, a poem indebted to the complaint form, Shakespeare interestingly
describes rape in terms that conflate writing, silencing, sheepfolds, echoes, and imprisonment: Tarquin uses Lucrece's nightgown to "pen her piteous clamors in her head" (line
681). Of course, Lucrece was a more ambiguous figure morally than Rosamond or Jane
Shore for Renaissance readers. She was, for instance, held up as an emblem of modesty. In
As You Like It, when Orlando assembles the body of his beloved by collecting attributes from
mythological figures, he appropriates Lucretia's modesty. She is also an exemplum of female
behavior in Thomas Salter's *A Mirror mete for all Mothers, Matrones and Maidenes* (1574), which

Of course, Gascoigne could have stylized himself as Satyra, a second Philomene, without calling attention to the discrepancy in the gender of the
comparison. We need only look to Shakespeare's Sonnet 110 to see how
common it was for a poet to assume the persona of Philomela without noting the physical problems such a transformation could cause. But Gascoigne
makes gender an issue in his figuration of his authorship as a socially victimized position: do not laugh, he warns, I am a she. Gascoigne craftily re-gen-
ders himself to discredit charges that he has despoiled his female readership; instead, he offers for his male audience's pleasure the "joke" of his
double gender. His effeminization may open him up to a figurative critical
rape by the Renaissance public, but it safeguards him from appearing as a
lascivious and amorous writer. Gascoigne's introductory metaphor thus
functions, like E.K.'s gloss or Rosamond's commands, to distance the poet
from the morally problematic position of courtier-lover.

After railing at drunken soldiers, corrupt priests, and arrogant gentlemen, Gascoigne concludes his satire with an epilogue that labels society's
villains as "monsters . . . With Angels face and harmefull helish harts"
(173), a duplicity he then refigures as courtly effeminacy:

> What should these be? (speake you my lovely lord)
> They be not men: for why? they have no beards.
> They be no boyes, which ware such side long gowns.
> They be no Gods, for al their gallant glosse.
> They be no divels, (I trow) which seme so saintish.
> What be they? women? masking in mens weedes?
>
>   .   .   .
>
> They be so sure even Wo to Men in dede.
>
>   (2:173-74)

Gascoigne's pun suggests that the term "women" has buried within it a
definition of sexual difference because the female sex is that which gives
"woe" to "men." This last satire thus creates a formal symmetry in *The Steele
Glass*. Gascoigne concludes his poem by righting the sexual inversion created by his assumption of the female subject position in the opening lines.
In other words, he reasserts his own manliness by naming everything against
which he inveighs as "feminine." "Woe" is contained within the very word
and meaning of woman; the poet must speak her voice in making his

---

condemns the reading of lascivious material but recommends the lives of virtuous women
such as Claudia, Portia, and Lucretia. Some texts, however, which follow Augustine's reading
of the myth, condemn Lucrece's overvaluation of reputation; and a few including Juan Luis
Vives, accuse her of wantonness in acquiescing to the rape. Through the character of
Lucrece, Shakespeare extends and modifies the politics of the female complaint.

social complaint, but he cannot, finally, be completely woeful—cannot be a woman or "Wo to Men." If Philomene "wraies [the lover's] woes," she does so to become the object, not the subject, of satire. At the text's conclusion, Gascoigne abandons the female role that he so fully assumed and suggests instead that such a colonization was at best a joke, and at worst a sign of degeneration. Gascoigne thus steps forth as a "true" author by figuring both his formal progression from amorous to didactic poetry and his personal conversion from wayward youth to serious author as a metamorphosis from effeminization to the truly masculine subject position. Like Daniel, Gascoigne uses the victimized woman's voice to "[wraie] his woes," but he fashions a female complaint/satire that finally deflects the identification between victimized woman and abused writer. By doing so, he draws on the very language that constrains him and fashions it for his own career needs. In essence, he reformulates the anxieties of publication in terms of a mythological female victim. His attached poem, *The Complaint of Philomela*, makes it more explicit that the female complaint serves as a trope for authorship, for in this text the narrator interprets Philomela's tragic tale as a sign of the dangers of a broadly defined and unruly social and sexual desire. By displaying what happens when the author/ poet attempts to "leape . . . beyond . . . lawful reache," the poem conventionally uses erotic desire to signify the dangers of overreaching in general (*Works*, 2:206). Gascoigne's use of the Philomela myth reveals one more instance in which the sixteenth-century writer drew on a highly gendered language to express and combat the anxieties surrounding authorship.

I argue that these writers undertake various female impersonations as a means of paradoxically defending themselves against the pervasive threat of effeminization that amateur writing was seen to pose. In a culture in which effeminacy was equated with weakness, it seems bizarre for writers to stage their own sexual disempowerment publicly. But when we realize that writing always harbored the threat of emasculation in the sixteenth century, these strategic and gendered tropes of the authorial career become more explicable. Numerous Renaissance prefaces, tracts, and apologies indicate that poets and courtiers endangered themselves because they catered to female tastes and desires. In *The Schoole of Abuse* (1579), Stephen Gosson describes at length how poetry and theater could wreak havoc on one's morals, particularly because they could "effeminate" the mind."[36] In *Playes Confuted* (1582), he mentions that while dressing as a woman on stage was horrific, adopting "not the apparell onely, but the

---

[36]Stephen Gosson, *The Schoole of Abuse* (1579; reprint, London: Shakespeare Society, 1841), 19.

gate, the gestures, the voyce, the passions of a women" was even more abominable.[37] Certainly Gosson is talking about actual, not textual, impersonations. But can these writers be completely exempt from such a taint in their assumption of the woman's passions?

Barnabe Rich's *Farewell to the Military Profession* opens with an address to a female audience that suggests that both courtiership and writing constitute a retreat to a female domain: "Gentlewomen I am sure there are many (but especially of suche as beste knowe me) that wil not a little wonder to see suche alteration in me, that havyng spent my yonger daies in the warres, emongest men, and vowed my self onely unto Mars: Should now in my riper yeares, desire to live in peace emongst women, and to consecrate my self wholy unto Venus."[38] Rich's consecration is delivered sarcastically, as he resigns himself to a social world that dictates that he "followe a Fiddle in a gentlewomans chamber" rather than "marche after a Drumme in the feeld" (4).[39] Throughout his preface, Rich suggests that men are forced into the company of women because society fails to esteem military action: "therefore to fitte the tyme the better, I have putte forthe these lovying Histories. . . . I truste I shall please Gentlewomen, and that is all the gaine that I looke for. And herein I doe but followe the course of the worlde" (10).

In describing "the course of the worlde," however, Rich registers quite markedly his hostility toward the task of pleasing gentlewomen. The preface openly scorns the feminine manners and apparel currently in vogue at the court: "For many now adaies goe aboute by as great devise as maie bee, how thei might become women theimselves. How many Gentlemen shalt you see at this present date, that I dare undertake, in the wearying of their apparell, in the settyng of their Ruffes, and the freselyng of their heire, are more new fangeled and foolishe, then any curtisan of Venice" (10). Playing at courtly fashions and fictions endangers foppish writers, threatening to make men "become women theimselves." When Rich resignedly urges his fellow soldiers to "laie aside your weapons, hang up your armours by the walles, and learne another while . . . to Pipe, to Feddle, to Syng, to Daunce, to lye, to forge, to flatter, to cary tales, to set Ruffe, or to dooe any

[37]Gosson, *Plays Confuted* . . . (1582), ed. Arthur Freeman (New York: Garland Press, 1972), 175.

[38]Barnabe Rich, *His Farewell to the Military Profession* (1581), ed. Thomas Mabry Cranfill (Austin: University of Texas Press, 1959), 3.

[39]Juliet Fleming makes this point in "George Pettie, Barnabe Rich, and the Delights for Women Only," in the forthcoming book *Sexuality and Gender in Early Modern Europe: Institutions, Texts, Images*, ed. James Turner (Cambridge: Cambridge University Press). My thanks to Juliet Fleming for sharing her ideas about Rich's work with me.

thing that your appetites best serves unto" (12), his ironic tone is quite biting. Rich's *Farewell* thus stands as an emblem of his loss, a textual sign of his effeminate ability to "please gentlewomen" by carrying tales rather than weapons.

Although Rich and Gosson are radically different writers—one presenting a collection of imaginative stories in hopes of courtly preferment, the other writing a didactic tract that condemns courtliness—both indicate that courtiership in general and poetic production in particular could effeminize the male subject. Both nostalgically long for the time when savagery and physical daring were lauded instead of the new-fangled fashions and fanciful games of gentlemanly play. Richard Helgerson observes, "From the repudiation of love and women to the repudiation of romantic fiction is a short way. . . . An attack on one is likely to be an attack on the other" (*Elizabethan Prodigals*, 96).

Although the act of wooing should, it seems, confer masculinity and enable the man to establish a clear difference between the participants in the game of courtly love, Elizabethans saw poetry and courtship as something that potentially destabilized gender. The wooer could become his "other", tainted by catering to the tastes of women. In Sidney's *Arcadia*, Musidorus offers this exact argument to the cross-dressed Pyrocles, who stands as a sign of this very threat. Musidorus begs Pyrocles to take control of the unnatural rebellion called love that has altered his mind and appearance: "true love hath that excellent nature in it, that it doth transform the very essence of the lover into the thing loved. . . . and this effeminate love of a woman doth so womanize a man that, if he yield to it, it will not only make him an Amazon, but a launder, a distaff-spinner or whatseover other vile occupation their idle heads can imagine and their weak hands perform."[40]

In the preface to his sonnet sequence *Castara*, William Habington extends Musidorus's warning to poets as well as to practioners of love. Here he describes poetry as a Circe-like seductive mistress: "when it is wholly imployed in the soft straines of love, his soule who entertaines it, loseth much of that strength which should confirme him man. The nerves of judgement are weakened by its dalliance, and when woman . . . is the supreme object of wit, we soone degenerate into effeminacy."[41] The gentlemanly amorous love poet, then, lays himself open to threats against his masculinity when he sets out to fulfill the demands assigned to his class: to act the part of the courtier.

[40]Philip Sidney, *The Countess of Pembroke's Arcadia* (1590), ed. Maurice Evans (New York: Penguin, 1984), 133–34.
[41]William Habington, *Castara*, STC 12585 (1640), sig A4[v].

By portraying the author as one who throws off female clothing and heroically enters a male martial arena (combating the "womanly humor" Harvey saw as evident in Spenser's earlier poems), *The Faerie Queene* obviously defends against this threat of effeminization. W.L. uses the distinction between poetic forms as the ground for establishing the "manly" Achillean writer. Gascoigne controls such a threat by scripting the kind of woman he will allow himself to be, and then ridiculing the conflation of male satirist and the feminized object of his satire. But in the related narrative of authorship, class, and gender that I trace in the creation of the literary pseudomorph, Daniel's complaint text and its imitators seem an aberration. Because Daniel's ventriloquization of the female voice is never thoroughly renounced, his work seems merely to analogize, rather than stay, the downward mobility threatened by publication. After all, the power of W.L.'s allusion rests in Achilles' final rejection of the discredited state of femininity. In Ovid's telling of the episode, Achilles' costuming is made to seem ridiculous and comic, a provisional dislocation of sexual identity that is told only because it inevitably is discovered and righted. Gascoigne's very warning—"(Laugh not good Lord) I am in dede a dame"—implies the inevitable comedy of sexual inversion. Because the male-authored female complaints employ the voice of the woman without statedly renouncing that position or rendering it comic, it seems that they unwittingly further the writers' descent into baseness without staging completely their triumphant rehabilitation.

One way that we can begin to disentangle this apparent contradiction is by turning to a pervasive theme within the complaints: the fallen woman's obsession with fame. Both Rosamond and Elstred spend a good deal of time meditating on the power of rumor and the problems generated by the circulation of texts, names, and reputations. The opening lines of Rosamond's complaint, for instance, introduce us to a woman grappling with the horrors of being a public figure. Her voice rises, projected from the hellish depths of the underworld: "A sheete could hide my face, but not my sin," she cries, "For Fame finds never tombe t'inclose it in" (*Poems,* 11.6–7). The first stanza centers around the unwilling publication of Rosamond's sin, which is written upon her body and which necessitates her tale. Rosamond's ever-shifting and often illogical identification of the source of her fall points to her ambivalence about how she should be known. Her text thus foregrounds the problem of controlling one's history and one's name.[42]

---

[42]Part of this ambiguity is obviously the poet's, as evidenced by Rosamond's contradictory speaking positions throughout the poem: she switches between the sorrowful and repentent

When calling out that "Rosamond hath little left her but her name, / And that disgrac'd, for time hath wrong'd the same. / No Muse suggests the pittie of my case," Rosamond contradictorily suggests that she is alternately dissatisfied with notoriety and anonymity (20–21). She begs for someone to circulate the correct story of her life: "Time hath long worn out the memorie / Both of my life, and lives unjust depriving" (17–18). She makes clear that her disgrace has not been forgotten; only the contingencies of her tale have been erased from cultural memory. Therefore, although she condemns *fama*, she needs a poet to publish her tale and redeem her reputation. Such a redemption is predicated on the very power of poetry, a power that is necessarily problematic for the textual subject when the work is made available for public scrutiny.

Her dependence on the public nature of her narration ironically subtends her strident condemnation of public exposure throughout the work. Rosamond rails against the power of projected language, complaining that "nothing can be doone but Fame reports" (560). She compares fame to an intrusive beastly bird, associated interestingly with the figure of the uncontrollably loquacious woman who dares to reveal the secrets of the elite courtier:

> Fame doth explore what lyes most secret hidden,
> Entring the closet of the Pallace dweller:
> Abroad revealing what is most forbidden,
> Of truth and falsehood both an equall teller:
> Tis not a guarde can serve for to expell her,
>   The sword of justice cannot cutte her wings,
>   Nor stop her mouth from utt'ring secrete things.
>   (561–67; emphasis mine)

Rosamond's denunciation of these invasions on her privacy is particularly interesting when read in terms of the preface to *Delia*, which we read in Chapter 3 as a powerful moment of eroticized disclosure. Here Daniel states that his published text registers the fact that his own "private" and secret passions were wrongly made public. His stylized and highly conventional indictment of publication is echoed by Rosamond's criticism of "utt'ring secrete things." Rosamond's fear of exposure points uncomfort-

---

heroine, the enraged victim of social and sexual abuse, and the coy paramour who boasts of her willful pride. Although righteously pointing to the snares of sin and worldly pleasure, Rosamond recounts with equal indignance the injustice of her imprisonment and her murder. In making her story immortal, Rosamond wants to vindicate her name and brag about her power. The effect is that the reader is made to sympathize with the plight of Rosamond's life, but finally to question the grounds on which she justifies herself.

ably back to the moment of textual betrayal that Daniel narrates in the introduction to this book. Daniel's reluctance to "shame" himself by publishing, then, is powerfully recast as the shame of sexual licentiousness in the course of the text. The poem's conclusion marks the affinity between the writer and his female subject, as it reminds the reader of the narrator's own woes ever present behind Rosamond's complaint. Because the poem itself testifies to Daniel's prodigality, he must cover his shame by refusing to write any more. The sonnet speaker in *Delia* finalizes this silence: "I say no more, I feare I saide too much" (Sonnet 50). At the end of *Rosamond*, Daniel echoes this sentiment:

> But ah the worlde hath heard too much of those,
> My youth such errors must no more disclose,
>   I'll hide the rest, and greeve for what hath beene
>   Who made me knowne, must make me live unseene.
>   (741–42)

In these moments, the female speaker's fall from grace becomes strangely conflated with Daniel's youthful errors, mistakes bound up both with public display and erotic desire. The woman's shame and her bold justification for her promiscuity become associated with the waywardness of publishing itself, the textual promiscuity of appearing in public. Rosamond's narrative of the loss of chastity reframes the language of exposure that Daniel uses in describing the publication of his work and his own passionate desires.

Lodge's Elstred concocts a peculiar and hideous image in her similar diatribe against fame, one that exaggerates Rosamond's description of the feathered, garrulous creature that threatens to disclose elite secrets to the world. Fame is represented here as a pastiche of body parts that burst strangely from Elstred herself "through continual motion growing great":

> The fame that should present my facts to view,
> As I from cradle crept, so gathered wing:
> As grew my beauties, so his feathers grew,
> As waxt my worth, so was he prest to spring,
>   As yeeres increast, from earth to trees he sprung,
>   From trees to towers, from whence my fame he sung.
>
> Thus through continuall motion growing great,
> His many feathers hatcht as many eyes,
> His eyes, as many tongues for to intreate,
> His tongues, as many eares to harken cryes.
>   Which feathers, eyes, tongues, eares, he ever frames
>   To paint our praise, and bruit our endlesse blames.
>   (60–61)

In describing this sprouting creature made of ears and eyes that turns against its own source, Elstred aligns herself with the stereotype of the grotesque and uncontainable woman. According to the female speaker, fame produces an inhumanly assorted beast that thrives on excess communication. With its multiple eyes, tongues, and ears, this bird becomes a figure for the horrors of exorbitant and ungovernable representation. Furthermore, Elstred figures her emergence into the public eye as a maternal dismemberment; fame is a "monstrous babe (that rents his mothers brest, / To fill the world with tragick historie)." Because she calls for her story to be told publicly, these words transform Elstred into her own hostile double, an identification that is extended when the poet becomes aligned with both woman and monster. After all, Lodge's text does seek to fill the world with Elstred's "tragick historie," and thus his own narration and publication become written as a "monstrous" rent in the fabric of female modesty and privacy.

B[arnabe] R[ich]'s *Greene's Newes both from Heaven and Hell* (1593) shows us how the narrative of the unchaste woman can express the author's own particular cultural problems. In this work, Robert Greene speaks from the grave, explaining how his status as an author has exiled him from both heaven and hell. Heaven rejects him because of a wanton and dissolute life that is evidenced in particular by his "writing of books."[43] Like Rosamond, the author exists in a state of limbo, mourning his fall into a salacious life. His voice emerges from hellish depths to lament the suffering he endures for his fiction-writing. A popular text, written one year after *Delia* and in the same year as *Phillis*, *Greene's Newes* shows how the same structure could serve as a vehicle for repenting both sexual and authorial indiscretions. The *Newes* demonstrates how the popular literary pattern of the woman's fall from grace could easily be appropriated to tell the story of authorial repentance. Here the writer's social and professional fall necessarily taints him. This stigma is everywhere apparent: Henry Chettle, for instance, notes that "To come in print is not to seeke praise, but to crave pardon."[44] Gabriel Harvey testifies to the prevalent fears of publicity when he mentions the "odious infamye" that could be incurred by stepping into the public eye.[45] George Puttenham also acknowledges

---

[43]B. R. [Barnabe Rich], *Greene's Newes both from Heaven and Hell*, STC 12259 (1593), title page.

[44]Henry Chettle, *Kind-Hartes Dream* (1592), reprinted in Bodley Head Quartos, ed. G. B. Harrison (London: John Lane, 1923), 5.

[45]Gabriel Harvey, *The Letter-Book of George Harvey, 1573–80*, ed. Edward J. L. Scott, 2d ser., 33 (Westminster: Nichols and Sons for the Camden Society, 1884), 59–60.

this social stigma when he urges poets not to feel "ashamed to bewray their skills" by publishing works under their own names.[46]

When poets become preoccupied with telling, rumor, slander, and fame in these complaint texts, they give voice to the anxieties surrounding public writing. The complaining woman's status as a tainted and sexually polluted *woman* is crucial for this displacement. For these figures absorb and re-present the shame of publication by translating it into terms to which male writers could not be equally vulnerable. The woman acts as the "other" from which the author promotes his own fame by publicly reporting her private shame, a peculiar type of violation that a man could not suffer in the same way: the loss of chastity. Juan Luis Vives makes this double standard clear in his *Instruction of a christen Woman* (1523) when he describes at length the cost a woman paid for sexual indiscretion. Men, he explains in a chapter devoted to the important of virginity and chastity, are judged on a variety of qualities, but "in a woman the honestie is in stede of all."[47] "Take from a woman her beautie," he continues, "take from her kynrede, ryches, comelynes, eloquence, sharpenes of wytte, counnynge in her crafte, gyve her chastitie and thou hast gyven her al thynges" (sig. G4v). It is no wonder that Ruth Kelso summarily notes that sexual purity was *the* key to proper womanhood: "Enough could not be said of [chastity] as the foundation of womanly worth. . . . Let a woman have chastity, she has all. Let her lack chastity and she has nothing."[48] When the poet becomes the monstrous beast that publicizes the experiences of his female

---

[46]Puttenham, *The Arte of English Poesie*, 22–23. In one of her poems, Isabella Whitney interestingly comments on the complex connections between fame and shame that are so densely interlaced in these complaint poems. The speaker in her female complaint compares her lover's betrayal to that of Sinon, Aeneas, and Theseus: "For they, for their unfaithfulness, / did get perpetuall fame: / Fame? wherefore dyd I terme it so? / I should have cald it shame." As she shifts the meaning of the word from a positive to a negative one, Whitney calls attention to the tenuous syntactical difference between the two sounds that marks their difference. The very magnitude of the word "fame" and the problematic within it arrest Whitney's lyrical complaint as she self-consciously interrupts herself to disclose, through a rhyme, the perjorative connotation of the word she has uttered. This conventional linguistic play becomes a register for the uneasy but prevalent connections between publicity and ignominy in the Renaissance. Isabella Whitney, "The Copy of A Letter lately written in meeter, by a yonge Gentilwoman: to her unconstant lover," STC 25439 (1567), sig. A3v.

[47]Juan Luis Vives, *Instruction of a christen Woman*, trans. Richard Hyrde, STC 24857 (1540); sig. G4. He goes on to say that "chastitie is the principall vertue of a woman and counterpeyseth with all the reste" (sig. L4v).

[48]Ruth Kelso, *Doctrine for the Lady of the Renaissance* (Urbana: University of Illinois Press, 1956), 24. Elaine Beilin seconds this assessment: "where chastity for men was by no means central, for women it was prescribed as the preeminent goal for all, whether celibate, maiden, wife, or widow" (*Redeeming Eve*, 6). See also Valerie Wayne, "Some Sad Sentence: Vives' *Instruction of a Christian Woman*" in *Silent But for the Word*, ed. Margaret Hannay (Kent, Ohio: Kent State University Press, 1985), 15–29.

subject, he uses the woman's complaint about her sexual fall to express the contradictory benefits and dangers in publishing courtly writing. By meditating so persistently on publication and publicness—on its hazards, its importance, and its follies—these female characters self-consciously disclose their strange role in articulating and holding at bay their authors' anxieties about appearing in the literary marketplace.

In his address to the Countess of Cumberland prefacing his *Letter from Octavia to Marcus Antonius* (1599), Daniel calls attention to the very substitution that I have outlined. Here he acknowledges that female grief is an important resource for the male writer:

> Although the meaner sort (whose thoughts are plac'd)
> As in another Region, farre below
> The sphere of greatnesse) cannot rightly taste
> What touch it hath, nor right her passions know:
> Yet haue I here aduentur'd to bestow
> Words vpon griefe, as my griefes comprehend;
> And made this great afflicted Lady show,
> Out of my feelings, what she might have pend
> And her the same I bring forth, to attend
> Upon thy reuerent name, to live with thee
> Most vertuous Lady, that vouchsaf'st to lend
> Eare to my notes, and comfort unto mee,
> That one day may thine owne faire vertues spread,
> B'ing Secretary now but to the dead.[49]

Daniel sets up a hierarchical social geography of readers that stretches from the "meaner sort," whose thoughts cannot rise to understand female passion correctly, to the truly enlightened who are sensitive to affliction and pain. The afflictions of Octavia become a touchstone for testing the worth of readers and writers. In fact, Daniel sets up this geography to herald the power of his own literary feat in transforming her suffering into language. By doing so, Daniel identifies his own sorrows and griefs with those of Octavia: he forms her words "out of my feelings," he states, articulating what his own personal "griefes comprehend." While he describes himself merely as a mediator, a secretary through which the dead speak, his own stake in this secretarial work is clear; for in asking for comfort from his potential patroness, he assumes that his text has exposed his own vulnerabilities and problems. The reader sees that Daniel is able to disclose and combat the stigmatization that he feels in publicly authoring lit-

---

[49]Samuel Daniel, *Works*, ed. Alexander B. Grosart, 5 vols. (London: Hazell, Watson, and Viney, 1885–1896; reissued, New York: Russell and Russell, 1963), 1:116.

erary works by ventriloquizing the female complaint. Her woes bespeak his own while displaying his distance from the "meaner sort" of literary clientele.

Many writers therefore confront the social problem of authorship by staging it as a cross-dressing, and they stay the articulated threat of effeminization by wearing out the metaphor, actually speaking through the woman's voice. The impersonation makes it clear that although poet and woman share one type of "shame," there is ultimately a crucial difference: he is the writing author, and she the fallen woman. Her victimization and/or violation not only supersedes the poet's own, but it also serves to set up his more serious, didactic authorial role. Thomas Middleton's *The Ghost of Lucrece* ironically discloses the vastly different repercussions of authorial and sexual shame when the title character indicts her rapist as an author:

> Loe under that base tipe of Tarquins name,
> I cypher figures of iniquitie,
> He writes himselfe the shamer, I the shame,
> The Actor hee, and I the tragedie
> The stage am I and he the historie.[50]

The vivid narration of the loss of chastity, then, constructs a pattern whereby the writer establishes an identification with and a renunciation of femininity. The Renaissance writer uses this technique to represent his shamed position as a public writer—at the same time, minimizing it by comparison to the wayward woman. In this sense, cross-dressing ironically marks more clearly the distinction between genders. In complaint texts, fallen women tell of the affinities between sexual and authorial indiscretions only, in the end, to vivify the absolute difference within that seeming analogy. The highly gendered rhetoric and the literary forms that these writers use, then, serve to manage and obscure the social fissures surrounding public writing. After all, Achilles' transvestism is recounted as a temporary "other" position that must eventually dissolve when his essential manliness becomes apparent to the smart reader.

The Rape of Lucrece allegorizes this emergence when Brutus capitalizes on Lucrece's rape and death to prove himself an orator and authoritative leader. Brutus's emergence is interestingly figured as the act of changing clothes:

---

[50]Thomas Middleton, *The Ghost of Lucrece* (1600), facsimile ed. Joseph Quincy Adams (New York: Scribner's, 1937), lines 337–41.

Brutus, who pluck'd the knife from Lucrece's side,
Seeing such emulation in their woe,
Began to *clothe* his wit in state and pride,
Burying in Lucrece's wound his folly's show.
He with the Romans was esteemed so
    As silly jeering idiots are with kings,
      For sportive words and utt'ring foolish things.

But now he throws that *shallow habit* by,
Wherein deep policy did him *disguise,*
And arm'd his long-hid wits advisedly . . .
         (lines 1805–16; emphasis mine)

Formerly regarded as a jester, Brutus makes his debut by taking advantage of the outrage generated by the tale of the violated woman. He thus becomes a figure for Shakespeare, whose emergence as an important author rested, in part, on his creation of <u>Lucrece</u>. Generally seen as a rhetorical masterpiece, *Lucrece* was the "graver" piece (more serious, printed, and memorializing) that Shakespeare, in his dedication to <u>Venus and Adonis,</u> had promised to deliver to the public. The poem was read as a sign of poetic seriousness, a work that could confer moral and poetic authority for the writer because it appealed to the "wiser sort."[51] In *The Steele Glass*, Nicholas Bowyer uses the same terms to praise Gascoigne's transformation from amorous lover to didactic writer: "now he seeks the gravest to delight." Having controlled his effeminization through the mythological figure of the complaining Philomela, Gascoigne emerges with a more worthy authorial identity.[52] The construction of authority rests on a now familiar pattern of disclosure and revelation, gendered in various ways by each career trajectory.

The packaging of the printed text of *The Complaint of Rosamond* is interesting because it charts the way in which writers used their female complaint poems to shape authorial roles. The title page of this text displays an arch in which are inscribed the words "the complaynt of Rosamond." The title is framed within an elaborate and ornate textual edifice that in-

---

[51]We can recall here Gabriel Harvey's famous comment: "The younger sort takes much delight in Shakespeares Venus, & Adonis: but his Lucrece, & his tragedie of Hamlet, Prince of Denmarke, have it in them, to please the wiser sort." Cited in *The Complete Works of Shakespeare*, ed. David Bevington, 3d ed. (Glenview, Ill.: Scott Foresman and Company, 1980), 1544.

[52]Gascoigne, *Works*, 2:139. A commendatory poem to Drayton's complaining Matilda activates this pun in a different context when the poem says of Drayton's female character: "Shee by thy Muse, her fame from grave doth rayse, / And hie conceit, thy lines doth dignifie" (Drayton, *Works*, 2:212).

troduces the printed work (fig. 6). The format for this display of Rosamond's complaint is retrospectively given meaning in the poem when the character describes her forced enclosure within the labyrinthine palace constructed by her kingly lover. We know that this connection is not haphazard because Rosamond explicitly compares the durability of this palace with Daniel's poem. The title page solidifies this identification by transforming her story into the palatial artifact that announces her author. We see the ominous character that this pictorial space exudes when we attend to the poems' prevalent thematic associations between imprisonment, entombment, reputation, and structural edifice. In one passage, Rosamond begs that her submission not "intombe with blacke reproch a spotted name" (319). Although ostensibly an attempt to erase the "blacke reproch" that Rosamond has suffered, Daniel's text reinscribes her ignominy by submitting it to the press, intensifying its magnitude by making it more public. Rosamond's violation not only absorbs the authorial breach of making private passions public, but it also becomes the physical and monumental sign that en-"tomes" Daniel's book. Not surprisingly, later writers simultaneously criticize Rosamond's ill repute and note Daniel's skill in redeeming and immortalizing her through poetic skill.

Daniel's title page plays out what Abbe Blum sees as the moments of "commemoration" and "monumentalizing" that Shakespeare stages in his works. Blum provocatively traces Shakespeare's impulse to fix value on that which is deemed inaccessible and unattainable by appealing to the body of the woman.[53] In *Lucrece*, for instance, the gaze of the intruder renders Lucrece immobile and inanimate, transporting her into the distanced realm of sanctified death at the moment of erotic violation. In increasingly complex variations, Blum surveys this gesture in numerous plays, seeing how they "demonstrate the coincidence of the heroine's death, effacement, physical or visual violation with the imagery of funereal, sexual, and idolatrous monument" (100). While Blum sees monumentalizing as a moment of circumscription/possession enacted on the bodies of women, her analysis can be reimagined so as to incorporate the textual-monumentalizing process that occurs when female complaints are translated into published works and made to figure their author's career development. In the female complaint, dead, unavailable, or repressed female subjects are brought back from the dead and then reentombed within the printed edifice of the text. Daniel's prefatorial icon inscribes Rosamond as

---

[53]Abbe Blum, "'Strike all that look upon with with mar[b]le': Monumentalizing Women in Shakespeare's Plays," in *The Renaissance Englishwoman in Print: Counterbalancing the Canon*, ed. Anne M. Haselkorn and Betty S. Travitsky (Amherst: University of Massachusetts Press, 1990), 99–118.

an ornate and somewhat inanimate figure who monumentalizes her author through her laments from the dead.

When Richard Barnfield celebrates the fact that Daniel's fame "was grav'd on Rosamonds blacke hearse," he puns on the multiple associations that this visual icon represents: the poet's reliance on his female subject's textual/funereal entombment. The pun on "grave" conflates Rosamond's physical death in the poem with her transformation into a printed, engraved, textual subject. In this sense, she is monumentalized twice: her body is carried to the grave while her story is disseminated as a book artifact to a larger reading public. Both transitions contribute to Daniel's sense of "gravity" as an author. We must remember that he promised to turn to more "tragicke notes" in his 1594 text as proof of his poetic seriousness. Daniel himself trades on the language of material structure when he styles himself a "curious builder" in the 1607 verse preface to *Delia* and *Rosamond*. He explains his revisions by noting that he has "refurnisht out this little frame," making "some rooms inlargd" (*Poems*, 3). As builder of the structure of poetic reputation as well as his own particular text, he can state conclusively: "Howsoever be it well or ill / What I have done, it is mine owne I may / Do whatsoever therewithall I will" (3). The presentation of himself as an unwilling author (seen so clearly in the 1592 version) has clearly disappeared as Daniel projects his voice comfortably within the now authorized work. In his complaint text, Daniel raises the question of poetic reputation by hinting that his renown is deeply interwoven with the lasting power of Rosamond's notoriety and beauty. In this later edition, he completes the process of naming his own authority by boasting assuredly, "I know I shalbe read, among the rest, / So long as men speake english" (4). Although Daniel was known for other works as well, Barnfield singles out his female complaint as a marker of this enduring fame. His reputation is seen as "grav'd on Rosamonds blacke hearse," a signifying crypt curiously figured by the spatial and architectural designs of the title page itself. Rosamond, in fact, uses the vocabulary of building when she tells Daniel that his "favourable lynes, / Reedified the wracke of [her] decayes" (716). The role of wayward woman may offer the sixteenth-century male writer a voice through which to bewail his precarious position within the culture, but that voice must be metamorphosed into a proper material surface—the edifice, monument, tomb—that can support his signature and announce his more "grave" authorial identity.

As a pseudomorph, the complaint poem thus sends out contradictory signals about the text's status as manuscript and printed object. We remember that formally these texts work to contain the stigma that they belie in their concern with reputation. By deferring to the variety of inscribed privileged readers who establish a multivocal quality for the text, writers fashion published books that bear the mark of things elite, private, and proper. Using amorous love poetry as a springboard, these poets rewrite their cultural place by creating texts that openly debate and interpret the status of poetry. The complaint text becomes one form through which the writer responds to the problems attached to courtly love and gentlemanly amateurism. Daniel's and Lodge's female complaint poems more overtly attend to issues of gender than Spenser's and Gascoigne's pre-texts do, but they can be seen as playing out similar ambivalences and concerns about the role of authorship in a newly popular print culture. The complaint texts thus offer courtly writing without the threat of effeminization, publication without the threat of class slippage. Just as prefaces became an important channel through which the legitimacy of publication could be strengthened, the physical composition of these pseudomorphs allowed the writer to reshape the authority of manuscript writing.

It is telling, then, that in *Colin Clouts Come Home Againe* (1595), Spenser encourages the promising "shepherd" Daniel to elevate his "lowly flight" and to try his hand at more noble forms of writing. He urges Daniel to abandon "soft laies" and turn to "tragick plaints." This is, of course, the familiar and seductive trajectory that Spenser and Daniel followed. But it is more interesting that Spenser makes the shepherd and lover into interchangeable speaking positions. If Spenser the shepherd is feminized by W.L., Daniel the lover is, in this reference, pastoralized. The ambitious humility that we know exists in the pastoral form becomes easily blurred into the lowly "soft laies" of femininity and love. As both writers seek to name a humble aesthetic status from which they will start their ambitious careers, they displace problems of downward social mobility onto literary genres themselves—the lowly pastoral and the morally inferior love song. Writers and publishers stylize this descent so prevalently because it was important in securing a narrative of the writers' progression to more noble and hence more masculine concerns.

I am suggesting, then, that the issues of class and form that surround public authorship become deflected in pseudomorphs onto constructions of gender, that the precarious position of the writing author motivated the conflation of transvestism with public appearance, and that gender difference was manipulated in order to articulate cultural concerns about the social place of the publishing writer. The rhetoric of cross-dressing and the genre of female complaint generated useful ways for expressing and managing these social problems. Critics such as Phyllis Rackin, Catherine Belsey, and Jean Howard have suggested ways that cross-dressing on the stage placed pressure on stable identity in the Renaissance.[54] This practice

[54]Phyllis Rackin, "Androgyny, Mimesis, and the Marriage of the Boy Heroine on the

critiqued an essentialist view of subjectivity, such critics argue, opening it up to the possibility of negotiating new gender roles in the ongoing reconstitution of the family. I am suggesting that colonizing the voice of the disenfranchised woman, a less threatening practice, rehearsed the threat of sexual dislocation experienced in early modern England—not necessarily to ensure its containment or liberation, but to tap into the charged nature of that anxiety to address the tricky dilemma of the poet caught between manuscript and print cultures. I narrate the historical particularities of how the female complaint was subsumed into the folds of another story in order to critique, rather than to further, the woman's tacit erasure as she became a trope for the insecurities of a male social order and its literary institutions.[55]

In analyzing this moment of displacement through the local context of Renaissance publication, we see that these multivocal and pseudomorphic texts are not signs of heteroglossia's anti-authoritarian impulse but ironically are imitations of more elite modes of writing. Writers created these impersonations and masquerades to shape a narrative of authorship that can gloss the possible social transgressions incurred by appearing in print. Helgerson's narrative of the emergence of the laureate poet as a reconception of the national, aesthetic, and philosophical place of writing helps us to see the more particularized struggle in which the writer engaged in defining authorship within this specific social milieu. The "self-crowning" in which the laureates engaged, I argue, involved juggling the problems of

---

English Renaissance Stage," *PMLA* 102 (1987): 29–41; Catherine Belsey, "Disrupting Sexual Difference: Meaning and Gender in the Comedies," in *Alternative Shakespeares*, ed. John Drakakis (London: Methuen, 1985), 166–90; and Howard, "Crossdressing, the Theatre, and Gender Struggle in Early Modern England."

[55]By placing representations of the female body and voice within the specific cultural configurations of sixteenth-century England, I hope to localize the common and transhistorical practice in which women serve as a trope for men's problems. Locating the particular contours of these representations, we avoid positing an unchanging patriarchy estranged from specific social solutions. While I argue that gender here negotiates class issues, I do not mean to suggest that Renaissance writers subordinate gender to class in all cases. Certainly, the reverse is true in other texts—for instance, in the massive displacement of sexuality onto economics in *The Merchant of Venice.* Critics such as Walter Cohen, Lynda E. Boose, and Carol Thomas Neely have charged historicists with perpetuating the subordination of gender to more "male" kinds of political power when they read Renaissance literary works and cultural practices. Keeping in mind their important cautions, I argue that it is vital that we examine the sexual politics of erasure within the socioliterary system of the Renaissance. Cohen, "Political Criticism of Shakespeare," in *Shakespeare Reproduced: The Text in History & Ideology,* 18–46; Boose, "The Family in Shakespeare Studies; or—Studies in the Family of Shakespeareans; or—The Politics of Politics," *Renaissance Quarterly* 40 (Winter 1987): 707–42; and Neely, "Constructing the Subject: Feminist Practice and the New Renaissance Discourses," *English Literary Renaissance* 18 (Winter 1988): 5–18.

gender and class that writers faced when they sought to break into print. The writers that I have discussed responded to these problems by devising diverse textual shapes and rhetorical stances that allowed them to forge a concept of authorship from within the codes of manuscript writing. In this combined formal and rhetorical fashioning, writers rehearsed and replicated other unauthorized but authorizing voices—the shepherd, the commonplace book writer, the female complaint speaker. In order to prove their skills at gentlemanly amorous manuscript writing, they created multivocal texts that were made to seem occasional and collective, and then they cast off that role and aligned themselves with the moral role established by their editorial pronouncements. These published works also flirted with the possibility of their own transgressive status by calling forth other violations to absorb the problematic issues of writing. It is no wonder that such serious and monumental works became associated with the naughtiness of gender blending. Gascoigne's and Spenser's careers were invested in female difference because such an association set the ground from which they rose into the sphere of transcendent poetry. Because Daniel actually colonized the female voice as part of his creation of a more serious poetic persona, he had to create a narrative of fall and redemption that distinguished him from the woes of female promiscuity. We find that the marginal poem attached to *The Faerie Queene* is not merely the product of a perverse and eclectic mind. Instead, W.L's trope is writ large in the careers of writers who cross-dressed downward to stage their ascent to literary fame. Pseudomorphs allowed these writers to cross gender, genre, and class in an attempt to produce elite-looking texts that negotiated a place for authorship in the realm of print.

CHAPTER FIVE

DANCING IN A NET:

The *Problems* of
Female Authorship

[She] takes great libertie or rather licence to traduce whom she please,
and thincks she daunces in a net.
—John Chamberlain, about Lady Mary Wroth

You presse the Presse with little you have made.
—John Davies to the Countess of Bedford,
the Countess of Pembroke, and Elizabeth Cary

WHEN JOHN DAVIES ADMONISHED three of the prominent women writers of his day because of their reluctance to enter into the world of print, he ironically used a language that would have had particularly threatening resonances for virtuous women: the phrase "to presse the Presse" inscribed print with an air of scandal by hinting at a bawdy, masculinized sexual position.[1] Davies's contradiction of his own ostensible encouragement through an unwitting innuendo only points to the prevalent and subtle cultural codes that privatized women. Women in early modern

---

[1] *The Muses Sacrifice, Works of John Davies*, ed. Alexander B. Grosart, 2 vols. (London: Cherlsey Worthies Library, 1878), 2:1, 4. Chamberlain's quote is found in "To Sir Dudley Carleton," 9 March 1622, in *The Letters of John Chamberlain*, ed. Norman Egbert McClure (Philadelphia: American Philosophical Society, 1939), 2:427. My title not only alludes to Chamberlain's striking criticism, but also echoes two contemporary feminist works engaged in ongoing revisionary projects: Annette Kolodny's "Dancing Through the Minefield," an important early work which theorizes the practice of feminist criticism in the academy (*Feminist Studies* 6 (1980): 1–25); and Ann Rosalind Jones's "Nets and Bridles: Early Modern Conduct Books and Sixteenth-Century Women's Lyrics," which explores the relationship between Renaissance women and the current ideologies of gender (*The Ideology of Conduct*, ed. Nancy Armstrong and Leonard Tennenhouse [New York: Methuen, 1987], 39–72). Jones's work, which is central to my reading of Renaissance women writers, posits that these women "reveal the ingenuity that was required to divert early modern controls upon women into channels for their survival through literary self-representation" (67). Although my chapter will uncover moments in which women represent themselves in less than celebratory ways—as dying martyrs and ghostly spirits, for instance—I choose this title because it accentuates that even these constructions could be affirmative.

England faced tremendous obstacles in establishing themselves as public figures of any kind. Literary and historical scholars have dramatized these prohibitions quite glaringly in past years, as they have documented restrictions on female education; the link between public speech and harlotry; the definition of the woman's domain as that of domestic piety; the identification of silence as a feminine ideal; and the mastery of rhetoric as a male puberty rite.[2] Constrained by the norms of acceptable feminine behavior, women were specifically discouraged from tapping into the newly popular channel of print; to do so threatened the cornerstone of their moral and social well-being. The rampant idealization of chastity acted as a linchpin that precariously linked female bodily and spiritual integrity with a coherent cosmic and social order that was continually threatening to slip into chaos.[3] An outpouring of published injunctions sought to secure that order by privatizing women, directing them to remain safely enclosed within the home rather than engaged in the circulation of social signs or events. In his *Instruction of a christen Woman,* Juan Luis Vives, tutor to Catherine of Aragon, suggests that "it neither becommeth a woman to rule a Schoole, nor to live amonge men, or speake abroad, and shake of her demurenesse and honesty: . . . it were better to be at home within and unknown to other folkes, and in company to hold her tongue demurely,

---

[2]For general discussions of restrictions on women, see Ruth Kelso, *Doctrine for the Lady of the Renaissance* (Urbana: University of Illinois Press, 1956); Elaine Beilin, *Redeeming Eve: Women Writers of the English Renaissance* (Princeton: Princeton University Press, 1987); Ann Rosalind Jones, *The Currency of Eros: Women's Love Lyric in Europe, 1540–1620* (Bloomington: Indiana University Press, 1990); Mary Ellen Lamb, *Gender and Authorship in the Sidney Circle* (Madison: University of Wisconsin Press, 1990); and Constance Jordan, "Feminism and the Humanists: The Case of Sir Thomas Elyot's *Defence of Good Women,*" in *Rewriting the Renaissance: The Discourses of Sexual Difference in Early Modern Europe,* ed. Margaret W. Ferguson, Maureen Quilligan, and Nancy J. Vickers (Chicago: University of Chicago Press, 1986), 242–58.

On the issue of women's education see Mary Ellen Lamb, "The Cooke Sisters: Attitudes toward Learned Women in the Renaissance," in *Silent But for the Word: Tudor Women as Patrons, Translators, and Writers of Religious Works,* ed. Margaret Hannay (Kent, Ohio: Kent State University Press, 1985), 107–25. For analyses of how women's genitalia and mouths were socially encoded as equivalents, see Peter Stallybrass, "Patriarchal Territories: The Body Enclosed," in *Rewriting the Renaissance,* 123–42; and Lisa Jardine, *Still Harping on Daughters: Women and Drama in the Age of Shakespeare* (1983; reprint, New York: Columbia University Press, 1989), Chap 4. For the male mastery of rhetoric, see Walter Ong, "Latin Language Study as a Renaissance Puberty Rite," *Studies in Philology* 56 (1959): 106–24.

[3]*The Mirrhor of Modestie,* a conduct book written by Giovanni Bruto and translated into English by Thomas Salter in 1579, warned, for instance, that educating women could turn them into "subtile and shameless Lovers, as connyng and skillfull writers, of Ditties, Sonnettes, Epigrames and Ballades." The text continues: "How far more convenient the Distaffe, and Spindle, Nedle and Thimble were for them with a good and honest reputation, then the skill of well using a penne or wrighting a loftie vearce" (sig. C5ᵛ).

and let few see her, and none at all heare her."[4] A woman's decision to "presse the Presse," to venture far from her place "at home within" and from her passive and pressed silent "feminine" role, could be seen as a sign of her refusal to respect sanctioned cultural boundaries.

Despite these overt gestures toward exclusion, it would be unfair to say that women's anxieties about appearing in print (and thus their labored justifications for their publications) were solely the product of their gender. As I have pointed out, writers both male and female risked estrangement from the social sources of power when they chose to publish. Because print publication was rhetorically scripted as a lower-class activity, writers of both genders had to counter the force of this stigma. This is not to say, however, that gender was not an issue. In a world in which privilege was attached to coterie circulation and published words were associated with promiscuity, the female writer could become a "fallen" woman in a double sense: branded as a harlot or a member of the nonelite.[5]

More vexed, however, was the problem posed when restrictions marked by gender and class became interwoven—that is, when Renaissance writers used a gender exclusive idiom to negotiate the myriad social problems of public authorship. Throughout the course of this book I have pointed out ways in which writers combated the social problem of publication by drawing on and accentuating the male-coded dynamic found in literature. One such dynamic existed in the potent cultural and literary discourse of Petrarchism, where the woman often functioned as a trope for social prestige and poetic laurels. Enacting the reflexes of reification and fragmentation, sixteenth-century coterie sonneteers established poetic authority, as Nancy Vickers has demonstrated, by linguistically dismembering the female body through the blazon.[6] Writers and publishers seized on the logic

---

[4]Juan Luis Vives, *Instruction of a christen Woman*, trans. Richard Hyrde, STC 24862 (1585) (sig. C6). Although Vives wrote during an earlier era, his conduct book was highly influential during Elizabeth's reign; it was reprinted more than forty times throughout the sixteenth century. Mary Ellen Lamb cites this dictate by Vives in "The Cooke Sisters," 114. For discussions of Vives's theories of women's education, see Gloria Kaufman, "Juan Luis Vives on the Education of Women," *Signs* 3 (1978): 891–96; Valerie Wayne, "Some Sad Sentence: Vives' *Instruction of a Christian Woman*," in *Silent But for the Word*, 15–29; and Beilin, *Redeeming Eve*, 4–8.

[5]In "A Hostile Annotation of Rachel Speght's *A Mouzell for Melastomus* (1617)" (*English Studies* 68 [1987]: 490–96), Cis van Heertum describes the anonymous glosses in one edition of this defense of women, annotations that persistently sexualized Speght's authorial presentation by attributing bawdy and scurrilous meanings to her words. Heertum observes: "This reader for one clearly felt that the author of *A Mouzell for Melastomus* had cheapened herself by appearing in print because he notes the she is 'by reason of [her] publique booke now not soe good as com[m]on' (sig. B2ᵛ)" (493).

[6]Nancy Vickers, "Diana Described: Scattered Woman and Scattered Rhyme," in *Writing and Sexual Difference*, ed. Elizabeth Abel (Chicago: University of Chicago Press, 1986), 95–110.

of the blazon (meaning in one definition "to publish") as a means of presenting their printed works. By using the female body as a metaphor for the newly commodified book, both became defined as unruly objects in need of supervision and governance. When they imagined the female body as a medium for articulating power, whether dismembered in poetic fragments or as a corporeal sign for the text, writers consolidated their shaky social status as publishing writers. One result was the creation of a masculinized notion of authorship. For women, then, the general cultural problems of public writing were compounded by the restrictions on their gender, by what Gary Waller describes as the "structures of power within the language these women use and that create them as subjects, denying them any owned discourse," and by the fact that these structures informed the economy of book publication.[7] Some English women did contest these explicit prohibitions polemically, but in responding to implicit exclusionary practices, they were given the trickier task of finding alternative modes of expression and self-authorization.

If women were tropes necessary to the process of writing, if they were constructed within genres as figures for male desire, with what authority could they publish? How could a woman become an author if she was the "other" against whom "authors" differentiated themselves?[8] In this chapter, I would like to address this broad range of inquiry by discussing several distinct but interrelated strategies that women used within their restricted position in the culture to fashion or adapt social and political written forms. I say fashion *or* adapt because women writers both created new genres and gestures to counter Petrarchan representations of power and exploited existing forms used by their male counterparts. Ann Rosalind Jones notes that women "wrote within but against the center of the traditions that surrounded them, using Neoplatonic and Petrarchan discourse in revisionary and interrogatory ways."[9] It seems crucial that we under-

[7]Gary Waller, "Struggling into Discourse: The Emergence of Renaissance Women's Writing," in *Silent But for the Word*, 246.

[8]A wave of dynamic Renaissance scholars are beginning to shape the vocabulary with which we can tackle these questions. See Jones, *The Currency of Eros*; Maureen Quilligan, *The Allegory of Female Authority: Christine de Pizan's "Cité des Dames"* (Ithaca: Cornell University Press, 1991); Beilin, *Redeeming Eve*; Gwynne Kennedy, "Lessons of the 'Schoole of Wysdome,'" in *Sexuality and Politics in Renaissance Drama*, ed. Carole Levin and Karen Robertson (Lewiston, New York: Edwin Mellen Press, 1991), 113–36; Lamb, *Gender and Authorship in the Sidney Circle*; Margaret W. Ferguson, "Running On with Almost Public Voice: The Case of 'E.C,'" in *Tradition and the Talents of Women*, ed. Florence Howe (Urbana: University of Illinois Press, 1991), 37–67; and Ferguson's "A Room Not Their Own: Renaissance Women as Readers and Writers," in *The Comparative Perspective on Literature*, ed. Clayton Koelb and Susan Noakes (Ithaca: Cornell University Press, 1988), 93–116.

[9]Ann Rosalind Jones, "Assimilation with a Difference," *Yale French Studies* 62 (1981): 135.

stand how existing discourses could be used by women to attend to female concerns—for instance, how Amelia Lanyer could use the Passion, a topic popular with male Protestant writers, to register her own peculiar predicament as a writer. While moments of open challenge to social restriction were rare, many women did create what Jones calls a "bricolage with social dictates"; thus, prohibitions on women's relationship to public writing did not necessarily effect their silence, but rather provoked them into "complex forms of negotiation and compromise."[10]

One writer who pushed negotiation to its outer limit was Mary Wroth. John Chamberlain, in fact, complained about the license she took with her speech when he ridiculed Wroth's works as mere slander. She "takes great libertie or rather licence to traduce whom she please," he protested, "and thincks she daunces in a net."[11] "To dance in a net" meant to render oneself invisible, and thus Chamberlain expresses his specific irritation that Wroth believed herself free to speak her mind publicly and escape repercussions. But his words also call to mind a particularly compelling image, one that registers the precarious freedom most female writers had when they sat down to compose their literary works. Women might have been caught in legal, social, and economic nets, but some found a way to dance within them quite visibly, to piece together discursive forms that circumvented restrictions on their public appearances. The strict limitations placed on women's social and mental activities only make their literary experiments more impressive; and the overwhelming weight of prohibitions against authorship compels us to look carefully at the forms women did choose, and the images women did construct, in these difficult and transgressive forays into print.[12]

The Female Legacy

In 1624 *The Mothers Legacie to her unborn Childe* . . . was published posthumously. Elizabeth Joceline issued this advice book as the final legacy of a

[10]Jones, "Surprising Fame: Renaissance Gender Ideologies and Women's Lyric," in *The Poetics of Gender*, ed. Nancy K. Miller (New York: Columbia University Press, 1986), 80, 92.

[11]Gwynne Kennedy offers an excellent reading of the specific meaning attached to Chamberlain's phrase, in "She 'thincks she daunces in a net': The Reception of Lady Mary Wroth's *Urania*" (Paper delivered at the Third Pennsylvania Symposium on Medieval and Renaissance Studies, Philadelphia, 1989).

[12]An affirmative reading of women's writing, however, should be wary of what Barbara Newman terms the "hermeneutics of sympathy" that often guides feminist interpretations, one that can be too easily set in distinction to the "hermeneutics of suspicion" employed when reading male-authored texts. In her brief discussion, Newman warns against the various "temptations" that feminist criticism faces. "On the Ethics of Feminist Historiography," *Exemplaria: A Journal of Theory in Medieval and Renaissance Studies* 2 (1990): 702–6.

mother to her unknown child, written as she anticipated the possibility of dying in childbirth (an anxiety that proved quite prophetic). Joceline is given license to author such a book because of the pressing possibility that her written maternal advice to her child may have to substitute for her living guidance. "I could not chuse but manifest this desire in writing," she explains, "lest it should please God to deprive me of time to speake."[13] The power implicit in her role as moral instructor stems from the impending threat of absence, the deprivation of "time to speake." Imminent danger allows her to offer what she terms "a few weake instructions comming from a dead mother" (sig. C5). The editor of the text, Thomas Goad, assures readers that the writer is both virtuous and dead, her work published only through the efforts of her devoted, grieving husband. The transgression of a woman's exposure in print is thus mitigated by Joceline's death, which both protects her reputation and gives her permission to speak. After all, she is merely doing her duty: instructing her child in the only way that circumstances will allow. The specter of death and the gravity of maternity join to produce a powerful counterforce to the culture's exhortations to silence.[14]

In his preface, Goad expresses how puzzled he is that Joceline was so obsessed with the possibility of dying: "the course of her life was a perpetuall meditation of death, amounting almost to a propheticall sense of her dissolution, even then when she had not finished the 27. yeere of her age, nor was oppressed by any disease, or danger, other than the common lot of child-birth, within some months approaching" (sig. A4ᵛ). Contrary to Goad's assessment, the possibility of death in childbirth was a real, everpresent danger for women of all ranks in the culture. Even the mortality rate for married aristocratic women was double that of their husbands;

---

[13]Elizabeth Joceline, *The Mothers Legacie to her unborne Childe* . . . , STC 14624 (1624), sig. C3ᵛ. Her text is excerpted in Betty Travitsky, ed., *The Paradise of Women: Writings by English-women of the Renaissance* (Westport, Conn.: Greenwood Press, 1981), 61–62. In this seminal anthology, Travitsky provides excerpts of writing by Elizabeth Grymeston, Dorothy Leigh, and Elizabeth Cooke Russell, all mother's legacies that I discuss in this chapter.

[14]In *The Paradise of Women,* Travitsky comments on the construction of the "new mother" in early modern England (49). Mary Beth Rose also comments on this phenomenon: "It is crucial to recognize that English Renaissance culture during and after the Reformation was in the throes of reconceptualizing issues of family and gender, and of redefining the significances of public and private life. Once this historical phenomenon is acknowledged, it becomes necessary to explore the ways in which representations of family and gender were being altered and shaped as part of a public, discursive process through which artists, lawyers, theologians, politicians, and mothers themselves contributed to a reconstruction of motherhood." "Where Are the Mothers in Shakespeare? Options for Gender Representation in the English Renaissance," *Shakespeare Quarterly* 42 (1991): 295.

one out of every four women died in the early years of marriage.[15] Pregnant women could, as did Joceline, anticipate the potential finality of this liminal period; indeed, many diaries and letters prior to *The Mothers Legacie* testify to the Renaissance woman's realization of the peril of childbirth and her efforts to come to terms with that peril during the period of pregnancy. Patricia Crawford documents how women took pains to finalize their lives by buying winding sheets and stoically professing their readiness for the life to come.[16] The title page to one tract of spiritual counsel recommends itself specifically to groups of persons at great risk in the culture: "Mariners when they goe to sea," "Souldiers when they goe to battell," and "Women when they travell of child."[17] Pregnancy presented, then, a demarcated and culturally acknowledged time of jeopardy that made it natural for women to be both the authors of and the audience for articulations of wisdom and counsel. When the mother-to-be undertook the travail to produce the heir and sustain the generation of the family, she placed her life in jeopardy. Renaissance women found that they could take advantage of these special circumstances by constructing final legacies as pre-texts to the hazardous event of childbirth. We need only note two other books presented as last will and testaments—*Praiers made by the right Honorable Ladie Frances Aburgavennie, and commited at the houre of hir death to Ladie Marie Fane (hir only daughter . . .)* (1582) and *The honour of vertue. Or the monument erected . . . to the immortall memory of . . . Mrs Elizabeth Crashawe Who dyed in childbirth* (1620)—to find evidence that this type of publication was becoming common.

The will is a peculiar document: it is written in the present tense and includes its imagined enactment in the future, but it is authorized by a past voice. It is because of the strange time frame involved in the concept of the will, that the writer is able to express, sanctify, and preserve his or her immediate desires. The voice that speaks is strangely present and absent, a ghostly corpse that undergoes a reckoning and asserts fervently held beliefs and desires. The very power of this speaking position rests in its doubleness: in the anticipated movement toward death, in the sanctity

[15]Rose cites this statistic from Lawrence Stone's *The Crisis of the Aristocracy, 1558–1641* (Oxford: Clarendon Press, 1965), 590, in "Where Are the Mothers in Shakespeare?" 294.

[16]Patricia Crawford, "From the Women's View: Pre-industrial England, 1500–1750," in *Exploring Women's Past: Essays in Social History*, ed. Patricia Crawford et al. (Boston: George Allen and Unwin, 1983), 74.

[17]William Perkins, *A Salve for a Sicke man, or . . . the right manner of dying well*, STC 19742 (1595). Mary Ellen Lamb mentions this fascinating title page in "The Countess of Pembroke and the Art of Dying," *Women in the Middle Ages and the Renaissance: Literary and Historical Perspectives*, ed. Mary Beth Rose (Syracuse, New York: Syracuse University Press, 1986), 212. This essay appears in revised form as Chapter 3 in *Gender and Authorship in the Sidney Circle*.

of the final departure. It is a strangely performative and self-constituting gesture dependent on the erasure of the subject at the very moment of powerful self-assertion. As grieving husbands and relatives published these private legacies posthumously—presenting public texts from the socially acceptable public position of mourning—they cleared a space in which women could legitimate their own break into print.

Of course, the culture's general approbation of moral instruction from mother to child sanctioned the publication of these advice tracts even when the woman was not at risk specifically from pregnancy. Because a woman's "natural" province was the home, she could speak more publicly in her role as nurturer. Advocates of the humanist program of learning, in fact, argued for the education of women on the grounds that mothers should be trained to inculcate religion in their children. In contrast to secular writers, who could tout their urbane wisdom through biting social and moral satire, women were allowed the spiritual and moral force possessed by the teacher. It is not surprising, then, that when Elizabeth Grymeston wrote one such counseling tract, *Miscelanae, Meditations, Memoratives* (1604), she justified her work as a mother's legacy. Although her text was not necessitated by the hazard of pregnancy, she nevertheless represented her maternal affection by looking toward the possibility of death. She tells her son Bernye: "I resolved to breake the barren soile of my fruitlesse braine, to dictate something for thy direction; the rather for that as I am now a dead woman among the living . . . I leave thee this portable *veni mecum* for thy Counseller, in which thou maiest see the true portraiture of thy mothers minde."[18] Her claim to imminent death and her special maternal relationship with her son give Grymeston the ground for transforming her "fruitlesse braine" into a productive medium. She begins to offer what she terms her "last speeches" by explaining her prerogative in offering advice: "My dearest sonne, there is nothing so strong as the force of love; there is no love so forcible as the love of an affectionate mother to hir naturall childe & there is no mother can either more affectionately shew hir nature, or more naturally manifest hir affection, than in advising hir children out of hir owne experience" (A3). Writing here is naturalized as prescribed maternal instruction (in a time when affective bonds between mother and child had to be constructed within texts rather than assumed) and legitimated as a final legacy. The *Miscelanae* was printed one year after Grymeston died. A tract that devotes one of its chapters to the power and finality of death, it seems especially resonant because her voice

---

[18]Elizabeth Grymeston, *Miscelanae, Meditations, Memoratives*, STC 12407 (1604), sig. A3–A3ᵛ.

reaches from the grave ("a dead woman among the living"), asserting her right to use her mind in the service of domestic duty.[19]

Grymeston labors to show her children a visible sign of herself as a speaking subject. The form dictates that she create, of course, a riven subjectivity: a "true portrait" predicated on her own bodily erasure. If we accept Catherine Belsey's argument that male bourgeois subjectivity fashioned itself by creating a radically unstable speaking position for the female subject, we must ask if such representations constitute another register of the Renaissance woman's discontinuous identity. Or we could posit that her ever-shifting position in the discourse of patriarchy—as childlike in her subordination to husband and as mother coequal to father in the hierarchical structure—makes the will an appropriate mode for displaying the absent/present, undecidable subject.[20] I argue that the woman's unstable speaking position is not merely a sign of her culturally circumscribed subject position, however, but a carefully formed *re-presentation* of that problematic position, a crafted self-portrait through which women rhetorically recast their riven subjectivity. In other words, these female legacies do not merely make visible women's disenfranchisement, but also act as a complex form in which a provisional self-authorization is made possible from within cultural restrictions. In Jones's terms, these mothers' legacies constitute a "bricolage" of social dictates because, if for no other reason, they expose the absent/present subjectivity of all women by taking it to an extreme.

These ostensibly private instructions from mother to child were often remarkably self-conscious about their public audience. Elizabeth Grymeston's epistle to her son, for instance, is prefaced by a commendatory poem by Simon Grahame that praises her immortal fame. Grymeston's text is not only a handbook for her son, Grahame tells us, but also a general guidebook for the Christian wanderer. Similarly, Frances Aburgavennie's maternal advice to her daughter becomes, as the title page tells us, "a Jewell of health for the soule, and . . . verie profitable to be used of everie faithfull Christian man and woman."[21] When publishing Joceline's work, Goad explains that he found it compelling and necessary to preserve this

[19]Rose reads these mothers' texts in light of the conflict of maternal ideology brought on by the Protestant revaluation of the family, which "gradually elicits a discourse in which motherhood begins to be construed in the language of power as well as desire" and thus destablizes established gender hierarchies ("Where Are the Mothers in Shakespeare?" 313). In this essay, Rose explains both the disruptive power mothers had on the stage, and the way in which Shakespeare neutralizes or ignores their problematic representational status.

[20]Catherine Belsey, *The Subject of Tragedy: Identity and Difference in Renaissance Drama* (New York: Methuen, 1985), 149–91.

[21]Frances Aburgavennie's work was published as part of *The Monument of Matrones: conteining seven severall Lamps of Virginitie . . . compiled . . . by Thomas Bentley*, STC 1892 (1582), 139.

mother's virtuous instruction by placing it "among the most publique Monuments" (A4ᵛ). Strikingly, the language that Joceline uses reveals that she anticipated this public placement; for she rationalizes her writing in terms that assume public censure: "I may perhaps bee wondred at for writing in this kinde, considering there are so many excellent bookes, whose least note is worth all my meditations. I confesse it, and thus excuse my selfe. I write not to the world, but to mine own childe" (C4ᵛ). This self-defensive claim to privacy contradicts itself by positing public critics who are wondering about her violation. Like the structure of confession, a performative act that depends on an oppositional public, her rationalization constitutes her authorial role against a fantasized disapproving public. The fact that Joceline continues to justify her work well into the body of the text vivifies her clear sense of its future exposure to a public audience. When women created these "intimate" legacies, their writing was often informed by the possibility of future appearances in print, appearances that could transform their private precepts into "publique Monuments."

These public/private declarations, eased into print through the authority of death, provide a vocabulary through which women could offer their words to the public. Women writers, then, developed a tradition based on the female legacy, drawing on the rhetoric of will-making as they fashioned many types of texts. Dorothy Leigh's *The Mothers Blessing: or The godly Counsaile of a Gentle-woman, not long since deceased, left behind her for her Children, containing many good exhortations and godly admonitions, profitable for all Parents, to leave as a Legacy to their children* (1616) was written specifically for publication, as the author made apparent by her appeal to Princess Elizabeth to protect the book as it circulated and her lengthy self-justification for her public appearance.[22] Leigh explains to her children that she writes to provide moral instruction for them in her last moments, a task that necessitates her emergence as an author: "seeing my selfe going out of the world and you but comming in, I know not how to performe this dutie so well, as to leave you these few lines" (A6ᵛ). After calling attention to the reciprocity in this moment of exchange—one person entering, the other exiting the world—she continues her justification: "I could not see to what purpose it should tend, unlesse it were sent abroad to you: for should it bee left with the eldest, it is likely the yongest should have but little part in it. Wherefore, setting aside all feare, I have adventured to shew my imperfections to the view of the World, not regarding what censure for this shall bee laid upon me, so that herein I may shew my selfe a loving

---

[22]Dorothy Leigh, *The Mothers Blessing: or The godly Counsaile of a Gentle-woman, not long since deceased, left behind her for her Children . . .* , STC 15402 (1616).

Mother" (A7–A7ᵛ). According to Leigh, the revelation of her "imperfections" is the price paid for the more important display of herself as "a loving Mother." In her second chapter, she restates her reasons for writing:

> But lest you should marvaile, my children, why I doe not according to the usual custome of women, exhort you by words and admonitions, rather then by writing, a thing so unusuall among us . . . know therefore, that it was the motherly affection that I bare unto you all, which made mee now (as it often hath done heretofore) forget my selfe in regard of you: neither care I what you or any shall thinke of mee, if among many words I may write but one sentence, which may make you labour for the spiritual food of the soule.
>
> (3–4, new pagination)

Her role as nurturing provider of spiritual food empowers her to speak, allowing her to "forget" the self dependent on the "usual custome" of textual silence and offering another, more authorized self in its stead. Leigh's words comprise a self-constituting gesture based on self-annihilation as she constructs an identity precisely through the erasure of her body. Forgetting is a necessary gesture (the "selfe going out of the world") that allows the production of the strangely present and absent voice that desperately hopes to find a local habitation in one effectual sentence. Clearly Leigh herself was not forgotten; *The Mothers Blessing* rapidly went through fifteen editions. She successfully exploited the rhetoric of the deathbed legacy as a means of presenting her work "abroad," as her preemptive arguments persuade us; "can any man blame a Mother" for writing, she asks coyly. Just in case someone dares to answer her rhetorical question positively, she offers a rebuttal: "will not a Mother venture to offend the world for her Childrens sake?" (11).

The license of leave-taking seen in these texts is reinforced by the highly public cultural narratives of female deathbed scenes. *The Autobiography of Alice Thornton* (1645), for example, richly dramatizes the power held by dying women later in the century. In this work, Thornton describes how her sister's ill health during the course of pregnancy leads to a lengthy and theatrical farewell, one that allows her to gather the family around her sickbed and lead them in numerous exhortations. Thornton first describes her sister's agony in pregnancy and childbirth, how she was "exceeding tormented with pains," and then elaborates on her final words:

> Yet still did she spend her time in discourse of goodness, excellently pious, godly, and religious, instructing her children and servants, and preparing her soul for her dear Redeemer. . . . [S]he poured out her soul in prayer with such comprehensive and good expressions that could be for her own soul, for pardon and remission of her sins . . . and then for her husband, children,

mother, and all her relations and myself; for the restoration of the king, the church and the kingdom's peace; with such pathetic and zealous expressions that all did glorify God for [the] things He had done for her. After which, she did in a manner prophesy that God would humble the kingdom by afflictions for their sin and security.[23]

In this scene, Thornton reveals how her sister's concerns gradually evolve from internal and private issues—namely, the well-being of her soul—to the familial and domestic, and finally to politics and the public world. Her sickness allows her to inhabit the privileged moral stance of divine prophet as she sees into the future (denied to her in body and thus accessible to her in vision) and strays into the social domain to makes pronouncements about its shortcomings. When Thornton goes on to say that her sister "was kind and dearly affectionate to her husband, to whom, under God, she left the care of her seven young children" (36), she makes clear that the wife here takes spiritual and domestic control of the family, instructing her husband by expressing her "will" for her children's guidance. Her ill health, the text mentions, even allows her to demand her husband's release from his civic duties; although she had wanted him to return home to attend to her pregnancy, the text states, "he, being engaged in his king's service, was not permitted to leave it . . . till she fell sick" (34). We might think back to Goad's astonishment that Joceline was obsessed by her own death. Here the woman's bodily dissolution gives her the power to usurp the prerogative of the Crown and venture social commentary. Thornton concludes this episode by describing the poignant moment in which her sister commends her soul to Christ, issuing her spirit in a final sweet breath.

Mary Sidney, mother of the Countess of Pembroke, experienced a similarly dramatic farewell transformation, as Raphael Holinshed's *Chronicles* (1587) recounts:

In this hir last action and ending of hir life (as it were one speciallie at that instant called of God) she so farre surpassed hir selfe, in discreet, wise, effectual, sound, and grounded reasons, all tending to zeale and pietie, as the same almost amazed and astonished the hearers to heare and conceive such plentie of goodlie and pithie matter to come from such a creature. Who although for a time she seemed to live obscurlie, yet she ended this life, and left the world most confidentlie.[24]

---

[23]Alice Thornton, *The Autobiography of Alice Thornton*, reprinted in *By A Woman Writt*, ed. Joan Goulianos (Indianapolis: Bobbs-Merrill, 1973), 35, 36.

[24]Raphael Holinshed, *The Third Volume of Chronicles* (1587), fol. Liiiiii2. Quoted by Lamb, *Gender and Authorship in the Sidney Circle*, 122–23. In her chapter entitled "The Countess of

Like *Macbeth*'s treacherous Cawdor, who exceeds his life in "the leaving of it," Sidney is shown to have "farre surpassed hir selfe" in her final moments, moving from obscurity to the striking visibility of a chronicled report. She possesses at this time a heretofore invisible moral authority that astonishes her auditors. (Holinshed's term "a-stone-ish" unwittingly has special resonances of a Medusa-like female power). While Belsey points to visual representations of deathbed scenes to illustrate the lack of a stable space for female subjectivity, we may read these narrative accounts instead as moments in which women controlled their riven subjectivity. To be sure, such narratives construct a "true" self only by framing it as a provisional and excessive one made visible at the threshold moment of death. Dying mothers, like confessing witches, were on the social margins, and thus they could speak from the privileged position associated with demonic power or imminent spirituality. Both had an elocutionary power that astonished audiences even more because of the taint generally associated with female discourse.[25]

Farewell scenes could be textualized as apologies for presenting highly publicized final legacies. Elizabeth Cooke Russell employs the language of the will to authorize her translation of John Poynet's *A way of reconciliation of good and learned man* . . . (1605). "Most vertuous and worthilie beloved daughter," she begins, "Even as from your first birth and cradle I ever was most carefull . . . to have you sucke the milke of sincere Religion: So willing to ende as I beganne, I have left to you, as my last Legacie, this Booke. A most precious Jewell to the comfort of your Soule . . . now naturalized by mee into English."[26] M.R.'s *The Mothers Counsell, or, Live within Compasse. Being the last Will and Testament to her dearest Daughter which may*

Pembroke and the Art of Dying," Lamb focuses on the appeal that the *ars moriendi* literature had for women: "The scene of the noble death repeatedly portrayed in the *ars moriendi* tracts offered a model of heroism that women might emulate without violating the dominant sexual ideology" (119). Lamb's project is somewhat different from mine; she sees the "art of dying" as a private task that women mastered in order to assuage their sense of exclusion. I attempt to outline how women could draw on that art as a means of rhetorical presentation. Thus, I see such forms not only as a means by which some "held forth mirrors in which women could be perceived as heroic" (145), but also as a language by which women authorized their own risky breaks into print.

[25]In *The Subject of Tragedy*, Belsey discusses the power of the witch's confession (185–91). For an analysis of the different issues raised by farewell addresses at public executions, see J. A. Sharpe, "'Last Dying Speeches': Religion, Ideology, and Public Execution in Seventeenth-Century England," *Past and Present* 107 (May 1985): 144–67. The confession of guilt, although tempered by its own distinct moral codes, carries a power similar to a mother's dying moral counsel.

[26]Elizabeth Cooke Russell, Preface, in John Poynet, *A way of reconciliation of good and learned man* . . . , trans. Elizabeth Cooke Russell, STC 21456 (1605), sig. A2–A2ᵛ.

The Mothers Counsell
O R,
Liue within Compasse.
Being the laft Will and Teftament to her
deareft Daughter.

wanto-
neffe.

Chaftity of body is the key to Relig.

In Chaftitie.

Temperance is the mother o...

In Temperance

Ma
ne.

Modefty

Humilitie is a womans beft Armor.

In Humilitie.

In Beautie.

...ty is a womans Golden Crowne.

Pride.

Odio
nell

Printed at *London* for *Iohn Wright*, and are to be fold at his Shop in
fpur ftreet without Newgate, at the figne of the Bible. 1 6

Figure 18. The Mothers Counsell, or Live within Compasse . . . , STC 20583 (1630?). By permission of the British Library.

{292}

serve for a worthy Legacie to all the Women in the World . . . (1630?, see fig. 18) and Elizabeth Richardson's *A ladies legacie to her Daughters* (1645) contribute as well to this curious pattern of female publication.

In the cases of Joceline and Grymeston, the price a woman paid for the authority of authorship was a large one: her life. But as women began to assume control of their own textual presentations, they found that the legacy's enabling vantage point outweighed its morbid associations. Not merely a technique manipulated by husbands, it became a more general cultural script for empowerment. By evoking the horizon of death, the Renaissance woman writer had a chance to undertake what was considered an exceptional feat: to take control of the frighteningly precarious circumstances of her life, to articulate her beliefs and desires, to display her mastery of moral precepts and knowledge, and to claim the power to show publicly, in Grymeston's words, "the true portraiture of [her] mother's minde." These textual displays fashioned women as writing subjects whose identities were consolidated by a mortality everywhere linked to the tremendous risk of childbirth. This perilous event thus became a touchstone that shaped women's conceptualization of their own mortality and allowed them to utter prophetic words to a future public and offer moral instruction.[27] The legacy was transformed, it seems, into a more general permission to speak.

It is peculiar, then, that this seemingly successful rhetorical strategy granted mothers testamentary powers that were highly contested in the culture. In the "Approbation" prefacing Joceline's book, Goad explicitly calls attention to the discrepancy between the author's public speech and her actual legal rights. He remarks that while a woman could not dispose of her real possessions, she could bequeath the wisdom she had garnered from life's experiences: "Our lawes disable those, that are under covert-baron, from disposing by Will and Testament any temporall estate. But no law prohibeth any possessor of morall and spirituall riches, to impart them to others, either in life by communicating, or in death by bequeathing" (A3). Goad's words are intensified by Joceline's own identification of her parental role as a spiritual husbandry: "It may peradventure when thou comest to some discretion, appeare strange, to thee to receive these lines from a Mother that died when thou wert borne; but when though seest men purchase land, and store up treasure for their unborne babes, won-

[27]For references to wills and women in other texts, see, for instance, Shakespeare's *King John* (2.1.193–94) discussed later in the chapter; see as well the contradiction in the father's and daughter's will in *The Merchant of Venice* (1.2.22–25), and the defamation of the mother's "will" as infanticide in *Titus Andronicus* (4.2.84). William Shakespeare, *The Complete Works of Shakespeare*, ed. David Bevington, 3d ed. (Glenview, Ill.: Scott Foresman and Company, 1980).

der not at mee that I am carefull for thy salvation" (C4). Both Goad and Joceline indicate an intriguing connection between the material and the spiritual, the woman's textualized advice springing from, and referencing, her inability to purchase and bequeath worldly treasure. In *The Mothers Blessing*, Leigh also promotes her own moral admonitions by comparing them favorably to mere material wealth. She tells her children: "I thought good (beeing not desirous to inrich you with transitory goods) to exhort and desire you to follow the counsell of Christ" (3). In these moments, mothers' legacies test the limits of their own metaphor, paradoxically authorizing a woman's right to speak by appealing to a legal power that was exposed finally as an inappropriate trope.

The cultural subtext of these self-conscious meditations on property and authorial propriety was a dispute about a woman's right to own and dispose of material goods. Women in early modern England waged arduous legal battles against fathers and husbands in their attempts to establish a claim to property; Ann Clifford's fifty-year struggle against Crown and family is perhaps the most notable legal domestic contestation. But more particularly, the woman's right to dispose of her own goods became a vexed issue during the 1550s. Local custom and common law had weakened the prohibition against married women who made wills without the permission of their husbands.[28] According to Pearl Hogrefe, however, the state began to crack down on the wife's right to make her own will at mid-century: "In the sixteenth century the inability of married women to make a will was given a renewed emphasis. Parliament in 1544 enacted this statute: 'Wills or testaments made of manors, tenaments, or other hereditaments, by any woman covert, by a person under twenty-one, by an idiot, or by any person not sane, shall not be good under law.' About the same time also . . . men were extending their control over movable or personal property and denying the right of a wife to make it the subject of a bequest."[29] The effect of this statute was to reinforce the lines of power that had been blurred by common law in the earlier part of the century. Although widows had more leeway in the matter, the property and goods of maids and wives (like that of idiots and madmen) belonged by law to the men who "covered" them. As Mary Beth Rose eloquently argues, there was an ongoing struggle in the sixteenth century about a married woman's legal rights because written law was often in conflict with her customary

---

[28]Susan Amussen discusses the complications in women's legally determined patterns of inheritance in *An Ordered Society: Gender and Class in Early Modern England* (Oxford: Basil Blackwell, 1988), 76–94.

[29]Pearl Hogrefe, *Tudor Women: Commoners and Queens* (Ames: Iowa State University Press, 1975), 31.

practices of exercising legal agency, bequeathing property, and managing family business. Not only were there sharp class differences in a woman's testamentary powers, but even within a given rank, women were constantly negotiating these powers.[30] We find, then, tremendous discrepancies between stated law and real experience, a problem that the 1544 statute attempted to resolve. This controversy becomes quite central to our understanding of the early modern female subject, for the ability to make a will constitutes one of the significant legal rights that historians identify in determining the gendered power relations within the culture.[31]

When Goad suggested that women bestowed the bounty of their intellectual riches because they were unable to control their material wealth, he highlighted a substitution that may account for the flourishing of the legacy form. In these mother's "wills," we see the way in which the form of the last testament allowed women to participate in generational transmission and thus to imitate the legal/economic power denied by the culture. Perhaps by showing the ease with which women could bandy and rehearse the language of legacy, fictional wills tested those restrictions discursively or called attention to the places where common practice did not square with legislative prohibition. In either case, the language of will-making clearly foregrounded a heated socio-legal controversy. Writing in this form created a dialectic in which women tested the power of a public language usually reserved for men; at the same time the use of the form pointed to the unsettled nature of the controversy over women's exact legal rights. As Leigh, Joceline, and Grymeston imitate the language of legal bequeathal, they implicitly establish a discursive domain that can be managed through the same terms. Mothers' legacies emphasize what is at stake—my child, my advice, my riches—as they meditate on what they can transmit to whom at the moment of death.[32]

Of course, men wrote tracts for their children as well. The advice epistle from father to son was so common that it was viewed as a traditional

[30]"Where Are the Mothers in Shakespeare?" 293. Rose suggests that we compare recent historical work on Renaissance women's extensive legal activities with the harsh and restrictive legal dictates expressed by, for example, T. E., *The Lawes Resolution of Womens Rights* (1632). For discussions of women's legal status as testators, see Mary Prior, "Women and the Urban Economy: Oxford, 1500–1800," in *Women in English Society, 1500–1800*, ed. Mary Prior (London: Methuen, 1985), 93–117; and Amussen, *An Ordered Society*, 81–85, 91–93, 119–123.

[31]In "Spinning Out: Women's Work in the Early Modern Economy," Merry Weisner, for instance, lists will-making as an important variable in assessing women's role in Renaissance culture. In *Becoming Visible: Women in European History*, ed. Renate Bridenthal and Claudia Koonz (Boston: Houghton Mifflin, 1977), 228.

[32]Rose comments: "While not practicing mimicry in Irigaray's self-conscious sense, the mother-authors disrupt male sexual discourse with their ambivalence at the same time that

puberty rite, the sign of the father's rhetorical skill in marking his son's coming of age.[33] Fathers generally wrote these moral and cultural guides in the present tense, however, as the current will of the father handed down to the son. As the preface to *Groats-Worth of Witte* (1592) shows us, men also drew on the language of will-making to present other kinds of works; this fictional publication is advertised as the author's "last birth," his deathbed text.[34] Rather than suggesting that this rhetoric conditioned a defiantly female form (created, used, and dispensed solely for one gender), I would like to argue that this cultural form particularly appealed to the women who dared to imagine venturing into the threatening arena of public authorship. The sudden and prolific production of female-authored tracts couched in the language of will-making creates a tradition of female legacy, a form crucial not because it revealed feminine difference or marked a female consciousness, but because it provided the ground from which women publicly challenged cultural demands for their silence.

Whitney's Fictional Will: Things Blazoned and Bequeathed

In light of this unfolding tradition, I would like to look at a fictional work by Isabella Whitney, sister of Geoffrey Whitney (the author of *A Choice of Emblems*) and one of the earliest female writers to publish secular verse. Whitney contributes a different, more lighthearted strain to this emerging legacy pattern as she combines the rhetorical strategy of will-making with others shared by male writers in authorizing her literary break into print. Whitney's first published work, "The Copy of A Letter lately written in meeter, by a yonge Gentilwoman: to her unconstant lover" (1567), was a complaint about sexual infidelity and a warning to

---

earnest attempts to reconcile their self-assertion with the sacrificial constructions of the oedipal plot, in which the best mother is an absent or a dead mother" ("Where Are the Mothers in Shakespeare?" 312). It is true that these mothers' advice books often partake of the patriarchal language that has made their publication so difficult. Rose interprets their mimicry as potentially unsettling the strictures against female speech. I agree with her assessment and add that when we interpret the content of these texts, we should keep in mind how transgressive it was for these women to think of publishing textual monuments and how controversial it could have been for them to draw on this particular principle of authorization.

[33]For a sampling, see the collection *Advice to a Son: Precepts of Lord Burghley, Sir Walter Raleigh, and Francis Osborne*, ed. Louis B. Wright (Folger Library; Ithaca: Cornell University Press, 1962). Marianne Novy discusses these tracts in her introduction to *Love's Argument: Gender Relations in Shakespeare* (Chapel Hill: University of North Carolina Press, 1985). I thank Greg Bredbeck for calling these works to my attention.

[34]Robert Greene, *Groats-Worth of Witte* (1592), reprinted in Bodley Head Quartos, ed. G. B. Harrison (New York: E. P. Dutton, 1923).

maidens about male flattery and deceit.[35] In this text, the narrator mourns the fickleness of her lover by comparing him to mythological unfaithful figures and thus giving voice retrospectively to legendary abandoned women. Her poems are published with two other verses written by men, each of whom complains about the inconstancy of his female mistress. The effect of the work is a set of reversals, her text a revision of the role of female temptress in the newly popular Heroidean complaint form.

In her second publication, *A sweet Nosegay, or pleasant Posye, contayning a hundred and ten Phylosophicall Flowers* (1573), Whitney extends the genre of the complaint by piecing together a more heterogeneous and complex material artifact.[36] The body of Whitney's text consists of more than one hundred versified imitations of the Senecan prose writing of Hugh Plat. As exemplary mid-century Tudor moral advice verse, these poems offer conventional wisdom on such subjects as friendship, moneylending, youthful inclination, and social honor. Preceded by a dedication, an author's address, and a commendatory verse, the poems are curiously followed by letters written by Whitney to family members that lament her loss of health and position. Those letters are succeeded by prose and verse epistles exchanged between herself and friends, letters in which each writer confides his or her woes and offers comfort or advice. Her complaints against fortune are thus cast and recast in various textual forms: verse epistles, dedicatory letters, sententious aphorisms, conventional complaint. The *Nosegay* provides an experimental foray into a more internally differentiated complaint form. While male writers link their complaint poems to sonnet sequences in order to fashion a more serious authorial role, Whitney produces her own authority by framing the complaint within a montage of autobiographical, moral, and fictional forms.

Through the *Nosegay*, Whitney counters the anxieties of print publication by presenting a book that replicates private textual circulation. Her inclusion of letters sent between family members and friends and her reference to the text's place in a gift/patronage cycle set up an internal textual exchange system within the work. Through these devices, she informs the print commodity with the reciprocity of social exchange at the very

[35]Isabella Whitney, "The Copy of a Letter lately written in meeter, by a yonge Gentilwoman: to her unconstant lover," STC 25439 (1567). Jones discusses "The Copy of a Letter" in *The Currency of Eros*, 36–52.

[36]Isabella Whitney, *A sweet Nosegay . . .* , STC 25440 (1573), facsmile reprint in *The Floures of Philosophie (1572) by Hugh Plat and A Sweet Nosgay (1573) and The Copy of a Letter (1567) by Isabella Whitney*, ed. Richard J. Panofsky (Delmar, New York: Scholars' Facsimiles and Reprints, 1982). References to the *Nosegay* are cited from the 1573 edition. Travitsky has made the final poem more accessible for scholars and students in her reproduction, "The 'Wyll and Testament' of Isabella Whitney," *English Literary Renaissance* 10 (1980): 83–94.

moment that she bewails her exclusion from the prestigious circles in London where such trafficking could occur. By writing of her loss of position and begging for aid in remedying her dire circumstances, Whitney, in fact, injects material circumstances fully into the realm of the abstract complaint. One effect is that the book not only registers the disparate voices that can give her various kinds of moral and material comfort and advice, but it also identifies itself as located squarely within a network of social relationships. She offers the work to her cousin, for instance, as recompense: "This simple verce: content you for to take / for answer of your loving letter lardge, / For now I wyll my writing cleane forsake" (sig. E2). The book seems to be produced multiply: as recompense to a specific patron, as needed advice to a sibling, as a response to a friend's letter of encouragement. It is not surprising that Whitney would produce a textual artifact like *Tottels Miscellany* or Gascoigne's *Flowres*, which showed her familiarity with the practices of more elite circles; while she belonged to a middle-ranking family, she had connections to aristocratic households. Her book uses the contextualizing layers of personal narrative to locate its poetic precepts within a manuscript environment. As in miscellanies such as *The Gorgeous Gallery of Gallant Inventions* and *A Handful of Pleasant Delights*, the book's very title offers a metaphor for its textual diversity. Like a nosegay, the book is a flexible arrangement of poetic works loosely gathered and provisionally bound.

The miscellaneous and multivocal textual pieces finally become anchored, however, to Whitney's personal narrative of economic disenfranchisement and spiritual sickness. Her book thus relies on an unconventional authorizing strategy: she steps forth as a publishing author by presenting a set of texts seemingly dispersed and multiple in their sites of production, but that multiplicity is finally governed by the overarching genre of the individual complaint and the authority of the sick (but curative) writing subject. Troped as a recipe for personal preservation (a "soveraigne receypt"), her text comes to life through the account of her unfortunate personal circumstances. Whitney initially justifies both her self-absorbed narrative of illness and her text itself by expressing her concern for the reader's well-being: "For these be but to keepe thee sound," she writes of her poems, "which if thou use them well: / (Paynes of my lyfe) in healthy state / thy mind shall ever dwell" (sig. A7ᵛ). Rather than fashioning a pseudomorph grounded in metaphors of femininity, sexual loss, or cross-dressing, Whitney frames her moral epigrams within metaphors of spiritual and social "dis-ease."

Whitney's anxieties about publication take the form of tropes of contagion in the *Nosegay*. The text is riddled with references to corrupt and noxious routes of circulation that pose a danger to both the spiritual soul and the wandering book. Whitney explains that she writes her book after a friend warns her of the danger of pestilent public avenues. Her work thus simultaneously defies and complies with this injunction: she sends out her moral *Nosegay* as preventive medicine against "stynking streetes" and "lothsome Lanes" (sig. A6ᵛ), but her book necessarily exposes itself to the infectious dangers of publication as it journeys to a public audience The author's introduction links infection to circulation "abroad," a word that was commonly used to describe publication, travel, and harlotry. If the heterogeneous form of the *Nosegay* reveals Whitney's concern with the social place of print, her use of the related metaphor of contagion suggests that gender is a complicating factor in the text's politics. In an epistle to her two younger sisters who are servants in London, Whitney uses the word "infection" to indicate the threat posed to sexual reputation. "All wanton toyes, good sisters now / exile out of your minde," she warns,

> I hope you geve no cause,
>   whereby I would suspect:
> But this I know too many liue,
>   that would you soon infect.
>   (sig. C8)

Drawing on the flexible metaphor of contamination, Whitney sets up a series of contradictory stances—as confined within the home, as exiled because of her loss of position. These stances generate interior/exterior oppositions that express the anxiety of publication and its concomitant problems of social exclusion and sexual libel. The *Nosegay* becomes a sign of—even as it acts as a talisman to ward off—the moral, physical, social, and sexual dangers of circulation.

The metaphor of sickness is pushed to its logical extreme in the *Nosegay's* final poem. Forced to leave London because she has lost her employment, Whitney assumes the persona of the dying citizen, who anticipating her own mortality, utters a poetic final farewell. *A sweet Nosegay*, published in the thick of England's ongoing struggle to determine a woman's testamentary rights, strikingly concludes with a versified last will and testament. Implicitly establishing an estate for herself through her own imaginative fiction, the speaker takes possession of her experiences, body, and text through a staged dispossession, a bestowal of her wealth onto the city of London and her body into the grave.[37] In representing the text as a medicinal nosegay of flowers that she has merely gathered from other textual

---

[37]In suggesting a link between Whitney's fictional will and the legal controversy that inspired the mothers' advice books, I obviously disagree with Richard Panofsky, Isabella

gardens, Whitney calls attention to her work's provisional coherence and dispersed authority. In representing the text as a legacy, however, she reclaims that dispersed authority and establishes the book as her property to be bequeathed.

What may at first seem to be merely a clever literary device for invoking strong closure for the book seems more resonant in light of the tradition of the mother's advice legacy. Although Whitney was not a mother, was not dying, and perhaps was not even actually in severe financial straits, she found it advantageous to draw from the same authorizing strategies used by sober and morbid mothers. Like them, Whitney reveals her spiritually healthy and exceptionally agile mind by articulating her "will" in the face of an anticipated dissolution of her ailing body. As we look at the logistics of desire in Whitney's "Wyll," we can begin to investigate how this genre allowed Renaissance women writers to come forth as authors within a culture that denied them public expression.

Whitney's literary "Wyll" playfully transforms legal language into an ironic meditation on property, power, and desire. She writes of her alienation from a position of power by simultaneously bewailing her loss of worldly goods and exercising control over the "common wealth." The power of her "will" is derived from the reverence exacted by the anticipated final departure. When the introduction to this final poem states that the author "fayneth as she would die" (E2), it both dramatizes her farewell in terms of a final ending and calls attention to the act of imagining involved in this dramatization. A fictional will is a doubling of its own logic of imagining: a future event (always imagined) is relegated even further into the realm of projection when it is fictionalized. The writer's voice emerges in this space of double mediation (a fictional approximation of an imagined possible future event). The text, then, revolves around the disjunction between the speaker's status as "whole in body, and in minde" (E3) and the imagined vacancy that gives her cause to speak.

Whitney expresses this paradoxical subjectivity through a legalistic language that allows her to display her competence as a speaking subject and demand an acknowledgment of her capabilities:

> I trust you all wyll witnes beare,
>   I have a stedfast brayne.
> And now let mee dispose such things,
>   as I shal leave behinde:

Whitney's twentieth-century editor, who states in his introduction that Whitney has "no special claim as a women author" (*The Floures of Philosophie*, xix).

> That those which shall receeve the same,
>   may know my wylling minde.
>
>   (E3v)

The pun implied by the phrase "wylling minde" suggests that the text acts as a testimony to her power and volition, a strong avowal of her "stedfast brayne." Through this pseudo-legal document, Whitney attempts to control the unfortunate circumstances so elaborately and poignantly articulated in the previous part of the text. Having opened her poem with a simple statement of loss—"This harvest tyme, I harvestlesse"—Whitney attempts in her "Wyll" to enact a fictional possession by dispossession (A5ᵛ). While thoroughly surveying the streets of London, describing the teeming activity and the bounty they offer, she casts this world as the object of her own generous bequest. She thus creates a myth of ownership to which she asks her readers to bear witness. In this vast anatomy, the city's fashion, food, habits, and prisons are resituated as her "Treasurye" to be distributed (E3). The legal allegory bolsters her claim to command language and property: "[I] did write this Wyll with mine owne hand," she boasts, "and it to London gave, / In witnes of the standers by, / whose names yf you wyll have, / Paper, Pen and Standish [inkwell] were: / at that same present by" (E8ᵛ). By anatomizing the urban environment around her in the presence of her dutiful witnessing writing instruments, she throws into relief a self "whole in body, and in minde." The world is reprocessed according to her coherent and "wylling minde."

Whitney makes clear that the legacy functions as a strategic bid for empowerment when she utters a threat in the poem's conclusion. While her power to speak is predicated on her feigned demise, the final effect of the will, as she reveals in the final lines, is a warning of her mortality and a plea for sustenance:

> And unto all that wysh mee well,
>   or rue that I am gon:
> Doo me comend, and bid them cease
>   my absence for to mone.
> And tell them further, if they wolde,
>   my presence styll have had:
> They should have sought to mend my luck:
>   which ever was too bad.
>
>   (E8)

These words indict those people who failed to help her acquire the bounty that she fictionally disperses. Her material needs thus find expression within the display of her psychic will; she uses her corporeal and textual "presence" as leverage in negotiating for her recovery. By denying her imaginary survivors the position of mourners, Whitney's reprimand also shores up her role as a complaining speaker.

Whitney squarely places her text within the tradition of the erotic complaint poem. In the opening lines, she explicitly addresses London as an ungrateful lover who has treated her with cruelty and contempt:

> The time is come I must departe,
>   from thee ah famous Citie:
> I never yet to rue my smart,
>   did finde that thou hadst pitie.
> Wherefore small cause ther is, that I
>   should greeve from thee go:
> But many Women foolyshly,
>   lyke me, and other moe,
> Do such a fyxed fancy set,
>   on those which least desarve.
>   (E2-E2v)

Whitney depicts her relationship with her social environment as a stormy and turbulent love affair. Although she realizes that it is unreasonable to mourn for a world that failed to welcome her, she justifies such feelings by appealing to a stereotypical love/loss situation: other women have developed a "fyxed fancy" for undeserving men. When accusing the city of "great cruelnes" because it failed "to ease [her] distres," she echoes the sonneteers' complaints against the ungratefulness of the hard-hearted mistress (E2v). Whitney's object of complaint is the city itself—London recast in the erotic language of desire. In *Still Harping on Daughters*, Lisa Jardine argues that male dependency on women in inheritance patterns in the Renaissance was ritually exorcised in fictional works through a demonization of women as sexually voracious. Here Whitney takes the opposite tack: she expresses and subordinates sexual desire to more material needs and dissatisfactions by making love the analogy for the more real problem of property.[38]

In Whitney's text, the speaker playfully manipulates the roles of deserted lover and dying woman as tropes for the exiled citizen. London becomes the erotic "other" on display, as it is dissected, anatomized, and described. Through the combined operations of mourning and celebration, Whitney produces an intricate blazon of the city. In doing so, she expands on her analogy of London as a stingy lover, whose bounty she never enjoyed

---

[38]Jardine, *Still Harping on Daughters*, 68–102.

except now in this written act of (dis)possession. She thus imitates the sonnet speaker's blazon of the mistress's body by using reification, commodification, and display as a means of establishing authority. Instead of the
glimpse of hands, eyes, and lips tantalizingly displayed in the blazons that
pervade Tudor poetry, Whitney's work makes us privy to a charting of the
streets, a detailing of cloaks, food, booksellers, and mints.

By blazoning the city of London, Whitney replicates the oppositional
subject/object relationship constructed by the Petrarchan poet's gaze on
his mistress's inaccessible body. For the blazon, as described by Vickers,
constitutes both a gesture of display and an assertion of possession used to
bridge a predominantly male community through a triangulated median
term. Patricia Parker's extension of Vickers's germinal work is here important; Parker brings the blazon to bear on the rhetorical tradition of amplification, specifically showing the trope's relationship between linguistic
and economic partition and distribution. Verbal division and expansion
allow a speaker to produce and control copiousness and plenitude. Francis Bacon, Parker notes, argues for a link between this figure and the production of property itself: "So when a great moneyed man hath divided his
chests and coines and bags, hee seemeth to himselfe richer then hee was,
and therefore a way to amplifie any thing, is to breake it, and to make an
anatomie of it in severall partes."[39] The speaker of the "Wyll," then, becomes "richer" through an exhaustive language of anatomization and
description. Whitney has already made it clear that her circumstances, not
love, frustrate her and cast her as a pawn to fortune. By creating the fiction that she designs the entire city, she fashions a potent myth that is bolstered through her poetic classification and amplification. She engages
the logic of the blazon—accounting and naming within the complaint's
language of praise and blame—in scripting her text of loss and "will"
power. Through this accounting, London becomes the median object that
solidifies Whitney's relationship with her urban audience. The speaker becomes empowered specifically by her role as social commentator. Because
her leave-taking constitutes a stroll through London's streets, it serves to
display her knowledge of urban life. Like the travel literature of the time
that exuberantly staged the exotic, her inventory of London reveals her
mastery of a public world often denied to more privatized aristocratic

[39]Francis Bacon, "Of the colours good and evil" (1597), in *The Works of Francis Bacon*, 10
vols. (London: C. Baldwin Printer, 1826), 2:229. Patricia Parker cites Bacon's remark in her
discussion of rhetoric and property, in *Literary Fat Ladies: Rhetoric, Gender, Property* (New York:
Methuen, 1987), 128. She draws on Nancy Vickers,"Diana Described"; and "'The blazon of
sweet beauty's best': Shakespeare's *Lucrece*," in *Shakespeare and the Question of Theory*, ed.
Patricia Parker and Geoffrey Hartman (New York: Methuen, 1985), 95–115.

women. Men may have had to travel to the New World to discover an exciting new life, but women could still marvel at the somewhat forbidden public world outside their door. Whitney's "Wyll" thus grants to her the privileged vantage point of social and moral satirist seen in popular poetic and prose works, and it does so, in part, through a blazoned legacy that smacks of the postures of erotic display and pursuit.

In one sense, Whitney's playful bequest brings to the fore the connections between objectification and description, making unabashedly evident the proprietary claims buried within this Petrarchan structure of representation. Whitney's description and display, however, take on markedly different characteristics from those found in this structure. The inherent contradictions in *her* proprietary powers are made clear, for instance, by the poem's fluctuating use of a particular word. Appearing twenty-two times in the space of the poem's 378 lines, the word "will" is used both as an auxiliary verb indicating future action and as an indication of desire. When the speaker says, "I yet wil leave him more" or "'Thus being weake, and wery both / an end heere wyll I make," she employs the word simply to indicate an anticipated action (E3ᵛ; E8). Yet in other declarations, "I wyll my friends these bookes to bye" or "By Thames you shal have Brewers store, / and Bakers at your wyll," the word names a preference, wish, or command (E6ᵛ; E3ᵛ). The instability of this word becomes important because it extends to the proclaimed "will" of the text, its raison d'être. For Whitney's legacy is portrayed alternately as a generous endowment and as a mere statement of what is and what will be. She offers both a celebration of abundance and an ironic compilation of social deprivation within London society, a documentation of poverty and plenty. This duality is particularly marked when the text shifts from its catalog of the fashion and food of the city to its long description of the various prisons. There is a striking difference, for instance, in leaving food for the hungry and leaving the criminal to the gallows. After saying of the citizens, "for their foode, I Butchers leave, / that every day shall kyll" (E3ᵛ), Whitney indicates that she merely "leaves" the rest to their fate. To the felons at Newgate, Whitney "leaves" a session in which some will suffer their thumbs to be branded; she "leaves" Holborne Hill as a spot for prisoners to go to be executed (E5ᵛ). In short, to the dispossessed, she leaves their raw, unmitigated fate. These mock bequests disclose a social world harshly indifferent to the desires of its individual citizens. The text stands poised, then, between the speaker's possession and her longing, as she alternately represents herself as conferring wealth and railing at fortune's inequities. Her poem may construct the presence and plenty of London; but because what she bequeaths is what she obviously cannot control, her verse is ultimately riddled with the harsh comic edge of bestowing London to London.

Whitney thus critiques the Petrarchan topos of plenty and lack by rendering it more starkly material. As the speaker unfolds the copious and manifold treasures of the city, she assures her readers/survivors that "in many places, Shops are full, / I left you nothing scant" (E5). But this plenty is poised against her own sense of deprivation:

> Yf any other thing be lackt
> in thee, I wysh them looke:
> For there it is: I little brought
> but nothyng from thee tooke.
> (E5)

The speaker's admission recasts the disposal of her properties in terms of loss. We can read these words, as we can the entire poem, as her possession rhetorically (in the space of the poem) of material things that were denied in reality, or we can see her poverty as a trope employed within this fictional myth of empowerment:

> Now London have I (for thy sake)
> within thee and without:
> As coms into my memory,
> dispersed round about
> Such needfull thinges, as they should have
> heere left now unto thee;
> When I am gon, with conscience
> let them dispearsed bee.
> (E7v)

Because it catalogs the speaker's lack of property and merely designates public goods as belonging the public domain, Whitney's "Wyll" directly contradicts the claims made by a legal will. Her poem exploits the absent/present speaker posited by any will-text as a means of pushing the Petrarchan paradox of loss and fulfillment to its extreme limit. Her legacy finally only documents her economic disenfranchisement through a feigned poetic possession. The book, figured as a legacy, both articulates and calls into question her authorial status. The contradiction in "leaving" London (exiting and bequeathing it) provocatively figures the woman's dubious speaking position within the culture.

Although the poem engages the logic of the blazon, it does not merely reverse genders, having the woman long for and master the male lover who is cast as the city. Instead, this particular trope for loss and desire foregrounds the peculiarities of the poetic strategy of anatomizing the object of display and desire; for Whitney's mapping of the overtly proprietary material world transforms the blazon into a spatial or cartographical catalog. In an earlier epistolary poem to her sister, Whitney states that her writing substitutes for the security of the domestic:

> Had I a Husband, or a house,
>   and all that longes therto
> My selfe could frame about to rouse,
>   as other women doo:
> But till some houshold cares me tye,
> My bookes and Pen I wyll apply.
>
> (D2)

Certainly, this is a legitimating posture designed to negotiate the conflict between domestic, propertied wife, and public writer. Her words also figure writing, however, as an act of loss, the trope for loss being architecture, space, the home. In her "Wyll," she rewrites the role of abandoned lover into that of evicted citizen who is unanchored to social stability and property. By casting the city as her possession through the blazon, the poem discloses and magnifies the rhetorical transformations that are always hidden within the Petrarchan speaker's act of wooing. For if the poetics of display involve a transformation of the gendered "other" into the mediating object to be owned and bartered, then Whitney's playful bequeathal foregrounds the objectifying component of description. Her poem makes unabashedly evident the advantages of this structure of representation: the sonnet speaker's assumption of ownership buried within the posture of adoring, feudal slave. Whitney thus participates in making and unmaking a poetics of display, as she writes from within, but against, a dominant poetic framework.

By framing her revision of the complaint and the blazon within the rhetoric of will-making, Whitney reinforces a tradition tied to women's contested rights to dispose of property. The *OED* lists one of the definitions of "will" as "the desire to do something when the power is lacking." The formation of the female "will" in nonlegal texts such as fictions. and advice books is bound up both with the "wylling minde" of Renaissance women and with those restrictions that prevented their desires from being expressed. Whitney's fictional text ironically becomes part of the body of literature in which mothers spoke from the grave. Although not proffering wisdom with moral certitude as those women did, and certainly departing from the doomed and tragic framework from which many of those writers spoke, Whitney nevertheless foregrounds their technique of transforming loss into a means of authorial empowerment. Her ironic claims to property, however, more fully underscore women's exclusion from the system of property transmission.

The social contestation over testamentary power complicates Whitney's authorizing gesture. Even as she seeks to establish a commodifiable textual terrain, her book-as-female-legacy ironically figures the ambiguity of her own authorial command. She draws on the debate about the rights and restrictions of female testators as a means of articulating her ambiguous relationship to the forms of public writing. We know that male writers also had to devise elaborate authorizing strategies because the culture did not have available an established role for the author in print. Whitney's *Nosegay*, however, imagines the relationship between author and public text in terms quite different from those employed by other poets. Her book thus marks an interruption in the gender ideology of authorship that was emerging in other literary works in the latter half of the century.

The printer of Whitney's fictional will, Richard Jones, went on to publish *The Gorgeous Gallery of Gallant Inventions* three years later. As Robert J. Fehrenbach has speculated, one of the poems in this work may have been authored by Whitney, a poem attributed to, or cast within the persona of, a gentlewoman poetically writing her will.[40] At least, the epigraph claims that attribution, although the body of the poem reveals a standard elegy rather than a poetic legacy. The argument for Whitney's authorship is heightened by the fact that the poem is written to William Gruffith; her first publication, "The Copy of A Letter," includes a response poem by a writer identified as "W. G." The authorship of this *Gallery* poem is a matter for speculation. But if this second poem is indeed by Whitney, it is certainly provocative that she chose once again to write through the overlaid frame of the legacy. If the work belongs to some other writer, it is still of interest because of the text's close association with, and apparent reference to, Whitney's previous poem. This repetition merely confirms that the form had become part of a cultural script that was frequently linked to female expression.

I think it no coincidence, then, that when John Webster's Duchess of Malfi sets forth to disobey her brother's demand for chastity, and instead to marry Antonio, she courts him through the rhetoric of will-making. Calling him before her, the Duchess engages her steward in a provocative bantering that ends with a triumphant bestowal of her ring on his finger. "I am making my will," she greets him, "were not one better make it smiling, thus? / Than in deep groans, and terrible ghastly looks."[41] After obtaining his approval in this endeavor, she reveals his real role in the pro-

[40]R. J. Fehrenbach, "Isabella Whitney (fl. 1565–75) and the Popular Miscellanies of Richard Jones," *Cahiers Élisabéthains* 19 (1981): 85–87.

[41]John Webster, *The Duchess of Malfi* (1623), in *John Webster: Three Plays* (New York: Viking Penguin, 1956), 1.2.298–301.

ject: "If I had a husband now, this care were quit: / But I intend to make you overseer" (1.2.304–5). The suggestive implications of assigning Antonio the role of surrogate husband are not lost on the steward. His equally flirtatious response generates an exchange that teases out the erotic resonances within the Duchess's declaration of her intent to make her will:

Antonio:	I'ld have you first provide for a good husband, Give him all.
Duchess:	All?
Antonio:	Yes, your excellent self.
Duchess:	In a winding sheet?
Antonio:	In a couple.
Duchess:	St. Winifred! that were a strange will.
Antonio:	'Twere strange If there were no will in you to marry again.

(308–13)

The reversal of the typical gendered power dynamic is visually highly determined in this scene, as the Duchess literally lifts Antonio from his knees on the stage to a more powerful position. She grandly instructs him, "raise yourself, / Or if you please, my hand to help you: so" (338–39); and a few moments later, she revels in her power to offer him more than her literal or figurative hand: "You may discover what a wealthy mine / I make you lord of" (348–49). Although the Duchess justifies her aggressive behavior by necessity ("The misery of us that are born great, / We are forc'd to woo, because none dare woo us," [360–61]), the witty conversation in this scene reveals her pleasure in this forward act, the act of "making" Antonio lord of her goods and herself. The language that she chooses to use when she transgressively and scandalously asserts her own erotic desire draws on one of the widow's few consolidated powers, the ability to fashion her "will." Like Whitney, who was unmarried, the Duchess's rights to testate were more defined than those of legally "covered" married women. Even so, the assertion of her sexual will has horrific consequences in the play, bringing on an orgy of bloodshed and mutilation. But while the play may be said to make highly problematic its own representation of this moment of female control, it nevertheless makes visible the terms through which such a moment can be imagined and staged.[42]

---

[42]See Mary Beth Rose, *The Expense of Spirit: Love and Sexuality in English Renaissance Drama* (Ithaca: Cornell University Press, 1988) for a discussion of how *The Duchess of Malfi* explores the contradictions of sexual ideology in a time when the family was being reconstituted. Rose notes that the play offers a blend of female heroism and the bourgeois desire for social mobility before it reinscribes those values in nostalgic and tragic terms at the conclusion (155–72).

Webster's play is not the only text to point out the intertwined psycho-logical, erotic, and legal meanings of the female will during this period. One scene from Shakespeare's *King John*, for instance, dramatizes two characters' argument over John's claim to the throne. When Elinor points to Richard's will as support for John's reign, Constance responds by delib-erately misunderstanding the word "will" as meaning obstinate; she then pathologizes it as something feminine: "a will, a wicked will, / A woman's will, a cank'red grandam's will!" she furiously terms it (2.1.193–94). Con-stance's outburst points to the cultural anxieties concerning the legal and psychological force of female volition. Prescriptive literature singled out female willfullness as one of the most alarming moral flaws; and a wo-man's power to testate, as I have noted, was constantly in dispute in the late sixteenth century. I suggest that the *Nosegay* registers the threat and power of the female will in its concern to reshape the book commodity and its relationship to its writer. By employing the tropes of "nosegay" and "legacy" as variations on the central metaphor of disease, Whitney is able to pose a proprietary claim for the writing subject's "will" over and against the privileged codes of manuscript exchange. She thus offers an alternate means of authorization, a new rhetoric through which women could nego-tiate their public exposure. The *Nosegay*'s attention to the uneasy connec-tion between women and property articulates the shaky claim that women, and men, had to public writing. Whitney playfully introduces her work by stating that the public should receive her work with good "wyll," she being "willing" to bestow it to her readers and to "expresse the good wyll" that rests in country folk. In establishing the work as the product of her "wylling minde," Whitney creates, from amid her manuscript-identified, collective work, a viable authorial position.

If critics have been slow to read the Duchess's rhetorical will-making, they have not missed the erotic, elusive wordplay within Shakespeare's pervasive "will," a multivalent word that simultaneously acts as his signa-ture, a sign of the bawdy entangling of the two sexes' genitalia, and the site of a virtuoso performance of rhetorical command. Stephen Booth refers to the group of "will" sonnets as "festivals of verbal ingenuity in which much of the fun derives from the grotesque lengths the speaker goes to for a maximum number and concentration of puns on *will*."[43] Cri-

---

43Stephen Booth, ed. *Shakespeare's Sonnets* (New Haven: Yale University Press, 1977), 466. For a discussion of Shakespeare's verbal puns on "wills" and "William," see Joel Fineman, "The Sound of O in *Othello*: The Real of the Tragedy of Desire," in *Psychoanalysis and . . .*, ed. Richard Felstein and Henry Sussman (New York: Routledge, 1990), 33–46; and Phyllis Rackin, *Stages of History: Shakespeare's English Chronicles* (Ithaca: Cornell University Press, 1990), 244–47.

tics have been interested in pursuing the thematic as well as rhetorical use of the male will, noting in particular the various configurations of the daughter's relationship to her father's testament. This is represented in strong form in Theseus's famous statement of filial imprintation and dramatized through Portia's binding to the father's word through the elusive caskets. But Whitney's farewell complaint makes visible an alternate working of the will, one linguistically playful although couched in tropes of death and absence. Her text participates in a tradition in which women negotiated their public exposure by calling attention to their controversial place within Renaissance inheritance practice and extrapolating from particular female associations with mortality. By reading her poems within this context, we are allowed to see how Whitney's strategies problematized an authorial role predicated on the exclusion of a speaking position for the female subject. The female legacy thus forms a trajectory, significant not merely because it rivals and intervenes in emerging masculine paradigms of authorial presentation, but also because it throws into relief the strategies of exclusion generated by those paradigms. My own critical uneasiness with the trope of inheritance—as a metaphor used to validate a literary heritage that excludes women writers—makes me particularly drawn to Whitney's brand of legacy. Cast as the product of a woman's "wylling minde," Whitney foregrounds a volatile and highly ironic female legacy while bestowing on readers and future writers an alternate language of authorial command.

Authorial Mourning and the Poetics of Display

Constructing the female legacy was just one avenue that women writers took in legitimating their right to speak publicly in fictional and nonfictional texts. In *A sweet Nosegay*, Whitney departs from these mothers' texts by revealing her knowledge of such "inappropriate" subjects as classical mythology, city satire, and Ovidian complaint. Women were generally given more cultural license, however, to study religious works, as many of these writing mothers evidently did. Because of their guilty lineage from Eve, women were frequently exhorted to meditate, pray, and study the Bible. As Elaine Beilin has demonstrated so fully, Renaissance women took these injunctions to heart, publishing works that sought to define the ideal of Christian life and to glorify "female" Christian virtues (*Redeeming Eve*). The title of Margaret Hannay's collection devoted to Renaissance women's writing, *Silent but for the Word*, encapsulates the exceptional nature of religious writing as legitimate projects for women. Hannay's observation was noted by a contemporary Renaissance writer as well. In the introduction to her sixteenth-century translation of French romance, Margaret Tyler calls attention to the genre-specific interdictions on women's writing. She denounces the detractors who would, she suggests, "enforce me necessarily either not to write or to write of divinitie."[44] Although Mary Sidney and Amelia Lanyer were very different kinds of writers, one an exceptionally powerful and learned aristocrat and the other a middle-class woman of dubious repute, both women appealed to the sanctioned symbolic mode of religious poetry as a means of grappling with the problematic metaphors subtending literary authority. Sidney, in her more private manuscript work, and Lanyer, in her published narrative poem, respond to the same set of prohibitive codes by devising authorizing strategies that could present them as writers. Like Whitney, these women tapped into the power implicit in the role of mourner, but they positioned that role in the discourse of religious poetry.

Sidney chose to create a manuscript text that was not only traditional in its religious subject, but also less of a cultural threat because it so evidently mediated a more male and authoritative text.[45] By translating the divine Psalms, Sidney located her authorial role within prescriptions of female piety; she further protected her writing by linking it to the authority of her source text. Although Sidney also translated works by Philip de Mornay, Robert Garnier, and Petrarch, the *Psalmes* are the only text in which we see how she intended to present her writing for her readers.[46] Though the work was never published, she carefully designed it for presentation to the queen at court, and thus she constructed a version of authorship that would not have been needed for a manuscript designed for private perusal. She articulated her own role in writing the poems through two verse dedications, "To the Angell spirit of the most excellent Sir Philip Sidney" and "Even now that Care which on thy Crowne attends" (also referred to

[44]Margaret Tyler, trans., *A Mirrour of Princely Deedes and Knighthood*, STC 18859 (1578), sig. A4ᵛ.

[45]See note 78 where I discuss John Florio's assessment that "all translations are reputed femalls, delivered at second hand." For discussions of Mary Sidney's *Psalmes*, see the pioneering introductory essay by John Rathmell in his edition, *The Psalms of Sir Philip Sidney and the Countess of Pembroke* (Garden City, N.Y.: Doubleday, 1963); Gary Waller, "The Countess of Pembroke and Gendered Reading," in *The Renaissance Englishwoman in Print: Counterbalancing the Canon*, ed. Anne M. Haselkorn and Betty Travitsky (Amherst: University of Massachusetts Press, 1990), 327–46; Waller's *Mary Sidney, Countess of Pembroke: A Critical Study of Her Writings and Literary Milieu* (Salzburg: Universität Salzburg, Institut für Anglistik und Amerikanistik, 1979); Beth Wynne Fisken, "Mary Sidney's *Psalmes*: Education and Wisdom," in *Silent But for the Word*, 166–83; and Coburn Freer, "Mary Sidney: The Countess of Pembroke," in *Women Writers of the Renaissance and Reformation*, ed. Katharina M. Wilson (Athens: University of Georgia Press, 1987).

[46]Sidney's other works include a translation of Philip de Mornay's *A Discourse on Life and Death* (1592), Robert Garnier's *Tragedie of Antonie* (1595), and Petrarch's *Triumphe of Death* (mss).

as "To the Thrice Sacred Queen Elizabeth"). These poems explained and justified Sidney's status as an author. The *Psalmes* went on to become highly public texts, circulating widely enough to be read by contemporaries such as Donne, Lanyer, and Herbert, and enduring to uphold her literary reputation in the next century. Sidney became identified with these poems more than any of her other works. Writers such as Thomas Moffett, Nicholas Breton, Henry Constable, and Edmund Spenser praised her success in these poetic texts; and when Simon van de Passe painted Sidney's portrait, he chose to represent her with *Davids Psalmes* clutched to her breast. Her other works, those without prefatorial justifications, interestingly did not achieve such fame.[47]

The Psalms were a particularly appropriate text for Sidney because they both signaled an allegiance to her brother and provided a religious version of secular literary forms associated with the Sidney family. Mary Sidney coauthored the text with Philip, revising his forty psalms and writing ninety of her own after his death. She obviously was attracted to the complaints of David because she wanted to finish the masterful project that her brother had begun. Certainly, these poems showed her inclination to fortify the Sidney family's reputation as a militant Protestant force and literary center, and they may have been presented to the queen as a political reminder of that force.[48] Combining her politics and her faith, Sidney sought to carry on the Genevan tradition established by Philip.[49] But she also could have seen the Psalms as offering a mode of literary authority distinct from that generated by popular courtly lyric poetry. In the poetic and formal challenges they offer, the Psalms can be said to constitute a religious version of the Petrarchan love complaint popularized largely by Philip Sidney's *Astrophel and Stella*. David's poems not only provided a discourse mobile enough for probing a range of intense emotions—joy, grief, exaltation, desolation, misery—but they also allowed the writer to experiment with various metrical and stanzaic arrangements.

[47]In "Mary Sidney: The Countess of Pembroke," Freer explains that the *Psalmes* were "known to a good number of churchmen, and selections were reprinted in anthologies of religious lyrics during the eighteenth and nineteenth centuries. Her other works fell into comparative obscurity" (489). The critical consensus to date is that the *Psalmes* are Sidney's most important works.

[48]Margaret Hannay makes this point in "'Doo What Men May Sing': Mary Sidney and the Tradition of Admonitory Dedication," in *Silent But for the Word*, 149–65.

[49]Hannay discusses Sidney's important role as Philip's political and literary executor. Her biography of Mary Sidney has enabled literary critics to comment more fully on this extraordinary woman's works. *Philip's Phoenix: Mary Sidney, Countess of Pembroke* (Oxford: Oxford University Press, 1990). Mary Ellen Lamb discusses Sidney's influence in "The Countess of Pembroke's Patronage," *English Literary Renaissance* 12 (1982): 162–79.

The Psalms' disjunct textual form offered a spatial arrangement in which the speaker could disperse emotions onto a serial plane through multiple personae. In this work, Sidney perhaps found a legitimate means of imitating the language, patterns, and images often used to construct a masculine paradigm of authorship.

By rehearsing the eloquent and often eroticized submission to a higher authority found in David's language, Sidney could also explore the vexed issues of sovereignty and subjection central to the discourse of love. David's poems reveal his negotiation for divine recognition and his articulation of loss, a poetic description of what he calls the "downcast state." It is telling that Philip Sidney turned to these translations when the queen banished him from court. The Psalms offered him a vehicle for expressing his sense of social estrangement and anxiety, while they also promised a rescue from hostile authority. The mingled voices of Sidney/David vividly describe the plagues sent by bitter enemies as they pray for God's help in developing weapons for combating these assaults. Through this highly mediated voice, Sidney imitates the speaking position in "male" symbolic modes, a position that turns on controlled subjection and embattled rescue through the appropriated weapon of language.

In her introductory poems, Sidney makes clear that the authoritative ground for the text is not its divine subject, but its author. Philip's hand in the project sanctioned the collaborative enterprise; as she states: "hee did warpe, I weav'd this webbe to end" (27).[50] Through the metaphor of weaving, she names her role as perfunctory, his as imaginative. She further effaces her authorial role by lauding Philip as the true source of the translations:

> To thee pure sprite, to thee alones addres't
> this coupled worke, by double int'rest thine:
> First rais'de by thy blest hand, and what is mine
> inspird by thee, thy secrett power imprest.
> ("To the Angell spirit," 1–4)

---

[50]Mary Sidney, "Even now that Care. . . ," (also known as "To the Thrice Sacred Queen Elizabeth") in *The Triumph of Death and Other Unpublished and Uncollected Poems*, ed. Gary Waller (Salzburg: Institut für Englische Sprache und Literatur, Universität Salzburg, 1977), 88–91. I cite all references to this poem and "To the Angell spirit of the most excellent Sir Philip Sidney (92-95) by line number from this edition. In order to make these poems more accessible, I should note that "To the Angell spirit" is included in Rathmell's edition of the *Psalms*, and "To the Thrice Sacred Queen Elizabeth" is reprinted in *The Female Spectator: English Women Writers Before 1800*, ed. Mary Mahl and Helene Koon (Bloomington: Indiana University Press, 1977), 66–69.

The work is doubly Philip's, Sidney claims, because he is its coauthor and sole inspiration. Although Philip did not publish his own works when he was alive, his death authorized the publication of his texts as well as those of others who discursively mourned his demise. Here Mary Sidney uses that authorization in her more private and circumscribed text. As female legacies demonstrate, the apocalyptic moment of the final departure overshadows and outweighs the social problems bound up with public display. Absence, death, and grief justify the spread of truth to a wider audience. Thus, while her insistence on a circumscribed audience is reiterated in her declaration to Philip that her work "hath no further scope to goe / nor other purpose but to honor thee," her modest claims ironically prove her an accomplished and public poet, "imprest" with secret power and a broad "scope" (29–30).

Sidney's prefatorial poems name Philip both as the origin of the *Psalmes* and the rationale for their circulation. When she admits to the queen that the "coupled work" is now a solo performance, "Which once in two, now in one Subject goe / the poorer left, the richer reft awaye," her words call attention to the trace of a "richer" and more legitimate voice embedded within her text (21–22). Her allusion to Penelope Rich, or at least to Astrophel's playful use of that name, locates Sidney as the stellar inspiration for her work. From the grave, "reft awaye," Philip is distanced enough from the material world to allow her to project his (and her own) voice to a larger audience. Sidney appropriates the "secrett power" of her fantasized and ethereal projection of her brother as a means of vindicating her literary endeavor and covering the transgression of her boldness in writing.[51] Philip gives her permission to speak.

In casting Philip as the text's "richer" origin, Sidney regenders and literalizes the concept of the muse itself, an icon that was often used to eroticize the moment of literary production. The eroticization of the relationships between writer, commodified book, and reader that I have described in previous chapters is intensified by the sexualization of the *very process of writing.* When Milton notes that his heavenly muse visits him nocturnally in his bed, he plays on a traditional depiction of literary texts as the progeny of male writer and female muse. Ben Jonson amplifies this notion when he guardedly praises the writings of his contemporary Cecilia Bulstrode as

---

[51]Donne described the *Psalmes* by reemploying Sidney's language, noting that the "cloven" nature of the work (union of God/man) is carried through in the double authorship: "'so thou hast cleft that spirit, to performe / That worke againne and shed it, here, upon / Two, by their bloods, and by the Spirit one; / A Brother and A Sister, made by thee / the Organ, where Thou art the Harmony." *The Poems of John Donne*, ed. Herbert J. C. Grierson, 2 vols. (Oxford: Clarendon Press, 1912), 1:348.

"equall with the best" although "with Tribade lust she force a Muse."[52]
"Tribade," according to the *OED*, means "the unnatural acts women perform on one another." Jonson's use of this homoerotic term marginalizes
the female writer into a socially awkward position. If the writer and muse
dally together in authoring a text, then the conventional gender of the
muse makes authorship a masculine undertaking. By making Philip her
muse, Sidney disrupts and restructures conventional sexual metaphors for
textual production, particularizing quite explicitly the abstractions that
fueled writing.

"To the Angell spirit" plays on this tradition by depicting the muse as
interactive; the ensuing work is cast as the product of an erotic entangle-
ment. Her muse and Philip's "combine" to produce a child: the text that is
"rais'de" by Philip's hand and later described as well "borne" (in the sense
of carried forth and birthed). The elegaic mode allows Sidney to define
her place in the writing process through an impassioned outpouring of
love. By tantalizingly troping her muse as a conjugal duo, Sidney attaches
free-floating anxieties about the sexualizing effects of writing to this barely
suppressed promiscuous mingling. The issue of her own desire is preemp-
tively raised and contained within the sibling relationship. She hints at the
provocative nature of this coupling: "So dar'd my Muse with thine it selfe
combine" (5). The muse not only is humanized and literalized, but its textual erotics are staged within the family relationship. Sidney thus cagily
reconstructs a potential problem rhetorically so that it serves to empower
her function as a writer.

Much of this address is couched in amplified Petrarchan language: the
poet gathers her thoughts like tributaries to the sea; she performs an
accounting of the "strange passions" in her heart; she protests against the
limits of language. "To the Angell spirit" blends broken bodies, monetary
expenditure, emotional reckoning, eternizing conceits, and hyperbolic
praise—in short, it trades heavily on typical Petrarchan poetic conventions. Like many other Renaissance writers, Sidney also offers a corporeal
metaphor for her text. But her analogy does not identify the work as a ravished or wounded maiden who requires editorial attention, a tactic that
many other sixteenth-century writers and publishers took in presenting
their authority through a corporeal trope.[53] Her text sallies forth as a
wounded body, painfully aware of the loss of its male author. In calling

[52]Ben Jonson, "Epigram on The Court Pucell," from *Under-Wood*, in *The Works of Ben
Jonson*, ed. C. H. Herford Percy and Evelyn Simpson, 11 vols. (Oxford: Clarendon Press,
1925–1952), 8:222.

[53]For examples of other works that are described as wounded or maimed, see the prefatory
material to Francis Beaumont's and John Fletcher's *Philaster* (which is subtitled *Love lies a
bleeding*). Here the publisher states that the main characters have "laine so long a-bleeding,

her work a "half maim'd peece" with "deepe wounds enlarg'd, long fes-
tered in their gall / fresh bleeding smart," Sidney draws on the conventional body metaphor for the text, one not unconnected with the violent
metaphors of Petrarchan emotion (19–20). But her language is peculiarly
emphatic about the text's injuries and its physical corporeality:

> . . . theise dearest offrings of my hart
>   dissolv'd to Inke, while penns impressions move
>   the bleeding veines of never dying love:
> I render here: these wounding lynes of smart
>   sadd Characters indeed of simple love
>   not Art nor skill which abler wits doe prove.
> Of my full soue receive the meanest part.
>   (78–84)

Combined with the image of the "half maim'd" poem, her evocation of
"wounding lynes" conflates her own grief at her brother's loss with David's
grief, Philip Sidney's wounds on the battlefield, and her own text. Using a
string of adjectival clauses, the poem creates a set of imprecise grammatical associations, a cluster of modifiers that refers back to Philip's body. His
anatomy blends with the very text of the *Psalmes* because both are wounded,
bereft, and incomplete. Rather than making way for the mastery of a curative editor, this trope authorizes the work as an emblem of the piecemeal
body of a culturally resonant, dead male. Philip's death enables his representation as a physical and textual commodity. Mourning is the public
operation, one perhaps even more authorized for women than men, that
allows Sidney to rewrite Petrarchan codes of power. She thus revises the
strategy of presenting the displayed "weak" text by holding up her martyred brother's heroic wounded body to deflect attention from her bravado
in daring to undertake such an ambitious project. Philip's body stands as a
sign of her ambivalent position as a female writer, registering as well as
assuaging the anxiety of writing.

Another of Sidney's central tropes for the text—that of cloth and cloth-

---

by reasons of some dangerous and gaping wounds which they received in the first
Impression, that it is wondered how they could go abroad so long or travel so far as they have
done." He then announces the authority of his own work by noting that he seeks to "bind up
their wounds" so that they may not be "so maimed and deformed as they at the first were,"
but appear in a state "suitable to their birth and breeding." In *Philaster*, ed. Andrew Gurr
(London: Methuen, 1969), 4. Like the 1623 Shakespearean folio, which presents a
Shakespeare "cur'd and well limb'd" (to replace the "maimed and deformed" pre-texts),
Philaster is authorized by being made healthy. The rhetoric of healing became one trope
among many in imagining the authority for the printed text.

ing—alters the resonances of the body metaphor. As a series of "holy garments" (alternately worn by David, the reader, and Elizabeth) and a "liverie robe" stitched, warped, woven, and attired, the text seems to shroud the
broken body, to drop a veil over the corporeal object through a craft that
is decidedly aristocratic, domestic, and female. Sidney revels in her ability
to call forth the body and then to make "peec't" cloth from pieces of
limbs. In this way, the work presents and conceals the wounded body, narrating but clothing its own textual lack. Sidney's formulation is particularly
interesting given the Freudian gloss on weaving as the labor of compensa-
tion for the "lack" inherent in woman. The work may manipulate the
readerly gaze in displaying the aristocratic male body, but it problematizes
that staging by enshrouding the body in elegaic text. Through alternating
self-referential metaphors, the poem both regenders and disrupts the
poetics of corporeal display central to male writers' self-authorizing
rhetoric. The poem may represent "the gratitude and discomfort [Sidney]
felt at having to use [Philip's] example to find her own means of expression," as critic Beth Wynne Fisken notes;[54] but it also reveals how Sidney
draws on a debilitating discourse for her own purposes. As Sidney expresses
the powerful emotions of piety and grief, she clears a space within the ideology of authorship for an alternative poetics of display.

Her poignant self-erasure in this process of revision may seem disturb-
ing to readers with a feminist sensibility. In one moment, for instance, she
claims that her project is to immortalize Philip by making him a twinkling
star—her "stella," in effect—and by relegating herself to blackness: "thou
art fixt among thy fellow lights: / my day put out, my life in darkenes cast"
(58). Sidney's self-abnegation, however, takes on new meaning when it is
stylistically dramatized in the next stanza. As if to demonstrate this erasure, the stanza omits the subject "I," instead piling up a stack of language
that finally artfully reveals, rather than renders invisible, her place in the
process of building Philip's corpus:

> As goodly buildings to some glorious ende
>   cut of by fate, before the Graces hadde
>   each wondrous part in all their beauties cladde,
> Yet so much done, as Art could not amende;
>   So thy rare workes to which no witt can adde,
>   in all men's eies, which are not blindely madde,
> Beyonde compare above all praise, extende.
>
> (94)

54Beth Wynne Fisken, "'To the Angell Spirit . . . ': Mary Sidney's Entry into the 'World of
Words,'" in *The Renaissance Englishwoman in Print*, 266.

The last verb hangs alone, demanding that the reader retrospectively apply a subject into the stanza that can govern these clauses. Although ambiguously related to the subject "rare workes" (words that enact a moment of self-extension), this verb points as well to the subject "I." "I" is never spoken, but it governs the act of poetic extension and the stanza's grammatical structure: I extend these works, which seem sufficient so as to need no aid, but only a mere expansion. The dislocated final verb forces the reader to reconstruct the dense grammatical organization of the stanza to *find* that subject. The deftness of this stylistic erasure and disclosure paradoxically serves to foreground her poetic presence. Philip's absent body, like his missing poems (both cut off by fate, both full of "wondrous parts"), enables her mystified but persistent presence. Her prefatorial poem tellingly ends with an expression of her desire to join her brother in the ranks of heaven; Philip's legacy seemingly inspires her desire for a leave-taking (Mary Ellen Lamb, *Gender and Authorship*, 115–18).

As in Whitney's text, sorrow becomes the trope through which Sidney's authorial and public identity can be formulated, not only through the *Psalmes*, but also through her role in making Philip's works public and fashioning his image. Sidney garnered authority from the cultural legend that she helped to create, a legend that authorized her production of Philip's works as well as her own. After his death, Mary Sidney became his literary executor, the recipient of praise heaped on him, and the director of his extant works. In revising and presenting publicly the text he named for her, *The Countess of Pembroke's Arcadia*, Mary Sidney apparently carried out Philip's intentions by erasing the main characters' unlicensed lust: she deleted Musidorus's attempted rape and Pyrocles's adulterous night of passion. Whether "bowdlerizing" the romance or merely making its plot more consistent, the countess certainly exercised considerable editorial power by making these changes.[55] In the preface to the 1593 edition, Hugh Sanford writes that the work is "now by more than one interest *The Countess of Pembroke's Arcadia*: done, as it was, for her: as it is, by her."[56] Through the eyes of this Renaissance publisher, we see that by editing the work, the Countess became more than merely the text's dedicatee. If manuscript circulation fostered a view of textuality that generally granted wide powers to the reader, the female writer capitalized on this view by extending it to the economy of publication.[57] She simultaneously scripted an

[55]For the publishing history of the *Arcadia*, see William Ringler, notes to *Sir Philip Sidney: Poems* (Oxford: Clarendon Press, 1962); and Hannay, *Philip's Phoenix*, 71–78.

[56]Hugh Sanford, "To the Reader," in Sir Philip Sidney, *The Countess of Pembroke's Arcadia*, ed. Maurice Evans (New York: Penguin, 1984), 60.

[57]Samuel Daniel, for instance, tells Mary Sidney that his text *Delia* is "begotten by thy hand

authorial and cultural role—in Hannay's terms, the role of the "Phoenix rising from her brother's ashes" (ix).

In his history of Wiltshire, John Aubrey claims that Mary Sidney wrote the poems in the *Arcadia* because "they seem to have been writt by a woman."[58] While we find Aubrey's comment hardly convincing, we may note that his confusion stems from the unique authority that Mary Sidney had over the text, authority that she exercised by appropriating her brother's work after his death. Aubrey's further salacious speculations, that the siblings' devotion extended to the bedroom, seem a perverse but not unsolicited response to the "coupled work" that inscribed a brother into the discourse of Petrarchan love.[59] Aubrey's words are ironic; for from her stance as a religious devotional poet and a mourning sister, Sidney established a dialogue with the textual mechanisms used in the fashionable poetics of erotic writing. In her prefatory poem she offered a modification of the embodied figures that kept becoming visible when writers and publishers placed their commodities in print. She was "coupled," not sexually perhaps, but textually, as Philip's body became a central icon in her construction of authorial and cultural identity. Sidney's legacy for women writers was, finally, an elegaic poetic corpus created from within sanctioned religious meditations and predicated on the absent and therefore representable male body.

The Body of Christ: Amelia Lanyer's Passion

In 1611, Amelia Lanyer, the middle-class daughter of a court musician, published a religious poem, *Salve Deus Rex Judaeorum*, which enacted its own brand of corporeal representation and its own complex authorizing strategies. In this text, Lanyer poetically presents the Passion of Christ while actively counteracting popular condemnations of women.[60] Expli-

---

and my desire." The exchangeability of her hand and his points to a conception of poetic property in which the dedicatee can "own" the work. *Delia,* STC 6254 (1594).

[58]John Aubrey, *The Natural History of Wiltshire* (1847; reprint, New York: Augustus M. Kelley, 1969), 89. In *Gender and Authorship in the Sidney Circle,* Lamb discusses the more common reverse charge, that Mary Sidney was not competent enough to have translated the Psalms so excellently (30). John Harington, for instance, attributed them to her chaplain.

[59]John Aubrey, *Brief Lives,* ed. Oliver Lawson Dick (Ann Arbor: University of Michigan Press, 1949), 139.

[60]Amelia Lanyer, *Salve Deus Rex Judaeorum,* STC 15227 (1611). I reluctantly cite this poem from A. L. Rowse's edition, which reproduces the text only to put forth the ludicrous and sexist argument that Lanyer's importance rests in her having been Shakespeare's frustratingly resistant "dark lady." Rowse's edition is valuable, however, because it is accessible and preserves the original text with its apparatus. Therefore, all references to *Salve Deus Rex Judaeorum* are to *The Poems of Shakespeare's Dark Lady,* ed. A. L. Rowse (New York: Clarkson N. Potter, 1979).

citly naming Mary Sidney as a literary precursor, Lanyer draws on the position of virtuous mourner in writing her *Salve Deus*. Like Sidney, Lanyer produced a religious work that responded to the poetics of corporeal display built into the gender ideology of sixteenth-century authorship. Unlike Sidney's poems, the *Salve Deus* foregrounds gender; in fact, Lanyer explicitly offers a defense of women as she revises traditional myths that fuel misogynist views of women's weakness. Although she admits a "Womans writing of divinest things" is "seldome seene" (41), she boldly offers a polemical counternarrative to biased accounts of women and biblical history: "I have written this small volume, or little booke, for the generall use of all virtuous Ladies and Gentlewomen of this kingdome . . . And this have I done, to make knowne to the world, that all women deserve not to be blamed" (77). Lanyer forges her defense by portraying biblical women as instruments of God sent out to counter sinful men. Pontius Pilate's wife serves as one of the text's central emblems of spiritual virtue, for she heroically attempts to prevent the crucifixion. Pilate's wife assumes the voice of the text, digressing into a polemic that judges the sin of Eve (foremother of female weakness) to be less egregious than that of Christ's male crucifiers. That murder, she announces, comprised a second fall ("men's fall"), one that was more horrendous than the initial loss of Eden and powerful enough to re-gender that first transgression.

In describing the crucifixion, Lanyer classifies the spectators' responses according to sexual difference: thieves, sergeants, and hangman stood passively while, she states, "the women cri'd" (109):

> When spightfull men with torments did oppresse
> Th'afflicted body of this innocent Dove
> Poore women seeing how much they did transgresse,
> By teares, by sighes, by cries intreat, nay prove,
> What may be done among the thickest presse,
> They labour still these tyrants hearts to move;
>   In pitie and compassion to forbeare
>   Their whipping, spurning, tearing of his haire.
>   (110)

Although the women try to soften the hearts of "tyrants," their labors are in vain; the men's "malice hath no end." This passage presents a group huddled around the cross, divided into camps by gender: the men inflict pain on Christ's body while the daughters of Jerusalem beg for his release from persecution. The crucifixion, then, becomes the site of contestation between the sexes, an agonistic moment in history that makes women's virtue visible. This scene of sorrow empowers women not only as historical figures, but also as agents within the immediate polity. Indeed, Lanyer's own break into print is legitimated by the virtue of these women's tears.

In a review of Spike Lee's *Do the Right Thing*, a controversial film about racial tensions in twentieth-century urban America, one critic complained about the absence of the "female viewpoint" within the debate about racially motivated violence. She concluded: "women are often victims of one kind or another. They may be perpetrators as well but for the most part they suffer the losses. Murder may be the greatest cause of death among young African-American men. But women are the mourners, the mothers, the sisters, the wives."[61] While I hesitate to essentialize the female position as that of the victim (as does this critic), it seems evident that women have historically been forced into, and thus subsequently allowed, the social position of mourning. Often excluded from public violence, women instead attend to the ensuing domestic casualties. Lanyer taps into this ascription of gender difference, as does Sidney in mourning Philip's death. Both women speak from the socially approved female role of mourner in their attempts to publicize and legitimate female speech.

Lanyer's intentions seem evident from the proto-feminist statements in her work.[62] Through the heterogeneous portions of the text—the eleven dedications, the meandering poetic narrative written in eight-line stanzas of iambic pentameter, and the concluding "Description of Cooke-ham," the first English country-house poem ever published—Lanyer variously configures women's relationships to mythology and each another. Her list of female dedications becomes a litany of the most learned aristocratic women of her time; her discussions of biblical women provide a mythohistorical basis for a defense of women's nature, and her nostalgic view of her childhood home portrays an Edenic environment in which girls frolic in harmony with nature. By representing the community of women in childhood, the heroism of women in history, and the virtues of Renaissance women, the *Salve Deus* generates a heterogeneous document that makes women central to the moral and social fabric of sixteenth-century culture. Lanyer thus goes far in accomplishing what Margaret Ferguson also sees in Elizabeth Cary's *Mariam*: "unravelling the logic which binds 'chastity' to 'silence' and 'obedience'" ("Running On," 41). Through her

[61]Ellen Goodman, "Missing: The Influence of Black Women. . . ," *Boston Globe*, 18 July 1989.

[62]On the controversy over the status of women, see Linda Woodbridge, *Women and the English Renaissance: Literature and the Nature of Womankind, 1540–1620* (Urbana: University of Illinois Press, 1984), who argues that the debates about women were part of an elaborate rhetorical game; and Constance Jordan, *Renaissance Feminism: Literary Texts and Political Models* (Ithaca: Cornell University Press, 1990), who places English defenses of women within the context of European and classical "feminism."

interwoven claims of past and present female virtue, Lanyer makes her biblical subject matter inextricable from the preliminary addresses that situate the text for her community of readers. At the same time, she implicitly fashions her own role as a public religious visionary. In her frame of reference, public speaking is an ethical and moral imperative for virtuous women.

The numerous dedications to women that preface the text, as Barbara Lewalski points out, create a female community of readers that is poised against this flawed community of biblical men.[63] Like the *Nosegay* and popular male-authored texts, the *Salve*'s copious preliminary material announces the text's site of production as collective and socially collaborative. Her multiple dedications inform the work with a reciprocity that reproduces in print the community of the patronage system. But Lanyer's particular representation of this community interestingly turns on the trope of the mirror, which had, as Karen Newman observes, deeply engrained special associations for women.[64] Lanyer locates its points of intersection as a complex presentation of mirroring, looking, and gazing; she invites the various dedicatees to see themselves in her textual glass (42, 48, 63, 72), to cast their eyes on her book (52), and to act as glasses reflecting the glory of God (53). Her work is figured almost obsessively as an interactive mirroring of female virtues, a redemptive textual space in which women might find the image of themselves and other devout women, and in which they, by looking, might purify their sight (67). When Christ is called the "mirrour of Martyrs" (99), it becomes apparent that Lanyer offers female readers the story of Christ as a model for, and an extreme example of, female piety. Christ and Lanyer's dedicatees blend into a space of refraction and community. Her pious subject matter thus becomes inextricably linked to her defense of good women.

The power of this textual community seemingly compensates for Lan-

---

[63]Barbara Lewalski, "Of God and Good women: The Poems of Aemilia Lanyer," in *Silent But for the Word*, 203–23. But Anne Baynes Coiro rightly cautions against reading Lanyer's addresses as constituting an unqualified affirmation of female community. In a talk entitled "Print and Manuscript as Gendered Performances," Coiro points out both harsh criticisms and subtle ironies that reveal the class tensions within Lanyer's praise of women. (Paper delivered at the Twenty-seventh International Congress on Medieval Studies at Kalamazoo, Michigan, Renaissance English Texts Society Panel, May 1992.)

[64]"The link between women and the mirror is, of course, an ancient commonplace, part of a complex articulation of women as objects of male desire and dependent on that desire for their status, livelihood, even their lives," Karen Newman argues. "Derided for her preoccupation with the material, the woman before the mirror epitomizes the memento mori. . . . Beside this long tradition is another, rival tradition derived from an ancient topos found in Plutarch. . . . There the metaphor of the glass is a site of ethical exampla." *Fashioning Femininity and English Renaissance Drama* (Chicago: University of Chicago Press, 1991), 7–8.

yer's sense of social alienation, which she presents in a Petrarchan complaint of loss and desire. She describes herself as someone

> Whose untun'd voyce the dolefull notes doth sing
> Of sad Affliction in an humble straine;
> Much like unto a Bird that wants a wing,
> And cannot flie, but warbles forth her paine:
>   Or he that barred from the Suns bright light,
>   Wanting daies comfort, doth comend the night.
>
> So that I live clos'd up in Sorrowes Cell,
> Since great Elizaes favour blest my youth;
> And in the confines of all cares doe dwell,
> Whose grieved eyes no pleasure ever view'th:
>   But in Christs suffrings, such sweet taste they have,
>   As makes me praise pale Sorrow and the Grave.
>
>   (44)

Initially, she sets up the analogy between her suffering and Christ's to differentiate them (his pain relieves hers), but this fleeting identification is
consolidated later in the work. The Petrarchan image of the wounded
bird with "untun'd" voice is here employed to connect Christian suffering
with political disenfranchisement and to hold up Christian devotion as a
remedy for a specifically social distress. Lanyer poignantly tells about her
embrace of redemptive suffering and vacuous night as antidotes to her
devastating exclusion from the court.

Lanyer's public narrative work, obviously quite different from Sidney's
more privatized lyric translation, nevertheless sees Sidney's "holy sonnets"
as an important literary precursor. Lanyer praises Sidney's *Psalmes* in a
dedication to the countess, the longest prefatory address she offers. It is
thus no coincidence that Lanyer also draws on and revises the rhetoric of
embodiment in her presentation of her work. She grounds her poetic
authority in her divine subject, which she metamorphoses into her animate text. She positions the body of Christ strategically in her presentation of her book. In explaining the "poverty" of her skill to Ladie Margaret, Lanyer sees fit to quote Peter: "Silver nor gold have I none, but such
as I have, that give I you: for having neither rich pearles of India, nor fine
gold of Arabia, nor diamonds of inestimable value . . . I present unto you
even our Lord Jesus himselfe" (66). The lavish materials she evokes in this
statement of humility are resonant when we consider that these were the
typical objects of comparison used in poetic descriptions of the mistress's
body. Her gesture of rejecting foreign tropes and commodities in the service of presenting the "natural" and Englished truth of experience was

one popularized by Sidney's *Astrophel and Stella*. Lanyer creates an antiblazon to present the unblemished rich jewel of Christ, who surpasses all metaphors of wealth:

> No Dove, no Swan, nor Iv'rie could compare
> With this faire corps, when 'twas by death imbrac'd;
> No rose nor no vermillion halfe so faire
> As was that pretious blood that interlac'd
> His body.
>
> (70)

This technique of negation harkens back to her previous affirmative presentation of "even our Lord Jesus himselfe." Christ's body, first offered as a substitute for poetic and material riches, becomes defined by what it is not: gold, ivory, jewels. Lanyer thus presents her book by inverting and critiquing the blazon.

The corporeal metaphor commonly used by writers in packaging their books becomes transformed under Lanyer's pen. Her text becomes the Word Incarnate, an unstable blend of total corporeality and transcendent spirituality. When she tells Mary Sidney that "it is no disparagement to you / To see your Saviour in a Shepheards weed, / Unworthily presented in your view / Whose worthinesse will grace each line you reade," she humbly suggests her own inadequacy in presenting such an important subject (64). But in conflating Christ with the poorly dressed pastoral book, Lanyer indicates the divinity within her own work that immediately offsets her self-deprecation. Her words thus ambitiously protect and announce her project by creating a religious version of the Virgilian progression—from pastoral to Passion. The incarnation is the Word made flesh; Lanyer strategically plays on this embodiment by calling attention to the fleshliness of her own representation of the Word. She carries the text-as-body metaphor, a staple of Renaissance prefaces, to one logical extreme.

We see Lanyer's use of personification again when she instructs Ladie Arabella:

> Come like the Morning Sunne new out of bed,
> And Cast your eyes upon this little Booke,
> Although you be so well accompan'd
> With Pallas, and the Muses, spare one looke,
> On this humbled King, who all forsooke.
>
> (52)

The audacity of suggesting that her reader merely "spare" a look for Christ (a rhetorical device seen as well when she presents "our Lord Jesus himselfe" because she lacks other gifts of value) inscribes the importance of her "little Booke," which is imagined as the animate "King." Through this language, her published text *becomes* Christ. She solicits Ladie Susan to do more than cast her eyes on this kingly text:

> Receive your Love whom you have sought so farre,
>> Which heere presents himselfe within your view;
>> Behold this bright and all directing Starre,
> Light of your Soule that doth all grace renew:
>> And in his humble paths since you do tread,
> Take this faire Bridegroome in your soules pure bed.
>
> (54)

Here agency is redirected from the displaying author to the divine subject who "presents himself." What better way to guarantee a good reception for the published work than to defer responsibility to the savior? By figuring the book as the incarnated, spiritualized, and eroticized body of Christ, Lanyer forges a vocabulary through which she can present her work.

By couching the presentation of her book in language that suggests that she is delivering the savior to her female readers, Lanyer inverts the mistress/mastery textual dynamic in which the writer establishes control over his work by figuring it as in need of governance. Deriving authority from the commodified presentation of the animated text, she draws on the text's superior matter rather than its unruly or deficient nature. The savior-as-book—walking, embracing, knocking on the reader's heart—should by definition be accepted and admired. Lanyer's indebtedness to Sidney is thus made apparent, for Sidney justified her work by pointing to the inevitability of its receipt by Queen Elizabeth:

> A King should only to a Queen be sent.
> Gods loved choise unto his chosen love:
> Devotion to Devotions President.
>> ("Even not that Care," 53–55)

Sidney here imagines a royal marriage between text and reader. The site of textual reception is a moment of embrace between actual and textual sovereigns. In fact, the queen's acceptance, named as "devotion," echoes the "president" (precedent) set by David's devotion to God. Sidney dramatizes this reciprocity through the chiasmic structure ("loved choise"/"chosen love"). Drawing on Sidney's mode of presentation, Lanyer personifies her text as the ultimate "president." Both women's texts come to life in the interconnected language of salvation and marriage.

The *Salve Deus* is represented not merely as animate, but more specifically as a physically desirable lover. Lanyer exhorts her female readers not
only to feast in a female community, but also to join in marriage: "Put on
your wedding garments every one, / The Bridegroome stayes to enter-
taine you all" (48). This erotic metaphor, common to medieval and Renaissance devotional works, is amplified throughout the text to the point of
acting as a central trope for her book, a metaphor especially resonant
when accompanied by proto-feminist polemic. As in Sidney's and Whitney's works, death, desire, and the blazon are intertwined in presenting
female poetic authority. Christ becomes the erotic "other" on display.
Lanyer thus demonstrates her command over the Petrarchan techniques
of reification, commodification, and display as she controls the alien force
that is written as a desirable object. Here Christ's body is lovingly detailed
in a blazon—his face compared to snow, his eyes to doves, his head to
gold, and his lips to dripping honey:

> This is that Bridegroome that appeares so faire,
> So sweet, so lovely in his Spouses sight,
> That unto Snowe we may his face compare,
> His cheekes like skarlet, and his eyes so bright
> As purest Doves that in the rivers are,
> Washed with milke, to give the more delight;
>   His head is likened to the finest gold,
>   His curled lockes so beauteous to behold;
>
> Black as a Raven in her blackest hew;
> His lips like skarlet threeds, yet much more sweet
> Than is the sweetest hony dropping dew,
> Or hony combes, where all the Bees doe meete;
> Yea, he is constant, and his words are true,
> His cheekes are beds of spices, flowers seet:
>   His lips like Lillies, dropping downe pure mirrhe,
>   Whose love, before all worlds we doe preferre.
>
>   (120)

Of course, the Song of Songs is the urtext for describing the union of
Christ and Church in erotic terms. In fact, because the secular and erotic
blazon is an offspring from the Canticles, Lanyer's revision returns the
love lyric to its sacred history. In the vocabulary of the Canticles, Lanyer
figures her readers as members of the holy Church, who accept Christ by
discovering his "rare parts" (71). "This rich jewel," the speaker tells her
female patron, "I present (deare Lady) to your view" (118). In a characteristically Petrarchan reflex, the speaker admits her failure in describing

ineffable experience and exhorts her reader to find Christ's image engraved *within* the heart: an icon that should be read, kissed, and lovingly admired.

The power of assuming this position is tempered, although enabled, by the stance of mourning that takes place in the moment of death. The language of eroticism evident in this scene pervades the texture of the entire poem. Christ is described as a "dying lover" (65), a "Lover much more true / than ever was since first the world began" (69), "the husband of [the reader's] Soule" (87), and the subject who "imbrace[s]" the soul of Ladie Arabella "in his dying armes" (52). The female reader is exhorted to welcome "this faire Bridegroome in [her] soules pure bed" (54). In making his way into the spiritual bedroom, Christ is portrayed as a lover, whose attempt to "unlock" the door to the Countess of Bedford's heart is fraught with sexual overtones. The erotic nature of salvation is made unabashedly explicit when the narrator advises Ladie Margaret not to feel ashamed because she is "inflam'd" with the "sweet love" of God. Throughout the poem, Lanyer figures spiritual transformation as courtship, and she urges her readers to evaluate Christ as a potential suitor: "if deserts a Ladies love may gaine, / Then tell me, who hath more deserv'd than he?" (76); "judge if ever Lover were so true" (118); he is "all that Ladies can desire" (71). At the poem's conclusion, she contrasts Cleopatra's faulty love for Antony with the Countess of Cumberland's virtuous desire for Christ, a comparison that acts merely as the culmination of the representation of spiritual grace as physical consummation. Redemption is persistently figured in sexual terms. While Mary Sidney attaches her free-floating anxiety about the sexualizing effects of writing to a promiscuous muse, Lanyer exhausts erotic possibilities within the sanctioned discourse of the Song of Songs.

It would be a mistake to think that Lanyer's work was blasphemous or sacrilegious. Leo Steinberg has shown us that erotic Renaissance pictorial representations of Christ were quite common. These depictions, he argues, were part of a sanctioned theological discourse on the Incarnation. Hundreds of Renaissance works stress Christ's sexuality both as an infant and during the crucifixion, Steinberg argues, in order to exempt him from genital shame and emphasize his humanity. Interestingly, these postures occur particularly at moments of threshold—the incarnation and Passion—moments when the mystery of a divine body would need to be fully articulated.[65]

[65]In *The Sexuality of Christ in Renaissance Art and in Modern Oblivion* (New York: Pantheon, 1983), Leo Steinberg documents the hundreds of pious works that accentuate the unveiling of Christ's sexual organs—the groin touching by the dying or dead Christ, the outlined erection of Christ in moments of suffering, the erotic "chin chuck" between infant and Mary, and

Lanyer's portrayal of Christ as a lover and her focus on his body's "rare" and eroticized parts draws on this pictorial tradition, but in doing so, it destabilizes the Petrarchan dynamic dear to Renaissance writers' self-authorizations. In *Salve Deus*, subject and object blend; the speaker does not merely derive power by differentiation—by gazing on the reified body of Christ—but she also labels that position as female. In this way, the positions of "other" and "self," encoded male and female, collapse. While obviously following traditional devotional poetry in depicting the particulars of Christ's body, Lanyer rhapsodically describes his dismembered and bloodied "feeble limbs":

> His joynts dis-joynted, and his legges hang downe,
> His alabaster breast, his bloody side,
> His members torne, and on his head a Crowne
> Of sharpest Thorns, to satisfie for pride:
> Anguish and Paine doe all his Sences drowne.
>
> (115)

The reader realizes that Lanyer is self-conscious about making Christ a staged display when the text retreats to frame this poignant scene as the object of the Countess of Cumberland's gaze:

> This with the eie of Faith thou maist behold,
> Deere Spouse of Christ, and more than I can write;
> And here both Griefe and Joy thou maist unfold,
> To view thy Love in this most heavy plight.
>
> (115)

Through this framing device, Lanyer foregrounds her construction of Christ as the (feminized) scene of grief. Her particular representation complicates the secular model of gazing and display because she evokes an empathic bond for the "heavy plight" of this tragic death. This tableau seems a powerful if not perverse answer to the images of female dismemberment and display layered within idyllic praise in secular love poetry. Lanyer offers a religious version of the blazon through the anatomized but heroic body of Christ.

The *Salve Deus* does not merely reverse the dynamics of the blazon (female dissecting male), but also destabilizes the subject/object relationship

---

the general gestures that emphasize the body and sexuality of Christ. Steinberg argues that this unveiling was a part of mainstream theology concerned to show that Christ was fully human. The particularities of his embodiment show that Christ was exempt from genital shame and could master his own (evident) sexual desire. See 84–87 for erotic illustrations of the incarnation in Christology.

inherent in that specific strategy of representation. The speaker and displayed subject exchange positions throughout the text, so that the eroticized "other," Christ, *also* occupies the same position of powerlessness as the speaker. In other words, Christ is represented in the socially inscribed female position as well as the eroticized position of "otherness." Both martyred saviour and cloistered female share the space of restriction and virtue, so that the speaker cannot derive authority merely from gazing on a reified linguistic object. Instead, these gendered oppositions break down. Lanyer makes this breakdown clear when she details Christ's virtues in terms of the values specifically prescribed to women in contemporary conduct books—constancy, faith, patience, sobriety, grace, piety, chastity, meekness, obedience. Even the title page's inventory of contents insists on this conflation as it lists the poem's compatible subjects: "The Passion of Christ," "Eves Apologie in defence of Women," "The Teares of the Daughters of Jerusalem," and "The Salutation and Sorrow of the Virgine Marie" (40). In her prose address to the reader, Lanyer explicitly calls attention to such a shared victimization, linking the men who criticize women with those who put Christ to death (77). By associating women's struggle against misogynist traditions with Christ's entrapment by male authorities, she feminizes Christ and renders women holy.[66] Christ becomes a sign for female authorial identity, a sign that destabilizes the gender codes of popular secular poetic traditions. If Whitney relies on the metaphor of sickness to draw her heterogeneous text into a coherent medicinal curative, Lanyer relies on the homology between text and Savior to express her political and moral authority. In the *Salve Deus*, she restructures the relationships among writer, text, and reader by figuring Christ as a commodified text and naming the reading public as women who righteously seek the printed object of their spiritual and textual desire.

Salve Deus Rex Judaeorum thus shows us one strategy by which a woman writer combined the stances of religious devotee, mourner, and apologist in creating an authorial role in print. Implicitly critiquing Petrarchan strategies, Lanyer provides an alternative to the authorial and social codes that alienated women from publication and the social sphere. In her choice of religious subject and her explicit reference to the "holy sonnets," Lanyer identifies Sidney as a model for her writing and, I argue, for her authorial presentation as well. Both Lanyer and Sidney offset the visibility of their literary enterprises by deflecting corporeality onto a male figure who cannot be reprimanded for public display; in this way they pre-

---

[66]Elaine Beilin notes that "Lanyer actually reveals [Christ] as the true source of feminine virtue: he appears not as a masculine warrior-hero" (183). Beilin makes this observation in her argument that Lanyer feminizes the discourse of praise (*Redeeming Eve*, 177–207).

empt the issue of sexual libel by foregrounding the eroticized male body. Lanyer carries Sidney's techniques further, employing them to counter the class stigma of print. In her direct, public, and polemical religious work, Lanyer draws from Sidney's more private writing a revisionary technique for elasticizing and contesting the authorial codes in the late sixteenth century.

Wroth's Defacement of Authority

We see that many women who published were quite familiar with the secular love poetry so powerful in cementing sixteenth-century social relations, but they looked instead to other genres for expressing their literary talents. These writers published works that reflected their identification with the mother's tradition of advice writing, for instance, or the more sanctioned works of religious meditation. Mary Wroth, a member of the Sidney family, however, placed herself within the vogue of literary production, however, by daring to write within the popular Petrarchan secular genres of the romance and sonnet. Rather than appealing to radically different forms in her confrontation with the cultural and literary paradigms set up by other writers, Wroth belatedly participated in the fashion for sonnet writing by creating her own sequence, a form that was everywhere coded as male.[67] The reader of her text has the rare opportunity to hear the silent mistress of the sonnet sequences finally speak.

Wroth's *Pamphilia to Amphilanthus* is unusual because of the invisibility of the addressed lover. Her sonnet speaker constructs an identity by thematizing negation rather than by creating a male equivalent of the female mistress. As Josephine Roberts notes, Wroth "deliberately subordinates the role of the beloved."[68] Amphilanthus's name is never mentioned except in the title of the work, and Pamphilia addresses her lover only three times in the 103 poems.[69] Departing from the sonnet tradition so evidently in place in the works of her uncle, Philip Sidney, Wroth never directs her readers to gaze on the body of the beloved. Her sequence refuses to blazon the male

[67]See Josephine Roberts, "Lady Mary Wroth's Sonnets: A Labyrinth of the Mind," *Journal of Women's Studies in Literature* 1 (1979): 319–29.

[68]Roberts, introduction to Mary Wroth's *The Poems of Lady Mary Wroth*, ed. Josephine Roberts (Baton Rouge: Louisiana State University Press, 1983), 48.

[69]Sonnets xxiv (21), xxx (26), and xci (song 1). She also addresses his eyes in sonnets ii (2), ⸱ ⸱), and l (43). I cite from Gary Waller's edition of *Pamphilia to Amphilanthus* (Salz-
⸱itut für Englische Sprache und Literatur, 1977), because he draws from the pub-
of 1621 rather than the autograph copy at the Folger (which never appeared in
hich serves as the basis for Roberts's edition). Because Wroth begins renumber-
ldle of the text, I use both of Waller's poem numbers (the Roman numerals to
text as well as the Arabic numbers that serve as titles).

lover, to produce him for display, or to anatomize him through metaphors of comparison. The pages of the text give us no glimpse of a hand, leg, or eye tantalizingly half-concealed and revealed for our readerly pleasure. Indeed, Wroth seems to expel almost completely the realm of the visible and public world.

By refusing to display the beloved, Wroth exempts herself from what Roberts calls the "rhetoric of wooing" or what I have termed the poetics of exchange. In other words, she does not represent her poems as manuscript works sent through an eroticized textual transmission to persuade a frustratingly elusive reader, nor does she stage her fickle lover's various refusals and emotions. Instead, the speaker focuses her attention almost entirely on the complex feelings of love and jealousy that plague her. Wroth creates a sequence that Ann Rosalind Jones characterizes as having a "nocturnal and hibernal mood" (*Currency*, 145). Of course, other sonnet sequences concentrate as well on the speaker's tumultuous emotions, and they include conventional apostrophes to sleep, death, absence, and night. Wroth, however, redirects the gaze created by Petrarchan poems so that it rarely leaves the speaking subject or the personified emotions she experiences.[70] Instead, the text magnifies and intensifies another traditional sonnet trope, the antitheatrical metaphor. Ironically, through recurring poems delineating a withdrawal from the public world toward an elusive interior, she stages her own private "show" of Petrarchan love.[71]

This staging is created largely through terms of negation, as Wroth creates a sphere for Pamphilia that is cast not only as private, but as privative. Wroth's sequence does seem inordinately preoccupied with the two Petrarchan subjects of absence and night. There are eighteen sonnets that detail possible ways in which the changing of night to day exemplifies the lover's grief-stricken mind.[72] In some, the speaker celebrates night because it refuses

---

[70]Samuel Daniel's frequently anthologized "Care-charmer Sleep" (*Delia*, 45) relies on the conventional appeal to night and absence, themes that characterize Wroth's sequence more definitively. Daniel's poem is interestingly followed by a renunciation of the powers of darkness, which become a figure for "times consuming rage."

[71]In "'Shall I turn blabb?' Circulation, Gender, and Subjectivity in Mary Wroth's Sonnets," Jeff Masten argues for the text's construction of a female "promissory" subjectivity, noting not only the gestures toward interiority in *Pamphilia*, but also Wroth's refusal to circulate her manuscript and Pamphilia's withdrawal from the traffic in men in the *Urania*. Wroth, he concludes, stages her own noncirculation formally and thematically, and in doing so, privatizes the sonnet genre and clears a space for a nascent female subjectivity. In *Reading Mary Wroth: Representing Alternatives in Early Modern England*, ed. Naomi J. Miller and Gary Waller (Knoxville: University of Tennessee Press, 1991), 68–87. See also Nona Fienberg's essay in the same volume, which argues in stronger terms that Wroth reclaims poetic invention for women ("Mary Wroth and the Invention of Female Poetic Subjectivity," 175–90).

[72]Including those that explore darkness and sleep, the following poems invoke night: Sonnets i (1), iv (4), xiii (12), xvii (15), xviii (16), xix (17), xx (18), xxii (19), xxiii (20),

to misrepresent itself hypocritically, but in most passages, she calls on darkness because it serves as an apt correlative to her own grief:

> Come darkest Night, becomming sorrow best,
>   Light leave thy light, fit for a lightsome soule:
>   Darknesse doth truely sute with me opprest,
>   Whom absence power doth from mirth controule.
>
>   (xxii, 19)

> Night, welcome art thou to my minde distrest,
>   Darke, heavy, sad, yet not more sad then I:
>   Never could'st thou finde fitter company
>   For thine owne humour, then I thus opprest.
>
>   (xliii, 37)

> I love [night's] grave and saddest lookes to see,
>   Which seemes my soule and dying heart entire,
>   Like to the ashes of some happy fire,
>   That flam'd in joy, but quench'd in misery.
>
>   (xvii, 15)

The speaker's invocation of "clowdy Night" with its "thickest mists" becomes a vivid temporal image of grief itself, one that is summed up by her cry: "Let me be darke" (c, 6). Kim Hall argues that in such moments Wroth attempts to become her own "dark lady," a figure who, in Sidney's and Shakespeare's sonnets, requires the attention of the talented poet to render her beautiful.[73] Whatever the racial coordinates of this self-blackening, Wroth's desire to mark herself visibly as "opprest" suggests a particular technique for authorization. While her invocations to night certainly intensify the complaints of melancholy uttered by other frustrated sonnet lovers, they also revise the meaning of this common Petrarchan trope and carry it to a logical extreme. Wroth severs darkness from codes of beauty,

---

xxiv (21), xxxiii (29), xxxiv (30), xliii (37), l (43), lxiii (1), lxv (3), and c (6). In *The Currency of Eros*, Jones suggests that the darkness of Wroth's sequence acts as a reference to her past courtly activity (namely her role in Jonson's "Masque of Blackness"). They also function as signs of a "dazzling asceticism, through which she demonstrates her superiority to the shallowness of court amours and the triviality of the lyrics in which they are encoded" (145 and 141 respectively). Waller sees Wroth's preoccupation with melancholia and interiority as part of her critique of the "glittering amorality of the Jacobean court" (introduction to *Pamphilia to Amphilanthus*, 12).

[73]Kim Hall states that "sonneteers establish their power over female matter and their poetic prowess by drawing on the dismembering power of the blazon . . . and by grounding relations between the White, European male and the foreign female through a metaphoric politics of color which permeates the sonnet cycle." "Acknowledging Things of Darkness: Race, Gender, and Power in Early Modern England" (Ph.D. diss., University of Pennsylvania, 1990), 63.

hints of sexual infidelity, and signs of vengeful cruelty, meanings that infiltrate the sonneteers' reading of the emblematic "dark lady." Instead, she associates it fully with high moral seriousness and the sorrow of unreciprocated fidelity. Her speaker is not the dark "other" from which the male writer establishes his stellar and enlightened poetic powers, for she over-represents herself until this darkness becomes the sober and abstract force of absence itself.

Like the sonneteers, who frequently play with the fruitful contrasts of blackness and brightness, Wroth's speaker sees paradoxes in the icon of night. The speaker acknowledges that night causes emotional pain because it creates delusive fantasies and fond tricks that can produce jealousy in the lover (xviii). It can also plunge her into a psychic grief more severe that she wishes to feel. When her "sun" left her, the speaker claims, "a night came cloath'd in absence darke; / Absence more sad, more bitter then is gall, / Or death" (xxxiii, 29). The speaker vividly calls attention to the problems of her own metaphor, however, when she marvels at how day and night fail to generate static meanings: when her beloved is absent, day is only darkness and misery, while night affords the fantastic light of his image. Wroth goes on to activate this contradiction as a trope for her speaker's internal confusion: "I sit and wonder at this day-like night" (xxvi, 23). Because the sequence originates with her voice calling on "night's blacke Mantle," it seems evident that the vacancy, blackness, and delusion of night offer us a continuous and self-conscious commentary on the authority formulated within the structure of erotic pursuit. The emerging subject is constructed through an "absence more sad, more bitter then is gall," but she registers the contours of that construction when she points out collapses in its meaning.

Throughout the entire poetic sequence, Wroth attempts to exhaust the possible ways of writing about the negative. She expels the material world in order to reveal the evacuated territory that she inhabits. Rather than demonstrating a self-scrutiny punctuated by a focus on the eroticized and displayed "other," her poems show us someone who labors to construct a linguistic plenitude from within a deathlike void. The speaker does define herself against the alterity of the Indian in Sonnet xxv (22), but her most characteristic formulation of subjectivity is in contradistinction to emptiness, or as an embodiment of it. This formulation is most striking when she feigns a demonic possession:

> Good now be still, and doe not me torment,
>   With multitude of questions, be at rest,
>   And onely let me quarrell with my breast,
>   Which still lets in new stormes my soule to rent.

Fye, will you still my mischiefes more augment?
   You say, I answere crosse, I that confest
   Long since, yet must I euer be opprest,
With your tongue torture which wil ne're be spent?

Well then I see no way but this will fright,
   That Deuill speech; alas, I am possest,
   And mad folkes senseles are of wisdomes right,

The hellish spirit, Absence, doth arrest
   All my poore senses to his cruell might,
   Spare me then till I am myselfe, and blest.

                      (lii, 45)

In what is arguably the only poem in which she responds to an interlocutor, Pamphilia speaks only to shun external debate. Instead, she opts for her own private internal division (the "rent" soul, the storms of interior quarreling). In order to silence her detractor's speech, she asserts, or perhaps admits, her own demonic possession. The poem makes clear that the speaker takes her terms of identification from her outer public, appropriating their phallic "Deuill speech" and "tongue torture" as a means of describing her private unblessed state. The poem is riddled with the language of demonry and religious exorcism ("crosse," "confest," "hellish," "blest"), but the force that controls her and makes her "not herself" is absence, a demonized spirit of vacancy. Although the speaker implies that she merely feigns this vacuous madness as a mechanism of self-defense ("this will fright"), she goes on to write many more poems concerned with the theme of absence, which suggest that this strange possessed dispossession *is* a vital part of her "quarrell" within her breast.[74] The ambiguity of this position is underscored by the fact that absence *arrests* her senses: it both obstructs her presence and apprehends her fully. While one subtext for this poem could be the witch hunts that raged in the early seventeenth century, another is clearly Petrarchan poetry's conventions for constructing a speaking subject.[75] This poem, characteristic of her sonnets and songs in general, refuses to pit speaker against the beloved's rhetorically controlled and displayed body; instead, it discloses the rent and vacant subjectivity that defines the speaker's identity.

   When addressing the problems raised in interpreting Renaissance wom-

---

[74]In addition to those that explicitly deal with night, Sonnets xxix (25), xliv (38), and xci (Song 1) treat the general theme of absence.

[75]See Alan Macfarlane, *Witchcraft in Tudor and Stuart England: A Regional and Comparative Study* (New York: Harper and Row, 1970).

en's writing, Gary Waller emphasizes the importance of determining the linguistic and discursive structures that were available during the time. He states of Sidney: "We look not only to the ways Mary Sidney tried to be faithful to her task and articulate what was 'there' in her text; we must also pay attention to the dislocations and gaps in her writing, to the *silences* (what she chose not to say) and the *absences* (what she could not say). . . . As with so much writing by women in this period, it is the struggle from *silence*—a struggle that often ends in *absence*—that is most characteristic" ("Struggling into Discourse," 252). The thematization of absence in Wroth is particularly interesting given Waller's formulation of women's relationship to the male-coded language of Renaissance poetry. Here the speaker's silence about Amphilanthus and her inscription of absence as the central force in the sequence indicates that Wroth transforms the restrictions of poetic discourse into its very theme. Thus, we can unearth what Wroth chose not to say (she chose not to represent the male lover), but we see as well that her poetry self-consciously meditates on the dilemma of what cannot be said. The sequence's intensification of the theme of negation and its peculiar representation of absence in "Good now be still" as a powerful and demonic force calls attention to the violent omissions evident in her own writing. As readers, we are directed not only to discover and give voice to silences within the work, but also to understand how silence, absence, and vacancy themselves define both text and speaking subject.

To understand Wroth's revision of the poetic techniques of corporeal display, we might look to the Renaissance editor of Anne Cooke Bacon's sermon translations. In the introduction to this learned text, the editor confusingly asserts the exceptional nature of the project by declaring that it is not like most works by women, who, it seems, usually warble in an inhuman and beastly way: "Speakying in prynt lyke Parates with solemne countenaunces, [they] debate matters of importaunce. . . or els warbling words of Scripture in all their doings, [they] deface the thing they most bable of."[76] Instead of commanding language, he suggests, women write only through their own ignorance; as a result, they "deface" the spirit of their texts. Here, "speakying in prynt" brings up associations far from those of being "a man in print," for the phrase signifies repetitive and unenlightened speech. Although this editor refers specifically to injuries done to biblical meanings, his criticism could have been levied at all types

---

[76]Anne Cooke Bacon, trans., *Certayne Sermons of the ryghte famous and excellente clerk Master Bernardine Ochine*, STC 18767 (1550), sig. A2ᵛ. Mary Ellen Lamb cites this declamation in "The Cooke Sisters," in *Silent But for the Word*, 117. We might recall here Lanyer's allegorization of the difficulty of female speech in her self-comparison to a wounded bird that "warbles forth her paine" (44).

of writing. Mary Wroth, writing an imaginative work of fiction rather than a polemical religious tract, ironically defaces the text that she speaks "in print": by rehearsing a male paradigm with a vengeance, she alters and "defaces" it, both through her broad revisions of poetic tradition and her specific erasure of the "face" of corporeality. She presents not an absent/ present Stella, but a personified motivating force labeled as absence; her text expels materiality itself and leaves instead the trace of the dark lady who has vanished into an abstraction. By "parroting" Petrarchan language, Wroth restructures and defaces a poetics that derived authority from a masculinized gaze.

Wroth's poetic innovations were packaged for the public in a way that further mitigated the transgression of her appearance in print. When it was published, *Pamphilia to Amphilanthus* was appended to her six hundred-page compendium romance, *The Countess of Montgomeries Urania* (1621). The presentation of this text was impressive; it appeared in a beautiful folio adorned with an engraved title page that landscaped the scope of her sweeping romance.[77] While this format certainly imitates the posthumous publication of Sidney's *Astrophel and Stella* (which was printed with his *Arcadia*), it marks a departure from its textual precursor by presenting a sonnet speaker derived from the romance it follows. Stella was not a character in Sidney's pastoral world. Pamphilia emerges from her longer narrative story to lament her betrayal; her poetic text seems to be produced from the realm of fiction itself. While other writers used the appended female complaint as a means of revising the perception of the poet-as-lover, Wroth's combined genres establish a different structure of representation: the female poet-as-character-as-lover. The poetic speaker is thus protected from sexual libel through the romance's explicit characterization of Pamphilia's chastity and through the mediating layer of fiction that places Wroth at a distance from her work. Although Wroth's sonnet sequence situates a woman in the position of Petrarchan lover, the text's architectonics intervene so that the reader identifies the speaker as merely a fictional character. Certainly by isolating Pamphilia from a cast of characters, the sequence belatedly establishes her as a focal point of the heterogeneous and digressive romance structure; therefore, the replication of her story in sonnet form has the effect of framing the larger work in terms of female authority and female desire. The retroactive creation of authority and the intensification of female desire effected by the concluding sequence, however, are alleviated by the text's foregrounding of its fictional and secondary status. If Wroth's sonnet speaker claims that her identity has been evacuated and replaced by absence, she also hints at the

---

[77]Mary Wroth, *The Countess of Montgomeries Urania*, Part 1, STC 26051 (1621).

exact effect produced by the sequence's form of publication: its institutionalization of its own literariness, which frames the sonnets squarely in the realm of monumentalized fiction.

The framing of Wroth's sequence, however, did not mitigate completely the effect of her revisionary paradigm of authorship. Her publication of the *Urania* and *Pamphilia and Amphilanthus* met with scandal when Lord Edward Denny accused her of libel and demanded that the text be withdrawn. Interestingly enough, his charge was couched in language that made transparently clear that her topical allusions were not all that were at issue. He attacked Wroth by criticizing female authorship in general, branding her a "monstrous hermaphrodite." Denny's words were particularly resonant given John Florio's gender-specific, though perhaps eclectic, designation of original texts as masculine and translations as "reputed femalls, delivered at second hand."[78] If original texts were gendered male, as Florio claims, then Wroth inadvertently re-gendered herself when she published her ambitious, unmediated fictions. The content of her publication—her staging of female desire—merely rendered this feat more transgressive; it intensified her encroachment, by the fact of publishing, on a male-defined preserve.[79] Denny held up Mary Sidney as a proper female example for the wayward Wroth to follow: "[I] pray that you may repent you of so many ill spent yeares of so vaine a booke and that you may redeeme the tym with writing as large a volume of heavenly layes and holy love as you have of lascivious tales and amorous toyes that at the last you may followe the rare, and pious example of your vertuous and learned Aunt, who translated so many godly books and especially the holy psalmes of David."[80] Denny made clear that Sidney's *Psalmes* were exemplary

---

[78]John Florio, in the introduction to his translation of Montaigne's *Essaies*, STC 18041 (1603), sig. A2. Florio's assessment, however, seems to be unusual in that humanist education encouraged translation and imitation as important modes of discursive learning. In fact, the opposition between original and secondary or imitative works is a categorical opposition largely absent in the Renaissance; the notion of original writing became valorized only later in literary history. Florio's statement nevertheless points to the "coveredness" that translation offered male and female writers. And while his negative comment may be exceptional, his use of gender as a means of denigrating translation's autonomous status certainly was not; after all, women legally were *femmes coverts*, "covered" by a male guardian. My thanks to Elaine Beilin for cautioning me about this point.

[79]Much later in the century (and published in the next), Anne Finch would verbalize her sense that female writing encroached on a decidedly male realm: "Alas! a woman that attempts the pen," she says in one of her poems, "Such an intruder on the rights of men." (Anne Finch, *Miscellaneous Poems on Severall Occasions*, 1713) reprint, Anne Finch, Countess of Winchilsea, *Selected Poems* (New York: Fyfield Books, 1987), 26.

[80]Edward Denny, "To Lady Mary Wroth," printed in the appendix to Roberts, *The Poems of Lady Mary Wroth*, 239. Gwynne Kennedy offers a fascinating analysis of how Wroth answered Denny's charges of aberrant sexuality by holding up her birth and rank. "She 'thincks she daunces in a net.'"

because of their moral subject matter, but he obviously responded to the decorum of their more private circulation and their "femall" (covered and mediated) status. Wroth, on the other hand, created a controversy because she wrote as a woman and as a transvestite author, generically cross-dressing as a male sonneteer. This transgression—read by Denny as the pluralization of gender—probably forced her out of the arena of authorship; she did not publish the second half of her *Urania*, and her first text might have been withdrawn. Because her public texts did not work within sanctioned and decorous paradigms, such as that of religious piety or maternal legacy, Wroth was silenced. Ironically, of course, silence and absence had been the devices she used thematically in establishing her own authority. In literary history and in the public arena, she became, at least for a while, her own dispossessed sonnet speaker.

Dancing in a Net

By analyzing ways in which Whitney, Sidney, Lanyer, and Wroth constructed alternative tropes of authorship, I do not mean to lump these diverse writers into an undifferentiated group. Rather, I hope to show a sampling of the wide range of strategies that women writers developed in describing their relationship to their texts and reading public, and I assume that further critical studies of these women will detail more particularly the social problems and literary solutions unique to each. These women were from very different social classes, and they obviously did not have the same interests in mind when creating poetic works. They did respond, however, to a shared set of prohibitions and exclusions. In other words, the culture's strictures against female education and its exhortations to privatization interpellated these women as a single group whose commonalty rested in the problem of their shared gender. While Whitney and Lanyer obviously did not have the material resources nor the strict dictates of their more upper class counterparts, their works reveal that they were not educated in drastically different ways. Each of these women was familiar with Petrarchan poetry, Ovidian complaint, moral satire, mythology, and the Bible; each recognized how exceptional it was for a sixteenth-century woman to write; and each experienced the fact that female authorship was a tricky business.

It was tricky because male writers and publishers were unwittingly fashioning a gendered ideology of authorship as they created techniques for grappling with the politics of publication. Petrarchism was, as many critics have pointed out, a political, social, and cultural force, not just a literary fad; and it offered a suitable discourse for scripting literary authority. The subject positions available in Petrarchan discourse saturated the most important cultural controversies—seeping into debates over family reorganization, battles over legal rights, and negotiations of class identities in early modern England.[81] These Renaissance women, enjoined to remain silent and to stay within enclosed and private walls, mobilized the Petrarchan forms and tropes that they everywhere encountered, forging an alternate discourse of power and the body to counter the gendered idiom used by other writers in expressing authorial power. Peter Stallybrass's investigation of the idealized female body as a patriarchal enclosed territory suggests that Renaissance bodies acted as critical pressure points for class negotiations. When women began to write publicly, they had to sidestep representations of their own scattered and reified corporeality—what Waller calls "the logic of love poetry," which is, he explains, "that of the gaze . . . the rendering open and passive of the beautiful object" ("Struggling into Discourse," 250). In Whitney's, Lanyer's, and Wroth's works, we see the disparate ways in which women writers challenged the tropes and cultural logic widely used to construct authorial identity in the realm of print. If laureate poets had to narrate their ascension from lowly poetic play into the more serious and transcendent realm of authorship, these women writers had to stay the threat of a double "fall" (both sexual and social) when they chose to wander transgressively into the literary marketplace.

Just as Spenser, Gascoigne, and Daniel reshaped authorship by restructuring its relationship to femininity and love, these women writers enlarged the emergent concept of authorship by situating it within the tradition of female legacy, biblical sanction, and family lineage.[82] In this way, they disrupted the logic of contemporary love poetry that informed the economy of book publication and recoded the sexualized language used to discourage women from "pressing the press." Ironically, by creating complex representations that orchestrated their exclusion from writing, these women found ways to legitimate their move "abroad" into the public wilderness. We see various ways in which the "private" became resituated within the public world: from the mother's posthumous private addresses to children came the rhetoric of the legacy; from Mary Sidney's privately

---

[81]For an overview of these social contestations, see the editors' introduction to *The Ideology of Conduct*, ed. Nancy Armstrong and Leonard Tennenhouse (New York: Methuen, 1987), 4–10.

[82]Tilde Sankovitch's discussion of French Renaissance women's str̶̶̶̶ ̶̶̶̶ "̶̶̶̶ ̶̶̶̶ the Book" helps us to contextualize these English women's quest for ̶ particular, her discussion of Catherine and Madeleine des Roches sho̶ quite different from Sidney's sibling-oriented authorization of her wri̶ *Writers and the Book: Myths of Access and Desire* (Syracuse, N. Y.: Syra̶ 1988); and Sankovitch's "Inventing Authority of Origin: The Difficul̶ *in the Middle Ages and the Renaissance*, ed. Mary Beth Rose (Syracuse, N.̶ Press, 1986), 227–43.

circulated and personified devotional poems came the polemical religious writing of Lanyer. It may not agree with modern tastes to read Sidney's stylization of her career in self-deprecating terms, Lanyer's identification with female martyrs and her praise of "pale sorrow and the grave," Wroth's description of herself as a possessed absence, or Whitney's imagination of her death in such evocative and rich language. These works depict women as mourners, exiles, and outcasts, even though such representations are rendered with varying degrees of levity and irony. But seen "situationally" within the perimeters of publication at the end of the sixteenth century, these noncanonical poetic wills, legacies, meditations, and elegies are astonishing not only for their poetic accomplishment, but also for the imaginative ways that they confront the social and sexual stigma of print. Renaissance literary works testify to the fact that women writers redefined the rhetorical codes and literary forms used to present authorship in print, and in doing so, women proved that they could dance in the textual and cultural nets that threatened to confine them.

THE POLITICS OF PRINT

IN WRITING THIS BOOK, I have had to guard against a nostalgic impulse to idealize preprint culture and thus subscribe to a "fall" into print. It is tempting to see authorship, which registered a rigid enforcement of social and sexual difference, as a consequence of this fall. I have also had to refrain from adhering too closely to the equally popular counternarrative that identifies print technology primarily as an instrumental force in the redemptive democratization of culture itself. To use my own shorthand here, I have tried to avoid making either Jack Cade or John Wolfe the singular representative emblem for the politics of print in the Renaissance. It is true that these two names figure centrally in crucial and compelling explanatory accounts of the social force of print. My reservations about such narratives have only to do with the temptation to tell one side of the story without seeing how the other serves as an important qualifier. The very fact that historians and literary scholars are pulled in opposite directions when describing print's place on the political spectrum testifies, I think, to the genuinely contradictory historical effects that print had on literary discourse and on Renaissance culture.

To explain my cryptic shorthand. When I evoke Jack Cade, I refer, of course, to the extraordinary figure in *2 Henry VI* who leads a rebellion against, among other things, literacy and (anachronistically) print. Jack Cade voices sentiments about reading and power that can be heard by critics who argue that writing, education, and printing are exclusionary practices used by a hegemonic Renaissance state to protect the privileges of the rich and powerful. Certainly, the fact that Tudor and Stuart English law allowed literacy as an exemption from trial suggests one of the more unfair social functions of reading. Until a time later than we care to imagine, a defendant could plead benefit of clergy simply by virtue of being able to read and thus could draw on class privilege to escape the full force of the law. When Renaissance writers proudly declared that print facilitated the nationalist project of establishing the English vernacular, they noted a separate but related boundary addressed by publishing. Print technology fed into this dynamic by giving the government a more effective medium for propaganda and control. In blending two historical revolts—the Peasants' Revolt of 1381 and the Cade Rebellion of 1350—into the story of Jack Cade, Shakespeare gives voice to a critique of that abuse of power. In Act 4, Cade and his followers set out to invert social norms, one of which is the value of writing and literacy. "Is not this a lamentable thing," Cade asks, "that of the skin of an innocent lamb should be made parchment? that parchment, being scribbled o'er, should undo a man?" (4.2.71–74).[1] He goes on to accuse Lord Say of such atrocities as "causing printing to be used," building a paper mill, and hanging men "because they could not read" (4.7. 32–39).[2] Cade's sense that printing is bound up with social tyranny and political repression is heard in critical accounts that associate publishing with the oppressive measures used to secure a hierarchical social order. Shakespeare's representation of the rebellion finally contains Cade, Phyllis Rackin argues, by making him subject to the very ideological force of writing/history/print that he fears. Cade thus becomes a sign of the authoritarian function print could be made to serve, and he is Shakespeare's most eloquent critic of that function.[3]

In this reading, "authorship" signifies a corresponding textual restraint, as the collective and collaborative nature of manuscript culture gives way to the more proprietary system of the marketplace. We find striking evidence for this view of print in Renaissance texts, for we stumble across numerous representations that show public writing to be a totalizing force that swallows polyvocality and difference into uniformity. When Cade's critique is tailored specifically to address textual issues, it suggests a link between the text's status as commodified property, its enclosure to fit the needs of a marketplace, and the restrictions that print could serve on a people. Print becomes a sign

---

[1] *The Complete Works of Shakespeare*, ed. David Bevington, 3d ed. (Glenview, Il.: Scott Foresman and Company, 1980). All references to Shakespeare's dramatic works are to this edition.

[2] In "The Peasants' Revolt and the Writing of History in 2 *Henry VI*," Geraldo Sousa discusses the relationship between writing and tyranny. His talk called this play to my attention. (Paper delivered at a meeting of the Shakespeare Association of America, Kansas City, 1992.)

[3] Phyllis Rackin, *Stages of History: Shakespeare's English Chronicles* (Ithaca: Cornell University Press, 1990), 203–17.

of corresponding textual and political regulatory systems. Throughout this book, I have described ways in which the seemingly innocent literary category of authorship did register nonliterary and political modes of authorization and authority. I am fully aware of how the distinct realms of textual authority and cultural authority can shade into one another. My hesitations about this conflation stem from the fact that the two are not naturally or necessarily linked: "policing" a text obviously does not imply an authoritarian politics, nor does linguistic instability imply a radical agenda. Thus, when the realms of the textual and social are made to correspond, that linkage is never simple, immediate, or inherent. Rather than importing a monolithic social power into the text, authorship acts as a contested site in which various politics are expressed. The politics of print are no exception.

From the opposite tangent, we find compelling arguments about print's impetus for progressive social change. In this reading, print technology is seen centrally as a democratizing force that improved the lives of human beings, specifically subordinate groups like women, by fostering an increase in the literacy rate. The press is portrayed as fundamental to the development of a public sphere that was set in distinction from dominant court culture and thus historically important to the rearrangements in political rule in the seventeenth century. This particular innovation in technology can be seen as providing new channels through which a repressive state apparatus could be challenged, for it created a public forum in which political debate could occur. Within the broad rubric of this story is the Renaissance subnarrative of the squabble between the state and those who used the print industry to challenge regulations set by the government. In this account, the press offered a medium for cultural expansion and increased the population's potential for self-determination. Our liberal investment in the "freedom of the press" partakes of this mythologization of its power.

Certainly, it is true that the press did lend an important tool to emergent clusters of power that began to rival Renaissance state authority. These clusters were mobilized in response to the queen's attempt to control the medium by censoring materials and regulating the daily operations of the printing business. Certainly, it is true that the sixteenth-century powers enacted a series of laws designed to control publishing. Stationers had to register materials to be printed; patents for specific types of texts were granted to printers by the Crown; presses were limited in number, and output and had to be licensed by the state. No printing press could be established outside the confines of London, save in the two universities. These regulations underscored the potential for transgression bound up in this technology, as the words of the 1586 Star Chamber Decree suggests:

> No printer of bookes, nor any other person or persons whatever, shall sett up, keepe, or mayntein, any presse or presses, or any other instrument or instru-

ments for imprinting of bookes, ballades, chartes, pourtraictures, or any other thing or things whatsoever, but onely in the cittie of London or the suburbs thereof . . . and that no person shall hereafter erect, sett up, or maynteyne in any secrett or obscure corner, or place, any such presse.[4]

This decree made it illegal simply to hide a press. The grimy machine of the press itself thus became represented in official language as a symbol of a volatile cultural power.

John Wolfe is perhaps the most famous Renaissance printer to rebel against the state control of publication, specifically against the system of granting patents. "It is lawfull for all men to print all lawfull books," he declared, and then indicated that he wanted to "reforme the government with this trade."[5] Ironically, Wolfe's fate was not to reform the government at all because he was bought off by the Committee of the Star Chamber and made a beadle to hunt down unlawful printers. Wolfe's legacy lived on, however, when Roger Ward continued the fight for more freedom in publishing; Ward was even imprisoned for violating a government ordinance designed to supervise the print industry. The skirmishes between printers and the Crown tell us that the business of printing offered numerous paths for subversion: one could print heretical or treasonous matter, publish a text patented to someone else, or simply run a press in a place that seemed designed to avoid the surveillance of the state. The cumulative effect of these disparate regulations was an acknowledgment that the press harbored the tremendous power of rerouting the flow of information and realigning factions within the culture. Instead of destroying the comradery of manuscript exchange, publishing here puts into the hands of the middle class an extraordinary means for voicing public dissent. Despite his ultimate shift in allegiances, Wolfe becomes emblematic of the democratizing possibilities of this medium. Literary scholars have thus echoed his claim that publishing could "reforme the government" by challenging parliamentary and monarchal authority. The advent of publishing does not offer a tale of woe.

This story is very seductive. Here print allows a resistance to nondemocratic social forces by challenging the very way in which politics at court are created. And again we find in Renaissance poems, plays, and prefatory materials evidence that publishing destabilized fixed authorities by giving

---

[4]Cited by Colin Clair, *A History of Printing in Britain* (New York: Oxford University Press, 1966), 110.

[5]Edward Arber, *A Transcript of the Registers of the Company of Stationers of London, 1554–1640*, 5 vols. (London: privately printed), 2: 781. Marjorie Plant describes the labor organization of the stationer's company and John Wolfe's attempts at revising regulations, in *The English Book Trade: An Economic History of the Making and Sale of Books* (London: George Allen and Unwin, 1939), 105–8.

writers a more potent weapon for social critique. But again, this view must be positioned against the foiled rebellion led by Cade and his sense that printing was ultimately a tool for political repression. Both narratives offer us rebels who use the site of print to fight seemingly unjust authorities, but each story emphasizes a different outcome: Cade is absorbed into the repressive force of writing, while Wolfe inspires a resistance that ultimately leads to the English revolution. Ideally, my study of the rhetoric of Renaissance authorship and its relationship to the social anxieties of print allows for the possibility that both of these characterizations capture some truth about the contradictory politics of print as they surfaced in various local practices. The formation of authorship reflects neither view exclusively: print did not vanquish an exclusive aristocratic manuscript culture, nor did it repressively stifle the free play of textuality by channeling words into the marketplace. While I do stress that the rhetoric of publication turned on formulations of class and gender that often reinforced, rather than questioned, normative social order, I bear in mind that print technology impacted its culture in ambiguous ways, the sum of which resists easy mapping onto ideological binaries. Instead, I claim more modestly that authorship traces for us one part of a rich and heated debate about how issues of rank fed into the making of books.[6]

Renaissance authorship is thus complicated by the contradictory politics of print that are played out in the physical features of the book, the gendered rhetoric that attends to those features, and the strange overlay of sexual and social authorizations onto the domain of literary textuality. In order to sort out our thinking about the relationship between authorship, print, and political structures, it is important, as we have seen, to take into consideration the variable of women's writing, which, when not ghettoized into a separate sphere of literary history, allows us to flesh out more fully the range of positions open to all writers in early modern England. By locating an analysis of women's anxieties about publication within the context of the general political climate of writing, we are able to identify more carefully ways in which gender affected women's status as publishing authors. In writing this book, I have been amazed to find how often gender was employed as a mode of organizing the requisite categories for assessing social and literary problems. We need to acknowledge this fact in

---

[6]For a reading that demonstrates how Francis Bacon negotiated the complicated politics of print in forging a path for the scientific author, see Martin Elsky, "Print and Manuscript: Bacon's Early Career and the Occasions of Writing," Chapter 6 in *Authorizing Words: Speech, Writing, and Print in the English Renaissance* (Ithaca: Cornell University Press, 1989). Elsky develops his discussion of the social relationship between authorship and publication from his more metaphysical discussion of the spatializing effects of print.

order to chart the myriad ways in which Renaissance textual media were invested unevenly with political and sexual significances. And in doing so, we see that gender difference itself was being produced in the debate surrounding authorship.

In closing, I should note that while it is tempting to allow the well-known and highly arguable story about the Renaissance birth of the individual to seep into my account of emergent authorship, I have been constantly reminded of the importance of keeping these arguments distinct.[7] The author that we see in early modern England is not the same entity as the bourgeois subject, although it can be said to share certain techniques of authorization with that being as it emerges in history. Instead of providing a literary counterpart to a Burckhardtian argument, I found, during my foray into the rhetoric of publication, another truism: that authorship bears the mark of things unauthorized. In the case of Renaissance authorship, what is "unauthorized" is an unwieldy and curious mass that includes manuscript coterie texts and unstable courtly pageants as well as more expected cultural staples of unruly women and transvestite prodigals. These unauthorized elements are made to coalesce into a shared discursive field, one in which various and sundry illicit, horrific, scandalous, and vulgar entities are suggestively aligned. In the subtle and startling rhetoric of publication, we see clearly how anxieties about disparate sites of disorder were enmeshed and condensed into the figure of the printing press.

In *The Merry Wives of Windsor*, Mrs. Page offers us a prime example of how print could be represented as a potent force that could occlude difference itself. "I warrant he hath a thousand of these letters, written with blank space for different names—sure, more—and these are of the second edition," Mrs. Page exclaims on seeing the duplicate letters that Falstaff has used in his double courting. "He will print them," she continues, "out of doubt; for he cares not what he puts into the press, when he would put us two. I had rather be a giantess, and lie under Mount Pelion" (2.1.71–78). Mrs. Page, herself a self-reflexive metaphor for the text, imagines the pressing of the man on the woman as that of ink on to paper, a sexualized printing metaphor that intensifies culturally widespread ideas about female impressionability. Her speculation that Falstaff will print his letters of seduction serves to accuse him of wantonness: he will press anyone. "Well, I will find you twenty lascivious turtles ere one chaste man," she concludes. In this figuration, the act of printing is an amplification of

[7]I bear in mind here Lee Patterson's warning about the dangers of positing the invention of subjectivity at all, particularly his sharp critique of Renaissance critics' accounts of emergent individualism. "On the Margin: Postmodernism, Ironic History, and Medieval Studies," *Speculum* 65 (1990): 87–108.

the already eroticized act of writing; if putting ink to paper constitutes a sexual act, then printing signifies a promiscuity that threatens property transmission and the status of the family, among other things (2.1.67). The multiplicity that the press offers becomes associated here with the duplicity of infidelity, an uncontrollable and wanton repetition that de-authenticates writing and creates an unauthorized mingling of distinct elements. Mrs. Page senses that multiple reproduction makes one "common," and thus she provides one articulation of what in other registers is a more explicit class issue. Her words testify to the precarious but recurrent sexual, social, and textual meanings attached to the word "press." But this passage also shows us how difficult it is to assess the political functions that printing was seen to play in Renaissance culture. In a comedy concerned with middle-class mobility, this reference to the sexual politics of printing opens up a set of complicated political tensions. In the context of the plot of *Merry Wives*, Mrs. Page's protestation signals a host of things awry in the social order, for her association between inauthentic reproduction and the vexed game of Falstaff's courtship raises the issues of inheritance practices, bourgeois female roles, shrinking aristocratic coffers, rituals of courtship and courtiership, and the truth of writing—issues that do not line up along a set political axis. Neither a revolutionary force that unfetters a newly literate populace nor a repressive force enclosing the page as commodified property, print can assuredly be said only to re-encode the already gendered cultural politics of manuscript writing in a way that produces new authorizations and authors.

To be represented as "a man in print" in the Renaissance, as the phrase implies, belied a nervousness about one's ability to be perfectly and completely a man at all. To be "a woman in print" was to call into question the logic that shifts social and class issues easily into the frame of sexuality and gender. Because no equivalent phrase exists, a woman in print unsettled the very categories by which manuscript and print media, and their attendant authorities, were expressed. When analyzing the sexual politics of authorship and print in the sixteenth century, we discover not only the diverse ways in which print was made to serve various political purposes, but also the slippage between those politics and their manifestation in literary representations of books themselves. In tracing these textual and social authorities, I cannot finally help but register the sheer force of Mrs. Page's words. For she makes visible a process in which authorship is engendered and women pressed into service as interchangeable tropes for a politically fraught and erotically charged book circulation: "he cares not what he puts into the press, when he would put us two." Such a context gives the phrase "publish or perish" a new meaning.

SELECTED BIBLIOGRAPHY

Renaissance Texts

Aburgavennie, Frances. *Praiers made by the right Honorable Ladie Frances Aburgaven-nie . . . .* In *The Monument of Matrones: conteining seven severall Lamps of Virgini-tie . . . compiled . . . by Thomas Bentley.* STC 1892. 1582.

Advice to a Son: Precepts of Lord Burghley Sir Walter Raleigh, and Francis Osborne. Edited by Louis B. Wright. The Folger Library. Ithaca: Cornell University Press, 1962.

The Arbor of Amorous Devices. STC 3631. 1597.

The Arundel Harington Manuscript of Tudor Poetry. Edited by Ruth Hughey. 2 vols. Columbus: Ohio State University Press, 1960.

B. R. [*See also* Barnabe Rich.] *Greene's Newes both from Heaven and Hell.* STC 12259. 1593.

Bacon, Anne Cooke, trans. *Certayne Sermons of the ryghte famous and excellente clerk Master Bernardine Ochine.* STC 18767. 1550.

Barnes, Barnabe. *Parthenophil and Parthenophe.* STC 1469. 1593. Edited by Victor A. Doyno. Carbondale: Southern Illinois University Press, 1971.

Barnfield, Richard. *Cynthia, with Certaine sonnets.* STC 1483. 1595.

———. *The Poems of Richard Barnfield.* London: Fortune Press, 1936.

Beaumont, Francis, and John Fletcher. *Philaster.* Edited by Andrew Gurr. London: Methuen, 1969.

Bodenham, John. *Belvedere, or the garden of the Muses.* STC 3189. 1600. Reprinted. New York: Burt Franklin, 1967.

Breton, Nicholas. *No Whipping, but a Tripping.* In *Works.* Edited by Alexander B. Grosart. 2 vols. Edinburgh: Chertsey Worthies, 1879.

Brittons Bowre of Delights. STC 3633. 1951. Edited by Hyder E. Rollins. New York: Russell and Russell, 1968.

Chamberlain, John. *The Letters of John Chamberlain.* Edited by Norman Egbert McClure. Philadelphia: The American Philosophical Society, 1939.

Chettle, Henry. *Kind-Hartes Dream.* 1592. Reprinted. Bodley Head Quartos. Edited by G. B. Harrison. London: John Lane, 1923.

Churchyard, Thomas. *Churchyards Challenge.* STC 5220. 1593.

Colin Clouts Come Home Againe. STC 23077. 1595. In *The Works of Edmund Spenser.* Edited by Edwin Greenlaw, Charles Osgood, Frederick Padelford, and Ray Heffner. Baltimore: Johns Hopkins University Press, 1932–1949.

Constable, Henry. *Diana, or, The excellent Conceitful Sonnets of H. C.* STC 5637. 1592. STC 5638. 1594. In vol. 2, *Elizabethan Sonnets: An English Garner.* Edited by Sidney Lee. New York: Cooper Square Publishers, 1964.

Daniel, Samuel. *Delia.* STC 6243.2–6243.4. In *Samuel Daniel: Poems and A Defence of Ryme.* Edited by Arthur Sprague. Chicago: University of Chicago Press, 1930.

——. *The Whole Workes of Samuel Daniel Esquire in Poetrie.* STC 6238. 1623.

——. *Works.* Edited by Alexander B. Grosart. 5 vols. London: Hazell, Watson, and Viney, 1885–1896. Reissued. New York: Russell and Russell, 1963.

Davies, John. *The Muses Sacrifice.* In *The Complete Works of John Davies.* Edited by Alexander B. Grosart. 2 vols. Edinburgh: Chertsey Worthies' Library, 1878.

——. *The Poems of Sir John Davies.* Edited by Robert Krueger. Oxford: Clarendon Press, 1970.

Davison, Francis. *A Poetical Rhapsody.* 1602. Edited by Hyder E. Rollins. Cambridge, Mass.: Harvard University Press, 1931.

Dekker, Thomas. *The Gull's Hornbook.* London, 1609. Edited by R. B. McKerrow. London: Chatto and Windus, 1907.

——. *The Wonderfull Year.* STC 6535.3. 1603. In *The Plague Pamphlets of Thomas Dekker.* Edited by F. P. Wilson. Oxford: Clarendon Press, 1925.

Donne, John. *The Poems of John Donne.* Edited by Herbert J. C. Grierson. 2 vols. Oxford: Clarendon Press, 1912.

Dowland, John. *The first book of songes or ayres.* STC 7091. 1597.

Drayton, Michael. *Idea.* STC 7202. 1593.

——. *Ideas Mirror.* STC 7203. 1594.

——. *Minor Poems of Michael Drayton.* Edited by Cyril Brett. Oxford: Clarendon Press, 1907.

——. *Poems by Michael Drayton Esquire.* STC 7218. 1608. Reprinted. STC 7223. 1619. Reprinted. STC 7225. 1623.

——. *Poly-Olbion.* 1622. Reprinted. Publications of the Spenser Society, n.s., 3 vols. Manchester: Charles S. Simms, 1889.

——. *The Works of Michael Drayton.* Edited by J. William Hebel. 5 vols. Oxford: Basil Blackwell, 1931–1941.

Elizabethan Sonnets: An English Garner. 3 vols. Edited by Sidney Lee. New York: Cooper Square, 1964.

England's Helicon. 1600. Edited by Arthur Bullen. London: Lawrence and Bullen, 1899.

Fletcher, Giles. *Licia, or Poemes of Love.* STC 11055. 1593? In *The English Works of Giles Fletcher, the Elder.* Edited by Lloyd E. Berry. Madison: University of Wisconsin Press, 1964.

Fraunce, Abraham. *Arcadian Rhetorick.* Edited by Hyder E. Rollins. Cambridge, Mass.: Harvard University Press, 1936.

Gascoigne, George. *A Hundreth Sundrie Flowres.* Edited by B. M. Ward. London: Frederick Etchells and Hugh MacDonald, 1926.

———. *The Princely Pleasures at Kenelworth Castle.* Reprinted. *The Complete Works of George Gascoigne.* 2 vols. Edited by John W. Cunliffe. Cambridge: Cambridge University Press, 1907–1910.

———. *The Spoyle of Antwerp.* STC 11644. 1577.

———. *The Whole woorkes of George Gascoigne Esquyre: Newlye compyled into one Volume.* STC 11638. 1587. Reprinted. *The Complete Works of George Gascoigne.* 2 vols. Edited by John W. Cunliffe. Cambridge: Cambridge University Press, 1907–1910.

Geminus, Thomas. *Compendiosa totius anatomie delineatio.* STC 11714. 1545.

Golding, Arthur. *The .xv. Bookes of P. Ovidius Naso, entytuled Metamorphosis, translated oute of Latin into English meeter, by Arthur Golding, gentleman.* 1567. In *Shakespeare's Ovid.* Edited by W. H. D. Rouse. London: Centaur Press, 1961.

Googe, Barnabe. *Eclogues, Epitaphs, and Sonnets.* STC 12048. 1563. Edited by Judith M. Kennedy. Toronto: University of Toronto Press, 1989.

Gosson, Stephen. *Plays Confuted . . . .* 1582. Edited by Arthur Freeman. New York: Garland Press, 1972.

———. *The Schoole of Abuse.* 1579. Reprinted. London: Shakespeare Society, 1841.

Greene, Robert. *Groats-Worth of Witte.* 1592. Reprinted. Bodley Head Quartos. Edited by G. B. Harrison. New York: E. P. Dutton, 1923.

Greville, Fulke. *Cælica.* In *The Poems and Dramas of Fulke Greville, first Lord Brooke.* Edited by Geoffrey Bullough. New York: Oxford University Press, 1945.

Griffin, Bartholomew. *Fidessa, more chaste then kinde.* STC 12367. 1596.

Grymeston, Elizabeth. *Miscelanae, Meditations, Memoratives.* STC 12407. 1604.

Guazzo, Steven. *The Civile Conversation of M. Steeven Guazzo.* STC 12422. 1581. Translated by George Pettie. Reprinted. Edited by Charles Whibley. 2 vols. New York: Alfred A. Knopf, 1925.

Habington, William. *Castara.* STC 12585. 1640.

Harington, John. *Letters and Epigrams of Sir John Harington.* Edited by Norman Egbert McClure. Philadelphia: University of Pennsylvania Press, 1930.

———. *Orlando Furioso.* Trans. edited by Robert McNulty. Oxford: Clarendon Press, 1972.

Harvey, Gabriel. *The Letter-Book of George Harvey, 1573–80.* Edited by Edward J. L. Scott. 2d. ser., 33. Westminster: Nichols and Sons for the Camden Society, 1884.

Heywood, Thomas. *The Dramatic Works of Thomas Heywood.* New York: Russell and Russell, 1964.

———. *England's Elizabeth: Her Life and Troubles.* 1631. Edited by Philip R. Rider. New York: Garland, 1982.

Holland, Philemon. Introduction. In Pliny. *The Historie of the World.* STC 20029. 1601.

Il Schifanoya. Elizabeth's Procession. In vol. 7, 1558–1580, *The Calendar of State Papers and Manuscripts, Relating to English Affairs . . . .* Edited by Rowden Brown and Cavendish Bentinck. London, 1890.

J. C. *Alcilia, Philoparthens loving folly.* STC 4274.5. 1595. Reprinted. STC 4275. 1613.

Joceline, Elizabeth. *The Mothers Legacie to her unborne Childe. . . .* STC 14624. 1624.

Jonson, Ben. *The Works of Ben Jonson.* Edited by C. H. Herford Percy and Evelyn Simpson. 11 vols. Oxford: Clarendon Press, 1925–1952.

Lanyer, Amelia. *Salve Deus Rex Judaeorum.* STC 15227. 1611. In *The Poems of Shakespeare's Dark Lady.* Edited by A. L. Rowse. New York: Clarkson N. Potter, 1979.

Leigh, Dorothy. *The Mothers Blessing: or The godly Counsaile of a Gentle-woman, not long since deceased, left behind her for her Children.* . . . STC 15402. 1616.

Lloyd, Ludwick. Preface. In *The pilgrimage of princes.* STC 16624. 1573.

Lodge, Thomas. *The Complete Works of Thomas Lodge.* Vols. 5–8 in the Hunterian Club Series. Glasgow: Robert Anderson, 1883.

———. *Phillis.* STC 16662. 1593.

———. *Scillaes Metamorphosis.* 1589. In *Glaucus and Silla with Other Lyrical and Pastoral Poems.* Chiswick: C. Whittingham, 1819.

Loves Martyr. Edited by Robert Chester. STC 5119. 1601.

M.R. *The Mothers Counsell, or, Live within Compasse. Being the last Will and Testament to her dearest Daughter which may serve for a worthy Legacie to all the Women in the World.* . . . STC 20583. 1630?

Martine, R. W. *Mar-Sixtus.* STC 24913. 1591.

Middleton, Thomas. *The Ghost of Lucrece.* 1600. Edited by Joseph Quincy Adams. New York: Scribner's, 1937.

The Mirror for Magistrates. Edited by Lily B. Campbell. 1938. Reprinted. New York: Barnes and Noble, 1960.

Mulcaster, Richard. "The Passage of our most drad Soveraigne Lady Quene Elizabeth through the Citie of london. . . ." In John Nichols. *The Progresses and Public Processions of Queen Elizabeth.* Vol 1. New York: AMS Press, 1823. In *The Quenes Maiesties Passage Through the Citie of London* . . . . Edited by James Osborne. New Haven: Yale University Press, 1960. Also in Arthur F. Kinney. *Elizabethan Backgrounds.* Hamden, Conn.: Archon Books, 1975.

Nashe, Thomas. *Works.* Edited by R. B. McKerrow. Revised by F. P. Wilson. 5 vols. Oxford: Basil Blackwell, 1958.

Nichols, John. *The Progresses and Public Processions of Queen Elizabeth.* 3 vols. 1823. Reprinted. New York: Burt Franklin, 1966.

Northbrooke, John. *A Treatise wherein Dicing, Dauncing, vaine playes or Enterludes* . . . *are reproved.* STC 18670. 1577.

Ovid. *The .xv. Bookes of P. Ovidius Naso, entytuled Metamorphosis, translated oute of Latin into English meeter, by Arthur Golding, gentleman.* 1567. In *Shakespeare's Ovid.* Edited by W. H. D. Rouse. London: Centaur Press, 1961.

———. *Metamorphoses.* Translated by Mary M. Innes. Harmondsworth: Penguin Books, 1955.

———. *Ovids Metamorphosis Englished, Mythologiz'd and Represented in Figures.* Translated by George Sandys. Oxford: I. Lichfield, 1632. Reprinted. Edited by Karl K. Hulley and Stanley Vandersall. Lincoln: University of Nebraska Press, 1970.

———. *Tristia.* Translated by Arthur Leslie Wheeler. The Loeb Classical Library. Cambridge, Mass.: Harvard University Press, 1965.

The Paradise of Dainty Devices. Edited by Hyder E. Rollins. Cambridge, Mass.: Harvard University Press, 1927.

The Passionate Pilgrim. 1599. The Folger Library. New York: Scribner's, 1939.

Percy, William. *Sonnets to the Fairest Coelia.* STC 19618. 1594.

Perkins, William. *A Salve for a Sicke man, or . . . the right manner of dying well.* STC 19742. 1595.

Petrarch. *Petrarch's Lyric Poems.* Edited and translated by Robert Durling. Cambridge, Mass.: Harvard University Press, 1976.

Pettie, George. *A petite Pallace of Pettie his pleasure.* STC 19819. 1576. Edited by Herbert Hartman. London: Oxford University Press, 1938.

The Phoenix Nest. Edited by Hyder E. Rollins. Cambridge, Mass.: Harvard University Press, 1961.

Propertius. *The Poems.* Edited and translated by W. G. Shepherd. New York: Penguin, 1985.

Puttenham, George. *The Arte of English Poesie.* 1589. Edited by Gladys Doidge Willcock and Alice Walker. Cambridge: Cambridge University Press, 1936.

Ralegh, Sir Walter. *The Poems of Sir Walter Ralegh.* Edited by Agnes M. C. Latham. London: Routledge and Kegan Paul, 1962.

Rich, Barnabe. [*See also* B.R.] *His Farewell to the Military Profession.* 1581. Edited by Thomas Mabry Cranfill. Austin: University of Texas Press, 1959.

——. *My Ladies Looking Glasse.* STC 20991.7. 1616.

Rowlands, Samuel. *Tis Merrie when Gossips meete.* STC 21409. 1602.

Russell, Elizabeth Cooke. Preface. In John Poynet. *A way of reconciliation of good and learned man. . . ,* translated by Elizabeth Cooke Russell. STC 21456. 1605.

Sabie, Francis. Preface. In *Flora's Fortune.* STC 21536. 1595.

Sackville, Thomas, and Thomas Norton. *Gorboduc.* Retitled in this edition as *The Tragidie of Ferrix and Porrex.* STC 18685. 1570.

Scoloker, Anthony. *Daiphantus, or The Passions of Love.* STC 21853. 1604.

Shakespeare, William. *The Complete Works of Shakespeare.* Edited by David Bevington. 3d ed. Glenview, Ill.: Scott Foresman and Company, 1980.

——. *Shakespeare's Sonnets.* Edited by Stephen Booth. New Haven: Yale University Press, 1977.

Sidney, Mary. *The Triumph of Death and Other Unpublished and Uncollected Poems.* Edited by Gary Waller. Salzburg: Universität Salzburg, 1977.

Sidney, Philip. *Astrophel and Stella.* In *Sir Philip Sidney: Selected Poems.* Edited by Katherine Duncan-Jones. Oxford: Oxford University Press, 1973.

——. *The Complete Works of Sir Philip Sidney.* Edited by Albert Feuillerat. 4 vols. Cambridge: Cambridge University Press, 1923.

——. *The Countess of Pembrokes Arcadia.* STC 22541. 1598. Reprinted. STC 22543. 1605.

——. *The Countess of Pembroke's Arcadia.* 1590. Edited by Maurice Evans. New York: Penguin, 1984.

——. *The Lady of May.* In *The Miscellaneous Prose of Sir Philip Sidney.* Edited by Katherine Duncan-Jones and Jan van Dorsten. Oxford: Clarendon Press, 1973.

——. *Sir Philip Sidney: Poems.* Edited by William Ringler. Oxford: Clarendon Press, 1962.

——. *Syr P.S. his Astrophel and Stella.* STC 22536. 1591.

Smith, William. *Chloris, or the complaint of the passionate despised shepherd.* STC 22872. 1596. In *The Poems of William Smith.* Edited by Lawrence A. Sasek. Baton Rouge: Louisiana State University Press, 1970.

Spenser, Edmund. *Amoretti and Epithalamion.* STC 23076. 1595.

——. *The Faerie Queene.* Edited by Thomas P. Roche. New York: Penguin, 1987.

——. *The Poeticall Workes of Edmund Spenser.* Edited by J. Payne Collier. 5 vols. London: Bickers and Son, 1873.

——. *The Yale Edition of the Shorter Poems of Edmund Spenser.* Edited by William A. Oram, Einar Bjorvand, Ronald Bond, Thomas H. Cain, Alexander Dunlop, and Richard Schell. New Haven: Yale University Press, 1989.

Thornton, Alice. *The Autobiography of Alice Thornton.* In *By A Woman Writt.* Edited by Joan Goulianos. Indianapolis: Bobbs-Merrill, 1973.

Tofte, Robert. *Laura the Toyes of a Traveller.* STC 24097. 1597.

Tottels Miscellany (Songes and Sonettes). STC 13860. 1557. Edited by Hyder E. Rollins. 2 vols. Cambridge, Mass: Harvard University Press, 1928–1929.

Vesalius, Andreas. *De humani corporis fabrica libri septem.* 1543. Reprinted. Brussels: Gabriel Lebon, 1964.

Vives, Juan Luis. *Instruction of a christen Woman.* Translated by Richard Hyrde. STC 24857. 1540. Reprinted. STC 24862. 1585.

Watson, Thomas. *The Hekatompathia, or Passionate Century of Love.* STC 25118a. 1582. Edited by S. K. Heninger, Jr. Gainesville, Fl.: Scholars' Facsimiles and Reprints, 1964.

——. *The Tears of Fancie.* STC 25122. 1593.

Webster, John. *The Duchess of Malfi.* 1623. In *John Webster: Three Plays.* New York: Viking Penguin, 1956.

Wheeler, John. *A Treatise of Commerce.* 1601. Reprinted. New York: Columbia University Press, 1931.

Whitney, Isabella. "The Copy of A Letter lately written in meeter, by a yonge Gentilwoman: to her unconstant lover." STC 25439. 1567.

——. *A sweet Nosegay, or pleasant Posye, contayning a hundred and ten Phylosophicall Flowers.* STC 25440. 1573. In *The Floures of Philosophie (1572) by Hugh Plat and A Sweet Nosgay (1573) and The Copy of a Letter (1567) by Isabella Whitney.* Edited by Richard J. Panofsky. Delmar, N.Y.: Scholars' Facsimiles and Reprints, 1982.

——. "The 'Wyll and Testament' of Isabella Whitney." Edited by Betty Travitsky. *English Literary Renaissance* 10 (1980): 76–94.

Whythorne, Thomas. *Autobiography.* Edited by James Osborn. London: Oxford University Press, 1962.

Willobie his Avisa. STC 25755. 1594. Reprinted. Bodley Head Quartos. Edited by G. B. Harrison. New York: E. P. Dutton, 1926.

Wilmot, Robert. *The Tragedies of Tancred and Gismund.* 1591. Edited by W. W. Greg. The Malone Society Reprints. London: Oxford University Press, 1914.

Wroth, Mary. *The Countess of Montgomeries Urania.* Part 1. STC 26051. 1621.

——. *Pamphilia to Amphilanthus.* Edited by Gary Waller. Salzburg: Institut für Englische Sprache und Literatur, 1977.

——. *The Poems of Lady Mary Wroth.* Edited by Josephine Roberts. Baton Rouge: Louisiana State University Press, 1983.

Zepheria. STC 26124. 1594. Reprinted. Publications of the Spenser Society. Manchester: Charles S. Simms, 1869.

Selected Bibliography

Critical, Theoretical, and Historical Texts

Agnew, Jean-Christophe. *Worlds Apart: The Market and the Theater in Anglo-American Thought, 1550–1750.* Cambridge: Cambridge University Press, 1986.

Alpers, Paul. "Pastoral and the Domain of Lyric in Spenser's *Shepheardes Calender.*" *Representations* 12 (1985): 83–100.

Amussen, Susan. *An Ordered Society: Gender and Class in Early Modern England.* Oxford: Basil Blackwell, 1988.

Anglo, Sydney. *Spectacle, Pageantry, and Early Tudor Policy.* Oxford: Clarendon Press, 1969.

Arber, Edward. *A Transcript of the Registers of the Company of Stationers of London, 1554–1640.* 5 vols. London: privately printed, 1875.

Armstrong, Nancy, and Leonard Tennenhouse, eds. *The Ideology of Conduct.* New York: Methuen, 1987.

Aubrey, John. *Brief Lives.* Edited by Oliver Lawson Dick. Ann Arbor: University of Michigan Press, 1949.

———. *The Natural History of Wiltshire.* 1847. Reprinted. New York: Augustus M. Kelley, 1969.

Axton, Marie. "The Tudor Mask and Elizabethan Court Drama." In *English Drama: Forms and Development.* Edited by Marie Axton and Raymond Williams. Cambridge: Cambridge University Press, 1977.

Barkan, Leonard. "Diana and Actaeon: The Myth as Synthesis." *English Literary Renaissance* 10 (1980): 317–59.

———. *Nature's Work of Art: The Human Body as Image of the World.* New Haven: Yale University Press, 1975.

———. *Transuming Passion: Ganymede and the Erotics of Humanism.* Stanford: Stanford University Press, 1991.

Barker, Francis. *The Tremulous Private Body: Essays on Subjection.* London: Methuen, 1984.

Barroll, Leeds. "A New History for Shakespeare and His Time." *Shakespeare Quarterly* 39 (1988): 441–64.

Barthes, Roland. *Image, Music, Text.* Edited by Stephen Heath. New York: Hill and Wang, 1977.

———. *The Pleasure of the Text.* Translated by Richard Miller. New York: Hill and Wang, 1975.

Beilin, Elaine. *Redeeming Eve: Women Writers of the English Renaissance.* Princeton: Princeton University Press, 1987.

Belsey, Catherine. "Disrupting Sexual Difference: Meaning and Gender in the Comedies." In *Alternative Shakespeares.* Edited by John Drakakis. London: Methuen, 1985.

———. *The Subject of Tragedy: Identity and Difference in Renaissance Drama.* New York: Methuen, 1985.

Benjamin, Walter. "The Work of Art in the Age of Mechanical Reproduction." In *Illuminations.* New York: Harcourt Brace and World, 1969.

Bennett, H. S. "The Author and His Public in the Fourteenth and Fifteenth Centuries." *Essays and Studies by Members of the English Association* 23 (1938): 7–24.

———. *English Books and Readers, 1475–1557.* Cambridge: Cambridge University Press, 1952.

——. *English Books and Readers, 1558–1603*. Cambridge: Cambridge University Press, 1965.

——. *English Books and Readers, 1603–1640*. Cambridge: Cambridge University Press, 1970.

Bentley, Gerald Eades. *The Profession of Dramatist in Shakespeare's Time: 1590–1642*. Princeton: Princeton University Press, 1971.

Bergeron, David. *English Civic Pageantry, 1558–1642*. London: Edward Arnold, 1971.

Berlant, Lauren. "The Female Complaint." *Social Text* 19/20 (Fall 1988): 237–59.

Blum, Abbe. "'Strike all that look upon with mar[b]le': Monumentalizing Women in Shakespeare's Plays." In *The Renaissance Englishwoman in Print: Counterbalancing the Canon*. Edited by Anne M. Haselkorn and Betty Travitsky. Amherst: University of Massachusetts Press, 1990.

Boose, Lynda E. "The Family in Shakespeare Studies; or—Studies in the Family of Shakespeareans; or—The Politics of Politics." *Renaissance Quarterly* 40 (Winter 1987): 707–42.

Booth, Stephen. *An Essay on Shakespeare's Sonnets*. New Haven: Yale University Press, 1969.

Bordieu, Pierre. "Forms of Capital." In *Handbook of Theory and Research for the Sociology of Education*. Edited by John G. Richardson. New York: Greenwood Press, 1986.

Breitenberg, Mark. "'. . . the hole matter opened': Iconic Representation and Interpretation in 'The Quenes Majesties Passage.'" *Criticism* 28 (1986): 1–25.

Bruns, Gerald L. "The Originality of Texts in a Manuscript Culture." *Journal of Comparative Literature* 32 (Spring 1980): 113–29.

Cain, Thomas. *Praise in "The Faerie Queene."* Lincoln: University of Nebraska Press, 1978.

Campbell, Marion. "Unending Desire: Sidney's Reinvention of Petrarchan Form in *Astrophil and Stella*." In *Sir Philip Sidney and the Interpretation of Renaissance Culture*. Edited by Gary Waller. Totowa, N.J.: Barnes and Noble, 1984.

Cixous, Hélène. "The Laugh of the Medusa." Translated by Keith Cohen. In *New French Feminisms*. Edited by Elaine Marks and Isabelle de Courtivron. Amherst: University of Massachusetts Press, 1980.

Clair, Colin. *A History of Printing in Britain*. New York: Oxford University Press, 1966.

Cohen, Walter. "Political Criticism of Shakespeare." In *Shakespeare Reproduced: The Text in History & Ideology*. Edited by Jean Howard and Marion F. O'Connor. London: Methuen, 1987.

Coiro, Ann Baynes. "Milton and Class Identity: The Publication of *Areopagitica* and the 1645 *Poems*." *Journal of Medieval and Renaissance Studies* 22 (Spring 1992): 261–89.

——. "Print and Manuscript as Gendered Performances." Paper delivered at the Twenty-seventh International Congress on Medieval Studies, Kalamazoo, Michigan, May 1992.

Corbett, Margery, and Ronald Lightbown. *The Comely Frontispiece: The Emblematic Title Page in England, 1550–1660*. London: Routledge and Kegan Paul, 1979.

Crawford, Patricia. "From the Women's View: Pre-industrial England, 1500–1750." In *Exploring Women's Past: Essays in Social History*. Edited by Patricia Crawford, Margaret Anderson, Raelene Davidson, Patricia Jalland and Margaret Ker. Boston: George Allen and Unwin, 1983.

Cressy, David. *Literacy and the Social Order: Reading and Writing in Tudor and Stuart England.* Cambridge: Cambridge University Press, 1980.

Davis, Lennard. *Factual Fictions: The Origins of the English Novel.* New York: Columbia University Press, 1983.

Davis, Natalie Zemon. "Printing and the People." In *Society and Culture in Early Modern France: Eight Essays.* Stanford: Stanford University Press, 1975. Reprinted. Ithaca: Cornell University Press, 1982.

Davis, Walter. "Actaeon in Arcadia." *Studies in English Literature* 2 (1962): 95–110.

De Grazia, Margreta. *Shakespeare Verbatim: The Reproduction of Authenticity and the 1790 Apparatus.* Oxford: Oxford University Press, 1991.

Derrida, Jacques. "Structure, Sign, and Play in the Discourse of the Human Sciences." In *Writing and Difference,* translated by Alan Bass. Chicago: University of Chicago Press, 1978.

Dolan, Frances. "'Gentlemen, I have one thing more to say': Women on Scaffolds in England, 1563–1680." Forthcoming in *Modern Philology.*

Dollimore, Jonathan, and Alan Sinfield, eds. *Political Shakespeare: New Essays in Cultural Materialism.* 1985. Reprinted. Ithaca: Cornell University Press, 1987.

Donaldson, Ian. *The Rapes of Lucretia: A Myth and Its Transformations.* Oxford: Clarendon Press, 1982.

Eisenstein, Elizabeth. *The Printing Press as an Agent of Change.* Cambridge: Cambridge University Press, 1979.

Elsky, Martin. *Authorizing Words: Speech, Writing, and Print in the English Renaissance.* Ithaca: Cornell University Press, 1989.

Esler, Anthony. *The Aspiring Mind of the Elizabethan Younger Generation.* Durham, N.C.: Duke University Press, 1966.

Febvre, Lucien, and Henri-Jean Martin. *The Coming of the Book: The Impact of Printing, 1450–1800.* Translated by David Gerard. London: Verso, 1990. Originally published as *L'apparition du livre* (Paris, 1958).

Fehrenbach, Robert J. "Isabella Whitney (fl. 1565–75) and the Popular Miscellanies of Richard Jones." *Cahiers Élisabéthains* 19 (1981): 85–87.

Ferguson, Margaret W. "A Room Not Their Own: Renaissance Women as Readers and Writers." In *The Comparative Perspective on Literature.* Edited by Clayton Koelb and Susan Noakes. Ithaca: Cornell University Press, 1988.

——. "Running On with Almost Public Voice: The Case of 'E.C.'" In *Tradition and the Talents of Women.* Edited by Florence Howe. Urbana: University of Illinois Press, 1991.

Ferguson, Margaret W., Maureen Quilligan, and Nancy J. Vickers, eds. *Rewriting the Renaissance: The Discourses of Sexual Difference in Early Modern Europe.* Chicago: University of Chicago Press, 1986.

Ferry, Anne. *The "Inward" Language: Sonnets of Wyatt, Sidney, Shakespeare, Donne.* Chicago: University of Chicago Press, 1983.

Fienberg, Nona. "Mary Wroth and the Invention of Female Poetic Subjectivity." In *Reading Mary Wroth: Representing Alternatives in Early Modern England.* Edited by Naomi Miller and Gary Waller. Knoxville: University of Tennessee Press, 1991.

Fineman, Joel. "Shakespeare's *Will*: The Temporality of Rape." *Representations* 20 (Fall 1987): 25–76.

Fisken, Beth Wynne. "Mary Sidney's *Psalmes*: Education and Wisdom." In *Silent But for the Word: Tudor Women as Patrons, Translators, and Writers of Religious Works.* Edited by Margaret Hannay. Kent, O.: Kent State University Press, 1985.

——. "'To the Angell Spirit . . . ': Mary Sidney's Entry into the 'World of Words.'" In *The Renaissance Englishwoman in Print: Counterbalancing the Canon.* Edited by Anne M. Haselkorn and Betty Travitsky. Amherst: University of Massachusetts Press, 1990.

Fleming, Juliet. "*The French Garden*: An Introduction to Women's French." *ELH* 56 (1989): 19–51.

——. "*Ladies' Men, the Ladies' Text, and the English Renaissance.*" Ph.D. diss., University of Pennsylvania, 1991.

Foucault, Michel. *The Archeology of Knowledge.* New York: Pantheon, 1972.

——. *Discipline and Punish: The Birth of the Prison.* Translated by Alan Sheridan. New York: Vintage, 1979.

——. "What Is an Author?" In *Textual Strategies: Perspectives in Post-Structuralist Criticism.* Edited by Josué Harari. Ithaca: Cornell University Press, 1979.

Fraistat, Neil, ed. *Poems in Their Place: The Intertextuality and Order of Poetic Collections.* Chapel Hill: University of North Carolina Press, 1986.

Fraser, Russell. *The War against Poetry.* Princeton: Princeton University Press, 1970.

Freccero, John. "The Fig Tree and the Laurel: Petrarch's Poetics." *Diacritics* 5 (1975): 34–40.

Freer, Coburn. "Mary Sidney: The Countess of Pembroke." In *Women Writers of the Renaissance and Reformation.* Edited by Katharina M. Wilson. Athens: University of Georgia Press, 1987.

Fumerton, Patricia. "'Secret' Arts: Elizabethan Miniatures and Sonnets." *Representations* 15 (Summer 1986): 57–97.

Gebert, Clara, ed. *An Anthology of Elizabethan Dedications and Prefaces.* Philadelphia: University of Pennsylvania Press, 1933.

Geertz, Clifford. "Centers, Kings, and Charisma: Symbolics of Power." In *Local Knowledge.* New York: Basic Books, 1983.

Girouard, Mark. *Life in the English Country House: A Social and Architectural History.* New Haven: Yale University Press, 1978.

Goldberg, Jonathan. *James I and the Politics of Literature: Jonson, Shakespeare, Donne, and Their Contemporaries.* Baltimore: Johns Hopkins University Press, 1983. Reprinted. Stanford: Stanford University Press, 1989.

——. "The Politics of Renaissance Literature: A Review Essay." *ELH* 49 (1982): 514–42.

——. "Textual Properties." *Shakespeare Quarterly* 37 (1986): 213–17.

——. *Voice Terminal Echo.* New York: Methuen, 1986.

——. *Writing Matter: From the Hands of the English Renaissance.* Stanford: Stanford University Press, 1990.

Goody, Jack, and Ian Watt. "The Consequences of Literacy." In *Literacy in Traditional Societies.* Edited by Jack Goody. Cambridge: Cambridge University Press, 1968.

Greenblatt, Stephen. Introduction. In "The Forms of Power and the Power of Forms in the Renaissance." *Genre* 15 (1982): 3–6.

——. *Renaissance Self-Fashioning: From More to Shakespeare.* Chicago: University of Chicago Press, 1980.

——. *Shakespearean Negotiations.* Berkeley: University of California Press, 1988.

Hall, Kim. "Acknowledging Things of Darkness: Race, Gender, and Power in Early Modern England." Ph.D. diss., University of Pennsylvania, 1990.

Halpern, Richard. *The Poetics of Primitive Accumulation: English Renaissance Culture and the Genealogy of Capital.* Ithaca: Cornell University Press, 1991.

Hannay, Margaret. "'Doo What Men May Sing': Mary Sidney and the Tradition of Admonitory Dedication." In *Silent But for the Word: Tudor Women as Patrons, Translators, and Writers of Religious Works.* Edited by Margaret Hannay. Kent, Ohio: Kent State University Press, 1985.

———. *Philip's Phoenix: Mary Sidney, Countess of Pembroke.* Oxford: Oxford University Press, 1990.

Harcourt, Glenn. "Andreas Vesalius and the Anatomy of Antique Sculpture." *Representations* 17 (Winter 1987): 28–61.

Hart, E. F. "The Answer-Poem of the Early Seventeenth Century." *Review of English Studies* 7:25 (1956): 19–29.

Haselkorn, Anne M., and Betty Travitsky, eds. *The Renaissance Englishwoman in Print: Counterbalancing the Canon.* Amherst: University of Massachusetts Press, 1990.

Helgerson, Richard. *Elizabethan Prodigals.* Berkeley: University of California Press, 1976.

———. *Self-Crowned Laureates: Spenser, Jonson, Milton, and the Literary System.* Berkeley: University of California Press, 1983.

Hogrefe, Pearl. *Tudor Women: Commoners and Queens.* Ames: Iowa State University Press, 1975.

Howard, Jean. "Crossdressing, the Theatre, and Gender Struggle in Early Modern England." *Shakespeare Quarterly* 39 (1988): 418–40.

———. "Renaissance Antitheatricality and the Politics of Gender and Rank in *Much Ado About Nothing.*" In *Shakespeare Reproduced: The Text in History & Ideology.* Edited by Jean Howard and Marion F. O'Connor. New York: Methuen, 1987.

Howard, Jean, and Marion F. O'Connor, eds. *Shakespeare Reproduced: The Text in History & Ideology.* New York: Methuen, 1987.

Hull, Suzanne. *Chaste, Silent, and Obedient: English Books for Women, 1475–1640.* San Marino, Cal.: Huntington Library Press, 1982.

Hulse, Clark. "Stella's Wit: Penelope Rich as Reader of Sidney's Sonnets." In *Rewriting the Renaissance: The Discourses of Sexual Difference in Early Modern Europe.* Edited by Margaret Ferguson, Maureen Quilligan, and Nancy J. Vickers. Chicago: University of Chicago Press, 1986.

Innis, Harold. *Empire and Communications.* Oxford: Clarendon Press, 1950.

Jacobus, Mary. "Is There a Woman in This Text?" *New Literary History* 14 (1982): 117–54.

Jardine, Lisa. *Still Harping on Daughters: Women and Drama in the Age of Shakespeare.* 1983. Reprinted. New York: Columbia University Press, 1989.

Jed, Stephanie. *Chaste Thinking: The Rape of Lucretia and the Birth of Humanism.* Bloomington: Indiana University Press, 1989.

Jones, Ann Rosalind. "Assimilation with a Difference." *Yale French Studies* 62 (1981): 135–53.

———. *The Currency of Eros: Women's Love Lyric in Europe, 1540–1620.* Bloomington: Indiana University Press, 1990.

——. "Nets and Bridles: Early Modern Conduct Books and Sixteenth-Century Women's Lyrics." In *The Ideology of Conduct*. Edited by Nancy Armstrong and Leonard Tennenhouse. New York: Methuen, 1987.

——. "Surprising Fame: Renaissance Gender Ideologies and Women's Lyric." In *The Poetics of Gender*. Edited by Nancy K. Miller. New York: Columbia University Press, 1986.

Jones, Ann Rosalind, and Peter Stallybrass. "The Politics of *Astrophil and Stella*." *Studies in English Literature* 24 (1984): 53–68.

Jones, Whitney. *The Tudor Commonwealth, 1529–1559*. London: Athlone Press, 1970.

Joplin, Patricia. "The Voice of the Shuttle Is Ours." *Stanford Literature Review* 1 (1984): 25–53.

Jordan, Constance. "Feminism and the Humanists: The Case of Sir Thomas Elyot's *Defence of Good Women*." In *Rewriting the Renaissance: The Discourses of Sexual Difference in Early Modern Europe*. Edited by Margaret Ferguson, Maureen Quilligan, and Nancy J. Vickers. Chicago: University of Chicago Press, 1986.

——. *Renaissance Feminism: Literary Texts and Political Models*. Ithaca: Cornell University Press, 1990.

Kahn, Coppélia. "The Rape in Shakespeare's *Lucrece*." *Shakespeare Studies* 9 (1976): 45–72.

Kaufman, Gloria. "Juan Luis Vives on the Education of Women." *Signs* 3 (1978): 891–96.

Kegl, Rosemary. "'Those Terrible Aproches': Sexuality, Social Mobility, and Resisting the Courtliness of Puttenham's *The Arte of English Poesie*." *English Literary Renaissance* 20 (Spring 1990): 179–208.

Kelly, Joan. *Women, History, and Theory*. Chicago: University of Chicago Press, 1984.

Kelso, Ruth. *Doctrine for the English Gentleman in the Sixteenth Century*. Gloucester, Mass.: Peter Smith, 1964.

——. *Doctrine for the Lady of the Renaissance*. Urbana: University of Illinois Press, 1956.

Kennedy, Gwynne. "Feminine Subjectivity in the Renaissance: The Writings of Elizabeth Carey, Lady Falkland, and Lady Mary Wroth." Ph.D. diss., University of Pennsylvania, 1990.

——. "Lessons of the 'Schoole of Wysdome.'" In *Sexuality and Politics in Renaissance Drama*. Edited by Carole Levin and Karen Robertson. Lewiston, New York: Edwin Mellen Press, 1991.

——. "She 'thincks she daunces in a net': The Reception of Lady Mary Wroth's *Urania*." Paper delivered at the Third Pennsylvania Symposium on Medieval and Renaissance Studies, Philadelphia, 1989.

Kennedy, William J. "Petrarchan Audiences and Print Technology." *Journal of Medieval and Renaissance Studies* 14 (1984): 1–20.

Kernan, Alvin. *Printing Technology, Letters, and Samuel Johnson*. Princeton: Princeton University Press, 1987.

Kinney, Arthur F. *Elizabethan Backgrounds*. Hamden, Conn.: Archon Books, 1975.

Kolodny, Annette. "Dancing through the Minefield." *Feminist Studies* 6 (1980): 1–25.

Lamb, Mary Ellen. "The Cooke Sisters: Attitudes toward Learned Women in the Renaissance." In *Silent But for the Word: Tudor Women as Patrons, Translators, and Writers of Religious Works.* Edited by Margaret Hannay. Kent, Ohio: Kent State University Press, 1985.

———. "The Countess of Pembroke's Patronage." *English Literary Renaissance* 12 (1982): 162–79.

———. *Gender and Authorship in the Sidney Circle.* Madison: University of Wisconsin Press, 1990.

Lanham, Richard A. "*Astrophil and Stella*: Pure and Impure Persuasion." *English Literary Renaissance* 2 (1972): 100–115.

Laslett, Peter. *The World We Have Lost.* New York: Scribner's, 1971.

Leinwand, Theodore. "Negotiation and New Historicism." *PMLA* 105 (May 1990): 477–90.

Lewalski, Barbara. "Of God and Good Women: The Poems of Aemilia Lanyer." In *Silent But for the Word: Tudor Women as Patrons, Translators, and Writers of Religious Works.* Edited by Margaret Hannay. Kent, O.: Kent State University Press, 1985.

Lewis, C. S. *English Literature in the Sixteenth Century (Excluding Drama).* Oxford: Clarendon Press, 1954.

Loewenstein, Joseph. *Responsive Readings: Versions of Echo in Pastoral, Epic, and the Jonsonian Masque.* New Haven: Yale University Press, 1984.

———. "The Script in the Marketplace." In *Representing the English Renaissance.* Edited by Stephen Greenblatt. Berkeley: University of California Press, 1988.

Lucie-Smith, Edward. *Eroticism in Western Art.* New York: Praeger Publishers, 1972.

MacArthur, Janet. *Critical Contexts of Sidney's "Astrophil and Stella" and Spenser's "Amoretti."* Victoria: University of Victoria, 1989.

McCanles, Michael. "*The Shepheardes Calender* as Document and Monument." *Studies in English Literature* 22 (1982): 5–19.

McCoy, Richard. "Gascoigne's 'Poëmata castrata': The Wages of Courtly Success." *Criticism* 27 (Winter 1985): 29–55.

———. *Sir Philip Sidney: Rebellion in Arcadia.* New Brunswick, N.J.: Rutgers University Press, 1979.

Macfarlane, Alan. *Witchcraft in Tudor and Stuart England: A Regional and Comparative Study.* New York: Harper and Row, 1970.

McGann, Jerome. *A Critique of Modern Textual Criticism.* Chicago: University of Chicago Press, 1983.

Macherey, Pierre. *A Theory of Literary Production.* Translated by Geoffrey Wall. London: Routledge and Kegan Paul, 1978.

McLeod, Randall. "UnEditing Shak-speare." *Sub-Stance* 33/34 (1982): 26–55.

McLuhan, Marshall. *The Gutenberg Galaxy: The Making of Typographic Man.* Toronto: University of Toronto Press, 1962.

Mahl, Mary, and Helene Koon, eds. *The Female Spectator: English Women Writers Before 1800.* Bloomington: Indiana University Press, 1977.

Marcus, Leah. *Puzzling Shakespeare.* Berkeley: University of California Press, 1988.

Marotti, Arthur. "John Donne, Author." *Journal of Medieval and Renaissance Studies* 19 (1989): 69–82.

———. *John Donne: Coterie Poet.* Madison: University of Wisconsin Press, 1986.

——. "'Love is not Love': Elizabethan Sonnet Sequences and the Social Order." *ELH* 49 (1982): 396–428.

——. "Patronage, Poetry, and Print." *The Yearbook of English Studies* 21 (1991): 1–26.

——. "Shakespeare's Sonnets as Literary Property." In *Soliciting Interpretation: Literary Theory and Seventeenth-Century English Poetry.* Edited by Elizabeth D. Harvey and Katherine Eisaman Maus. Chicago: University of Chicago Press, 1990.

——. "The Transmission of Lyric Poetry and the Institutionalizing of Literature in the English Renaissance." In *Contending Kingdoms: Historical, Psychological, and Feminist Approaches to the Literature of Sixteenth-Century England and France.* Edited by Marie-Rose Logan and Peter L. Rudnytsky. Detroit: Wayne State University Press, 1991.

Masten, Jeff. "Beaumont and/or Fletcher: Collaboration and the Interpretation of Renaissance Drama." *ELH* 59 (1992): 337–59.

——. "'Shall I turn blabb?' Circulation, Gender, and Subjectivity in Mary Wroth's Sonnets." In *Reading Mary Wroth: Representing Alternatives in Early Modern England.* Edited by Naomi J. Miller and Gary Waller. Knoxville: University of Tennessee Press, 1991.

Mazzotta, Giuseppe. "The *Canzoniere* and the Language of the Self." *Studies in Philology* 75 (1978): 271–96.

Merrix, Robert. "The Vale of Lillies and the Bower of Bliss: Soft-core Pornography in Elizabethan Poetry." *Journal of Popular Culture* 19 (Spring 1986): 3–16.

Miller, David Lee. "Authorship, Anonymity, and *The Shepheardes Calender.*" *Modern Language Quarterly* 40 (1979): 219–36.

Miller, Edwin Haviland. *The Professional Writer in Elizabethan England: A Study of Nondramatic Literature.* Cambridge, Mass.: Harvard University Press, 1959.

Miller, Jaqueline. "'What May Words Say': The Limits of Language in *Astrophil and Stella.*" In *Sir Philip Sidney and the Interpretation of Culture.* Edited by Gary Waller and Michael D. Moore. Totowa, N.J.: Barnes and Noble, 1984.

Miller, Naomi J., and Gary Waller, eds. *Reading Mary Wroth: Representing Alternatives in Early Modern England.* Knoxville: University of Tennessee Press, 1991.

Mohl, Ruth. *The Three Estates in Medieval and Renaissance Literature.* New York: Columbia University Press, 1933.

Moi, Toril. *Sexual/Textual Politics: Feminist Literary Theory.* New York: Methuen, 1985.

Montrose, Louis. "Celebration and Insinuation: Sir Philip Sidney and the Motives of Elizabethan Courtship." *Renaissance Drama* 8 (1977): 3–35.

——. "'Eliza, Queene of Shepheardes,' and the Pastoral of Power." *English Literary Renaissance* 10 (1980): 153–82.

——. "The Elizabethan Subject and the Spenserian Text." In *Literary Theory/ Renaissance Texts.* Edited by Patricia Parker and David Quint. Baltimore: Johns Hopkins University Press, 1986.

——. "Gifts and Reasons: The Contexts of Peele's 'Araygemement of Paris.'" *ELH* 47 (1980): 433–61.

——. "Of Gentlemen and Shepherds: The Politics of Elizabethan Pastoral Form." *ELH* 50 (1983): 415–59

——. "'The perfecte paterne of a Poete': The Poetics of Courtship in *The Shepheardes Calender.*" *Texas Studies in Literature and Language* 21 (1979): 34–67.

——. "Professing the Renaissance: The Poetics and Politics of Culture." In *The New Historicism.* Edited by H. Aram Veeser. New York: Routledge, 1989.

——. "The Purpose of Playing: Reflections on a Shakespearean Anthropology." *Helios* 7 (1980): 51–74.

——. "Shaping Fantasies: Figurations of Gender and Power in Elizabethan Culture." *Representations* 2 (1983): 61–94.

Mullaney, Steven. *The Place of the Stage: License, Play, and Power in Renaissance England.* Chicago: University of Chicago Press, 1988.

Mumford, Lewis. *Technics and Civilization.* New York: Harcourt, Brace, 1934.

Murray, Timothy. *Theatrical Legitimation: Allegories of Genius in Seventeenth-Century England and France.* Oxford: Oxford University Press, 1987.

Neale, John. Introduction. In *The Quenes Maiesties Passage Through the Citie of London . . . .* Edited by James Osborne. New Haven: Yale University Press, 1960.

——. "Sayings of Queen Elizabeth." *History,* n.s. 10 (October 1925): 212–33.

Neely, Carol Thomas. "Constructing the Subject: Feminist Practice and the New Renaissance Discourses." *English Literary Renaissance* 18 (Winter 1988): 5–18.

——. "The Structure of English Renaissance Sonnet Sequences." *ELH* 45 (1978): 359–89.

Newman, Barbara. "On the Ethics of Feminist Historiography." *Exemplaria: A Journal of Theory in Medieval and Renaissance Studies* 2 (1990): 702–6.

Newman, Karen. *Fashioning Femininity and English Renaissance Drama.* Chicago: University of Chicago Press, 1991.

——. "Portia's Ring: Unruly Women and the Structures of Exchange in *The Merchant of Venice.*" *Shakespeare Quarterly* 38 (Spring 1987): 19–33.

Newton, Judith. "History As Usual? Feminism and the 'New Historicism.'" In *The New Historicism.* Edited by H. Aram Veeser. New York: Routledge, 1989.

Newton, Richard. "Jonson and the (Re-) Invention of the Book." In *Classic and Cavalier: Essays on Jonson and the Sons of Ben.* Edited by Claude Summers and Ted-Larry Pebworth. Pittsburgh: University of Pittsburgh Press, 1982.

Novy, Marianne. *Love's Argument: Gender Relations in Shakespeare.* Chapel Hill: University of North Carolina Press, 1985.

O'Malley, Charles D. *Andreas Vesalius of Brussels: 1514–1564.* Berkeley: University of California Press, 1964.

Ong, Walter. *Interfaces of the Word.* Ithaca: Cornell University Press, 1977.

——. "Latin Language Study as a Renaissance Puberty Rite." *Studies in Philology* 56 (1959): 106–24.

——. *Orality and Literacy: The Technologizing of the Word.* New York: Methuen, 1982.

——. *The Presence of the Word.* New Haven: Yale University Press, 1967.

——. *Rhetoric, Romance, and Technology.* Ithaca: Cornell University Press, 1971.

Orgel, Stephen. "The Authentic Shakespeare." *Representations* 21 (1988): 1–25.

——. *The Illusion of Power: Political Theater in the English Renaissance.* Berkeley: University of California Press, 1975.

——. *The Jonsonian Masque.* Cambridge, Mass.: Harvard University Press, 1965.

——. "Sidney's Experiment in Pastoral: The Lady of May." *Journal of the Warburg and Courtauld Institutes* 26 (1963): 198–203.

——. "What Is a Text?" *Research Opportunities in Renaissance Drama* 2:4 (1981): 3–6.

Parker, Patricia. *Literary Fat Ladies: Rhetoric, Gender, Property.* New York: Methuen, 1987.

——. "Shakespeare and Rhetoric: 'Dilation' and 'Delation' in *Othello*." In *Shakespeare and the Question of Theory*. Edited by Patricia Parker and Geoffrey Hartman. New York: Methuen, 1985.

Patterson, Annabel. *Censorship and Interpretation: The Conditions of Writing and Reading in Early Modern England*. Madison: University of Wisconsin Press, 1984.

——. *Fables of Power: Aesopian Writing and Political History*. Durham, N.C.: Duke University Press, 1991.

——. "'Under . . . Pretty Tales': Intention in Sidney's *Arcadia*." *Studies in the Literary Imagination* 15 (1982): 5–21.

Patterson, Lee. *Negotiating the Past: The Historical Understanding of Medieval Literature*. Madison: University of Wisconsin Press, 1987.

——. "On the Margin: Postmodernism, Ironic History, and Medieval Studies." *Speculum* 65 (1990): 87–108.

Plant, Marjorie. *The English Book Trade: An Economic History of the Making and Sale of Books*. London: George Allen and Unwin, 1939.

Pomeroy, Elizabeth. *The Elizabethan Miscellanies: Their Development and Conventions*. Berkeley: University of California Press, 1973.

Porter, Carolyn. "Are We Being Historical Yet?" *South Atlantic Quarterly* 87 (Fall 1988): 743–86.

Prior, Mary. "Women and the Urban Economy: Oxford, 1500–1800." In *Women in English Society, 1500–1800*. Edited by Mary Prior. London: Methuen, 1985.

Prouty, C. T. *George Gascoigne: Elizabethan Courtier, Soldier, and Poet*. New York: Columbia University Press, 1942.

Quilligan, Maureen. *The Allegory of Female Authority: Christine de Pizan's "Cité des Dames."* Ithaca: Cornell University Press, 1991.

——. *Milton's Spenser: The Politics of Reading*. Ithaca: Cornell University Press, 1983.

——. "Words and Sex: The Language of Allegory in *De planctu naturae*, *La Roman de la Rose*, and Book III of *The Faerie Queene*." *Allegorica* II (1977): 195–216.

Rackin, Phyllis. "Androgyny, Mimesis, and the Marriage of the Boy Heroine on the English Renaissance Stage." *PMLA* 102 (1987): 29–41.

——. *Stages of History: Shakespeare's English Chronicles*. Ithaca: Cornell University Press, 1990.

Rathmell, John. Introduction. In *The Psalms of Sir Philip Sidney and the Countess of Pembroke*. Garden City, N.Y.: Doubleday, 1963.

Roberts, Josephine. "Lady Mary Wroth's Sonnets: A Labyrinth of the Mind." *Journal of Women's Studies in Literature* 1 (1979): 319–29.

Root, Robert K. "Publication before Printing." *PMLA* 28 (1913): 417–31.

Rose, Mary Beth. *The Expense of Spirit: Love and Sexuality in English Renaissance Drama*. Ithaca: Cornell University Press, 1988.

——. "Where Are the Mothers in Shakespeare? Options for Gender Representation in the English Renaissance." *Shakespeare Quarterly* 42 (1991): 291–314.

Rubel, Vere L. *Poetic Diction in the English Renaissance from Skelton through Spenser*. Oxford: Oxford University Press, 1941.

Rubin, Gayle. "The Traffic in Women: Notes on the 'Political Economy' of Sex." In *Toward an Anthropology of Women*. Edited by Rayna R. Reiter. New York: Monthy Review Press, 1975.

Saenger, Paul, and Michael Heinlen. "Incunable Description and Its Implication for the Analysis of Fifteenth-Century Reading Habits." In *Printing the Written Word: The Social History of Books, Circa 1450–1520*. Edited by Sandra L. Hindman. Ithaca: Cornell University Press, 1991.

Sankovitch, Tilde. *French Women Writers and the Book: Myths of Access and Desire*. Syracuse, N.Y.: Syracuse University Press, 1988.

———. "Inventing Authority of Origin: The Difficult Enterprise." In *Women in the Middle Ages and the Renaissance*. Edited by Mary Beth Rose. Syracuse, N.Y.: Syracuse University Press, 1986.

Saunders, J. W. "From Manuscript to Print: A Note on the Circulation of Poetic MSS. in the Sixteenth Century." *Proceedings of the Leeds Philosophical and Literary Society* 6 (1951): 507–28.

———. *The Profession of English Letters*. London: Routledge and Kegan Paul, 1964.

———. "The Stigma of Print: A Note on the Social Bases of Tudor Poetry." *Essays in Criticism* 1 (1951): 139–64.

Scott, Joan. "Gender: A Useful Category of Historical Analysis." *American Historical Review* 91 (December 1986): 1053–75.

Sedgwick, Eve. *Between Men: English Literature and Male Homosocial Desire*. New York: Columbia University Press, 1985.

Sharpe, J. A. "'Last Dying Speeches': Religion, Ideology, and Public Execution in Seventeenth-Century England." *Past and Present* 107 (May 1985): 144–67.

Sheavyn, Phoebe. *The Literary Profession in the Elizabethan Age*. Manchester: Manchester University Press, 1909.

Shumaker, Wayne. *English Autobiography*. Berkeley: University of California Press, 1954.

Sinfield, Alan. "Power and Ideology: An Outline Theory and Sidney's *Arcadia*." *ELH* 52 (1985): 259–77.

Skretkowicz, Victor. Introduction. *The Countess of Pembroke's Arcadia: The New Arcadia*. Edited by Victor Skretkowicz. Oxford: Clarendon Press, 1987.

Smith, Hallet. *Elizabethan Poetry*. Cambridge, Mass.: Harvard University Press, 1952.

———. "*A Woman Killed With Kindness*." *PMLA* 53 (1938): 138–47.

Southall, Raymond. *The Courtly Maker: An Essay on the Poetry of Wyatt and His Contemporaries*. New York: Barnes and Noble, 1964.

Stallybrass, Peter. "Patriarchal Territories: The Body Enclosed." In *Rewriting The Renaissance: Discourses of Sexual Difference in Early Modern Europe*. Edited by Margaret Ferguson, Maureen Quilligan, and Nancy J. Vickers. Chicago: University of Chicago Press, 1986.

Stallybrass, Peter, and Allon White. *The Politics and Poetics of Transgression*. Ithaca: Cornell University Press, 1986.

Steinberg, Leo. *The Sexuality of Christ in Renaissance Art and in Modern Oblivion*. New York: Pantheon, 1983.

Stone, Lawrence. *The Crisis of the Aristocracy, 1558–1641*. Oxford: Clarendon Press, 1965.

———. *The Family, Sex, and Marriage in England: 1500–1800*. London: Weidenfeld and Nicolson, 1977.

———. *An Open Elite? England, 1540–1880*. Oxford: Clarendon Press, 1984.

Strong, Roy. *The Cult of Elizabeth*. London: Thames and Hudson, 1977.

———. *Splendour at Court*. London: Weidenfeld and Nicolson, 1973.

Suleiman, Susan. "Pornography, Transgression, and the Avant-Garde: Bataille's

Story of the Eye." In *The Poetics of Gender*. Edited by Nancy K. Miller. New York: Columbia University Press, 1986.

Summit, Jennifer. "The Gloss That Mars: Gabriel Harvey's Marginalia." Paper delivered at the Twenty-seventh International Congress on Medieval Studies. Kalamazoo, Michigan. May 1992.

Svensson, Lars-Hakan. *Silent Art: Rhetorical and Thematic Patterns in Samuel Daniel's "Delia."* CWK Gleerup, 1980.

Tennenhouse, Leonard. *Power on Display: The Politics of Shakespeare's Genres.* New York: Methuen, 1986.

Thompson, John. *The Founding of English Metre.* New York: Columbia University Press, 1961.

Traub, Valerie. "Desire and the Difference It Makes." In *The Matter of Difference.* Edited by Valerie Wayne. Ithaca: Cornell University Press, 1991.

Travitsky, Betty, ed. *The Paradise of Women: Writings by Englishwomen of the Renaissance.* Westport, Conn.: Greenwood Press, 1981.

Tyson, Gerald P., and Sylvia S.Wagonheim, eds. *Print and Culture in the Renaissance.* Newark: University of Delaware Press, 1986.

Vance, Eugene. "'Love's Concordance': The Poetics of Desire and the Joy of the Text." *Diacritics* 5 (1975): 41–8.

Van Heertum, Cis. "A Hostile Annotation of Rachel Speght's *A Mouzell or Melastomus* (1617)." *English Studies* 68 (1987): 490–96.

Vickers, Nancy. "'The blazon of sweet beauty's best': Shakespeare's *Lucrece.*" In *Shakespeare and the Question of Theory.* Edited by Patricia Parker and Geoffrey Hartman. New York: Methuen, 1985.

——. "Diana Described: Scattered Woman and Scattered Rhyme." In *Writing and Sexual Difference.* Edited by Elizabeth Abel. Chicago: University of Chicago Press, 1986.

Wall, John N. "The Reformation in England and the Typographical Revolution: 'By this printing . . . the doctrine of the Gospel soundeth to all nations.'" *Print and Culture in the Renaissance.* Edited by Gerald P. Tyson and Sylvia S. Wagonheim. Newark: University of Delaware Press, 1986.

Waller, Gary. "Acts of Reading: The Production of Meaning in *Astrophil and Stella.*" *Studies in the Literary Imagination* 15 (1982): 23–35.

——. "The Countess of Pembroke and Gendered Reading." In *The Renaissance Englishwoman in Print: Counterbalancing the Canon.* Edited by Anne M. Haselkorn and Betty Travitsky. Amherst: University of Massachusetts Press, 1990.

——. *Mary Sidney, Countess of Pembroke: A Critical Study of Her Writings and Literary Milieu.* Salzburg: Universität Salzburg, Insitut für Anglistik und Amerikanistik, 1979.

——. "The Rewriting of Petrarch: Sidney and the Languages of Sixteenth-Century Poetry." In *Sir Philip Sidney and the Interpretation of Renaissance Culture.* Edited by Gary Waller and Michael D. Moore. Totowa, N.J.: Barnes and Noble, 1984.

——. "Struggling into Discourse: The Emergence of Renaissance Women's Writing." In *Silent but for the Word: Tudor Women as Patrons, Translators, and Writers of Religious Works.* Edited by Margaret Hannay. Kent, Ohio: Kent State University Press, 1985.

Warkentin, Germaine. "'Love's sweetest part, variety': Petrarch and the Curious

Frame of the Renaissance Sonnet Sequence." *Renaissance and Reformation* 11 (1975): 14–23.

——. "The Meeting of the Muses: Sidney and the Mid-Tudor Poets." In *Sir Philip Sidney and the Interpretation of Renaissance Culture*. Edited by Gary Waller and Michael D. Moore. Totowa, N.J.: Barnes and Noble, 1984.

Warner, Michael. *The Letters of the Republic: Publication and the Public Sphere in Eighteenth-Century America*. Cambridge, Mass.: Harvard University Press, 1990.

Wayne, Don. "Drama and Society in the Age of Jonson: An Alternative View." *Renaissance Drama* 13 (1982): 103–29.

Wayne, Valerie. "Some Sad Sentence: Vives' *Instruction of a Christian Woman*." In *Silent but for the Word: Tudor Women as Patrons, Translators, and Writers of Religious Works*. Edited by Margaret Hannay. Kent, Ohio: Kent State University Press, 1985.

Weisner, Merry. "Spinning Out: Women's Work in the Early Modern Economy." In *Becoming Visible: Women in European History*. Edited by Renate Bridenthal and Claudia Koonz. Boston: Houghton Mifflin, 1977.

Welsford, Enid. *The Court Masque*. New York: Russell and Russell, 1962.

Whigham, Frank. *Ambition and Privilege: The Social Tropes of Elizabethan Courtesy Theory*. Berkeley: University of California Press, 1984.

——. "Interpretation at Court: Courtesy and the Performer-Audience Dialectic." *New Literary History* 14 (1983): 623–39.

Wickham, Glynne. *Early English Stages, 1300–1660*. 3 vols. New York: Columbia University Press, 1959–1981.

Williams, Raymond. *Keywords*. 3d ed. New York: Oxford University Press, 1984.

——. *Marxism and Literature*. Oxford: Oxford University Press, 1977.

Wilson, Luke. "William Harvey's *Prelectiones*: The Performance of the Body in the Renaissance Theater of Anatomy." *Representations* 17 (1987): 62–95.

Withington, Robert. *English Pageantry: An Historical Outline*. Vol. 1. Cambridge, Mass.: Harvard University Press, 1918.

Woodbridge, Linda. *Women and the English Renaissance: Literature and the Nature of Womankind, 1540–1620*. Urbana: University of Illinois Press, 1984.

Woodmansee, Martha. "The Genius and the Copyright: Economic and Legal Conditions of the Emergence of the 'Author.'" *Eighteenth-Century Studies* 17 (1984): 425–48.

Wrightson, Keith. *English Society, 1580–1680*. New Brunswick, N.J.: Rutgers University Press, 1982.

Yates, Frances A. *Astraea: The Imperial Theme in the Sixteenth Century*. Harmondsworth: Penguin, 1977.

INDEX

Absence, as trope, 331–36
Achilles, 227–30, 266
Actaeon. *See* Diana-Actaeon myth
Agnew, Jean-Christophe, 54n
Alpers, Paul, 243n
Amussen, Susan, 54n, 295n
Anglo, Sydney, 120, 125n
Anonymity, staged, 238–40
Arbor of Amorous Devices, The, 103, 105
Attribution, 23–24, 97–102, 238–40, 243–45
Aubrey, John, 319
Author function, 11, 50–53, 82–87, 112, 116

Barkan, Leonard, 190–91, 192n, 212, 225–26, 229n
Barnes, Barnabe, 68, 187, 199, 205–7
Barnfield, Richard, 65–66; *Cynthia,* 64, 71, 74, 213n
Barroll, Leeds, 111
Barthes, Roland, 11, 52–53, 93
Bastard, text as, 16, 206–7, 234–36
Beaumont and Fletcher (*Philaster*), 315n
Beilin, Elaine, 270n, 310–11, 329n
Belsey, Catherine, 6, 7n, 193n, 277–78, 287, 292
Bennett, H.S., 14, 210n
Bergeron, David, 119n, 121n, 125n
Berlant, Lauren, 251n
Blazon, 67–70, 190, 281–82, 302–6, 326–30

Blum, Abbe, 274
Bodenham, John (*Belvedere*), 103–4, 147n, 178
Body, as metaphor for text, 60–70, 180–88, 202–9, 315–17, 323–27
Book commodity, 5, 57–62; surveillance of, 208–9
Boose, Lynda, 277n
Booth, Stephen, 51, 196–98, 309
Breitenberg, Mark, 119n, 124n
Breton, Nicholas, 98–99, 208–9
Brittons Bowre of Delights, 98–99, 100–101, 105
Bruns, Gerald L., 9n, 106–7

Campbell, Marion, 51n, 94n
Chamberlain, John, 279, 283
Chastity. *See* Female reputation
Chettle, Henry, 187n, 269
Childbirth, risks of, 284–85
Christ, body of, 323–30
Churchyard, Thomas, 66, 163–64, 252
Class, use of term, 11n
Cohen, Walter, 4n, 277n
Coiro, Ann Baynes, 14n, 59n, 322n
Commonplace books, 31–34, 231, 243–45
Constable, Henry (*Diana*), 194, 221–22
Contagion, as a trope, 298–300
Coterie writing. *See* Manuscript texts
Cressy, David, 16n
Cross-Dressing: Achilles', 227–30, 266; Daniel's, 253; practice of, 224n, 266,

Cross-Dressing, (*cont.*)
275–78; Spenser's, 232, 240–43

Daniel, Samuel: *The Complaint of Rosamond*, 250–60, 266–68, 273–75; *Delia*, 34, 43–44, 47, 71–75, 175–76, 193–94, 199–201, 331n; *Letter from Octavia to Marcus Antonius*, 271–72; preliminary apparatus to his works, 74–79, 185
Davies, John, 15–16, 279
Davis, Lennard, 161n
Davis, Walter, 71n
De Grazia, Margreta, 5n, 82n, 83
Dekker, Thomas, 1, 2–3
Denny, Edward, 337–38
Derrida, Jacques, 124
Diana-Actaeon myth, 190–91, 198–202, 207–8, 211–14, 225–26
Dolan, Frances, 161n
Dollimore, Jonathan, 4n
Donaldson, Ian, 217–18
Drayton, Michael, 180; *Ideas Mirrour* and *Idea*, 43, 79–80, 90–92; *Matilda*, 252; preliminary apparatus to his works, 79–87
Duchess of Malfi, The. See Webster, John

Effeminization, 263–72
Eisenstein, Elizabeth, 9n, 20n
Elizabeth I: coronation procession, 117–26; progress pageants, 126–60; representation of her desire, 133–37, 146–47, 159; sayings, 64–65, 111, 122–24, 221
Elsky, Martin, 9n, 345n
England's Helicon, 104–5, 224
Exclusivity, construction of, 96–97, 177–80, 222–26
Executions, accounts of, 161–62

Female body, 169–70, 179–88, 199–208, 220–22, 226
Female complaint poems, 250–60, 263, 274–76, 296–97, 302–3
Female legacy. *See* Women, legacies of
Female reputation, 266–72

Ferguson, Margaret, 321
Ferry, Anne, 178, 195n
Fienberg, Nona, 331n
Fineman, Joel, 219, 309n
Fisken, Beth Wynne, 317
Fleming, Juliet, 224n, 264
Fletcher, Giles (*Licia*), 209–10, 251
Foucault, Michel, 11, 52–53, 100, 112–13
Foxe, John, 15n
Fraistat, Neil, 23
Fraunce, Abraham, 225
Freccero, John, 93–94
Freer, Coburn, 312n
Fumerton, Patricia, 194, 195n

Gascoigne, George, 223; "The Adventures of Master F.J.," 38, 132; *A Hundreth Sundrie Flowres*, 243–45; *The Posies*, 34, 245–50; presentation of authorship and career, 138–40; *The Princely Pleasures at Kenelworth Castle*, 127–40, 145–46; *The Steele Glass*, 140, 227, 260–63, 273; *The Tale of Hemetes the Heremyte*, 128–32, 137
Gender, 3, 7n, 50, 69–70, 159, 272, 276–77, 345–46; and class, 277n; and historicist studies, 6–7
Girouard, Mark, 177
Goad, Thomas, 284–85, 287–88, 293–95
Goldberg, Jonathan, 47n, 53n, 113n, 225n, 239
Goldwell, Henry, 163–64
Gorboduc, 182–84
Gosson, Stephen, 263–65
Grafton Bible, 120
Greenblatt, Stephen, 112, 113n, 121–22, 195n
Greene, Robert, 177–78
Griffin, Bartholomew (*Fidessa*), 44–45, 195, 199
Grymeston, Elizabeth, 286–87

Habington, William (*Castara*), 57, 265
Hall, Kim, 332

Halpern, Richard, 238n
Handful of Pleasant Delights, A, 103
Hannay, Margaret, 312n, 319
Harington, John, 15–16, 57–58, 60–61, 105
Harvey, Gabriel, 66, 241, 269, 273n
Helgerson, Richard, 6n, 17, 56, 131n, 142n, 233–34, 248n, 265, 277–78
Heywood, Thomas, 123–24
Hogrefe, Pearl, 294
Homosocial rivalry/bonding, 38–40
Howard, Jean, 222n, 233, 276–77; and Marion F. O'Connor, 229n
Hull, Suzanne, 225n
Hulse, Clark, 48

Il Schifanoya, 122–23, 125
Intellectual property, 87n

Jardine, Lisa, 12n, 280n, 302
J.C. (*Alicilia*), 92
Jed, Stephanie, 183n, 218n
Joceline, Elizabeth, 283–84, 287–88, 293–95
Jones, Ann Rosalind, 7, 279n, 282–83, 287, 331, 332n; and Peter Stallybrass, 178n
Jones, Richard, 101, 104, 105, 307
Jonson, Ben, 18–19, 184–85, 314–15
Jordan, Constance, 280n, 321n

Kahn, Coppélia, 184n, 218
Kegl, Rosemary, 12n
Kelso, Ruth, 270, 280n
Kennedy, Gwynne, 282n, 283n, 337n
Kennedy, William, 42n
Kolodny, Annette, 279n

Lamb, Mary Ellen, 154n, 280n, 285n, 290n, 312n, 318
Laneham, Richard, 135–36
Lanham, Richard, 48
Lanyer, Amelia, 319–30
Lee, Spike, 321
Leigh, Dorothy, 288–89, 294–95
Leinwand, Theodore, 113n
Lewalski, Barbara, 322

Lewis, C. S., 105
Literacy, 16n, 341–42
Lodge, Thomas: *Complaint of Elstred*, 258–59, 268–69; *Phillis*, 44, 46n, 62–63, 203–4; *Scillaes Metamorphosis*, 185–87
Lloyd, Ludwick, 210
Loewenstein, Joseph, 18, 134n
London, as lover, 302–3
Love's Martyr, 66–67
Lucie-Smith, Edward, 211
Lyly, John, 165n

M.R. (*The Mothers Counsell*), 291–93
MacArthur, Janet, 95n
MacCaffrey, Wallace, 224
McCanles, Michael, 238
McCoy, Richard, 128n, 129n, 148n, 247, 249–50
McGann, Jerome, 10
Manuscript texts: class politics of, 25–29, 53–55; "closed" and "open" nature of, 8–10, 11, 106–7; collaborative nature of, 31–34; erotics of, 41–50; features in print, 55–57, 95–97, 231–32, 240, 297–98
Marotti, Arthur, 9–10, 30n, 31–34, 102, 115n, 188, 208n, 243n, 245
Marcus, Leah, 5n, 87n
Masten, Jeff, 18n, 331n
Middleton, Thomas, 272
Miller, David Lee, 143n, 234–35, 237–38
Miller, Jacqueline T., 51n
Mirror for Magistrates, 250–51
Miscellanies, 95–107; format for poetry, 101, 103–5; preliminaries, 97–99, 103, 224; politics of, 96–97, 107–8, 224
Montrose, Louis, 4n, 6, 13n, 56n, 141–43, 160–61n, 234n, 238
Moi, Toril, 21n
Mother's texts, 283–96
Mourning, 316–17, 320–21, 327, 329–30
Mulcaster, Richard, 117–26
Mullaney, Steven, 18n
Mumford, Lewis, 231–32

Murray, Timothy, 5n, 19, 20n, 116n

Nashe, Thomas, 13, 170–72, 208
Neale, John, 119
Neely, Carol Thomas, 277n
New bibliography, 30
New historicism, 4–5n; and feminism, 6–7
Newman, Barbara, 283n
Newman, Karen, 6, 170n, 322
Norton, Thomas, and Thomas Sackville. *See Gorboduc*

O'Connor, Marion. *See* Howard, Jean
Ong, Walter, 20n
Orgel, Stephen, 10n, 18, 94, 136, 141, 145, 148–49
Ovid, 225n, 228n, 252

Pageantry: and authorship, 114–17; censorship of, 134–35; courtly erotics of, 135–37, 158–59; and interpretation, 124–26; politics of, 116–17
Paradise of Dainty Devices, The, 98
Parker, Patricia, 172n, 226, 303
Passionate Pilgrim, The, 98–100
Pastoral, 141–43, 227–31, 324
Paternity, as trope, 16, 153–56, 206–7, 235–36
Patterson, Annabel, 5–6n, 134n, 155n, 238n
Patterson, Lee, 5n, 346n
Percy, William (*Coelia*), 41–42, 174–75, 194–95
Petrarchan poetics, 188–89, 190n; fragmentation and unity, 67–70, 91–93, 303–6; and Amelia Lanyer's writing, 323–30; and pageantry, 136–37, 146–47, 158–59; and Mary Sidney's writing, 315–17; and Mary Wroth's writing, 331–35. *See also* Blazon
Pettie, George, 27–28, 174–75, 209
Philomela, 260–62
Phoenix Nest, The, 67n, 100, 157n
Plant, Marjorie, 62n, 210, 344n
Poetical Rhapsody, A, 98, 209, 224

Pomeroy, Elizabeth, 102n
Porter, Carolyn, 4–5n
Prefaces and preliminary matter, 1–3, 128–32, 138–40, 148–58, 169–88, 207–8, 227–36, 273–75, 312–18, 322–23
"Press," erotic implications of, 1–3, 182, 219–20, 279–80, 346–47
Print, 7–9, 20–21; and authorship, 21–22; "closure" of, 71, 93–95, 106–7; culture, 10–11; erotics of, 15–16, 219–20, 345–47; increases in, 14; objectivity of, 59–60, 93, 164–65; politics of, 11–12, 341–47; regulation of, 343–44; stigma of, 2–4, 5–6, 14–15, 17, 25–26, 173, 230, 267–69, 281
Privacy, construction of, 176–78, 188–90
Prodigality, 245–47
Psalms. *See* Sidney, Mary: writings of
Pseudomorph, 231–32, 276–78
Puttenham, George, 240–41, 269–70

Quenes Maiesties Passage . . ., The. See Elizabeth I: coronation procession
Quilligan, Maureen, 67n, 212n, 282n

Rackin, Phyllis, 276–77, 309n, 342
Reagan, Ronald, 123n
Rich, Barnabe, 221, 264–65, 269
Roberts, Josephine, 330
Rollins, Hyder E., 107n
Rosamond, The Complaint of. See Daniel, Samuel
Rose, Mary Beth, 6, 7n, 284n, 285n, 287n, 294–95, 308n
Rowlands, Samuel, 204–5
Russell, Elizabeth Cooke, 291

Saenger, Paul and Michael Heinlen, 88
Sandys, George, 225
Sankovitch, Tilde, 339n
Saunders, J. W., 2n, 13, 145n, 179
Scoloker, Anthony, 1–3, 68, 182
Scott, Joan, 3n
Sedgwick, Eve, 38n

Shakespeare, William: *2 Henry VI*, 341–42; *King John*, 309; *A Lover's Complaint*, 259–60; *Love's Labour's Lost*, 36–37, 99, 165, 172n, 189; *Merry Wives of Windsor*, 98, 346–47; *The Rape of Lucrece*, 34, 213n, 214–20, 261–62n, 272–73; *Romeo and Juliet*, 35–36; *Sonnets*, 195–98

Sharpe, J. A., 161n

Shore, Jane. *See* Churchyard, Thomas

Sidney, Mary: dedication to, 153–56, 323; and mother's deathbed, 290–91; writings of, 311–19, 325

Sidney, Philip: *The Arcadia*, 67, 68n, 151–58, 212–14, 265; *Astrophel and Stella*, 40, 42–49, 55, 70–72, 170–72, 195; critique of Elizabeth, 141–47; *The Lady of May*, 140–58; literary reputation of, 147–59, 228

Sinfield, Alan, 142n

Smith, William (*Chloris*), 33n, 63–64, 199, 203

Sonnets, 39–57; commodification of, 57–95, 202–11; exchange of, 29, 31–50; lack of closure in, 50–52; mistresses in, 40–42, 50, 61–63, 68–70; rhetoric of disclosure in, 188–202; and sight, 190n; title pages and book layout, 70–89; titles, 61–70, 203–4

Speakes, Larry, 123n

Spenser, Edmund: *Amoretti*, 43–47, 71, 73, 191–93; *Colin Clouts Come Home Againe*, 157, 276; *The Faerie Queene*, 55n, 67n, 150–51, 210–11, 227–33; *The Shepheardes Calender*, 233–43

Spiritual erotics, 323–30

Stallybrass, Peter, 6, 216, 220–21, 222n, 280n, 339; and Allon White, 6n, 19, 163n

Steinberg, Leo, 327

Stone, Lawrence, 54, 176

Suleiman, Susan, 169, 92n

Summit, Jennifer, 71n

Tennenhouse, Leonard, 113, 222n

Theatricality, commodification of, 112–14, 159–67

Theatrical Scripts, 88–89

Thornton, Alice, 289–90

Title pages, 74–89, 273–75

Tofte, Robert (*Laura*), 175n

Tottels Miscellany, 23–30, 97–98, 107, 151, 170

Traub, Valerie, 7n

Travitsky, Betty, 284n, 297n

Tyler, Margaret, 311

Vesalius, Andreas, 169–71, 184n, 202–3

Vickers, Nancy, 38–39, 190–91, 215, 281, 303

Virgilian formal progression, 230, 254

Vives, Juan Luis, 270, 280–81

Waller, Gary, 51, 94, 159n, 283, 332n, 335, 339

Warkenten, Germaine, 32

Warner, Michael, 20n

Watson, Thomas, 201–2

Webster, John, 307–8

Whigham, Frank, 144

White, Allon. *See* Stallybrass, Peter

Whitney, Isabella: "The Copy of A Letter . . .," 270n, 296–97; fictional will of, 299–310; *A sweet Nosegay*, 297–310

Whythorne, Thomas, 35, 37–38, 177n

"Will," 307–10

Williams, Raymond, 108n

Will–making. *See* Women: testamentary powers of

Willobie His Avisa, 207–8

Wilmot, Richard, 66–67, 179

Wolfe, John, 344–45

Women: legacies of, 283–95; religious works of, 310–30; restrictions on, 279–83; testamentary powers of, 294–95

Woodbridge, Linda, 321n

Woodmansee, Martha, 21n, 87n

Wrightson, Keith, 12n, 54n

Wroth, Mary, 330–38

Zepheria (Anon.), 199